A SURVEY OF
EUROPEAN
CIVILIZATION

Editor • First Edition
CARL L. BECKER
Late John Stambaugh Professor of History, Cornell University

Editor • Fourth Edition
LEO GERSHOY
Professor of History, New York University

Part One · To 1660 · by Wallace K. Ferguson

Wallace K. Ferguson
The University of Western Ontario

Geoffrey Bruun

A SURVEY OF

EUROPEAN CIVILIZATION

Fourth Edition

HOUGHTON MIFFLIN COMPANY / BOSTON

New York   Atlanta   Geneva, Ill.   Dallas   Palo Alto

EDITOR'S FOREWORD

THE GENEROUS ACCLAIM ACCORDED A SURVEY OF EUROPEAN CIVILIZA-
TION *and its wide and long adoption in undergraduate courses clearly attest its
merits. In this edition, as in earlier revisions, the two authors working in close
and critical collaboration have pushed their narrative back to early origins in
pre-history and forward to the troubled present. Within the long span of the
centuries that they cover they discern neither decisive breaks nor permanent
dislocations to destroy the continuity of the history of Western man. While
each of them has amplified his part of their common enterprise by introducing
new data and, where he felt it needed, shifted his emphasis, they have adhered
to their integral conviction that the progressive evolution of European civilization constitutes the hard core of a slowly emerging global order.*

*Fully aware that a shift is taking place in the center of gravity, they remain
persuaded — and correctly so — that through its long ascendancy Europe
remains, in their own words, "the logical center and European history the
logical axis for what is now almost a world civilization." Many of us well,
others ill, but all of us, are enmeshed in a common pattern of institutions,
interests, aspirations — and frustrations too — that is the collective heritage of
this Europe-centered culture.*

*The obligations that the authors incurred to others for scholarly assistance,
together with relevant details concerning the successive revisions, they themselves state in their preface. Two distinguished historians, the late Carl Becker
and William L. Langer, have written luminous introductions to earlier editions.
From his own review of the* Survey *in this Fourth Edition the present editor is
convinced that it offers a meaningful dialogue between the authors and their
intellectually inquisitive readers.*

*It is a rich panorama, selective in its data and coordinated in presentation;
distinguished, too, in felicity of expression which links the writers, this editor
nostalgically likes to think, with Carl Becker, who influenced them early in
their professional careers. A text full enough to be self-sufficient, it does not
overwhelm its readers with ponderous details. More than ever the* Survey *is a
valuable instrument of teaching in our era of the "paperback revolution," giving
to undergraduates the structure of historical development without which the
now available miscellany of source material may well become a distracting
embarrassment of riches.*

LEO GERSHOY

New York University

AUTHORS' PREFACE

OUR RESPONSIBILITY FOR THE PREPARATION *of this Fourth Edition of A SURVEY OF EUROPEAN CIVILIZATION has once more been divided, with Wallace K. Ferguson in charge of Part One and Geoffrey Bruun of Part Two, and once more we have benefited by the generous help of many friends and colleagues. In Part One Professor Lionel Casson of New York University contributed materially to the revision of the chapters on the Ancient World, and Professor Bryce Lyon of Brown University read the chapters on the Middle Ages and made many valuable suggestions. Professors William H. Stockdale and John Rowe of the University of Western Ohtario assisted in the task of bringing the Suggestions for Further Reading in Part One up-to-date. To all of them our most hearty thanks. An especial debt of gratitude is due to Margaret Ferguson who read both manuscript and proof of Part One with an alert and meticulous eye.*

The Part Two text benefited in equal measure from the critical readings given it by Professor Herbert H. Rowen of Rutgers University, Professor Boyd C. Shafer of Macalester College, and Professor Leo Gershoy of New York University. Throughout the process of revising earlier chapters and adding new material on recent history the many thoughtful suggestions of these tactful colleagues have been a constant help and stimulus. Our thanks are also due Joseph Bernard, David Redmond, and Edwin Self for aid with the Part Two Suggestions for Further Reading. It has been a special pleasure to find ourselves working in concert with our old friend Leo Gershoy as general editor. Finally, to our associates at Houghton Mifflin Company, those vigilant, talented, and tireless experts on editorial, art, and production problems, we offer our admiration and our gratitude.

WALLACE K. FERGUSON
GEOFFREY BRUUN

CONTENTS

A SURVEY OF
EUROPEAN
CIVILIZATION

Part One — To 1660

> "What seest thou else
> In the dark backward and abysm of time?"
> • Shakespeare, *The Tempest,* Act I, scene 2

Introduction

In SURVEYING the history of European civilization, we shall be in fact tracing the origins and development of our own culture, for, when European colonists first settled on these shores, they brought with them their cultural traditions to lay the foundation of Western civilization in the New World. Transplanted to a new environment, European civilization developed along partially independent lines, but there was no real break in continuity. Generation after generation, the influence of European culture on the shaping of America has been reinforced by successive waves of immigration as well as by constant intellectual and commercial intercourse between the lands lying on both sides of the Atlantic. Nor is this the only reason why European history should be of interest to American students today; for, with the development of rapid transportation and almost instantaneous communication between distant lands, the histories of the two continents which form the North Atlantic community have become more closely interrelated than seemed possible in the days of American isolation.

But before beginning our historical survey we may well pause to consider some rather more fundamental problems than those posed by the relation of European to modern American civilization. In the first place, what is history, and of what use is it to us? And, since men have not always held the same opinions concerning these questions, how did the modern conception of the nature and purpose of history develop? Finally, when did history, properly speaking, begin, and what was its background in prehistoric time?

1. The Study of History

What is history? Ideally the subject matter of history is man and all that man has thought, said, and done since the dawn of civilization. For practical purposes, however, history cannot include every thought, every word, every action or event in which man has been involved. For of all the thoughts, words, and actions of millions of men through countless generations, only a minute fragment can be known today. And even that minute fragment can be known only imperfectly through such written records as survive, and through the mute evidence of those things man has made which have withstood the ravages of time. The history that we can know, the history that we can learn and study, is, therefore, something much less comprehensive than history considered as the sum of all past events. It is recorded history. It differs from history as we first defined it in much the same way that our present memory differs from the sum total of the innumerable and largely forgotten thoughts, words, and actions of our entire life. It includes only those things the memory of which has survived and is still available today. History, then, might be defined by analogy as the recorded memory of mankind.[1]

The value of history. This brings us to the second question. What is the use of history?

---

[1] This definition, and much of the following argument, was suggested by the late Carl Becker's presidential address to the American Historical Association in 1931, published in *Everyman His Own Historian* (New York, 1935), pp. 233–255.

If, instead, we ask: what is the use of memory? the answer is obvious. Without memory we would be unable to meet the simplest problems of daily life. We would be strangers and afraid in a world we never made. We would have no means of anticipating the probable results of any action or of calculating what other people might do. We would, in short, be unable to act intelligently. That extension of memory which is history may not be as immediately and constantly necessary in the conduct of our daily lives as is personal memory; but without it we would be unable to orient ourselves or to act intelligently in the larger context of national or world affairs. This does not mean that a knowledge of history, however extensive, will enable us to forecast with certainty the course of future events, any more than our memory of personal experience will enable us to say exactly what will happen tomorrow. In either case, however, a knowledge of what has happened in the past may afford us a clue to what is likely to happen in the future. It makes us better equipped to assess probabilities. And it enables us to understand better the situation in which we find ourselves by making it possible to see how it came to be what it is. To think of the practical use of history solely in these terms is, however, to take too limited a view of its value. It is also the key to an understanding of past culture, to the appreciation of those works of philosophy, religious inspiration, literature, art, and music which form our most precious legacy from the generations of men who have gone before us.

Written history. To make this cumulative memory of mankind available is the primary function of the historian. The process by which this end is achieved is a complex one and involves the labors of many different kinds of historians. First of all, it is essential that as much as possible of the surviving evidence of man's activity should be brought to light and studied with critical care. During the past century and a half, countless historians have devoted their lives to detailed research in archives and libraries or to examining with the aid of archaeologists the remains of long-buried civilizations. The results of their labors, published in collections of sources or in monographic studies, may then be used by less specialized historians as the material from which to write histories on a larger scale covering, perhaps, the whole history of a country or of an age. Finally, from these more generalized histories it is possible to construct surveys of still larger areas of historical time and space. As a rule it is only in the second and third of these stages, at more than one remove from direct contact with the sources, that history reaches the reading public. Even professional historians, though they may be specialists in their own field, are dependent on the work of other historians for their knowledge of the greater part of history.

The interpretation of history. At each stage of this process, the historian has at his disposal more facts than he can work into his written account. He must therefore select those which seem to him most significant. Unless he is satisfied with the barest narrative, he will also try to explain them and to show relations between cause and effect. In other words, he will interpret history, and the picture he presents will inevitably be colored by the experience, the interests, and the prejudices of his own age and his own society. For this reason history, written history, does not remain the same from generation to generation, but must be constantly rewritten. What seems significant and worth recording at one time may not seem so at another, and what may seem a valid explanation of historical events to one generation may not seem so to men of a later time whose experience of economic, political, or social movements has been different. This does not mean that historians wilfully distort history, although some historians have done so in the interest of political or social propaganda. Rather it means that the historian is striving to make history not only available but also useful to his own time. It is his duty not only to record history but also to think about it and to make the results of his thought available to the public. At its best, written history is more than the recorded memory of mankind. It is man's thoughtful consideration of his past.

History as story. Full appreciation of the importance and scope of the historian's function as the interpreter of man's experience is a relatively recent development. Until the nineteenth century, history was primarily story, a narrative of events compiled largely from narrative sources. Moreover, it was limited almost exclusively to war and politics, with occasional

Stonehenge, a ring of giant monoliths in southern England, is evidence of religious observances in prehistoric times.

excursions into church history. When historians speculated about the value of history beyond its obvious interest as story, they concluded that it was useful chiefly as a storehouse of examples of good and bad behavior, of successful or unsuccessful actions, mostly on the part of statesmen or military leaders. Assuming men to be much the same in all ages, they argued that individuals might profit by these examples to guide their own actions in similar circumstances. If we now regard this as an inadequate view of the scope and purpose of historical writing, we must at the same time not forget that story is still an essential part of history. It provides the basic framework of chronological reference to which we can relate more general developments, as, for example, we might date the rise of English drama by relating it to the reign of Queen Elizabeth. It is through story, too, that we can make the acquaintance of great men in the past, the saints and sages, the prophets and poets, the heroes and statesmen who have made our civilization. And, last but not least, the story is interesting for its own sake.

History as development. In the troubled period following the French Revolution, historians began to take a more profound view of the nature of history. When so many age-old institutions had been violently overthrown, men began to place a new value on the continuity of historical tradition and turned to the study of the past as a means of diagnosing, and possibly finding cures for, their present ills. Out of this intensified interest in history there grew a deeper understanding of historical causes and a new appreciation of the principle of historical development. No longer satisfied to explain events by the workings of Providence or of chance or by the actions of individual men, historians began to examine the historical development of institutions, cultures, and political organizations and discovered that gradual evolution provided the most satisfactory explanation of their present character. As the nineteenth century progressed, with accelerated economic, social, political, and cultural change, the conviction that historical development furnished the essential clue to understanding any aspect of human society became stronger and more nearly universal. In mid-century, Ernest Renan wrote: "The characteristic trait of the nineteenth century is to have substituted the historical method for the dogmatic method in all studies related to the human mind. . . . History is, in fact, the necessary form of understanding everything that is subject to the laws of changing and successive life." Since then there have been occasional reactions against this view, but most historians remain convinced that, as Carl Becker once remarked, they can explain anything only by showing what it successively was before it became that which it will presently cease to be. The knowledge thus acquired may not be absolute and can scarcely be permanent; but what the historian seeks is not absolute knowledge as it may be sought in the physical sciences. What he seeks is understanding, and even a relative understanding of ourselves and other peoples may be of invaluable service to our troubled world.

The expanding scope of history. Having recognized the principle of historical development, historians necessarily took a much larger view of the scope of history. It could no longer be limited to the story of battles or the narrative of political events. It must include the study of all forms of human activity. And it must give due attention not only to the few outstanding men whose names are known, but also to the anonymous masses of mankind. To the older type of history as the story of war and politics, there has thus been added economic history, social history, cultural history, the history of ideas, and all the possible subdivisions of these categories; for all these different kinds of history contribute to our knowledge of how a civilization is formed and how it develops from age to age. They are all necessary to the making of a complete picture of our past. The developmental view of history, too, has turned the attention of historians to the earliest origins of civilization and has led them to press the frontiers of historical knowledge as far back as possible into the distant past.

Historical sources. This great expansion in the scope of history forced historians, among other things, to seek new kinds of sources of information about the past. They could no longer be content with earlier chronicles and narratives from which to compile their histories. Even the political historians of the nineteenth century began to search government archives and collections of family papers for all sorts of documentary evidence — state papers, diplomatic correspondence, diaries, and memoranda — with which to fill in and verify their narratives. Great masses of such documents have been edited and published, with critical care to establish their authenticity. But for economic, social, or cultural history such sources are not enough. It has been necessary to go further afield and to make use of any surviving evidence of the past, from an account book to a work of art, or from a rusty piece of ancient armor to the inscription on a tombstone. For the study of many of these sources, especially

those pertaining to the distant past, special training was needed, and historians had to acquaint themselves with a whole group of special disciplines: palaeography, the study of old forms of writing; epigraphy, the study of inscriptions; philology, the study of languages; numismatics, the study of coins; anthropology and sociology, the study of man and society; and, finally, archaeology, the study of old civilizations. It was only through a combination of these disciplines that scholars were able to decipher the inscriptions and written records of the ancient Egyptian, Mesopotamian, and Aegean civilizations and so recover some two thousand years of lost history. By studying and classifying broken pieces of pottery, tools, and weapons found buried beneath the sites of ancient cities, archaeologists have also been able to reconstruct in rough outline the development of civilization for some two thousand years preceding the beginnings of recorded history. And finally, in cooperation with geologists, who could furnish evidence of the age of rock formations in which signs of human life were found, and palaeontologists, whose field is the study of fossils, scholars have been able to reconstruct with approximate accuracy the general course of man's prehistoric development. Our survey of European civilization can properly begin only with the dawn of actual recorded history in the earliest known civilizations, but for the sake of perspective we must first pause to sketch briefly what is known of man's prehistoric background.

2. Before History

Our evidence for the first appearance of man or of man-like creatures, sometimes called hominids, and of their gradual evolution over hundreds of thousands of years is distressingly meager. A few widely scattered fossilized fragments of skulls and other bones are all that we have to work with in reconstructing the physical appearance of our most distant ancestors. There is, as a result, considerable difference of opinion among physical anthropologists as to just when and how recognizable human beings evolved, and new discoveries are constantly changing the picture. It seems fairly certain, however, that the earliest proto-human forms had already diverged from the ancestral primate stock by the beginning of the Pleistocene or

Glacial Epoch, a period which lasted about a million years and gradually came to an end some ten thousand years ago, when the climate became much as we know it today. During this long period there occurred a series of slow but extreme changes of climate, which exercised a profound influence on the development of man and his culture. Four times increasing cold pushed ice sheets down over the northern latitudes. Between these periods of glaciation there were long warm intervals when the ice caps receded. Each of these changes left its mark on the earth's surface, and it is by identifying the geological strata in which human remains have been found that we can give them approximate dates.

The Old Stone Age. Fossilized remains are not, however, the only evidence we have of the development of man. Much more numerous are the tools he made, roughly shaped from stone or flint. These tell us less about the physical evolution of man, but much more about the infinitely slow growth of his culture, that is, his use of techniques and forms of society that are not purely instinctive and biologically in-

Stone tools, some crude and some highly finished, have been found over wide areas of Europe and Asia. This hand axe, chipped out of flint, was held in the fist.

herited. It is the possession of culture, indeed, that sets man apart from the rest of the animal kingdom. Man, or his semi-human predecessors, had reached the first stage, the fashioning of crude stone tools, some 600,000 or 700,000 years ago. This marks the beginning of what archaeologists call the Palaeolithic or Old Stone Age. This era, which lasted till about 10,000 years ago, has been further divided into three sub-periods, the Lower, Middle and Upper Palaeolithic, marked by successive improvements in the variety of tools used and the skill with which they were shaped. During this whole period man was a hunter and food-gatherer, dependent for his subsistence on the pursuit of wild animals, birds, and fish, as well as on the collection of fruits, berries, and nuts. The first type of man for whom we have considerable quantities of fossilized remains appeared in Europe during the Third Interglacial Period and persisted into the first phase of the Fourth Glacial Period. This was the race known as Neanderthal. In archaeological terms these people belong to the Middle Palaeolithic. They had specialized weapons, such as spear-points and fairly sophisticated tools for scraping, chopping and digging, made of bone and antler as well as of stone and flint. As the advancing cold of the Last Glaciation drove them into caves and rock-shelters, they made semi-settled homes for themselves. They also developed some form of social organization, for they hunted large animals in groups. Authorities disagree as to their relation, if any, to Modern Man. All we know is that, after holding their own for thousands of years and having adapted to the sub-arctic conditions of the Last Glaciation, they disappeared completely, to be replaced by Modern Man.

Modern Man. The origins of Modern Man (*homo sapiens*) are shrouded in mystery. It seems fairly certain, however, that men of our own type took over the European scene during the interstadial period of relatively less severe cold between the two major divisions of the Last Glacial Period. He persisted throughout this time of markedly fluctuating climate, to which, with his greater physical adaptability, and greater mental and technological equipment, he was able to adjust himself. By the time the Upper Palaeolithic began (about 30,000 years ago), we know that men were living and hunting in fairly sizable groups.

This cave painting from the cavern of Lascaux, France, dates from the late Palaeolithic period. Like other paintings of animals from this period, it shows amazing artistic skill.

Caves and rock-shelters formed their seasonal abodes; in eastern and central Europe the earliest purposely constructed dwellings date from this time. A variety of animals — bison, wild cattle, horse, reindeer, mammoth, and wooly rhinoceros — were among the chief objects of their hunt. These Upper Palaeolithic men were highly gifted: they possessed an extraordinarily well developed aesthetic sense and a truly remarkable artistic skill.

Technological advance. It is estimated that the Lower Palaeolithic lasted some 400,000 years and the Middle Palaeolithic possibly another 150,000 years, but the entire Upper Palaeolithic probably covers a span of less than 30,000 years. Now the pace of man's cultural development shows a marked forward surge, as demonstrated by the fact that during this time the advances in technology were far greater than during the Lower and Middle Palaeolithic Periods combined. Apparently human culture, as manifested by technology, economy, art, religion, and social organization, became more complex and specialized as man's physique became more highly evolved. The tools are now more profuse, much finer and more specialized, and they cover an infinitely greater range of types. Beautifully manufactured blade, bone, and antler tools appear, as well as objects made of ivory and hafted implements. Hunting, in which missile weapons were now employed, was conducted on a communal basis. The new inventions include the needle and thread, skin clothing, specialized hunting and fishing equipment, and stone lamps for use in the dark caves where the earliest paintings and engravings are preserved. The location and arrangement of certain Upper Palaeolithic settlements reflect the increasing complexity of man's social organization.

Cave art. Above all, this is the great era of Palaeolithic cave art. It is found in the inner recesses of many caves in France and Spain, and includes finger-tracings, paintings, engravings, bas-reliefs and sculptures. Such magnificent carved and painted frescoes as those of the bison and bulls of Altamira in northern Spain, the bulls, bison, reindeer, and horses of Lascaux and Cap Blanc in France, and many others, were created by Upper Palaeolithic Man at this time. It is thought that this was not, however, art for art's sake, but was the product, as is the case with primitive hunting peoples of today, of the magico-religious rites connected with hunting. Whatever the reason for its birth and growth, it is art in its finest creative form, and represents at the same time an incredible victory of man's technological skill over his environment and available resources. Because of its remarkable realism and vividness, it has won the unqualified admiration of modern artists.

The New Stone Age. With the final retreat of the ice sheet following the Last Glaciation, the climate and shape of the lands surrounding the Mediterranean Sea began to assume something of their modern character. Man had to adjust to the new conditions and in doing so produced new and more refined tools, so that archaeologists regard this period as marking the end of the Old Stone Age. There followed a transitional period, varying in duration from place to place, which archaeologists identify as Mesolithic, before the emergence of the Neolithic or New Stone Age. These names were given to the successive periods by the pioneer archaeologists who judged cultural progress primarily by the methods of working stone tools. The revolutionary change in man's way of life which marked the beginning of the New Stone Age was, however, infinitely more important and comprehensive than the mere production of polished stone axes. This change began in the Middle East, possibly as early as 8000 B.C. The essential element in the change, the most revolutionary in the whole cultural history of mankind, was that men gradually ceased to be food-gatherers or hunters and became food-producers. They learned, in short, how to raise crops and domesticate animals. Having become farmers, they ceased to wander in search of game, or such scarce food as un-aided nature provided, and settled down. A settled existence necessitated the development of more complex forms of social organization, as men clustered together in village communities and learned to cooperate for defense or for the irrigation and working of their fields. For the first time it became possible to produce a surplus of food, so that some men could devote themselves to specialized crafts and exchange their products for the surplus food grown by others. The result was an amazingly rapid technological advance. Neolithic men not only developed all the basic forms of farming and animal husbandry, but also invented spinning and weaving, stone hand-mills for grinding grain into flour, and, one of the most important inventions of all, the shaping and firing of clay

Recent excavations have bared the Neolithic stone walls of Jericho, built about 7000 B.C. So far as is known it is the world's earliest walled city.

pottery. They also learned to build houses of mud brick and to build walls around their villages for defense.

It was from such Neolithic village communities in the fertile river valleys of Egypt and Mesopotamia that cities gradually developed and with them the earliest civilizations. By about 3000 B.C., with the invention of writing, they had entered the period of recorded history, and it is here that our survey of European civilization may begin.

SECTION A

THE ANCIENT WORLD

The Athenians built their finest temples on the top of the Acropolis, a commanding hill in the center of Athens.

(c. 3000–31 B.C.)

The course of history is an unbroken stream, flowing steadily from obscure or unknown sources in that distant age when mankind was young. As it enters those chronological periods for which our knowledge of events is more complete, the stream seems to broaden and deepen. It flows serenely through the open daylight of the Greek and Roman world, to dwindle into comparative obscurity as it enters that darker period that followed the barbarian conquests, and to emerge again into plainer view in the High Middle Ages, whence it flows with ever-increasing volume down to our own time. Its character changes gradually. There are no sharp breaks. There is no place where one may say: Here history changes; here an age ends and another age begins. To divide history into periods is, therefore, in a sense meaningless and may be misleading. Yet the historian finds it convenient, indeed indispensable for purposes of discussion, to isolate and name certain large chronological periods, which seem to have a measure of unity and a character that differentiate them from the ages before and after. He must never forget, however, that his divisions are artificial and the chronological limits vague and uncertain. The first such period, starting from the beginning of recorded history, might be conveniently regarded as ending with the establishment in 31 B.C. of the Roman Empire, which was to unify the varied cultures of the ancient world within its frontiers.

The earliest sources of that broadening stream of historical development which culminates in our modern occidental civilization are to be found in the lands bordering the eastern Mediterranean. In the fertile valleys of the Nile, the Tigris and Euphrates, and in the islands of the Aegean, appeared the first evidences of civilization among the peoples of the Western world thousands of years before the beginning of the Christian era. We can trace these early civilizations in their major outlines through archaeological remains and, after a time, through the writing that has been preserved. Much of their content and character seems strange and foreign to us, for, though we owe to the ancient Eastern cultures many of our conceptions of religion and morality, we have a more direct legacy from the people of ancient Greece and Rome. The influence of their original thought in the fields of philosophy, literature, art, science, and law was of decisive importance in shaping the later culture of western Europe and America and forms an integral part of our contemporary civilization.

1

The Ancient Middle East (c. 3000–c. 500 B.C.)

THE TWO EARLIEST known civilizations were cradled in fertile river valleys in the Middle East, one in the broad and easily accessible basin formed by the Tigris and Euphrates rivers in lower Mesopotamia, the other in Egypt in the long narrow valley of the Nile. Progressive desiccation, which followed the last Ice Age, made the higher lands less habitable and partially dried the swamps of the river valleys. In these watered lowlands (as well as in northern Palestine) the first known village communities made their appearance, in Mesopotamia as early as c. 7000 B.C., in Egypt possibly two thousand years later. During the following two or three thousand years, these nascent civilizations passed through the transitional stage from Neolithic village culture to a well-developed political organization. Since we have no written records, this early period is known to us only through the material remains which archaeologists have discovered. Progress during these millenniums was slow, but its cumulative effect was revolutionary. Both Mesopotamia and Egypt could support a growing population only by the use of intensive irrigation, and an economy involving irrigation demands intensive social organization as well as technological knowledge. When both civilizations emerged with the invention of writing into the full light of recorded history, about the year 3000 B.C., they possessed urban centers, religions, and governmental systems. They had also acquired impressive craft techniques, and considerable engineering skill. Both were now in the Bronze Age and boasted some metallurgy. Before long other centers of civilization came into existence in neighboring lands — in the islands of the Aegean and in the strip of fertile land that runs up the Mesopotamian valley and then westward and southward down the Syrian coast, completing what has been called the Fertile Crescent.

1. Mesopotamia: The Land of the Two Rivers

The Tigris-Euphrates Valley. The two great rivers, the Tigris and the Euphrates, between which lies the land of Mesopotamia (modern Iraq), rise in the mountains of Armenia and flow southeastward for more than a thousand miles to empty into the Persian Gulf. In a land that had far too little rainfall to support farming, the rivers furnished a plentiful supply of water — once the inhabitants learned to contain it with dikes and to distribute it through irrigation canals. To the south of the valley are open grasslands and desert, while on the northern side are sloping plains and mountain ranges. The lands on both sides of the valley were occupied largely by peoples who, living

12

the lives of nomadic herders, were less civilized than the farmers in the basin, more barbaric and aggressive. This sets a pattern: Mesopotamia has ever been a prey to the hill men and desert tribes who have struggled for possession of the rich valley land, while its internal history has been marked by wars between rival city-states and the rise and fall of successive kingdoms. The political history of Mesopotamia is a complex tale, and can be summarized here only very briefly.

Sumer and Akkad. The first people to emerge from the shadows of Mesopotamian prehistory were the Sumerians, who occupied the lower Mesopotamian valley some time before 3000 B.C. In all probability they were not the first inhabitants of the land but were preceded by several older cultures between about 5000 and 3000 B.C., which laid the foundations upon which the Sumerians built. These forerunners, however, remain anonymous, whereas the Sumerians are known not only through archaeological remains but written records as well — the earliest so far known. The language in which their legacy has been preserved can be read with a high degree of accuracy; yet it remains mysterious in that it stands alone, having no demonstrable relation to the Semitic, Indo-European, or other known language groups. As the population increased, a number of city-states were formed in the Sumerian land. These states were frequently at war, and one after another conquered its neighbors and managed for a time to maintain an ascendancy. Meanwhile their neighbors in northern Mesopotamia, the Akkadians, were growing in strength. About 2350 B.C., this Semitic people, led by Sargon, the first great conqueror known to history, overpowered the Sumerians and made themselves masters of the whole Mesopotamian valley. In the following generations, under the dynasty founded by Sargon, Akkadian culture and political power extended from western Persia to Asia Minor.

Babylonia. After various vicissitudes, the land of Sumer and Akkad was conquered by another group of Semites, the Amorites, about 1900 B.C. Their best-known king, the great Hammurabi (1728–1686 B.C.) made Babylon, his capital, the cultural center of Mesopotamia. Hammurabi's reign marked a high point of able and unified government. Shortly there-

Hammurabi, the Babylonian king famed for his conquests and legal code, here stands before the sun-god.

after less civilized peoples, not only Semites but also Indo-Europeans,[1] broke into the Land of the Two Rivers. Northern Mesopotamia was overrun by the Mitanni, a people whose ruling element was most probably Indo-European. Southern Mesopotamia, including Babylon, was taken over by the Kassites, who were in large part Indo-European. These conquests, however, did not materially change the culture of Mesopotamia. Art, religion, and literature still continued to bear the distinctive stamp of the Sumerians. And this culture attained a new flowering after Mesopotamia had been invaded once more, this time by the Assyrians.

Assyria. The Assyrians were Semites, a hardy hill folk from the lands bordering the upper Tigris. By about 1000 B.C. they controlled most of Mesopotamia, and by the second quarter of the first millennium they reached

[1] The terms "Semitic" and "Indo-European" refer to peoples speaking a language belonging to one of these language groups. The Semitic languages are mostly concentrated in the Middle East. The Indo-European group includes most of the languages of Europe as well as Armenian, Persian, and Sanskrit, the ancient language of India. The languages in each group share a similar grammatical construction and have a vocabulary with many common roots.

the zenith of their power. Under Esarhaddon (680–669 B.C.) Assyria boasted a world empire which included Egypt among its dependents. But the end of Mesopotamian supremacy was not far off. Nineveh, the last important capital of Assyria, fell in 612 B.C. to forces composed partly of resurgent Babylonians. During the reign of Nebuchadnezzar (604–562 B.C.), the awesome figure of Biblical history, Babylon recaptured for a time the ancient glories of the age of Hammurabi, but the end came soon after with the capture of the city by the Persians in 539 B.C.

Writing. The cultural history of Mesopotamia presents a very different picture from the political story, for, despite frequent conquests and the rise and fall of states, a common civilization developed and was carried on by peoples of different origin and different languages. The decisive step in this process was the invention of writing about 3000 B.C., the essential medium for the preservation and diffusion of man's intellectual achievements. There is still much about the origin of writing that has not been fully explained. What is clear, however, is that it came about gradually as the by-product of a society that had a compelling need for order and neatness in its business transactions, whether private or communal. This need resulted in the use of distinctive and recognizable pictorial symbols to identify objects, owners, and places. These symbols in turn became the specific graphic reflections of the names for which they stood and could thus be sounded accordingly. Once the gap between picture and sound had been bridged, the sounds for specific concrete things could be employed for like-sounding terms, much in the manner of our rebus principle. Just as our "eye" can stand for "I," so Sumerian *ti,* "arrow," could be and was used for *ti,* "life." Soon means were devised to direct the reader to the particular word and the precise form intended. Before long a flexible device was at hand for the accurate recording of anything that human speech can convey. The device spread rapidly to neighboring lands, becoming more and more abstract in form, until most of the signs bore little resemblance to the original pictures. Wherever Mesopotamian influence prevailed, these signs came to be made up of wedges — hence the modern name "cuneiform" or wedge-

shaped — normally formed by impressing the angle of a square-shaped stylus onto a clay tablet. Moreover, the basic idea of writing, as distinct from the actual script itself, traveled still farther afield; this is perhaps how writing came to Egypt. The eventual introduction of the alphabet, which came about in the second millennium B.C. along the Syro-Palestinian coast, is no more, in effect, than an extreme simplification of the original idea of writing.

Literature and science. The significant contributions of Mesopotamia to world civilization did not stop with the discovery of writing. This new and revolutionary device was in itself a medium for carrying other cultural products of Mesopotamia to other lands and cultures. In literature, for example, Sumerian and Akkadian epics, such as the story of the great Sumerian hero Gilgamesh, traveled not only to Iran, Syria, and Palestine, but also to Egyptian and Hittite centers. The Greeks, too, may well have borrowed from Mesopotamia the outward form of the epic, and they certainly imported and translated Mesopotamian animal fables. In the sciences, the pioneering achievements of Babylonia in mathematics and astronomy have received due appreciation in modern times. To Babylonia we owe the beginnings of algebra, the division of the circle into 360 degrees, the division of the day into hours of 60 minutes, and the twelve signs of the zodiac.

Law and government. Among the most fruitful and far-reaching attainments of Mesopotamia were those in the fields of law and government. Law was to the Mesopotamians at once the expression and the safeguard of the cosmic order. Under it, the mortal ruler was not an autocrat, not a god as he was in Egypt, but a servant of the higher powers to whom he was accountable for his lowliest subjects. Mesopotamia produced a succession of legal codes, of which the celebrated Code of Hammurabi is by no means the oldest. Fragments of three collections of laws considerably earlier than the work of the great Babylonian legislator are now available, and the existence of still older laws may be confidently assumed. Moreover, hundreds of thousands of cuneiform legal texts have been recovered amid the archaeological remains.

The great vitality of the Mesopotamian way of life is best attested by its broad and abiding

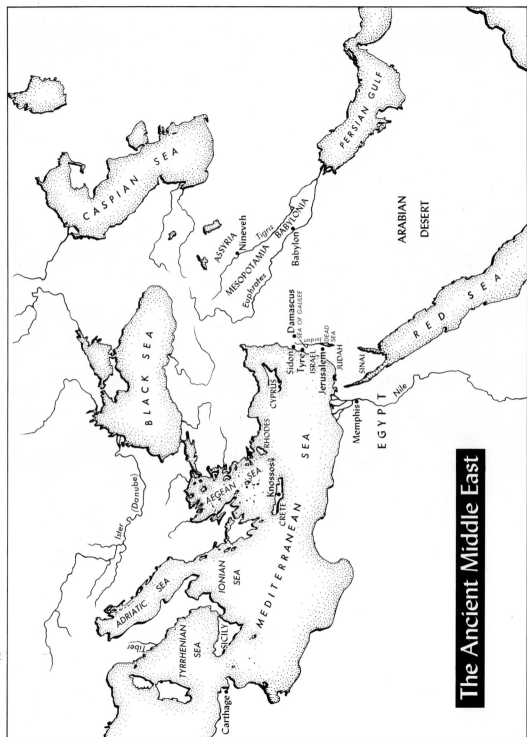

The Ancient Middle East

CASPIAN SEA

ASSYRIA
Nineveh
Tigris
MESOPOTAMIA
Euphrates
BABYLONIA
Babylon

ARABIAN
DESERT

RED SEA

BLACK SEA

Damascus
SEA OF GALILEE
Sidon
Tyre
Jordan
DEAD SEA
ISRAEL
Jerusalem
JUDAH
SINAI

Nile
Memphis
EGYPT

CYPRUS
RHODES

AEGEAN SEA

MEDITERRANEAN SEA

Knossos
CRETE

Ister (Danube)

ADRIATIC SEA

IONIAN SEA

TYRRHENIAN SEA

SICILY

Tiber

Carthage

Cuneiform writing was done by pressing a square stylus against a wet clay tablet. This example is part of a Mesopotamian code of laws which shows many resemblances to the Hebrew laws recorded in the Old Testament.

appeal. Embodied in it is a particular solution of the problems of the individual and of society which enabled Mesopotamian civilization to triumph over the obstacles of race, language, and geography and to remain for 2500 years a positive cultural factor in the face of incessant political rivalries. The whole of western Asia was profoundly affected by its contribution, not only in law but in art and literature and religion as well. Indeed, since the Bible enshrines much of Mesopotamian culture, it has, in a way, lasted to our own times.

2. Egypt: The Land of the Nile

The Nile Valley. Egyptian civilization, like that of Mesopotamia, was born in a river valley and nourished on the rich alluvial soil

washed over the land by annual floods. But, although the geographical factors which brought these two oldest civilizations to birth were in many ways similar, the peculiar character of the Nile Valley gave to Egyptian civilization a unique form. The Nile River rises in the mountains of equatorial Africa, but reaches Egypt proper only after it has passed a series of cataracts which prevented navigation. From the last cataract (or the first, as it is generally called, counting from the Egyptian side) the Nile cuts its way northward through a desert plateau for some six hundred miles until, about a hundred miles from the Mediterranean coast, it fans out into a triangle or delta of natural waterways. Until it reaches the flat and heavily irrigated delta country, the Nile Valley is a narrow trough, ten to twenty miles wide, between limestone cliffs flanked by arid desert. The teeming life of Upper Egypt was crowded into the thin ribbon of land in the valley bottom, where the soil was fertilized by annual deposits of silt brought down in the Nile floods, and where, despite a rainless climate, intensive agriculture was made possible by irrigation. Although Lower Egypt, the Delta, is open to the sea and lies close to the western horn of the Fertile Crescent, ancient Egypt was free from the threat of invasion during the greater part of its history. North Africa was not as arid in the early Egyptian period as it is today, but even the coastal area was not thickly populated, so that Lower Egypt had no really dangerous neighbors, while the whole length of Upper Egypt was protected on both sides by the desert. Egyptian civilization was thus able to develop more or less independently, though not untouched by outside influences.

Pre-dynastic Egypt. The beginning of the historical era in Egypt, as in Mesopotamia, was preceded by a period of some two or three thousand years during which village communities grew into larger states and undertook the task of harnessing the Nile and using its water to irrigate their land, a task requiring a high degree of cooperative effort. Satisfactory control of the river on which the life of Egypt depended, however, could not be achieved without a centralized authority over the whole land. This final step was taken about the year 3000 B.C., when the rulers of the so-called First Dynasty united Upper and Lower Egypt and welded the whole Nile Valley from the First Cataract to the sea into a single political unit.

The Old Kingdom. The unified system of government introduced at this time reached its fullest development in the period from about 2700 to 2200 B.C., which is generally called the Old Kingdom and which lasted from the Third through the Sixth dynasties or ruling families. Religious ideas and practical needs combined to give the pharaohs, as the rulers were called, a degree of absolute authority unparalleled in any other civilization. The pharaoh was not merely an absolute monarch; he was a living god, the son of Ra, the sun god. In practice his supernatural authority was largely delegated to officers of the royal household and to the governors of the *nomes* or provinces into which Egypt was divided, but the pharaoh was the source of all power. He was also in theory the owner of the entire land, and the surplus wealth of the state was at his disposal. The peasants, who made up the mass of the population, lived strictly regimented lives and were liable to service at any time on the

great engineering and monumental projects undertaken by the government. Agriculture formed the basis of the Egyptian economy, but there was a middle class of skilled artisans living in cities, a large part of whose labor was required to supply the needs of the pharaoh and his court. To the modern mind the ancient Egyptian state seems appallingly despotic, but it evidently suited the land and the people. It gave them both material and emotional security. And since it was a god they obeyed, a god on whose magic powers the prosperity of the land depended, they probably did not resent the lack of a freedom they had never known.

Religion. Convinced that their existence in this life and after death depended on supernatural forces, the Egyptians were an extremely religious people, if in a somewhat materialistic fashion. Much of the wealth of the state went to the support of the temples of the gods, and the priests who served them formed a rich and powerful class. Aside from the pharaohs, the Egyptians worshipped a great variety of gods, with the most important of whom the pharaoh

Seen from the air, the pyramid of Cheops demonstrates the geometrical accuracy achieved by the Egyptian engineers.

was himself associated. The most striking characteristic of Egyptian religion, however, was the obsession with immortality which was one of the most important factors in shaping the civilization of Egypt for thousands of years. It was believed that the soul would continue to live as long as the body remained intact and was supplied with the necessities of life. A great deal of public and private wealth, therefore, went to constructing stone tombs to preserve the mummified bodies of kings and nobles. These tombs were furnished with miniature replicas or painted reliefs which represented the food, servants, and furniture that might be needed to keep the soul comfortable, and which, incidentally, furnish the best source for our knowledge of Egyptian life.

The pyramids. Since all Egyptian life revolved around the person of the divine king, it was natural that special attention should be given to preserving the mortal remains of the pharaohs. The construction of tombs drained the resources of the state through the whole period of the pharaohs' rule, but none of the later tombs equaled in magnitude the immense pyramids constructed by the pharaohs of the Fourth Dynasty. Two thousand years later, the Greek historian, Herodotus, was told that it took 100,000 men twenty years to build the pyramid of Khufu (or Cheops, as Herodotus called him), and the estimate seems not improbable. This vast pile, 755 feet square at the base and 481 feet high, contains over two million blocks of stone, each weighing about two and a half tons. It is a masterpiece of engineering skill and at the same time a striking testimonial to the administrative efficiency required to feed and supply such a large army of workers.

Hieroglyphic writing. So complex an administrative system as that of the Old Kingdom would be almost inconceivable without some means of keeping written records, and it is probably no coincidence that the earliest known Egyptian writing dates from the First Dynasty. From the beginning, Egyptian writing appears in two forms, the hieroglyphic picture-writing

The colossal statue of Ramses II is part of the façade of the temple at Abu Simbel. Such statues, reflecting through their size the superhuman power of the pharaohs, were typical of Egyptian sculpture.

used for monumental inscriptions and the simplified cursive script used by scribes. As was noted in the previous section, the basic conception of Egyptian writing was similar to the Mesopotamian and was probably borrowed from it. The actual form of Egyptian script, however, was original. It was not intended to be impressed upon clay tablets, but to be carved on stone or written with pen and ink on papyrus. From at least as early as the Second Dynasty, papyrus rolls made from strips of the papyrus reed glued together were in common use as writing paper. Thanks to the dry Egyptian climate, vast numbers of these rolls have survived and are constantly being deciphered.

The Middle Kingdom. The Old Kingdom came to an end with the passing of the Sixth Dynasty about 2200 B.C. The growing independence of the provincial governors had fatally weakened the central government, and a period of confusion and civil strife followed. From this dark period Egypt was rescued by

the pharaohs of the Eleventh and Twelfth dynasties, who formed what is called the Middle Kingdom from about 2000 to 1785 B.C. Prosperity returned with strong government, and the tombs, temples, and colossal statues dating from this period are evidence of a great revival of social and cultural energy. The years of chaos, however, had left their mark. The pharaohs' power was not as absolute as it had been. They did, however, succeed in extending their sphere of influence far beyond the old frontiers of Egypt, throughout Palestine to the north and Nubia to the south. Under the pharaohs of the Twelfth Dynasty Egypt became wealthy and powerful, and wealth was no longer monopolized by the royal family as in the days of the Old Kingdom, but was more widely spread among the nobility and a very small middle class. Egypt was moving away from the identification of the entire people with the personality of the divine king which had marked the Pyramid Age. In the literature of this period, too, there was a new emphasis on humanitarian ethics and individual morality. A more spiritual conception of immortality was fostered by the cult of Osiris, the dying and rising god, who judged the souls of men in accordance with their conduct in this world.

The New Kingdom. A second period of disorder followed the brilliant age of the Twelfth Dynasty. Written records became scarcer and it is difficult to reconstruct the events of the next two centuries. Lower Egypt was eventually conquered by invaders from Syria, known as the Hyksos, who, however, apparently left little permanent impression on the culture of that conservative land. About 1580 B.C. they were driven out, and Egypt was once more united under a family of native rulers, the Eighteenth Dynasty. The New Kingdom which they established and which lasted till about 1085 B.C. was a militaristic state, more totalitarian than the Middle Kingdom. The governmental bureaucracy grew more complex, and the pharaoh as owner of all the land collected rents in the form of one-fifth of the produce. The new monarchy not only restored order at home; it also made Egypt a power in the Mediterranean world by conquering Syria and establishing an empire that stretched from the fourth cataract of the Nile to the Euphrates. Detailed accounts of military expeditions and diplomatic

Although almost too well known, the limestone head of Queen Nefertiti (c. 1360 B.C.) is too beautiful to be omitted.

correspondence with the potentates of the Middle East enable us to relate the history of this last great age of ancient Egypt to that of the neighboring countries. The ruins of magnificent temples and colossal portrait statues also remain as mementos of the power of the last great pharaohs. At its best the portrait sculpture of the New Kingdom, as for example the head of the lovely Queen Nefertiti, has seldom been surpassed. The jewelry and furniture found in the graves of this period are also distinguished by exquisite workmanship.

During the last two or three centuries of the New Kingdom, however, there were increasing evidences of both political and cultural decline in Egypt. The authority of the pharaohs was rivaled by that of the priests whose temples had acquired great wealth and vast quantities of land. The fighting spirit of the people, too, seems to have been weakened by long years of easy living. Egypt's hold on her conquered territory on the Asiatic mainland was shaken. Finally, about 1200 B.C. a mass invasion of Indo-European peoples streamed down through the Middle East, and Egypt was forced to give up her foreign possessions and retire within her ancient frontiers. Thereafter she was no more than a third-rate power, no longer in the mainstream of history.

3. *The Aegean, Asia Minor, Syria, and Palestine*

Minoan civilization.   During the third and second millenniums B.C., while Mesopotamia and Egypt were passing through the great period of their civilization, another rich and vigorous civilization arose in the island of Crete. Completely unknown until the present century, this flourishing civilization is generally called Minoan from the name of Minos, the great Cretan king of Greek legend. Here archaeologists have uncovered the remains of a people who were every bit as advanced and sophisticated as those of Mesopotamia and Egypt, yet whose culture was totally different. At Knossos, their capital, Cretan kings lived in an enormous palace, one so sprawling and complicated that it gave rise, among later generations of Greeks, to the myth of the Labyrinth. No walls surrounded it — or, for that matter, any of the palaces in any of the other towns of Minoan Crete; apparently the Minoans were secure in their island isolation and the possession of a strong navy. The palace at Knossos knew such creature comforts as baths with water piped in; an abundance of underground storerooms served to preserve the royal taxes (paid, of course, in kind) and keep the larders well stocked. Chamber walls were decorated with paintings utterly unlike those found in Egypt or Mesopotamia, paintings that are characterized above all by movement, by a love for living things, particularly sea creatures. The same qualities appear in the sculptures and reliefs that have been found. The Minoans had their own form of writing, and archaeologists have brought to light hundreds of clay tablets inscribed with their distinctive script; unfortunately we have not yet solved the secret of how to read it. This impressive civilization seems to have begun its growth about 3000 B.C. and to have reached its height between 2000 and 1500 B.C., after which it was dominated by the people to whom we must turn next.

The Mycenaeans.   A day's sail northward from Crete lies the Greek peninsula. Here arose the only civilization that was the cultural heir of the Minoans. Around 2300 or 2200 B.C. the peninsula was invaded by the first of that group of Indo-Europeans who were destined to make so great an impression on the history of the world: the Greeks. Historians, however, are careful to distinguish these Bronze Age Greeks from those who appear later in Greek history proper by referring to them as "Mycenaeans" (so called from Mycenae, the first of their towns to be excavated) or, as Homer called them, "Achaeans." They settled in towns which, unlike the Minoan, were protected by massive walls. Primitive at the outset, they raised their culture to a higher level by borrowing heavily from their more sophisticated Minoan neighbors to the south. In time the Mycenaeans grew so strong that by about 1400 B.C. they dominated the Aegean and even exercised a kind of overlordship of Minoan Crete. Tablets dating from this time have been found in the ruins of the palace at Knossos, written in the Minoan script, but in an early form of

This inlaid bronze dagger, found in Mycenae, shows the vivid portrayal of figures in motion characteristic of Minoan art.

Fragments of pottery, which are indestructible, furnish some of our best examples of very early art. The above vessel, now reconstructed, was found in Mycenae. It dates from c. 1200 B.C.

Greek rather than in the mysterious Minoan language. Since the secret of deciphering this writing, known as Linear B to distinguish it from the still undeciphered Minoan Linear A, was discovered in 1952, it has become clear that the Mycenaeans were Greek-speaking but had borrowed the art of writing from the Minoans. A great seafaring people like the Minoans before them, the Mycenaeans carried on a flourishing maritime commerce that extended westward to Italy and eastward to the shores of the Levant and to Egypt. Some time around 1200 B.C. they also launched an attack on the prosperous city of Troy in western Asia Minor, an event immortalized in Homer's epic poems.

The Hittites. Between the Aegean and the Mesopotamian cultural centers, several minor civilizations flourished on the Asiatic mainland during the second millennium B.C. Syria and Palestine were inhabited by the Canaanites, a Semitic people who shared the Sumero-Semitic culture of Mesopotamia. Farther north, in Asia Minor, the Hittites had founded a kingdom which by the middle of the second millennium stretched down into Syria and threatened Mesopotamia. These were an Indo-European people who had invaded Asia Minor some time before 2000 B.C. and formed a ruling class, dominating the indigenous population they found there.

Save for some cryptic references in the Old Testament and in Egyptian sources, the Hittites were virtually unknown to history until the early years of this century, when archaeological excavations brought to light the ruins of their cities and thousands of clay tablets, inscribed in both cuneiform and hieroglyphic scripts, from their governmental archives. Through these it has been possible to reconstruct the outlines of their history. They were a warlike people and at the height of their power, in the fourteenth century B.C., they were serious rivals to the Egyptian New Kingdom for the control of Syria. Although the Hittites had reached a fairly advanced stage of culture, it was largely derivative and dependent on borrowings from Mesopotamia.

Such borrowings were facilitated by the fact that during the second millennium the various centers of civilization we have discussed were in more or less constant commercial contact with one another. Throughout the Fertile Crescent goods traveled by caravan, while Minoan and Mycenaean ships spread them far and wide through the Mediterranean and the Aegean.

New Indo-European invasions. About 1200 B.C. the prosperous civilizations of the Middle East suffered a rude, and in some places disastrous, shock. A new wave of Indo-European invaders poured down from the lands north of Greece, through the Greek peninsula and through Asia Minor into Syria. In Asia Minor the invaders wiped out the Hittite empire and drove south to the borders of Egypt. There they were checked by the heroic resistance of the Egyptians, but thereafter, as we have already noted, Egypt remained confined within her own frontiers and ceased to be a power in Middle Eastern affairs. The movement eventually played itself out, leaving pockets of the invaders settled here and there. Among the best known of these were the Philistines who, after being turned back from their attempted invasion of Egypt, settled in Palestine and played an important role in Old Testament history. In Greece itself the invaders, here traditionally called Dorians, swept across the peninsula and the islands of the Aegean, destroying the Mycenaean towns and with them much of Mycenaean civilization. Much less civilized than their Mycenaean predecessors, these new

Greeks introduced a dark age in which for centuries Greece remained cut off from the outside world and even lost the art of writing.

The Phoenicians. The disruption caused by the invasions, and the resulting power vacuum in the Middle East, presented opportunities which were exploited by two small but very important nations: the Phoenicians and the Hebrews. The Phoenicians, as the Greeks called them, were a Semitic people, mostly of Canaanite origin, settled along what is today the Lebanese coast. Taking advantage of the economic void created by the destruction of the Mycenaean maritime trade, they took to the sea and founded a commercial empire based on Tyre, Sidon and other coastal towns. Although they had highly skilled industries, the Phoenicians were primarily merchants. They sailed to every part of the Mediterranean world and by 800 B.C. had established trading colonies, some of which grew to be powerful cities, as far west as Carthage and Cadiz. Their culture was borrowed largely from the Egyptians and Mesopotamians, but their contribution as disseminators of civilization throughout the Mediterranean was extremely important. It was through them that the alphabet was introduced into Europe and spread throughout the Middle East, replacing the cumbersome cuneiform and hieroglyphic scripts. They did not themselves invent the idea. Earlier experimental alphabets can be dated back several centuries. But the Phoenician alphabet, using only twenty-two signs, each representing a consonantal sound, was so simple and easily learned that it was widely adopted. The Greeks founded their own alphabet upon it and, directly or indirectly, it has fathered most of the alphabets of Western civilization.

The Hebrews. Of still greater importance for their influence on Western civilization were the Hebrews, who lived to the south of the Phoenicians in Palestine. Their history is told in the Old Testament and is therefore more familiar than that of any other ancient people. The earlier part of their story is traditional and largely unverifiable, but from about the end of the second millennium it becomes more clearly historical and can be checked and supplemented from other sources. The Hebrews were basically a Semitic people, originally nomadic, who had emigrated from Mesopotamia about the twentieth century B.C. Later some of the Hebrews migrated to Egypt, where they were oppressed by the pharaohs until they were rescued from captivity by Moses, probably in the thirteenth century B.C. In Palestine the Hebrew tribes fought among themselves and with their warlike neighbors, especially the Philistines, until they were united under Saul and his successor, King David (c. 1010–970 B.C.), who conquered the Philistines and other surrounding peoples and ruled a strong kingdom from his capital at Jerusalem. Under David's son, Solomon (c. 970–930 B.C.), the Hebrew state reached the peak of its wealth and power, but it was soon weakened by civil strife and became divided into two kingdoms. During the eighth century the northern kingdom, Israel, was conquered by the Assyrians and many of its inhabitants were forced to emigrate, thus disappearing from the biblical story. A second disaster occurred in 586 B.C. when the Babylonian king Nebuchadnezzar captured Jerusalem, the capital of the southern kingdom of Judah, and took the people into captivity in Babylon, where they remained for fifty years until they were freed by the Persian king Cyrus and permitted to return to Palestine.

Hebrew religion. It is not, however, the story of the wanderings, the triumphs and tribulations of the Hebrew people that makes the Old Testament the most significant collection of writings produced by the ancient world. Its contents include, beside the historical books, the moral and religious teaching of the prophets, the glorious collection of hymns and prayers known as the Psalms, some of the finest poetry and story in world literature, and the accumulated wisdom of a thoughtful and highly ethical people. The unique contribution of Hebrew thought was an exclusive monotheism, a profound faith in the existence of one all-powerful and benevolent God, Yahweh, or Jehovah as he is called in the English translation, who watched over the fortunes of his chosen people but demanded of them, on pain of severe punishment, exclusive devotion and a high standard of moral and ethical conduct. Nowhere else in the ancient world was religion so closely related to morality and to an ethical system based on principles of justice and mercy. Founded upon the Ten Commandments, which Moses is said to have received from Yahweh

Reliefs, showing soldiers, courtiers, and conquered peoples bearing tribute to the Persian king, decorate the stairway of the palace of Darius at Persepolis.

on Mount Sinai during the exodus from Egypt, and upon the laws and ceremonial regulations laid down in the first books of the Old Testament, the Hebrew religion was rigid and formal in its earliest manifestations; but it developed in breadth and depth through centuries of adversity, as generations of prophets contemplated the problems of man's relation to God and to his fellow men and spoke in tones of inspired authority to the conscience of the Hebrew people. Out of the religious and moral thought of this small and frequently afflicted people eventually grew both Christianity and Mohammedanism, the two greatest monotheistic religions of the modern world.

Persian Empire. Before concluding this survey of the ancient Middle East, we have still to mention the last and greatest in extent of the Asiatic states in the period that preceded the conquests of Alexander the Great. In the sixth century B.C. the Persians, an Indo-European people from the land to the east of Mesopotamia (modern Iran), began to expand their domain and, under the leadership of their great king Cyrus, drove westward to the Mediterranean and eastward to the borders of India. After the death of Cyrus in 529 B.C., his son Cambyses added Egypt to his domains, thus rounding out an empire that included the whole Middle East. Though the Greeks scornfully referred to them as the "barbarians," the Persians were a civilized and tolerant people with a genius for government. So vast an empire under an absolute monarchy could not permit the independence of such restless neighbors as the Greeks, and the next king, Darius the Great (521–485 B.C.), determined to conquer them.

"Ours is a constitution which does not imitate those of our neighbors, but is rather a pattern to others. Because power rests with the majority and not with the few, it is called a democracy." • Pericles of Athens (490–429 B.C.)

2

Ancient Greece   (c. 1000–338 B.C.)

GREAT AS IS our debt to the early civilizations of Egypt, Mesopotamia, and the eastern shores of the Mediterranean, these civilizations produced forms of culture, of political and social organization, of religion and ethics, that are largely foreign to us. This, of course, was not true of the Hebrew people, whose history has been made familiar to us through the Old Testament and many of whose religious and ethical ideas were absorbed into Christianity. But with that single exception, no ancient people seems closely akin to us until we come to that group of tribes who by the year 1000 B.C. had settled Greece, the islands of the Aegean, and the coastline of Asia Minor, and who called themselves Hellenes. Even their earliest surviving literature, dating probably from the eighth century B.C., speaks directly to us. And by the fifth century there was in the Greek city-states a civilization in which we can feel ourselves at home. The Greeks are more to us than dim figures reflected in the poetic imagery of an epic story. Their human forms are preserved in imperishable marble, and their ways of thinking in equally imperishable poetry and prose. Here we find poetry, drama, art, philosophy, scientific speculation, and political institutions that we can comprehend because they are the forerunners of our own. We are bound to these Greeks by a cultural tradition that has never been broken. When we trace any branch of our secular culture back to its roots, these roots will be found in the rocky soil of Hellas.

1. The Formation of Greece (c. 1200–500 B.C.)

The story of the successive Indo-European invasions of Greece has been told briefly in the preceding chapter. Historic Greece was founded by the second wave of invaders, who entered the peninsula about 1200 B.C., wiped out or subjugated their Mycaenean predecessors, and introduced a dark age in Greek history which lasted for several centuries. Formed by the fusion of successive groups of invaders with the indigenous peoples of the peninsula, the historical Greeks were at no time a united or homogeneous nation, although when Greek met Greek they recognized in one another certain common cultural traits which differentiated them from the "barbarians," as they called the non-Greeks of the Asiatic mainland. The topography of the lands they settled was partly responsible for this lack of unity. The Greek peninsula is mountainous, with a deeply indented coastline, and beyond it are the innumerable islands of the Aegean archipelago. Divided from its neighbors by mountain ridges, or isolated on tiny islands, each community

24

became a separate political unit. For centuries these little communities were largely agricultural, but the cultivators, instead of living on their farm plots, clustered their homes about strong points or fortresses and so created small cities which eventually grew into city-states, thus forming political institutions markedly different from those in the kingdoms of the East.

The Homeric Age. Our first literary evidence regarding the life of the early Greeks comes from the two great epic poems ascribed to Homer, the *Iliad* and the *Odyssey,* composed probably in the eighth century B.C. Scholars have long debated whether these epics were the work of one poet or an amalgam of poems composed over many centuries. According to the most recent theory, many poems composed by bards to be sung at banquets and festive

occasions were passed on orally by one generation of bards to the next, until finally one poetic genius, drawing upon the whole oral tradition as so much raw material, created the two epics more or less in the form in which we have them now. The length and carefully worked out structure of the poems suggest that they were written down when composed, and by the eighth century the Greeks had adapted the Phoenician alphabet to their use, adding the necessary vowel sounds and so creating the form of writing they were to use thereafter. In any case, the *Iliad,* the story of the siege of Troy by Agamemnon, king of Mycenae, and the Achaean princes, refers to events which probably took place some three hundred years before the date of the poems. Both the *Iliad* and the *Odyssey,* which tells of the wanderings

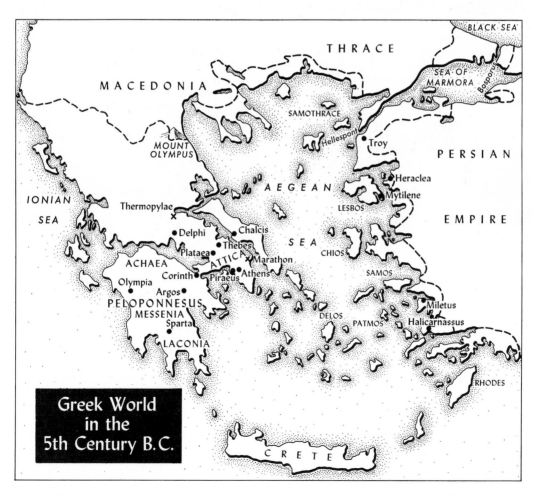

Greek World
in the
5th Century B.C.

of Odysseus (Ulysses), thus refer to an earlier Mycenaean society, but they also tell us much about conditions existing in the poet's own time. The framework of the society Homer depicts is the tribe, and within the tribe the patriarchal family. It was a decidedly aristocratic society. The king or *basileus* was the most powerful chieftain and claimed descent from a god — usually Zeus, "father of gods and heroes." He was the commander in war, the chief judge, and the high priest who performed sacrifices to appease the gods. But he was not an absolute ruler. Surrounding him were lesser kings, tribal chiefs and heads of great families, whom he consulted on affairs of state and especially on military matters, for these small kingdoms were often at war with one another. Those of the people who had a tribal and a family status also had a voice in decisions affecting the whole community, for on such occasions the king would call an assembly and the nobles would debate the problem before the people. No vote was taken and rarely did the commoners speak, but they could express their opinions by ominous silence or shouts of acclamation.

Economic growth.   The economic as well as the political life of Homeric Greece was simple and primitive. Each family produced the necessities of life on its own estate, and even the nobles took part in working the fields. There was little industry or commerce, since commerce was still largely in the hands of the Phoenicians. From about the end of the ninth century, however, an economic development began, slowly at first, which in the next three hundred years created the flourishing prosperity of Greece's Golden Age. More land was brought under cultivation and the wealthier families enlarged their holdings. No significant improvements were made in farming methods, but there was more extensive cultivation of vineyards and olive groves. The Greeks were also turning more and more to the sea, first as pirates and later as traders, thus regaining from Phoenicia the hold they had had on maritime commerce in the Mycenaean age. Active commerce began earlier and progressed more rapidly in the Greek cities of Asia Minor than on the Greek mainland. These cities were advantageously situated for trade and had the additional advantage of closer contact with the economically advanced countries of the Middle East. Taking the products of these eastern countries as models, they also began to develop their industries. Wool from the flocks which grazed the plateaus provided material for textiles; clay offered an opportunity for the further development of ceramics; wood and leather lent themselves to the growing skill of craftsmen. As early as the eighth century coined money was introduced which greatly facilitated exchange and gave an added impetus to commerce.

The era of colonization.   Although commerce and industry became increasingly important features of Greek life from the eighth century on, the great majority of Greeks still derived their living from the land. The growth of population, the relatively poor soil, and the encroachments of great estates seriously threatened the livelihood of the small holders who made up the greater part of this majority. The large landholders had enough income to invest in improvements and in lucrative vineyards and olive groves, but the peasants were often without means to tide them over a bad season. When disaster ruined his crops, or when some improvement was necessary, the small holder might borrow from the owner of a large estate, but as security he had to pledge not only his land but himself and his family. Failure to repay the loan meant slavery. Peasant holdings became smaller, the number of those in bondage increased, and the ranks of the landless were enlarged. It was, in large part, to alleviate these conditions and to diminish the danger of revolt that colonies were founded. From the eighth century to about the end of the sixth, groups of colonizers went forth from the older communities, from those of Asia Minor first and later from Greece, to form new and independent city-states along the shores of Thrace and the Black Sea and westward to southern Italy and Sicily. In the history of Greece these colonies played no small part: they were involved in political struggles, they took part in the cultural achievements of Greece, and they contributed mightily to the development of trade and industry, at first as the recipients of Greek manufactured goods for which they offered food and raw materials. Later some of them developed their own industries, others became centers of exchange. Some, indeed, were founded as trading posts. Foremost in colonization was the Ionian city, Miletus, whence bands of settlers went to the Black Sea region. Chalcis and Eretria rivaled each other in establishing colonies in Thrace. Corinth looked farther westward; her most famous daughter city was Syracuse in Sicily.

Growth of city-states. The political structure of the Greek communities began to assume its distinctive form during the seventh and sixth centuries. Ancient Greece was never a unified country, but was made up of a number of small, independent states, each of which was composed of a city and its surrounding territory. The city-state or *polis* was the framework within which the political, religious, and cultural life of the Greek people was formed, as well as the sole focal point of their patriotism and loyalty. Even the Greek colonies, once founded, became city-states almost entirely independent of the mother city. To this unique form of state the modern world owes many of its traditions of government, citizenship, and justice. Most city-states were small enough so that the citizens from the surrounding countryside could easily gather in the city. Here was the market place, and here the shops of the craftsmen, the temples, and the seat of government. With the growth of great estates, the wealthy landowners gained an increasing control of the government of the city-states. The kings of the Homeric age disappeared or were left with only their religious functions. The extent to which power was concentrated in the hands of a few varied from city to city, but, in general, the right to vote was confined to citizens with a certain amount of landed property, and the right to hold office was limited to members of a few families or at most to the wealthiest citizens. Monarchy was thus followed by aristocracy or by oligarchy, i.e., the rule of a few.

Tyranny. In many cities of Greece, especially those near the coast, the oligarchies were threatened by the growing demand of the rest of the citizens for a voice in the government. The small landholders resented the rule of their creditors; the citizens whose wealth, derived from commerce and industry, was in money rather than in land demanded the revision of property qualifications. Leaders arose who offered to redress these grievances in re-

Our best examples of Greek painting come from pieces of pottery like this amphora, which, since it portrays men picking olives, was probably designed to store olive oil.

turn for popular support in deposing ruling families. Having seized power, the popular leader ruled illegally as a dictator or "tyrant." Thus, oligarchy was in many instances succeeded by tyranny, which, in turn, paved the way for democracy; for to maintain power the tyrants had to make concessions to the people.

Two city-states played such an important role in Greek history that they deserve special attention. They are interesting, moreover, as representing two markedly different types of government and two even more strongly contrasted types of culture. Sparta became, by the seventh century B.C., and remained to the end, a conservative military state ruled by an aristocracy devoted to "Spartan" discipline, and contemptuous of intellectual or aesthetic culture. Athens, on the other hand, by the end of the sixth century had passed through every phase of political change from monarchy to democracy. Her citizens were incurable individualists, and in war as in peace they never lost their creative enthusiasm for art, literature, and philosophical speculation. The glory that was Greece was to a very large extent the glory that was Athens.

military

Intellectual

Sparta. From its earliest appearance in history, Sparta was a powerful military state which met the problem of scarcity of land by conquering its neighbors rather than by overseas colonization. By the year 800 B.C., the Spartans had conquered Laconia and Messenia and held the entire southern part of Greece. The lands around Sparta itself were divided up and assigned to individual Spartans, while the conquered people on these lands were impressed as state slaves — helots, as the Spartans called them — who were forced to cultivate the land for its Spartan owners. The more distant areas were given control of their own local affairs, but in all other matters were strictly subject to Sparta. Only the Spartans had any voice in the government of the state. Nominally at the head of the government were two kings, but the real power was in the hands of five magistrates elected for a year and a Council of Elders elected for life from among Spartans over sixty years old. All Spartans might vote for the magistrates and the members of the Council and sit in the Assembly to which major decisions were referred, but only to be accepted or rejected without discussion. Such a government guaranteed stability, while to assure the continuous military power on which their domination of the conquered lands depended, the Spartans developed a social organization that was in many respects unique. The state assigned to each Spartan a section of land and a number of helots. Until he was thirty years old he lived in barracks; until he was sixty he took his meals with his fellow warriors in the common mess to which he contributed a fixed amount from the produce of his land. The Spartan's education, designed to make him a hardy and disciplined soldier and an efficient member of a military aristocracy, was begun at the age of seven, when he was taken from his home to join a troop of youngsters of his own age. His training was almost entirely physical, combined with rigid discipline. It bred in the Spartans the essential military virtues, but it left them conservative, unimaginative, narrow-minded, and suspicious of all outsiders.

Athens. While Sparta was hardening into conservatism, Athens was passing through a period of rapid change and was soon to emerge as Sparta's chief political rival in Greece. Un-

like most Greek cities, the evolution of her political institutions had been accomplished with little bloodshed. From the middle of the seventh century the power of her king had been severely curtailed. Indeed, kingship became an elective office with purely formal duties, held for only a year. The customary law of the land was committed to writing. To Solon, elected chief magistrate in 594–593 B.C., is attributed a series of fundamental reforms including the division of the population into classes based on property, each with its political privileges and obligations, the grant of citizenship to the poorest classes, and the prohibition of slavery for indebtedness. Under the tyrant Pisistratus, land was taken from the old noble families and given to the poor, and tenant farmers were given ownership of their land. Then at the end of the sixth century came Cleisthenes, whose reforms laid the firm foundation of Athenian democracy and determined the form which the political institutions of Athens retained during the period of her greatest power.

Athenian democracy. As a means of checking factional feuds and breaking the power of the old aristocratic families, Cleisthenes redivided the population into territorial groups which cut across the old units. Ten new tribes were created with equal representation in a Council of Five Hundred. Membership in the Council was open to all citizens over thirty years of age. To insure its being a fair sample of the citizen body, the requisite number were chosen by lot, and men who had held the office twice were ineligible. The Council did not make the final decision in legislation, but it prepared the bills to be brought before the Assembly, issued decrees to facilitate the execution of decisions made by the Assembly, and negotiated with the representatives of foreign powers. The Council also collaborated with the magistrates in the work of administration. Cleisthenes allowed the old magistracies to remain, but a large part of their political power passed to a new board of ten *strategoi* (generals) who were elected annually. Originally created to command the army, the *strategoi* soon became the chief executive officers of the state and could be re-elected year after year. Pericles, for example, held the office for many years.

The Assembly. All Athenian citizens over eighteen years old were members of the Assembly, although in practice only a fraction of the citizen body attended its meetings. Most Athenian citizens were farmers, and, while the seasonal nature of their work left some free to engage in politics, others were too busy or too far away. In the Assembly any member might express his opinion of the proposals submitted to it by the Council or move an amendment, although usually the party leaders monopolized the discussion. The Assembly was the supreme legislative body and its jurisdiction was wide: it passed on the proposals of the Council, and occasionally its members suggested measures; it had the final word in the disbursement of state funds; it elected some magistrates and subjected all of them to examination; and it formed a court to judge cases involving important crimes against the state. To it also belonged the power of ostracism, an institution which gave the assembled citizens an opportunity to vote for the exile of a leader suspected of tyrannical designs. By a later extension it was applied to men whose policies they wished to reject. The victim of ostracism had to go into honorable exile for ten years.

Justice. The administration of justice was the province of the *Heliaea,* a large jury numbering about six thousand in the fifth century. The members were chosen by lot, six hundred from each tribe, and divided into tribunals. There were no state prosecutors and no lawyers in Athens, nor were there presiding judges to interpret the law. The injured party brought suit and the defendant had to present his own defense. The decision rested with the *heliasts,* who voted by secret ballot for condemnation or acquittal. Although a trial had to be completed in a day, the tribunals were overwhelmed with work and trials might be delayed for months.

Exclusiveness. Broad as the base of Athenian democracy seems to have been, it was actually restricted to a part of the population of the state, to those whose ancestors had been Athenian citizens. Although in the sixth century some aliens long resident in the city and others who were only partly Athenian were enfranchised, citizenship became increasingly exclusive. In the middle of the fifth century, when Athens was at the peak of her power and leader of a federal empire, citizenship was limited to those both of whose parents were citizens. This jealous guarding of the privileges of citizenship, which was characteristic of other Greek states as well as Athens, was one of the major weaknesses of the city-state system. It prevented Athens from strengthening her citizen body by taking in the numerous and prosperous *metics,* as the resident aliens were called, who carried on a large part of Athenian commerce and industry. And it prevented any city-state from expanding except by conquest and by treating the conquered peoples as subjects rather than citizens. In short, Greek democracy was for citizens only. It was founded on no doctrine of the equality of all men, and it was not incompatible with the oppression of subject peoples or with the institution of slavery.

Archaic culture. The centuries in which the classic civilization of Greece was taking shape and which historians call the Archaic Period (c. 800–500 B.C.) were filled with poetry, for it was in poetry rather than prose that the early Greeks found the medium that best suited them for the expression of thought and emotion. Unfortunately, only fragments of this fund of poetic writing remain, enough to stimulate without satisfying our curiosity. That there was a great deal of lyric poetry of a very high order is evident, but the scattered fragments that have survived are only enough to tell us something of what we have lost through the destruction of the works of Sappho of Lesbos and others whose names and bits of whose poetry have come down to us. There were epic poets, too, though none who rank with Homer. Fortunately we have two long poems by Hesiod, whom the Greeks themselves regarded as the greatest epic poet after Homer. Though epic in form, they are very different in spirit from Homer's heroic tales. The *Works and Days* is a sober didactic essay in verse on all sorts of subjects, from an account of the fall of man, moral admonitions, and praise of honest labor, to practical advice to farmers for conducting their year's work. In the *Theogony,* Hesiod tells at length the story of the loves and the conflicts of the Olympian gods. Later Greek writers quoted him almost as frequently as they did Homer, but for his instructive content rather than for his poetic quality. Hesiod was trying to explain the universe and establish

Painting of a youth playing a lyre, from a red-figured amphora of the early fifth century B.C.

moral values in terms of myth; but by the sixth century there were a number of speculative philosophers who were not satisfied with mythology and who were beginning to seek a reasoned and scientific explanation of the universe. The theories they evolved, preserved for the most part in fragmentary form or through the comments of later writers, may not have supplied any final answers, but their insatiable curiosity prepared the way for the splendid philosophical and scientific activity of the Greek mind in later centuries.

2. *The Persian and Peloponnesian Wars*

Persian threat. Until the opening of the fifth century, the Greek city-states were left free to develop their political institutions, and, unhappily, to war incessantly among themselves without serious interference from any foreign power. The rise of the great Persian Empire in the sixth century, however, presented an in-

creasingly grave threat to Greek independence.[1] Before the end of the century the Persians had subjugated the Ionian Greek cities on the coast of Asia Minor. When these rebelled in 499 B.C. and Athens sent them aid, inadequate but still enough to irritate the Persian king, Greece itself fell under the Persian threat. The revolt of the Ionian cities was crushed, but it had made the Persian king, Darius, aware of the dangerous spirit of independence among his Greek subjects, allied as they were by many cultural ties with the free Greek cities beyond his frontiers. To prevent further rebellion or challenge to his authority, Darius determined to conquer the independent cities of the Aegean islands and the Greek mainland. The stage was thus set for a life and death struggle between the small Greek city-states and the great "barbarian" empire of the Persians.

Persian War. The Persian War was an important event in the history of Western civilization, for, had the Persians been successful, the brilliant culture of Greece might have been crushed just as its Golden Age was dawning. Persia and Greece represented two distinct types of culture, and the threat to Greek culture was all the greater because the Persian attack was directed primarily against Athens, the vital center of Greek civilization in the fifth century. In 490 B.C. the Persian fleet landed a large army on the plain of Marathon, about twenty-four miles across the hills from Athens. Although aid from Sparta was on the way, the Athenian generals decided not to wait, but to risk everything on a battle before the Persian army and navy could lay siege to their city. The Athenian army was no more than half the size of the Persian host, but the concentrated fury of its attack brought a decisive victory. The battle of Marathon not only ended the Persian threat for the time but also gave the Athenians, and indeed all the Greeks, a new confidence in their ability to resist. A revolt in Egypt prevented the Persians from renewing the attack for several years. Darius, the Great King, died and it was not till 480 B.C. that his son Xerxes was prepared to invade Greece once more, this time with a much larger army. To meet the new threat Athens built an effective navy and joined with other Greek cities in a

[1] See above, page 23.

defensive league under Spartan leadership. This time the Persian army came by land from Asia Minor around the north shore of the Aegean and so down into Greece, with a large Persian fleet off shore keeping in touch with it on the way. A small Spartan force which attempted to stop the Persian host in the narrow pass at Thermopylae was wiped out, fighting to the last man, and the Persians marched on to take Athens and to devastate the surrounding countryside of Attica. The Athenian navy, however, won a great victory over the Persian fleet in the straits of Salamis and forced it to withdraw to Asia Minor. A second Persian invasion was repulsed the following year by the combined Greek armies at Plataea and by a second naval victory at Mycale.

Athenian Empire. After the war with Persia, Athens rose to a position of leadership among the Greek cities. She had now become one of the most prosperous cities in Greece. Her port, Piraeus, connected by long, fortified walls with the city itself, was a thriving commercial center; the work of her craftsmen was famous; and by the end of the sixth century she had outstripped Corinth, her chief economic rival in Greece, in industry and trade. During the Archaic Period the Greek cities in Asia Minor had been economically more advanced than those in Greece proper; but their prosperity had been damaged by the Persian domination, and in the fifth century Greek trade with the western Mediterranean was growing. The result was to shift commercial leadership from Asia Minor to the cities of the Greek mainland. The fleet which the Athenians had built to meet the Persian invasion put them in a position to take advantage of this shift. To wrest from Xerxes those Greek cities still under his domination, to prevent Persia from resuming power in the Aegean, and to insure mutual defense, the cities of Asia Minor and the islands agreed, in 478 B.C., to form a maritime confederacy with Athens at its head. Headquarters were established at Delos, an island centrally located in the middle of the Aegean, and a constitution was formed giving each member representation on the Council and demanding from each ships or money in proportion to its wealth. Athens, strongest and wealthiest of the cities, dominated the confederacy and gradually transformed it into an empire. In 454 the treasury of the confederacy was moved from Delos to Athens and its contents thereafter were handled by the Athenian government. The allies who resented Athenian domination and attempted to withdraw from the confederacy were brought back by force. Athens interfered in the internal affairs of these cities, favoring the democratic parties and encouraging the election of magistrates who would be subservient to her will.

Peloponnesian War. During the half-century following the Persian War, Athens was not only the most powerful city but also the intellectual and artistic center of Greece. Under the brilliant administration of the great Pericles, who was elected *strategos* year after year from 461 to 430 B.C., Athenian culture reached the peak of its development. But the very success of Athens and the arrogance it bred in her citizens made her powerful enemies. Her subject cities were restless; Corinth resented her intrusion into the trade between Greece and the western Mediterranean; and Sparta, at the head of a league of Peloponnesian cities which included Corinth, watched the growth of the Athenian Empire with sullen jealousy. Sooner or later a clash between Athens and Sparta and their respective allies seemed almost bound to occur, if only because of the mutual antipathy of two powerful, arrogant, and fundamentally different peoples. The great Peloponnesian War which grew out of that mounting antagonism lasted from 431 to 404 B.C., and involved nearly all the Greek states on one side or the other. It was a disaster from which Greece never fully recovered. The story of the war, told in vivid detail by the Athenian historian Thucydides, is too long and complex to retell fully here. For over a dozen years Athenian sea power balanced Sparta's superiority on land. The balance was upset when an Athenian expedition sent to conquer Syracuse in Sicily in 415 was totally destroyed. Nevertheless, Athens was able to maintain the struggle for another decade, until a Spartan navy, built with Persian aid, decisively defeated the Athenian fleet. The grim war, which had lasted twenty-seven years, finally came to an end with the surrender of Athens in 404. The conditions of peace imposed by Sparta included the break-up of the Athenian Empire, the destruction of the long walls between Athens and

Piraeus, the surrender of the Athenian fleet, and the establishment of an oligarchy in Athens in the hands of thirty men approved by Sparta.

Political weakness of Greece. But Greece was not thereafter at peace. Sparta and Persia were engaged for fourteen years in conflict over the Ionian cities which Persia expected to receive in return for the assistance she had given Sparta during the Peloponnesian War. While Sparta was thus occupied, Athens, Thebes, Corinth, and Argos formed an alliance (395 B.C.) to resist her domination in Greece. Athens, meanwhile, had quickly restored her democracy and had re-established some of her alliances. An effort was made in 386 to assure peace: the Ionian cities were ceded to Persia, and the autonomy of all Greek city-states was proclaimed. But alliances and counter-alliances were formed none the less, and their conflicts told eloquently of the inability of the Greek cities to unite as a nation. This lack of unity was not a serious danger so long as there was no threat to Greek independence from a strong foreign power. In the second half of the fourth century such a threat did arise in the growing military strength of the kingdom of Macedonia, and this threat the Greek states failed to meet as they had met the Persian menace. The story of the Macedonian conquest, however, must be left to the next chapter.

3. *Greek Economy in the Fifth and Fourth Centuries, B.C.*

The vigorous civilization of Greece in the fifth and fourth centuries was based upon a prosperous economy. Even the devastation caused by the Peloponnesian War brought no more than a temporary depression. Athens and the other states recovered rapidly, and in the following century the generally healthy state of Greek economic life was in marked contrast to the political weakness which left the Greek city-states helpless before the Macedonian conqueror.

Agriculture. Agriculture furnished a broad base for Greek prosperity, although it made few large fortunes. In the democratic states in particular, where legislation discouraged the accumulation of large estates, farms were usually small and were owned and worked by citizens.

Resident aliens, who controlled some of the largest commercial enterprises, were forbidden to buy land, and in general there seems to have been little tendency to invest commercial capital in large landed estates. The soil of Greece is poor, but it lends itself to the production of olive oil and wine, so that the small farmers could produce crops for which there was a profitable commercial market.

Industry. Industry, too, furnished a living for a large number of workers, rather than large fortunes for a few capitalists. Although industrial enterprises multiplied during the fifth and fourth centuries, industry never attained large-scale organization. The typical shop was composed of a master craftsman, a few slaves and hired assistants, and perhaps an apprentice. The outstanding exception was mining; for mines belonged to the state. Citizens, and occasionally *metics,* were granted concessions to extract the metal in return for rent and royalties. Concessionnaires hired gangs of slaves to work the mines, and the lot of these slaves was hard indeed, for the heavy manual labor was not lightened by machinery. Some division of labor was effected during the fifth and fourth centuries, especially in those industries making goods for export. In the manufacture of ceramics the tasks of firing, shaping, and decorating were early distinguished. These however, were exceptional cases. In most industries, the workers manufactured their products from beginning to end, as, indeed, was true of most industries until the introduction of power-driven machinery in modern times.

Commerce. With the rise of urban centers devoted to commerce and industry, the demand for foodstuffs increased. It has been estimated that by the fourth century Athens had to import seventy-five per cent of the grain she consumed. Grain and livestock came to Athens from Thrace and the Black Sea region. Corinth imported these necessities from the West, and when Athens attempted to tap this source Corinth took steps to exclude her. The problem of the food supply was of such importance that states passed laws to limit re-exportation of grain brought to the ports and to insure distribution at low prices, especially in times of distress. In addition to grain, Athens imported fish, salted meats, fruit, and wine. Raw materials were another large item in Athenian imports: metals, wood and pitch, wool and flax were needed by her craftsmen. From the East came luxury goods. Slaves, too, were brought from the East as well as from Thrace and the Black Sea region. In exchange Athens exported olive oil, silver, marble, lead, manufactured products, and works of art. Trade, except in grain, was free. The state levied only a small export and import tax. By far the greater part of commerce was carried on by sea, since roads were generally poor and the cost of inland transportation was well-nigh prohibitive.

Investment and banking. One of the most important developments in Greek economy was the use of commercial loans. A merchant might borrow funds to purchase a cargo; but because the risks were great, interest rates were very high. Not all investments, however, were in trading ventures. Men with surplus funds could invest in industrial enterprises, or buy houses in Athens and lease them, or purchase slaves for hire. By the end of the fifth century another field for investment was opened to citizens and *metics* alike — banking. The banks of the fourth century B.C. did not employ credit instruments to the extent that modern banks do, but they effected the exchange of money without the actual transfer of coin. They also received deposits and acted as agents in investing other people's money.

Slaves. During these centuries slaves played a more important part in the economic and social life of Greece than hitherto. In Athens, the most economically advanced city of Greece at this time, it is possible that more than half of the population were slaves. Since many of the slaves were originally prisoners of war, while others had been captured and sold by pirates, and still more had been imported by slave-traders from among the less civilized peoples on the periphery of the Mediterranean world, their abilities and hence the nature of their employment varied widely. The most unfortunate were the gangs of slaves who worked in the state-owned mines and quarries, but this kind of gang labor was exceptional. The great majority were employed as household servants or as workers in commerce or industry. As craftsmen, clerks, or even business managers, they worked side by side with free men, and under much the same conditions. Those who came from the more economically advanced

Pericles, the great statesman of the Athenian Golden Age, a period that has often been called "The Age of Pericles."

centers of the Middle East might, indeed, be more highly trained and more generally competent than their masters and so might make themselves indispensable. Such slaves might eventually secure their freedom.

4. The Civilization of the Golden Age

The Golden Age. The Golden Age of Greek culture has frequently been identified with the period in the middle of the fifth century when Pericles led the Athenian democracy; but in a broader sense it covered the greater part of the fifth and fourth centuries, beginning before the Persian War and outlasting the Macedonian conquest. In these years Athens and the other Greek cities produced the finest works of classical art, art which, characterized above all by simplicity, clarity, and proportion, has remained for all time the norm of classical beauty. The literature of the Golden Age, too, demonstrates the classic virtues, dealing simply and clearly, yet with high seriousness, with human problems that have eternal validity. And through the whole period the Greek mind was striving through philosophical and scientific speculation to understand man and nature in the light of pure, unaided human reason.

Religion. In mythology Greek art of the classical period found inexhaustible inspiration. Temples were built to house the gods, hymns were composed in their praise, festivals were held in their honor. The gods of the Greeks were anthropomorphic. Though superhuman in power and beauty, they were not above such human motivations as jealousy and favoritism. Their characters and functions overlapped to some extent, but the major attributes of the more important deities were distinguished. Thus, Zeus was the king of the gods, mighty in rage and firm in justice; Athena, sprung from the head of Zeus, goddess of wisdom; Aphrodite, born of the sea foam, goddess of love; Apollo, especially dear to the Greeks, was the god of light and healing, the patron of music and the arts. The worship of these gods in-

This sixth-century B.C. *statue of a young woman, from the Athenian Acropolis, wears the "archaic smile" characteristic of pre-Golden Age sculpture.*

volved no dogma, no systematized theology. Even the ritual attending their worship was not the special office of a priestly caste; in some city-states priests were elected like other magistrates. Each city claimed a god or goddess as patron, and the worship of this deity was fraught with keen patriotism. The adventures of the gods formed a rich mythology; their spiritual attributes were identified with moral laws; but as an outlet for religious feeling the mystery cults were more satisfactory. The worship of Dionysus, "the beautiful, weeping creature, vexed by the wind, suffering, torn to pieces, and rejuvenescent again at last," and the Eleusinian mysteries dedicated to Demeter and Kore were of great antiquity. Both cults sprang from a deep awareness of the mystery of the seasons, the death of the earth in winter, its rebirth in spring. To the initiate both promised personal immortality and purification from sin.

Architecture. Nowhere was the Greek sense of form more clearly displayed than in architecture, and, of all public buildings, it was the temples upon which the Greeks concentrated to the greatest effect their artistic skill and their feeling for restrained beauty. Religion and civic patriotism combined to make the temple the symbol of all that the Greeks cherished most highly. Greek architecture was a unique achievement. No other ancient civilization produced buildings of such perfect harmony and proportion, and the prevalence of modified versions of the Greek style in our own public buildings, notably in Washington, attests its survival value after more than two thousand years. Greek temples were rectangular structures containing a main room, or *cella,* and perhaps an additional small room, a porch in the front and sometimes one in the back, a roof sloping slightly from the center and a row of columns in front. Columns might also be built along both sides, and some temples had a double row at one or both ends. The frieze and pediments of the temple were decorated by groups of figures carved in relief, usually representing scenes from mythology. Wars and the ravages of time have destroyed most of the temples and public buildings built by the Greeks. Those which still stand are in ruins. But from these ruins we can reconstruct the harmonious lines and excellent proportions of the original edifices; from the fragments of sculpture that remain we can glimpse the strength and beauty of the figures that adorned the temples. In contrast to their temples and public buildings the private homes of the Greeks were insignificant. Simply designed, these dwellings lined narrow, crooked streets. Occasionally a wealthy citizen would build a more imposing house in the country, or even in the city, but these were relatively scarce.

The Acropolis. The most famous examples of Greek architecture are the buildings on the Acropolis in Athens. The Persians had demolished the original temples and the work of reconstruction was begun under Pericles. Here on a hill were built the Parthenon, magnificent tribute to Athena; the exquisite Ionic temple of Athena Nike; the Erechtheum with its Porch of the Maidens; the Propylaea, a gateway cut into the wall at the entrance to the Acropolis. The Parthenon, designed by the architect Ictinus, was the supreme achievement of Greek architecture. It had seventeen columns along its sides and eight in front and behind. On the west pediment was depicted the struggle of Athena and Poseidon for control of Athens; on the east the birth of Athena; around the outer walls of the *cella* a continuous frieze portrayed scenes from a great festival in honor of Athena.

Sculpture and painting. The statue of Athena in the Parthenon and the figure of Zeus in the temple at Olympia were the works of the great sculptor, Phidias. It was he, too, who designed the frieze and pediments of the Parthenon. Phidias fixed forever in their full dignity and grandeur the forms of the gods whose statues he shaped. Two other Athenian sculptors of the fifth century, Polyclitus and Myron, excelled in the portrayal of athletes as they appeared in the Olympic games. Myron's well-known discus-thrower, in particular, is an unrivaled study of an athlete in motion. Portraits of living men now took their place beside idealized statues of the gods. In the fourth century Praxiteles, whose Hermes has survived in the original, endowed his statues of the gods with a life-like grace which contrasted strongly with the rigid pose characteristic of early Greek sculpture; and Lysippus, famous for his bust of Alexander the Great, also fashioned a

The Discus-thrower is a copy of a lost original by Myron, an Athenian sculptor of the fifth century B.C.

Hermes, holding the infant god Dionysus, is one of the finest works of Praxiteles (fourth century B.C).

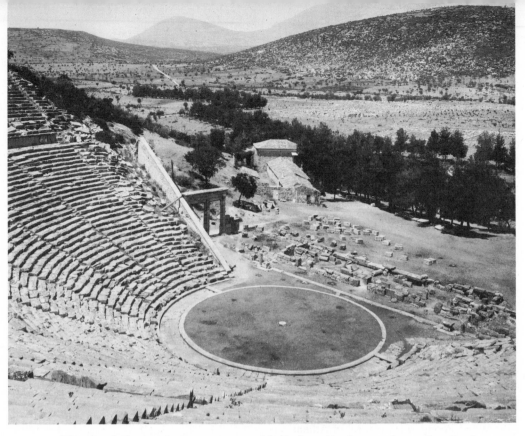

This Greek theater, built into a natural hillside at Epidaurus, shows that Greek drama must have been performed before a vast audience.

vigorous statue of Poseidon, which fixed for all time the image of the God of the sea. The Greeks were skillful painters as well as sculptors, but since paintings, particularly murals, are perishable, hardly a trace has survived. We can judge the quality of their painting only by their beautifully decorated vases depicting scenes from mythology or from daily life.

Lyric poetry. Lyric poetry, which had played such a large part in the literature of the Archaic Period, seems to have been relatively rare during the Golden Age. One lyric poet of this period, however, was of such outstanding importance, both for the artistic quality of his work and for his influence on later poets, that he cannot be ignored. Pindar was born about 522 B.C. in Thebes and lived through the first half of the fifth century. He was the supreme master of the ode, the poetic form later adapted to the Latin tongue by Horace. Here is perfection of form, but to the modern mind relatively little important poetic content, for most of his odes were written to honor the victorious athletes in the Olympic games. For the greatest

Greek poetry of the Golden Age, as well as for the most profound contemplation of human life, we must turn to the dramatists.

Tragedy. Drama was born and flourished in Athens. Its beginnings are shrouded in mystery. All that we can be sure of is that it arose in connection with the worship of Dionysus. In its earliest form the plot seems to have been unfolded by a single narrator, together with a chorus which sang and performed solemn dances. When, early in the fifth century, Aeschylus (525–456 B.C.) introduced a second actor and unfolded his story through dialogue, the dramatic form emerged. Only seven of his plays have come down to us. Chief among them is the *Oresteia,* a trilogy which is considered by many to be the greatest work of any Greek dramatist. Sophocles (496–406 B.C.), the most popular dramatist of his day, was Aeschylus' younger contemporary and rival. Building on the foundation laid by Aeschylus, he refined the technique of tragedy. The number of actors was now increased, while the chorus played a less important role, in general merely commenting on the action of the plot or expressing the emotions of the spectators. In the plays of Sophocles the characters are more sharply delineated; the structure of the plot is more complex and is concentrated more exclusively on one tragic issue. In the greatest of his plays, *Oedipus the King,* character and fate cooperate to bring about the inevitable tragedy. Oedipus is enmeshed in a web of circumstance which leads him to fulfil his prophesied destiny by unwittingly killing his father and marrying his mother. In the tragedies of Euripides (c. 480–406 B.C.) the characters are more human, and passion spins the plot. Two of his most famous plays, *Medea* and *Hippolytus,* are studies of the tragedy caused by women scorned. Less popular than Sophocles in his own day, Euripides has won for himself a lasting place in the world's literature through his psychological insight into female character. Phaedra, the heroine of *Hippolytus,* became the subject of one of Racine's greatest plays, while another of his heroines, Iphigenia, inspired plays by both Racine and Goethe.

Comedy. Comedy developed later than tragedy. Its materials were drawn from everyday life: current movements were satirized, well-known men ridiculed. Only the work of Aristophanes (c. 448–c. 388 B.C.) has come down to us, and of his forty-four plays only eleven have survived. The plots of Aristophanes' comedies are wildly fantastic and the treatment is raucous and witty. Beneath the fantasy, however, there is a vast amount of realistic, albeit satirical, comment on the contemporary scene. It is from Aristophanes rather than from the great writers of tragedy that we learn about the real, living, human society of fifth-century Athens. Many of his comedies, notably *The Wasps, The Frogs,* and *Lysistrata,* are still played and make good theater. The popular success of modern performances of the great tragedies of Aeschylus, Sophocles, and Euripides is also proof of the lasting vitality of Greek drama.

History. The interest in man which is evident in all Greek art, and pre-eminently in Greek drama, showed itself also in the writing of history. Prose chronicles, of which only fragments have survived, were written in the sixth century, but history in the modern sense

Sophocles, one of the three Greek tragedians whose works survive.

of the word dates from the generation of the first Greek dramatists. Herodotus (484–425 B.C.) has been called with good reason "the father of history" and also "the first great European prose writer." The theme of his *History* is the story of the Persian War. His vivid narrative of this stirring event has kept alive the memory of the Athenian victory at Marathon and the last heroic stand of the Spartans at Thermopylae. But although the Persian War furnishes his central theme, he wandered from it repeatedly to give discursive accounts of the geography, social customs, religion, and ethnic character of almost all the peoples of the ancient world from Egypt to the Black Sea. He had traveled widely and wherever he went he had observed and listened. He had an insatiable curiosity and an inexhaustible interest in his fellow men. And he could make a good story out of everything he saw or heard. The second great Greek historian, Thucydides (c. 460–c. 400), wrote history of a very different kind, much closer to the scholarly or "scientific" history of recent times. His account of the

Peloponnesian War was written with a passion for accuracy and objectivity and with a conviction that, since human nature is everywhere pretty much the same, his analysis of the motives and actions of the leaders on both sides of the conflict would prove a useful guide to future statesmen and generals for all time. The care with which his work has been studied throughout the centuries goes far to prove the truth of his conviction. If he lacked the story-telling art and the leisurely charm of Herodotus, he set a standard for thoughtful, accurate, and impartial historical scholarship that has seldom been surpassed. Compared with Thucydides, Xenophon (c. 430–355 B.C.), the outstanding Greek historian of the next generation, seems scarcely more than a competent war correspondent. Still, his *Anabasis,* which tells the story of the retreat to the sea of ten thousand Greek mercenaries in the service of Persia after their leaders were killed, is an exciting piece of reporting and the first preserved example of autobiography.

Science and medicine. One of the strongest traits in ancient Greek thought was a desire to find rational explanations of things. By the fifth century, educated Greeks were beginning to lose faith in the gods of Homeric mythology and to seek elsewhere the answers to fundamental questions concerning the nature of man and the universe. Having few instruments of precise measurement and hence few accurately ascertained facts, they were forced to rely on pure speculation, with generally erroneous results. Yet their attempt to find rational explanations was itself a superb achievement and an inspiration to future generations. For two thousand years European scientific thought was founded upon the legacy of Greece, including such mistaken hypotheses as that of Empedocles (c. 490–430 B.C.) that the whole universe is composed of four elements, fire, air, water, and earth. The science of medicine attracted some of the best minds of the fifth century, and though here, too, they were hampered by lack of reliable knowledge, their approach to the problem of healing at least was scientific. Hippocrates (c. 460–370 B.C.), the most famous physician of this period, rejected supernatural explanations and cures, and observed and recorded symptoms carefully. His theory that the liquid parts of the body are composed of four "humors," blood, phlegm, bile, and black bile, and that disease is caused by a disturbance of the equilibrium between these, was commonly accepted until the beginning of the modern age. But though his physiological theory was erroneous, his prescriptions for careful nursing were sound enough, and his devotion to the welfare of his patients is still echoed in the Hippocratic Oath taken by every American medical student on graduation.

Philosophy. The greatest triumphs of the Greek mind in this period were achieved in philosophy rather than in science, although a good deal of natural science was included in philosophy. The Greek philosophers of the fifth and fourth centuries, however, were interested not only in attempting to explain the nature of the universe, but also in the ethical and moral problems of men, and in the means of reaching the most perfect form of life for the individual and for society. These were all problems that they believed could be solved by clear, logical thinking. We cannot here examine the ideas of those professional teachers of philosophy, who were known as Sophists, except to note that many of them came to the disillusioned conclusion that no really valid knowledge was possible. The philosophers of lasting importance were those who believed not only that knowledge was possible but that its pursuit was the noblest function of man. The method they used was logical analysis directed toward the definition of universal truths, and both their method and their conclusions have exerted a profound influence on European thought down to the present time.

Socrates. The pioneer in a new direction taken by Greek philosophy in the fifth century was Socrates (469–399 B.C.). Since he himself wrote nothing, we know his teaching and his amiable personality only through the works of Plato and other disciples. He was a stonemason by trade, a fantastically ugly little man who by sheer charm, character, and intelligence attracted about him a group of the most brilliant young aristocrats in Athens. Socrates was primarily interested in the ethical and moral problems that are common to all men. His method was not to lecture but to ask questions, demonstrate the logical fallacies in the answers, and then ask more questions, thus forcing his disciples to clarify their own ideas and define what they meant by such concepts as temperance, courage, or justice. It was a technique peculiarly suited to the discussion of ethics since the data could be drawn from every man's personal experience. Few philosophers have ever examined human motives more closely than Socrates or set a higher standard of ethical conduct. His association with the aristocratic faction in Athens, however, and perhaps his habit of questioning accepted opinions, aroused suspicion and he was condemned to death on a charge of impiety and corrupting the youth of the city.

Plato.   Plato (427–347 B.C.) was one of the young aristocrats who fell under the influence of Socrates, but he both altered and added to his master's teaching. His philosophical writings took the form of dialogues, like those conducted by Socrates, and in many of them Socrates is represented as the chief interlocutor. The early dialogues are Socratic inquiries into the essential characteristics of the good life, but from there Plato went on to construct a theory of knowledge applicable to all reality. What Plato sought to discover by rational thought were the eternally valid universal "forms," or as he called them "ideas," of which individual actions or things are but imperfect and transitory manifestations. These ideas, for example the idea of man or horse as distinct from individual men or horses, he thought to have a real existence and to be the only perfect realities. They were the "universals" which so profoundly influenced the thought of medieval schoolmen. Through knowledge of these universal ideas man could discover the rational order which Plato believed existed throughout the cosmos. Plato's faith in reason as the necessary guide to the highest form of life also led him to propose a theory of the ideal state as one in which the ruling class would be composed of philosophers. This conception, discussed in his famous dialogue, *The Republic,* has always held a strong appeal for those who distrust democracy and would prefer government by an aristocratic *élite.*

Aristotle.   The third of the great Greek philosophers, Aristotle (384–322 B.C.), adapted the ideas of his predecessors and applied them to a far wider range of subject matter. His interests, indeed, were very different from theirs, for much more than Socrates and Plato was he concerned with the natural sciences and with factual knowledge of the workings of the material universe. He rejected the belief that universal ideas had a real existence apart from the individual objects they represented, though he did not abandon them. His study of the biological sciences, too, made him more aware of the constant process of change in nature than was indicated by Plato's unchanging ideas. Finally, he abandoned Plato's poetic use of myth and dialogue as a means of conveying truth, in favor of sober, scientific prose. In the form in which they have come down to us, at least, Aristotle's writings have nothing of the superb literary style that distinguished Plato's dialogues. The range of Aristotle's work was encyclopedic, covering the fields of physics, astronomy, biology, psychology, metaphysics (i.e., the study of first principles and basic ideas about nature), formal logic, ethics, politics, and the theory of rhetoric and poetry. Aristotle's logic was a system of deductive reasoning, which is still regarded as basic to any study of formal logic, but in his scientific work he recognized the value of observation, experiment, and inductive thinking. Much of his science, indeed, seems based on little more than common-sense explanations of things he had observed. For two thousand years many of his theories were accepted because they appealed to men's common sense, even when they were totally wrong because based on erroneous premises. To the medieval schoolmen, as we shall see, Aristotle was not only the authoritative master of logic and metaphysics, but also the supreme source of scientific knowledge, "the master of those who know," as Dante called him.

"Would that the people of India may believe me to be a god. For wars depend upon reputation, and often even what has been falsely believed has gained the place of truth." • Alexander the Great (336–323 B.C.)

3

The Hellenistic Age

THROUGH most of the fourth century B.C., wars and social struggle were sapping the strength of the Greek city-states. Persia, the old enemy of the Greeks, watched this internal disintegration with avid interest, awaiting the time when Greece would be too weak to resist her armies. And, in the second half of the century, Macedonia, a young and vigorous state newly united under her far-sighted king, Philip II, watched both Greece and Persia. Greece was too weak to meet the new Persian threat; Macedonia was too strong not to meet it. But to enter the lists with Persia, Philip had first to bring Greece under his control. This he accomplished. But the task of fighting Persia was left to his son, Alexander, a young and brilliant general who conquered the whole Eastern world from Egypt to India. Alexander's empire did not long endure, but in the brief span of its existence it opened the East to the Greeks and their culture, and in the two centuries from the death of Alexander to the time when Rome secured domination of the East, a new civilization flourished, an international civilization founded on Greek culture, but with a super-structure reflecting the conditions under which it was shaped. The city-state was no longer the only unit of political, social, economic, and cultural life. Great kingdoms ruled by absolute monarchs dominated the scene, and smaller kingdoms imitated their structure. Old values and old loyalties faded; citizenship lost its meaning; cosmopolitanism replaced localism. New values emerged, but they were related to the needs of the individual rather than the community. A new class arose to fashion the life of the new age, a Graeco-Oriental upper class, speaking the Greek language and imbued with Greek culture. In these centuries the civilizations of Greece and the Orient met to form a new combination in which, however, the dominant elements were essentially Greek, and which historians have generally called Hellenistic. This was the civilization which Rome took over and adapted and passed on to the Western world.

1. *Macedonian Conquests and the Hellenistic Kingdoms*

Rise of Macedonia. Macedonia, to the north of Greece, was a relatively backward country still no more than semi-civilized in the fourth century B.C. Although kin to the Greeks, the Macedonians had been very little influenced by Greek culture. They had never developed city life or the city-state system. They still retained much of their tribal organization under a landholding aristocracy. Although the monarchy was growing stronger during the first half of the fourth century, it was not till the accession of Philip II in 359 B.C. that Macedonia was welded into a strong state. Philip had spent three years of his youth as a hostage in Greece, where he had learned something of Greek culture and military organization and had also had an opportunity to observe the lack of unity among the Greek city-states. Two years after his accession Philip invaded Thrace and seized the gold mines of Mount Pangaeus. With the wealth drawn from these mines he organized a professional army, recruiting foot soldiers from among the free peasants and shepherds of the Macedonian hills and cavalry from the landed aristocracy. The foot soldiers he trained to fight in the tactical formation known as the *phalanx,* a massed body of pikemen eight to sixteen ranks deep. Rigidly disciplined and kept in constant training, the Macedonian troops were the most effective standing army the ancient world had yet seen.

Conquest of Greece. During the first twenty years of his reign Philip advanced slowly toward the conquest of Greece. Playing one city off against another, gaining adherents through bribery or threats, he moved steadily southward. At last in 338 B.C. he was ready for the final stroke. For years the great Athenian orator and statesman, Demosthenes, had warned his fellow Greeks against the approaching menace. His warnings went largely unheeded, and at the last moment only Athens and Thebes and a handful of smaller states rallied to meet the invader. They were decisively defeated by the Macedonian army at Chaeronea, and Philip was master of Greece. Before the year was over, Philip called a council at Corinth which Sparta alone refused to attend. There a Hellenic League was organized with Philip at its head. Philip was no ruthless conqueror. Each city-state within the league was to remain autonomous, although each was expected to furnish contingents to an army of which Philip was to be the commander. At the meeting of the Council in the following year, Philip announced his intention of going to war against Persia.

Alexander's conquests. Before he could carry out his plans, Philip was assassinated in 336 B.C. and his son, Alexander, only twenty years old, succeeded to the throne. Athens, taking advantage of the temporary confusion caused by the death of Philip, planned revolt and Thebes actually revolted. Alexander replied by destroying the city of Thebes. Then

he turned to Persia. Most of the Greek cities of Asia Minor accepted him without a struggle. To undermine the effectiveness of the Persian fleet, Alexander determined to take its bases. This he accomplished by defeating the Persian army at Issus and, after a seven months' siege, capturing Tyre. These victories gave him possession of the coasts of Asia Minor, Syria, and Phoenicia. Next he added Egypt to his domains, an easy conquest, for the Egyptians had long resented Persian rule, and Egypt was far from the center of Persian power. Returning to Asia, Alexander inflicted a crushing defeat on the Persian forces in Babylonia in 331 B.C. But still he was not satisfied. In a triumphant march eastward, he led his army into India, coming to a halt only when his weary soldiers refused to go deeper into an area of intolerable climate and deadly fevers.

Spread of Greek culture. Alexander's conquests were more than a series of military victories, brilliant though these were; they were also the medium through which Greek culture was to be disseminated throughout the ancient world. Alexander himself had a deep-seated admiration for the cultural achievements of the Greeks: it was not for nothing that Aristotle had been his tutor. Following each successful campaign he founded cities in the newly conquered territory, cities which served a military purpose, but which also attracted emigrants from Greece, and became centers for the dissemination of Greek culture.

Alexander the Great, as portrayed on a silver tetradrachm coined by Lysimachus, one of Alexander's generals who became king of Thrace.

Alexander's government.   When Alexander returned from India, the great problem which confronted him was that of administration. How was he to govern his vast domains? The question can never be adequately answered, for Alexander died before he could effect a permanent solution. But from his temporary measures we can infer something of his intent. As he went from conquest to conquest, he left the recently acquired territory in the hands of Macedonian generals, who were to exercise a general authority, but he apparently made no effort to alter the existing forms of local government. There is reason to believe, indeed, that what Alexander had in mind was the fusion of Greek and Persian elements throughout his realm. He adopted Persian dress and manners, married a Persian princess, and encouraged his followers to marry Persians. He also introduced Persians into the administration and the army. But this policy was too liberal to be readily accepted by his Macedonian followers, and it did not outlast his lifetime. What did last was the infusion of Greek culture throughout the Middle East, which resulted from the founding of cities colonized by Greeks and from the creation of a Greek-speaking upper class.

Deification of Alexander.   To strengthen his position in these diverse realms, Alexander resorted to an expedient which has occasioned much comment and not a little controversy — he declared himself a god. This act was differently interpreted in various parts of his empire. The Macedonians did not accept him as a deity, but, since he was their legitimate king, their refusal had no serious consequences. In Egypt the pharaohs had always been worshipped as gods; each was the son of Ra. So when Alexander became their ruler the Egyptian priests solemnly proclaimed him to be the son of Ra. The Persians and other Middle Eastern subjects did not look upon their kings as gods, but they believed them to be divinely appointed and divinely inspired. Thus they readily accepted Alexander as their god-appointed king.

Hellenistic kingdoms.   When Alexander died in 323 B.C. at the age of thirty-three, there was no one who could fill his place. His Macedonian generals carved up the newly conquered empire among them, and for more than forty years they and their successors fought over the division of the spoils. From this long conflict three large kingdoms emerged: Syria, including Persia and part of Asia Minor, under the rule of the Seleucid dynasty; Egypt under the Ptolemies; and Macedonia under a new dynasty founded by Antigonus, who was, like the founders of the other dynasties, one of Alexander's Macedonian generals. There were also several smaller kingdoms, the only important ones being the wealthy little kingdom of Pergamum in Asia Minor and the kingdom of Bactria to the east of Persia. With the exception of Macedonia, these Hellenistic kingdoms were in reality oriental despotisms, though ruled by Macedonian dynasties, which depended upon the support of a Greek or Greek-speaking upper class.

Greece.   Greece meanwhile maintained a shadow of independence under the control of Macedonia. The Macedonian kings kept garrisons in Greece until Antigonus Gonatas adopted the alternative policy of establishing tyrants favorable to him in as many as possible of the Greek cities. The city-states in the third century were losing much of their distinctive character and exclusive patriotism. The great age of the city-states, indeed, was past, but no satisfactory substitute had been found. An interesting experiment in federation, however, was made during the middle years of the third century in the formation of two large leagues, the Aetolian League, which included most of the cities, with the exception of Athens, in northern and central Greece, and the Achaean League, which included most of the south except Sparta. These were more closely integrated federations than the leagues of the fourth century, but they failed to take the additional steps that might have led to national unity. Quarrels between the Achaean League and Sparta, and later between the two leagues, opened the way for Macedonian intervention, and by the end of the third century Philip V of Macedonia was for all practical purposes the ruler of Greece. However, the new Macedonian domination of Greece did not last long; it was overthrown within a half-century by the intervention of a more dangerous power, the rising Roman Republic. The story of Roman expansion, however, must be left to the following chapter.

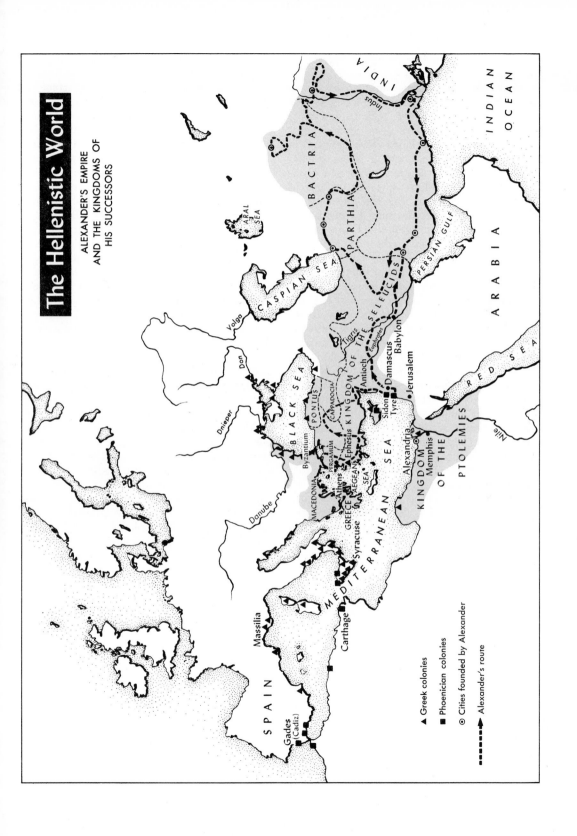

The Hellenistic World

ALEXANDER'S EMPIRE
AND THE KINGDOMS OF
HIS SUCCESSORS

▲ Greek colonies
■ Phoenician colonies
⊙ Cities founded by Alexander
▰▰▰▶ Alexander's route

INDIAN OCEAN

ARABIA

INDIA

BACTRIA

PARTHIA

KINGDOM OF THE SELEUCIDS

PERSIAN GULF

Indus

CASPIAN SEA

ARAL SEA

Volga

Don

Dnieper

Danube

BLACK SEA

PONTUS

CAPPADOCIA

KINGDOM OF

Tigris

Euphrates

Babylon

Antioch

Damascus

Jerusalem

Sidon

Tyre

RED SEA

Nile

Alexandria

Memphis

KINGDOM OF THE PTOLEMIES

MEDITERRANEAN SEA

AEGEAN SEA

Byzantium

PERGAMUM

Ephesus

Athens

GREECE

MACEDONIA

Syracuse

Carthage

SPAIN

Massilia

Gades (Cadiz)

2. Hellenistic Institutions

Alexander's successors continued his policy of founding new cities and attracting Greeks to come and settle in them. Great numbers of enterprising Greeks flocked to Syria, Egypt, and other Hellenistic kingdoms to engage in trade or to acquire positions in the royal bureaucracy, and everywhere they formed a ruling class. Their culture was the nucleus of Hellenistic civilization. But the line between Greeks and non-Greeks was not sharply drawn. Descendants of those whom the Greeks had once called barbarians, educated in Greek schools and speaking the Greek language, now took their places in the ranks of the true Greeks to form a Graeco-Oriental upper class. There remained, however, a cleavage between the Hellenized upper classes and the natives who retained their traditional speech and customs.

Absolutism. In Macedonia the traditional concept of kingship long persisted: the monarch was neither divine nor absolute, and he depended upon a national army, not a mercenary force. The kings of Egypt and Syria, on the other hand, claimed absolute authority, although in practice the power of the monarch was at times more limited. In Syria, particularly, the existence of old Greek cities, on which the prosperity of Syria largely depended, made absolute government difficult. The Greeks, living in what had once been city-states, were accustomed to managing their own affairs, and the Seleucids were forced to grant these municipalities considerable independence, at least in local government.

Royal control in Egypt. Absolutism found its most complete expression in Egypt. There autocracy extended to economic as well as to political life. The Ptolemies took advantage of the traditional prerogatives of the pharaohs in ordering economic activity to bring agriculture, commerce, and industry under their control. Vast royal estates, scattered through the country, were worked by tenant farmers directly for the benefit of the king. Since the cultivation of most of the land in Egypt was directly or indirectly under government supervision, the inefficient traditional agriculture that obtained under the pharaohs could be replaced by the latest, most scientific methods, thereby ensuring a maximum output. This enabled Egypt, particularly in the third century B.C., to become the greatest single supplier of grain in the eastern Mediterranean. Her wealth, however, did not depend solely on this commodity. The Ptolemies saw to it that her industries were developed as well. Under a royal monopoly, workshops turned out fine linens, glass, cosmetics, and above all, papyrus. From now until the end of the ancient world, Egypt was practically the sole supplier of cheap writing paper.

Commerce and industry. The fifth century B.C. had developed a network of trade that, though covering the whole of the Mediterranean area, was conducted on a relatively small scale. The Hellenistic Age not only extended that network farther eastward to include the new areas opened by Alexander, but conducted trade on the grand scale. Commercial enterprise was now in good part in the hands of kings who could command the total resources of a country: the Ptolemies sold grain by the fleetload, not merely the shipload. Internationally minded businessmen appeared on the scene with head offices in Ephesus or Syracuse or Alexandria — the vast new entrepôt founded by Alexander and lavishly built up by the Ptolemies to serve as their capital — and with branch offices in any number of key ports. In addition to the basic commodities — grain, olive oil, wine, salted fish — that criss-crossed the Mediterranean, there arose a brisk trade in exotic luxuries to satisfy the taste of the increasing number of people who now had the money to afford them: spices and perfumes from India, silks from China via India, perfumes from Arabia, and ivory and gold from Africa. Goods from the Far East were sometimes brought overland by caravan to the coastal cities of Asia Minor. More frequently they were carried by water from India through the Indian Ocean and then either through the Red Sea to Alexandria or through the Persian Gulf to Mesopotamia and thence overland to the ports of Asia Minor and the Levant. Not all luxuries, however, came from so far away. Fine woolens were woven in Miletus and Pergamum, and the Ptolemies' workshops in Alexandria produced glass, jewelry, and cosmetics. Improvements in navigation aided this far-flung commerce. Ships were made larger and more efficient; ports were given facilities to handle the increased volume; and lighthouses and other navigational aids were set up. The most famous was the Pharos, the great lighthouse of the harbor of Alexandria, which served as a model for all subsequent ones.

The Hellenistic Age, particularly during the third century B.C., was unquestionably prosperous. But the prosperity did not reach all levels of society. The upper class, largely Greek or at least Greek-speaking, of merchants and manufacturers, government officials and landowners, flourished, but peasants and artisans and unskilled labor stayed in their traditional poverty. The result was an ever-widening gap between rich and poor, between the ruling class and the ruled, which, unhappily, was to plague the eastern Mediterranean lands for the rest of their history.

Decline of Greece. Greece itself suffered seriously as a result of the new shift in the political and economic center of gravity. The city-state patriotism, which had been the mainspring of Greek culture, was fading, if it had not entirely disappeared, and many of the most energetic Greeks had migrated to seek their fortunes in the new Hellenistic states in the East. Athens was still a center of culture frequented by students from all parts of the ancient world, but the leadership in science and learning had passed to Alexandria. Greece had Hellenized the whole of the Middle East, but she herself was no longer a great productive cultural force.

3. Hellenistic Culture

Cosmopolitanism and individualism. The civilization of the Hellenistic Age marks a transitional stage from the city-state culture of classical Greece to the universal and composite culture of the Roman Empire. Rome could not so easily have absorbed the ancient civilizations which clustered about the eastern end of the Mediterranean had they not already been fused into a common cosmopolitan civilization by the Hellenizing influence of Alexander and his successors. And with cosmopolitanism came a rootless individualism very different from the spirit of the small, exclusive, and tightly organized city-states in the Golden Age of Greece. Greek culture dominated the new and larger world: the Greek tongue became the language

Mosaics, made by cementing together small pieces of colored stone, glass, and similar materials, are more durable than paintings. This example, showing the god Dionysus riding a panther, is part of a floor uncovered on Delos in 1939.

of all educated men, with some modification Greek art forms persisted; Greek economic developments were the bases of Hellenistic organization. But the *milieu* in which the Greeks had fashioned this culture was gone. The place of the city-state, with its laws and its mores and the demands which it made upon the loyalty of its citizens, was taken by vast and impersonal kingdoms. And, lacking the close identification with the community characteristic of the old city-states, men sought the reason and the source and the end of their being within themselves.

Philosophy. The dominant philosophies of the age reflected this deeply rooted individualism. The schools founded at Athens by Plato and Aristotle continued to teach the philosophical systems of the masters with great ingenuity, but with little originality. In this unsettled age the search for first principles and basic understanding was losing its appeal. Men were now more concerned with the personal and practical problem of how to rationalize their lives, how to find happiness or at least contentment in a life that had lost its framework of piety and patriotism. The original thinkers of the Hellenistic Age were seeking a way of life rather than the solution of metaphysical problems. Epicurus (340–270 B.C.), who taught a pleasantly casual school of philosophy in his garden at Athens, found the secret of the good life in the intelligent pursuit of pleasure. Taking as his basic premise the assumption that everything in the universe, including the soul of man, is made up of a fortuitous accumulation of material atoms in a state of constant motion, Epicurus denied both the existence of any divine or supernatural power and the immortality of the soul. It followed that man need not regulate his life with reference to the will of the gods or to fear or hope of a life after death. He has but this life to live and might as well enjoy it. To gain the maximum of pleasure and avoidance of pain, however, requires wisdom and self-control. Sensual indulgence, if carried to excess, defeats its own ends. The most lasting pleasure is to be found in a simple, quiet life of moderate indulgence and mental activity, among pleasant companions and far removed from the ambitions, worries, and hazards of public life. Epicureanism was a completely self-centered philosophy, tolerating no emotion strong enough to disturb the serene detachment of the happy sage. Zeno (c. 350–c. 258 B.C.), who founded the Stoic school at Athens, sought the same goal as did Epicurus — the attainment of the good life — but the road he found to it was very different.

The secret of contentment or happiness, he taught, was not to be found in pleasure but in duty, in the pursuit of virtue, and in the complete mastery of the passions by reason. The Stoics believed that the universe is governed by "natural law," the primary characteristics of which are order, reason, and justice. The highest aim of man should be to live in harmony with this law and thus to achieve inner strength and peace. To do so requires rigid self-mastery. The sage's reward is the clear conscience that comes from having done one's duty and from having lived uprightly, unswayed by passion. Stoicism was individualistic, but not anti-social. It was, in fact, cosmopolitan in its teaching that all men are equal in their relation to the rational universe, and it was public-spirited in its emphasis on duty and justice. Although its rigid morality was too demanding to be widely practiced, it had an important influence, particularly in the following age, on the ruling class of the Roman Empire, on Roman law, and on much Christian thought.

Science.   While philosophy became increasingly a matter of ethics and personal morality, science became more impersonal, more exact. Scientists sought to discover the precise nature of phenomena in the external world rather than to find man's place therein, or even to set forth an explanation of the entire universe. And the science of the Hellenistic Age was truly brilliant. In the field of mathematics Euclid's work was momentous; his system of pure geometry written early in the third century is studied

The Dying Gaul, a tragic gladiator drooping over his broken sword, is one of the most effective examples of Hellenistic realism.

today. Archimedes (c. 287–212 B.C.), also a mathematician, made discoveries of far-reaching importance in mechanics and hydrostatics. One of the most significant of his contributions was the discovery that when a body is immersed in a fluid, it loses weight equal to the weight of the fluid it displaces. This is still known as Archimedes' principle. In the second century Hipparchus made some very important astronomical calculations, including his discovery of the precession of the equinoxes and an almost accurate estimate of the distance between the earth and the moon. Eratosthenes (c. 273–192 B.C.) estimated the earth's circumference and reached a figure only about four per cent less than that accepted today. These are but a few of the scientists of this age whose names, and fragments at least of whose works, have come down to us. A large part of their contribution consisted in collecting and classifying data rather than in discovering new principles. They thus played an important part in the transmission of ancient science to the medieval world, but since, like the earlier Greeks, they had no clear understanding of the experimental method, much of what they taught had to be unlearned before the principles of modern science could be discovered.

Scholarship. The Museum at Alexandria, supported by the state and dedicated to research, was the scene of most of the scientific investigation of this period. Here doctors wrote the textbooks that were to influence the study of medicine until modern times. Here, too, were performed vast labors in literary scholarship. The Museum library was the largest and most complete that the world had yet seen. Scholars pored over its manuscripts, deciphering, determining authorship, deciding on the correct version, and compiling grammars and dictionaries.

The New Comedy. But the literary endeavor of the Hellenistic Age was not confined to scholarship, although this was, on the whole, a scholarly rather than a creative age. All the older forms of Greek literature were practiced assiduously and a new type of pastoral poetry, which influenced Virgil and many later writers, was created by Theocritus (c. 270 B.C.). There were no great writers of tragedy after Euripides, but in the third century comedy

flourished for a while in the expert hands of a few outstanding dramatists. The New Comedy of the third century stemmed indirectly from Euripides. Because he had brought to his writing a brooding realism which questioned the old heroic values and which probed the human heart, Euripides had not been accepted in his lifetime. But a later day, bereft of those very values which he had questioned, and like him concerned with the complex nature of man, applauded his genius. In the comedies of Menander (c. 342–291 B.C.), chief exponent of the New Comedy, complicated plots, usually dealing with love affairs that have run into difficulties but that in the end are happily resolved, served as vehicles for subtle analysis of character and an astute examination of ideas and motives.

History. In the writing of history the Hellenistic Age found a medium for the exercise of both literary form and scholarship. Yet, so far as we can judge from the fragments that have survived, most of the histories of this period lacked the vigor and the thoughtful analysis that had characterized the work of Herodotus and Thucydides. Some were mere compilations, scholarly but uninspired; others sacrificed accuracy and analysis to dramatic effect and rhetorical embellishment. And most of them were designed to please the despotic rulers of the Hellenistic states and so suffered from the distortion of fact which is almost unavoidable in an official history. Moreover, in the large cosmopolitan states of the Hellenistic Age citizenship had ceased to have any real meaning and there was none of that active political life which had made the Greek city-states such interesting subjects for historical study. One exception to this general statement, however, must be noted. The Roman Republic in the third and second centuries B.C. was still essentially a city-state although rapidly expanding to imperial proportions. The story of its vigorous political development and of its growing domination of the Mediterranean world was a theme that might well inspire a thoughtful observer, and it is not surprising that it called forth the most important historical work since Thucydides. Polybius (c. 205–c. 120 B.C.) was a Greek aristocrat who had had a good deal of political and military experience before a series of events brought him to Rome as a

Laocoön, priest of Apollo, warned the Trojans against the wooden horse. As punishment the gods sent sea serpents to devour him and his sons. The Hellenistic original, now partially restored, was discovered in 1506.

hostage. There he became intimate with some of the leading senatorial families and was able to observe the growth of the Roman state from the inside. His history of the rise of Rome, with special emphasis on the period from 221 to 146 B.C., was thus written from the vantage point of an experienced foreign observer, who admired Rome but was not personally involved in Roman politics. Like Thucydides, he hoped that his history would furnish valuable lessons for future statesmen; to serve that purpose it must be accurate, and the true causes of events must be made clear. The result was one of the most thoughtful histories of ancient times.

Sculpture. In the arts the individualism and the restless vitality of the Hellenistic Age were expressed most clearly in sculpture, at least so far as we can determine, since almost all Hellenistic painting has disappeared. Hellenistic sculptors produced thousands of statues for royal and other wealthy patrons, and many of these have survived either in the original or in later Roman copies. They cover an amazing range of subject matter, from gods and goddesses, through various human types, to realistic portraits. The restraint and serenity characteristic of the classical age has given way to a new feeling. Hellenistic sculpture is more naturalistic, more highly individualized, more intensely emotional. The Dying Gaul is a brilliant embodiment of human suffering executed in realistic detail. The Nike of Samothrace, the Winged Victory, portrayed at the moment of alighting on the prow of a hard-driving warship, is a superb study in motion. The Laocoön group, of the first century B.C., is an example of the later art of the period, when naturalism gave way to exaggerated realism and emotion to theatricality.

Etruscan painting shows a decided Greek influence. This example is a detail from a wall painting in the Tomb of the Leopards at Tarquina, c. 490 B.C.

Roman culture and institutions. Meanwhile, during the seventh and sixth centuries, Italy was brought into still closer contact with the civilization of the East as Greek colonies were planted in Sicily and on the southern coast of the peninsula.

The republic: government. The sixth century was drawing to a close when the Romans rose in rebellion against the Etruscan kings and established an independent republic. The traditional date, 509 B.C., is probably fairly correct. The constitution of the new republic was essentially conservative and aristocratic. The existing social distinction between the wealthy "patrician" families and the "plebeian" mass of the people was given legal sanction and formed the basis of a political caste system. Intermarriage between the two classes was forbidden, while all offices, as well as membership in the Senate, were reserved for the patricians. The executive and legislative branches were carefully balanced so as to prevent radical action. Full executive authority, including command of the army and, in the early period, large judicial powers, was shared by two consuls elected for a year at a time. These were advised by the Senate, a body of three hundred elder statesmen appointed for life, at first by the consuls, later by the censors. The constitutional powers of the Senate were rather vague, but their practical influence was always great. As the republic expanded in later centuries, new offices were created to take over parts of the consuls' duties and it became the custom to appoint all who had held offices to the Senate. It thus became a body of experienced administrators whose advice the short-term magistrates could scarcely reject. The legislative power and final sovereignty theoretically rested not with the Senate but with the citizens, who, operating through a number of legislative bodies, expressed their will and elected the magistrates. The voting procedures of these bodies, however, were such that only during certain limited periods did the political decisions reflect the views of the people at large. For most of the time government remained safely in the hands of the landed aristocracy.

Social and economic life. The aristocratic constitution of the young republic reflected the social and economic organization of the Roman people. The political caste system was based on wealth, mostly in the form of land, and on a very strong family organization. As with many primitive agricultural people, the family was a much larger and more significant unit than its modern counterpart, including, as it did, dependents and slaves, and the head of the family had an unlimited authority. Every effort was made to perpetuate the family fortunes, and the recurrence of the same family names in political office, generation after generation, attests the success of the patricians in keeping their family estates and the political position that went with them intact. Indeed, the economic developments of the first two centuries of the republic favored the growth of large patrician estates, though they were hard times for the poor. Rome had little commerce in this period and no more industry than the production by small artisans of articles of daily use. Agriculture formed the basis of Roman wealth. But during the fifth and fourth centuries, the rich volcanic topsoil of the Campagna was becoming exhausted as the result of overcropping and the deforestation of the neighboring hills. By the fourth century, grain raising in the lowlands of Latium was becoming unprofitable

4

The Roman Republic

AT THE END of the sixth century B.C., when
the vigorous city-states of Greece were already
emerging from the archaic period of their civilization, the little Italian city-state of Rome
was just beginning her career as an independent republic. Compared to the Greeks of that
age, the Romans were little better than barbarians. Sturdy and strong-willed they were,
but with small aptitude for abstract speculation and with still less of the creative originality
in literature and art that was the glory of ancient Greece. Three centuries later, when
Greece had passed her golden age, the Romans
appropriated the Greek heritage and used it as
the foundation for a great and lasting culture
of their own; but their most original and characteristic achievements were of a different kind.
They demonstrated over a period of centuries
their possession of a legal and political genius
such as the world has seldom seen. And these
qualities, so sadly lacking among the more
subtle and speculative Greeks, carried the little
city-state on the Tiber from triumph to triumph
until she had become the undisputed mistress
of the Mediterranean world. Alone among the
ancient city-states, Rome was able to evoke a
legal and political system that could survive the
strain of territorial expansion and bridge the
gap from city-state to empire.

1. The Early Republic and the
First Period of Expansion

The Italian background. We have little historical knowledge of Italy prior to the foundation of the Roman Republic. For the earlier
period we must depend chiefly on the evid[ence]
supplied by modern archaeology. The maj[ority]
of the Italian people were evidently descer[ded]
from tribes of mixed ethnic origin who [had]
drifted down from the north across the Alp[s in]
successive waves during the second millenn[ium]
before Christ. Of these the most important [in]
Roman history were the kindred Latin peo[ple]
who settled the fertile plain of Latium on [the]
western coast south of the Tiber. They w[ere]
already well established when the neighbor[ing]
district of Tuscany to the north of the Ti[ber]
was conquered by the Etruscans some ti[me]
prior to 800 B.C. The Etruscans were a sea[far-]
ing people of mysterious but probably East[ern]
origin, more highly civilized than the Itali[ans]
among whom they settled. Their langua[ge,]
which is not Indo-European, still baffles sch[ol-]
ars, although their alphabet is adapted fr[om]
the Greek and their culture shows strong e[vi-]
dence of Greek influence. With them came t[he]
first elements of the highly developed civili[za-]
tion of the eastern Mediterranean, includi[ng]
the political form of the city-state. Their i[n-]
dustrial and artistic products, brought to lig[ht]
by the excavation of thousands of Etrusca[n]
tombs, follow Greek models too closely to clai[m]
much originality, but they show a high degre[e]
of technical skill, while the remains of thei[r]
roads, bridges, and tunnels give evidence o[f]
remarkable engineering ability. In the seventl[h]
century they began to spread their territoria[l]
domination southward among the poorly or[-]
ganized tribes of Latium. Throughout most o[f]
the sixth century Etruscan kings ruled Rome
and the neighboring Latin cities, contributing
in no small degree to the development of

and was being replaced by cattle and sheep grazing. In this less intensive use of the land the small farmer was at a distinct disadvantage. More and more, small farms were bought up to be incorporated in large estates, while the discontented plebeians organized their political strength in the hope of securing relief from debt, or allotments of public land from conquered territory.

Rise of plebeian power. The struggle between the classes, which formed the underlying *motif* of Roman politics for centuries, began early in the history of the republic. Until much later times it was a very orderly struggle. With characteristic Roman tenacity and respect for law, the plebeians kept up a steady political pressure, and during the course of little more than a century and a half they succeeded in bringing about a gradual and bloodless democratic revolution. Early in the fifth century they gained the right to elect tribunes to protect their interests. Then a plebeian assembly was created, and its authority was steadily increased until, by 339 B.C., it was recognized as a law-making body with full powers, subject only to the formal assent of the Senate, and even this check was removed before long. Meanwhile the plebeians had secured the right of intermarriage with the patricians and eligibility to nearly all state offices. They had also secured some economic relief by a modification of the laws regarding debt and through small allotments of public land. These had been dangerous years for Rome, during which she was forced to lead the group of Latin communities which formed the Latin League in a series of defensive wars against warlike neighbors until the nearest and most threatening of these had been defeated. It was to the indispensable part they played in the army during these wars that the plebeians owed much of their political success. When Rome entered on a period of more rapid expansion in the latter part of the fourth century, the plebs had thus secured an active share in government and the power to control legislation when they chose to do so. With that for a long time they remained content. Inevitably, however, it was the more wealthy among the plebeians who had the means and leisure to undertake public office. In the course of time these tended to become almost indistinguishable from the patricians in both political point of view and social standing,

thus reopening the gap between the ruling class and the mass of the people.

Expansion in Italy. From about the middle of the fourth century B.C., Rome was drawn into one war after another, each of which brought further territorial expansion. First she fought a series of successful battles against her former allies of the Latin League in Latium, the district immediately around Rome, with the result that the population of Latium was absorbed into the growing Roman state as partial citizens. Then followed a long and bitter struggle against the Samnites, a group of hardy and courageous tribes inhabiting the area now known as the Abruzzi. Thanks to their superior military organization, the Romans were eventually able to conquer the Samnites and the other Italian tribes who had allied themselves with them. By 290 B.C., Rome dominated all of Italy south of the Po Valley, with the exception of the Greek cities scattered about the southern tip of the peninsula. And these she conquered within the next two decades.

Results of expansion. With rare political wisdom, the Romans refrained from reducing the conquered Italians to complete subjection, as was the habit of ancient conquerors. She left the defeated cities and tribes an almost complete local autonomy, contenting herself with control of their military force and foreign policy. Separate treaties with each welded the Italian peoples into a firm federation under Roman leadership. The terms of the treaties varied with varying conditions, thus making possible more satisfactory relations than could have been established under any one consistent scheme. In addition, Roman and Latin colonies with full or partial Roman citizenship were founded at strategic points throughout Italy. This accomplished the dual purpose of accelerating the Romanization of the peninsula and of supplying the poorer Roman and Latin citizens with much-needed land. These colonies had also the important economic effect of turning the surplus Roman population back to the land instead of into industry or commerce. The Romans remained a nation of farmers and landowners.

First Punic War. Rome was soon to have need of her allies, and her wise treatment of them was to be amply justified by their loyalty during the long struggle with Carthage, which began scarcely more than a decade after the

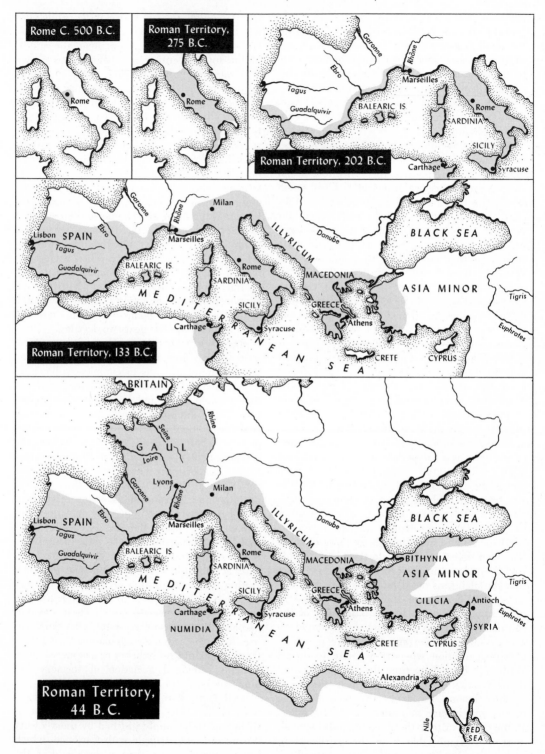

Rome C. 500 B.C.

Roman Territory, 275 B.C.

Roman Territory, 202 B.C.

Roman Territory, 133 B.C.

Roman Territory, 44 B.C.

last wars in Italy. Carthage, founded by Phoenician traders perhaps as early as 800 B.C., had long been a wealthy state. It had conquered an empire extending along the North African coast from what is now Libya westward to the Straits of Gibraltar and including also southern Spain, Sardinia, the Balearic Islands, and more than half of Sicily. It had a powerful navy and its wealth enabled it to hire large armies of well-trained mercenaries. Although the Carthaginians had rich landed estates on the fertile African coast, which they worked with slave labor, their wealth came mostly from commerce and depended on their control of the western Mediterranean trade. Hitherto Rome and Carthage had been friendly enough, for Rome was a land power interested chiefly in agriculture, and there was no sufficient point of contact to arouse enmity. The Roman conquest of the commercial Greek cities in southern Italy altered this situation, making the two powers dangerously close neighbors. The first Punic War (so called from the Roman name for the Phoenician people of Carthage) began in 264 B.C. when the Carthaginians threatened to occupy Messina and close the narrow straits between Sicily and Italy. Most of the fighting occurred in Sicily, and the Romans soon realized that they could never succeed in an overseas war without a navy strong enough to meet the Carthaginian fleet and keep sea communications open. This was a new venture for the Romans and proved immensely expensive in both money and men. During the next few years they built two complete fleets, totaling more than five hundred ships, and lost both as the result of battle and shipwreck. The Roman treasury was exhausted and the people were already taxed to the limit of endurance, but Rome would not admit defeat. Private contributions raised the money for a new fleet. Finally, in 242 B.C., after more than two decades of incessant fighting, Rome won a decisive naval victory and took command of the seas. Carthage had no alternative but to abandon Sicily, and the following year sued for peace.

The first Roman province. The war left Rome exhausted, but she was able to recoup part of her losses by exacting a large indemnity from Carthage and by levying an immense tribute of grain from the newly acquired territory in Sicily. The conquest of Sicily marked the beginning of a new policy for Rome, the first step toward empire. A few friendly cities were treated as liberally as the Italians had been, but the greater part of the island was made into a Roman province governed by a Roman official and obliged to pay a tithe of its produce to the Roman people. A few years later Rome acquired still more territory by taking Sardinia from Carthage.

Second Punic War. The peace that followed the first Punic War was no more than a truce of exhaustion. The military party in Carthage, led by Hamilcar Barca, was determined on revenge and the recovery of Sicily and Sardinia. Meanwhile, Hamilcar attempted to compensate for these losses by founding commercial colonies in Spain. After his death his brilliant son, Hannibal, continued his work until he had an army in Spain which he felt was strong enough to invade Italy. The story of the second Punic War (218–202 B.C.) is one of the most dramatic in military history. Traveling at incredible speed, Hannibal marched through southern Gaul and struggled across the Alps into Italy in mid-winter before the Romans were well aware of their danger. The Carthaginian commander had no intention of besieging the city of Rome, which was much too strongly fortified, but pinned his hopes to defeating the Roman army in open battle, thus providing Rome's subject Italian allies with an opportunity to rebel and assert their independence. Had this happened, the power of Rome would have been permanently broken. So far as Hannibal's own part of this plan was concerned, his hopes were realized. In one battle after another he defeated the Romans, finally wiping out almost the entire Roman army at Cannae in 216 B.C. But Rome's Italian allies failed to live up to his expectations. They remained stubbornly loyal to Rome. During the next few years the Roman army, under the canny leadership of Quintus Fabius, surnamed Cunctator (the Delayer), adopted the exasperating policy of refusing open battle, so that Hannibal was forced to waste his strength in futile maneuvers. He could neither capture the city of Rome nor crush the elusive Roman army, and, though he could lay waste large sections of Italy, the Roman state remained intact. In these years the tenacious courage of the Romans and their allies was tried to the utmost.

The loss of men and of material wealth had been tremendous. Yet Rome was still capable of taking the offensive. In 204 B.C. an expeditionary force under Scipio Africanus was sent to Africa, and Hannibal was forced to return to defend Carthage. The war ended with his decisive defeat at Zama in 202. By the terms of peace, Spain became a Roman province, while Carthage was forced to pay a huge indemnity, surrender her fleet, and accept Roman dictation of her foreign policy. There could no longer be any doubt of Rome's complete domination of the western Mediterranean.

2. *Expansion and Civil War*
(*202–31* B.C.)

The Senate. The devastating struggle with Carthage and the final victory, which made Rome the strongest power in the Mediterranean world, wrought great changes both in the internal politics of the republic and in her relations with other states. The conflict between the democratic and aristocratic parties had been thrust into the background by the stress of war. The plebeians had already gained sufficient voice in government to satisfy their most pressing demands and, while the state was in danger, were willing to entrust the conduct of affairs to the more experienced senatorial class, which now included many of the richer plebeians who had gained admission to the Senate by way of public office. The Senate, indeed, had gained almost complete control of policy, especially in foreign affairs, for it was a continuing body and its members were more thoroughly conversant with the complicated problems of state than the yearly magistrates or the occasional popular assembly could be. As a result, the foreign policy of Rome in the years following the second Punic War naturally reflected the interests of the senatorial aristocracy. The senators were mostly great landowners, trained in public service. They would have little interest in gaining commercial advantages from Rome's growing power, but would be keenly sensitive to anything that affected the prestige or honor of the state. Moreover, as the most cultured group in Rome, many of them had been strongly influenced by the recent introduction of Greek literature and art and had acquired a great admiration for Greece.

Eastward expansion. It was this combination of pride in the power of Rome and interest in Greek culture that motivated the foreign policy of the Senate in the opening years of the second century. Hitherto, Rome had preserved a strict neutrality in the quarrels of the Hellenistic kingdoms which had emerged from Alexander's empire, but she could no longer ignore the responsibilities of power. When the alliance of Philip V of Macedonia and Antiochus III of Syria threatened to upset the balance of power in the East and destroy the independence of the Greek states, the Senate felt called upon to interfere. After defeating Philip in 197 B.C. and Antiochus in 191, Rome guaranteed the freedom of the Greek states and assumed a benevolent protectorate over them. There seems at first to have been little imperialistic intention in Roman policy. Once having entered Greek politics, however, Rome was forced, step by step, into deeper and deeper involvement. A second war had to be fought with Macedonia (171–167 B.C.), after which Rome cut Macedonia into four republics and reduced the Greek states to the position of dependent allies. When even this failed to keep the peace, Rome took over Macedonia as a tribute-paying province (146 B.C.), and tightened her hold on the Greek allies so that they became completely dependent on her. Meanwhile the growing determination of the Romans to tolerate no rivals in the Mediterranean led Rome into an unprovoked assault on Carthage (149–146 B.C.). The ancient city, which had made a remarkable economic recovery since the end of the Punic Wars, was destroyed and the Carthaginian territory became the Roman province of Africa. A few years later, 133 B.C., Rome acquired still another province, that of Asia, by the testament of the dying king of Pergamum. The Roman Republic was rapidly acquiring an empire.

Economic and social developments. Rome's expansion, whether imperialistic or accidental, left her with a sizable overseas empire and made her the sole dominant state in the contemporary world. This situation inevitably had repercussions on the social and economic life of the Roman people. Wealth flowed to Rome from the plunder and tribute of the provinces, greatly increasing both public and private capital. Very little of this new capital, however, was invested in industry or commerce, so that there was less change in the character of Roman economy than might have been expected. Industrial production, it is true, was increasing in volume with the growing demands of a wealthy class of consumers, but it was still limited largely to manufacture by small artisans of goods for daily use, with little or no surplus for export. The most significant change was the introduction of large quantities of slave labor as the result of the number of prisoners taken during the decades of continuous warfare. This naturally tended to drive free labor out of competition and had the undesirable effect of adding to the number of poverty-stricken and discontented city plebeians. Commerce, too, was growing in volume, but, except for army and state contracts let out to citizens, the greater part of this was left to the more commercially experienced Eastern peoples who had now been drawn into Rome's expanding orbit. Among the Romans themselves financial affairs were now largely in the hands of the increasingly important class of *equites* or knights, so called because in earlier times they had been distinguished from the poorer plebeians by being able to afford the expense of maintaining a horse and serving in the cavalry. By the second century B.C., however, they had ceased to be a military class and had become simply businessmen with a special interest in banking and finance. In general they found safer and more substantial profits from investment in contracts for public works or army supplies or for the exploitation of state mines and forests than in competition with the skilled merchants of the East. The knights, too, enjoyed a privileged position in the provinces as bankers and as contractors for the collection of the provincial taxes. By the end of the second century many of them were very wealthy and were becoming a power in politics.

Agriculture. The greater part of Roman capital was still invested, as of old, in land. The second Punic War had greatly accelerated the growth of large estates. Whole sections of Italy had been deserted following their devastation by Hannibal's armies, and after the war these lands were taken over by the government as public land to be leased to anyone who could invest the necessary capital to restore it to use. Roman senators, who as a class were barred by tradition and also by actual law from engaging in trade, took advantage of this situation to acquire large estates from the public land. Later the capital obtained from exploitation of the provinces enabled many senators to expand their estates still further. The possession of capital also permitted the owners of large estates to combine scientific methods of cultivation with slave labor to produce cash crops such as wine, olive oil and wool. Such estates were operated with the sole aim of making a profit for their owners, who, more often than not, were absentee landlords living in Rome and devoting themselves to maintaining their political and social status. It required considerable capital to plant a vineyard or olive orchard or to stock a sheep ranch, and there was a long delay before vines and orchards began to bear fruit. The initial cost of a large number of slaves to work the estate was also considerable. But once established, the large estate produced a steady and handsome income. Small farmers could not compete with these new methods, and, as more and more of them were forced to give up their land, the social discontent of the earlier period rose again to a dangerous pitch.

Gracchan reforms. It was the hope of reestablishing the class of small landowning citizens, who had been the military and political backbone of the republic during the first period of expansion, that inspired the reforms proposed by Tiberius Gracchus. As one of the tribunes for the year 133 B.C., he proposed to the popular assembly a law for the redistribution of all public lands held in excess of the legal limit set for individuals by laws which in fact had been ignored for many years. Since lands leased from the public domain still legally belonged to the state, Gracchus proposed that the state should take back land from the owners of great estates who had obtained more than their allowance and give it to needy citizens, thus drawing the restless mass of the unemployed away from Rome and resettling them on the land. The law was violently opposed by the Senate, not only because most of its members were large landowners, but because Gracchus had secured its passage by the popular assembly, which had taken no initiative in politics for nearly a century. This was a revolutionary move and posed an immediate threat to senatorial authority. When the idealistic reformer stood for election again the following year, riots broke out in which Gracchus himself was killed. The redistribution of public land was continued for some years after his death, then came to a standstill, until, ten years later, his unfinished task was taken up by his younger brother, Gaius Gracchus. The reform program of the younger Gracchus was much more extensive, and given time he might have accomplished much good. Like his brother, however, he was defeated and killed while his reforms were still in their initial stage.

War with the allies. The Gracchan dream of restoring democratic government by a free and vigorous citizenry was impossible of fulfillment at this late date. The Roman plebeians, living on the dole and including among their number a growing proportion of freed slaves of foreign extraction, were not the citizens who had made Rome great. Yet the Gracchi had shown them their political power and under any leader who could catch their fancy by bribes or promises they might yet be a disturbing factor in politics. A new spirit of violence filled the political conflicts of the rest of the century and spread eventually to the Italian allies. These, despite their loyalty in time of desperate danger, had never been admitted as a body to Roman citizenship. In 91 B.C. they rebelled and were pacified by the long-desired gift of citizenship only after three years of destructive warfare (91–88 B.C.). Under other circumstances this act might have furnished the republic with a broader and more stable political base, but the new citizens, like the old, were not allowed to vote unless present in person in Rome. They merely added to the number of discontented citizens who might follow a demagogue.

Early civil wars. To this unstable political situation, the army added a new element of danger. During an otherwise unimportant war in Africa against the Numidian king Jugurtha, the army had been reorganized by Marius, the democratic consul for 107 B.C. Instead of drafting the property-owning citizens as was the ancient custom, he recruited a volunteer army composed mostly of landless men, who served as professional soldiers for pay. The new army represented the irresponsible and discontented elements in Roman society and might prove a dangerous weapon in the hands of an unscrupulous general. This was demonstrated in 88 B.C., when Sulla, a general of aristocratic background, marched on Rome at the head of his own army and drove out Marius and the democratic leaders. It was an armed coup d'état. Sulla then left to carry on a war with the Eastern king, Mithridates of Pontus, while Marius returned with an army, seized the capital and massacred hundreds of his senatorial enemies. During the next few years the violence of party strife grew into civil war, accompanied by wholesale proscription and massacre of the defeated parties. Sulla returned in 84 B.C. and, after heavy fighting, once more occupied Rome and killed or exiled thousands of the democratic party. It has been reckoned that during the decade of the war with the Italian allies and the early civil wars at least half a million Romans and Italians perished.

Rome and the provinces. The evident disintegration of republican government in the first century B.C. was closely connected with economic and social developments in Italy, but in a more fundamental way it was the result of Rome's expansion and of the exploitation of the conquered provinces. Irresponsible senatorial governors and the financiers who held contracts for the collection of provincial taxes cooperated to fleece the helpless provincials. Both the upper classes, senators and *equites*, were rapidly adopting a policy of barefaced imperialism, motivated by no more altruistic aim than to rob the conquered peoples of the East. In 63 B.C. the brilliant Roman general, Pompey, opened up new fields for plunder by adding the rich provinces of Bithynia, Cilicia, and Syria to Rome's growing empire. Rome had now become a parasitical state, draining the provinces of their wealth with disastrous results for herself as well as for the unfortunate provincials. The great fortunes made by conquering generals, senatorial governors and tax-collecting *equites* went to increase the size and number of large estates in Italy. And this in turn swelled the number of small farmers who, having lost their land, were forced to join the degraded city populace that lived on the dole from the provincial revenues. The final result of imperialism seemed to be the ruin of the provinces and the demoralization of the Roman citizens of every class. The republican government of a small city-state was proving totally inadequate for the administration of an empire. The only solution seemed to be the dictatorship of some man strong enough to suppress party strife by force and to restore honest and efficient government. And the necessary force could be provided by the great professional armies which had been created as a result of the military reforms of Marius.

Julius Caesar.   Half a century of civil wars between rival leaders elapsed, however, before a permanent dictatorship was established. For a time, Julius Caesar seemed destined to accomplish this result. He was the most able politician of his generation and won a great reputation and the loyalty of his army in a long series of wars which ended with the conquest of Gaul and the invasion of Britain. Returning in 49 B.C., he entered on a civil war with his old ally, Pompey, who had ruled Rome in his absence. The defeat of Pompey left him master of the state. Caesar's power was that of an armed dictator, though he exercised his authority through the old republican offices and institutions. He instituted a number of admirable reforms and, given time, might have reconstructed the state on a permanent basis and won the loyalty of the Roman people. But Caesar was ambitious. The belief that he intended to establish himself as a king of the Hellenistic type aroused intense opposition among the old senatorial aristocracy, and on the Ides of March, 44 B.C., he was assassinated.

Antony and Octavian.   The murder of Caesar did not restore free republican government. His place was taken by a triumvirate, composed of Mark Antony, Lepidus, and Caesar's grandnephew and heir, Octavian. A civil war with the senatorial party led by Brutus and Cassius followed. The triumvirs were victorious, but the selfish bond that held them together could not withstand the strain imposed by the necessity of sharing power. While Octavian earned the confidence of the Romans by just government in Italy, and rid himself of one rival by forcing Lepidus to retire to private life, Antony followed his own designs in the East, where he married Cleopatra, the Queen of Egypt. Charging him with a treasonous plan to carve out for himself a kingdom among the Eastern provinces, Octavian marched eastward, defeated Antony in 31 B.C., and annexed Egypt. Octavian was now master of the state as his great-uncle had been before him. But his dictatorship was a permanent one. Though he asserted his in-

The commanding personality of Julius Caesar is reflected in this portrait bust, an art form at which the Romans excelled.

tention of restoring the republic and though he retained the Senate, the consuls, and the old machinery of government, he kept control of the government in his own hands during a long lifetime and passed on his power to the emperors who succeeded him. In 27 B.C. the Senate conferred upon him the name of Augustus, and it was under that name that he proceeded to organize the Roman Empire and establish the great period of Augustan peace.

3. Roman Culture in the Republican Age

Influence of Greek culture.   Of the early literature, art, and philosophy of Rome almost nothing remains, and historians entertain a probably well-founded suspicion that very little existed. The interests of the sturdy farmers, soldiers, and statesmen of the early republic did not run naturally in those directions, while their remarkable lack of commercial contact with the outside world kept them for a long time insulated against the influence of more advanced civilizations. The conquest of the Greek cities of southern Italy and Sicily brought the Romans into direct contact with Greek culture, but it was not until toward the end of the third century B.C. that they seem to have become fully aware of its charm. Having become aware of it, however, the educated class in Rome set about absorbing Greek literature and thought with all the enthusiasm of the recent convert. During the second century, as the eastward trend of foreign policy brought the republic into ever closer relations with the Greek world, a knowledge of Greek became a necessary part of a Roman gentleman's education and, by the following century, it had become a second mother tongue to the Roman literati. Greek slaves and freedmen swarmed into Rome, bringing the artistic techniques of the Hellenistic East and, in many instances, serving as tutors to the sons of wealthy families. The earliest Roman literature and philosophy date from the beginning of the Greek influence and, throughout, they retained the character imprinted upon them by Greek forms and Greek thought. But, as they developed, they became adaptations rather than imitations of the Greek models. Roman culture was built upon a Greek foundation, but the structure was Roman, and it had the lasting quality peculiar to Roman buildings. It still stands today as one of the great monuments of human civilization, preserving for us not only much Greek thought

that would otherwise have been lost, but also much that was the original expression of Roman genius.

Latin drama. The drama dominated the early period of Latin literature. Plays adapted from the Hellenistic New Comedy or the older Greek tragedies brought entertainment and intellectual stimulus to a public not yet fully accustomed to reading in any extensive fashion. The first dramatist of whose quality we can judge from plays that have survived intact was Plautus (c. 254–184 B.C.), who wrote boisterous, rollicking comedies based on Greek plots. In the next generation, the more subtle shadings of Greek comedy were presented in an infinitely more refined, literary Latin by Terence (c. 195–159 B.C.), a member of the aristocratic circle of the younger Scipio, though born a slave in Africa. At the same time Ennius (239–169 B.C.) reproduced in Latin the best tragedies of Sophocles and Euripides, with variations that brought them into harmony with the characteristic Roman conceptions of morality. Drama continued to be the most prolific form of Latin literature through most of the second century. As the educated Romans developed more consistent reading habits, however, it declined, its place being taken by other types of poetry and prose.

Poetry. The early imitations of Greek poetry were rendered somewhat awkward by the intractability of the Latin tongue. Long practice under Greek guidance was needed before it acquired the flexibility that would enable the Roman poets to rival their Greek models. By the middle of the first century it had reached that stage, and the Roman writers had by then so thoroughly absorbed the spirit and forms of Greek literature that they were able to work freely, without the cramping effect of too close imitation. The lyric poetry of Catullus (c. 84–54 B.C.) has all the spontaneity and ease of a native literature despite his use of Greek forms. The charming lyrics addressed to Lesbia, in particular, have a youthful freshness that makes them more appealing than any of the Hellenistic poetry that has survived. The men of this generation perfected the poetic vocabulary, the meters and rhythms of Latin

The individualistic realism of this bust of an unknown Roman shows the strong Hellenistic influence on late republican sculpture.

poetry and prepared the way for the great poets who would give the Augustan Age its exceptional brilliance.

Prose. While the Golden Age of Latin poetry was yet to come, the prose writers of the late republican era created a Latin style that has never since been surpassed. Latin oratory flourished in these years under conditions similar to those which had developed the rhetorical style of republican Athens, and partly under the influence of Greek models. The hectic political life of the dying republic placed a premium on oratory, and every young Roman aristocrat devoted himself to the study of rhetoric as the essential training for a career in public office, in the Senate, or in the law courts. Cicero (106–43 B.C.), the unrivaled master of Latin prose, had a long and distinguished career in public office and was one of the most intransigent leaders of the conservative senatorial party in opposition to the dictatorial ambitions of Caesar and the triumvirate. His rhetorical style was developed in the heat of political controversy. His orations against Catiline, whom he prosecuted for conspiracy against the state, are models of their kind. Cicero's fame as a prose writer, however, does not rest solely upon his orations. His familiar letters show a more amiable side of the great controversialist's character and are filled with priceless reflections of the social life of republican Rome. Finally, in the philosophical treatises *On Friendship, On Duty, On Old Age,* etc., he demonstrated the capacity of the Latin language to express the finest shades of meaning, while at the same time transmitting to the Latin world the best moral teaching of the Greek philosophers. Julius Caesar, too, was a master of prose style, although of a more simple and direct sort. His *Commentaries on the Gallic Wars,* a report to the Roman people on his conquest of Gaul, have served as an introduction to Latin prose for countless schoolboys. They constitute also a masterpiece of historical literature. This same generation of politically active writers produced one other popular historian, Sallust (86–34 B.C.), whose account of the Catiline conspiracy, from a point of view very different from that of Cicero, and of the war against the Numidian king Jugurtha, have been greatly admired for their vigorous style, if not always for their reliability.

Religion. The religion of Rome was native to the country, but like other aspects of Roman culture it was transformed by Greek influence, while Roman philosophy was in origin an importation from Greece. The early Roman religion consisted of a formalized worship of *numina* or spirits who pervaded the household, the fields, and the woods. Later, as the state developed, the conception of household gods was adapted to the needs of the state and a ritualistic state religion evolved as a significant factor in practical politics. It was only after the Greek cultural invasion, however, that the impersonal *numina* or gods acquired an anthropomorphic character and a mythology. By the simple expedient of identifying the native gods with their Olympian prototypes, the Romans took over the literary heritage of Greek mythology. As a result of this process, Latin literature was greatly enriched, but the Roman religion lost its indigenous character and much of its hold on the faith of the educated classes. By the Age of Augustus it had degenerated into a literary convention, a "poets' religion," while the religious emotions of the mass of the people were being fed by Hellenistic cults that were beginning to be imported from the East.

Philosophy. The most cultured of the Roman aristocrats were turning meanwhile from religion to philosophy for comfort and guidance. As a rule they lacked the interest in metaphysical speculation about the nature of the universe which was characteristic of the Greeks of the classical age, but like the later Hellenistic philosophers they were greatly concerned with practical morality. They asked of philosophy how a man should live so as to achieve peace and the good life; and many of them found satisfactory answers according to their temperament in either Epicureanism or Stoicism, both of which had originated in Greece in the third century B.C. and have been discussed in the preceding chapter. Epicureanism gained many adherents among the wealthy Romans who were disillusioned and repelled by the violence of republican politics. Stoicism, on the other hand, made its strongest appeal to the conscientious statesmen, public officials, and judges who were the mainstay of the Roman state. It was a stern and somewhat arid philosophy, but for centuries it inspired the men who gave just rule to the Roman Empire and fashioned Rome's great code of law.

SECTION B

THE ROMAN EMPIRE AND

The Arch of Titus was erected to celebrate the emperor Titus' defeat of the Jews and the destruction of Jerusalem. The Roman Forum can be seen in the background.

ITS DECLINE (31 B.C.-c. 500 A.D.)

A generation before the birth of Christ, there occurred an event which gives a double significance to our conception of that period as the beginning of a new chronological era. The founding of the Roman Empire by Augustus was the decisive step in the creation of a world-state in which were gathered together under one ruler and under the protection of the *Pax Romana* the civilized peoples of all those lands that border on the Mediterranean. During the first five centuries of our era, the Roman Empire supplied the framework of civilization. Within that framework the various ancient cultures interacted upon one another and became more cosmopolitan, while to the evolution of Western civilization were added two new ingredients of lasting importance — the Christian religion, and the conception of a universal, international world-state with laws that were the common possession of all civilized peoples. The Mediterranean peoples enjoyed two centuries of unprecedented prosperity within the protecting frontiers of the empire, but these were followed by three troubled centuries of economic and cultural decline. When the empire finally collapsed in the West, ancient civilization in that area had already been greatly transformed. The whole western half of the empire was overrun by vigorous Germanic tribes from the northern forests beyond the Rhine and the Danube. These barbarian conquerors trampled Roman civilization underfoot, but they did not entirely destroy it. Despite internal decay and external violence, a vital remnant remained, reinvigorated by Christianity and preserved within the framework of the Christian church. As had happened so often before in the history of civilization, the conquerors were themselves conquered by a superior culture which they would in time absorb to the limit of their capacity and adapt to their own character and needs. The history of the following centuries is the history of the reconstruction of Western civilization from Roman and Germanic materials, shaped by the dominating influence of Christianity.

5

The Roman World in the

First Two Centuries of the Empire

FOR TWO glorious centuries, from 31 B.C. to 180 A.D., the ancient world enjoyed peace and prosperity such as it had never known. It was not a large world by today's standards, but it comprised all the lands that had as yet attained any degree of civilization, save for those distant countries in the Far East which were little more than names to the Roman citizen, known to him only through the luxuries imported from India by Alexandrian merchants. Various types of culture were included within this great empire, Middle Eastern, Greek, and Latin, their roots striking deep into the past. Now, with no political barriers to keep them apart, and with easy intercourse guaranteed by the protection of the Roman government, they met and, though each retained in part its own identity, they gradually fused to form a new composite, which, for lack of a better name, we may call Roman civilization. It was not, however, Roman in the narrower national sense in which the culture of the republic was Roman, i.e., the product of the Roman or Italian people; for to the civilization of the Roman Empire all the more civilized peoples within its borders contributed, the provincials no less than those who could claim descent from the citizens of the old republic. Neither the "Roman peace"

nor Roman civilization was destined to last. When the former was broken, the latter declined. But what was left of Roman culture was to form a major part of the legacy of the past to the people of medieval and modern Europe.

1. Organization of the Empire

The principate. The greater part of the lands included in the Roman Empire had been conquered by the Roman Republic. But, though the republican government succeeded in conquering the Mediterranean world, it proved unable to rule it. The attempt to rule a great empire with the governmental machinery of a city-state republic resulted in civil war and anarchy, in the economically ruinous exploitation of the provinces and the corruption of the Roman people. The new wine could not safely be contained in the old bottles. When, therefore, Augustus seized control of the empire in 31 B.C. with an authority backed by a victorious army, the majority of the people, Roman and provincial alike, were prepared to accept him as the savior of the state. And Augustus made it as easy as possible for the Romans to accept his authority. He avoided all

62

unnecessary offense to their republican sentiments. Claiming for himself only the military title of *Imperator* and the civil title of *Princeps,* or first citizen, he exercised his authority through the old offices and institutions of the republic. But, though the Senate still met and passed resolutions, and the popular assembly still elected officers, there is no doubt that the will of Augustus controlled every decision. He was commander of the army and navy; his was the final authority in the provinces; he had absolute control of finance; in short, by virtue of a long list of special powers formally or tacitly delegated to him, he was the actual ruler of the state.

Growth of absolutism. During a long reign, dating for all practical purposes from his defeat of Antony in 31 B.C. till his own death in 14 A.D., Augustus made very intelligent use of his practical control of government to reorganize the administration of the empire and to create an efficient governmental system. His reign marked the first essential steps from republic to empire. What remained for his successors was to transform his practical absolutism into an openly constitutional absolutism and to complete the evolution of Rome from a city-state to a world-state with universal citizenship and political unity. It was a very gradual evolution, extending over more than two centuries, and was scarcely completed before the empire began to decline.

The Senate. The first step in strengthening the emperor's position was to undermine the status of the old senatorial families and to nullify the authority of the Senate. The chief danger from these representatives of the old republic lay in the fact that there was no established rule of imperial succession. On the death of an emperor the Senate became the governing body of the state and had, theoretically, the right to choose his successor, although, as events were to prove, the deciding voice was likely to be that of the army. Augustus himself secured a peaceful succession by adopting his step-son Tiberius as his heir. The three following emperors — Caligula, Claudius, and Nero — were also connected by family ties with Augustus and owed their position largely to the loyalty of the army to the family of the great founder of the empire. The fact that any member of the senatorial aristocracy

Although Augustus is here somewhat idealized, much of the true character of the founder of the Roman Empire is revealed as well.

could, in theory, aspire to the principate, however, bred suspicion in the minds of these emperors and led to wholesale prosecutions which thinned the ranks of the old senatorial families. After the death of Nero in 68, the army revolted and created four emperors in one year, but fortunately the last of these, Vespasian (69–79), was able to restore order and reestablish a constitutional principate. He was, indeed, the first of a series of strong rulers who gave the empire more than a century of good government. Under their rule the Senate came to represent the whole empire rather than the exclusively Roman aristocracy and was brought firmly under the emperor's domination. During most of this period the emperors happened to be childless, and so solved the question of succession, as Augustus had done, by adopting the ablest man available and naming him his heir. Unfortunately the last of the "good emperors," the philosopher Marcus Aurelius (161–80), did have a son whose feeble reign opened the way to the military anarchy that was to plague the empire for another hundred years.

Imperial administration. The second step in establishing the imperial authority over a united empire was the development of an efficient, centralized administrative system. The irresponsible provincial governors of the republican regime were replaced by officers appointed by the emperor and directly responsible to him. Even the worst emperors of the first two centuries generally gave good government to the provinces. Two centuries of unbroken peace and security amply justified the imperial system in the minds of the provincials and secured their unquestioning loyalty.

Municipal government. The powers of these imperial officials stopped short of local government. In this sphere, which most closely affected the lives of the people, the emperors wisely allowed almost complete freedom. For administrative purposes, Italy and the provinces were divided into *civitates* or municipalities. In the eastern part of the empire, these represented survivals of the ancient city-states, with their traditions of self-government and civic patriotism. In the newer barbarian West, tribes or cantons were organized into municipalities with a city as the capital. The citizens (not as a rule including the poorest classes) elected their own officers and their own *curia* or council, chosen from a local aristocracy of wealth corresponding to the senatorial class at Rome. In each municipality the old republican government of Rome was reflected in miniature, with variations depending on the ethnic origins and traditions of the individual city.

Extension of Roman citizenship. This free municipal citizenship did much to keep the provincials contented. But the empire could never become a truly united world-state so long as the invidious distinction between Roman citizens and all others remained in force. Roman citizenship carried with it important legal privileges, as the career of St. Paul indicates (cf., Acts 22:27 and 25:12 ff.), which were not shared by the provincial subjects of Rome, even though these might be citizens of their own municipalities. These privileges included the right to appeal to the emperor from the sentence of a local court, and exemption from degrading punishments such as scourging.

Rome, unlike the Greek city-states, was relatively liberal in granting citizenship to conquered peoples, and the emperors early realized the advantages to be gained from extending citizenship to the provincials. It would level all classes under their authority, broaden the foundations of their power, add to the loyalty of the provincials, and weld all parts of the state more closely together. Hence, despite the opposition of the Italians, who were unwilling to share their special privileges as Roman citizens, they gradually extended citizenship to the most influential classes in the provinces, until by the *Constitutio Antoniana* of 212 all free-born citizens of the municipalities throughout the empire were made Roman citizens.

The army. The army played an important part in the dissemination of Roman citizenship. The legions, which formed the bulk of the standing army, were recruited by voluntary enlistment from the body of Roman citizens. When these proved insufficient, provincials were admitted and by virtue of their military service received citizenship. The number thus honored was greatly increased by the military reforms of Vespasian (69–79), who barred Italians from service in the legions. The aristocratic youth of Italy might still serve in the praetorian cohorts, the picked imperial bodyguard, and after training there might be transferred as officers to the legions or auxiliary troops. But the rank and file of the legionaries were now mostly provincial. The army, some 400,000 strong, was usually stationed at strategic points along the frontiers, where there was most to fear from invasion. The term of service was from twenty to twenty-five years, after which the retired soldier was often granted land near his old camp. Many of the legions' camps became permanent centers of Roman influence and formed the nucleus of new provincial towns. Some of these towns, formed around the *castra* or camp of the legions, still exist, as is shown by such English names as Chester, Lancaster, Manchester.

Emperor-worship. We have seen how the imperial administration and the spread of Roman citizenship tended to solidify the empire, while the free municipal government gave an outlet to local initiative. More than this was needed, however, to complete the evolution of the empire into a strongly coherent world-state.

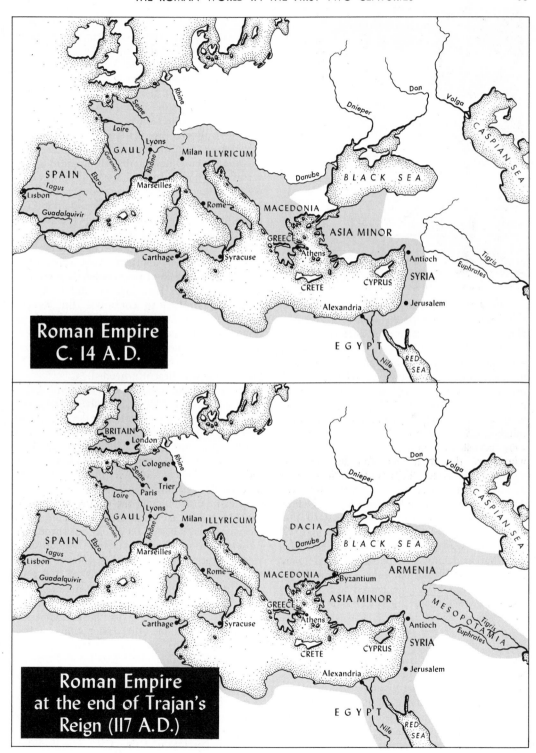

Roman Empire
C. 14 A.D.

Roman Empire
at the end of Trajan's
Reign (117 A.D.)

The Praetorian Guard, depicted here in a relief sculpture now in the Louvre, formed an élite military corps stationed in Rome.

Imperial patriotism had to replace, or be superimposed upon, local civic patriotism. This result was accomplished in part through the institution of emperor-worship. In the ancient world every city-state had had its own peculiar religion, closely bound up with the state. Men were accustomed to worship gods or heroes who were the traditional founders or protectors of the state. This tradition was inherited by the Hellenized monarchies that followed Alexander's empire, and in turn by the Roman conquerors. It was the grateful eastern provincials who first hailed Augustus as a god and savior. He was quick to realize the value of a cult that made imperial patriotism a religion, and one in which the emperor was himself the central figure, though he barred it from Italy lest it offend the old republican sentiment of the Romans. Even in Rome, however, Augustus was deified after his death, and during his lifetime was hailed as *divus* if not as *deus,* a divine hero if not a living god. Many characteristics of the old Roman religion prepared the way for the acceptance of emperor-worship in the West, and, as the eastern influence grew with the further unification of the state, it became firmly established. Domitian (81–96) was the first emperor to claim the title

Dominus et Deus in Rome during his own lifetime. Under his successors, emperor-worship became a recognized state religion, in which all citizens took part, whatever their other religious traditions might be. There was little protest, since few of the ancient religious cults were exclusive or debarred their followers from the worship of other gods.

Roman law. Even more important than emperor-worship for the unification of the state was the development of Roman law into a universal civil code. Indeed, its legal system was perhaps Rome's greatest contribution to civilization. It was more just and humane than any previous code, and it has formed the foundation for the civil law of most modern European countries. Republican Rome had from the first its own civil code, applying exclusively to Roman citizens. Each of the conquered territories had also its own legal system, and these the Romans permitted to continue. But as the Roman Empire assumed world proportions, as commerce between the provinces increased, some body of law with common jurisdiction over subjects as well as citizens in all parts of the empire was urgently needed.

As early as the second century before Christ, such a body of law was evolved from the praetors' edicts and from the decisions and comments of jurists in individual cases tried in the Roman courts. This collection of praetors' law and of the precedents established by judges' decisions was strongly influenced by the best local laws and the current practices of businessmen throughout the empire. In time it came to form a common code applicable to all freemen everywhere. Based on jurisprudence rather than on legislation, the Roman code was constantly reinterpreted to keep it in harmony with the changing needs of the age. The great value of this reinterpretation by edict and precedent lay in the general recognition by Roman jurists of the fundamental principles, based on Stoic conceptions of justice and human brotherhood, that equity is more important than strict legality and that all free men are equal before the law. About the beginning of the second century A.D., the emperors' rescripts and decrees, or "constitutions" as they were called, began to replace the praetors' edicts, thus continuing the construction and reinterpretation of the code. The tradition of jurisprudence also continued unbroken. Even during the troubled third century a series of distinguished jurists made invaluable contributions to the elucidation and systematization of law.

2. Society

Importance of cities. By the second century, the Roman Empire had become a vast commonwealth of self-governing municipalities, whose local freedom was protected rather than disturbed by the imperial administration. Stimulated by the security and prosperity that accompanied the "Roman peace" and by the policy of the emperors, old cities took on a new life and new ones sprang up to rival them in all parts of the empire. For, where there were no cities, as in Spain or Gaul, the emperors created them. As in the old city-state, the political, social, and cultural life of each municipality was focused on the city which was its center, and this preponderant importance of the cities lent to the whole of Roman civilization a strongly urban character.

Luxury of city life. In the prosperous years of the first two centuries, the urban upper classes possessed great wealth, and they spent it freely in adding to the beauty and dignity of their native cities. Rome was proverbial for the splendor of its temples, theaters, circuses, forums, public baths, and palaces, while in the provincial cities the same magnificent buildings were to be found in proportionately lesser degree. Even the smaller towns of Gaul and Britain were well planned, well kept, and sanitary. The streets were wide, straight, fully paved, and clean. Great aqueducts brought water to the cities in plentiful supply. There were statues and monuments everywhere. Private houses, too, were built with every facility needed to make life pleasant and agreeable. They had shaded central courts in which fountains played to cool the midday heat. They had running water and, in some cases, central heating. The ruins of Pompeii, preserved intact by their covering of volcanic ashes, show a degree of comfort and convenience in public and private life not to be experienced again until relatively modern times. And Pompeii was little more than a third-rate town.

Liberality of citizens. Many of the buildings and public works were constructed by the emperors or by the municipal governments. The majority, however, owed their existence to the civic pride and generosity of wealthy citizens. Markets, bridges, roads, and aqueducts, as well as all kinds of public buildings, were

The Roman Forum was originally a market place and the center of public life in the ancient city. Now only fragments remain of the temples, basilicas, and shops that lined its paved streets and squares.

The Pont du Gard, a triumph of Roman engineering skill, combines a bridge on the lower level with an aqueduct on the upper level. It is located near Nîmes in southern France.

donated to the city by men who had been honored with public office in the local government, or by men who hoped to be so honored, or by others motivated simply by that passionate love of their native city which was so strong a force in the ancient municipality. The circuses, banquets, and other public amusements of that sociable age were also due in many cases to private liberality. Social standing and civic honors were alike the monopoly of wealth; but wealth carried with it also heavy duties of service and generosity, rigidly enforced by public opinion.

Social classes. The municipal aristocracy was made up of the wealthier citizens who had sufficient property to qualify for offices in the local government or for membership in the *curia*. The list of *curiales,* as those eligible for membership in the *curia* were called, was revised every five years. From this group men of servile birth were usually excluded. Yet former slaves, "freedmen," often rose to positions of wealth and power. Many a highly educated Greek slave, or Syrian who had inherited the commercial genius of his people, was able to acquire sufficient money to buy his freedom and afterwards to make a great fortune in trade. The mass of the citizens, shopkeepers, artisans, and so forth, and the poorer proletariat, who were sometimes excluded from citizenship, led obscure lives of little or no social or political importance, as did also the peasants who lived outside the cities. There were, however, frequent public amusements, gladiatorial shows, chariot races, games, and pantomimes, to break the tedium of their lives, and most of them belonged to some club which organized banquets and social gatherings and afforded them the comforting sense of belonging to an exclusive society. The slaves were the lowest social class. They were the property of their masters, without social or civil rights, though a growing humanitarian spirit was mitigating the brutality with which many were treated in the early days of Rome's conquests. They were also becoming less numerous because of the frequency of manumission and because the empire now fought only defensive wars and was no longer taking great numbers of prisoners.

Imperial aristocracy. Superimposed upon the municipal aristocracy, and recruited from it, was an imperial or Roman aristocracy. This was made up of two classes, the senators and the knights or *equites*. By the second century these classes had lost their purely Roman character and included provincials who had risen in the imperial service. The *equites* were mostly men of moderate wealth, who had held offices in the imperial administration or the army. The senatorial aristocracy, as its numbers dwindled, was recruited in turn by the emperor from the *equites* who had won his gratitude by faithful service. Both the imperial and municipal aristocracies were clearly defined castes, based partly on heredity, partly on wealth. Class distinctions were sharply drawn, but were not permanent. Few noble families lasted for many generations. The birth rate in aristocratic families seems to have been generally low, and the families soon died out. Their places were taken by men from the lower classes.

3. Economic Life

When Augustus ushered in the two centuries of Roman peace, he introduced also an era of unprecedented prosperity to Italy and the provinces. The wars which had devastated the empire were ended. The civilized world had been united in a single state, under a government strong enough to guarantee peace and security. Merchants might carry their wares freely from the Black Sea to Spain, from the Nile to the Thames, without crossing a frontier. And wherever they went they found the same laws, the same coinage, the same privileges, and the protection of the same government. During the first two centuries, the emperors allowed full freedom to commerce, barring slight interprovincial duties, and abstained from governmental interference in industry. New and safe markets were established in the barbarian provinces. Everywhere new cities were founded, providing at once the supply and the demand for a new economic life.

Communications. A good share of the amazing revival of commerce must be credited to the ease and security of communications within the empire. The Mediterranean Sea, though stormy and treacherous, was a broad highway through the center of the Roman world, and the imperial fleet kept it clear of pirates. In each province the emperors repaired or constructed a skillfully planned network of roads, connecting all the important cities. These roads, stone-paved and permanent, were built originally for the legions, but they served the merchants equally well. Over them messengers of the imperial service, equipped with relays of horses, could average fifty miles a day. Ordinary travelers could maintain an average speed of five miles an hour in districts where a thousand years later roads were almost impassable or nonexistent. Communications in Europe and the Middle East were probably never so rapid or so safe until the coming of the railroad as

they were in the first two centuries of the empire.

Foreign commerce. Commerce with lands outside the empire flourished, but was of secondary importance. From the East, the traditional source of luxuries, came perfumes, spices, ivory, precious stones, and silk, and from eastern Africa ivory, gold, and condiments, to be paid for in manufactured goods or coin. Furs, amber, wax, and slaves were imported from Germany and Russia, in return for oil and wine. It was a colorful trade, but it was almost entirely in luxuries and its importance cannot be compared with that of the trade within the frontiers.

Interprovincial commerce. Within the empire, the most important articles of interprovincial commerce were raw materials and manufactured goods for everyday use, the prime necessities of life. It was from these rather than the luxuries that great commercial fortunes were made. Grain, olive oil, wine, timber, metals, hemp, and flax could not be produced in all parts of the empire and so had to be shipped to the consumer. Some manufactured articles, too, could be produced only, or to better advantage, in certain localities. With these exceptions, goods were usually manufactured in the town where they were to be sold. Egypt had almost a monopoly on the production of linen and paper. Asia Minor, Italy, and Gaul produced quantities of woolen goods. Syria alone held the secret of Tyrian purple dyes and also led in the manufacture of fine glassware. Italian glazed pottery was unrivaled till the second century, when it was driven from the markets by the superior products of Gaul. These and other articles, specialties of certain regions, were shipped freely and in great quantities to all parts of the empire.

Industry. Though great fortunes were made from commerce, much of the wide prosperity of the Roman world resulted directly from manufacturing. Industry was mostly in the hands of small independent artisans. It contributed to the livelihood of the masses rather than to the fortunes of the few capitalists. When the goods manufactured were intended for the local market, as was most often the case, the artisan was merchant as well as manufacturer, selling his wares to the consumer in

The Appian Way, a famous Roman road, runs southward from Rome to Brindisium. The ruins of an aqueduct run parallel to the road at this point.

his own little shop. Only in the case of goods intended for a distant market was there any attempt at mass production. Wealthy men sometimes employed large numbers of slaves or free workers in their shops. However, this differed from our own factory system in that each worker completed the article he was making, from beginning to end, and there was little use of machinery of any but the simplest sort. But even goods intended for export were often produced by independent workers.

Agriculture. Roman society was so characteristically urban, and commerce and industry played so important a part in economic life, that we are in danger of forgetting the country and the products of the soil. Yet the fact remains that the majority of the population worked on the land, and agriculture formed the broad base on which the economic structure of the empire rested. The great fortunes accumulated through commerce or imperial favor were mostly invested in land; for land-ownership provided a safe, respectable income with a minimum of risk and worry, which was always the ideal of the wealthy aristocracy. Men of great wealth bought up large estates, which they cultivated by slave labor or let out to small tenants. Free peasants with small holdings were unable to compete with cheap labor and scientific methods of agriculture, and many were forced to sell their land, which went to swell the already large estates of the rich. The peasants themselves were faced by the melancholy alternative of joining the poor city proletariat or becoming tenants on the land they once had owned. The wealth resulting from agriculture, then, was becoming concentrated in the hands of a relatively small class of landed proprietors.

4. Culture of the Empire

The Augustan Age. The Golden Age of Latin literature began amidst the political tumult, the wars of conquest and the civil strife of the dying republic; but it reached its full development in the tranquillity of the Augustan Age. By that time the Latin writers had learned what Greece could teach them, and the classical Latin style had been formed by such masters as Cicero and Catullus. When Augustus seized control in 31 B.C., a brilliant group of poets and prose writers were ready to begin their mature work under the favorable conditions which his rule was to provide. The dictator himself was eager to promote a Latin literature that would serve to reawaken Roman patriotism and reflect glory upon the Augustan state, and at his court there were liberal patrons, like the wealthy Maecenas, who gave encouragement and material support to writers ready to carry out the emperor's program.

Virgil. Roman patriotism, pride in the past and hope for the future, is the constant theme which runs through the poetry of Virgil (70–19 B.C.), the greatest of all Latin poets, who has been called "the voice of Rome incarnate." This theme, less pronounced in his early poems, the *Eclogues,* which are rather stylized and conventional pastorals, became obvious in the *Georgics,* a " farmer's handbook" in verse, which expresses the poet's deep love of the Italian land and the sober virtues that had carried a nation of farmers to world empire. In the *Aeneid,* the magnificent epic which connects the origins of Rome with Homeric Troy, the theme of Roman virtue and Roman glory swells into a vast peal of organ music. The *Aeneid* is modeled on the Homeric epics, to which it is related as a kind of sequel, but it is never slavishly imitative. Its spirit is essentially Roman.

Horace. Virgil's great epic stands alone. The other poets who graced the court of Augustus for the most part cultivated the shorter lyric forms. Of these the best beloved throughout the centuries has been Horace (65–8 B.C.), whose *Odes* and other poems have been read, translated, and imitated by poets of every European language down to the present. If he lacked the prophetic grandeur of Virgil, Horace was equally typical of the Roman character at its best. Clarity, moderation, and balance, always combined with flawless form, make him the most perfect example of the classical Latin ideal. There is in all his work a genial understanding of people and a loving appreciation of natural beauty. Whether singing of his love for Lydia or of the contentment he found on his little Sabine farm, whether urging the enjoyment of the good things of this world or gently moralizing, Horace speaks with the directness of a contemporary to men of kindred temperament throughout the ages.

The elegiac poets. A more limited form and a more limited mood characterized those poets of the late republic and the Augustan Age who adapted the structure of the Greek elegy and used it for love poetry of a very personal kind. The elegiacs of Tibullus (c. 55–19 B.C.) and Propertius (c. 50–16 B.C.) celebrate the delights and torments of love, its triumphs, frustrations, and ultimate disillusionment. Ovid (43 B.C.–18 A.D.), too, used the elegiac form in the light-hearted poems addressed to Corinna and also in the *Ars Amatoria.* The latter is a book of practical advice, often ironical and always witty, on the art of love. Ovid was the most fluent versifier as well as the most cheerful hedonist of all the Augustan poets. He seems incapable of the tenderness of Tibullus or the passion of Propertius, whose Delia and Cynthia were undoubtedly real women, whereas Ovid's Corinna is almost certainly synthetic; but he very probably knew more about women than either of them. In his greatest work, the *Metamorphoses,* Ovid abandoned both the frivolity and the elegiac form of his earlier verse and allowed his amazing fluency and gift for poetic imagery full rein. Here in a sustained poem of nearly twelve thousand hexameter lines, he wove his way through some two hundred and fifty stories drawn from classical mythology. It is a storehouse from which medieval and modern men have drawn poetic inspiration as well as a large part of what they know of ancient myth.

Livy. Patriotism and the belief in the virtues that made Rome great found more explicit expression in the greatest prose writer of the Augustan Age, the historian Livy (59 B.C.–17 A.D.). Like the *Aeneid,* Livy's history of Rome *ab urbe condita* (from the founding of the city) was designed to promote the program of patriotic and moral revival, by which Augustus hoped to repair the damage done by the civil wars. And, like Virgil, Livy needed little urging from his imperial patron, for his patriotism and his pride in the old Roman virtues arose from a deep personal conviction. Only thirty-five of the hundred and forty-two books that made up the original history survive, but we have summaries of nearly all of them. Judged by modern standards, Livy leaves much to be desired in the way of accuracy and critical sense. He accepted legendary stories at their face value when there were no other sources available. But judged by any standard, the history is a literary masterpiece. It shaped the conception of Roman history and influenced the Latin prose style of European scholars for many centuries.

The Silver Age. The period from the death of Augustus to the death of Marcus Aurelius in 180 A.D. is generally referred to in histories of Latin literature as the Silver Age. Compared with the creative vigor of the Golden Age, the literature of this period seems thin and self-conscious, artificial and pedantic. There are erudite compilers like the elder Pliny

(23–79 A.D.) whose *Natural History* is an encyclopedia of ancient knowledge. And there are a host of society poets and satirists, like Juvenal (c. 50–c. 130 A.D.) and Martial (40–104 A.D.), who commented upon the manners and morals of contemporary society in epigrammatic verse. The verbal economy of the Latin language lends itself to this kind of writing. At its best it was used with telling effect; at its worst it descended to the level of artifice for artifice's sake. Among the prose writers the most distinguished practitioner of the epigrammatic style was the historian Tacitus (c. 55–c. 117 A.D.). A good illustration of his style is the famous comment on the Roman conquest of Britain: *Solitudinem faciunt pacem appellant* ("They make a wilderness and call it peace"). His sharply etched portraits of the principal figures at Rome from 14 to 96 A.D., contained in the *Annals* and the *Histories,* are our most vivid source for the history of the first century. In contrast to his somewhat jaundiced view of Roman society under the tyrannous emperors, his ethnographic account of the early Germans in the *Germania* presents those barbarian people in a favorable light.

Trajan's Column in Rome, 125 feet high and covered with a spiral band of carving in relief, was erected in the years 106–13 to commemorate the emperor's victory over the Dacians. The bands shown here begin a continuous pictorial narrative.

Greek literature. So much of the important literature of this period was written in Latin that we are apt to forget that it was not the only language of the empire. It was, indeed, rapidly becoming the only literary language of the western half of the empire, spreading with Roman civilization to the provinces of Africa, Spain, Gaul, and Britain, where no old established culture existed to combat it. The number of writers of the Silver Age who were born in the provinces, especially in Spain, is proof that mastery of Latin was no longer an Italian monopoly. The eastern half of the empire, however, remained, as it had been throughout the Hellenistic period, predominantly Greek-speaking. Alexandria continued to be an active center of Greek scientific and philosophical thought. There, in the second century A.D., Ptolemy wrote the works on astronomy and geography that were to be accepted as authoritative till the sixteenth century. Greek literature in this period was, however, generally more distinguished for learning than for creative imagination. Plutarch (46–c. 120 A.D.), indeed, is almost the only Greek man of letters in these years whose name is widely known today, but his great series of biographies of Greek and Roman personalities arranged in pairs, the *Parallel Lives,* are an enduring part of the world's literature.

Roman sculpture. The development of Roman art parallels in many ways that of Latin literature. In both fields, the Romans owed much original inspiration to Greek models, but they adapted these to express their own character. The sculpture of the later republican period was clearly an importation from the Hellenistic East, but the portrait busts and statues which are the most characteristic form of Roman sculpture have a realism that reflects the Roman interest in individual personality rather than in idealized representations of human types. Realism and individuality continued to characterize Roman sculpture through the first two centuries of the empire, though in many of the statues of the emperors, as in those of Augustus and Claudius, a new emphasis on the imperial dignity lends a touch of idealization. The emperor had become the symbol of empire, and the tendency to idealize him became more pronounced with the growth of the cult of emperor-worship. Glorification of the

The huge basilica built by Constantine at the edge of the Roman Forum furnishes an excellent example of the use of the rounded vault as a structural principle.

emperors and of the empire led also to the development in this period of a special type of monumental sculpture: the decoration of altars, columns, and triumphal arches with scenic reliefs depicting imperial triumphs and achievements.

Architecture. The grandeur of Rome found expression as well in the magnificent buildings erected in the first two centuries of the empire, not only in Rome but also in many provincial cities. Greek influence is evident in the use of columns, though seldom in the pure Greek form, but the limited spatial range of the low rectilinear Greek temple could not meet the Roman demand for grandeur of design. The most characteristic Roman contributions to architecture, which continued to influence western European architecture for centuries, were the arch, the vault, and the dome. These forms enabled the Romans to build on a grand scale buildings which expressed the spirit of the Roman Empire just as the perfect proportions of the Greek temple had expressed that of Greece.

6

Decline of the Roman Empire

To the student who has studied the history of the Roman Empire during her two glorious centuries of peace, prosperity, and highly cultivated civilization, the three centuries that followed must come as a disheartening anticlimax. The decline of the empire, and its disappearance in the West before the end of the fifth century, will seem inexplicable and almost incredible. Generations of historians, both before and after Gibbon wrote *The Decline and Fall of the Roman Empire,* have offered their explanations. But no single explanation will entirely suffice. Each factor in the situation seems to be at once cause and effect of the general tendency. We can only conclude that there were hidden elements of weakness in the structure of the Roman world which were not apparent so long as everything went smoothly, but which combined to cripple society once the peaceful course of prosperity and good government was broken. Whatever the ultimate causes may have been — and at this distance of time we cannot identify them with any certainty — it is clear that once the decline had begun, the economic, social, and political ills from which the empire suffered interacted upon one another to hasten the disintegration. And, finally, all of these ills were increasingly aggravated by the growing pressure of the barbarian tribes along the northern frontier and, eventually, by their invasion of the empire and

the resultant political break-down of its western half. This last factor in the situation must, however, be reserved for fuller discussion in Chapter 7. Here we will be concerned chiefly with the internal causes or symptoms of decline.

1. Beginning of the Decline: The Third Century

Economic causes. Symptoms of a general decline in the vitality of the empire were already apparent in the third century. Among these some of the most significant were economic changes that were undermining the prosperity of the empire and producing a social situation that was both materially and spiritually unhealthy. It is difficult to isolate the causes of the economic regression, since they were intimately related, as we shall see, to the effects of civil war and the burden of taxation which, in the two following centuries, became ever more crushing as the defense of the empire made increasing demands on its wealth and manpower. There is, however, positive evidence that agricultural production, on which so much of the empire's economy depended, was declining, thus decreasing the food supply of the cities and also the buying power of the landowning classes. In parts of Italy and North

74

Africa, and possibly in other areas as well, deforestation had resulted in soil erosion, or overcropping of marginal land had led to soil exhaustion. A more important factor, however, was the widespread decline of scientific farming on the great estates which had largely replaced small independent farms throughout the empire. By the third century, slave labor was becoming scarce, and owners of large estates were giving up the attempt to make a profit by supplying produce to the city markets. Instead they rented the land out to small tenants, who lacked the capital, equipment, and skill to farm in the most productive way. Moreover, as we shall see, a combination of economic factors and imperial laws bound these tenants to the land so that they lost their freedom and much of their incentive to vigorous enterprise. The great estates, like the later medieval manors, were beginning to produce largely for their own consumption, and so the mutually profitable economic exchange between country and city gradually died out.

Equally significant is the fact that Roman commerce and industry apparently faced a declining rate of growth after the second century. The inclusion of the half-barbaric and economically undeveloped provinces of the West within the empire had at first opened up a great field for commercial and industrial exploitation on the part of the more highly developed East. Furthermore, the advance of these western provinces from semi-barbarism to a standard of living comparable to that of the rest of the empire helped to maintain a steady rate of expansion in the economy of the empire as a whole. By the second century, however, the West was fully developed and the last economic frontier had vanished. Thereafter further expansion would have to come largely within the existing limits of a stable society. New methods of cheaper mass production might have maintained the rate of growth by lowering the price of goods and increasing the quantity that could be sold. Or a more equable distribution of wealth and higher wages might have had a similar effect by increasing the buying power of the population. But neither of these things happened. The Romans made

Marcus Aurelius is remembered as the philosopher-emperor and author of Meditations.

no significant inventions of machinery to speed up production; the competition of slave labor tended to keep wages at a very low level; and an increasingly large proportion of the wealth of the state was being concentrated in a relatively small aristocratic class, who invested their wealth in large landed estates rather than in commerce or industry. As a result, the economy of the ancient world lost the stimulus of expansion, and a capitalist economy that has ceased to grow is in imminent danger of decline.

Failure of government. While it is clear that many of the causes of the empire's decline were inherent in the economic structure and possibly could not have been avoided, it is also true that some of the most serious economic and social evils can be traced more or less directly to the failure of the imperial government in the third century and to the policies of the later despotic emperors. Throughout the second century the emperors had become steadily more autocratic. Until the death of Marcus Aurelius in 180 A.D., however, they had mostly been men of unusual ability, capable of discharging their enormous duties. Good

government might not have been able to maintain prosperity much longer, but bad government certainly hastened the decline. And bad
government began with the reign of Com-
modus (180–92), the son of the philosophical
Marcus Aurelius, nor did it end with his assassination at the hands of mutinous soldiers.

Military anarchy. There followed a century
of chaos and anarchy, in which the army took
government into its own hands. Imperial power
had always depended essentially on the support of the legions, but hitherto the emperors
had been able to control them. Now the army
assumed control of the emperors, creating and
destroying them at will. Recruited largely from
the least civilized parts of the empire and stationed permanently on the frontiers, the legions had lost all sense of responsible citizenship and were ready to follow any commander
who chose to make a bid for the imperial title.
Between the years 192 and 284, there were
thirty-three emperors, most of whom died by
violence. During all that time, the empire was
more or less constantly a prey to revolution,
civil war, and the threat of foreign invasion.
Troops marched and countermarched through
all the provinces, plundering as they went and
rendering the roads unsafe for merchants. To
make matters worse, the emperors, in order
to satisfy the demands of the mutinous soldiers
who had created them, were forced to impose
crushing taxes, thus striking a direct blow at
trade by sapping the buying power of the citizens. They also adopted the ruinous policy of
raising money by debasing the coinage. This
combination of disorder, heavy taxation, and
military tyranny was all that was needed to upset the delicate economic equilibrium of the
Roman world.

Once started on the downward path, the
Roman Empire declined steadily. Roman society had apparently no longer the inherent
strength necessary for recovery. It yet remained
to be seen what the government could do, once
the military anarchy was brought to an end.
In the last years of the third century, the emperor Diocletian made a desperate effort to restore the strength of the empire by the brute
force of a despotic government. He reorganized
the empire in the most arbitrary fashion, and
for a time succeeded in checking the most obvious signs of disintegration. But in the long
run, the expedients of autocratic government

were among the most potent factors in perpetu-
ating the general economic and social decline.

2. Reforms of Diocletian

Diocletian establishes an autocracy. The
reign of Diocletian (284–305) marks a turning point in the history of the empire almost as
significant as the change from the republic to
the empire under Augustus. Like Augustus,
Diocletian was faced with the task of preventing the disintegration of the state, and he strove
to solve the problem in the arbitrary fashion
that came most naturally to a half-civilized
soldier who had fought his way up from the
ranks by sheer force of will. His first step was
to assume all power in the state and to free
himself from all constitutional checks. The
emperors had been gaining steadily in power
since the days of Augustus; but hitherto the
old forms of senatorial government had been
preserved. Diocletian abandoned all such fic-
tions. He reduced the Senate to the status of a
municipal council for the city of Rome and
declared the emperor to be the supreme ruler
of the state, with no constitutional limits to his
power. The emperor was now the sole source
of all law and authority and was himself above
all law. He was the divine ruler, surrounded
by all the pomp and ceremony of an eastern
despot, demanding servile obedience from his
subjects. This was a far cry from the days
when Augustus had posed as the first citizen of
Rome, to whom the body of citizens had delegated imperial authority. The very idea of
Roman citizenship now disappeared. There remained only subjects.

Administration centralized. The second step
was to centralize imperial administration so as
to bring the whole system of government more
directly under the emperor's control. Diocletian realized, however, that the task of personally governing so vast a state would be beyond
the powers of one man. He recognized also that
the Greek East and the Latin West were drifting apart. He therefore chose a colleague in the
year 286, a trusted general named Maximian,
who was to share with him the title of Augustus or emperor and govern the western
half of the empire. Further, to avoid interference on the part of the army with the succession to the throne, each of the two Augusti
adopted a younger man, who took the title of

Diocletian, the emperor who reorganized the Roman Empire, was a man of strong will and commanding personality.

Caesar. The Caesar was to assist in the task of governing and to succeed to the title of Augustus on the death or abdication of his superior. To systematize the civil administration, Diocletian then divided the empire into four great prefectures, each governed by a prefect who was directly responsible to the emperor of his half of the empire. The prefectures in turn were divided into a varying number of dioceses (there were seventeen in all), each administered by a vicar who was responsible to the prefect. The dioceses also were divided into provinces, much smaller than the old provinces (there were one hundred and one in the whole empire), each under a governor who was responsible to his vicar. Instructions could thus be passed down from the emperor, or cases could be referred back to him, through a regular chain of command. Each of these officers was assisted by a host of civil servants and special agents. There were also scores of officials attached to the imperial courts to assist in the central administration. This highly organized system took over all the duties of local as well as imperial government. The municipalities lost their free self-government and the municipal *curiales* became merely unpaid servants of the state, who carried out the dictates of the imperial officers.

Army reorganized. The third step in reform was to reorganize the army so as to make it more efficient, more dependent on the emperor, and entirely separated from the civil administration. Senators and citizens were gradually excluded from the army, as they had other services to perform for the state, and they soon lost all military spirit or ability. The old legions were posted along the frontiers as hereditary guards, while a new and more mobile force was recruited from German barbarians and the most uncivilized subjects of the empire. This barbarous army served only for pay and had no interest in the welfare of the state. Its officers rose from the ranks by a regular system of promotion, the highest office being that of *magister militum* or master of the soldiers. In the late fourth and fifth centuries even this office was usually held by a German of barbarian origin, Romanized though he might be.

Reform of taxation. These changes immediately strengthened the imperial authority. But the elaborate imperial courts, the numerous administrative officials, and the large mercenary army were very expensive. The emperors needed money and still more money, while at the same time the waning economic prosperity of the empire made the collection of taxes more difficult. To secure a sufficient income, Diocletian instituted a new system of taxation, which was simple, uniform, and efficient from the government's point of view, but deadly in its effect upon the people. It was to be responsible for many of the economic and social ills of the later empire. The principal tax was on land. All the land of the empire was divided into units of varying size according to their fertility, each unit in the municipality to pay an equal tax. There was also a head tax on the workers of the land. Merchants and artisans who had no land paid a special and very heavy tax. Each year the emperors calculated the amount of taxes needed. This sum was divided and subdivided among the various administrative divisions of the empire until the process ended by the assignment of a definite sum to each municipality. The municipal *curia* or council was held responsible for the collection of that sum. The system seems reasonable enough, but it left too many opportunities for graft and oppression on the part of the administrative officials, and its enforcement had, as we shall see later, most unfortunate effects on Roman society.

Constantine completes the reform. Diocletian's system was somewhat modified by his successors, but in the main it remained in force till the fall of the Western Empire. The practical working-out of many details was left to Constantine the Great (313–37), who after some years of civil war between rival Augusti and Caesars reunited the empire under his single rule. Diocletian's plan for dividing the administration of the empire and controlling the succession had not worked very well, but the actual division between East and West was growing too strong to be ignored. Constantine himself demonstrated this by founding a new capital at Constantinople in the East. After his death the empire was again divided, and there were nearly always two emperors thereafter, though it must not be forgotten that the division was solely for administrative purposes. In theory the empire remained one and united, under two rulers of equal power. At times, however, one must for convenience refer to the different parts as the Eastern and Western Empires, and this usage is further justified by the very real and growing cleavage between them in language and culture, the West having become completely Latinized while the East remained Greek.

3. Social Decline

In the society of the early empire there had been elements of weakness that tended to sap the vigor and vitality of the people, but these were counterbalanced by the individual freedom and opportunity for advancement enjoyed by all except the slaves. Roman society under the empire was never democratic. It was divided into classes, jealous of their rights; but in the first two or three centuries these classes were constantly recruited from below. There was no legal check on the ambition of the individual to improve his social or economic position. Peasants might move to the city, or artisans might become small landowners. Any worker, except the slave, was free to choose whatever occupation seemed to offer the greatest reward. Even the slave might buy his freedom and go into business for himself. Many freedmen rose to positions of wealth and influence. Any freeborn man, including the children of ex-slaves, of unusual thrift, industry,

or initiative might make sufficient money to join the curial class, the local aristocracy, and be eligible for membership in the municipal council. And any *curialis* might hope for promotion to the imperial aristocracy and the senatorial rank. The incentive to ambition provided by these opportunities for advancement was responsible for much of the vigorous economic life and the social vitality of the first two centuries. All this was changed by the autocratic emperors who followed Diocletian and who, in applying his system of government, were forced to bind men to their class or occupation in hereditary castes.

Workers bound to their land. The success of Diocletian's reform of the administration and the army depended on the collection of sufficient taxes to pay for their upkeep. The most important tax was that on land and on the agricultural workers. This tax weighed most heavily on the small landholders and the tenant farmers, who either paid the tax directly or had it passed on to them by their landlords in the form of rent. Many of these, unable to make a living after paying the taxes or heightened rents, were forced to abandon their land, either drifting to the cities to join the host of unemployed living on the dole, or seeking the protection of some great landlord who needed workers. As a result a good deal of marginal land was deserted and went out of cultivation, thus reducing the amount of taxable property. To check this development, which would prove disastrous to the imperial income, Constantine issued laws binding the agricultural worker, and his children after him, to the land he worked. The tax on the land and that on the worker were now united and became an hereditary obligation. No matter who owned the land, the workers remained as hereditary tenants, still legally free men except that they could not leave their land. They were called *coloni*. Slaves could no longer be sold off the land, and as their value as saleable property disappeared they were given the partial freedom of the *coloni*. All farm workers, then, were leveled to the same condition of partial servitude. A series of severe laws punished the *colonus* who left his land as rigorously as though he were a runaway slave. Great numbers of the population were thus forced to give up all hope of changing their economic or social status.

Tradesmen bound to their trade. The merchants and artisans in the city met the same fate. They had to pay a special tax, heavy enough to be ruinous in a time of constant economic depression. Certain necessary trades were being deserted since there was no longer any profit in them. The autocratic emperors could think of no way of improving conditions except to issue new laws forcing the merchant or artisan to continue in his occupation. The workers in each trade formed an hereditary caste. A baker must remain a baker, and all his sons must become bakers. There was no legal escape, even though it might become impossible to make a living, and though there might be better opportunities in other occupations.

Curiales ruined. But of all the people of the empire, the once well-to-do upper and middle classes of the municipalities, the *curiales,* suffered most, being reduced to universal and perpetual bankruptcy by the disastrous system of taxation. The *curiales* had been the mainstay of the flourishing municipal life of the early empire. Membership in the *curia* had been an honor eagerly sought. Now it became a ruinous burden. For the *curia* was made responsible for the collection of all taxes in the municipality. If it could not collect the full amount assigned to it, the members had to make up the deficit, and there usually was a deficit, from their own pockets. To keep the *curia* filled, the emperors issued strict laws forcing all men who had sufficient property to enroll in the curial class, and forcing all *curiales* to take their turn in office. In 336 Constantine made the curial position hereditary. It was still possible for a *curialis* who had sufficient wealth left after having filled all the offices a number of times to purchase senatorial rank which granted exemption from curial duties. But few were able to avail themselves of this privilege, and the sons of those who did, if born before their father's elevation, remained in the curial class. The *curiales* sought desperately to escape, and many succeeded, despite the harsh laws, thus making the burden heavier for those who remained. By the beginning of the fifth century men of curial descent were barred from the army, the administration, and the priesthood. They could not leave their cities, even for a short trip, without permission; they could not reside in the country; and they could not sell or dispose of their property by will without the permission of the governor of the province. Many were reduced to such despair that they forfeited their property and sought to hide themselves as *coloni* on senatorial estates. Occasionally the emperors tried to alleviate the condition of the *curiales* in individual cases, as when Julian in 363 granted immunity from service in the *curia* to the fathers of thirteen or more children, who might be considered to have done enough for the state. But on the whole the laws regarding the *curiales* became steadily more oppressive and their condition ever more hopeless.

Senatorial aristocracy. The senatorial aristocracy was the most fortunate class, a wealthy, privileged group, riding securely on the surface of a sea of destitution. Its members no longer had any necessary connection with the Senate, and their numbers had greatly increased since the early days of the empire. Their wealth was invested in land, since they were barred by law from engaging in commerce, and most of them were owners of great estates that were steadily crowding out the small landowners, many of whom had been forced to abandon their land and seek the protection of powerful neighbors from the inexorable demands of the tax collectors. As a rule their fortunes had been made originally in the imperial administrative service, and were being constantly increased by the unlimited opportunities for graft which they enjoyed. For, despite all the good intentions of the emperors, it proved impossible to enforce honest administration in the provinces. Governors and the higher officers, all of the senatorial class, were able to cheat the people on the one hand and the government on the other; while the senatorial landowners were often able to evade the taxes or to use their wealth and connection with the administration to defraud their poor neighbors or their tenants.

Effect of taxation. As was pointed out at the beginning of this chapter, there were weaknesses in the economy of the empire which might have led to a decline under any circumstances. It is nevertheless true that the crushing burden of taxation imposed by the autocratic emperors was a major factor in accelerating the decline and making recovery impossible. It was the government's insatiable demand for taxes that was responsible for the arbitrary laws which froze society in hereditary castes and which contributed to the decline by paralyzing individual initiative. The exactions of corrupt tax collectors, whose demands were limited only by the ability of the individual to pay, robbed the people of all incentive toward enterprise or thrift. Finally, in a more direct way, excessive taxation was crushing commerce, industry, and agriculture by absorbing the profits, while at the same time by impoverishing the mass of the people it reduced the market for goods.

Conclusion. To summarize the course of social decline: the fourth and fifth centuries witnessed the ruin and degradation of the worker on the land and the merchant and artisan in the city, and, above all, of the upper and middle classes of the municipalities, who had been the backbone of old Roman society; while the only group that was still prosperous was the selfish, parasitical, and unproductive senatorial aristocracy, made up of corrupt administrative officials and great landed proprietors. With the decline of industry and commerce, the economic center of gravity was shifting from the city to the country, where the great estates worked by semi-servile *coloni* were becoming increasingly isolated and self-sufficient communities. In the western half of the empire in particular, where the Germanic invasions hastened the decline, the provinces were sinking into a simpler, more restricted, and largely agrarian economy, although the process was not completed until some three centuries after the collapse of the imperial government.

4. Decline of Roman Culture

Roman civilization emerged from the fiery ordeal of the third century, its metal not purified but debased. The general level of culture was distinctly lower than it had been, and it was given no opportunity to recover, but rather sank with increasing rapidity during the fourth and fifth centuries. It is not surprising that a period of general decline should be accompanied by a corresponding decay of culture. Literature and art, science and philosophy, and all the workings of the human mind must always be strongly influenced by the conditions

under which men live. Some of the inevitable results of the political, social, and economic developments we have outlined are too obvious to demand comment; others deserve some further explanation.

Literature and art. The most striking characteristic in the mental attitude of fourth- and fifth-century Romans was apathetic resignation. The great majority of the population had lost all individual liberty and all hope of improving their economic or social position, while the condition of the empire as a whole grew steadily worse. With no hope of improving conditions, men came to accept them passively. Such a state of mind was fatal to originality or creative energy. Abundant evidence of this can be found in the literature of the period. Pagan writers seemed able to do no more than imitate the classics of the Augustan Age without producing anything new or significant. The sober military historian, Ammianus Marcellinus (c. 330–c. 392), indeed, is almost the only pagan writer of the fourth century who can hold our respect. Only the Christian theologians were able to build upon the foundation of classical culture, though transforming it in the process, to create a vigorous literature, for they had new sources of inspiration and hope for the future — if not in this world, then in the next. In almost all forms of art there was a general lowering in the standards of taste and in creative vigor. Architecture alone continued to thrive under the later emperors, utilizing the arch, the vault, and the dome to create buildings of monumental size. Here, too, Christianity brought new inspiration. The need for churches which, unlike the pagan temples, could contain a large congregation led to the adaptation of the form of the Roman basilicas — rectangular barn-like structures intended for legal and administrative business — to new religious purposes. Some of the most magnificent surviving churches in Rome, like that of Santa Sabina and Santa Maria Maggiore, date from the last days of the Western Empire.

Decay of official religions. The gradual loss of hope and confidence that characterized pagan literature in the third and fourth centuries was accompanied by the decay of the old official religions, which had emphasized the duties of the citizen to the state, and by the spread of mystery religions originating in the Middle

East, which offered personal comfort in this world and the hope of a happier life after death. Even before the end of the republic, the old pagan religion of Rome was losing its hold upon the educated classes. The emperors from Augustus to Marcus Aurelius strove to revive the official cults, but with little real success, and thereafter they became increasingly empty formalities. Until the triumph of Christianity in the fourth century, the emperor was worshipped from the Euphrates to the borders of Wales, but nowhere was his cult more than a formal patriotic rite. The ancient gods of Greece and Rome, enshrined in the epics of Homer and Virgil, were also worshipped, but in much the same formal way. There were temples everywhere to Jupiter, Juno, Minerva and the other gods who sat upon Mount Olympus, watching with impartial interest the destinies of men, though interfering now and then for the salvation of the state. But there was nothing left in the old mythology to give inspiration, hope, or comfort to the individual, nor to answer his anxious queries concerning his fate after death had overtaken him. Even before the disastrous third century, when public and private calamities caused men to seek more eagerly than ever for supernatural comfort, the twilight had begun to settle over Olympus. It was soon to darken into night, though the old gods long maintained a shadowy existence through official practice and in literary tradition.

Eastern mystery religions. For the majority of the people of the empire, the vacuum left by the decay of classical paganism was filled by mystery religions, which had spread through the Hellenistic East during the three centuries before Christ and which began to penetrate the West in the last years of the Roman Republic. Thereafter, aided by the unification of the Mediterranean world under the empire, they spread rapidly through the western provinces, following the lines of trade and the march of the legions. By the third century, they were the dominant religious force in the West as well as in the East. The most important of the mystery religions were those of the Great Mother (Magna Mater) from Asia Minor, of Isis from Egypt, and of Mithra from Persia. Of these, the cult of Magna Mater was the oldest and least spiritual. It was in essence a

A relief from the triumphal arch erected in honor of the emperor Constantine in 312 shows the emperor burning incense at an altar while slaves bring an ox, a sheep, and a pig for an official sacrifice. The emperor is surrounded by the standard-bearers of the victorious legions.

nature myth, its ceremonies celebrating the annual death and rebirth of vegetation, but also by extension promising its initiates a second birth. Isis, too, was a mother goddess who typified the life force and held forth a hope of immortality to her devotees. Her cult, served by shaven and tonsured priests, and characterized by colorful ritual, solemn processions, and sacramental ceremonies, was especially popular among women. Mithraism, on the other hand, appealed more strongly to men, and temples of Mithra were to be found in every camp. Its teachings, based on a dualistic conception of the universe and the soul of a man as torn by perpetual strife between light and darkness, good and evil, stressed the masculine virtues and a rigorous morality. As the god of light or the sun, Mithra fought against the powers of darkness and evil and aided men in their struggle to avoid the temptations of the flesh and to pursue a virtuous life, which would be rewarded by a happy existence after death. The cult of Mithra included a baptismal rite, the eating of a sacred meal of bread and wine which identified the devotee with the savior god, and the celebration of the birthday of Mithra on the twenty-fifth of December, the date on which the lengthening day announced the rebirth of the sun.

Common characteristics. Despite great variety of ceremony and belief, the mystery religions had many characteristics in common, and all satisfied much the same human needs. Each cult centered upon a divine savior, but all recognized the existence of a supreme divine force, which might be worshipped through the medium of other deities as well. Their primary appeal was that they satisfied the universal desire for individual salvation. They offered purification from sin and freedom from the sense of guilt, and they promised immortality to those who had been initiated into the mystery. Through participation in their sacred rites, the initiate was brought into mystic union with the divine being and thereby exalted above the miseries of mortal life. The ceremonies themselves, performed by a professional priesthood, made a strong appeal to men and women wearied with a drab and hopeless existence. Since they placed their major emphasis on immortality rather than on life in this world, they did little

to encourage the vigorous performance of worldly tasks, though in this respect Mithraism is a partial exception. Some historians have, therefore, regarded the spread of the mystery religions as one of the causes for the decay of the ancient civilization.

Neoplatonism. The adherence of the more highly educated classes to the eastern cults was gained through the support given them by the dominant philosophical system of the third century, Neoplatonism. This was a late revival of the philosophy of Plato, though in a debased form and intermixed with oriental ideas and superstitions. To the Neoplatonist, the chief aim of all thought and aspiration was to bring the individual soul into closer communication or harmony with the great spiritual force which rules the universe, whatever man may call it. And he recognized the gods of the various religions as partial and imperfect manifestations of that divine force. Neoplatonism, then, was a kind of vague monotheism, or belief in one god, who, however, might be worshipped under many forms and in many ways. As this philosophy became popular, the devotees of the various mystery religions came to accept their gods as personifications of one divine power, and many, if not most of them, joined more

This relief, showing a procession in honor of Isis, was taken from a temple to Isis in the city of Rome. The Egyptian origin of the cult of Isis is evident in the costume of the participants and the oriental character of the whole composition.

than one cult, seeking in each a different aspect of the one truth. The belief in one god, fostered by Neoplatonism, in a measure prepared the way for Christianity, as did the ceremonies, the teachings, and the emotional atmosphere of the mystery cults. On the other hand, the acceptance of all gods made Neoplatonism the most dangerous enemy to the exclusive monotheism of Christianity, which branded the worship of other gods as idolatry and a deadly sin.

In this depressing chapter, we have tried to picture Roman society in the centuries of decline, and to show as far as possible why it had lost its earlier strength and prosperity. Two great movements, however, of vital importance to any study of the fourth and fifth centuries, we have neglected so far, reserving them for special treatment in the following chapters. They are, first, the triumph of Christianity and its adoption as the state religion of the Roman Empire, and second, the invasion of the empire by hordes of Germanic barbarians. Both had a great immediate influence on the history of the dying empire, but an even greater effect in shaping the civilization of medieval Europe.

Mithra, the god of the sun, whose worship was widespread among the Roman legions, is shown here killing a bull. The ceremonial killing of a bull, reenacting a legendary episode, was part of the cult of Mithra.

"The brethren ought to be occupied at specified times in manual labor, and at other fixed hours in holy reading." • St. Benedict of Nursia (c.480–c.527)

7

The Christian Church in the Roman Empire

As THE OLD PAGAN Roman Empire decayed, there grew up in its midst a new spiritual empire, which in course of time was to replace it in the West and to carry on in western Europe the Roman tradition of unity in administration, law, language, and culture through the long chaotic centuries of the Middle Ages. Christianity was the one vital force and the church the one living organism in the Roman world during the last two centuries of the Western Empire. When that empire disappeared, the church, so far as was possible, took its place; the popes took over the universal authority of the emperors; and the episcopal hierarchy filled the void left by the withdrawal of the imperial administration. Throughout the Middle Ages the unity of the Roman Catholic Church was the bond that held together the various peoples of western Europe. Christianity had made profound changes in Roman thought, ethics, and morals; it had helped to destroy much of pagan culture; yet it was through the church that such elements of Roman civilization as it could assimilate were preserved and handed on to the Germanic peoples who swept over the Western Empire, burying it beneath the flood tide of barbarism.

1. Origin and Spread of Christianity

Origin. The Roman Empire was no more than two generations old when the foundations of the Christian religion were laid by the teaching of Jesus of Nazareth, whom his followers hailed as Christ, the son of the living God. Christ and his earliest disciples were Jews, and Christianity inherited from Judaism the exclusive, monotheistic belief in one God and the preoccupation with moral and ethical problems that were the unique characteristics of the ancient Hebrew religion. But, although rooted in Judaism, Christianity was original, not only in the belief that Christ was the long-awaited Messiah, the savior of mankind through whose redeeming sacrifice the faithful might obtain eternal salvation, but also in the quality of its ethical teaching, a quality perhaps best represented by Christ's Sermon on the Mount (Matthew, chapters 5–7). Later, as the new religion spread to the Jews beyond Palestine and to the other peoples of the empire, its development was influenced by Greek philosophy and by some of the concepts and practices common to the mystery cults. St. Paul, who was well educated and trained in Greek philosophy, was the most influential figure in the first period of expansion, both for the contributions he made to the growth of Christian theology and for the incentive he gave to missionary work among the Gentiles. It was he, more than any of the other apostles, who freed Christianity from Jewish national exclusiveness and made it a world religion.

The New Testament. Along with much else drawn from ancient Judaism, Christianity inherited the Hebrew Scriptures as a repository of

84

divinely revealed truth, and to these, during the century or so after the death of Christ (30 A.D.), were added a number of new and distinctively Christian works, which came to be regarded as the New Testament. It is characteristic of the increasing cosmopolitanism of Christianity that these Christian Scriptures were written in Greek, the international language of the Hellenistic world. To the first four books of the New Testament, the Gospels ascribed to Matthew, Mark, Luke, and John respectively, we owe most of what we know about the life and teaching of Christ. Although written probably between the years 60 and 110, they were evidently founded upon a well-established oral tradition. In the Gospels, and especially in the first three, the story of Christ's life — his birth, his mission, his death and resurrection — is told with unparalleled vividness, to which no summary account can do justice. The fifth book, the Acts of the Apostles, tells the story of the early missionaries with special attention to St. Paul and the mission to the Gentiles. The remainder of the New Testament, except for the final book, the visionary Book of Revelation, is composed of pastoral letters. Nearly half of these are from St. Paul and were written between the years 50 and 62. These twenty-one epistles, which discuss problems of doctrine, ethics, and church organization, contributed strongly to the development of a systematic theology and to the conception of a universal Christian Church.

Spread of Christianity. For three centuries after its foundation, Christianity spread slowly and was apparently only one, and by no means the most popular, of a number of cults of eastern origin. Slow as its progress was at first, however, it gained ground steadily, and by the middle of the third century there were well-organized Christian communities in every city of the empire. The fact that the new religion was long regarded by outsiders as no more than a fanatical Jewish sect undoubtedly hindered its growth. The exclusive monotheism of the Jews, as well as their persistently rebellious attitude toward the imperial government, had made them generally unpopular, and the Christians, while breaking with the national exclusiveness of the Jews, were as rigidly monotheistic. Their refusal to participate in the official cults or to recognize the validity of other religions antagonized both government officials and the devotees of the mystery cults. Moreover, Christianity spread at first most rapidly among the underprivileged classes, including the slaves, and was regarded as socially disreputable. The fact that the Christians held their meetings in secrecy also aroused the suspicion of government officials and enabled their enemies to circulate wild stories ascribing to them horrible orgiastic rites.

Factors favoring it. Yet, despite all the disadvantages under which it labored, there were elements in Christianity which made it irresistible. The figure of Christ loomed large in the thought of the early church. His followers had as the central fact of their religion a definite personal Savior, who supplied that connecting link between man and God for which the philosophers and the devotees of the pagan cults were blindly groping. This faith in a personal Savior, whom his first disciples had known in the flesh and whose words they reported, carried with it a definiteness of conviction in the reality of salvation, of the expiation of sin, and of the immortality of the soul (all questions that obsessed the mind of the ancient world) far greater than was possible for the mythological pagan or mystery cults. At the same time, Christianity gave men hope for the future, not only for themselves as individuals, but for the world. Where the pagan looked back with nostalgic longing to a mythical golden age, the Christian, especially in these first centuries, looked forward with confident expectation to a future golden age when the second coming of Christ would herald the establishment of the Kingdom of God on earth. The closely-knit organization of the church, too, which bound together Christians from all parts of the empire in bonds of brotherhood, gave the church an advantage over the mystery religions, which never attempted more than local organization. Finally, Christian ethics and morals, difficult though they were for the pagan to accept, bore fruit that could not be ignored in the admirable lives led by the early Christians. Nor could the pagans fail to see that they had peace of mind, hope, and certainty, strong enough to carry them through the fires of persecution, when for the rest of the world there was no peace, when hope was dying, and certainty unattainable.

2. *Persecution and Triumph*

Early persecutions. Christianity as a religion and the church as an association were banned by the imperial government as soon as they became strong enough to attract the attention of the emperors. About the year 111, the Emperor Trajan issued a rescript to provincial governors instructing them to prosecute those openly charged with adherence to the new religion, but not to seek them out nor continue the prosecution if they were willing to take part in the ceremonies of the official cult. For the following century and a half, this rescript may be taken as a fair enough definition of the imperial policy. Christianity was not a legal religion and its members might be punished even by death, but there was no general or systematic attempt to suppress them. The initiative was left to the provincial governors, who enforced the law with more or less severity as they chose. By the middle of the third century, however, conditions had changed and reforming emperors were forced to take stronger action.

Reasons for persecution. One may well ask why the imperial government, usually so tolerant of all religions, should have maintained so hostile an attitude toward Christianity over a period of two centuries. Yet there was reason enough, and from their own point of view the emperors were amply justified. Christianity was opposed to the whole spirit of Roman civilization and of imperial government. The most serious specific charges brought against the Christians were that they were stubborn and consistent law-breakers, that they refused to discharge the duties of a citizen toward the state, and that they were organized in illegal, seditious societies. And these charges were well founded. The Christian, strict monotheist as he was, was forbidden to take part in the emperor-worship which was the patriotic duty of all citizens. He could not accept public office or serve in the army without violating his principles, as both demanded participation in certain official and, to the Christian, idolatrous ceremonies. His attitude toward the whole governmental system, so closely bound up with paganism, was one of suspicion if not of actual hatred, and in any case he felt that he owed his first loyalty to a higher fatherland than the worldly empire.

Such an attitude in individuals was sufficiently dangerous. It was made more objectionable by the compact and efficient organization of the church. In nearly every community the Christians had a strong, corporate organization, under recognized bishops. And they were in constant communication with the other churches throughout the empire. Christianity was becoming a state within and opposed to the empire. No autocratic ruler could afford to ignore it. As their numbers increased, especially after the beginning of the third century, when they were joined by many members of the upper classes, the Christians became an ever greater menace to the state.

Persecution under Decius. In the year 250, the Emperor Decius undertook a vigorous program of reform to check the alarming decline, and as part of that reform instituted the first thorough attempt to crush Christianity in all parts of the empire. All citizens were commanded to take part in the ceremonies of the official religions. Those who refused were liable to various punishments, including the death penalty. Great numbers of the Christians complied with the law, while others bought certificates asserting that they had done so. But there were also many who remained true to their faith and suffered martyrdom. The persecution raged for about a year, until it was cut short by the death of the emperor.

Last persecution. During the remainder of the third century, the Christians were alternately persecuted and tolerated, according to the policy of the various emperors. From each persecution they emerged with numbers greatly diminished, but with their organization still intact; and at the first sign of toleration, the apostates, as the deserters were called, returned, and with them came new converts, won over by the example of the martyrs. Despite persecution, Christianity was growing stronger and more popular. It was also becoming more inimical to the government, and hence more dangerous. The last and most thorough attempt to stamp it out was begun in 303 by Diocletian, the great reformer and reorganizer of the empire, and was continued by his successors till 311. They succeeded only in proving that the Christians could not be crushed. The next great emperor was to seek their support and to found his government on a close alliance with the once outlawed church.

Christianity freed by Constantine. Diocletian abdicated in 305, and this act was followed by years of bitter civil strife. By 312 there were four rival emperors, of whom one was Constantine the Great. Supported only by the legions of Gaul and Britain, he was the least powerful of the four. His rival in the West was Maxentius, who held Italy, Spain, and Africa, while Licinius and Maximus divided the East between them. His position was very uncertain, but he was able to form an alliance with Licinius to defeat their respective opponents in the West and East. Like himself, Licinius had taken a neutral stand during the late persecution, while Maxentius and Maximus had actively oppressed the Christians. Gathering his legions, Constantine marched swiftly into Italy, staking his whole career on the chance of victory against greatly superior forces. It was probably during that daring march that he decided to seek the support of the Christians. At any rate, to that period belongs the story, so variously interpreted, of his vision of a fiery cross in the sky and the words *Hoc vince* ("By this conquer"), which he took as his standard. At Saxa Rubra, a few miles from Rome, he met the army of Maxentius, destroyed it completely, and became sole emperor of the West.

Edict of Milan (313). The following year he met his colleague Licinius, who had also been successful, at Milan, and there issued an edict of general and complete toleration of all religions including Christianity. Licinius was unwilling to go farther than that, but in 323 Constantine defeated him and united the whole empire under his rule. From that time on Constantine's attitude toward the Christians became steadily more favorable, until he was finally baptized into the faith a few days before his death in 337. He took no action against paganism, but his patronage of the church set Christianity well on its way to becoming the state religion.

Constantine's motives. That Constantine's policy was inspired to any great degree by religious motives seems most unlikely. He was no doubt drawn toward the idea of monotheism, as were so many intelligent pagans, and in his later years came to consider Christianity its truest expression. But his action was that of a keen and farsighted statesman rather than a convert. The Christians were still a minority in 312 (probably not more than one-tenth of the population of the empire), but they were a very determined and well-organized minority, settled for the most part in the cities and wielding far more influence than their numbers would indicate. Constantine had seen the failure of Diocletian's attempt to crush them. Where Diocletian had failed, he himself could have little hope of success; and if the Christians could not be crushed, it would be better to have them as allies rather

The catacombs in Rome and elsewhere were extensive underground vaults and galleries constructed as tombs for early Christians. Some of the chambers, especially those containing the body of a martyr, were also used as tiny churches. The wall paintings are the earliest surviving Christian art.

The colossal marble head of Constantine the Great, the emperor who freed the Christians from persecution, now stands imbedded in the wall of the Palazzo dei Conservatori in Rome.

than as enemies. In 312 he had needed the support of the Christians against Maxentius, and after 323, when he was emperor of both East and West, he needed the aid of any organized force that would help to hold the empire together. The compact organization of the Christian Church appealed strongly to Constantine's political sense. It had shown its power in the days of persecution, when it had threatened to disrupt the state. Now it might be equally effective in helping to unify and preserve the empire.

3. Church and State: The Struggle Against Heresy and Paganism

The fourth century. The fourth century was a period of astounding growth in the Christian Church. The century opened with the persecution of the Christians, still a small minority of the population, by a pagan emperor. At its close, Christianity was the sole official religion of the empire, claiming at least the formal adherence of the great majority of the population, and protected by a Christian emperor who issued persecuting laws against pagans and all who departed in any way from the accepted doctrines of the state church.

Lowering of standards. But this rapid growth was not all pure gain to the church. The influx of great numbers of the indifferent or self-seeking inevitably lowered the general average of morality and religious zeal in the church, while at the same time introducing non-Christian elements into its doctrine and practice. Before the Edict of Milan, the Christians had been a picked group of earnest believers who were prepared to sacrifice a good deal, even if not all were prepared to face death, for their faith. Now it was to the advantage of all to join the triumphant religion. The easy conversion of those who were merely following the line of least resistance or of personal advantage signified no very vital change in their method of life or in their thought. They clung stubbornly to ancient superstitions, translating them into terms of the new religion. The cult of a host of saints and martyrs sprang up to take the place of the many local gods of pagan mythology. The pagan who had relied on the protection of the homely gods of the hearth found similar comfort from the adoption of a patron saint. Christian celebrations were created to replace the feasts and holidays of the older religions. The assimilation by Christianity of so much of popular belief and practice was in no small degree responsible for its almost universal acceptance during this period, but at the sacrifice of its early purity and simplicity.

Church and state. The change made by Constantine in the status of the church raised several vexing problems, among them that of the relation of the state to the church, which was to trouble the peace of Christendom for centuries. Hitherto the church, being outside the law, had been left free and independent of governmental interference, except for the attempts to suppress it. Would it retain that freedom after Christianity had become the official religion of the empire? And further, would the emperor, himself a Christian, submit his conscience to the guidance of the church in matters of faith and morals, terms that might be extended to include almost any political act? Or would the emperor insist on controlling the policies of the church, which was growing rapidly in wealth and political influence, on the ground that an absolute ruler could not afford to give up his hold on so powerful an institution? The solution of these problems varied with the centuries, but in the fourth century and thereafter in the East, with few exceptions, the emperors asserted a practical control over the church.

Growth of dogma. Another problem which, though not new, took on a new significance with the official recognition of Christianity, was the necessity of defining Christian belief or dogma in an authoritative way so as to preserve the unity of the faith. In the early days of the church, Christian belief had been relatively simple, dominated by the personality and teaching of Christ. But, as time passed, it became necessary to state more clearly certain points not fully explained in the Scriptures, in order to defend Christianity against pagan attacks and also to preserve the purity of the faith, which was in constant danger from the ideas brought in by new converts from the mystery cults and the pagan religions. Most of the early controversies over points of dogma arose in the East. The Greek mind, trained in philosophy and metaphysical speculation, was forced by its very nature to work out clear logical statements of all debatable questions, no matter how abstract. Out of the innumerable controversies resulting from this urge toward speculation and definition, there grew up a body of recognized dogma, accepted by the universal church and called orthodox. The opinions of the minority in each case, which were condemned by the dominant party in the church, were called heterodox or heretical. The distinction between orthodoxy and heresy, between opinions accepted or rejected by the church authorities, was often decided partly by political considerations and after a bitter struggle between the opposing parties.

The Arian heresy. Both problems, the authoritative definition of dogma and the relation between church and state, arose in an acute form in the decade following the Edict of Milan as the result of a controversy, the so-called Arian heresy, which for some sixty years threatened to break up the unity of the Christian body. This heresy, like most early heresies, arose from the dilemmas presented by the doctrines of the Trinity and the Incarnation, which obsessed the minds of Greek Christians. Was Christ, the Son of God, fully divine, of the same nature as God? Were the Father and the Son, the first two persons of the Trinity, one, or were they distinct and the latter a creature, created in time and hence on a lower order than the former? Had Christ become fully human? If not, how could his suffering save and redeem mankind? Stripped of all its involved subtleties and distinctions, the doctrine brought forward by Arius, a priest of Alexandria, about the year 318 was a denial of both the absolute divinity and the complete humanity of Christ. His argument was logical in a literal-minded way, but it would have robbed Christianity of its essential meaning. Both his supporters and his opponents, feeling the question to be of vital importance, took firm stands in the controversy.

Council of Nicaea. When Constantine took over the government of the East after his defeat of Licinius in 323, he found the church divided into apparently irreconcilable parties. The emperor never did understand just what the argument was about, but he was quite certain that it must be stopped. He had favored Christianity and was prepared to support it still further in the hope that the well-organized church would help to unify the empire. It would have just the opposite effect, however, if the church were split into two antagonistic parties. The unity of the church was a vital political issue. To preserve that unity, one side of the argument or the other (Constantine did not greatly care which) must be established as orthodox, and those who would not accept it of their own free will must be forced to do so by the state. As a means of reaching an authoritative decision, the emperor called the first general or ecumenical council of the church to meet at Nicaea in 325. All the bishops were invited to attend, but only seven delegates came from the West. The majority of the bishops were opposed to Arius, and the emperor used all his influence to make the decision unanimous. The council condemned the Arians and drew up the Nicene Creed, which asserted both the full divinity and humanity of Christ.

The Nicene Creed.   Since the Nicene Creed not only defined orthodox belief in opposition to Arianism, but also provided one of the clearest brief statements of basic Christian doctrine and has been accepted with minor variations by most Christian churches, it is worth quoting in full. The following translation is that made familiar to English-speaking people by its inclusion in the Book of Common Prayer.

I believe in one God, the Father Almighty, Maker of heaven and earth, and of all things visible and invisible; and in one Lord Jesus Christ, the only-begotten Son of God, begotten of his Father before all worlds, God of God, Light of Light, very God of very God, begotten not made, being of one substance with the Father, by whom all things were made; who for us men, and for our salvation, came down from heaven, and was incarnate by the Holy Ghost of the Virgin Mary, and was made man, and was crucified also for us under Pontius Pilate. He suffered and was buried, and the third day he rose again according to the Scriptures, and ascended into heaven, and sitteth on the right hand of the Father. And he shall come again, with glory, to judge both the quick and the dead, whose kingdom shall have no end. And I believe in the Holy Ghost, the Lord and giver of life, who proceedeth from the Father and the Son, who with the Father and the Son together is worshipped and glorified, who spake by the prophets. And I believe one Catholic and Apostolic Church. I acknowledge one Baptism for the remission of sins. And I look for the Resurrection of the dead, and the life of the world to come.

Arian reaction under Constantius.   After the Council of Nicaea, Arius and his followers were banished from the empire by imperial decree. But Arianism was by no means dead. It continued to spread through the East and among the Germanic tribes north of the frontier. Most of the later invaders of the empire were Arians. The prolonged life of the heresy was largely due to the continued interference of the imperial government in church affairs. The next emperor in the East, Constantius (337–61), the second son of Constantine, who for a time shared the empire with his brothers Constantine II and Constans, became a convinced Arian and entered the struggle with partisan enthusiasm. The Arian bishops were recalled while the orthodox were deposed, and Athanasius, the leader of the opposition to Arianism, was forced to flee to the West. Council followed council with bewildering and contradictory results. Heresy seemed about to triumph, but after the death of Constantius the Christians were temporarily reunited in opposition to a last desperate revival of paganism.

Pagan revival under Julian.   There were still many pagans in the empire. The government had taken no action against them, though Constantius had issued some oppressive edicts which were never enforced. The Roman Senate and aristocracy were still predominantly pagan, and most of the teachers in the schools carried on the old tradition. In fact, patriotism and literature were the strongest supports of the old religions, and many of the highest social and intellectual classes longed for a return to

Christ as the Good Shepherd was one of the favorite themes of early Christian art. The painting at the left, dating from the early third century, is in the Catacomb of Callixtus in Rome.

the ancient gods of the golden age, when Greece and Rome had been truly great. One of these, and the most ardent, came to the imperial throne in 361, Julian (called by Christian historians "the Apostate"), a nephew of the great Constantine. With the reunited empire under his rule, Julian disowned the Christianity he had been forced to profess, and spent his brief reign in a vain attempt to revive all that was best in paganism and to make it the state religion. Julian was in many ways one of the noblest spirits of his age, but he was running counter to the current of the times. The Christians were not so hopelessly divided, nor the pagans so zealous, as he had hoped. He died knowing that he had failed and, according to a legend that is too good to be true, murmuring, "Galilean, thou hast conquered!" His own legions chose a Christian, Jovian, as his successor.

Arianism under Valens. After the failure of the pagan revival, Christianity became again the imperial religion, and again the Arian controversy tore the eastern churches. On the death of Jovian after one year's reign, the generals of the army chose as emperor one of their own number, Valentinian I (364–75), who immediately gave the rule of the East to his brother Valens (364–78). Valentinian in the orthodox West could afford to ignore the dogmatic controversy, but in the East it was impossible for the emperor to stand aside. Valens followed the example of Constantius and gave his support to the Arians, who nevertheless were losing ground through divisions and quarrels among themselves. Unlike the orthodox, they had no definite statement of their faith to hold them together. The year 378 was a momentous year for the Roman Empire. Valens fell in battle against the Goths, the first of a long series of successful invaders of the empire,[1] and with him perished the last hope of Arianism.

Triumph of orthodoxy. Gratian, the son of Valentinian, had already succeeded his father in the West. He now chose as his colleague in the East a Spanish count, Theodosius I (379–95). Both had been reared in the West and were strictly orthodox. As Arianism was mostly an eastern problem, it was left to Theodosius

[1] See below, page 102.

to crush it. In 380 he issued an edict threatening all heretics with legal punishment, and the following year summoned the second ecumenical council of the church at Constantinople, which confirmed the Nicene Creed and condemned Arianism. Further imperial edicts restored all orthodox bishops and forbade the Arians to hold services or build churches. Arianism was suppressed, as it had been fostered, by the power of the state. It still continued strongly among the barbarians, but within the empire its cause was lost. Meanwhile, Gratian was taking steps to stamp out paganism, and in 391 and 392 Theodosius issued stringent laws against idolatry. Sacrifice to pagan gods, whether in public or private, was to be regarded as treason, and paganism gradually died out during the following century. The legal triumph of the church over heresy and paganism and its evolution from a persecuted sect to a persecuting state church were complete.

4. The Latin Church: The Rise of the Papacy

The fifth century. The center of interest in religious history during the fifth century shifts to the West. The church in the East had conquered its most dangerous heretical opponent, though other heresies arose in profusion, springing for the most part from the attempt to define further the exact nature of the union of perfect God and perfect man in Christ. Political rivalry between the patriarchs of Alexandria, Antioch, and Constantinople, who were all fighting for supremacy in the Eastern Church, added bitterness to these controversies. But in the long run peace was restored, the primacy of the Patriarch of Constantinople, the imperial capital, was recognized, and through the patriarchs who were their creatures the emperors maintained their control of the church, which gradually sank into a stagnant and somewhat servile quiet. In the West, on the other hand, where the imperial power was being weakened and finally destroyed under the shock of successive barbarian invasions, the Latin Church was growing rapidly in organization, independence, and authority. With a theology peculiarly its own, it came under the leadership of the bishops of Rome, who fell heir to the universal authority abdicated by the emperors.

The Latin Church.   The church at Rome and in the West generally during the first two centuries after its foundation was predominantly Greek, Christianity having spread first among the Greek-speaking commercial classes. As it was adopted more widely, however, by all classes, it necessarily drew its adherents from the Latin-speaking majority of the population. Before the end of the persecutions, the Western Church was almost entirely Latin, and the difference in language was significant of other and more important differences between the Christians of the West and their Greek brethren. The very small delegation sent by the western bishops to Nicaea in 325 shows how little interest they took in the problem which was threatening to disrupt the Eastern Church. Throughout the fourth century the gap between East and West was slowly widening. The administrative division of the empire and the founding of a new capital for the East at Constantinople were both cause and result of an actual diversity of interest. After the death of Theodosius in 395, under whom the empire had been briefly reunited, the division into two empires was final and complete. In theory, of course, the unity of the empire was still maintained, but in actual practice East and West went their separate ways independently. And this division in the state was strengthened by a similar split in the church, though it, too, maintained its theoretical unity. The knowledge of the Greek language, essential to communication with the East and to an understanding of Greek ideas, was dying out in the West. At the same time there grew up, in the last years of the fourth century and in the fifth, a school of Latin theology and church policy, quite different from the Greek, and destined to shape the thought of Western Christendom for more than a thousand years.

The Latin Church Fathers.   The leaders of this movement were three men, Ambrose, Jerome, and Augustine, who, together with Pope Gregory the Great, have been accorded the title of Fathers of the Church in Latin Christendom. Though differing widely in character and in the nature of their contributions, they were all three stoutly orthodox, doughty champions of the unity and authority of the Catholic Church.

Ambrose.   St. Ambrose (c. 340–97) was a practical administrator. From his father, the prefect of Gaul, he inherited the tradition of Roman government. In 374 he was elected Bishop of Milan, where the emperor was then residing, and soon became the most influential official in the Western Church. In all his relations with the government he insisted on the maxim that the emperor is *in* the church, not *over* it, and he had the courage and character to force even the great Theodosius to submission, refusing to administer the sacraments to him until he had done full penance for massacres he had ordered at Thessalonica. Ambrose is also credited with introducing the singing of hymns into the Western Church and himself wrote several. He has, indeed, been called the virtual founder of Latin hymnody. In his writings and his example, he left to the Western Church a priceless tradition of discipline and independence.

Jerome.   His contemporary, St. Jerome (c. 340–419) was the most learned of the three, a masterly scholar and linguist. Aside from his numerous works against heresy and his active promotion of monasticism at Rome (of which more hereafter), his great service was the translation of the Bible from the original Hebrew and Greek into forceful and eloquent Latin. This arduous task, which occupied twenty years, was completed in 405. The Vulgate, as this version of the Bible is called, was soon accepted as the authoritative text by the Latin Church, as it still is by Roman Catholics, and had an incalculable influence on ecclesiastical literature during the following centuries.

Augustine.   St. Augustine (354–430) was the real founder of Latin theology and the most powerful mind in the history of the Western Church. Born in the Roman province of Africa, he was trained in philosophy and classical literature and much influenced by Neoplatonism before he fell under the influence of Bishop Ambrose and was converted in middle age to Christianity. In 395 he was made Bishop of Hippo in Africa and spent the rest of his life in active pastoral work and in writing. His *Confessions,* written about the year 400, rank high among the world's great autobiographies, as well as among the finest works of religious inspiration. His longest work, *The City of God,* was undertaken after the sack of Rome in 410 to demonstrate that the calamities which had overtaken the empire were not due to its desertion of the ancient gods, but were merely signs that the old worldly empire was passing, to be replaced by a new spiritual empire, the Christian Church. A large part of *The City of God* deals with the history of mankind since the Creation, drawing largely upon the Old Testament for the history of the period before the birth of Christ, and representing all human history as the working out of a divine plan. All worldly states Augustine believed to be founded in sin and doomed to pass away. Only the city of God is eternal and destined to triumph. It is a conception of history which influenced nearly all historical writers for a thousand years. Augustine also wrote numerous works in which he constructed a dogmatic system, in opposition to such heretics as the Pelagians, who held that human nature is not essentially evil and that men are able to seek the good of their own free will, and the Donatists, who believed that the validity of the sacraments depended on the moral character of the priest. Typically Latin, Augustine was not vitally interested in the metaphysical speculations that so attracted the Greeks. On the contrary, his thought revolved about the more human problem of how the individual Christian obtains salvation. And this problem he resolved into a logical and almost legal system of divine justice, in which he pictured all men as damned by the original sin inherited from the fall of Adam, were it not that some have been predestined or chosen from the beginning for salvation through Christ's sacrifice, which salvation comes to them, not by virtue of any action of their own will, for the human will is powerless, but through the working of divine grace upon those who are chosen. This was the orthodox belief, though the church never fully accepted the extreme statement of Augustinianism.

Organization of the Latin Church. The period which marked the growth of Latin theology witnessed also the completion of a centralized system of government in the Western Church. The building of a clerical hierarchy of ascending offices was a matter of slow growth, in which the church followed the lines of imperial administration. Within each Roman municipality since the second century, the bishop had been recognized as the head of the local church, having authority over the priests and deacons. The next step was to create some higher authority that could establish uniformity in belief and practice and enforce discipline over these isolated communities. In the third century, councils of all the bishops in a given province of the empire were fairly common. By the end of the fourth century the bishop of the provincial capital, who presided at these councils, had been recognized as the superior of the bishops in his province, with the title of Metropolitan or Archbishop. The Latin genius for government, however, and the need for a centralized administration in a time of frequent heresies and barbarian invasions, demanded some still higher authority over the whole church. This led to the elevation during the fifth century of the Bishop of Rome to a position of supremacy in the Latin Church, comparable to that of the emperor in the civil government.

The Bishops of Rome. As head of the Christian community in the ancient capital of the empire, the Bishop of Rome occupied a position of great political influence at home and of prestige abroad. Already in the fourth century, the pagan Ammianus Marcellinus had noted, with a mixture of admiration and contempt, the wealth, pomp, and power of the Roman bishops. Their importance was greatly increased after 402, when the emperor deserted the capital to establish his court in the impregnable city of Ravenna, sheltered by its impassable marshes.[1] Thereafter the bishops became the most powerful officials in the city. After the sack of Rome by the Visigoths in 410, Bishop Innocent I (402–17) took the lead in directing and aiding reconstruction. It was Innocent, too, who first definitely asserted his right to supremacy in the Western Church. From the beginning of his reign, he claimed that all the churches of the West owed obedience to the Roman bishop and that in all matters of discipline and usage they should accept his decisions and follow the custom of the Roman Church.

[1] See below, page 103.

Leo the Great.   From this point on, events moved rapidly. The bishops in all the provinces were assuming greater powers, due to the collapse of the imperial administration under the shock of successive invasions. In many cities they took over the duties of the imperial officers, acting as judges and governors and using their influence to protect the citizens from their barbarian conquerors. With these new responsibilities they felt more keenly the need of moral support from some higher authority and looked more eagerly to the Roman bishop for guidance. Thus by the middle of the century, Leo the Great (440–61) was able to exercise the full authority over the church to which as pope (for we may now use that term for the Bishop of Rome) he felt entitled, and that authority was given imperial sanction by a law of Valentinian III, conferring upon him jurisdiction over all the bishops in the Western Empire. Leo I was in many ways the most impressive figure of his generation, a man of remarkable energy, courage, and statesmanlike vision. When Rome was threatened by the Huns in 451 and sacked by the Vandals in 455, it was Leo who carried out the negotiations, successful in the former case, on behalf of the defenseless city. With inflexible purpose he forced the bishops of the farthest provinces to obedience, and in the heretical controversies of his time, he boldly asserted his right to settle the questions at issue as the final authority in matters of faith. The papacy had still to pass through many vicissitudes before it reached its full growth, but from Leo's time on, Western Christendom looked to Rome for leadership.

Theory of papal supremacy.   We have seen why some supreme authority in the church was necessary and have traced the steps by which it arose. Before leaving the subject, let us examine some of the reasons why that supremacy should have been given to the Bishop of Rome rather than to any other bishop, and also the theories which bolstered up his claims. From the first the Roman Bishop occupied a unique position in the church, as heir in a way to the authority both of Augustus, the founder of the Roman Empire, and of St. Peter, the traditional founder of the church in Rome. The dominant position of Rome in the empire, as the capital and center of imperial administration, gave to the head of the Christian community there a prestige which no other bishop could equal, and made it natural that he should become the head also of the ecclesiastical administration. Moreover, according to the tradition generally accepted in the church, the apostle Peter had been the first Bishop of Rome, and to him, as the Bible tells, Christ had given the care of his flock and the keys of heaven and hell, saying, "On this rock will I build my church." As successors to Peter, the Bishops of Rome claimed the full powers given to him by Christ. The Roman bishopric was generally known as the See of Peter or the Apostolic See. Finally their rise to supremacy was aided by the reputation for orthodoxy built up by a long line of Roman bishops, who, with the Latin instinct for law and authority, stood steadfastly by the letter of the orthodox creeds.

5. The Growth of Monasticism

The ascetic impulse.   One further aspect of Christian life and thought, and not the least important, came into existence during this period with the institution of monasticism. In almost every religion which has deeply touched the emotions of men, and where the ideal of spiritual communion with God has stirred the imagination, some earnest souls have felt an irresistible impulse to renounce all worldly or material pleasures, in order that they might concentrate their desires on the things of the spirit, and to undergo physical suffering, so that they might conquer their bodily appetites and give free play to spiritual aspiration. The practice of this renunciation and voluntary suffering is called asceticism. It was not a uniquely Christian impulse (indeed, there is no more than a suggestion of it in the teaching of Christ), but was common in other religions of eastern origins. During the third century, it was given strong support by the Neoplatonic philosophy, of which we have already spoken. In popular Neoplatonism there arose, as a sort of by-product, an oriental concept of two antagonistic forces at war in the universe, spirit and matter. This is known as dualism. It led to the idea that all material interests and all physical appetites or passions are by their nature evil, and that they must be overcome before the spirit, purified by that conquest, can

The earliest Christian churches in Rome were patterned after the Roman basilicas, which were designed for the conduct of business and legal affairs. The church of Santa Sabina, built in 425, has the long, rectangular shape, the rows of pillars marking off the side aisles, and the rounded apse characteristic of the basilica.

reach its desired harmony with God. This conception coincided with certain aspects of Christian thought and in turn had a powerful effect upon it. Dualism in greater or less degree remained a constant factor in Christianity until at least the end of the Middle Ages. Over against God and the spirit, it set up an unholy trinity of the world, the flesh, and the devil. Only by renouncing these three was it possible to live a truly religious life.

Monasticism. About the beginning of the fourth century, when the church had passed from persecution to triumph, this ascetic impulse took on a new and more definite form. The crown and rewards of martyrdom were no longer available. The church was no longer a community apart from the rest of society, but had embraced the world. The more deeply religious, then, who felt it necessary to withdraw from the world, were forced also to withdraw in a measure from the church and to seek in solitude, or in the company of an inner circle of the devout, that freedom from worldly contacts that had been enjoyed by the early church. These motives, strengthened by the growth of the ascetic ideal, drove men out into the desert to live as hermits and later to form communities with those of like mind. They were the first Christian monks.

In the East. Monasticism began, as was natural, in the East, the home of asceticism.

The first monk of whom we have definite knowledge was St. Anthony, an Egyptian, who in the last years of the third century fled to the Thebaid desert from the world that was too much with him. He lived as a hermit in constant prayer, fasting, and self-inflicted suffering. The tales of his holiness, his visions, and the miracles attributed to him spread through Egypt and attracted others in great numbers to follow his example. The natural instinct of men to live in some kind of organized society soon asserted itself, even among these hermits who had fled from society, and before 325 the monk Pachomius founded the first monastic community with a definite rule of government. As monasticism spread from Egypt throughout the East, thousands embraced it, the majority preferring the orderly communal life with provisions for daily labor prescribed by the rule of Pachomius. There were still many who preferred solitude, however, and among these asceticism was often carried to the most eccentric extremes. The classic example is that of St. Simeon Stylites, who in the fifth century spent thirty-six years on top of a pillar, exposed to the weather and without room even to lie down. But for the most part, the communal life triumphed over the solitary, and an improved rule written by St. Basil before his death in 374 was adopted by most monks in the Greek Church.

In the West. Western monasticism was originally an importation from the East, though it soon became acclimatized and developed along characteristically Latin lines. Introduced at Rome, apparently by St. Athanasius in 339, it soon attracted numbers of both men and women. At first there was some opposition to what seemed an antisocial movement, and St. Jerome, the most vigorous and influential champion of the monastic ideal in the West, aroused a good deal of antagonism by encouraging a number of noble Roman ladies to desert the world. But, once started, monasticism could not be checked. It became increasingly popular, spreading from Italy to all the provinces, and it attracted adherents for a variety of reasons. The ascetic impulse was still, of course, the strongest motive, but there were many who embraced monasticism as a means of escape from intolerable social or family obligations. The movement here passed through the same course of development from the solitary to the communal life as in the East, but western monasticism was always more practical and orderly, laying greater stress on the necessity of discipline and labor. The monks of the Latin Church, too, were much less interested than the Greeks in theological speculation and took less part in the controversies of the age.

St. Benedict. To trace the full development of monasticism in the West into a uniform and regulated order, we must go a little beyond the chronological bounds set for this chapter to the sixth century and the epoch-making work of St. Benedict of Nursia. Born about 480 of a wealthy and noble Italian family, Benedict fled at an early age from the temptations and distractions of the world and, like so many of his generation, sought salvation in a hermit's cell. For three years he lived a life of rigid asceticism and complete solitude, his home an almost inaccessible cave in a precipitous rock. But his very efforts to escape from the fellowship of men brought men to him. The fame of his holiness attracted numbers of monks to his vicinity, who begged him to be their leader. About the year 520 he founded the famous monastery of Monte Cassino, and some time later wrote for the guidance of his monks the rule which was to regulate monastic life for centuries. Wherever the rule was adopted, it checked the restless wandering and the dangerously irregular asceticism of the monks. It provided that the monk, after a probationary period of a year during which he had time to determine whether he was suited to the monastic life, should take the three fundamental vows of perpetual poverty, chastity, and obedience; thereafter he was bound to remain in the same monastery for life, to obey his superior with humility in all things, to give up all private property, and to cut himself off from all relations with people, even his own family, outside the monastery. Each monastery was a separate institution, ruled by an abbot who was elected by the other monks for life. His powers were limited only by the provisions of the rule and by the supervision of the bishop of the diocese.

Life in a Benedictine monastery. Each Benedictine monastery was a small self-contained community. Its members all lived under the same roof and shared the same food at a common table. St. Benedict had had personal experience of the dangers and temptations that accompanied too much solitude, idleness, and unbridled asceticism. He therefore provided for a full schedule of daily activity and forbade all unusual ascetic practices. Part of each day, a large part we would think, was devoted to prayer, meditation, and religious services at prescribed hours, while six or seven hours were to be spent in manual labor in the fields or about the house, or in reading and copying manuscripts. The monks were to produce their own food and other necessities as far as possible and so be free from dependence on the outside world. Food, though not of a luxurious sort, was to be provided in sufficient quantities to maintain health. There were also special rules for the care of the sick or aged. It was an austere, hard life, but not an impossible one.

The sanity, moderation, and orderly government of the Benedictine rule appealed strongly to the western mind, and in the following centuries it was adopted by all monasteries in the West. It was also applied to the nunneries. As a result of the provisions for labor in the fields and copying manuscripts, the monasteries became centers of civilization everywhere throughout the dark ages, and played an important part in cultivating waste land, improving agricultural methods, and preserving literature and learning.

1 *Bird hunting in a papyrus swamp, Egyptian tomb fresco, 18th dynasty, 1570–1349 B.C. By permission of the Trustees of the British Museum.*

The wall paintings found in many Egyptian tombs were not intended to serve a purely decorative purpose as were the Greek vase paintings. They usually represented things the soul would need in the afterlife, hence the effort to portray objects, like the birds being hunted in the picture above, with lifelike realism. Compared with the crowded Egyptian scene, the classically simple figure of the hunter decorating the Greek oil bottle has the clarity of a piece of sculpture.

2 *Hunter with dog, by the Pan Painter, Athenian red-figured lekythos, 470–460 B.C. Courtesy, Museum of Fine Arts, Boston. (George Cushing)*

The eruption of Vesuvius in 79 A.D., which buried Pompeii and neighboring towns under volcanic ash, preserved a number of Roman wall paintings. Many of them are realistic portraits that have an intimate, human quality in marked contrast to the rigid formality of later Byzantine mosaics.

3 *Portrait of a Roman couple, fresco from Pompeii, first century* A.D. *Museo Nazionale, Naples. (European Art Color, Peter Adelberg, New York)*

4 *Christ Pantocrator, Ruler of the Universe, Byzantine mosaic in the monastery at Daphni, Greece, c. 1100. (Colorphoto Hinz, Basel)*

Stained glass replaced mural painting in the Gothic churches, which left little wall space for pictures. The art of book illumination, however, continued throughout the Middle Ages. The miniature of the three wise men offering gifts to the infant Jesus is typical in its two-dimensional handling of space and figures.

5 *Notre Dame de la Belle Verrière, Gothic stained glass window, Chartres cathedral, 12th century.* (*Giraudon*)

6 *Adoration of the Magi, illumination from an 11th century Gospel. Biblioteca Queriniana, Brescia.* (*Fototecnica di Brescia*)

In the Later Middle Ages northern book illuminators and Italian panel and fresco painters influenced one another and thus developed an "International Gothic Style," combining aristocratic Gothic elegance of line with a more realistic handling of figures and landscape. Northern painters like the Limbourg brothers, however, were still confined to the illuminator's miniature art a century after Italians like Simone Martini were painting large murals.

7 *Illustration for the month of August, in the Très Riches Heures du Duc de Berry, by the Limbourg brothers, c. 1416. Musée Condé, Chantilly. (Giraudon)*

8 *Guidoriccio da Fogliano, by Simone Martini, fresco in the Palazzo Pubblico, Siena, 1328. (Scala)*

8

The Barbarian Invasions of the Empire

BEYOND THE frontiers of the empire lay the barbarian world, often hostile and always a menace to Roman civilization. Roman statesmen could never forget for long the danger threatening from the north, where restless and warlike German tribes milled along the Rhine-Danube border. Time and again, since before the days of Julius Caesar, the legions were called upon to expel barbarian invaders. Until the fourth century they were always successful, but the task became increasingly difficult, for the empire was fast weakening as a result of the general decline. Meanwhile, great numbers of Germans had entered the empire peacefully, in small groups, to take service in the army or to work on the large estates. Having settled within the empire, these barbarian immigrants were, in course of time, more or less Romanized, though as their numbers increased they undoubtedly helped to lower the general level of Roman civilization. But if the Roman melting pot could assimilate a slow barbarian infiltration, it could not absorb whole nations, when once the barbarians succeeded in making an armed invasion. And the mass invasions began in 376, when the Visigoths crossed the Danube frontier, setting an example that was soon followed by other tribes all along the northern border. In wave after wave, they broke across the shattered frontier, until within a century the Western Empire was submerged beneath the barbarian flood.

Thus was added to the basic Roman culture, modified by Christianity, the third ingredient which went to make up medieval civilization, the influence of the Germanic peoples who from this time on were the dominant force in western Europe.

1. The Early Germans

Origins. The original home of the Germans or Teutons was in all probability the northern part of modern Germany near the Baltic coast and across the sea in the southern portion of the Scandinavian peninsula. Here they may have remained for many centuries with a population held relatively stable by the even balance of their struggle for existence. The acquisition of better tools and techniques, however, probably from the more civilized south, in time gave them a little edge in their eternal conflict with the forces of nature so that the population began gradually to increase. They then began to expand slowly west to the North Sea, southwest, south, and southeast to the Rhine and the Danube, and east to the Vistula. In Caesar's time they occupied all the land he knew beyond the Rhine. Closer contact with Roman commerce now brought them still better tools and weapons, so that it became easier to maintain life, and the population thereafter increased more rapidly.

Sources of our knowledge. Our knowledge of the early Germans before they impinged upon the Roman Republic, and thus made their first tumultuous entrance upon the stage of history, is necessarily vague and uncertain. It belongs to the field of archaeology rather than of history. Yet from the implements and weapons, excavated from tombs and village sites, we can learn something of their daily life and trace the general trend of their civilization. For actual historical information we are indebted chiefly to a brief account in Caesar's *De Bello Gallico,* known to every student who ever studied Latin, and to a more full and circumstantial account of their manners and customs in the *Germania,* written by the Roman historian Tacitus in 98. The reliability of the *Germania* has been the subject of endless debate. But even if we accept it as reliable, it must not be forgotten that nearly three centuries of contact with Roman civilization and of development in social and political customs passed between the date of Tacitus' work and the first successful invasions of the empire. Some further information may be gleaned from the German laws, written down later but based on ancient custom. The mass of Anglo-Saxon, German, and Scandinavian folk literature, too, in its earliest origins dates back to the period of the invasions and supplies us with valuable material with which to reconstruct the characteristics of the Germans of that period.

Appearance and characteristics. The Germans were tall and powerfully built. To the small, though wiry, Roman they seemed veritable giants. Their fair skin, blue eyes, and long reddish or golden-blond hair were in equally strong contrast to the swarthy peoples of the Mediterranean basin. Hardy and robust they must have been, for none but the strong could survive in that land of forest and swamp, with heavy rain in summer and bitter cold in winter. Their temper reflects the stern conditions of their life. Though hard-headed and canny enough in many ways, they were of a moody and fitful temperament, given to fighting, hard drinking, and reckless gambling. Through all the earliest Germanic literature there runs a persistent strain of melancholy, illuminated by flashes of fierce delight in the heady joys of battle. Their virtues, like their vices, were those of a rough, primitive people. Physical courage, loyalty, and hospitality were their prime virtues as they have always been among men who are called upon daily to pit their strength against the forces of nature and who must depend on their fellows for existence amidst constant dangers from a hard climate, flood, famine, and hostile neighbors.

Manner of life. At the time of our first historical knowledge of them, the Germans had already reached the iron age of civilization and had begun the practice of agriculture, though Tacitus later describes them as still depending for the most part on hunting and on their herds of cattle and swine for their food. They lived in village communities and, as time passed, undoubtedly developed a more settled way of life with constantly increasing cultivation of the soil. Their agricultural methods, however, remained crude and wasteful. They had very few industries and those the most primitive. The smith, who made tools and weapons, practiced almost the only honored trade. The freeman preferred to devote his time to hunting and fighting, leaving to the women and slaves the work in the fields and the making of clothing from skins, wool, and linen.

Social organization. Tacitus divides the Germans whom he knew into four social classes: nobles, freemen (evidently the great majority), freedmen (who were little better than serfs), and slaves. Modern historians have disagreed violently as to the extent of the freedom enjoyed by the mass of the early German people. In all probability the gap between noble and freeman widened as the Germans became more civilized and gained a more coherent organization, with social and political power becoming more closely concentrated in the hands of the noble families. The family, as in most societies, was the social unit; but there was also a larger kinship group, the sib or clan, composed of families related originally by blood ties. Members of the clan felt a mutual responsibility for the welfare of their fellows, avenged the death of their kinsmen and supported them in lawsuits or in battle. This clannish loyalty was necessary for the protection of the individual at a time when central government was still loosely and ineffectively organized. Distinct from these family or kinship groups was the *comitatus,* a band of warriors who attached themselves voluntarily to some chief renowned for his courage and skill in war. These "comrades" were attached to their chief by a strong bond of personal loyalty; they fought at his bidding and considered it a disgrace to survive him if he were killed in battle.

This relief of about the year 700, portraying a mounted German warrior, is a good example of primitive German art.

In return he supplied them with arms, clothing, food, and opportunities for plunder.

Political organization. The smallest political unit was the village community, which enjoyed a considerable degree of self-government. The largest unit in the early days was the tribe. In the primitive state described by Tacitus the government of the tribe was in the hands of a council of chiefs, of noble family or distinguished by their courage or wisdom; but all important questions were discussed and decided in an assembly of all the freemen (that is, of the warriors) presided over by the chiefs. During the period of migration, many of the tribes united to form larger groups, and in the process the freemen apparently lost much of their earlier independence and share in the government. The dangers which attended the mass migration of a whole people demanded a more highly centralized government than had been needed in the early days. Before the age of the invasions nearly all the Germanic peoples were ruled by kings with the aid of an advisory council of chieftains. The development of kingship was by no means uniform among all the tribes, and the powers of the king were probably not clearly defined, but depended on the character of the individual king and on circumstances of stress or danger.

Law and justice. The social and political ideas of the early Germans were largely personal, having to do with family relationships or personal loyalties to a chief or king. The concept of a territorial state as a political entity had not yet arisen among them. This personal character is reflected in their laws, which dealt mostly with injuries or obligations between individuals. Their laws, moreover, unlike those of the Romans, were not the product of legislation on the part of the government plus the precedents established by the decisions of judges, but were made up of immemorial customs of the tribe, handed down from generation to generation, though not put into written form till after the invasions. A crime was considered, not as an offense against the state, but as an injury to an individual, for which the law gave him a means of procuring satisfaction. A trial or lawsuit, then, was a contest between two individuals, with the court merely acting as the arbiter and imposing the customary sentence. Its principal function, indeed, was to serve as a substitute for private vengeance, which might initiate an endless blood feud. There was no attempt to sift evidence, as was done in the Roman courts, in arriving at a decision. Instead, the court appealed to the gods — or, after the Germans were converted to Christianity, to God — to decide the issue. Normally the defendant was allowed to clear himself by taking a solemn oath that he was innocent, frequently aided by the oaths of a number of his friends. If he or any of his oath-helpers, or compurgators as they were called, hesitated or made the slightest slip in reciting the exact words of the oath, he was declared guilty on the assumption that God would not permit a guilty man to perjure himself successfully. Where the oath was judged insufficient to prove innocence, the accused man had usually to clear himself by undergoing an ordeal. This took various forms. He might, for instance, be required to pick a small object out of a pot of boiling water or to carry a red-hot iron in his bare hand for a certain number of paces. The arm was then wrapped up for three days or more and if it was then found to be healing cleanly he was adjudged innocent. Ordeal by combat, a formal duel between the contestants or their legally appointed champions, was also a common practice, founded on the belief that God would defend the right. The penalty imposed on the guilty was usually a fine paid as compensation to the injured party or, if he were killed, to his family. The amount to be paid for killing a man, the *wergeld* or man-money, or for any of a great variety of injuries was fixed by custom and varied widely in accordance with the rank of the injured man. Those collections of law which have survived are consequently valuable evidence regarding the relative status of the different classes in society. Crude as this judicial procedure was, it had the virtue of simplicity, and in the general barbarization of the empire that followed the invasions it gradually replaced the more rational and sophisticated practice of the Roman courts and continued to administer such justice as there was in western Europe for centuries.

2. The Migrations Before 376

Cause of the migrations. The *Völkerwanderung* or Wandering of the Peoples, as German scholars call the great migrations into the empire after 376, had in reality begun long before that date. For centuries the increase in population had driven German tribes to seek more fertile or less thickly populated lands, while the pressure of expansion from the interior of Germany piled up the southern tribes against the barrier of the Roman frontier. Germany was not densely populated according to modern standards, but the early Germans, with their primitive methods of agriculture and their reliance on herds and hunting for the greater part of their food, needed a great deal of land to support them. Their margin of subsistence was always small, and any increase in population soon caused overcrowding. The migration of a whole tribe or nation was made more easy by the fact that they were not entirely dependent on agriculture and had neither the settled habits nor the traditional attachment to their land of a race of farmers. Sometimes the migrations were peaceful and unopposed; more often they involved the conquest or expulsion of the tribes who occupied the new territory.

Germans filter into the empire. As the press of population increased outside the frontiers of the empire, great numbers of Germans drifted across the border to seek employment in the Roman army or to settle peacefully in the rich and protected provinces. By the time of Constantine, the barbarian element in the army had begun to predominate over the Roman, and during the following two centuries, in the West at least, the imperial soldiers and officers, including those of the highest rank, were mostly German. Of those who entered peacefully as farmers, some were given land by the state in deserted regions, while others became tenants on the large private estates. In either case they went to swell the class of half-servile agricultural workers. Still others were allowed to enter by tribes as *foederati* or allies, and were given grants of land by the government within the frontier on condition that they should aid in repelling further invasions. This gradual infiltration of barbarian elements into the empire played its part in lowering the level of Roman culture, but it also helped to ease the shock of the great invasions, for by that time the Roman provincials were already acquainted with German customs and the invaders found many of their own race, partly Romanized, already settled in the provinces.

The Germans in the fourth century. By the fourth century, the restless wandering of the German tribes, attended by conquests and alliances, had led to the formation of several more or less clearly defined peoples, each composed of an amalgamation or federation of smaller tribes. It will be of service in tracing their later history to note the position of the more important of these on the eve of the great invasions. Of the West German tribes (those whose original home was the central southern coast of the Baltic), two great confederations had formed along the Rhine, the Franks on the lower and the Alamanni on the upper part of the river. In the northwest, along the coast of the North Sea and in the Danish peninsula, were the Saxons, Angles, and Jutes who were later to invade England. Of the East Germans (those whose early home was apparently the southern part of the Scandinavian peninsula and the Baltic coast between the Oder and the Vistula), one group, the Burgundians, had drifted westward to the Main, between the Franks and the Alamanni. The rest had moved south and east, the Vandals to the upper reaches of the Oder, with the Lombards still farther east between the Oder and the Vistula, while far to the southeast were the two great Gothic peoples stretched all along the lower Danube and the Black Sea.

The Goths. By the middle of the third century, the Goths had completed their long migration from the Baltic shores and had divided into two separate units, the Visigoths or West Goths and the Ostrogoths or East Goths. The river Dniester formed the boundary between them. Of these the Visigoths were brought into closest touch with the empire, which lay just across the Danube from them. During the first three quarters of the fourth century, except for a brief period, 367–69, the Visigoths were on peaceful terms with the Romans, and a considerable trade sprang up between them.

Introduction of Christianity. It was during this quiet interlude that Christianity was first introduced among the Goths, gaining great numbers of converts. Credit for this must be given in large measure to Bishop Ulfilas, who began his forty years of active missionary work among the Visigoths in 341. He was not himself of pure Gothic blood, being descended from a Christian family of Cappadocia taken prisoner by the Goths in a raid of the preceding century, but he was a Goth at heart. As a young man he had been taken to Constantinople, apparently as a hostage, and there received a good education in Latin and Greek. Returning as a missionary to his people, he was amazingly successful. As part of his missionary activity, he translated the Bible into the Gothic tongue, inventing an alphabet modeled on the Greek for the purpose and thereby laying the foundation for a written Germanic literature. Hitherto the Germans had had no writing except the crude runic letters, suitable only for carving brief inscriptions on tools or weapons. The translation of so large a work as the Bible into a language which had no traditions of writing must have involved immense labor, even though the gentle bishop did quietly omit the more bellicose tales from the Book of Kings as an unnecessary stimulant to a people already too prone to war. Modern philologists owe a

The page shown here is taken from the New Testament in Gothic as translated by Ulfilas. The lettering in this beautiful manuscript, now in the University Library in Uppsala, is in silver.

great debt to Ulfilas for this specimen of one of the Germanic dialects three centuries earlier than any other that has survived. From the Visigoths Christianity spread before the end of the fourth century to the Ostrogoths, Vandals, and other Germanic nations. But it was the Arian form of Christianity, in which Ulfilas himself had been trained during the period of Arian domination in the East. As a result, almost all the barbarian invaders of the empire were either pagans or Arian heretics, a fact that further strained their relations with the orthodox Romans among whom they settled.

The Huns. The final invasion of the empire by the Visigoths was not undertaken of their own volition nor with the aim of conquest, but was forced upon them by fear of the Huns, a horde of Asiatic barbarians, new to Europe. For centuries these Mongolian nomads had driven their herds in yearly migrations from the northern to the southern steppes of central Asia, following the seasonal changes in pasture. Forced at last by some obscure disturbance among the peoples of the interior of

The panels of this Anglo-Saxon casket, c. 700, are carved from walrus ivory. The larger panel depicts a scene from the pagan myth of Wayland the Smith (left) and the Christian Adoration of the Magi (right). Runic writing runs around the edge.

Asia to seek new lands, they launched themselves westward into Europe, falling upon the flank and rear of the Ostrogothic kingdom about the year 371. Short, broad-shouldered, and bow-legged from much riding, with yellow skin and hideous, beardless faces marked by deep scars inflicted in childhood, unspeakably dirty, thus did the Gothic historian Jordanes later describe these fierce and untamed savages, who seemed more barbarous to the Goth than did the Germanic barbarian to the civilized Roman. The Huns lived, fought, ate, and even slept on horseback. They were far more mobile than the German tribes and their ability to cover great distances in an incredibly short time led the Goths to exaggerate their numbers. By 375 they had conquered the Ostrogoths. The following year the Visigoths, after a vain attempt to check them at the boundary line of the Dniester, turned in panic to seek protection within the Roman frontier.

3. *The Invasion of the Visigoths*

Invasion and war. In 376, when the Visigoths petitioned for permission to cross the Danube and settle within the empire, the imperial government had been seriously weakened by the recent death of Valentinian I, the able and energetic emperor of the West and the dominating spirit in the imperial partnership. His younger brother Valens, the Eastern emperor, was thus left to meet the crisis on his own responsibility, for he could not accept the guidance of his nephew, the youthful though brilliant Gratian, who had succeeded his father

in the West. The dilemma presented by the Goths might well have troubled a stronger man than the cautious and vacillating Valens. To refuse their petition was to risk a serious war; to grant it was to admit a potential enemy to the heart of the empire. After a long, and to the Goths a maddening, delay he decided to admit them on condition that they surrender their arms, give hostages, and settle as *foederati*. All might yet have been well had these terms, humiliating though they were to a warlike people, been strictly enforced. But the corrupt and avaricious officials who supervised the transportation of the barbarians across the Danube neglected to secure their arms, while at the same time plundering them and taking many of their young men and women as slaves. Moreover, no provision was made for feeding the host. Within a year the Visigoths, enraged by this treatment and made desperate by famine, broke their oath of allegiance and set out to plunder Thrace.

Battle of Adrianople. Meanwhile, in the West, Gratian was busy repelling an invasion of the Alamanni on the Rhine and was unable to bring aid to the East till late in the summer of 378. By that time Valens had finally arrived on the scene and had taken command of his army at Adrianople. Jealous of his nephew's victory in Gaul, Valens decided to engage the Gothic army himself without waiting for the reinforcements which Gratian was bringing from the West. It was a disastrous decision. Before nightfall the emperor and two-thirds of his army were slain and the remainder scattered. The battle of Adrianople marks the end of an epoch, for it broke the prestige of the hitherto invincible Roman army.

The Visigoths and Theodosius. The victorious Goths soon found that, though they could ravage the open country at will, they could not capture the walled towns nor consolidate their conquests. The new emperor of the East, Theodosius I, who had been chosen by Gratian as his colleague, was soon able to restore the peace. By 382 the Visigoths were settled in Thrace as *foederati* or allies, retaining their own customs and government. Under the firm rule of Theodosius, the East enjoyed a period of quiet, but in the West there was turmoil and confusion. Two successive revolts of the legions in Britain and Gaul led to the death of Gratian (383) and of his younger brother and successor, Valentinian II (392). After crushing the rebels, Theodosius reunited the empire under his rule; but it was divided again after his death between his two incompetent sons, Arcadius (395–408), who took the eastern half, and Honorius (395–423), who, though only ten years old, became the nominal ruler of the West.

Alaric and Stilicho. With the death of the great Theodosius, the Roman Empire fell upon evil times. The Visigoths, under the leadership of their young king, Alaric, immediately broke the peace and set out on a plundering expedition through Thrace, Macedonia, and Greece. Alaric was no wild barbarian chieftain, but a soldier trained in the Roman army. He had commanded the Gothic auxiliaries in Theodosius' last campaign. After ravaging the Eastern Empire, Alaric turned toward the West, but was repeatedly repulsed by the efforts of the commander-in-chief of the western imperial army, a Vandal named Stilicho, who acted as regent during the minority of Honorius and was for years practically the ruler of the Western Empire. Meanwhile, the western frontiers were falling, left unprotected as the legions were called in to defend Italy. In 406 the Vandals, with a host of allies from other tribes, swept across Gaul to the Pyrenees and later entered Spain. In 407 there was another revolt of the remaining legions in Britain and Gaul. And in 408, as though to complete the chaos, Honorius was persuaded to decree the death of Stilicho. The Vandal general had proved himself the one man who could hold the barbarians in check. His death opened the gates of Italy to the Visigoths.

Sack of Rome (410). Alaric met with little opposition as he led his people down into Italy. The emperor had taken refuge behind the marshes that surrounded Ravenna; the army was disrupted, and Rome was at the mercy of the Goth. By besieging the helpless city and cutting off supplies, Alaric soon wrung a large ransom from the terrified inhabitants. He then tried to make peace with the emperor, but Honorius, himself safe in Ravenna, refused to meet his terms. In disgust the Visigothic king again marched on Rome, captured it, and gave it over to his followers to plunder. The sack of Rome, the ancient capital of the world empire, shook the morale of the Romans as perhaps nothing else could have done. We have seen how it inspired St. Augustine to write a defense of Christianity against the charge that the disaster had been caused by the desertion of the old gods. After pillaging the city for three days, the Visigoths moved on to southern Italy laden with plunder. Alaric probably intended to cross to Africa, but his plans were cut short by his premature death late in 410.

Visigoths in Gaul and Spain. After the death of Alaric, the Visigoths wandered northward through Italy and thence into southwestern Gaul, where they established a kingdom between the Loire and the Pyrenees and were recognized by the imperial government as *foederati*. From there they later expanded into Spain and by about the middle of the century had occupied the whole peninsula, except the northwest corner. The Visigoth Kingdom continued in Gaul until the coming of the Franks in the early years of the sixth century and in Spain till the Moslem invasion of 711. In the part of Gaul ceded to them by Honorius, the Goths took possession of two-thirds of the land, leaving one-third of each estate to the original owners, who were also allowed to remain under Roman administration.

4. The Vandals and Huns and the Fall of the Western Empire

The Vandals invade Africa. The settlement of the Visigoths in Gaul was followed by a brief period of comparative stability, but it was soon

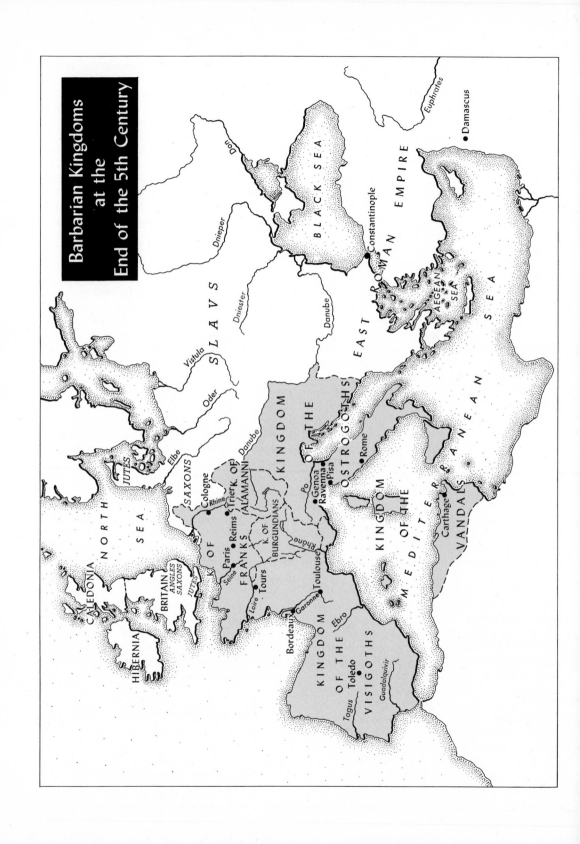

Barbarian Kingdoms
at the
End of the 5th Century

HIBERNIA

CALEDONIA

BRITAIN
ANGLES
SAXONS

JUTES

NORTH SEA

JUTES

Elbe

SAXONS

K. OF FRANKS

Cologne
Rhine
Trier
Reims
Paris
Seine
Tours
Loire
Bordeaux
Garonne
Ebro

K. OF ALAMANNI

K. OF BURGUNDIANS

Rhône

Toulouse

KINGDOM OF THE VISIGOTHS

Toledo
Tagus
Guadalquivir

SLAVS

Vistula

Oder

Dniester

Dnieper

Don

Danube

Danube

KINGDOM OF THE OSTROGOTHS

Po
Genoa
Ravenna
Pisa
Rome

MEDITERRANEAN SEA

KINGDOM OF THE VANDALS

Carthage

BLACK SEA

Constantinople

EAST ROMAN EMPIRE

AEGEAN SEA

Euphrates

Damascus

broken by the renewed migration of another Germanic nation. The Vandals, who had crossed from eastern Germany to Spain in the great invasion of 406, had finally been driven to the southern part of the peninsula by the combined force of the Visigoths and the imperial troops. Thence they cast longing eyes across the Straits of Gibraltar toward the rich grain fields and wealthy cities of the North African provinces. Hitherto the Vandals had met with no great success in their wanderings. On the eve of their departure from Spain, however, they acquired, in the person of the terrible Gaiseric (428–77), a king who was to infuse new life into his people and to lead them to victory for nearly half a century. Under his leadership the Vandals crossed the straits in 429 and overran the whole North African seaboard, devastating the land as they went. The death of the aged St. Augustine during the siege of Hippo is one of the memorable events of these tragic years. The emperor was powerless to stem the tide, and in 435 was forced to recognize the Vandals as *foederati*.

Vandal Kingdom in Africa. But Gaiseric was not long content with partial success. The capture of Carthage in 439, the largest city and most important harbor on the African coast, completed his conquests. Three years later the emperor ceded the North African provinces to him. The Vandals now turned to the sea in search of further plunder. Using Carthage as a naval base, their ships preyed upon Roman commerce and the unprotected coastal towns of the Mediterranean. This systematic piracy struck a crippling blow to the expiring commerce of the empire, while the loss of grain and taxes from the African provinces further depleted the already exhausted imperial treasury. The Vandal Kingdom continued to flourish for nearly a century, to be finally destroyed in 534 by the victorious armies of Justinian.[1]

Italy and Gaul. While Africa was being wrenched away, the empire maintained a precarious hold on Italy and part of Gaul, though all its powers were declining with ever-increasing rapidity. The death of Honorius was followed by the reign of a usurper, but in 425 the imperial line was restored in the person of Valentinian III (425–55), the dissolute and

incompetent grandson of Theodosius. During the greater part of Valentinian's reign, the outstanding figure in the Western Empire was the general Aëtius, who became commander-in-chief of the army in 429 and thereafter was the real ruler of the Western Empire. He showed little interest in Africa, but concentrated his attention on Gaul, where he succeeded in keeping the barbarians in check. He prevented the expansion of the Visigoth Kingdom, repelled the Franks, and crushed the Burgundians, transplanting the defeated nation to southeastern Gaul (443), where they founded a federate kingdom between the Rhône and the Alps.

The Huns under Attila. Meanwhile, the Huns, those fierce Asiatic nomads who had driven the Visigoths across the Roman frontier, had organized a great marauding empire to the north of the Black Sea and the Danube. Here they hung like a threatening cloud over the Eastern Empire, while Theodosius II (408–50), the son of Arcadius and almost as weak as his father, sought to placate them by the payment of tribute. About 433, the famous Attila came to rule over the united Hun tribes, the Ostrogoths, and the other subjugated European barbarians, increasing the menace by the force of a keen predatory mind and a dominating personality. Attila soon forced Theodosius to double the tribute, but for some years the relations between the powerful Mongol and Constantinople remained peaceful enough. After 440, however, the Huns began to threaten the Eastern Empire more seriously, and throughout the following decade repeatedly ravaged the provinces south of the Danube, exacting a higher tribute on each occasion. This systematic blackmail was brought to an end by the death of Theodosius. Marcian (450–57), his successor, refused to pay the Hun-money and Attila, perhaps judging the devastated eastern provinces scarcely worth further plundering, turned his attention westward.

Attila invades Gaul and Italy. The invasion of Gaul by Attila in 451 spread terror through the West, rousing Romans and barbarians to present a united front against the dreaded "Scourge of God." Having crossed the Rhine to the north of Mainz, Attila rode southwest into the heart of Gaul. Near Troyes he met an

[1] See below, page 114.

The warrior shown in relief on an ivory tablet probably represents Aëtius, the commander who defeated Attila's Huns, although some scholars have identified the figure as that of Stilicho.

allied army hastily gathered together by Aëtius and composed of Roman troops, Visigoths, Burgundians, and other *foederati*. In the bloody battle which followed (commonly but inaccurately called the battle of Châlons), neither side could claim a clear victory. It was generally recognized as a Roman triumph, however, as Attila withdrew from Gaul to his capital in what is now called Hungary. The following year he returned to the attack, this time swooping down over the Alps into Italy, where there were no German federates to aid the disorganized Roman army. After sacking several cities in northern Italy, Attila again retired without attempting to capture the defenseless city of Rome. Legend has accorded the credit

for saving the city to Pope Leo I, who held an interview with Attila and persuaded him to spare it. Famine and fever among his plunder-laden troops, however, probably weighed more heavily with the Hun than did the arguments of the good bishop. At any rate, he returned to the Danube and died there a year later (453).

Disappearance of the Huns. Attila's empire, which had been held together by his strong personality, fell to pieces immediately after his death. It had never become an organized territorial state, nor had it struck roots into the soil. The vassal tribes rebelled and the Huns themselves were soon divided. Within a few years they had broken up or drifted eastward, disappearing into the shadows that for the modern historian veil eastern Europe and the Asiatic steppes. They had passed through Europe like an evil wind, but left no permanent mark, save for the débris of the empire they had helped to destroy.

The Vandals sack Rome (455). With the retreat of Attila, the Romans breathed freely again, but not for long. Within two years Rome was in more serious danger than ever. Aëtius, who had never been fully trusted by the emperor, was assassinated by him in 454, and his murder was soon avenged by the assassination of Valentinian himself. So ended the dynasty of the great Theodosius, and in the paralysis of imperial government which followed, Gaiseric the Vandal saw an opportunity too promising to be ignored. Sailing across from Carthage, the Vandals entered Rome without opposition. Again Leo I interceded with the barbarian, gaining a promise from Gaiseric that the lives of the inhabitants would be spared. For two weeks the Vandals looted the still wealthy city at their leisure, after which they returned home, leaving Rome impoverished.

End of the Western Empire. The two decades following the sack of Rome saw the final disintegration of the empire in the West. Such vestiges of Roman administration as remained in the provinces practically disappeared, while in Italy the real rulers were the barbarian generals who not only controlled the imperial government, as their forerunners Stilicho and Aëtius had done, but created and deposed emperors at will. The fiction that the Western Empire was still ruled by its emperors was finally brought to an end in 476. In that year Odovacar, a general of German descent newly risen to command of the Roman army, deposed the last emperor of the West, Romulus Augustulus (satirically named "the little emperor"), and thereafter left the throne vacant, taking the government openly into his own hands, though recognizing the nominal authority of the emperor in the East. Theoretically, this meant that the Roman Empire was once more united under one emperor, who delegated power in Italy; actually Odovacar was the independent ruler of Italy, and the empire in the West had come to an end. This made relatively little change in the conditions of government, it is true, since the greater part of the Western Empire had long since fallen a prey to barbarian kingdoms, and Italy itself had been ruled for twenty years by barbarian generals. Still, the fact that there was no longer to be an emperor of the West makes the date 476 a significant one.

5. *The Ostrogoth Kingdom in Italy*

Ostrogoths invade Italy. After thirteen years of undisputed rule in Italy, Odovacar, like so many of the emperors whose place he had taken, found his position threatened by a new barbarian invasion. The Ostrogoths had freed themselves from the overlordship of the Huns after the death of Attila and had migrated into the Balkan provinces of the Eastern Empire, where they alternately ravaged the country and fought for the emperor as *foederati*. Under the vigorous leadership of their king, Theodoric, they became a serious menace to the empire, almost equally dangerous whether as friends or as enemies. Theodoric had passed most of his youth in Constantinople as a hostage. He had gained a thorough knowledge of Roman institutions, which showed him the weakness of the empire, though at the same time it aroused in him a great respect for Roman traditions and civilization. Oddly enough, he seems never to have learned to write, but merely traced his name with the aid of a gold plate in which the letters had been cut. In 488, the Emperor Zeno sought to rid himself of a dangerous ally by commissioning Theodoric to invade Italy and suppress Odovacar. After some delay, the Ostrogoths reached Italy

in 489. Odovacar was defeated in battle and took refuge in the impregnable city of Ravenna. For nearly three years the Goths besieged the city in vain. At last Theodoric resorted to treachery. Having tricked Odovacar into negotiating a peace treaty, he assassinated him. This act completed the conquest of Italy.

Theodoric, king and patrician. For thirty-three years Italy enjoyed the advantages of a just and moderate government under the Ostrogothic king. Despite occasional reversions to barbaric cruelty and treachery, Theodoric (493–526) proved a worthy successor to the best of the Roman emperors. We may discount the effusions of court poets, but the estimate of Procopius, the historian of the Eastern Empire, may be taken at its face value: "His manner of ruling over his subjects was worthy of a great emperor; for he maintained justice, made good laws, protected his country from invasion, and gave proof of extraordinary prudence and valor." He gave proof, too, of unusual wisdom and tact in handling a delicate situation, for although he was to all practical intents and purposes the independent ruler of Italy, his constitutional position was rather ambiguous. He was the legitimate king of his Ostrogothic people, but so far as the Italians were concerned his position was that of a nominal agent of the emperor, who had conferred upon him the title of Patrician. Realizing that this strengthened the legitimacy of his government without curtailing his real power, Theodoric continued to recognize the formal superiority of the Eastern emperor.

Romans and Goths in Italy. The dual character of Theodoric's government arose from the fact that he ruled two distinct peoples without making any attempt to draw them together or to encourage fusion. The Goths had appropriated about a third of the land (some scholars say of the public land) and had settled quietly among the resident Romans. Each people retained so far as possible its own legal and judicial system, though cases involving both Romans and Goths were apparently tried in the Gothic courts. The status of the two peoples was strongly influenced by the fact that the army was purely Gothic. The Goths remained the military caste; their courts were military courts; and their land was granted to them according to custom as federate soldiers. The civil government was as purely Roman. Theodoric made no change in Roman administration or laws in so far as they affected Roman citizens, and all civil offices were filled by native Italians. The old imperial officers, the consuls, and the Senate remained with remarkably little change and were among the most loyal supporters of the Gothic king. Even the difference in religion between the Arian Goth and the orthodox Roman, though it caused some friction, seems not to have placed any serious strain upon their relations. Theodoric made no attempt to force his own religion on his subjects, but maintained a policy of absolute toleration. "We cannot," he wrote through his secretary Cassiodorus, "impose religion, because no one can be compelled to believe against his will."

Revived prosperity. Perhaps the greatest change made by the Gothic king was the introduction of peace, security, and revived prosperity in Italy during his long reign. Agriculture and commerce flourished as they had not done for a century. Justice was administered with greater firmness and integrity. Long-neglected harbors, aqueducts, and public buildings were restored and new ones erected. Italy was still far removed from the good old days of Roman prosperity, but better off than she had been or than she was to be again for centuries to come. Unfortunately, Theodoric's work died with him. Factional strife broke out soon after his death, and by 555 the Ostrogothic Kingdom in Italy had been crushed by the armies of the great Eastern emperor, Justinian.[1]

Continued decline of culture. The brief period of peace brought with it a slight revival of intellectual life, but could not check the steady decline of Roman culture. Rather, the work of the Latin writers who flourished under Theodoric merely serves to demonstrate the drift toward barbarism in the West. The great age of classic literature was buried in the distant if unforgotten past, while the creative period of Christian writing had ended with Augustine, the last of the fourth-century Latin Fathers. The representative writers of this period, Boëthius and Cassiodorus, both Romans in the service of Theodoric, contented themselves with translations from the Greek, the knowledge of which was dying out in the West,

with slim commentaries on the work of earlier commentators, and with compilations and epitomes of earlier learning. The Roman mind, half-barbarized, could evidently no longer appreciate the full scope of antique thought, nor could it create an independent literature of its own. The most original work of this age, the *Consolation of Philosophy,* written by Boëthius in prison while awaiting execution as the result of a conspiracy against Theodoric, has charm and pathos, but it is no more than an eclectic echo of various ancient philosophical systems, in which the sole originality lies in the author's choice of such materials as suited his needs. Yet the labor of these scholars was not unimportant because unoriginal. By bringing the thought of the civilized past down to the level of a more barbaric age, they kept it alive and furnished the groping minds of a still darker period to come with materials not too far above their range of comprehension, so that they might in time recover something of the fading heritage of Greece and Rome. Boëthius and Cassiodorus were to rank high among the most popular authors of the Early Middle Ages.

Anglo-Saxons in Britain. In tracing the principal migrations of the barbarian peoples during this confused period, we have so far ignored the conquest of Britain, not because it is unimportant, but because it stands somewhat apart from the main current of events on the Continent. Early in the fifth century the Roman legions had been withdrawn from Britain for the defense of Italy and Gaul, leaving the Britons to their own devices. During the next two centuries the distant island province, almost unnoticed by Rome, was overrun by a group of Germanic tribes or coalitions of tribes, the Jutes, Angles, and Saxons, who sailed over from their home in northeastern Germany on the shores of the North Sea and laid in Britain the foundations of the English people. Little is known of the actual course of the conquest, save that it occupied a long period of steady migration and of thorough occupation of the land. Seriously begun probably about the middle of the fifth century, it was completed by the end of the following century. The Romanized Celts who made up the provincial population were either annihilated or driven back into the hills of Wales and Cornwall in the southwest corner of the island. They seem

[1] See below, page 114.

This solid gold belt clasp, with its intricately interwoven design, is one of the masterpieces of seventh-century Anglo-Saxon goldsmith work. It was found in Sutton Hoo, England.

to have had little or no influence on the religion, language, or manners of the invaders, who remained Germanic and pagan. It was the most thorough and complete conquest made by any barbarian nation.

The Franks. We have ignored the Franks too, in the long run the most important of all the barbarian invaders. For the conquest of Gaul by the united Frankish tribes, begun in the last years of the fifth century and completed early in the sixth, was but the beginning of a long story and one that forms the central theme of western European history for some centuries. It will be left to a later chapter for fuller treatment than could be afforded it here.

Summary. By the end of the fifth century Roman government had completely disappeared in the Western Empire, its place being taken by a number of barbarian kingdoms.[1] Italy was ruled by the Ostrogoths, North Africa by the Vandals, Britain by the Anglo-Saxons, southwestern Gaul and Spain by the Visigoths, and southeastern Gaul by the Burgundians, while the Franks had already conquered what remained of the latter province. Of these only the Franks and the Anglo-Saxons were to retain their conquests. The remainder were soon to lose their political identity and in time even their racial identity, having merged with the people among whom they had settled. For it must not be forgotten that, except in Britain, the invaders were never more than a minority of the population of the conquered provinces. Statistics as to their actual numbers vary so widely as to be obviously unreliable, but it has been suggested that none of the invading peoples numbered above one hundred thousand. At any rate, the numbers were small enough to permit the final absorption of the barbarian by the Roman stock to a very large extent. The fusion of the two peoples was accompanied by a fusion of cultures. The barbarian became more civilized through contact with the Roman, while on the other hand the Roman was drawn down closer to the level of the barbarian. The final result was a mixture of the Latin and Germanic past, welded together to make up medieval civilization.

[1] See map, page 104.

SECTION C

THE EARLY MIDDL

St. Philibert in Tournus, France, is a
Romanesque church dating from the
latter part of the Early Middle Ages.

With the disappearance of the Roman Empire in the West, Europe may be considered to have entered upon that period of its history vaguely known as the Middle Ages. It is a rather misleading term, but hallowed by centuries of use and difficult to replace. The term Middle Ages was first coined by Renaissance historians, who regarded the thousand years following the collapse of the Roman Empire as merely a middle period of Gothic barbarism, separating the glorious age of antiquity from their own great age of the revival of classic civilization. More modern historians have retained the term because it serves a useful purpose and has been so long accepted; but they have shown that its original meaning was based on a complete misconception of the nature of European history. The Middle Ages were much more than the name implies; for it was during those thousand years that the modern world was made, and they also produced a civilization different from that of the age before or after and well worthy of study in its own right. But if it is a mistake to treat the Middle Ages as a negligible period, it is equally misleading to treat the whole period as a single, coherent age. For even the most summary purposes of classification, ten centuries are too long a time, and they witnessed too many sweeping changes, to be grouped together under one name. For greater convenience, therefore, we have made further divisions, and will treat first under the heading of the Early Middle Ages the period extending roughly from the end of the fifth to the middle of the eleventh century. Changes in plenty occurred even within this shorter period, but it had certain characteristics that mark it off from the more settled age that followed. It was during these five and a half centuries that, in the almost purely agrarian society of western Europe and the more cultured East, the foundations were laid for that new type of civilization which we think of as typically medieval. It was in this period that the Roman Empire in the East became Byzantine, that Islam transformed the culture of a large part of the Roman world, that the Germanic and Scandinavian peoples settled down in their permanent dwelling places, that feudal society began to take definite shape, and that the feudal kingdoms on the one hand and a united Catholic Christendom on the other emerged from the tangled chaos of the barbarian conquests.

9

The Eastern Empire Becomes Byzantine

WHEN Constantine the Great by imperial decree established a "New Rome" on the impregnable site of the ancient town of Byzantium, calling it Constantinople, he gave to the eastern or Greek half of the Roman Empire a capital of its own and a focal center for its administration and its culture. Thenceforth, with occasional exceptions during the fourth century, the two parts of the empire were divided into separate administrative units. In theory the empire was still one and united, but as time passed the two sections drifted farther and farther apart, separated by differences in language and in religious and political interests, until at last the actual division assumed a greater reality than the theoretical unity. After the Western Empire was destroyed by the barbarian invaders, the last link connecting the Greek East with the Latin West was broken. Only the Eastern Empire remained, exclusively Greek in culture and inhabited by people of eastern origin. The old tradition of the Roman Empire, however, died hard. The emperor at Constantinople still claimed lordship over the lost provinces, and in the sixth century Justinian partially realized for a time the dream of restoring the West to imperial rule. Until its final collapse in the fifteenth century, the empire continued to call itself Roman. But even under Justinian the empire was drifting further from the Roman traditions, continuing

the steady development of social and political institutions, religious ideas, and a culture based on its Greek and oriental heritage rather than on that of Rome. To call this later empire Roman, as did the people of the empire themselves, leads to confusion and a misconception of its true nature. A better name is that commonly used by historians and derived from Byzantium, the original name of the city of Constantinople. Hereafter we shall call it the Byzantine Empire.

1. *Justinian's Dream of Restoring the Empire*

Justinian (527–65). For more than a century after the death of the great Theodosius in 395, the empire in the East was not distinguished by strong government. Its rulers were able to do little more than preserve their state from the assaults of barbarian enemies, while making little attempt to save the West from destruction or to reform conditions in their own empire. A new and more glorious era in the imperial annals opened with the proclamation of the Emperor Justin in 518. An Illyrian peasant, Justin had neither education nor experience in government beyond that supplied by his training in the army. But he had a nephew named Justinian, who soon became the power behind the throne and directed his uncle's government until the death of Justin in 527, when he succeeded him as emperor. Thanks to his uncle's generosity, Justinian had been given all the advantages of education and training that the older man lacked. Moreover, he had intelligence of a high order and an amazing capacity for work. His tireless attention to the details of administration caused one of his courtiers to describe him as "the emperor who never sleeps." On the other hand, there were weaknesses in his character that at times threatened to nullify the results of his labor. In moments of stress he sometimes showed a sad lack of firmness and decision.

Theodora. This weakness, however, was fortunately counterbalanced by the iron nerve of his wife Theodora, who more than once, as during the Nika riots in Constantinople in 532, bolstered up his failing courage and saved him and the empire from disaster. Theodora knew the people as Justinian never could. She was the daughter of a bear-keeper in the hippodrome and had herself been a popular actress there. All contemporary writers agree as to her charm and beauty, her keen intelligence, and her influence over Justinian, whom she

had married in the days before he was elevated to the throne. As empress her power was greater than that of any of her predecessors.

Justinian's aims. Throughout his reign, Justinian was inspired by one great ambition — to restore the Roman Empire to all its former greatness. Under the inspiration of that dream he undertook to reconquer the lost provinces of the West, to rebuild the fortifications and public buildings of the empire, and to dazzle the world with the splendor of his court and capital. It was an ambition noble in itself, but its fulfillment was beyond the powers of the state as he found it. A second ambition, which he thought to be a necessary part of the first, was to establish in the most complete way the absolute, autocratic power of the emperor as the sole source of authority. His exalted conception of the emperor's powers and duties led him to make much-needed reforms in the administration and the law, but it did not restore the imperial tradition of the great days of Rome. Though he may not have realized it, Justinian was merely following the tendencies of the later emperors since Diocletian, completing their work in making the empire an autocracy.

A mosaic in the church of San Vitale, Ravenna, showing Justinian and his courtiers, symbolizes the emperor's political and spiritual authority.

Reconquest of the West. Justinian's first opportunity for interference in the West was afforded by a dynastic revolution in the Vandal Kingdom in Africa. On the pretext of restoring the rightful ruler, Justinian sent an army under the command of the brilliant general Belisarius in 533. The Vandal resistance proved amazingly weak, and within a year Belisarius had completed the conquest of the kingdom. A similar dynastic dispute gave Justinian a pretext for invading the Ostrogothic Kingdom in Italy in 535. Belisarius again led the imperial troops to victory. By 540 he had conquered all of the peninsula south of the river Po. Continued Gothic resistance in the north, however, delayed the completion of the conquest of Italy until 555. In both North Africa and Italy the imperial administration and law were reintroduced — also, unfortunately, the imperial taxation which proved ruinous to the liberated provincials. Meanwhile, Justinian had also succeeded in reconquering southeastern Spain from the Visigoths and in recovering the islands of the western Mediterranean.[1]

Diplomacy and defense. In his zeal to restore the prestige of the Roman Empire, Justinian also sought by the use of skillful diplomacy to dominate the barbarian tribes beyond the frontiers — the Lombards and other Germans, the Slavs who had migrated from what is now Russia to the Danube, and the Bulgars, Avars, and other Mongolian peoples who had followed the Huns from Asia. This was necessary for defense as well. For the wars in the West and with Persia in the East had forced him to withdraw many of the troops from the frontiers, and though Justinian built or reconstructed at great expense a ring of forts about the empire (some six hundred in the Balkans alone), there was still serious danger of invasion. His principal aim was to gain allies among the neighboring tribes. Bribes, titles, and subsidies were scattered with a lavish hand. No expense was spared to advertise the splendor and power of the emperor. Barbarian chieftains were invited to Constantinople, where the magnificence of the court and the extravagant ceremony surrounding the person of the ruler made a profound impression on their simple minds. Finally, the imperial diplomats, with that unscrupulous subtlety for which Byzantine diplomacy became famous, stirred up strife among the barbarians in order that they might destroy one another for the good of the empire. This system as perfected by Justinian, though many of the methods were already familiar, continued in force for centuries. It was not always successful; it placed a heavy strain on the imperial treasury; and it aroused the cupidity of the barbarians. Even during Justinian's reign the Balkan provinces were repeatedly ravaged by the Slavs, and after his death they settled there in force.

Administrative reform. The fault inherent in all of Justinian's grandiose plans was that their fulfillment cost more than the empire could afford. His military and diplomatic operations were expensive enough. To them was added the ruinous expense of restoring and constructing roads, bridges, aqueducts, theaters, palaces, and churches, especially those in Constantinople, on a scale befitting the grandeur of the Roman Empire. Under such conditions the problem of filling the imperial treasury became one of the most vital concerns of the government. Justinian was sincerely anxious to be a good as well as a great ruler, but his constant need of money forced him to tolerate the methods of his hated minister, John of Cappadocia, who fleeced the people unmercifully. The Nika riots of 532 in the capital were a protest against his administration and were suppressed only after Belisarius had massacred some thirty thousand of the rioters. After this affair, Justinian undertook to reform the administration so as to protect the taxpayer from illegal exactions and at the same time to increase the income of the government by checking corruption and by making the civil service more efficient. The sale of offices, which led the men who had purchased them to recover their money at the expense of the people or the government, was abolished, and salaries were increased so as to make graft unnecessary. Regular steps of promotion in the service were instituted to encourage industry and efficiency. At the same time, a good many useless offices were done away with and the whole system was brought more directly under the control of the central government, thus increasing the absolute power of the emperor. The result was an administrative machine which preserved the

[1] See map, page 116.

Sancta Sophia, Justinian's great church in Constantinople, is a monument to Byzantine artistic and engineering skill. The minarets were added by the Moslem conquerors. The windows at the base of the dome which gave brilliant lighting to the interior are a striking feature.

empire through many a crisis in the following centuries.

Justinian and the church. As has been said, Justinian was determined to make the emperor the sole authority in the state, interpreting that authority to include every aspect of the people's life. Religion was too important a factor to be ignored by a ruler with such absolute claims and, besides, Justinian was a theologian at heart. Since the time of Constantine, the emperors in the East had exercised a greater control over the church than had their colleagues in the West. They had dominated church government and most of them had used their civil powers to crush opposition to the dogmas which the church had declared to be orthodox. Justinian, however, went one step further, and an important step it was to prove for the future of the Greek Church. He asserted the right of the emperor to decide disputed points of dogma himself and to force acceptance of his opinions on the church and the people. He thus became the effective head of the church in matters of faith as well as of government, while the church became practically a department of the state. The Greek Church was never after able to free itself altogether from this subservience to the emperors.

Justinian Code. One further task undertaken by Justinian, the most important in its permanent and far-reaching effects on later European civilization, remains to be mentioned. This was his codification of Roman law, the work with which his name is most commonly associated. There were two kinds of law recognized by the Roman courts. First, there was the direct imperial legislation, laws called "constitutions," issued by the emperors themselves. Then there was a great body of jurisprudence, composed of decisions handed down by authorized judges and lawyers. Through the centuries a huge mass of law had accumulated until it became unwieldy and confusing. Some attempt at straightening out this legal tangle had been made by Theodosius II, who in 438 had issued the Theodosian Code including the imperial constitutions since Constantine. However, much still remained to be done if Roman law were to be preserved. Justinian set himself to the task in the first year of his reign, appointing a committee of ten jurists to compile a new code. The *Codex Justinianus* or Justinian Code was completed the following year and given its final form in 534. It included all imperial legislation up to that time in condensed and simplified form, with everything that was obsolete, contradictory, or repetitious eliminated and the whole arranged in logical order. The still more difficult task of carrying out a similar condensation and simplification of jurisprudence was begun in 530 and completed in three years. It is known as the *Digest* or *Pandects*. To this was added a brief official handbook or text for the use of students, called the *Institutes*. These three works, together with the *Novels,* a collection

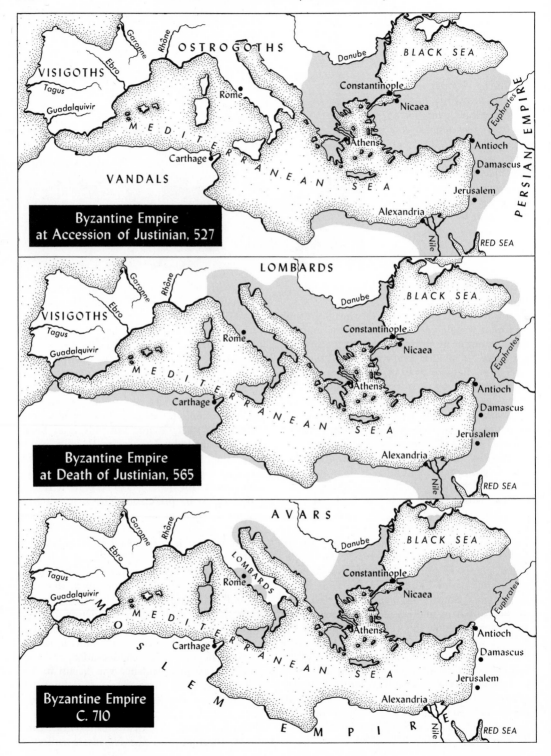

Byzantine Empire
at Accession of Justinian, 527

Byzantine Empire
at Death of Justinian, 565

Byzantine Empire
C. 710

of the laws issued by Justinian himself, are collectively known as the *Corpus Juris Civilis,* the body of civil law. In it was preserved all that was most valuable in Roman law in a clear and available form for the use of later generations. It forms the basis of civil law in most European countries today.

Failure of Justinian's dream. Justinian left the marks of his handiwork on many aspects of Byzantine life and government. The law, the church, the administration, diplomacy, and the position of the emperor in the state through the following centuries were all influenced in greater or lesser degree by his work, while the great public buildings he had erected remained a permanent memorial to his reign. But his greatest ambition, the dream of restoring the Roman Empire to its former size and grandeur, was doomed to failure. His plans for conquest and reconstruction had far exceeded the financial resources of the empire. On his death he left the state bankrupt and the people crushed by the weight of intolerable taxation. The empire was so exhausted that it was unable to hold the reconquered provinces of the West or to repel new invaders in the East. The following century saw the empire cut down to a mere fraction of its former size. Indeed, the conquest of the West had been a mistake. Had Justinian devoted his great powers to strengthening the empire in the East he would have deserved greater praise.

2. *The Byzantine Empire Survives*

Loss of territory (568–700). The reign of Justinian was followed by a period of repeated losses and disasters, during which the Byzantine Empire was reduced to the territory that, with some variations, it retained till the end of the Middle Ages. Within a generation the Lombards invaded Italy and conquered most of it;[1] the Visigoths recovered the part of Spain conquered by Justinian; the Slavs and other barbarians occupied all of the Balkan provinces except Thrace and the coastline of Greece; and the Persians began a war which left both Persia and the empire exhausted. After the death of Mohammed in 632, the Arabs, now welded into an aggressive nation and inspired by his teaching, set out on a career of conquest at the expense of the empire. By the year 700, they had wrested from it all the provinces in Africa and in Asia, except the peninsula of Asia Minor which lies between the southern shore of the Black Sea and the Mediterranean. Thus the Byzantine Empire was cut down to a comparatively small territory, part in Europe, part in Asia, centering on the city of Constantinople.[2]

Survival of the empire. Despite the loss of so many provinces and the almost continuous danger from Moslems and Slavs, the Byzantine Empire survived until the middle of the fifteenth century. More than once in that long period it seemed doomed to destruction; it suffered at times from revolution, anarchy, and bad government; but it always recovered. It has been said frequently enough that the most remarkable characteristic of the empire was its power of recuperation. Until fairly recent years, historians, following the example of Gibbon, have emphasized the weakness, corruption, and cultural sterility of Byzantium and have pictured the empire as in a state of perpetual decline. There were, indeed, elements of weakness, both political and social, in the Byzantine Empire. But there were also elements of strength and amazing vitality.

Elements of strength. The absolute powers enjoyed by the emperors who followed Justinian, though dangerous in the hands of a weakling, were a source of great strength when wielded by a strong ruler, and there were many strong rulers in Byzantine history. Time and again in moments of extreme danger a man of powerful personality fought his way to the throne and infused new life into the empire. His control of every department of state, including the church, made it possible for an able emperor to use all the powers of the state to the best advantage. Nor were the results of weak rule as disastrous as they might have been; for the administrative system as organized by Justinian was capable of carrying on the business of government even during a revolution. The imperial authority and the centralized administration gave a real political unity to the state, and this was further strengthened by the religious and cultural unity of Byzantine society.

[1] See below, page 137.

[2] See below, pages 125–126, and map, page 127.

Some of the finest surviving examples of Byzantine church architecture were built in Ravenna during the sixth century when it was the center of imperial administration in Italy. The church of San Apollinare in Classe, intended for the use of the fleet, marks the site of the ancient harbor, which is now silted in.

Economic strength. Through all its changes of fortune the Byzantine Empire also enjoyed an economic strength that enabled it to recover from the most serious reverses. The geographic position of the empire, and especially of the capital, gave it unequaled opportunities for trade. Straddling the narrow Sea of Marmora, between Europe and Asia, the Black Sea and the Mediterranean, the empire was the meeting place of trade routes running east and west, north and south. The commerce of the world was transshipped in the harbors of Constantinople, bought and sold in its markets. For centuries, it was one of the richest cities of the world, "the city of the world's desire." Stimulated by trade, the capital and other imperial cities became centers of thriving industry. Constantinople was especially famous for the manufacture of all articles of luxury.

The impregnable city. Nor was it only as a commercial and industrial center that Constantinople gave strength to the empire. Its site, chosen by the warrior Constantine, made it impregnable to attack. Open to the sea, it could not be starved into submission, and built as it was on a small peninsula, only the landward side needed defense. Here it was guarded by walls so strong and so well fortified that they could be held against any army not equipped with modern artillery. Wave after wave of invasion, which might have destroyed the empire, broke against the city walls. Only twice since the days of Constantine has it been taken by siege.

Elements of weakness. So much for the factors that helped the empire to survive. Let us now glance for a moment at the reverse side of the coin and note the evidences of weakness. There was one serious disadvantage in the imperial system. No fixed rule of succession had been worked out. A strong emperor might nominate his successor with a fair hope of his being accepted by the people, but the right of heredity was not legally recognized. If the late emperor's nominee were not accepted, the result was usually decided by intrigue and violence. Moreover, the absolute powers of the emperor invited revolution. So long as he ruled there was no check upon his authority. But any man who could gain the support of a powerful faction in the army, at court, in the church, or among the people of the capital might succeed, with luck, in assassinating the emperor and being proclaimed his successor. He would then enjoy all the powers that went with the imperial purple. It was a prize worth fighting for. True, many successful revolutions placed a strong man on the throne in place of a weakling, at a time when strong government was needed. Yet the system led to perpetual intrigue, plots, and riots, which threatened the security of the government and the state.

Social weakness. Part of the responsibility for this condition must be accredited to the character of the Byzantine people. Much has been written about the vices and weakness of that cultivated, luxurious, and pleasure-loving society, always excitable, capricious, and easily aroused to factional passion. No doubt these characteristics have been overemphasized; for as one historian remarks, "It may be doubted whether any empire can live by vice alone." There must have been counterbalancing qualities of thrift, industry, and tenacious courage. Yet it cannot be denied that the society of the later empire was politically unstable. Disputes over points of theological dogma, economic or political grievances, the ambitions of a popular leader or the unpopularity of a minister could stir feeling to fever heat. The hippodrome, center of Byzantine social life, was often the scene of popular riots that sometimes assumed dangerous proportions. Two rival parties, the Greens and the Blues, sponsored the chariot races which were the chief attraction of the hippodrome, and the victory of one or the other was a matter of state-wide importance. These parties included in their ranks almost the entire population, from the imperial family down to the poorest laborer. They were in reality political parties and furnished a ready-made organization for the popular leader.

The Greek Orthodox Church.   The Byzantine people were intensely religious and were always keenly interested in theological questions. Disputes over the most fine-spun differences in the statement of dogma could arouse fanatical passions which were often used by political leaders to gain the support of the populace for their own ends. The monks and the clergy could become dangerous enemies of the government. For the most part, however, the emperors were able to maintain their absolute control of the church, sternly suppressing all heresies or movements for independence, and they found in it a useful instrument for preserving the unity of the empire. The Eastern Church had become thoroughly Greek in spirit and tradition. Differences of language, culture, and interest had divided it since the fourth century from the Latin Church of the West. For years at a time all communion between them was broken off, until in 1054 the schism

or split between them became definite and permanent. Thereafter the Greek Orthodox Church, to which the Byzantine and Slavic peoples adhered, was separated by a barrier of theological belief and religious practice from the Roman Catholic world of the West.

Learning and literature.   The importance of religious interest can be clearly seen in its effect on Byzantine education and literature. The Bible and the works of the Fathers of the Greek Church occupied a prominent place in the curriculum of the schools, while theology was the subject of a good half of the literature produced under the empire. A second influence, equally strong, was that of Greek antiquity. Byzantine culture was essentially Greek, though it had absorbed much from the Middle East, from Syria, Persia, Egypt, and later from the Arabs. The people of the empire were very proud of their inheritance from ancient Greece. The Greek classics formed the basis of Byzantine education. Century after century the writers of Byzantium imitated the classics, wrote learned commentaries upon them, and strove to preserve the ancient Greek style. This led to a growing differentiation between the written language and spoken Greek. In the cultured society of Byzantium, laymen of the

Byzantine religious pictures, like this one from the sixth century which depicts the Virgin enthroned, surrounded by angels and saints, retained their traditional style for centuries. Such pictures in the Byzantine tradition are known as icons.

upper classes continued to be well educated through centuries when in the West only the clergy were literate. The Byzantine Empire was thus able to maintain an unbroken tradition of secular literature and learning, despite the strong religious preoccupation that characterized its culture. Most of the long line of competent historians who recounted its history were laymen. They were thus better equipped to write history in secular terms than were the monastic chroniclers of the West. They were generally careful in collecting their material and they strove to maintain the standards of accuracy set by Thucydides and their other ancient models. Nearly all the classical forms of poetry were also assiduously cultivated and, in the case of the epigram at least, with considerable verve and finesse. Byzantine literature was sophisticated and often brilliant; reverence for classical purity of form and diction lent it a superficial polish; but something of originality and spontaneity was lost through imitation of the classics and because the language of literature was no longer that actually used by men.

Art.   In the art of Byzantium many of the same elements were present as in its literature.

Religion played fully as important a part. The churches were the finest examples of Byzantine architecture, and the icons, or pictures of saints, and religious scenes were among the best works produced by the artists of the empire. Byzantine art has often been described as bound by tradition, formal and monotonous, incapable of originality, but this prejudiced view has been abandoned by most recent critics. It was, indeed, a traditional art in many ways, dominated by fixed religious conceptions; but it showed also great variety and versatility. Though drawing their inspiration from Greek, oriental, and Christian traditions, the Byzantine artists produced a style that was in reality original and characteristically their own.

Architecture.   The Byzantine architects adapted earlier Roman forms of construction for their churches, making much use of arches, vaults, and domes, although their lavish use of color in the interior decoration seems more characteristic of the Middle East than of Rome. The most magnificent of all the Byzantine churches was the great church of Sancta Sophia (Holy Wisdom), built by Justinian to grace his capital and still standing, little touched by time though somewhat marred by the hand of man.

This Byzantine mosaic portrays Christ entering Jerusalem. It belongs to the twelfth century, some six hundred years later than the mosaic shown on page 119, and illustrates the continuity of Byzantine tradition.

Sancta Sophia is at once the supreme expression of Byzantine religious aspiration, the most perfect example of Byzantine art, and a daring triumph of engineering skill. Here the architects used space, light, and color with unrivaled effect. The nave is 100 feet wide, and above it the great dome soars to a height of 179 feet. Light flows in from forty windows about the base of the dome. Before the Moslem Turks covered the Christian decorations with whitewash, the interior, thus lighted, must have glowed and sparkled, as the varicolored marbles and mosaics caught and reflected the light. Procopius, who saw it when it was new, wrote: "It is flooded with sunlight, both direct and reflected. You would imagine that it was not merely illuminated from without by the sun, but that radiance springs from within it, such a superabundance of light pours into this holy temple."

Mosaics. The colorful effect of the Byzantine church interiors was enhanced by the liberal use of mosaics as pictorial decoration. Although Byzantine artists practiced both fresco and panel painting, mosaics were the most characteristic form of Byzantine pictorial art. These were large mural pictures, made up of countless tiny bits of colored glass or stone set in cement. In many mosaics the background was composed of gold leaf set between pieces of glass. Some of the finest surviving examples of Byzantine mosaics are to be found in Italian churches built during the period of Justinian's reconquest of Italy, notably in the churches of San Vitale and San Apollinare Nuovo in Ravenna. Compared with the realistic art introduced during the Renaissance, the figures in Byzantine mosaics and paintings seem stiff and unreal. They are, indeed, flat, without modeling or depth. There is no suggestion of perspective in the scene, and convention demanded that all the figures face the front. They are transcendental figures rather than mortal creatures of flesh and blood, and the artists were bound by rigid iconographic traditions. The mosaics are, however, remarkably effective as mural decoration, for they lie flat against the wall rather than suggesting a three-dimensional space set into the wall. The polished surface of glass and stone, moreover, lends them a glowing vitality that no paint can equal. Although little appreciated for centuries after the Renaissance, the merit of Byzantine painting and mosaic has been reasserted by recent critics who have become accustomed to think in terms of abstract design and impressionistic forms.

Influence on the Slav nations. Byzantine civilization spread far beyond the narrow confines of the empire. It had a permanent influence on the growth of the Slavic countries of eastern Europe, as great as was the influence of Rome on the Germanic nations of the West. The Slavs who had settled in the Balkans, and the various Slavic peoples who combined to make Russia, looked to Byzantium for religious and cultural leadership. The church of the Slavs was the Greek Orthodox; their writing was based on the Greek alphabet and their literature on Byzantine models; their art and architecture were strongly Byzantine in character; and their foreign trade was mostly with the empire.

Influence on the West. But Byzantine influence was not limited to eastern Europe. Relations between Constantinople and the West were never entirely cut off. Till the middle of the eleventh century, the empire retained a foothold in Italy, and throughout the remainder of the Middle Ages there was constant commerce between Constantinople and Venice and other Italian cities. Byzantine art forms can be clearly seen in Italy, especially in Ravenna and the south, and to a lesser degree their influence can be traced in the other western countries. The extent of this influence has been hotly debated. It is, at any rate, a factor that cannot be ignored in any study of medieval culture. Above all, the Byzantine Empire performed a great service for European civilization by preserving the body of Roman law and the masterpieces of Greek literature, philosophy, science, and art, which might otherwise have been lost during the dark period of the Early Middle Ages.

10

The Rise of Islam and the

Expansion of the Moslem Empire

A FEW YEARS after the death of Justinian, a man was born in a little Arabian town near the Red Sea, who was to have a far wider influence on the history of the world than that exercised by the great Byzantine emperor. In the century following that which saw Justinian's attempt to restore the old Roman Empire, Mohammed founded a new religion that has ever since been the most powerful rival of Christianity, and at the same time laid the foundations for an empire that spread till it included the former Roman provinces in Syria, northern Africa, and Spain and extended eastward to the borders of India. In this empire, composed of many varied races held together by a common religion, there grew up in the following centuries a civilization higher and in many ways more enlightened than that of early medieval Europe, and one from which the peoples of the West learned much, despite the bar of religious antagonism. That empire has long since fallen to pieces and its civilization has decayed, but millions of men still follow the teaching of Mohammed and pray with their faces turned to the town in which he was born.

1. Mohammed and the Founding of Islam

Arabia. Arabia, the home of the new religion, forms a large peninsula between the Red Sea and the Persian Gulf, with the Indian Ocean to the south.[1] To the northwest lies Syria, in Mohammed's time a Byzantine province, and to the northeast the valley of the Tigris and Euphrates, then the richest part of the Persian Kingdom. For the most part, Arabia is a desert of rock and sand, where nomadic tribes of Bedouin, as the desert Arabs are called, still live in tents beside the oases where they water their herds. No settled or agricultural life is possible in desert Arabia, and until very recent times much of the interior was unexplored. Along the coastline, however, to east and west there is richer land.

The Arabs. The life of the seventh-century Arabs was not unlike that of the early Children of Israel as pictured in the Old Testament. The family or tribe was the social and political unit, under the authority of the head of the family. Their religion, however, was still a crude and superstitious paganism, in which idolatry played an important part, though Jewish tribes and Christian merchants had spread some knowledge of their religions in Arabia before the coming of Mohammed, and the idea of monotheism at least was apparently not unknown. Some vague unity was given to Arab religion by the common veneration of certain sanctuaries, of which the most important was a small temple, square in shape, called the Kaaba (Cube). This was situated in Mecca, a commercial town some fifty miles inland from

[1] See map, page 127.

the middle of the Red Sea coast. To Mecca Arabs came from all parts of the country in annual pilgrimages during the sacred months when tribal warfare was forbidden. The city of Mecca was, then, in some degree the center of Arab religion before the days of Mohammed.

Mohammed.   It was in Mecca that Mohammed was born about the year 570. Later tradition tells us a good deal about his early life, his appearance and character, but very little of it is trustworthy historical information. Though pious legend ascribed to him important family connections, he was probably of humble birth. He was left an orphan at an early age and lived in poverty till he was about twenty-four years old, when he entered the service of a wealthy widow named Khadija. While working for her, he led at least one caravan on a trading trip to Syria. About the year 595, he married his employer and for the next fifteen years lived the comfortable, if uneventful, life of the ordinary well-to-do Meccan merchant. He was described as a kindly man, gifted with a winning personality. His later career shows him to have had a strong will and ruthless determination, combined with sound practical sense and great ability in judging men.

The founding of Islam.   The beginning of Mohammed's prophetic mission is dated from his fortieth year, though there is good reason to believe that he had given much thought to religious matters before that time. Tradition tells us that he spent one month in every year in solitary meditation on a mountain near Mecca. Here occurred the first revelation. There seems to be no doubt that Mohammed suffered from some kind of nervous seizure of an hysterical nature, though we have not sufficient reliable information to warrant a clear diagnosis. At any rate, the revelations on which his teaching was based were produced after some kind of trance, which later, at least, the prophet could bring on at will. The first converts were members of Mohammed's own family or were close friends. Among them, his cousin Ali and his friends Abu Bakr and Omar later played important roles. Mohammed called his religion *Islam,* meaning "submission" — i.e., to the will of God — and his followers *Moslems,* those who had surrendered themselves. At first the Moslems formed a secret society. When at last they made their faith public, they met with opposition and persecution from the pagan Meccans, who feared that Mohammed's insistence that there was but one God, Allah, would destroy the faith of the people in idols and with it the profitable trade with the pilgrims who came annually to the Kaaba.

Hegira (622).   As Islam slowly gained ground at Mecca, the persecution became more severe. Finally, Mohammed decided to flee from the city and to seek a safer place of refuge for his followers. He found it in Medina, a city to the north of Mecca, where Jewish and Arab tribes had for some time been engaged in civil strife. The way was prepared by sending missionaries, and in 622 a delegation of some seventy converts from Medina invited Mohammed to come to their city. The flight of the prophet and his followers to Medina, known as the Hegira, marks the beginning of the Moslem calendar. Taking advantage of the feuds which divided the people of Medina, Mohammed soon became its ruler, making it the capital of a rapidly growing state.

Islam conquers Arabia.   In the years following the Hegira, the character of Islam changed materially. It became a fighting religion and the prophet a political leader. Forced to provide for the refugees in his care, Mohammed began to prey upon the caravans which passed near Medina on the way to Mecca. This led to a war with Mecca which dragged on for years. The Moslems continued to raid caravans and nearby villages and to plunder the Jewish tribes. As a victorious religion promising plunder and profit in this world, and the blessings of paradise after death, Islam attracted converts from many of the Bedouin tribes. By 630, Mohammed was strong enough to conquer Mecca almost without opposition. Henceforth Mecca was to be the religious center of Islam, toward which all Moslems turned to pray, and the Kaaba its most sacred *mosque* or temple though Medina remained for some time the political capital. By taking over the pilgrimages, the sacred city, and the sanctuary from Arab paganism, Mohammed made it easier for converts to join the new religion. Before his death at Medina in 632, he had succeeded in gaining at least the formal adherence of the greater part of Arabia.

The Koran.   From the beginning of his mission till his death, Mohammed continued to

This page from the Koran is from a parchment copy made in Morocco in the eleventh century.

publish a series of divine revelations, containing all his teaching on moral and theological questions, as well as his legislation on purely political matters and his comments on current events. Together they make up the Koran, collected and put in order soon after the prophet's death and since handed down with little or no change. The revelations were originally dictated by Mohammed to his friends or secretaries (it is very doubtful whether he himself could write), and were preserved as separate fragments with no attempt to keep them in chronological order. In the final edition of the Koran, they were arranged according to length, the longest chapters first, then the shorter in diminishing order. As Mohammed's ideas developed with experience or changed with the needs of the moment, the lack of dates makes it a very confusing book. Often later revelations modify or cancel earlier ones. The contradictions, however, seem to have aroused no skepticism. Despite difficulties of interpretation, the Koran has always been accepted by Moslems as the final authority on all matters of faith and morals.

The doctrine of Islam. The theological doctrines of the Koran are simple enough. There is but one God and Mohammed is his prophet. Other prophets there have been in the past,

Adam, Noah, Abraham, Moses, and Jesus. To each a part of the truth was revealed; but the final revelation was made only to Mohammed. After death there will be a bodily resurrection and a future life — for the faithful in a paradise of sensuous pleasures, for the infidel in a hell (gehennem) of perpetual fire. There are also many moral regulations. The prophet commands his followers to practice the virtues of charity, humility, and patience, and to forgive their enemies. He condemns avarice, lying, and malice, and prohibits drinking and gambling. Polygamy is permitted, the prophet setting the example himself by marrying several times after the death of Khadija, but in many ways the position of women was improved and their rights safeguarded. The practices and ceremonies of Islam are described in detail, including prayers at stated intervals during the day, pilgrimages to Mecca, and fasts from sunrise to sunset during the sacred month of Ramadan. For the rest, the Koran is occupied chiefly with legislation for the government of the Moslem state. For his ideas, Mohammed drew freely upon Christianity, Judaism, and Arab paganism, though his knowledge of the first two was uncertain and inaccurate, picked up apparently, from casual conversations rather than from reading. Yet the result of this mixture of ideas was a doctrine, original when taken as a whole, and designed to appeal to the simple Arab of the prophet's day, while at the same time capable of holding the faith of more civilized people.

2. *The Expansion of the Moslem Empire*

The crisis. The death of Mohammed came as a shocking surprise to his devout followers and precipitated a crisis which threatened to wreck the young Moslem state. The prophet had made no arrangements for the succession to his position as religious and political ruler. Ali, Mohammed's cousin and husband of his daughter Fatima, felt that his kinship to the prophet and his unequaled reputation as a warrior gave him a natural claim to leadership. The Medinese were jealous of the Meccan companions of the prophet and wanted one of their own number, though they might have compromised on Ali. Despite this strong opposition, however, Abu Bakr was finally chosen due to the aid of the redoubtable Omar. He took the title of caliph, held by all the later successors of Mohammed as religious and political rulers of the Moslem Empire. Meanwhile, the new state seemed to be falling to pieces, as tribe after tribe revolted. The Arabs had no tradition of political unity or government and resented the necessity of paying taxes. A year or more of constant warfare passed before Abu Bakr was able to reclaim the deserters and to complete the conquest of Arabia.

Motives of expansion. No sooner had the Arabs been united under the rule of the caliph than they launched upon that amazing series of conquests which in time was to extend their empire from the Indus to Spain. It has often been said that the motive which drove them forth to conquest was religious fanaticism, the determination to force Islam upon the infidel. Mohammed's teaching did, in fact, furnish a bond to hold the Arab tribes together and his promise of paradise to those who died fighting the infidel gave them a high fighting spirit. Actually, however, the Arabs made little or no attempt to force their religion upon conquered peoples. The motives which inspired the raids into foreign countries were really economic and political. Arabia had for some time been suffering from an economic decline, and the tribes were restless and discontented. The naturally

rich lands of Syria, Persia, and Egypt attracted them as the fertile provinces of the Roman Empire had attracted the Germanic barbarians. Only their lack of unity hitherto had prevented them from making the attempt. At the same time, the caliph realized that to hold the wild Bedouin tribes in subjection and to check their intertribal feuds, some outlet must be given them for their warlike energy. The conquest of the rich neighboring countries offered such an outlet, combined with the promise of plunder beyond the dreams of the simple Arab. Moreover, the Byzantine Empire and the Persian Kingdom had just completed a long and devastating war which had left both countries exhausted. The time was ripe for the venture.

First period of expansion. The first attack was directed against Syria, late in 633. Beginning as a plundering raid, it soon became an organized invasion. The victorious Arabs captured Damascus in 635, defeated the Byzantine army the following year, and by 637 had conquered all of Syria except Jerusalem and Caesarea. The former fell in 638, the latter in 640. The Syrian provincials, crushed by imperial taxation, seem rather to have welcomed than resisted the conquerors. A similar apathy, indeed, favored the conquerors in most of the parts of the Byzantine Empire and the Persian Kingdom which they invaded. To the people, conquest meant merely a change to a less oppressive government. Meanwhile Arab

The magnificent Great Mosque in Damascus was constructed by the Umayyad caliph, Walid I (705–15), on the site of the Byzantine cathedral of St. John the Baptist. Walid was noted for his lavish expenditure on buildings. This one cost the equivalent of seven years' revenue for the whole of Syria.

armies were carrying the banners of Islam to east and west. Abu Bakr had died in 634, to be succeeded by the vigorous Omar (634–44), who pushed forward the conquests with energy and foresight. Before his death, the Mesopotamian portion of the Persian Kingdom and also Egypt had been added to the growing Moslem state. Under the next caliph, Othman (644–55), the Arabs conquered the remainder of Persia to the east and drove westward as far as Tripoli on the African coast.

Civil war (655–61). Further expansion was checked for a time by civil war. Ali, proclaimed caliph at Medina, was opposed by the head of the Umayyad (or Ommiad) family, one of the leading families of the Meccan aristocracy. The assassination of Ali in 661 finally left the Umayyads supreme, and for nearly a century the caliphate was handed down in that family. As their strongest support was in Syria, the first Umayyad caliph moved the capital from Medina to Damascus.

Second period of expansion. A second period of expansion now began. The conquest of North Africa was a long, slow process, due more to the resistance of the Berber tribes than of the Byzantine government. By about 708, however, the Berbers were thoroughly conquered and they soon adopted Islam. The next step in the westward march of the Arabs was the conquest of Spain from the Visigoths, begun in 711 and completed with the aid of Berber allies within two years. From there they pushed on across the Pyrenees into southern Gaul in search of plunder, pressing steadily northward till they were turned back at Poitiers by the Franks under Charles Martel, of whom more will be said in the next chapter. Meanwhile the Moslem Empire had reached its farthest extent to the east, stretching as far as the river Indus in India and to the borders of China in central Asia.[1]

Decline of Umayyads. During the century of Umayyad rule, a considerable transformation took place within the Moslem Empire. The caliphs made little attempt to convert the conquered peoples, for so long as there were infidels to tax, the faithful could be relieved of financial burdens. But the taxes in themselves encouraged conversion, as did the desire of the conquered peoples to share in the political and other privileges reserved for the faithful, and by the end of the seventh century great numbers of the conquered had adopted Islam. The Arabs, meanwhile, though still the ruling class, had become scattered and were mingling with the other races of the empire. Thus, as the majority of the subject peoples became Moslem, the distinction between the conqueror and the conquered, the Arab and the non-Arab, was partially lost through the growth of common religious interests. Islam, then, rather than Arab nationalism, was becoming the important factor in Moslem patriotism. And the Umayyads, though acting as both religious and political rulers, had always represented Arabian rather than the broader Moslem interests.

Rise of the Abbasids. Discontented with Umayyad rule, the more devout Moslems, especially in Persia, turned to the Abbasid family for leadership. They were descended from Abbas, the uncle of Mohammed, and could rely on their relation to the prophet's family to attract the loyalty of devout Moslems of all races. After some years of political disturbance, the Umayyad dynasty was finally overthrown in 750 and the Abbasid dynasty took its place, though an Umayyad emir continued to rule in Spain, separating it from the rest of the empire. Persia now took the place of Syria as the center of the empire, and the capital was moved from Damascus to Bagdad on the Tigris. The Abbasids continued to stress their claims to Moslem rather than purely Arab loyalty. The Arab aristocracy were succeeded by a mixed official aristocracy drawn from all the Moslem races. The caliphs took on the character of oriental despots, with all the pomp and ceremony of the old Persian kings. And in this new Abbasid empire there grew up a composite Moslem civilization that was partly Arab, partly Persian, and partly Greek, the whole welded into a new synthesis by the doctrines of Islam and the common use of the Arabic tongue.

3. *Moslem Civilization under the Caliphate*

The caliphate. For about seventy-five years after the fall of the Umayyads, the Abbasid caliphs enjoyed an era of absolute power and

[1] See map, page 127.

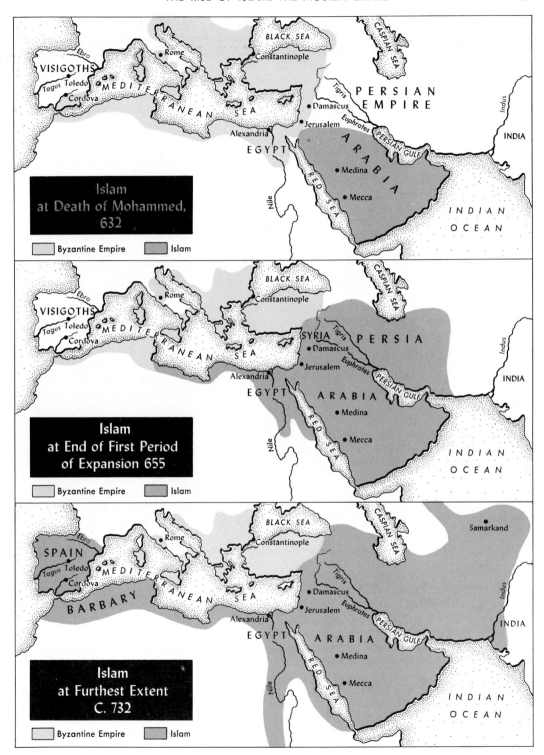

great prosperity. The reign of Haroun al Rashid (786–809), whose name is familiar to all who have read the *Arabian Nights,* marks the point of greatest power in the history of the caliphate. Bagdad was one of the richest cities in the world, the center of an empire stretching from central Asia to the Atlantic, for though Spain was now politically independent, it still recognized the religious authority of the successors of the prophet. But that empire was too large and composed of too many varied races to be held together for long under the despotic rule of one man, unless that man were a statesman of unusual strength and genius. Shortly after Haroun's reign, the powers of the caliph declined and the empire began to disintegrate. The tenth century saw a further disintegration. The Umayyad emir in Spain took the title Caliph of Cordova, and in Egypt a member of the Fatimite family, descended from Mohammed's daughter Fatima, founded the caliphate of Cairo, which later came to include Syria. From 945 to 1055 the caliphs of Bagdad were completely dominated by a Persian dynasty of emirs, from whom they were "liberated" by the Seljuk Turks, who had come originally from central Asia and had adopted Islam with fanatical zeal. For two centuries, Turkish emirs and sultans ruled in the name of the puppet Abbasid caliphs, reviving the political strength of the empire for a time and recovering Syria. It was with them that the crusaders had to deal. At last, in the middle of the thirteenth century, they, too, were overcome by a fresh invasion from Asia, that of the Mongol hordes, and with them the Abbasid caliphate finally disappeared.

Moslem civilization. Despite political divisions, however, the Moslem world retained throughout this period a strong economic, religious, and cultural unity. Mohammed had taught that all Moslems are brothers, equal in the sight of God. Conversion to Islam wiped out the differences between peoples of different ethnic origin. Moslem traded freely with Moslem from India to Spain, and, thanks to the common use of the Arabic language, ideas circulated as freely. The unifying force of the old Roman Empire had never succeeded in imposing a single language upon the people within its frontiers, but this Islam achieved by virtue of the Moslem's obligation to read the Koran and to pray in the language spoken by the prophet. The converts, who brought their inherited cultures into Islam, undoubtedly contributed more to its civilization than did the Arabs, who had little cultural tradition of their own; but, because it was expressed in the Arab's tongue, the resulting synthesis of cultures has often been referred to as Arabic. Under the favorable conditions created by a common religion, a common language, and an economic revival that concentrated great wealth in the cities throughout the Islamic empire, Moslem learning, literature, science, art, and technology far surpassed anything to be found in Western Christendom during the Early Middle Ages. The most brilliant period of Moslem culture extended from the eighth century through the eleventh, and coincided with the darkest period in the culture of the West. Thereafter, Moslem civilization declined as that of western Christian Europe took on new life, but, though past its peak, it continued to flourish for two centuries longer, during which time it served as a reservoir from which the Latin West drew material for its own cultural revival.

Education and learning. Religion furnished the basis and provided the framework for Moslem education. Reading and writing in Arabic, the study of the Koran, arithmetic and other elementary subjects were taught to children in schools attached to the mosques. In the large cities, well-endowed mosques offered more advanced instruction in literature, logic, philosophy, law, algebra, astronomy, medicine, and other sciences, as well as in the theology and tradition of Islam. There was evidently a large reading public, for books were produced in great quantities. Wealthy people collected extensive private libraries, and there were also large public libraries in the chief cities. Theology naturally attracted the attention of many Arabic scholars, and its development under the influence of Greek and Persian philosophy led to the rise of a number of sects, which correspond more or less to the heresies in the early Christian church. Orthodox reaction to these, in turn, led to conservatism and, after the eleventh century, to the effective shackling of free thought. Next to theology, the most common subject of Moslem scholarship was the law. Moslem law was founded upon general principles laid down in the Koran, but the needs of a highly developed economic, social, and political system could not be met satisfactorily by laws framed for primitive Arabia. The basic principles had to be developed and adapted to new circumstances, and in doing so the Moslem jurists drew heavily upon the practice of Roman law which they found in the lands taken from the Byzantine Empire.

Philosophy. More important for the history of European civilization than the work of the Moslem theologians and jurists was that of the students of philosophy, who translated the works of the Greek and Hellenistic philosophers into Arabic and passed them on, enriched with commentaries, to the schoolmen of Western Christendom in the twelfth and thirteenth centuries. The Moslem philosophers were transmitters of Aristotelian and Neoplatonic ideas rather than original thinkers; but there was originality in their effort, similar to that of the Christian scholastics, to harmonize rational Greek metaphysics with revealed religion. The Persian philosopher and scientist, Ibn Sina (980–1037), known to the Latin West as Avicenna, exerted a strong influence upon medieval Christian as well as Moslem thought. Still more influential was the Spanish Ibn Rushd (1129–98), called Averroës by the Christians, whose philosophical system was founded upon Aristotle, though tinged with Neoplatonism. Like Avicenna, Averroës denied the biblical story of the creation of the world, the immortality of the individual soul, and the possibility of God's interest in individuals, as contrary to Aristotelian metaphysics; but he seems to have felt that philosophical speculation could be kept from conflicting with what theology taught as revealed truth. Theology, he taught, is but a symbolical representation of the truth that the philosopher attempts to reach by reason. The Christian schoolmen who fell under his influence in the thirteenth century were accused of maintaining a double standard of truth, holding that different things could be true in philosophy and in theology. This is an oversimplification of their position;

but Averroism certainly contributed a skeptical and rational element to scholastic thought throughout the Later Middle Ages.

Science. Many of the Moslem philosophers were interested in the natural sciences, bringing to their study an eager curiosity and keen powers of observation. They not only absorbed the works of Greek scientists, including many since lost, but added discoveries of their own. In medicine, the works of the ancient Greek physicians, Galen and Hippocrates, were translated into Arabic in the early Abbasid period. To this body of medical knowledge Moslem physicians later added the results of their own valuable clinical experience, embodying the whole in great encyclopedic works on the subject. The works of Avicenna were later translated into Latin, and he was long recognized in western Europe as one of the great masters of medicine. In the fields of chemistry, physics, astronomy, geography, and mathematics, the Moslems also took over the legacy of Greece, adding to it from their own scientific observation. Their work in chemistry was both hampered and stimulated by the dominant interest in alchemy, that is, the attempt to transmute baser metals into gold. Nevertheless, much practical work was done in preparing and isolating chemical substances such as alkalis, sal-ammoniac, arsenious oxide, saltpeter, and crude forms of sulphuric and nitric acids. Finally, the Moslems made contributions of the greatest importance to the development of mathematics.

Miniature from a thirteenth-century Arabic manuscript of the De materia medica *of Dioscorides showing a Moslem pharmacist at work. The Moslems made notable contributions to pharmacy as well as to chemistry.*

Building upon the Greek heritage and borrowing from India the system of numerals still called Arabic, they laid the foundations for modern arithmetic, geometry, trigonometry, and algebra.

Literature. The Moslems also produced a highly developed and varied literature in prose and verse. The Arabic language proved extraordinarily flexible and well adapted to poetic writing, but it could also express fine shades of meaning in prose. A good deal of Arabic prose was devoted to scholarly subjects — theology, philosophy, science, and history; but there was also a more popular literature in the form of short stories. Not much of Arabic poetry or popular prose was carried over directly into western Europe, but there is evidence that

One of the finest examples of Egyptian Moslem architecture, the El-Azhar mosque, was built in 970. The minarets, first introduced by Caliph Walid I in the early eighth century, were a characteristic feature of the medieval mosques.

Arabic models influenced the development of Provençal lyric poetry as well as other forms of medieval European literature, although the extent of that influence is difficult to define. The collection of short stories known as the *Arabian Nights* and the poems attributed to Omar Khayyam (1050–1120) are among the few pieces of Arabic literature that have made a place for themselves in translation in the Western world.

Art and architecture. Moslem art and architecture showed a remarkable uniformity of style, although there were regional variations resulting from the influence of earlier local styles. Moslem artists and architects borrowed from Byzantine, Persian, and other sources, but the special requirements of Islam gave their work a new form. The ground plan of the mosques was usually based on that of Mohammed's house at Medina, a roofed rectangular building combined with a walled courtyard open to the sky. The most noticeable features of the exterior were the tall minarets from which the muezzins called the faithful to prayer. The inside was brilliant with colored tiles and decorated with complex designs of interwoven lines and geometrical figures, in low relief or color, of the type now known as arabesque. Mohammed's prohibition of paintings or images of living creatures banned representational art from the mosques, but human and animal figures were sometimes used in secular paintings and in the illustration of books. Much of the finest Moslem art, however, was in the form of objects of luxury — jewelry, carved ivory, ceramics, carpets, tooled leather, and other products of skilled craftsmanship.

Commerce and industry. This flourishing civilization rested on a solid foundation of commercial and industrial prosperity, and its spread throughout the whole Moslem world was due in large measure to the freedom of commercial intercourse from end to end of the Moslem Empire. Even after the political disintegration of the caliphate, commerce circulated freely wherever Islam was recognized, with a freedom reminiscent of the old Roman Empire. There was also a great foreign trade, especially to the East. Moslem captains sailed their boats down the Tigris from Bagdad or put out from Aden and other Red Sea ports and traded with

A pilgrim caravan on the way to Mecca as depicted in a thirteenth-century Persian painting.

all the lands bordering on the Indian Ocean. Here they met and exchanged goods with merchants from as far east as China. At the same time camel caravans struck out overland, eastward through central Asia to China and India, north into Russia, and south and west into Africa. At first trade with Christian Europe was very limited, but by the eleventh century a steady commerce had developed, mostly by way of Italy. For centuries the Moslem traders acted as intermediaries between the West and the Far East. It was through them that Europe acquired those eastern luxuries, which with the growth of a more refined taste became necessities, as well as those goods, silks, damask cloth (from Damascus), muslin (from Mosul), paper, glassware, swords, steel mirrors, etc., which were manufactured by the Moslems themselves.

Islam and the West. In this survey of the Moslem Empire and its civilization, we have traveled far ahead of our story into the later centuries of the Middle Ages. It will be necessary to turn back now to an earlier period and to trace the history of western Europe through the centuries following the Germanic migrations. As we follow the gradual development of medieval civilization, however, we must not forget the existence of the Moslem world beyond the confines of Christendom or the influence which it exerted on the formation of European culture.

11

The Franks, the Lombards, and the Papacy

IN THE THREE CENTURIES which followed the deposition of the last Roman emperor in the West in 476, the foundations of medieval civilization were laid in the blending of Roman, Germanic, and Christian elements that was to make up the composite culture of the Middle Ages. We have already seen how in that period the Eastern Roman Empire became Byzantine, how Justinian in the sixth century sought to make it once more a world empire, and how in the next century the rising power of Islam stripped it of all but a fraction of its provinces. In that same period the early Germanic kingdoms, Ostrogothic, Vandal, and Visigothic, were destroyed. Meanwhile, two new powers, which were to be of supreme importance in shaping the Middle Ages, were rising to dominate the West in close alliance with each other. They were the Franks, the only Germanic nation with the exception of the Anglo-Saxons to found a permanent kingdom, and the Roman popes, rulers of the Catholic Church and heirs to the tradition of the Roman Empire. And in between, exercising a strong influence on the destinies of both, were the Lombards, last of the Germanic invaders.

1. The Franks in the Merovingian Age

Franks in the fifth century. Early in the fifth century, when barbarian hordes were sweeping across the Roman Empire to found kingdoms within its frontiers, a loosely united group of German tribes, known collectively as the Franks, had established themselves on both banks of the lower Rhine. Their early history is very obscure. They were evidently one of the most backward and barbarous of the Germanic peoples. They were divided into a number of petty kingdoms, and at the time when the last emperor of the West was deposed they had expanded into the northern angle of Gaul between the Rhine and the sea. Between them and the Loire to the south, the Gallo-Roman provincials had formed an independent "kingdom" under the rule of a Roman patrician named Syagrius. Southern Gaul, between the Loire and the Pyrenees, was part of the Visigothic Kingdom. Eastern Gaul in the valley of the Rhône was occupied by the Burgundians, to the north of whom, in modern Alsace, lay the kingdom of the Alamanni.

Clovis (481–511). Such was the situation in Gaul in the year 481 when a fifteen-year-old prince named Clovis, grandson of that Merowech after whom the royal Merovingian family was named, became king of one of the Frankish tribes. He was a thorough barbarian, ruthless, treacherous, and avaricious, but endowed with great ability. He was not long contented with his little kingdom. Gaul was divided and weakened by war. It was his for the taking. In 486, he defeated Syagrius and conquered his territory south to the Loire. Ten years later, he crushed the Alamanni and added their lands to his growing kingdom. Meanwhile, he had married a niece of the Burgundian king, named Clotilda, who unlike most of the Burgundians was a Catholic. When the battle with the Alamanni was going badly and his heathen gods seemed unable to aid him, he prayed, so the legend tells us, to the God of Clotilda and promised allegiance in return for victory.

Conversion and further conquest. The conversion of Clovis and his followers to Christianity was in itself an important event, but it was his adoption of the orthodox Catholic form of Christianity that was most significant and destined to have far-reaching results. The story of the conversion is based on legend, none too trustworthy. It is suspiciously reminiscent of the legend regarding the conversion of Constantine the Great. In all probability Clovis, like Constantine, was motivated chiefly by political considerations. Certainly the baptism of the king with three thousand of his soldiers caused no real change of heart. All the other Germanic peoples which had settled within the empire were Arian Christians, that is, heretics in the eyes of the Catholic provincials. By embracing Catholicism, Clovis became the champion of orthodoxy and gained the support of the Gallo-Romans, who still formed the majority of the inhabitants, and especially of the powerful Catholic clergy throughout Gaul. Bishop Gregory of Tours, whose interesting *History of the Franks* (575–94) is almost our only source for early Frankish history, stresses the fact that Clovis made his attack on the Arian kingdoms of Gaul a holy war. Every historian of the period has quoted his report of Clovis's address to his soldiers on the eve of his campaign against the Visigoths in 507. "It grieves me that these Arians should hold part of Gaul. Let us march, with the help of God, and reduce them to subjection." They marched and, with the help of the Catholic population at least, conquered the Visigothic Kingdom as far south as the Pyrenees. In the remaining years of his life, Clovis consolidated the Frankish tribes. By a series of brutal and treacherous murders, he got rid of all the rival Frankish kings, leaving in 511 a united kingdom to his sons.

Conquests completed. The successors of Clovis for half a century continued his career of conquest. The kingdom was divided among his four sons according to the German custom, as though it had been a private estate. The theoretical unity of the kingdom, however, was preserved, and, though the kings quarreled and murdered freely among themselves, they cooperated in extending its boundaries. Burgundy

was conquered in 534, and Provence was taken from the Ostrogoths two years later. The Frankish kings now ruled all Gaul except a narrow strip of Visigothic territory on the Mediterranean. They also pushed across the Rhine and subjugated the Bavarians, Thuringians, and Franconians in central and southern Germany.

Civil war. The last surviving son of Clovis, Chlotar, had reunited the entire kingdom under his rule before his death in 561. It was then divided again among his four sons, as it had been on the death of Clovis. The next half-century was a period of anarchy and barbarous civil war, during which the conquests ceased while the Frankish kings wasted their energy in fratricidal feuds. The history of this period, as related by Gregory of Tours, is a tale of cruelty, avarice, and treachery, of debauched kings and vindictive queens, for whom Gregory sought excuses because of their defense of Catholic orthodoxy. These civil wars had one very important result. From the constantly shifting divisions and reunions of territory, three fairly distinct kingdoms emerged—Neustria, which included the whole of western Gaul, and Austrasia and Burgundy, which divided the east between them, the former to the north on both sides of the Rhine, the latter to the south on the Rhône.

Decline of the Merovingians. From 613 to 639, Chlotar II and Dagobert, the last of the actively ruling Merovingian kings, in turn reigned over the reunited Frankish Kingdom, but already the royal power was weakening. A century of absolute power and unrestrained debauchery had fatally weakened the health and character of the Merovingian stock. After Dagobert, the Merovingian kings became mere puppets, powerless in the hands of their chief ministers, the mayors of the palace, who now ruled the country in the king's name. For more than a century these pathetic "do-nothing kings" dragged out a useless existence, shut up in a villa in the country and brought out once a year, riding in an oxcart, to be seen by the people and to read an address prepared by the all-powerful mayor. Weak in mind and body, they made no attempt to assert their authority. Most of them died in their twenties.

Pepin of Heristal. For a generation or more after the death of Dagobert, the civil wars between Neustria, Austrasia, and Burgundy were begun again and carried on by the mayors of the palace of the three kingdoms. At last, however, the Mayor of Austrasia, Pepin of Heristal, decisively defeated the Neustrians at Tertry in 687 and reunited the whole Frankish realm under his rule. During his long reign of twenty-seven years (687–714), Pepin held the Frankish Kingdom together, repressed rebellious nobles and subjected the frontier duchies which had become almost independent. He has been called the "second founder of the Frankish Kingdom." He was also the first of a long line of able and statesmanlike rulers of the family known as Carolingians from the most famous of their number, Charles the Great.

2. Society and Institutions in the Merovingian Age

Fusion of German and Roman.   The gradual blending of the Roman and Germanic elements of medieval civilization took place for the most part under Frankish rule. Other barbarian peoples who settled in the Roman provinces were in time absorbed by the Roman population. Others again, like the Saxons in Britain, destroyed Roman civilization and remained stanchly Teutonic. The unique contribution of the Franks is that in their kingdom, which came to include almost all of Christian western Europe, they held the balance between the two great sources of European civilization, so that a fairly equal blending of the two was possible. Three things favored this development. First, their conquest of Gaul was an expansion of their original holdings, rather than a migration. They did not leave their ancient base to travel among an alien people, but spread their conquests while still keeping in touch with their original homeland. Second, their conquests spread in both directions, to the south and west into Romanized Gaul and to the east and north into Germany, so that the Roman and German elements remained evenly balanced. Third, the adoption of Catholic Christianity by the Franks, and the conversion of the Arian Germans whom they conquered, placed the German and Roman on the same religious plane and facilitated the fusion of their institutions.

Distribution of population.   The Franks were always a minority in Gaul, except in the northern angle which had been their home. To the south of the Loire they confiscated none of the land belonging to the Gallo-Romans, except in rare instances. They had conquered the Visigoths with the aid of the provincials and so dared not alienate them. They contented themselves, therefore, with taking the land of those Visigoths who retired to Spain, and especially of the Visigothic government. In Burgundy, too, they seem to have left private property untouched and to have taken only the lands of the Burgundian king, which in themselves were extensive enough. The population of Gaul, then, was not radically changed by the Frankish conquest. In western Gaul, which became the kingdom of Neustria, and especially in the part south of the Loire known as Aquitaine, the Roman population and culture predominated. Here the language remained essentially Latin in origin, developing in time into the French tongue. In Austrasia, the German element predominated, especially beyond the Rhine, where it was almost pure. Here the language remained Germanic. In Burgundy, which the Burgundians had already made half German before the Frankish conquest, the two elements were most evenly mixed. Throughout the Frankish realm the extent of Roman and German cultural influence varied like the colors in a spectrum, from the almost pure Roman of Aquitaine in the southwest to the almost pure German of the northeast end of Austrasia, passing through all the intermediate stages between. But because it was all under Frankish government, all parts were affected by the blending of Roman and Germanic institutions.

Merovingian kingship.   When Clovis became king, he was the military leader of a small tribe. Before his death he had become the absolute ruler of a large state, and this development was continued by his descendants. This naturally meant a great change in the position and powers of the king and in the theory of kingship. In some respects the Merovingian monarchy borrowed from Roman precedent, in others it retained German traditions, but the blend produced a new institution. The Merovingian king had the absolute authority of a late Roman emperor over all his subjects, but that authority was exercised purely by right of heredity, through his descent from the Merovingian line. The Franks never developed the conception of a state composed of citizens who had delegated supreme authority to their

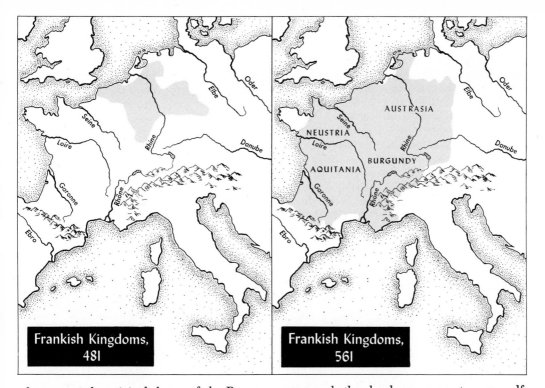

Frankish Kingdoms, 481

Frankish Kingdoms, 561

ruler, as was the original theory of the Roman empire. On the contrary, the Frankish king regarded his kingdom as a private domain, which he had inherited and which he divided among his sons according to the Germanic custom for the inheritance of private property. Yet even when divided, the kingdom remained theoretically united, ruled by members of the Merovingian family, each of whom kept the title, King of the Franks. The only limits to the king's authority were those imposed by the growing strength of the aristocracy, who might disregard his commands, revolt, or assassinate him. While he remained in power, however, he was the sole legislator, supreme judge, chief executive, commander-in-chief of the army, and practical head of the church. These powers, it is true, were gradually taken over by the mayor of the palace, but the theory remained the same, with the mayor exercising absolute authority in the name of the king.

Mayors of the palace. The administrative system of the Merovingians, if it can be called a system, grew up haphazardly to meet the needs of the moment in the most convenient way. The Roman system of taxation and of administration by a hierarchy of officers was too complicated for the German mind, and indeed had broken down before the Franks arrived in Gaul. The expenses of government were small. The army and the local government were self-supporting, and fines covered the expenses of justice. The expenses of the royal court were met for the most part by the income from the king's own extensive estates. No distinction was made between the king's private purse and the state treasury. The king's personal servants, then, who had charge of the king's estates and income, naturally took over the financial administration of the state as well. A corps of officials administered the business of the palace for the king, and since the king had no ready-made administrative system, it was easiest for him to extend their powers from the palace to the whole state. Thus the marshal, who had charge of the royal stables, became commander of the cavalry; the count of the palace, the king's legal adviser, became the head of the royal courts of justice; the referendary or royal secretary took charge of all documents of state. But of all these palace officials, the chief was the mayor of the palace, who had charge over all the others. It was he who became the king's chief minister and finally his master.

Counts and dukes. For local administration, the kingdom was divided into units which in Gaul usually corresponded to the Roman *civitates* or municipalities with their surrounding territory, and in Germany to the land occupied by a tribe. Over each of these divisions the king appointed a count, who had full jurisdiction as administrator and judge. After 614, the counts were chosen from the noble families in the county and the title tended to become hereditary. In some parts of the kingdom, especially along the frontiers, a number of counties were gathered together under the command of a duke whose duties were chiefly military. The counts and dukes were paid no salaries, but supported themselves by the income from land granted to them by the king as remuneration for their services, by judicial fines and fees of various kinds, and by exploiting the people. They were often half independent of the king and many of them oppressed the people cruelly. Throughout the whole of Frankish history they were a menace to king and people alike.

The church: bishops. The church played a tremendously important part in the life of the Merovingian age, barbarous and immoral though the age was in general. The bishops, who governed the church, were among the most important administrative officials in the state. The bishop's diocese was usually coextensive with the territory ruled by a count, and his political power within that territory was often

as great as that of the count. This was particularly true in the cathedral city where the bishop had his residence. The Franks, at first, cared little for town life and left the Gallo-Roman institutions of town government untouched. With the continuous decline of urban economy, however, the towns shrank in size; the old institutions withered away; and the bishop gradually took over the effective government. He had great wealth at his disposal, drawn from the numerous estates bequeathed to the church, and he had an immense moral and religious prestige. He acted as judge in many cases, supervised education, gave relief to the poor, kept up roads and public works, and protected the people from the exactions of king or count. Most of the bishops were of noble family, many of them Gallo-Romans. Unfortunately, the king often interfered in episcopal elections to nominate men of his own choosing, some of whom had little savor of sanctity about them. It was perhaps too much to expect of the king that he should leave such wealthy and powerful officials free from his control, and, indeed, it was important that the church should work in close alliance with the monarchy. The effect, however, was to make the church more worldly and to lower the general level of morality among the clergy. Still the bishops were usually far superior in character to the counts and were in many ways the strongest moral force in the kingdom.

Laws. The laws in vogue in the Frankish Kingdom provide us with one of the clearest examples of the way in which Roman and German traditions lived on side by side and eventually mingled. The Franks, like all early Germans, believed that every man had the right to be judged according to the traditional laws of his own people. Except for royal edicts dealing with specific problems, there was no uniformity of law. The Gallo-Roman retained his Roman law, while the Frank, Burgundian, or Bavarian had each his ancestral customary code. However, the German codes did not cover many cases arising from the new conditions in Gaul and so laws were borrowed from

This miniature of a monk writing, from the twelfth-century Canterbury Psalter, is unusual in including the name of the scribe, Eadwine, as well as a presumed self-portrait.

the Roman code. As the population became more mixed, the distinction between Roman and German gradually died out, and with it the distinction between the legal systems. The result was a residue of laws in which the Roman and German elements were preserved in proportion as they suited the needs of the people and the age.

3. *The Lombards and the Papacy*

Let us turn now to Italy, where events of great importance were taking place during this period. Part of the story has already been told. It was while Clovis was establishing the Frankish Kingdom in Gaul that Theodoric, the great Ostrogothic king, carved out for his people a kingdom in Italy, and while the sons of Clovis were conquering the remainder of Gaul, Justinian was making Italy once more a province under imperial rule. Within three years after the death of Justinian, another great change took place. A new nation of barbarian invaders, the Lombards, swept down into Italy and opened a new chapter in its history.

Lombard conquest. The Lombards were one of the East German peoples. Their original home was on the banks of the Elbe in northern Germany. Thence they migrated south and east to the Danube, where they were converted to the Arian form of Christianity. In 568, they followed the track of earlier Germanic invaders from the Balkans down into northern Italy. Meeting with little opposition, for the country had been ravaged by war and plague, they occupied the plain between the Alps and the Apennines, ever since called Lombardy. It was a thorough conquest. They made no pretense of alliance with the empire, as the Ostrogoths had done, nor did they leave the conquered Italians in possession of their estates. The continuity of Roman civilization, which had survived so many invasions, was at last broken, or at least severely strained. About 575, marauding bands of Lombards began to push farther south, and within a decade had occupied the center of Italy almost to the southern end of the peninsula. The emperors made some attempt to check the Lombards, but in vain. In 605, a truce was arranged between them. By that time, the Lombards had conquered all of Italy except the territories around Ravenna, Rome, Naples, and the extreme south. These were still ruled by representatives of the emperor, nominally under the Exarch of Ravenna, though Rome and the other imperial possessions were so cut off from the exarchate as to be left practically independent. The unity of Italy was completely destroyed, to be recovered only after thirteen centuries had passed. The Lombard Kingdom itself was not strongly united. The Lombard dukes were always half independent and often rebellious, especially in the two large duchies of Spoleto and Benevento in the center and south, which were never firmly attached to the kingdom and where the Lombards remained in the minority.

The papacy (to 590). Out of the chaos of this last barbarian invasion, one Italian power, the Roman papacy, rose with greater authority than ever before. The popes had lost much of their prestige since the days of Leo the Great, though they had gained much in wealth from estates bequeathed to them in all parts of Italy. The restoration of imperial rule in Italy had been a serious blow to their authority, for Justinian had introduced that domination of the church by the state which had long been recognized in the Eastern Empire, but had never been enforced in the West. Moreover, the pope's authority outside of Italy had suffered. The bishops of Gaul were controlled by the Frankish kings, and Spain under the Visigoths was Arian almost to the end of the sixth century. But the Lombard conquests broke the power of the emperor over the pope, and in 590 the Roman Church found in Pope Gregory the Great a leader who was to set the papacy back again on the road to independence and spiritual dominion in the West.

Gregory the Great (590–604). Gregory was a thorough Roman, born of a noble and wealthy Roman family. In early life he held some of the most important administrative posts in the city, but gave up his political career to retire to a monastery. He was called forth to serve the church, and finally, in 590, to become pope. In that difficult position he proved himself an able administrator, a diplomatic statesman, and a stanch defender of papal supremacy. He had an indomitable will, untiring energy, and the self-confidence of the born autocrat. And all of these qualities were needed by the man who

The Lombard historian, Paul the Deacon, tells the story of how Pope Gregory the Great was inspired by the Holy Ghost in the form of a dove. When Gregory was dictating, a curtain was drawn between him and his secretary. After one long silence the secretary looked through a hole in the curtain and saw a dove with its beak between the pope's lips. When the dove withdrew its beak, the dictation was resumed. The illustration is from a tenth-century manuscript.

occupied the chair of St. Peter in those troubled times. Rome was constantly in danger from the Lombards who surrounded the Roman territory. The imperial governor, cut off from his superior at Ravenna, was powerless. It was the pope who undertook the defense of the city, negotiated with the Lombards, and used his resources to maintain public works and relieve the poor. Though still recognizing the overlordship of the emperor, Gregory made himself the practical ruler of Rome and the land about it. At the same time he pressed his claims to universal authority over the Catholic Church with the greatest vigor. He was not always successful. The Frankish bishops were polite rather than obedient, but they learned to look more than before to Rome for guidance.

Mission to England. Gregory also extended the influence of the papacy by extending the boundaries of the Catholic Church. The Anglo-Saxons in England were still heathen, though missionaries from the Celtic church in Ireland, which had been isolated from the Roman Catholic Church since the Saxon conquest of Britain, had begun to work in the north. Gregory believed that the Saxons were ripe for conversion, and the result proved him correct. The mission headed by St. Augustine of Canterbury, which he sent to England in 596, met with extraordinary success. During the following century the whole of England was brought into the Roman Church.

Gregory's writings. In the midst of a busy life, Gregory found time to write, besides numerous letters, a long commentary on the Book of Job, called the *Moralia,* and a book of instructions to the clergy, entitled *Pastoral Care.* These works, widely read during the Middle Ages, earned for him the title of Father of the Church along with Ambrose, Jerome, and Augustine. Yet in style, erudition, philosophical background, and intellectual breadth, he cannot be compared to the earlier Fathers. He knew no Greek; his Latin style, though simple and forceful, was far from classical; and his thought was encumbered with superstitions. Nothing shows more clearly the cultural decline that had taken place in Italy in the past two centuries than the intellectual gap which separates Gregory from Augustine. His influence, nevertheless, was very great, all the greater perhaps because he was not too far above the intellectual level of the following centuries. Throughout the Middle Ages a persistent tradition ascribed to him the authorship of the Gregorian chant, the magnificent plainsong melodies that in the generations after his death became the universally accepted setting for the Roman Catholic liturgy. Modern scholars no longer accept his authorship, but there is evidence that he did contribute in some way to the codification of the music of the Roman liturgy. Certainly its adoption as the uniform practice throughout the church was in accord with his strong feeling for the unity of the Catholic Church under the primacy of the Roman papacy.

Popes, emperors, and Lombards. The seventh century passed with little change in the relative positions of the three powers in Italy:

the papacy, the Lombards, and the imperial government. The gradual conversion of the Lombards to Catholicism was the most important event. The emperors, absorbed in the struggle with the Persian Kingdom and later with the rising Moslem Empire, made no serious attempt to recover the land lost to the Lombards or to re-establish their control of the papacy. Early in the eighth century an imperial decree forbidding the presence of pictures or images (icons) of the saints in churches caused a break between the pope and the emperor. The decisive schism between the Roman Catholic and Greek Orthodox churches did not occur until 1054, but after the "iconoclastic controversy" in 725 the popes could no longer look to the emperors for protection. When the Lombards threatened to capture Rome and deprive the pope of his independence, he was forced to turn to the only other power strong enough to aid him, the ruler of the Frankish state.

4. The Frankish Kingdom and the Church

Charles Martel. On the death of Pepin of Heristal, the Austrasian mayor of the palace, in 714, his title was left to an infant grandson, under the guardianship of his grandmother. In those troubled times an infant and an old woman could not hope to rule, even had the child possessed the title of king and the loyalty of the people to a traditional house. Ruling merely as mayor of the palace, his position was untenable. Neustria rebelled, and the kingdom which Pepin had reunited threatened to fall once more into its component parts. It was saved by Pepin's illegitimate son Charles, later called Martel (the Hammer), who escaped in 715 from the prison where he had been confined by the infant mayor's guardian. He was then a man in his early twenties, strong, vigorous, and warlike, the obvious heir to his father's position. Gathering the Austrasian nobles about him, he crushed the rebellion in Neustria, deposed his nephew, and by 720 was recognized as mayor of the palace in all parts of the Frankish Kingdom. Charles was above all

A page from a medieval missal showing the musical notation for the Gregorian chant that took its name from the great pope.

a warrior, at a time when a fighting prince was needed. His reign was filled with campaigns, for the most part successful, against rebellious counts and dukes, against the heathen Germans to the north and the Moslems to the south. The latter had invaded Gaul as far as the Loire when Martel met them at Poitiers in 732. In that famous battle the Hammer of the Franks struck the decisive blow that checked the advance of Islam to the west. At the end of his reign he left the kingdom greatly strengthened and his family firmly established in their position as the real rulers of the Franks.

Missions in Germany: Boniface. One of the most difficult tasks Charles had to undertake was the subjection of the German tribes beyond the Rhine who were nominally under Frankish rule. The problem was made all the more difficult by the fact that many of them were still heathen. Charles realized that they could never be brought fully under the Frankish rule until they had adopted the religion of the Franks. He therefore gave enthusiastic support and armed protection to the missionaries who were working for their conversion. Of these by far the most important was an English monk, Winfrith, better known by his Latin name,

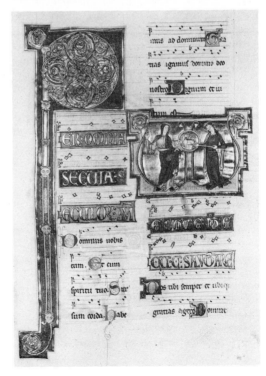

Boniface. Wherever his work progressed, this great missionary founded Benedictine monasteries as outposts of Christianity and organized the new church as part of the Roman hierarchy.

Pepin, mayor and king. On the death of Charles Martel in 741, the Frankish Kingdom was again divided between his two sons, Pepin (misnamed "the short") and Carloman. After six years, however, Carloman renounced the world and retired to a monastery in Italy, leaving the whole kingdom in Pepin's capable hands. The latter proved himself a true member of his illustrious family, ruling with wisdom and firmness, defending his kingdom and protecting the church. He crushed rebellions in the German duchies, defeated the "wild Saxons," and in the last years of his reign completely subjugated Aquitaine, which had made a strong bid for independence. For three generations now the Carolingian mayors had ruled as sovereigns in everything but name. By 751, Pepin felt that he was firmly enough established to risk deposing the puppet Merovingian and to assume the title of king. But he would need some sanction other than that of force to offset the traditional loyalty of the people to the ancient Merovingian house. He turned naturally to the church, the greatest moral force of the age, appealing to the pope for advice. The appeal reached Rome at a crucial moment. Ravenna had just fallen to the Lombards and Rome was threatened. Glad of the opportunity to win favor with the powerful ruler of the Franks, the pope replied that "it was better that he should be called king who had the power, rather than he who had none." Pepin, thus fortified, called an assembly of the nobles and clergy of the kingdom at Soissons in November, 751, and there proclaimed himself King of the Franks. The saintly Boniface, as representative of the papacy, consecrated him with holy oil. The consecration was a new departure and a significant one. It gave the king a special character and added a divine sanction to royal authority which served it well for centuries. It was also a recognition of papal supremacy over the Catholic Church. It bound church and state closer together, and it placed Pepin in the pope's debt. He was soon called upon to discharge that debt in full.

Donation of Pepin (756). Meanwhile, the pope's position was growing more desperate.

The Lombards were threatening to take from him his independent government of the land about Rome. In the winter of 753–54, Pope Stephen III journeyed to the Frankish court to make a personal appeal to Pepin for aid. There he reconsecrated Pepin, giving the Carolingian house the full sanction of the Roman Church. In return, Pepin made two expeditions against the Lombards in 754 and 756, both of which were successful. After the second, he forced the Lombard king to give up to the pope, not only the Roman lands, but also the land of the late exarchate. The gift of this land, stretching from Rome to Ravenna clear across central Italy, is known as "the Donation of Pepin." The keys to the cities included in it were laid upon the tomb of St. Peter, together with a deed giving them in perpetuity "to the Roman Church, to St. Peter, and his successors the popes." Thus was founded an independent principality in Italy under the rule of the pope and known as "the Papal States," or "the States of the Church." With minor changes it lasted until the unification of Italy in 1870 and during all the intervening centuries it played a very important role in the political history of Italy, as well as in shaping the course of papal policy.

Reform of the Frankish church. The close alliance between king and pope led to a much-needed reform of the church in the Frankish Kingdom. Under Pepin's direction, regular councils of the bishops were convened and steps were taken to raise the standards of education and morality among the clergy. The rule of St. Benedict was enforced in all the monasteries and the ecclesiastical hierarchy was reorganized to bring the clergy more directly under the authority of the pope.

The reign of Pepin was of great significance for the history both of the Franks and of the papacy. His fame has been somewhat obscured by the greater renown of his son Charlemagne. Yet in establishing the Carolingians as the royal family of the Franks, in suppressing rebellious nobles, in defeating the Lombards, in aiding missionaries, in reforming the church, and finally in building a firm alliance with a greatly strengthened papacy, he laid the foundations upon which Charlemagne was to build his empire. He also laid the foundations of the pope's temporal rule.

"He affirmed he would not have entered the
church that day, even though it was so high
a Church festival, if he had known what
the Pope intended to do." • Einhard, *Vita Caroli*

12

The Carolingian Empire and the Northmen

THE GREAT historical developments of the three centuries with which we have dealt in the last chapter: the expansion of the Frankish Kingdom, the conversion of the Germans to Catholic Christianity, the rise of the papacy to a position of unprecedented secular and spiritual authority in alliance with the Frankish rulers, all reached their culmination in the reign of Charlemagne. And in the Carolingian Empire, founded by the Frankish king and the Roman pope in the conviction that they were reviving the old Roman Empire in the West, the three elements of medieval civilization, the Germanic, Roman, and Christian traditions, were at last united. The Carolingian Empire lasted less than a century. It was too large for perfect cohesion. It was shaken by the assaults of the Northmen and torn apart by the rising feudal nobility. But the ideal of a united Christendom and of a universal empire remained. The nations which sprang from its ruins were Catholic and possessed of a homogeneity in which the distinction between Roman and barbarian no longer existed.

1. Charlemagne and His Empire
(768–814)

Charles the Great. Few names occupy so large a place on the pages of history and legend or in the minds of men as that of Charles, eldest son of King Pepin. Historians by common consent have called him Charles the Great,

Carolus Magnus, as the Latin chroniclers wrote it, and medieval legend has popularized the name in the Romance form, Charlemagne. When his father died in 768, Charles was not yet thirty. For three years he shared the kingdom with a younger brother, Carloman, but the unity of the kingdom was preserved by the death of the latter, as it had been in the generation before by the retirement of the elder Carloman. Thereafter Charles ruled alone until his death in 814. Much of the credit for his achievements during that period must go to the three generations of able rulers who preceded him and who laid the foundations; but he fully justified his title of "the Great" by his clear, statesmanlike perception of the needs of his age and of the course that must be taken to bring their work to completion, as well as by his untiring care for the material and spiritual welfare of his people.

Character. We are fortunate in possessing a contemporary description of Charles, which rescues him from the obscuring mists of medieval legend and romance. In his *Life of Charles,* the royal secretary Einhard has left us a vivid pen portrait of the genial giant who was his friend as well as his king. Here we see Charles as a tall, vigorous man, so well proportioned that his stoutness was not a noticeable defect. He was fond of hunting and swimming, temperate in his use of food and drink, though in his last years persisting stubbornly in his preference for roast meats against the advice of his physicians. He was an eager student, having acquired a fair knowledge of Latin and some Greek, but his studies had begun too late in life for him ever to have learned to write. Above all he was a tireless worker, with an inexhaustible interest in all the varied details of government. For the rest, Einhard pictures him as a kindly yet masterful man, a good companion and a fond father, whose only defect was the unrestrained interest in the opposite sex which gave rise to more than one scandal at court.

Conquest of Lombardy. One of the first important events of Charles's reign was the conquest of Lombardy. This might be classified as "unfinished business" left over from his father's time. So long as the Lombard Kingdom remained, the pope would never be secure in his government of the States of the Church in central Italy. After Pepin's death, the Lombard king, Desiderius, had retaken the cities of the exarchate which had been ceded to the pope, and in 773 Pope Adrian called upon Charles to rescue the papacy as his father had done before him. Charles marched into Italy with a large army, defeated and deposed Desiderius and, in 774, declared himself King of the Lombards. He celebrated Easter that year in Rome and there renewed the Donation of Pepin.

Conquest of the Saxons. Another important conquest made by Charles was that of the heathen Saxon land which extended from the Frankish frontier on the Rhine north to the borders of Denmark and east to the river Elbe. The "wild Saxons" had long been dangerous and lawless neighbors. They clung stubbornly to their pagan religion and their freedom, both endangered by the great Christian state to the south. They realized, as did Charles, that the two were inseparable. Whether the desire to protect and extend his frontiers or to convert the heathen weighed more strongly with the Frankish king cannot be determined. Certainly conquest and conversion went hand in hand, and the invaders came armed with both sword and cross. Charles led his first campaign against the Saxons in 772, but thirty-two years passed before the conquest was completed. During that time Charles directed eighteen campaigns into the Saxon land, pillaging, laying waste the country, and sometimes massacring or deporting part of the population. The "perfidious" Saxons would submit and swear allegiance, only to return to their religion and their free-

dom when the troops were withdrawn. By 804, however, the Saxons had at last become members of the Roman Catholic Church and subjects of the Frankish state.

Other wars. Meanwhile, other wars occupied a great deal of Charles's time and energy. He put down revolts in Aquitaine and Lombardy and conquered Bavaria. He also waged war with neighboring nations. In 778 he invaded Moslem Spain, taking advantage of a rebellion there to strike a blow against the powerful Umayyad emir, who might again become a menace to Frankish security as in the days of Charles Martel. This campaign was a failure, though Charles later secured a strip of territory to the south of the Pyrenees, known as the Spanish March. While returning through the Pyrenees, the rear guard of the Frankish army, led by a noble named Hruodland, was cut off and destroyed by Basque mountaineers in the pass of Roncesvalles. This event is of little historical importance in itself, but is famous because it gave rise to the greatest of medieval epics, the *Song of Roland*. Against the Mongolian Avars, who had established a kingdom in Hungary and threatened his eastern frontiers, Charles had better success. In 791 he marched through their kingdom, bringing back immense booty. Later they were forced to recognize him as overlord. The protection of the newly conquered Saxon land also forced Charles into wars with the Danes to the north and the Slavs to the east across the Elbe.

Charles crowned emperor. As the eighth century drew on to its close, the figure of Charlemagne more and more dominated the West. He was the acknowledged ruler of all Catholic Christendom except the British Isles, feared and respected by his heathen and infidel neighbors. Only the Moslem caliph at Bagdad or the Greek Orthodox emperor at Constantinople could rival him in power or prestige, and the latter had fallen upon evil times. Scholars at Charlemagne's court who had studied the classical literature began to compare him to the ancient Roman emperors. More than three centuries had passed since there had been an emperor in the West, but the ideal of a universal Roman Empire still cast its spell over the imaginations of men. Its memory had been kept alive by the Roman Catholic Church, a universal spiritual empire, ruled by the pope at Rome, employing Latin as

This bronze statuette of Charlemagne was made during the emperor's lifetime, or shortly after, and may have been a fair likeness. The horse is a sixteenth-century replacement.

its official speech and with a hierarchical government modeled after the imperial administration. The Church gave unity to Catholic Christendom, but many medieval thinkers felt that the divine scheme called for some secular counterpart, a political empire and a temporal ruler who would hold secular authority over all Christians (i.e., Catholic Christians) as the pope held spiritual authority. In actual fact, the King of the Franks held practically that position, yet to the medieval mind it was inconceivable that such a ruler should not be the Roman emperor. The obvious solution was to make the Frankish king emperor of a revived Roman Empire. Some such reasoning, more or less influenced by Charles's personal ambitions and by the pope's need for protection against seditious riots in Rome, must account for the amazing and epoch-making scene which occurred in Rome on Christmas Day of the year 800. As Charles knelt before the altar of St.

Peter's Church after the Christmas Mass, Pope Leo III placed an imperial crown on his head and hailed him emperor amidst the shouts of the people. Charles later denied any previous knowledge of the event. Perhaps he had not wished to receive the crown from the pope. If so, he was justified by the troubles arising from that act in future centuries. But the fact was accomplished. An empire had been created, Roman in name but more than half German in fact, and inseparably linked to the Catholic Church.

Carolingian administration. The general structure of government under Charles was much the same as that under the Merovingian kings, discussed in the preceding chapter. The addition of the imperial title made little difference. The monarch was absolute ruler of the state and exercised an extensive control of the church. The central administration was in his hands, assisted by the same palace officers as in Merovingian days, except that there was no longer a mayor of the palace and that the lay referendary had been succeeded by a chancellor who was usually a churchman. The counts were still in charge of the local administration, though more closely associated with the bishops, who had become recognized administrative officers of the state as well as of the church. Much of Charles's success in maintaining his authority throughout the realm depended on the close personal check he kept on these local officers. This was accomplished through the institution of the *missi dominici* ("those sent by the king"). The *missi* had been known in earlier times as representatives of the king on special missions. Charles now regularized their duties, sending them out each year in pairs to visit all parts of a given territory. The two *missi* traveling together were usually a layman and an ecclesiastic, a count and a bishop or abbot. It was their duty to examine the administration of both church and state in their territory, to see that the king's orders were carried out, to preserve close relations between the central and local administration, and to prevent injustice and oppression. This system checked the independence of the counts during Charles's reign, but it had no permanent value, for it was merely an extension of personal rule and its success in the long run depended entirely on the character and strength of the ruler.

The Palace Chapel of Charlemagne in Aachen has rounded arches in the Romanesque style, but the octagonal shape suggests Byzantine influence.

Capitularies. The whole conception of Carolingian government was paternal. As father of his people, Charles felt responsible for their welfare and issued innumerable decrees or "capitularies" dealing with the most varied aspects of public and private life, religious and moral as well as material, for church and state were so closely bound together that it was impossible to make any clear distinction between their respective jurisdictions. Those of the capitularies that have survived are of great value to the historian in helping him form a picture of the age. Some of them are detailed instructions for the management of the royal estates; others regulate the discipline and organization of the church; while still others are general decrees applying to the whole realm and published everywhere by the counts and bishops. Taken together they justify the description of Charles as one of the great legislators of the Middle Ages.

Economic conditions. Many of Charles's capitularies deal with economic problems. By far the greatest number of the people in this age were engaged in farming or drew their income from the land. The most interesting of the capitularies are those dealing with the management of the royal estates. These show a considerable improvement in agricultural methods, which were copied on the great villas or estates of the nobles and the church. The building-up of large estates went on steadily through this period, as the small landowners lost their land and freedom under the stress of compulsory military service, which often proved too great an economic strain on the small farmer. This, of course, added to the power of the nobles and the great churchmen, a fact that was to have important results in the next century. Industry was limited almost entirely to the production on the estate of the tools, weapons, clothing, and so forth needed by the people of the villa. Commerce of a general sort had declined greatly since the conquest of the Mediterranean by the Moslems, which hindered trade with the East. In fact, during the eighth century trade was limited more and more to the meeting of local needs, and barter (exchange of goods) was steadily replacing a "money economy" (the buying and selling of goods for cash).

Carolingian Renascence. Despite all the multifarious activities which we have outlined or suggested, Charles still found time to take a keen interest in the education of his people and especially of the clergy. As protector of the church — and in reality its master, whatever the theory of the relation of church and state might be — he felt responsible for the purity of its teaching. The religion of the people was steeped in superstition brought over from pagan days, and the majority of the clergy were too ignorant to instruct them. Charles realized that the better education of the clergy was a matter of supreme importance. Wherever possible he encouraged bishops and abbots to found schools for the training of priests. He himself founded a school at the palace to which he brought scholars from all parts of Europe. Paul the Deacon (Paulus Diaconus), the author of the famous *History of the Lombards,* came from Italy. Theodulphus, whom Charles made Bishop of Orléans, was a Spanish Goth. Einhard was one of the few Frankish scholars. But most important of all the teachers at the palace school was Alcuin, a Saxon monk from northern England who had received his education in the school founded by the Venerable Bede. These men devoted themselves to the study of Latin antiquity, both classical and Christian. They also stimulated the copying of ancient manuscripts and introduced a more legible style of handwriting, which set a standard followed for centuries. Their work has given to the age the somewhat exaggerated name, the Carolingian Renascence, or rebirth of culture. Actually they learned little more than the rudiments of the ancient culture. They found more that they could understand in the works of the scholars of the intermediate period, like Boëthius and Gregory the Great, than in the masterpieces of the golden age or in the works of the great fourth-century Fathers of the Church. Moreover, education in this age was limited exclusively to the clergy, and, except for bare literacy, to only a small minority of these. Laymen no longer knew Latin or were able to read even their own language. The Carolingian revival is important none the less, for it marks the beginning of the long process by which the German people assimilated the ancient classical and Christian learning and made it their own.

2. Break-up of the Carolingian Empire

Disruptive factors. The reign of Charlemagne was followed by a period of disaster, darkness, and chaos, and within three generations the Carolingian Empire had disappeared. Despite its apparent strength, there were elements of fatal weakness in Charles's empire, held in check only by the force of his powerful personality. The empire had in fact no real ethnic or political unity. It was held together only by loyalty to the ruler and by the common bond of membership in the Roman Church. The great size of the empire, in an age when communications were difficult and government crippled by lack of monetary income, made it almost impossible for any but a great administrative genius to govern all parts by the system of personal rule which was all that the German people had as yet been able to evolve. Most important of all the factors in the disintegration of the empire was the fatal weakness of the central government. And this was caused, not

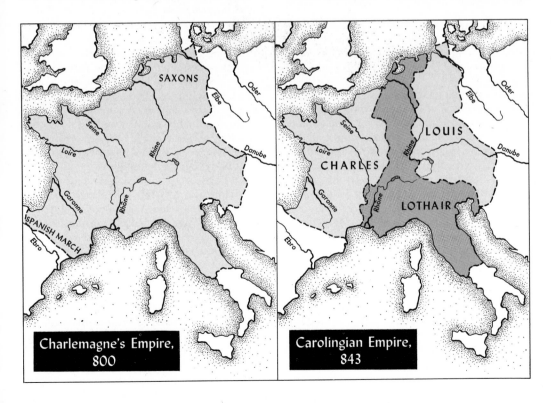

Charlemagne's Empire, 800

Carolingian Empire, 843

St. Mark is accompanied by the lion traditionally associated with him in this miniature from an evangelistary commissioned by Charlemagne in 781.

only by the difficulties inherent in personal rule, but even more by the growing power and independence of the aristocracy, the counts, bishops, and great landowners, who gradually took over the rights and duties of government into their own hands. All this was included in the development of that system of society known as feudalism, concerning which more will be said in the following chapter. Its earliest origins date back to the Merovingian period. Its development was controlled but not halted by the great Carolingians, and under the successors of Charlemagne it became stronger than the monarchy. The civil wars arising from the Frankish custom of dividing the realm among all the late ruler's heirs were also a seriously disruptive factor throughout the ninth century. Finally, as though its internal difficulties were not enough, the weakened and divided empire was subjected to a long series of devastating raids and invasions by hordes of Magyar horsemen from the east,

by Moslems from the south, and from the north and west by those fierce Scandinavian pirates, the Northmen. It may be that the growth of feudalism was as much a result as a cause of the inability of central government under these circumstances to perform its function of maintaining order, administering justice and guaranteeing protection to its subjects, and, indeed, it may have helped to prevent the total disintegration of the state. The fact remains, however, that in the kingdoms which emerged from the Carolingian Empire the authority of the monarchy had dwindled until it was little more than a legal fiction.

Louis the Pious. Charles the Great was survived by only one son, Louis (814–40), called the Pious because of his devotion to the church. The year before his death, Charles had himself bestowed the imperial crown upon Louis, in the hope apparently of breaking the tradition of papal coronation. This precaution was nullified, however, for Louis permitted the pope to crown him in 816. Thus far the unity of the empire had been saved, as in preceding generations, by the survival of only one heir. But almost at once the fatal principle of division began to cause trouble. In 817, Louis announced his plans for the division of the empire among his three sons after his death. Six years later these plans had to be rearranged to include a fourth son, Charles, born to Louis's second wife Judith. This strong-minded lady seems to have completely dominated her amiable husband and was determined to gain a fair share, or more, of the heritage for her son. The remainder of Louis's reign was filled with intrigues, rebellions, and civil wars, as each of the brothers strove to hold or extend his portion, while the country was ravaged, government neglected, and the imperial authority weakened. Under normal circumstances Louis would probably have been a good ruler. But he lacked the character or ability to control his family, not to mention the insurgent aristocracy and the ambitious princes of the church.

Division of the empire. When Louis the Pious finally died in 840, the question of division was still unsettled. One of his sons had died, but each of the remaining three was dissatisfied with his share. Lothair, the eldest, who had inherited the imperial title, hoped to extend his authority over the whole empire. The two younger brothers, Charles the Bald and Louis the German, as they were called, therefore united against him. In 841 they met in the deadly battle of Fontenoy. Great numbers of the Franks were slain, but neither side won a clear victory. Charles and Louis separated for a time, but were soon forced to reunite. They met at Strassburg in the following year and there each took an oath of perpetual loyalty to the other. The text of the oath has survived and gives interesting evidence of the development of separate languages within the Frankish Empire. Louis read the oath in the Romance tongue, the ancestor of modern French, so as to be understood by his brother's troops, most of whom came from western Gaul. Charles, on the other hand, took the oath in the German dialect which alone would be understood by the men who had followed Louis from the east. The alliance proved too strong for Lothair, and in 843 peace was concluded by a treaty arranged at Verdun. Lothair was given the imperial title and a strip of territory about a thousand miles long and rather more than a hundred wide, running from north to south through the center of the empire from the North Sea to Rome. It included most of the valleys of the Rhine and the Rhône and more than half of Italy. The portions assigned to the two younger brothers, with the title of kings, had a greater geographical and cultural unity. Charles received the Romance-speaking western kingdom, while Louis took the German lands to the east. The Treaty of Verdun did not create new nations, but it did mark off the territories which were to become the countries of France and Germany and the "middle kingdom," the debatable land over which the French and German nations have fought almost to the present time.

Dissolution of the empire.   During the remaining years of the Carolingian Empire, the chief historical interest attached to the western kingdom of Charles the Bald (843–77). They were years of anarchy and disaster. The Northmen plundered the towns and monasteries on the coast and along all the navigable rivers. The king was powerless to defend his people. Charles seems to have been a fairly capable and energetic person, but his every effort was defeated by the refusal of the nobles to cooperate or to obey his commands. He had weakened his position, as had his brothers also, by bribing the nobles with gifts of land, immunities,

and privileges, in order to retain their loyalty during the civil war. There were open rebellions in Brittany and Aquitaine, and everywhere the nobles were assuming greater independence, while the people were forced to turn to them rather than to the king for protection. The later Carolingians who followed Charles were short-lived and dogged by misfortune. In 884, Charles the Fat, son of Louis the German and the only surviving adult member of the Carolingian family, reunited the whole empire under his rule. But this weak and shiftless emperor was but a poor parody of his great namesake. During the two years following his accession, the Northmen besieged Paris in force. Charles proved utterly unable to cope with them and finally bought them off by offering them Burgundy to plunder. The nobles of the empire rose in indignation and deposed him. He died shortly thereafter, in 888, and with him perished the Carolingian Empire.

Formation of kingdoms.   The empire now broke up into separate kingdoms, one in Italy, two in Burgundy, one in Germany, and one in the west which from this time on may be

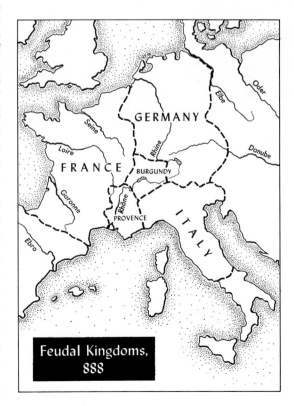

Feudal Kingdoms, 888

called France. Of these the latter two were to maintain their separate existences through the centuries till they formed nations in the modern sense. In Germany illegitimate Carolingians ruled till 911. In France the western branch of the Carolingian family lasted longer. But the history of the feudal kingdoms which rose from the ruins of the Carolingian Empire is another story and will be told later.

3. *The Coming of the Northmen*

The Northmen.   The Carolingian Empire, like its greater forerunner the Roman Empire, decayed largely because of internal weakness, but, as in the case of the older empire, the process of dissolution was accelerated by the impact of barbarian invaders from the north. These new invaders, the Northmen, who fell upon all the exposed coastline of western Europe with fire and sword in the ninth century, destroyed much of the civilization they found, as had their Germanic predecessors, but in the end they added new energy and vitality and new elements of culture to the formation of medieval civilization.

The Vikings.   The home of the Northmen was in the three Scandinavian countries of Denmark, Norway, and Sweden. There, cut off by the sea from the rest of Europe and hence from the influence of Rome and Christianity, they had retained their pagan religion and ancient customs, which in many ways resembled those of the early Germans to whom they were closely akin in race. Yet in one important respect they were different from their Germanic cousins in their manner of life. The rocky hills of Norway and Sweden and the marshy sandflats of Denmark afforded little room for agriculture, though the Northmen made good use of what land they had. The sea offered a better living, and the innumerable creeks and fiords provided perfect natural harbors. Of necessity, then, the Northmen had become amphibious. They were industrious farmers, but also daring sailors, fishermen, traders, and pirates, equally at home on land or sea. From this varied life they acquired remarkable versatility, reckless daring combined with sound practical sense. Above all, they were a hardy, vigorous people, toughened by the constant hardships of northern winters and storm-swept seas. Tall, blond men, vain of their gold ornaments and scarlet cloaks, their ringmail and carved sword hilts, never so happy as when their long-handled battle-axes clove through the ranks of their enemies — such were the Vikings, as those of the Northmen were called who set out on piratical raids in ever-increasing numbers from the end of the eighth century. What were the causes of this sudden activity? Probably much the same as for the migrations of the early Germans — lack of room at home due to increase in population. For centuries the sea had cut them off from the south. Now they discovered that it provided an open road for those who had the courage to take it.

Viking routes.   The first Viking raids were directed toward the British Isles. The *Anglo-Saxon Chronicle* mentions one as early as 787. But it was not till the beginning of the ninth century that they became general and assumed serious proportions. It was in the last years of Charlemagne that the Vikings first beached their long boats on the Frankish coast. Thereafter their raids continued, each year bringing more and larger boats, manned by more numerous, more experienced, and hence more dangerous crews. It is impossible to distinguish absolutely between the Vikings of the various Scandinavian countries. In general, however, those who sailed westward around the north of Scotland, to prey upon the coasts of Scotland, Ireland, and the smaller islands, were Norwegians. Later these sailed farther west to Iceland, Greenland, and the coast of North America. Both Norwegians and Danes harried the coast of western Europe, while the Danes seem to have been chiefly responsible for the invasion of England. The Swedes took the eastern route by river through Russia to the Black Sea and eventually to Constantinople, where they met other Vikings who had sailed eastward through the Mediterranean from the Straits of Gibraltar. No part of Europe that could be reached by water was safe from these far-wandering men.

Raids.   The seacoast towns were naturally the first objects of their raids. Masters of the sea, they struck where they chose with all the advantage that goes with a surprise attack. Their long open boats would appear unheralded out of the morning mist, and before a force could be collected to ward them off they would

The Oseberg ship, now in the Viking Ships Museum at Oslo, was large enough but probably not sufficiently sturdy to sail the open sea. The number of holes used as oarlocks shows that it was designed to carry more than thirty men.

have sacked the town and carried their plunder off to the safety of the sea. As they grew bolder, the Vikings struck inland, rowing their boats up the navigable rivers on which the most important towns were situated. For centuries these rivers had been the principal highways of trade. They now served the northern pirates equally well. Everywhere the Northmen sought out monasteries and churches, not so much through malice against the Christian clergy as because they had learned that there was always rich plunder to be found under the sign of the cross and that the monks and clergy had become too accustomed to the protection offered them by religious veneration to have taken the necessary precautions for defense. Great numbers of the monasteries were completely destroyed — a serious blow to learning, since they were the chief centers of education. The fear these rapacious pirates inspired is echoed eloquently in the prayer, introduced into the litany, "From the fury of the Northmen, good Lord, deliver us!"

Settlements in Europe. About the middle of the ninth century, the activities of the Northmen entered a new phase. No longer were they content to make annual expeditions in search of movable plunder. Instead they began to settle at strategic points along the coast and to carry on their depredations at closer range. The Frankish Empire had been sadly weakened by the civil war between the sons of Louis the Pious and by the resulting division of the empire. The Danish host took advantage of the weakness of the central government to found permanent camps at the mouths of the great rivers which empty on the western coast. Toward the end of the century, however, their raids were checked as the towns improved their fortifications and the nobles began to build strong castles for defense. In 891, the German king, Arnulf, defeated a large Danish army on the lower Rhine and drove them out of that district. Thereafter the settlements of the Northmen were confined to the lower reaches of the Seine, and the raids on other parts soon ceased. In 911 or 912, the land about the lower Seine, known thereafter as Normandy, was ceded to the Northmen by the Carolingian king, Charles the Simple. Their leader, Duke Rollo, became a vassal of the French king, though a very independent one, and was converted to Christianity. Further immigration continued for some time and Normandy occupied a rather anomalous position as at once a Scandinavian colony and a French duchy. But by the end of the tenth century, the Normans had adopted the religion, speech, and culture of the French people among whom they lived. By that time Normandy had become definitely French, though always more than half independent of the French king.

Settlement in England. In England much the same development had taken place about the middle of the ninth century. In 866, the Danes began a concerted invasion which threatened to overwhelm all England. Mounting themselves on horses stolen from the coast shires, they rode inland sweeping all opposition before them. Anglo-Saxon England was at this time divided into four separate kingdoms and failed to unite against the foreign foe. Within five years the Northmen conquered the kingdoms of Northumbria, Mercia, and East Anglia. In 871, they invaded the southern kingdom of Wessex, the last Saxon stronghold.

Alfred the Great. Here they were finally checked by the skillful and courageous leadership of the young Alfred (871–900), who succeeded his elder brother as King of Wessex in the midst of the invasion. Seven years later "the army," as the Saxons called the Danish host, again invaded Wessex and was again repulsed. Later Alfred reconquered London and part of Mercia from the Danes. England was now divided into two parts, the Saxon kingdom of Wessex south of the Thames and the "Danelaw" to the north. In the intervals between conflicts with his dangerous neighbors, Alfred turned his attention to strengthening his kingdom. He reorganized the government and the army along lines that were to be followed by his successors, fortified the towns, and created a fleet that could cope with the Danes in their own element. Like Charlemagne, to whom he has often been compared, Alfred was vitally interested in religion and education, though unlike the great Frankish ruler he was himself one of the finest scholars of his day. The heathen "army" had destroyed the greater part of monastic culture in northern England, including the school at York where a century earlier Alcuin had received the education which made him the foremost scholar at Charlemagne's court. Even in Wessex learning had declined. Both people and clergy were ignorant and were falling back into pagan superstition. Realizing the importance of educating the clergy, Alfred gave his personal attention to the founding of schools, while he himself undertook the translation of such works as the *Pastoral Care* of Gregory the Great, the *Consolation of Philosophy* of Boëthius, and Bede's *Ecclesiastical History,* from Latin to Anglo-Saxon. It was he, too, who was responsible for the institution of the *Anglo-Saxon Chronicle,* our best source for

the history of his age. As the founder of the English kingdom and of English literature, Alfred fully deserved his title, "the Great."

Reconquered Danelaw. Meanwhile, the Danes were settling everywhere north of the Thames, farming and building fortified "boroughs" as military centers. They were also gradually adopting the Christian religion. They failed, however, to develop any strong political organization. In the two generations following Alfred the Great, his son and grandsons were able to complete his work by reconquering the Danelaw and establishing a united kingdom in England. For a time the Danes retained their own laws; but as their language and customs were not radically unlike those of the Saxons, they gradually merged with them into one indistinguishable nation.

The Swedes in Russia. Of the Vikings from Sweden who struck out to the east and south by way of the rivers through Russia we know less than about those who went to the west. We know, however, that these Vikings, whom the Slavs called "Russ," occupied Novgorod and Kiev about the middle of the ninth century and under a leader named Rurik carved out some kind of kingdom for themselves — the first Russian state. They traded from the Baltic to the Black Sea, and kept up commercial relations with Constantinople and Bagdad. In the course of time, like those Northmen who had gone to England and Normandy, they adopted the speech, religion, and customs of the people among whom they lived and so disappeared as a people.

Contribution of the Northmen. The coming of the Northmen caused the partial destruction of civilization and learning in many parts of Europe, but their advent was not an unmitigated disaster. The outworn Carolingian Empire, which they helped to destroy, was succeeded by new kingdoms, the nations of the future. In England they made the union of the whole country into one kingdom possible. And everywhere they introduced new and vigorous blood. Moreover, they proved themselves capable of absorbing the culture of more civilized peoples and, in time, of adding to it. Above all, their keen interest in trade led to a revival of commerce and town life in the British Isles, Normandy, and Russia, for which later ages owe them a great debt of gratitude.

"Master: And which do you think among secular crafts holds the first place?

Councillor: Agriculture, because the plowman feeds us all." • Colloquy of Aelfric the Grammarian (c. 955–c. 1010)

13

The Feudal System

THE KINGDOMS which replaced the disrupted Carolingian Empire were feudal kingdoms; and medieval society, in which the Germanic and Roman elements had at last merged to form a new composite, was throughout a feudal society. It is feudalism that gives to the society of the Middle Ages its peculiar character, differentiating it clearly from that of Roman antiquity or of the modern age. It pervaded and gave form to every aspect of life and every institution. Economic, social, political, and judicial institutions were all parts of the feudal system — as was also the church. To understand the feudal system, then, is essential to an understanding of the life of the Middle Ages. It is difficult, however, for the modern man, with his conceptions of private ownership of land, to visualize a society in which no one, or at least very few, owned land outright, but instead held it as an hereditary right from some social superior in return for personal services. It is difficult, too, for us to imagine a society in which the great majority of the people, the workers, were only partly free, while the remainder formed a fighting and ruling aristocracy. It is still less easy, perhaps, to picture a state in which the body of the citizens had no direct connection with the central government and where the ordinary rights and duties of government, such as the prosecution of justice in the law courts, the enforcement of law and order, the coinage of

money, taxation, and the organization of the army, had passed into the hands of private individuals.

In this chapter we shall try to explain how such a system arose and how it functioned. But we can do so only in the most general way; for feudalism evolved gradually and according to no preconceived plan, so that what is true of one place may not be entirely true of another, and what applies to one time may not apply to another. All that we can attempt is to trace the main outlines of the feudal system and to describe what was most generally true. Broadly speaking, the eighth and ninth centuries may be taken as the age in which feudalism originated; the tenth and first half of the eleventh century as the period in which it took definite shape; and the next two hundred years as the time of its highest and most complete development, to be followed by centuries of slow decay as new forms arose to take its place.

1. Origins of Feudalism

Failure of central government. Feudalism arose because it was the only system that could satisfy the needs of the age. It came as a result of a vast number of bargains and arrangements between private individuals or between individuals and the monarch — bargains in which both parties made the best terms they could according to their needs and ambitions. The fundamental cause of feudalism, then, is to be found in the conditions of the period — roughly the eighth and ninth centuries — in which it arose. Of these conditions the most important was the weakness and eventual failure of the central government, which, in turn, was very largely the result of the economic conditions prevailing throughout western Europe. After the beginning of the eighth century, the western Christian lands were cut off from trade with the East by Moslem domination of the Mediterranean, while at the same time the commerce of the northern and western coasts was disrupted by the ravages of the Northmen. Lacking the stimulus of external trade, the commerce of Western Christendom, which had been declining for centuries, almost disappeared and city life of a normal kind disappeared with it. What was left was an almost purely agricultural economy carried on by barter and exchange of services, with very little money in circulation. Land became almost the sole source of wealth, and without markets there was no adequate means of turning its products into cash. Under such circumstances, taxes were difficult if not impossible to collect on any significant scale. As a result, the government, deprived of financial support, was forced either to pay for services with grants of land, which always tended to become hereditary, or to delegate its duties and privileges to those landholders who could exert effective authority over the people on their land. In addition, the Frankish government had always suffered from the weaknesses inherent in a primitive system of personal rule. Even in their best days, the Carolingian rulers had never provided a really adequate government. Yet feudalism made slow progress until the ninth century, when under Louis the Pious and his warring sons the central government gradually collapsed. Weakened by civil wars and rebellions, the later Carolingians were unable to protect their people from the raids of the Northmen and the violence of the nobles, and were forced to leave them, together with many of the privileges of government, in the hands of the fighting aristocracy, whom they could no longer control and to whom the people were forced to turn for the protection which the king could no longer offer. Let us

see how this change worked out in relation to the different classes of society.

Small landowners lose freedom. For the class of small landowners, the rise of feudalism meant the loss of free ownership of their land and with it the loss of freedom and independence. Since Roman times there had been many great estates worked by slaves and more or less servile *coloni*. Small farms were now added to these estates or were put together to form new ones, and their former owners sank to a position very like that of the *colonus*. One of the principal causes of this development during the eighth century, and especially under the warlike Charlemagne, was the heavy burden of compulsory military service laid on all freemen. During the summer months when his land needed the most attention, the freeman was often forced to go on campaigns at his own expense and without pay. For this and other reasons, great numbers of small farmers sank hopelessly into debt, and in order to cancel their debts or to escape military service they gave up their lands to some large landholder. Thereafter they worked the land as dependent tenants under his protection. Freemen also who had no land or had lost it, and hence had no way of making a living, "commended" themselves to a neighboring lord. Henceforth they were his "men" and usually were given some land to work. In either case they became dependent on the lord and lost their freedom. During the turbulent ninth century this process was greatly accelerated. The necessity of securing protection forced the remaining small freemen to put themselves and their land under the protection of the local lord, even though it meant the loss of ownership and liberty, for in that lawless age security was more important than freedom. At the same time, many great landowners took advantage of their power and the lack of governmental control to force their poorer neighbors into this dependent position. Whatever may have been the steps by which this process was completed, and they are none too clear, by the end of the ninth century almost all the workers on the land had become unfree tenants on large estates.

Rise of a military aristocracy. While the poorer citizens were sinking in the social scale, the wealthier or more fortunate were forming a military aristocracy. Since the early years of

Medieval scribes often decorated the margins of their manuscripts with tiny lifelike sketches from daily life. The two men shown here, one reaping, the other sowing seeds, are from a fourteenth-century breviary and psalter.

the eighth century, when Charles Martel had mounted part of the Frankish army in order to meet the Moslem cavalry on equal terms, military service had become more expensive. In the course of time practically the whole fighting force came to be made up of mounted men. As a result, only men with sufficient wealth to provide themselves with a horse as well as with armor and weapons could afford to fight. Hence the flight from military service, which so reduced the imperial army that Charlemagne issued edicts forcing the lords to equip and bring into the army, under their own leadership, at least some of the men dependent on them. Thus there grew up a class of military dependents, who, however, unlike the laborers, did not lose their status as freemen, since fighting was considered an honorable occupation. In the chaos of the ninth century, fighting men were at a premium. They were needed by the king and by the lords and hence were able to secure more favorable terms for themselves than were the laborers. The warrior who commended himself to a lord was not paid wages for his services, since lack of sufficient money in circulation made regular wages impractical, but would normally receive from him the use of enough land, together with the peasants to work it, so that the income would provide him with horse and armor and the leisure for fighting. Also the freeman who had land enough to maintain himself as a warrior, but who needed the protection of some great lord, would give up his land to the lord and be allowed to retain the income from it in return for military service. By the end of the ninth century, this reciprocal combination of landholding and

military service had become the general rule. There were some exceptions. Instead of granting land as payment for service, a lord might simply take a warrior into his household and provide him with food, clothing, weapons and armor. Also, in the unplanned development of the feudal system, some lands, called "allods," remained independent, being freely owned and not held from any lord. The number of these exceptional cases, however, decreased rapidly after the ninth century, and it became a recognized axiom in most parts of Europe that there should be no land and no man without a lord. Like the laborer, the fighter held his land from some lord whose man he was, but his position in the social scale was infinitely higher and tended to become hereditary, thus laying the foundation for a military aristocracy.

Powers of state in private hands. So far as the administration of the state as a whole was concerned, one of the most important factors in the rise of feudalism was the passing of many of the rights and privileges of government from the king to the great nobles. The steps by which this process took place are difficult to trace. The explanation of why they occurred is more clear. As the central government grew weaker, the nobles grew stronger and hence more independent. Since they were strong enough to assume one of the greatest responsibilities of government, that of granting protection and preserving order, it was only natural that the nobles should assume the other rights and privileges of government over their people. Even had they not been anxious to seize power, it would have been thrust upon them; for the people turned naturally to the local lord for protection and justice, rather than to the distant monarch. In an age of general anarchy like the ninth century, he ruled who had the power to rule, regardless of legal right. The counts and dukes of the Carolingian Empire, whose offices had become practically hereditary, were the natural leaders of their administrative districts. It was easy for them to establish themselves as rulers in their own right rather than as officers of the crown, though still recognizing the king as their superior. Similarly, lesser lords took over the actual government of their own districts, simply because they were strong enough to do so.

So far we have tried to show how feudalism came into existence. We must turn now to the description of the system in its completed form.

2. The Manorial System

The manor an economic unit. By the end of the ninth century, the manorial system of landholding and cultivation was almost universal throughout Europe. It should be clearly distinguished from the feudal system which, strictly defined, involved only the military and political organization of the aristocracy and in which the fief was the essential landed unit; but, since feudalism was based on landholding, the manorial system was closely related to it and, indeed, furnished the economic foundation on which the whole feudal structure rested. It also furnished the economic, social, and judicial framework within which the peasants lived and worked. With a few exceptions, chiefly in mountain country or in regions given over to sheep or cattle grazing, the land was divided into estates, called "villas" in France and "manors" in England, of which the owner was a lord or "seigneur" and the workers were peasant tenants, dependent on him. It was through the organization of the manor that the peasant laborers had their only contact with the military ruling class, which formed the upper ranks of feudal society. The lord of the manor was a member of the fighting aristocracy. He might have no more than a single manor, or he might hold hundreds. In any case the individual manor was an independent unit. We may confine our study of the economic base of feudalism, then, to the organization of a single manor.

The typical manor. No two manors were exactly alike. There were infinite variations in custom and practice. Yet the general characteristics of the manorial system were sufficiently alike in all parts of western Europe to justify the description of a typical manor, on the understanding, of course, that the details would vary widely in any given case.[1] At the center of the manor, on the highest point of land, stood the manor house, fortified to give protection to the lord and peasants in case of attack. If the manor was the home of a powerful baron, it would be a fortified castle — otherwise no more than a strongly built house. If the lord was absent or lived on another manor, the manor house would be occupied by the bailiff, who acted as his agent and managed the estate. Near the manor house clustered the huts of the peasants, each with a little land attached, forming the village which was an indispensable part of any manor. In the village there would also be a mill, a blacksmith's shop, a small church, and a house for the parish priest. Surrounding the village were the cultivated fields and the meadows, wastelands, and woods. Part of the cultivated land, perhaps a third, was set aside for the sole use of the lord. This was called the "demesne." It might be all in one block, or part of it might be scattered in small pieces throughout the manor. The remainder of the cultivated land was parceled out among the peasants of the village. The meadows, wastelands, and woods were not formally divided, but were considered common land, shared proportionately by lord and peasants.

Open-field system. On all sides of the village, the cultivated lands stretched in great open fields, each containing hundreds of acres. While the crops needed protection, the shepherds, cowherds, and swineherds kept their charges out of the fields by day and enclosed them at night, or the fields may have been protected by temporary fences during the growing season. After the harvest the livestock of the lord and the villagers was turned loose to graze on the stubble. This method of farming is called the "open-field system." For purposes of cultivation the land was usually divided into three fields to allow for rotation of the crops.

[1] See chart, page 155.

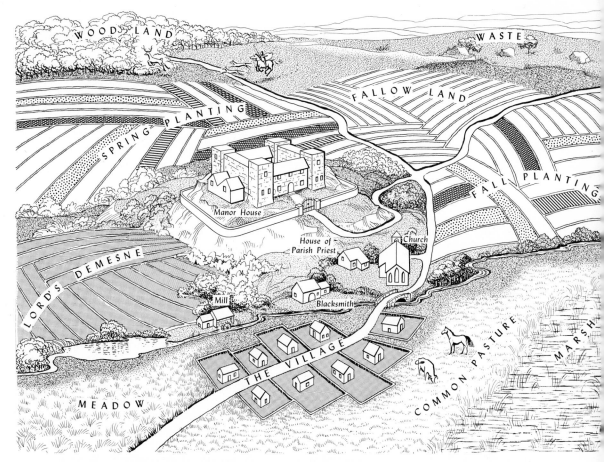

One field would be reserved for spring planting of oats or barley; the second for the fall planting of wheat or rye, to be harvested in the following summer; the third would lie fallow, that is, it would be allowed to rest without crop, though plowed twice during the year, while the young grass which sprang up served as pasture for the cattle. Each year the treatment of the fields shifted in steady rotation, so that each field lay fallow once in three years. This system was necessary at a time when methods of fertilizing were crude and unscientific. The land would soon have become exhausted if it had not been allowed time to recover or if the same crop had been planted on it year after year. On very poor land even one year fallow in three was not enough, and there, as also in Italy and parts of southern France where the hot summers made a spring planting impractical, a two year rotation was generally followed.

Intermixed tenure. Scattered through these open fields, and outside the demesne farm, were the small holdings of the peasants. Each field was subdivided into numbers of long narrow strips separated by thin ridges of grass. The shape of these strips was fixed by the plow. They were usually as long as the lay of the land would permit, so that the heavy plow, drawn by a team of four or eight oxen, would not have to turn too often. Every peasant held a number of these strips, scattered at random through each of the three fields. Sometimes the lord reserved some of them as demesne land, and some strips were assigned to the parish church as "glebe land," from which the priest received the produce. The amount of land held by a single peasant varied, depending on the number of strips he had inherited. This system of "intermixed tenure" may have originated as a plan for giving each of the peasants land of

Plowing with an ox-team, as pictured in a miniature from the Luttrell psalter (c. 1340).

equal value — allowing to none the advantage of having his whole plot in especially fertile soil or near the village. Whatever its origin, the system continued because it fitted into the method of working the land employed on the manor; for, though each peasant took the crop from his own strips, the whole village united their labor in the communal cultivation of the fields. Very few peasants could have been rich enough to own a plow and a complete team of oxen, or the still more costly horses that, after the tenth century, began to replace the oxen in some parts of northern Europe, so that it was necessary for the villagers to cooperate and pool their resources. The simplest method under the circumstances was for each plow team to work straight across the field, plowing each strip in turn. Thus the intermixture of the strips guaranteed the same treatment for all. At the same time, the cooperative system tended to check individual initiative and to prevent the peasant from trying new experiments.

The peasants. The inhabitants of the village who worked the fields were all members of the peasant class. They were all tenants, holding their land from the lord of the manor. They were all under the lord's jurisdiction and more or less dependent upon him. Yet within this class there were innumerable gradations and shades of social status and degrees of wealth and freedom — or perhaps it would be more accurate to say, of poverty and servitude. It is impossible to distinguish clearly between the various grades of peasants, as there was little uniformity throughout Europe, and even the names used to describe them are often confusing. The unfree tenants were generally called villeins or serfs. As a rule, they were bound to the land on which they were born and could not leave it without the lord's consent and the payment of a fine. The free tenants were not thus bound, but they were nevertheless under the lord's jurisdiction so long as they remained on the manor. The origin of these differences in status is probably to be found in the manner in which the peasants' ancestors first came under the jurisdiction of the lord and in the terms of the original bargain between them; for the contract between lord and tenant was hereditary, passed on with little change from generation to generation.

The manorial contract. The relation between the peasant and the lord of the manor can best be described as based on an unwritten contract, to which custom had given a legal sanction. It was not a one-sided bargain. The lord gave the peasant protection, established a court where he could appeal for justice, built a mill, and provided a church for the village. Above all, he furnished the land. All the land of the manor belonged legally to the lord; but custom forbade his taking the peasant's strips of land from him, provided the latter had fulfilled all his obligations. Nor could the lord prevent the peasant from taking his customary share of hay from the meadows or from pasturing his allotted share of cattle, swine, or geese on the common land. Thus the peasants, though in most cases not free to leave their land, had the security which came from the hereditary right to its possession.

In return for these privileges, the peasants owed certain payments and services to the lord. All but the freest peasants were obliged to work for the lord a certain number of days each week. This "week work" was utilized for the cultivation of the demesne land and for incidental tasks, such as carrying the lord's produce to market or to another of his manors. At certain times during the year when the pressure of work was greatest, as at harvest time, all the peasants on the manor were forced to work on the lord's demesne. These special services were called "boon works." Labor services were an essential part of the manorial system. Indeed, the whole system may be regarded as a method of securing labor for the lord's land without the payment of money wages. All the tenants, too, owed the lord payments as rent for their land. These were usually made in kind, that is, in produce, but might in exceptional cases be made in money. The amount of the payments was fixed by custom, though in some places the lord had the legal right to exact as much as he chose from his serfs. The villagers had also to pay for the use of the lord's mill and the great oven where all baked their bread. There were other occasional dues. On the death of a tenant his heirs had to make a special payment, called "heriot," as recognition of the lord's possession of the land and for the renewal of the hereditary contract. The unfree peasant, too, had to make a payment, called "merchet," if his daughter married outside the manor, as the lord was thus deprived of one of his serfs.

Self-sufficiency of the manor. The manor was a little economic and political world, complete in itself. The peasant had small contact with the world outside or with any higher authority than his lord. In the Early Middle Ages there was little commerce, and most of the peasant's needs — food, clothing, and tools — were produced on the manor. The produce of the fields was mostly consumed on the manor, though grain might be carried to another manor belonging to the lord or, after the revival of town life, might be sold in a nearby market. In short, the manorial system represented a very simple and primitive form of economy, wherein exchange of produce and services took the place of cash transactions. In the High Middle Ages, after the rise of the towns and the revival of trade had reintroduced money economy, the self-sufficiency of the manors was impaired. Buying and selling began to supersede the simpler forms of barter, and during the Later Middle Ages cash payments gradually took the place of services or payments in kind.

3. Military Feudalism and Landholding: The Fief

The military aristocracy. The peasants, laboriously tilling their strips of land, turning over part of their produce to the lord of the manor and cultivating his demesne farm, formed the foundation of feudal society. By their unremitting toil they made it possible for their lord to live without labor and to devote his energies to fighting, the only occupation suitable for a noble. The clearest distinction between social classes in the feudal era was that between the non-noble laborer and the noble warrior. Both held land in hereditary

A windmill, from a miniature in the margin of a fourteenth-century manuscript now in the Bodleian Library, Oxford.

tenure from some superior, it is true, but the tenure of the peasant was based on "ignoble" services, i.e., manual labor, whereas the feudal tenure of the noble landholder was based on "noble," i.e., military, service. The right to fight was a privilege reserved for the military aristocracy, from which base-born men were jealously excluded. To this military aristocracy belonged originally all who could afford to live without working, and who had sufficient income to provide them with the necessary war-horse, heavy armor, and weapons. That, of course, usually meant all who had sufficient land to provide such an income, for to this class almost the only possible source of income was land. We have already seen the ways in which this class arose through the combination of landholding and military service. Whatever the nature of the original bargain between the fighter and his lord, the amount of land was necessarily greater than that involved in the contract between the laborer and the lord of the manor; and the fighting man's relation to his lord carried with it no suggestion of servility, but was a free and honorable bargain between two members of the same military aristocracy.

The fief.   There were many variations in rank and wealth within the military class, extending from the poorest knight, who had barely enough land to furnish him with equipment, to the great count or duke, whose wide lands supported hundreds of knights who rode to battle at his command. But certain characteristics were common to them all. All were warriors, set apart by that honor from the base-born; almost all were in some degree lords with a greater or lesser number of dependents, for even the poorest knight was usually lord of at least a small manor; and each held a "fief" from some greater lord to whom he owed military service. The fief was the indispensable land unit of military feudalism. It varied in size with the wealth and importance of the holder — that of a poor knight being merely a single manor, that of a count or duke a great territory including hundreds of manors. In any case, the holder of the fief was the "vassal" of the lord from whom he received the fief and who might be a baron, count, duke, or king, or any other lord with land enough to grant part of it to a vassal in return for mili-

tary service. The vassal did not own the fief, just as the peasant tenant did not own the land he worked, but he had an hereditary right to the use of it and could not legally be deprived of it so long as he fulfilled his obligations.

Homage and investiture.   The relations between the vassal and his lord were based on a commonly understood contract, handed on with little change from generation to generation. This contract was formally renewed by a solemn ceremony, whenever the death of either party introduced his heir as a new personality into the relation. The vassal's part in this ceremony was called "homage." He knelt before his lord, bareheaded and unarmed, placed his hands between the hands of his lord, and declared himself to be his man (*homme*) and took an oath to be faithful to him. The lord then responded with the ceremony of "investiture," presenting to the vassal a spear, flag, or some other symbol representing the fief. The symbolical ceremony of homage and investiture constituted a binding agreement, defined by custom and enforced by public opinion. It could not be legally broken by either party unless the other had failed to live up to the terms of the contract.

Military duties of the vassal.   The feudal contract included a number of mutual obligations. For the vassal's part, the chief of these was to fight for his lord. Originally, no doubt, the vassal was expected to fight whenever and as long as the lord needed him. As society became more settled, however, and the need for military aid less constant, the amount of military service was usually fixed at a certain number of days (customarily forty) a year. The number of knights required to fulfill the vassal's obligation varied, of course, with the size of the fief. The holder of a single manor, rated at one knight's service, would be responsible only for his own service, whereas a baron whose fief was larger would be bound to answer his lord's call to arms accompanied by other knights, who in turn were bound to follow him because they held fiefs from him and were his vassals. Closely allied to this military obligation was the court duty. The vassal was obliged to attend the court of justice held by his lord on stated occasions, and also to do his lord honor by his presence at festive celebrations, where the number of vassals in his retinue was an indication of the lord's social importance.

Relief and aids. The vassal also owed his lord certain contributions in money or produce. These were not annual payments, but were made only on special occasions. The heaviest payment in most cases was the "relief," which sometimes amounted to as much as a year's income from the fief. It was paid whenever a vassal died and was succeeded by his heir. Like the "heriot" paid by the peasant tenant under similar circumstances, it was apparently a recognition of the lord's possession of the land and a fee for the renewal of the contract, which was considered to be temporarily broken by the death of one of the contracting parties. In addition to the relief, there were three generally recognized "aids." All the vassals were obliged to contribute to making up the lord's ransom if he were captured, to defraying the expenses of the ceremony of knighting his eldest son, and to providing a dowry when his eldest daughter married. The vassal was also expected to house and entertain the lord and his retinue whenever he chose to visit the vassal's fief.

Duties and privileges of the lord. The obligations of the lord, included in the feudal contract, were not so onerous as those of the vassal. This was natural enough, since, in theory, it was he who provided the land. The lord's most important duty was to protect his vassal from all enemies. He was also obliged to maintain a court where his vassals could appeal for justice, to act as guardian for a vassal's minor heirs, and to secure a suitable husband for the unmarried heiress of any of his vassals. These latter duties, however, were also privileges and often very remunerative. The fines imposed in his court added considerably to the lord's income. His right of wardship over minor heirs might be a still more valuable prerogative, since he was entitled to the full income from the fief, which he managed till the heir was old enough to assume the responsibility. The choosing of a husband for an unmarried heiress was also a jealously guarded right. It was important to find her a husband as soon as possible, as a woman could not perform a vassal's duties, and it was even more important to choose as her husband some man who would fulfill those duties adequately and faithfully.

In case there were no heirs, the fief returned or "escheated" to the lord. He could then retain it or grant it to another vassal at will.

Subinfeudation. The personal tie between lord and vassal was the cement that held feudal society together — if very imperfectly. The great nobles, who held fiefs directly from the king as his vassals-in-chief, split the greater part of their land into smaller fiefs, granted to vassals who thus became the subvassals of the king. These in turn might grant part of their land to vassals of their own, who would be subvassals of the king's vassal, and so on down to the fief so small that it could support only a single knight. This process is known as "subinfeudation." Had it worked out according to theory, the aristocratic feudal society would have taken the form of a symmetrical pyramid, of which the knights formed the base, the barons, counts, dukes, and other great nobles the higher ranks in diminishing numbers, and the king the apex. But feudalism had not grown up according to any preconceived theory. From the beginning, the steps in the feudal hierarchy had been uneven, and with the passage of time the natural shifts of family fortune introduced new complications with every passing generation, until the whole system was reduced to utter chaos. At the same time, western Europe was gradually becoming more civilized and settled, so that the mutual need for military service and protection was less vital and the personal tie of dependence and loyalty was weakened. In proportion as this occurred, landholding became the most important part of the feudal bargain. Thus it happened that, by marriage, conquest, purchase, or inheritance through the mother's family, nobles frequently acquired fiefs from several lords at once, to each of whom they would owe vassal's service. Again, part of such a vassal's fief might pass into the hands of a much more powerful lord, who would nevertheless become his vassal for that land. The duties of a vassal might thus become extremely complicated. Many were forced to introduce reservations into the oath of loyalty, "saving the rights of his other lords." These complications of subinfeudation destroyed all proportion and symmetry in the ranks of the feudal nobility. There were knights who held small fiefs directly from the king; counts who held fiefs from petty barons; and untitled lords whose

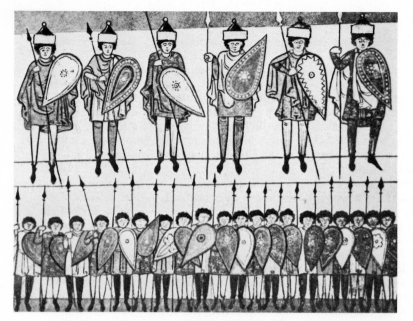

The great lords with the vassals under their command, shown here in a miniature from an eleventh-century manuscript, represent a segment of the feudal pyramid.

fiefs rivaled those of counts or dukes. The Count of Champagne, to cite a well-known example, was the vassal of the King of France for part of his lands and of nine other lords for the remainder, including the German emperor and the Duke of Burgundy.

4. The Church in the Feudal System

Extent of church land. Thus far we have discussed feudalism only as it affected laymen — the nobles and peasants. We must turn now to consider the position of the clergy in the feudal system; for it would be impossible to understand the history of the medieval church — or of feudalism — without an understanding of the intimate connection between the two. It was inevitable that the church should become feudalized, since it was a great landholder, and landholding on a large scale was possible only by feudal tenure. Landholding in the Middle Ages carried with it political, judicial, and military responsibilities and a complex of personal relations. As a landholder, then, the church became of necessity an integral part of feudal society, bound to the secular world by innumerable personal and economic ties. It has been reckoned that during the twelfth and thirteenth centuries approximately one-third of the usable land in western Europe was controlled by the church. Even as early as the ninth century, according to one historian's estimate, there were bishops and abbots whose lands covered more than one hundred thousand acres, while even the poorest held five thousand acres or more.

Ecclesiastical lords and vassals. These lands had been accumulated as the result of generations of pious gifts, inspired, more often than not, by the desire of a dying king or lord to reconcile himself with God and to throw some good deed into the balance to outweigh his sins. After the time of Charlemagne, most gifts of this kind were in the form of fiefs and were held in feudal tenure for the church by the bishops, as rulers of the dioceses, or by abbots, as the heads of monasteries. So much land could not be held without producing the military service expected from all vassals. Since the bishops or abbots, as churchmen, were not supposed to fight, they were forced to parcel out part of their lands to lay vassals who owed them military service, which in turn they could pass on to their lords. There was little to distinguish an ecclesiastical fief from any other. The bishop or abbot gave and received military service and the usual relief and aids like any lay noble, save that election took the place of inheritance, and land once acquired by the church could never be legally alienated from it. These ecclesiastical nobles were usually vassals-in-chief of the monarch, and their military support was often more important to the king than that of the lay lords, whose family ties and ambitions might interfere with their obedience.

Ecclesiastical nobles. Just as in lay society there was a clear distinction between peasant and noble, so in the ecclesiastical hierarchy there was a social distinction, though not so rigid, between the lower and the higher clergy. The parish priests were mostly of peasant stock, and those who served the manorial churches were almost as dependent on the lord of the manor as were the other peasants. The bishops, abbots, and other high officials of the church, on the other hand, were usually of noble birth. The younger son of a noble family might gain through such a position far greater wealth and power than he could hope for from his share of the family estates. As a result, the great nobles frequently interfered in ecclesiastical elections to secure a vacant bishopric or abbacy for one of their relatives, thus establishing him comfortably and gaining for themselves a wealthy and powerful ally. Still more frequently, the king would bestow an ecclesiastical office as a reward for service and in order to guarantee the faithful performance of the clerical vassal's duties by placing the office in trustworthy hands. The men who thus rose to influential positions in the church were not necessarily more religious in character or interests than the ordinary lay nobles. Their training and tastes were very similar to those of their brothers who had remained "in the world." They loved hunting and fighting and took an active part in feudal politics. Many a lusty bishop led his mounted vassals into battle, lightheartedly swinging a mace in place of a sword and thus avoiding the sin of shedding blood.

Their dual character. Yet, despite their worldly interests, these "ecclesiastical barons" had important spiritual duties to perform. The government of the church was in their hands. Their offices had in fact a dual character which led to innumerable complications and controversies. They owed vassal's allegiance to their overlords and at the same time owed obedience to their superiors in the church. Neither state nor church could afford to lose control over such powerful officials; yet they could not serve both God and Mammon — though the distinction between the two was sometimes none too clear. It was this conflict of interests and duties which caused the long struggle between church and state, between the papacy on the one hand and the emperors and kings on the other, that

for centuries disturbed the peace of Europe. The intrusion of the church into the feudal system resulted in a confusion thrice confounded.

5. *The Feudal State*

The monarchy. We have seen how the whole fabric of feudal society was woven together by a vast number of personal relations, wherein every man — peasants, nobles, and clergy — owed obedience to some immediate superior. In this complex and decentralized system the very idea of a state, composed of citizens ruled directly by a central government, ceased to exist. Yet, through all the feudal period, the kingdoms maintained their existence and kings continued to govern, though with powers sadly diminished. There was no state system of taxation, coinage, laws or law courts, and no national army. But there were the feudal equivalents, and the monarchy survived in the midst of feudalism because it had itself become feudalized. The theory of feudalism recognized the king as the supreme overlord of all lords and the final proprietor of all the land in the kingdom, though most of it was parceled out to his vassals-in-chief. He ruled, then, not as an absolute monarch, nor as a constitutional monarch like modern kings, but as a feudal overlord. In place of state taxation, the king had to depend for the expenses of government on the income from his own lands — the royal estates — and on the feudal aids and other perquisites involved in the feudal contract with his vassals. He could not raise a national army, but he could call upon his vassals to perform their military service, accompanied by their vassals and subvassals. He could not issue legislation binding on all members of the state, but he could command his vassals and issue edicts in the pious hope that his vassals would pass them on to the people they ruled. He had no jurisdiction over the majority of citizens, but he could hold a feudal court for the trial of his immediate vassals and dependents. In practice, it is true, the vassals-in-chief obeyed the kings and performed their duties only when they felt it expedient to do so, and they seldom brought more than a fraction of their own vassals with them when called upon for military service. More often than not, in the early period of feudalism, they felt strong enough to ignore the royal commands. Nevertheless, the kings had an inestimable advantage over the other feudal lords, by virtue of the theory of supremacy, which was always recognized as valid even when ignored in practice. With the passage of time the kings, first of England and later of France, were able to make that theory a reality. In Germany and Italy the rise of the monarchy was complicated by unusual problems which prevented the completion of the process.

Private jurisdictions.   Despite the theory of feudal supremacy of the monarch, however, feudalism was by its very nature antagonistic to central government. All local government was in the hands of the nobles. The king's direct authority ended with his own vassals; it could not reach beyond them to their dependents. Within his own fief, every noble had full jurisdiction and exercised all the powers of government. As a thirteenth-century jurist put it, "each baron is sovereign in his barony." He held courts for his dependents; levied a kind of taxation through tolls on roads and bridges; often he issued his own coinage; and he could always raise an army, composed of his vassals, to be used for any purpose he chose.

Private wars.   In no respect can the sovereign rights of the feudal lord be more clearly seen than in this recognized right to raise an army and to wage open war on other lords. Only in England, and even there not till the reign of Henry II in the twelfth century, was the monarchy strong enough to suppress private wars. The causes of feudal warfare were innumerable. Disputed boundaries, quarrels over the terms of vassalage, family feuds, personal antagonisms, greed, or sheer boredom were the most common. The nobles loved to fight. Fighting was not nearly so hazardous as in modern times, and it was often a very profitable occupation. The heavily armored knight was more likely to be captured than killed and could then be held for ransom. A further economic incentive to war was the hope of obtaining booty or land. Had there not been opportunities for profit without too great risk, the nobles would probably not have clung so tenaciously to their sovereign rights in this respect. On the whole it was the peasants who suffered most, because of interference with their work and destruction of their crops.

Peace of God.   The church, which despite its feudal character maintained a higher social conscience than the lay world, strove as best it could to curb the warlike ardor of the nobles, or at least to mitigate the evil effects of war on the poor and defenseless. In the last years of the tenth century, the clergy in many parts of Europe instituted the "Peace of God," requiring the nobles to take an oath not to harm the person or property of peasants, merchants, churchmen, or other noncombatants. The nobles themselves recognized the necessity of some such restriction, but old habits were too powerful to break and little good came of it. In the eleventh century a more effective check was applied by the church through the institution of the "Truce of God," which forbade the prosecution of private war during certain seasons — at first from Friday to Sunday of each week (the days of the death and resurrection of Christ) and during the forty days of Lent, from Ash Wednesday to Easter. Later this "closed season" was extended to include the time of harvest from the Feast of the Assumption (August 15) to Martinmas (November 11), and from sundown on Wednesday to sunrise on Monday of each week. The Truce originated in France where private wars were most frequent. Thence it spread to the other countries of Europe, except England, where its place was taken by the King's Peace. It was undoubtedly a beneficial institution, but it is difficult to determine how much of the gradual cessation of feudal warfare may be credited to the Truce and how much to the natural stabilization of society through the growth of royal power.

Estimate.   Feudalism has often been called a system of organized anarchy. The evils of the system are written plainly so that all who run may read. But in judging feudalism it must be remembered that organized anarchy is better than anarchy which has no organization, and that without it European society might have dissolved into complete chaos. Whatever its faults, the feudal system did at least give some order to society in a lawless age, and it held the kingdoms together until such time as the rising power of the monarchy could weld them into strong coherent states. It was a phase in the evolution of western Europe from barbarism to modern civilization.

14

The Founding of the Feudal Kingdoms

and the Revival of the Empire

IN THE LAST CHAPTER we studied the manner
in which feudalism functioned as the dominating force in the medieval state. In this chapter
we shall trace the history of the feudal kingdoms through the formative period of the tenth
and the first half of the eleventh centuries. It
was a stormy and chaotic period, the "iron
age" of feudalism. Wars, private feuds, rebellions, acts of violence and oppression were so
common as to be considered the normal state
of society. The menace of the Northmen subsided early in the tenth century, but the wild
Magyars from the Hungarian plains continued
to add the terror of barbarian raids to the
other perils of that turbulent age. In each of
the kingdoms, the monarchs struggled desperately and with varying success to control their
independent and warlike vassals and to establish royal authority. In Germany, during this
period, the kings were more successful than
elsewhere, gradually gathering the reins of
government into their own hands and suppressing the great nobles. In the second half of the
tenth century, they extended their rule to Italy
and refounded the empire. We may end our
study of them, for the time being, with the
death of Henry III in 1056, under whom the
imperial authority reached its greatest height.

In France, this period includes the century-
long struggle between the Carolingian and
Robertian families for the royal title, and the
founding of the Capetian dynasty in 987. During all this time the French kings were waging
a losing battle against the feudal lords. In
England this century and a half saw the uniting
of England under the descendants of Alfred the
Great, the second Danish conquest, the re-
establishment of Anglo-Saxon rule, and finally
the Norman Conquest, which introduced a new
era in the year 1066.

1. Germany, Italy, and the
Holy Roman Empire

The tribal duchies. Feudalism in Germany
during the tenth century was at once better
organized and more decentralized than in
France. This was due to the existence of the
great tribal duchies. The population of Germany was less mixed than that of Gaul, and
the ancient tribes had maintained something of
their old national traditions and coherence
under their own hereditary dukes. Toward
these tribal dukes the people felt a more direct
loyalty than they would have accorded to mere

163

feudal superiors. Each of the five great duchies, Saxony, Bavaria, Franconia, Swabia, and Lorraine[1] (the "stem" duchies, as they were called), formed a feudal state within the kingdom. The chief problem confronting the tenth- and eleventh-century monarchs was to control the duchies. Without such control, the king was powerless outside his own lands; with it, he had a more effective government than he would have had without the tribal organization. Even in the duchies, however, the disintegrating forces of feudalism were at work. The lesser nobles fought for independence of the dukes as the dukes sought independence of the king. Many of them succeeded in transferring their allegiance from their duke to the king, thus weakening the duchies, but adding little strength to the monarchy, since their very numbers made it difficult for the king to control them. The weakening of the monarchy after Henry III was at least partly due to the breaking-up of the duchies into smaller units.

Conrad I.   When the German branch of the Carolingian line ended with the death of Louis the Child in 911, the dukes and other magnates of Germany gathered to elect a new king. They chose Duke Conrad of Franconia (911–18). The nobles felt that it was necessary to have a king, but they were not prepared to surrender any of their authority to him. As a result, the royal title carried with it little more than honor — and none too much of that. As king, Conrad's authority scarcely extended beyond his own duchy. Realizing that the king, to make his rule effective, must have the support of more than one duchy, Conrad planned to improve conditions in the next reign. Before his death he made his son promise to give up his own claims to the crown in favor of his rival Henry, Duke of Saxony, and thereafter to support his government. Such at least is the story told by the contemporary chronicler, Widukind.

Henry I.   As a result Henry I, called Henry the Fowler, was elected in 919 and founded a dynasty that lasted for more than a century. Backed by Franconia as well as his own duchy of Saxony, Henry was able to force the other dukes to at least nominal submission. His success in defending the eastern frontiers against

barbarian invaders, too, added considerably to his prestige. He defeated and drove back the heathen Wends — the Slavic people to the east of the Elbe — and the Hungarians, who were ravaging the central part of Germany. Henry also forced the Duke of Bohemia to recognize him as overlord. On his death, Germany was still little more than a federation of duchies, but he had laid the foundation on which his brilliant son, Otto, was to build a stronger kingdom.

Otto the Great.   All the dukes concurred in the election of Otto I (936–73) and did homage to the new king. Almost immediately, however, his attempts to establish an effective authority over the dukes drove them into revolt. Within the next two years he had to suppress serious rebellions in Bavaria, Franconia, and his own duchy of Saxony, as well as to defend Lorraine against an alliance of its duke with the King of France. Following these revolts, Otto strove to bind the duchies more closely to himself by granting them to his own kinsmen and by making marriage alliances between his relatives and members of the ducal houses. This policy was none too successful even in his own lifetime, and it could have no permanent value. Even a king of so commanding a personality as the great Otto could not always depend on his kinsmen, and he had to put down another widespread and dangerous rebellion in 953–54. Rather more successful was his policy, followed by most of his successors for a century, of granting large tracts of land and great administrative powers to the archbishops and bishops. While still permitting the clergy to elect these officers in the usual manner, he reserved the right of approval and to all practical intents and purposes chose them himself. To make sure of their loyalty, he invested them not only with their fiefs, but also with the symbols of their ecclesiastical office. He thus surrounded himself with powerful and loyal vassals who, because of the rule of clerical celibacy, could not leave legitimate heirs and therefore could not establish an hereditary claim to their fiefs. For generations these ecclesiastical princes formed the strongest support of the monarchy. In these various ways, Otto gradually extended and consolidated the royal authority. Meanwhile, he was continuing his father's work in defending his eastern frontiers

---

[1] See map, page 165.

NORTH SEA

BALTIC SEA

POMERANIA

FRIESLAND

Hamburg

Bremen

NORD MARK

SAXONY

Brunswick

Hildesheim

Magdeburg

Goslar

Elbe

Oder

Vistula

POLAND

Aachen

Cologne

Liége

LOWER LORRAINE

Frankfurt

FRANCONIA

Prague

BOHEMIA

MORAVIA

Trier

Mainz

Nürnberg

F R A N C E

UPPER LORRAINE

Rhine

SWABIA

BAVARIA

Augsburg

Danube

AUSTRIA

Salzburg

TYROL

STYRIA

H U N G A R Y

K. OF BURGUNDY

Milan

LOMBARDY

CARNIOLA

Venice

Po

Genoa

Ravenna

Rhône

Avignon

Pisa

Florence

TUSCANY

PAPAL

STATES

A D R I A T I C   S E A

CORSICA

Rome

SARDINIA

NORMAN KINGDOM OF SICILY

MEDITERRANEAN

SEA

The Holy Roman Empire about 1050

The Emperor Otto III, enthroned and holding the symbols of imperial power, the scepter and orb, is flanked on his right by clerics and on his left by lay nobles. The painting comes from a tenth-century manuscript.

and conquering his heathen neighbors, thus laying the foundation for the permanent extension of Germanic rule and Christianity to the east. Still more important, he administered a crushing defeat to the Hungarian invaders near Augsburg in 955. Thereafter they ceased to trouble the western kingdoms.

Revival of the empire. Like Charlemagne, Otto kept an interested eye on Italy. This country had been for half a century in a condition of utter anarchy. The Lombard kings in the north were powerless against the great nobles; and in the central district, the Papal States, Roman nobles dominated the feeble popes and used the power of the papacy for their own ends. The country was ripe for conquest. In 951, Otto invaded Italy on the pretext of rescuing Queen Adelaide, the widow of the former king of Italy, who was being imprisoned and mistreated by her husband's successor, Berengar II. The expedition was successful so far as it went. Otto defeated Berengar and married the beautiful Adelaide, but was recalled

to Germany by a rebellion there. He contented himself for the time with forcing Berengar to recognize him as his overlord. Ten years later he again invaded Italy. This time he deposed Berengar and proclaimed himself king, as Charlemagne had done. Still following in the footsteps of the great Carolingian, he proceeded to Rome where, in February, 962, he was crowned emperor by Pope John XII.

Theory of empire. The Holy Roman Empire, founded by Otto the Great, was considered to be a revival of the Carolingian Empire, just as the latter in turn had been regarded as a continuation of the ancient Roman Empire. The new empire, however, was in reality quite different from its predecessor, as Charlemagne's empire had been different from that of the Caesars. Yet the theory which underlay and motivated the revival of the Roman Empire in the tenth century was much the same as that which brought it about in the year 800. Medieval people had inherited two great traditions from Roman antiquity — a universal empire and a universal church. The latter had survived, and was incomplete without its secular counterpart. In an age when men thought customarily in terms of logic and theology, it seemed essential that there should be a universal secular ruler who, like the pope, had received his authority directly from God. Such a ruler would be at once the protector and servant of the church, the secular counterpart of the pope, with different but parallel powers over all Christians. Feudal theory, too, fitted vaguely into this conception. There should be some one ultimate overlord from whom the various kings held their land in fief. The condition of anarchy prevailing generally throughout Europe made men long for some strong, divinely appointed ruler. In actual fact, the emperors were far from being universal rulers. Though they were recognized as of higher rank than the kings, their government was never extended beyond the two kingdoms of Germany and Italy, which Otto already held before his coronation, and Burgundy, which was added in the next century. The imperial title brought Otto no additional power, and future emperors were to pay dearly for that empty honor. The theory of the empire bound them to a close partnership with the papacy, which in time led to a disastrous struggle for supremacy with popes who were stronger than they.[1] Moreover, the imperial title committed them to an inevitably unsuccessful attempt to rule both Germany and Italy. As a result they finally lost what real power they would have had as kings of Germany had they concentrated their attention there instead of trying to extend their government over an alien and unwilling people, divided from Germany by the towering barrier of the Alps.

Otto II and Otto III.   The dangers inherent in the imperial claims were demonstrated in the reigns of Otto's son and grandson. The intervention of Otto the Great in Italy had been no more than an episode in his brilliant career. His power rested solidly on his control of the German Kingdom. Both Otto II (973–83) and Otto III (983–1002) wasted the results of his labor by following the lure of empire into Italy. Otto III, especially, neglected Germany in his attempt to realize a vain though glorious dream of restoring the ancient Roman Empire. He was but three years old when his father's death at Rome left him heir to three crowns. His mother, a Greek princess named Theophano, educated him in the Byzantine tradition, and as he grew up his tutor, the great French scholar, diplomat, and Archbishop of Reims, Gerbert, impressed his

1 See below, Chapter 15.

mind still further with the glorious legend of the ancient empire. Otto III made Rome the capital of his empire and exercised a strict control over the papacy, nominating three popes in succession, the last of whom was Gerbert (Sylvester II). He died in his twenty-second year, having lost control of Germany and with Italy rising in revolt about him.

Henry II and Conrad II.   The next two emperors, wiser than the erratic Otto III, turned their attention to the slow and difficult task of rebuilding royal authority in Germany and re-establishing peace and order. Henry II (1002–24), a great-nephew of Otto I, was a pious, well-educated, and conscientious monarch. He depended very largely on the support of the great ecclesiastical lords, the bishops whom he himself had chosen and invested with their offices. He gave them still more land and administrative authority, and with their aid gradually suppressed the rebellious lay nobles. On his death the crown passed to Conrad II (1024–39), Duke of Franconia, who founded a new dynasty. One event of Conrad's reign is of outstanding importance. In 1032, he fell heir to the kingdom of Burgundy, which thereafter was part of the Holy Roman Empire. It lay in the valley of the Rhône, including what is now part of eastern France and western Switzerland. It must not be confused with the duchy of Burgundy, which lay to the northwest of it and was a fief of France.

In this miniature from a contemporary manuscript, Christ crowns the Emperor Henry II and the Empress Kunigunde while St. Peter and St. Paul stand as witnesses. Actually they were crowned by the pope.

Henry III. Due to the work of these two emperors, Henry III (1039–56), the son of Conrad II, was able to gain a more complete control of Germany than had been possible for any previous emperor. So great was his power, indeed, that he was able to extend it successfully to Italy. Here the papacy had again fallen into a state of degradation in the hands of unworthy popes. In 1046 there were three rival popes at Rome, to the scandal of the faithful throughout Europe. As emperor, and therefore protector of the church, Henry claimed the right to depose these men who were disgracing the holy office. In their place, he secured the election of a series of reforming popes, the most important of whom was an earnest and high-minded German bishop who took the title Leo IX (1049–54). Emperor and pope now worked together for the reform, not only of the papacy, but of the whole church. It was a valuable and necessary work, but it had unfortunate after-effects for the empire. Henry succeeded in so strengthening the papal power that future popes were able to engage in a bitter and partially successful struggle with his son Henry IV for supremacy. But that is another story.

2. *France*

Robertians and Carolingians. In the Western Frankish Kingdom, which became the kingdom of France, the century following the death of Charles the Fat and the dissolution of the Carolingian Empire was one of turmoil and disintegration — disintegration of the kingdom and also of the larger fiefs — and of the most chaotic development of feudalism. Across the blurred pages of French history in this age pass the shadowy figures of the Robertian and Carolingian kings, good and able men some of them, but frustrated at every turn by the independence of their unruly vassals. Of these two royal families, the Carolingians depended chiefly on the traditional loyalty of the people to their house and on the respect of the clergy for the consecrated descendants of the great Charles. The Robertians, so called because they were descended from Robert the Strong, Count of Paris, had no long-established hereditary claim to the royal title and had therefore to depend on their personal ability and on their strength as the most powerful feudal family in France. For a full century after the deposition of Charles the Fat, Robertian and Carolingian kings alternated on the throne until the Carolingian line finally came to an end with the death of Louis V in 987. The next king, Hugh Capet, belonged to the Robertian family, but he has generally been regarded as the founder of a new dynasty which bore his name.

First Capetian kings. The election of Hugh Capet (987–96), then, marks the beginning of the famous Capetian dynasty. For over three centuries his descendants passed the crown on in unbroken succession from father to son, gradually changing the elective kingship to one clearly hereditary. During that period the average length of reign was nearly thirty years. The story of how the Capetians used their dual position as kings and feudal lords to increase their royal authority will be told in Chapter 16. For the present, however, they were merely nominal overlords of the feudal kingdom, actually less powerful than many of their vassals. Hugh Capet had been forced to give away a considerable part of his lands as bribes to secure his election. What little additional power he acquired through the royal title did not compensate for that loss. As king his authority scarcely extended beyond his own family land, shrunk now to a narrow strip of territory running north and south through central France, with Paris at its center. This was the beginning of the so-called Île de France, the land over which the king was the immediate lord. Hugh's successors, Robert II (996–1031) and Henry I (1031–60), were unable to control even this small territory. Unruly vassals, secure behind the walls of their fortified castles, defied the kings in their own domain. Throughout the remainder of the kingdom, the nobles went their independent way with no more than lip service to the king.

The great fiefs. Feudalism in France was less well organized than in Germany. There were no tribal duchies, unless Normandy with its Scandinavian tribal feeling might be so designated. There were innumerable great and petty fiefs, whose boundaries and interrelations shifted constantly with the shifts of family fortune. To draw a map of feudal France in the eleventh century would have been a superhuman task even for a contemporary, and, in any case, it would not have remained accurate for any length of time. There were, however, a few great fiefs which remained fairly constant, though tending to disintegrate as the subvassals became more independent.[1] To the north of the Île de France lay the half-independent counties of Vermandois and Flanders; to the west the great duchies of Normandy and Brittany and the rich counties of Anjou and Maine; to the east were the county of Champagne and the duchy of Burgundy. Southern France was far beyond the reach of the eleventh-century kings, and separated from the north by radical differences of language and culture. The largest fief here — and for that matter the largest in France — was the duchy of Aquitaine, which stretched right across the country south of the Loire. The dukes of Aquitaine occupied an almost royal position in southern France, but, like the Capetian kings, they had very little real power over their vassals. To the south of Aquitaine lay the duchy of Gascony and the county of Toulouse. Most of these great fiefs were as large as the royal domain. What chance had the king to assert his authority over such powerful vassals?

3. *Saxon England*

England united. While feudal kingdoms were being formed on the Continent from the wrecks of the Carolingian Empire, a united Anglo-Saxon kingdom was taking shape in the island across the Channel. By 954 the reconquest of the Danelaw [2] had been completed and the descendants of Alfred, the great King of Wessex, became in fact kings of England. The Danish conquest was in the long run a blessing to England, although at the time very effectively disguised, for it made possible the unification of the whole kingdom under a stronger monarchy and with a more systematic administration than had existed in the old Saxon kingdoms.

Government in Saxon England. The new English kingdom was not a feudal kingdom. Although it contained elements of feudalism, the king had more effective authority. His power, indeed, was limited only by his dependence on the support of the nobles who made up his council, the "Witan," with whom he was bound to consult on all important matters. For purposes of local government, the kingdom was divided into shires. This system, begun in Wessex, was introduced into the rest of England after the conquest of the Danelaw. It was retained by the Normans after they conquered England, and it has remained to the present the basic structure of English local government. The principal officer of each shire was the earl, usually a great noble, who was commander of the shire militia and who occupied a position similar to that of the Carolingian counts, showing a like feudal tendency to regard his office as an independent hereditary right. Royal authority was represented more directly by a less exalted but more useful officer, the sheriff, who took over more and more of the actual administration of the shire. He collected the rents due to the king from the royal estates and the fines assessed in the shire courts. He was also responsible for maintaining order and enforcing justice. Under both the Saxon and, later, the Norman kings, the sheriffs furnished a link between central and local government, between the king and his humbler subjects, that had no parallel in the early feudal kingdoms on the Continent. The shire court was an important institution of local government, which lasted through the period of Norman feudalism and had a permanent effect on the growth of English governmental and judicial practice. This was a periodic assembly of the more important landowners and freemen of the shire, presided over by the sheriff, in which administrative business was carried out and both criminal and civil cases were judged, the final judgment being given by the members of the assembly. Similar courts for less important cases were also held in each "hundred," the smaller areas into which the shire was divided for purely local affairs.

The second Danish conquest. The story of the last century of Anglo-Saxon England can be told very briefly. The second half of the tenth century was a period of unusual peace and restored prosperity. The church and the monarchy worked closely together, to their mutual advantage. The moral and educational standards of the monks and the clergy were raised by the efforts of the kings in cooperation

[1] See map, page 196.
[2] See above, page 150.

with Dunstan, the reforming Archbishop of Canterbury, and in turn the clergy gave their full support to the royal government. But the welfare of the kingdom depended on the character of the king, and at the end of the century England was left at the mercy of one of the most incompetent rulers in all its long history. The weak and misguided government of Ethelred the Redeless, i.e., the helpless (978–1016), so called because of his notable lack of common sense, aroused factional strife within the kingdom and opened the way to a new Danish conquest of England, completed by the Danish King Canute in 1017. This second Danish conquest meant no such mass migration into England as had the first conquest in the ninth century. It was little more than a political revolution — the replacing of a Saxon by a Danish king — and it left no very lasting impression on the development of England. After Canute's death in 1035, the line of Danish kings lasted for only a few years, dying out in 1042. The English were then free to return to their own native royal family.

Saxon restoration. After some indecision, the Witan bestowed the crown upon Ethelred's son Edward (1042–66), later called "the Confessor." He was a pious and peace-loving man, fitted by neither character nor training for his position. He had spent nearly all his life in exile in Normandy and was far more Norman than English in his sympathies and interests. He surrounded himself with Norman favorites, to whom he gave high offices in church and state, thus opening the way to Norman influence in England. The Saxon

nobles naturally resented this preferment of foreigners and, on occasion, expressed their resentment in open rebellion. Feudalism had been growing steadily during the recent troubled times when men could not depend on the king for protection. As on the Continent, the increasing power and independence of the nobles meant the weakening of royal authority.

The Norman Conquest. In January of the fateful year 1066, King Edward died, leaving no immediate heirs. The country needed a strong king, and one whose interests would be purely English. The Witan, therefore, gave the crown to Earl Harold of Wessex, as the strongest man in England, though not of the blood royal. His election did not go unchallenged. Across the Channel in Normandy, Duke William cast covetous eyes on the English throne. He was a distant relative of Edward the Confessor, and claimed that both Edward and Harold had acknowledged his right to the succession. His case was strengthened by the charge that Harold had broken a solemn vow to support him. Moreover, he was given the blessing and moral support of the pope, whom Harold had antagonized by exiling the Archbishop of Canterbury from England for political reasons. William was no mean antagonist, for Normandy had become the strongest duchy

William the Conqueror as depicted in the Bayeux tapestry.

in France in the century and a half since its foundation, and was now almost an independent state. Though French in speech and manners, the Normans still possessed the wandering instincts and the vigorous, adventurous spirit of their Viking ancestors. In the late summer of 1066, William crossed the Channel with an army of adventurers and landed near Hastings on the southern coast. King Harold, who had just defeated an invading army of Danes in the north, rushed south to meet him. The two armies met at Hastings in a hard-fought battle that decided the fate of England for centuries. The Saxons were defeated. That in itself might not have been fatal to their cause, but Harold and his brothers had fallen, and England was left without a leader. On

Mounted Norman knights are shown charging the Saxon foot soldiers at the battle of Hastings in this scene from the Bayeux tapestry. The famous tapestry, 230 feet long, tells the story of the Norman conquest of England.

Christmas Day, William the Conqueror was crowned king, and a new era in English history had opened. Thereafter, England, with a population still about ninety-nine per cent Anglo-Saxon, was to be ruled by a dominant minority of Norman and French conquerors. This small group could not materially change the racial stock of England; but they could, and did, introduce new elements of language and culture, together with new forms of government and administration, from the Continent.

THE HIGH MIDDLE AGES

Typical of Gothic sculpture are these four saints that
stand in the south portal of the cathedral of
Chartres. The statue on the right, clothed in chain
mail, represents the warrior saint, St. George.

c. 1050–c. 1270)

By about the middle of the eleventh century, western Europe had passed the first stage in its slow development of a new civilization. The wild days of tribal migrations and Viking raids had passed, as well as the most unsettled age of feudalism. Christianity had spread north and east to include all the German and Scandinavian peoples; the empire of Charlemagne had given place to feudal kingdoms and the Holy Roman Empire; and the reformed papacy was emerging from a period of weakness and degradation to assert its authority over all western Christendom. Everywhere there were signs of awakening energy, of spiritual and intellectual growth. Not all the causes of this great revival can be discerned. The most basic factor, however, was undoubtedly the reopening of trade with the Middle East and the growth of regular commerce along all the trade routes of western Europe. Reviving commerce brought old cities back to life and created new ones; and in these cities dwelt a growing class of merchants and artisans, who were neither noble nor peasant, a class new to feudal society. From the fruitful interchange of goods between the cities and the countryside, a new prosperity and the use of money spread as a vitalizing force throughout western Christendom, bringing with it new opportunities for social and cultural progress.

The period that followed the middle years of the eleventh century, a period of a little more than two centuries, witnessed the full development of that type of civilization which we think of as characteristically medieval. We shall call it the period of the High Middle Ages. It saw the long struggle between the empire and the papacy, the growth of royal authority in France and Norman England, the perennial warfare of Christian crusaders against the infidel, the expansion of Christian Europe into the Slavic lands to the east and into Moslem Spain, the rise of the papacy to the highest peak of its power and the full development of the church as a strongly organized universal institution, the revival of education, and the rise of the universities. It was a period of vivid life and restless energy, held within the framework of a more or less stable and integrated society. Above all, it was the great age of the *Respublica Christiana*, when all nations of western Europe formed parts of the commonwealth of united Christendom.

15

The Struggle Between the Empire and the Papacy

FOR NEARLY A CENTURY, from the imperial coronation of Otto the Great to the death of Henry III, the emperors were the dominant members of the papal-imperial partnership which claimed universal rule over all Christendom. Vigorous emperors of the Saxon and Franconian dynasties had patiently built up a strong monarchy in Germany in opposition to the independent interests of the nobles; they had asserted a spasmodic control over northern and central Italy; and they had more than once attempted to reform the papacy by deposing weak and unworthy popes and replacing them with men of character and ability. The popes, on the other hand, though strong in theoretical claims, were generally powerless to enforce their authority over the whole church, or even to maintain their independence from control by secular powers. Dominated by the unruly nobles and populace of Rome, they were rescued by the emperors only to fall under their more powerful control. The whole church, in fact, seemed dominated by worldly interests. The administrative officers of the church, the bishops and others, were so inextricably entangled in the feudal system that they could give no more than formal obedience to the pope, and often enough they took no more than a formal interest in their spiritual duties.

It was, indeed, a dark age for the church, reflecting the evils of a turbulent and disorganized feudal society. But there were signs of returning spring in this winter of the church's discontent. There was a rapidly growing demand for reform in many places, and the purification of the papacy under Henry III made Rome the center of the reform movement. Thereafter, for more than two centuries, the popes strove to strengthen the papacy and the church by freeing them from outside influence. This inevitably brought the papacy into conflict with all secular governments, for the attempt to gain independence soon forced the popes to claim supremacy over all worldly powers. It was with the emperors, however, whose empire included Italy and who shared with the popes a claim to universal rule, that the struggle for supremacy was most bitter and prolonged, ending only with the destruction of imperial authority. This conflict between the empire and the papacy is the central theme which gives continuity to the history of Germany and Italy throughout the High Middle Ages.

1. The Investiture Controversy

Minority of Henry IV. The death of Henry III in the prime of life was a disaster from which the empire never fully recovered. The centrifugal forces favoring local independence in Germany and Italy could be held in check only by the most alert watchfulness and by constant pressure on the part of the emperor.

174

With Henry's death that pressure was removed for a fateful period. Henry had planned to save the empire from the dangers of a disputed election and to confirm the hereditary principle of succession by having his infant son crowned king while he himself was still alive. Henry IV (1056–1106) thus succeeded peacefully to the throne, but at barely six years of age. For the next thirteen years, until the young emperor-elect took active control of the government, anarchy ran riot. Neither his mother, who acted as regent till 1062, nor the faction of ecclesiastical and lay nobles who then seized the government and the guardianship of the young monarch, could maintain the pressure necessary to preserve imperial authority in either Germany or Italy.

Germany. In Germany, the nobles, who were technically royal officials responsible for local government, had actually acquired a hereditary right to their offices and lands, and hence were ever ready to assert their independence of royal control. More and more the emperor was forced to rely for aid and counsel in peace or war on his great ecclesiastical vassals, the bishops and abbots. These the emperors had generously endowed with land, since their fiefs could not be made hereditary. They were still royal officers and it was tremendously important to the central government to secure the election of men who would be loyal to the emperor. The German towns, too, most of which were ruled by bishops, were usually loyal. But these supporters of the monarchy were useless unless led by a strong emperor.

Imperial Italy. Even more in Italy than in Germany the imperial authority depended on the constant activity of a vigorous ruler. It almost disappeared during the minority of Henry IV. In Lombardy, numerous towns, growing rapidly under the first impulse of reviving trade, were beginning to yearn for independence and were growing restless under the rule of their bishops, who represented the imperial government. Milan was especially restless. There the citizens gained a powerful ally in the pope by protesting against the emperor's interference in the election of their archbishop, thus giving a coloring of religious reform to their revolt. In central Italy the imperial problem was further complicated by the pope's claims to secular rule over the Papal States, dating back to the eighth-century Donation of Pepin.

The Normans in Italy. In the southern part of the peninsula and in Sicily a new menace to imperial rule in Italy had been slowly rising, to grow strong during the minority of Henry IV. Here, until recently, there had been a number of little independent states — Lombard, Byzantine, and Moslem — none of them strong enough seriously to trouble the emperors, though all attempts to conquer them had failed. In 1016, a band of Norman knights landed at Salerno on their way home from a pilgrimage and discovered the possibilities for fighting and plunder offered by the frequent wars between the rival states. Thereafter each year brought more adventurers of the reckless Norman breed, eager to fish in the troubled waters of southern Italy. In the course of time, as their numbers increased, their leaders built up small states of their own. At the opening of the reign of Henry IV, Robert Guiscard, perfect type of the Norman conqueror, dominated most of southern Italy. He was the terror of the native populations of the south and a constant menace to imperial Italy. In 1059 Pope Nicholas II invested him with land, and Robert replied by doing homage to the pope and assuming a vassal's obligation to protect him. By thus aiding in the establishment of a strong Norman state to the south, the pope hoped to free himself from the necessity of depending on the emperor for defense and, at the same time, to acquire an armed ally to use against him if necessary. Here, as elsewhere in Italy, the hostile attitude of the papacy was to prove the most serious obstacle to the re-establishment of imperial domination.

The Cluniac reform. The opposition of the popes to Henry IV grew out of a movement for the reform of the church, which had been active for some time before it gained weight at Rome. It had originated as a monastic reform in the Burgundian monastery of Cluny. This monastery, since its foundation in 910, had been exempt from the rule of the local bishop. Its abbot owned no superior except the pope. Under a series of able and pious abbots, it acquired a great reputation for holiness and strict observance of the monastic rules. It was joined by a number of other monasteries, new and old, in all parts of Europe, all of which were under

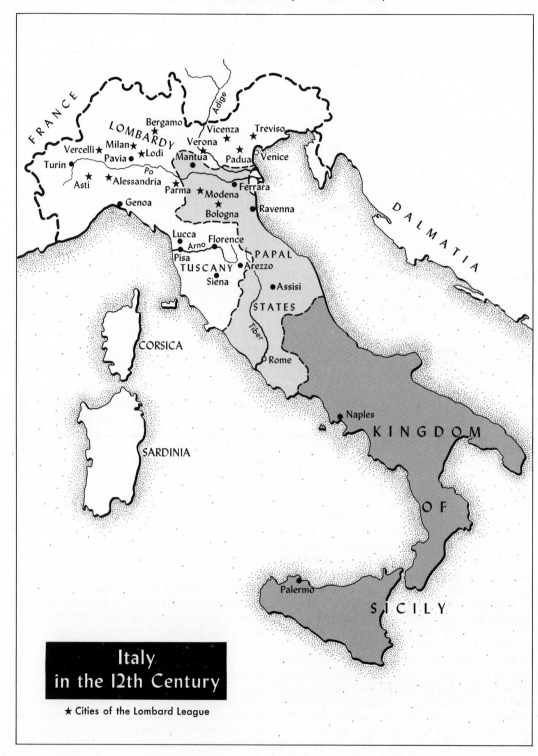

FRANCE

LOMBARDY

Bergamo
Vicenza
Treviso
Vercelli ★ Milan ★
Verona
Turin ● ★ Lodi
Pavia ● Po
Mantua
Padua
Venice
★ Asti ★ Alessandria
Parma ★
Modena ★
Ferrara
Genoa ●
Bologna ★
Ravenna

Lucca ●
Florence
Arno ●
Pisa
PAPAL
TUSCANY ● Arezzo
Siena ●
STATES
● Assisi

Adige

DALMATIA

CORSICA

Tiber

Rome

SARDINIA

Naples ●

KINGDOM

OF

Palermo ●

SICILY

Italy in the 12th Century

★ Cities of the Lombard League

the rule of the abbot of Cluny. This "congregation" of monasteries was a new departure in monastic organization. Through it the demand for reform, not only of the monasteries but also of the whole church, gained a wide hearing. The pious Emperor Henry III and his appointee Pope Leo IX took up the reform movement under papal direction, but with the emperor still in full control.

Hildebrand's reform program. After the death of Henry III, a succession of reforming popes carried on the work, but no longer in cooperation with the emperor. During all this time, till he himself was elected pope as Gregory VII, the monk Hildebrand was the most active agent of reform at Rome, the power behind the papal throne. It was he who formulated most perfectly the program for reform and finally put it into effect. The spiritual character of the church had suffered greatly through its close connection with feudal politics and worldly interests. The majority of the higher clergy were little more than royal officers or feudal barons, while the morals of all ranks of the clergy had degenerated deplorably. Any attempt to raise the general spiritual level of Christendom must begin with a reform of these blind leaders of the blind, to whom the care of souls was entrusted. This, as Hildebrand saw it, could be accomplished only by restoring papal authority and by preventing laymen, whether nobles or kings, from influencing the choice of ecclesiastical officers. Thus only could the church be emancipated from secular control and be left free to perform its true duties. The reformers concentrated at first on the suppression of two abuses: first, simony, that is to say, the sale of church offices or bribery in church elections (so called from Simon Magus who had attempted to buy the gift of the Holy Spirit from St. Peter); and second, the marriage of the clergy, which though commonly practiced was contrary to church law. Simony was often the means by which outsiders influenced clerical elections, while the marriage of the clergy tempted them to give more attention to providing for their children (often at the expense of the church) than to their religious duties. Further, the papacy must itself be freed from outside influence, especially from control by the emperor. It was for this reason that Nicholas II made his alliance with the Normans in 1059, and the same year issued the Election Decree, providing for the free and independent choice of future popes by the college of cardinals.

Gregory VII and lay investiture. When Hildebrand ascended the chair of St. Peter as Gregory VII (1073–85), the reform program was given a new impetus and wider scope. The character of Gregory dominates the history of Europe in these years. From a peasant home he had risen by sheer force of character and ability to the most important office in Christendom. Small and unprepossessing in appearance, he yet commanded respect by his integrity and the burning zeal that threatened to consume his frail body. He had an iron will and was inspired by an unshakable determination to do what he considered right for the church. For two years he strove without much success to force the bishops, especially of Germany and northern Italy, to strict obedience. Then, in 1075, he published the first papal decree definitely forbidding lay investiture. It had long been the recognized right of the feudal overlord of a bishop or abbot to invest him with the insignia of his fief, just as he would any other vassal. The insignia representing an ecclesiastical fief, however, had a spiritual significance, and the pope now claimed that no layman had the right to bestow them. There was, of course, more than a mere question of symbols involved. The right to confer the investiture carried with it the right to refuse it, and so to cancel the election of an unsatisfactory candidate. Gregory's prohibition of lay investiture struck at the heart of secular control over the church. It was bound to precipitate an open conflict with the emperor, for Henry IV was now of age and determined to recover his father's authority. Other rulers might compromise; the emperor could not afford to. More than any other ruler in Europe, the emperor depended on the support of his ecclesiastical vassals. To give up the right to choose them would have crippled his power beyond hope of repair, leaving him at the mercy of rebellious lay nobles. The crux of the difficulty lay in the fact that the loyalty and obedience of the bishops was of vital importance both to the pope as head of the church and to the emperor as ruler of the state.

Rival claims to supremacy. This practical issue brought to the fore the broader and more serious problem of supremacy, which had all along been present in the theory of the Holy Roman Empire, waiting only for an open conflict between a strong pope and a determined emperor to be brought out into the open. The emperor admitted the universal spiritual authority of the pope, while the pope, in turn, admitted the universal secular authority of the emperor. They had parallel powers, both divinely ordained. But in case of conflict, which had the higher authority? History favored both equally. The popes had always given the crown to the emperors, but the emperors, including the pious Henry III, as guardians of the church had frequently deposed bad popes and had chosen their successors. Faced by the necessity of establishing his supremacy in order to force the emperor to do his will regarding the investitures and other reform measures, Gregory took an exalted stand, asserting that, as the soul is more important than the body, so the spiritual is higher than the secular authority. Moreover, as the successor of St. Peter, the pope is responsible to God for the souls of all men, including kings, and it is his duty to admonish a wicked ruler and, if he is unrepentant, to free his subjects from their allegiance lest they, too, be led astray. With Gregory, the papal claim to supremacy may

have been largely a means to a practical end, but he nevertheless stated it firmly.

Gregory VII and Henry IV. Henry's attempts to re-establish imperial authority in Italy had already caused a breach with the papacy before Gregory was elected, but a rebellion in Saxony in 1073 forced him to make peace with the new pope. Henry did not re-open the conflict until two years later when he had restored peace in Germany. He then challenged the pope by investing his own candidate with the archbishopric of Milan, to which Gregory replied with the decree against lay investiture. With the aid of his bishops, most of whom were loyal and also opposed to the pope's strict reforms, Henry took the offensive and declared Gregory deposed. But he had reckoned without the restless lay nobles. When the pope replied by excommunicating the emperor and freeing his subjects from their oath of allegiance, many of the German nobles took the opportunity to rebel. Again Henry was forced to conciliate the pope in order to have a free hand against rebellion at home. Hastening to Italy, he sought out the pope in the castle of the Countess of Tuscany at Canossa in January, 1077. He pleaded for absolution as a penitent sinner, a plea that the pope, as a priest, could not refuse, especially when the

The pope is bestowing the crown upon the emperor in this thirteenth-century mosaic in the chapel of St. Sylvester, Rome.

emperor, as Gregory himself recounts, showed his contrition by standing for three days barefoot in the snow before the barred gates of the castle. The absolution of Henry, freeing him from the ban of excommunication, caused a strong reaction in his favor. The pious returned to their allegiance and the insurgent nobles lost their excuse for rebellion. Nevertheless, the emperor had set a dangerous precedent in his dramatic recognition of the pope's spiritual authority, a precedent that was to have more influence on later generations than in his own day. Still, it was an immediate victory for the emperor, though the disaffected nobles persisted in their rebellion and elected Rudolf, Duke of Swabia, as an anti-king.

Defeat of Gregory VII. It was the pope who reopened hostilities. Henry had continued to invest his ecclesiastical vassals, and in 1080 Gregory took the decisive step of definitely deposing him and recognizing Rudolf in his place. This time general public opinion was against the pope. He was the aggressor and it was generally considered that he had exceeded his powers. With the aid of German and Italian clergy, Henry deposed him and procured the election of an anti-pope. The emperor then besieged Rome and entered it in 1084. There he was crowned by the anti-pope Clement III. Gregory was forced to flee to his Norman allies in the south and died in exile.

The struggle continues. Gregory's successors, especially Urban II (1088–99), continued his program of reform and his struggle with the emperor. They were generally recognized in the lands outside the empire where reform had been effected without so much conflict. Henry's anti-pope was accepted only where the emperor could enforce obedience. Yet the schism (the split in the church between the adherents of the rival popes) continued until the emperor's death. Henry's life ended in tragedy. His last years were embittered by the treachery and rebellion of his son Henry, in alliance with the papal party.

Henry V. With the accession of Henry V (1106–25), the schism was ended and for a time pope and emperor were at peace. But the new emperor was no more ready than his father had been to give up the control of ecclesiastical elections, of which lay investiture was the symbol. Through the reigns of three popes

R̄ex rogat abbatem. Mathildim supplicat atqꝫ

The humiliation of Henry IV at Canossa made a strong impression on his contemporaries. Here the emperor is shown on his knees begging Countess Mathilda of Tuscany and the Abbot of Cluny to intercede for him with Pope Gregory VII. The miniature is from a manuscript life of Mathilda in the Vatican Library.

the controversy continued, often accompanied by violence. At last, worn out by the long strife, both parties agreed to settle the investiture question by a compromise, arranged at Worms in 1122.

Concordat of Worms. According to the Concordat of Worms, signed by both emperor and pope, bishops and abbots were to be invested by the emperor with the insignia of their secular office only (that is, their fief), not with the ring and the staff which symbolized their spiritual authority. In Germany the investiture was to precede consecration and the emperor was to be represented at elections. This left him still in practical control. In Burgundy and Italy, however, where the emperor had lost real authority, the imperial investiture was to follow consecration, and so was not a necessary preliminary to taking office. In France and England the question had already been settled by the monarch's giving up actual investiture, but retaining a dominant influence in elections. The emperor had retained what was most vital to him — control over the German clergy. But the compromise was really a papal victory. The emperor had given up a recognized right, while the pope had merely stopped short of the full assertion of his theoretical claims.

Papal gains. The papacy had, indeed, made great advances during the course of the controversy. The popes had strengthened their position as rulers of the international church and had made sweeping claims to universal authority. When the conflict with the emperors was revived, it was to be a struggle for supremacy, considered as an end in itself. Meanwhile, through his quarrel with the pope and the schism in the church, the Emperor Henry IV had lost a great opportunity in being unable to take his place as the leader of Christendom in the First Crusade, thereby surrendering that position to his opponent Pope Urban II.[1]

2. *The Struggle for Supremacy*

Welf and Hohenstaufen. During the three decades of uneasy peace between the empire and the papacy which followed the Concordat of Worms, the chief interest in German history centers in the rivalry of two great feudal families, the Welfs and the Hohenstaufens. Later this feud was to spread to Italy, where the party which favored the papacy and fought for local independence called themselves Guelfs from the German name Welf, while the imperial party were called Ghibellines from the German Waiblingen, the name of one of the Hohenstaufen family possessions. This Italian feud persisted for centuries, long after the rivalry of the two German families had subsided. The feud had its origin in 1125, when, on the death of Henry V without direct heirs, the nobles asserted their right to elect an emperor regardless of hereditary rights. Passing over Frederick of Hohenstaufen and his younger brother Conrad, nephews of Henry V, they chose a Saxon noble, Lothair III (1125–37), who had no shadow of hereditary claim. This election, incidentally, was a significant victory for the elective over the hereditary principle of succession. The Hohenstaufens were bitterly offended and were soon in open rebellion. They were thus brought into conflict with the Welfs, for Henry the Proud, head of that family, was the son-in-law and heir of Lothair. The rebellion was crushed, but the feud continued. By

the end of Lothair's reign, Henry the Proud was Duke of Bavaria, Saxony, and Swabia, and Count of Tuscany in Italy, in fact so powerful that the nobles feared he might dominate them too strongly if he were to become emperor. They therefore elected his rival, the Hohenstaufen Conrad III (1138–52). It was the Welfs who were now in opposition to the emperor, and throughout Conrad's reign Germany was kept in a turmoil. Innumerable family feuds and private wars added to the general anarchy. The disturbed state of the empire during the investiture controversy had given a new impetus to feudal independence. Strongly fortified castles had sprung up everywhere. Conrad's prestige was also shaken by his failure to accomplish anything in the Second Crusade. When he died, he left the imperial title almost completely stripped of its authority.

Frederick Barbarossa. The empire was rescued from disintegration by the next Hohenstaufen emperor, Frederick I, called Barbarossa (1152–90). From the first the new emperor inspired hope and confidence in all who longed for the restoration of peace, order, and strong government. Well-built, handsome, and genial, the red-bearded monarch charmed all who knew him. Frederick was, indeed, the perfect type of the chivalrous ruler of the Middle Ages. He was a first-class soldier, with a full-blooded love of battle, but he was also a just and conscientious monarch, bent on enforcing law and order in his harassed realm. In one respect only did he fail to appreciate the needs of his age. He failed to understand or to realize the importance of the growing commercial and industrial life in the towns. For feudal Germany, however, his reign marks an era of imperial authority and of comparative peace such as had not been seen for a century. The feud between Hohenstaufen and Welf was buried, to be resurrected for a brief period only toward the end of his long reign. Frederick was himself half Welf, a nephew of Henry the Proud through his mother, as of Conrad III through his father. The current head of the Welf family, his cousin Henry the Lion, Duke of Saxony and Bavaria, was his friend and comrade in arms for twenty years. Lesser feuds were suppressed, at least so long as the emperor was present in Germany, by the enforcing of a "land peace" forbidding private wars. Since, however, the emperor's activity could not be

[1] See below, page 204.

limited to Germany, his rule did not have as permanent results there as it might have had. He succeeded in re-establishing the overlordship of the emperor over his eastern neighbors, Poland, Bohemia, and Hungary. He also reasserted imperial authority in Burgundy, where it had long been ignored. Finally he strove to recover imperial control of Italy — there to meet the only failure of his career.

Frederick and the papacy. Frederick's first expedition into Italy in 1154–55, for the purpose of receiving the imperial crown, brought him face to face with two powers which were to unite in successful defiance of his authority — the papacy and the Lombard cities. With the former he was at first friendly enough, for the pope needed his aid against the citizens of Rome, who had tried to revive the ancient freedom of the city under the leadership of a reformer named Arnold of Brescia. Frederick showed his willingness to aid the pope by securing the execution of the heretical rebel before his own arrival in the papal city. The first meeting, however, between the ambitious emperor and the equally strong-minded and determined pope, Adrian IV (1154–59), proved that their friendship was no more than skin deep. Frederick haughtily refused to act as squire to the pope and to hold his bridle and stirrup. The two potentates almost parted in anger. Frederick finally submitted to what he considered an affront to the imperial dignity only when it was pointed out that there was ample precedent for the act.

Question of supremacy revived. Behind this apparently trifling incident lay the whole question of supremacy, which once more became a paramount issue. Both parties had greatly strengthened their theoretical claims since the days of Gregory VII, and the issue of supremacy as an end in itself was now more clearly stated. A host of writers on both sides had discussed the question thoroughly. The enthusiastic study of Roman law, which resulted from the great revival of learning during the twelfth century, afforded the emperor some telling arguments. Frederick based his claims to supremacy on historical precedent and on the Roman conception of the emperor's absolute authority. But the papacy, too, had been strengthening its claims by the development of a legal code, modeled after Roman law, based on the Scriptures and on the decrees of

Frederick Barbarossa and the Bishop of Freising are portrayed in a relief from the porch of the cathedral of Freising. The bishop, Otto of Freising, was the emperor's uncle and one of the greatest of medieval historians.

popes and councils. A full compilation of this "canon law" was completed during the reign of Conrad III by Gratian, a teacher of law at Bologna. It was known as the *Decretum* of Gratian. The church was rapidly becoming a great international state, of which the pope was the absolute ruler, with an administrative system, laws, and courts of its own, and basing its claims to supremacy over secular governments on legal as well as moral grounds.

The Lombard communes. The popes found allies against the emperor in the Lombard cities. Since the middle of the eleventh century, the Italian towns had been growing rapidly as the result of a great revival of international trade. The crusades had further stimulated trade, and by the middle of the twelfth century the numerous cities that dot the Lombard plain were busy centers of industry and commerce. Originally these cities had been governed by their bishops, acting as imperial officers. But with increasing prosperity, the citizens began to demand freedom and self-government. During the investiture controversy, both emperors and popes had sought their aid and had paid for it with concessions of liberty. When Frederick made his first expedition into Italy he found the cities, with the land around them, organized as "communes," practically self-governing republics. He found them also in a shocking state of anarchy, each city divided by turbulent political factions and engaged in feuds with other cities. The emperor was surprised to find these burghers as independent and as aggressively warlike as the feudal nobility. He realized that he must crush their independence before order and imperial government could be re-established in Italy.

The Lombard League. In 1158, Frederick made a second expedition into Italy with a large army. After capturing Milan, the strongest of the Lombard cities, he called an Imperial Diet at Roncaglia. There he publicly asserted his imperial rights, as defined by the jurists on the basis of Roman law and medieval prece-

dent. Disregarding the privileges of the communes, he claimed all rights of sovereignty, the "regalia" as they were called, including the appointment of officers and collection of taxes from tolls, markets, mints, law courts, etc. Never had the medieval empire seemed so strongly established in Italy. But the imperial officers were unpopular and taxes oppressive. Milan revolted and with her several other cities, supported by the pope. At this point Adrian IV died and there was a hotly disputed election. A majority of the cardinals elected Alexander III (1159–81), while a minority declared for Victor IV. It was the latter, more favorable to him, whom the emperor chose to recognize, thus assuring the continuance of the schism, since he was not accepted as pope anywhere outside the empire. Meanwhile, Frederick continued the war against the rebellious communes. In 1162 he completely destroyed Milan, banishing its citizens. But the discontent in Lombardy persisted. In 1166, Frederick had to make a third expedition to Italy to crush a league of cities, which had united against him and had so far forgotten their jealousy of Milan as to aid the Milanese in rebuilding their city. Alexander III, now in possession of Rome, was the heart and soul of the resistance to the emperor. Frederick, therefore, marched against Rome and captured it. His success was immediately followed by disaster, however, in the form of an epidemic that destroyed his army and forced him to retire to Germany, where domestic affairs kept him busy till 1174.

Triumph of Lombard League. The Lombard League, led by Milan, used the years while the emperor was in Germany to gain the adherence of nearly all the North Italian cities. The league also built a new and heavily fortified city, called Alessandria in honor of the pope, where it would command the Alpine passes into Lombardy. When Frederick returned, this city withstood all his attempts to capture it through the winter of 1174–75. The war dragged on till 1176, when the emperor was disastrously

The effigies of Henry the Lion, Frederick Barbarossa's cousin and head of the House of Welf, and his wife, who was the sister of Henry II of England, are from their tomb in the cathedral of Brunswick.

defeated by the Lombard army at Legnano. Frederick accepted defeat with as good grace as possible. He made peace with Alexander III, thus ending the schism, and the following year he arranged a truce with the Lombard League, which was later confirmed by the Peace of Constance, 1183. The emperor surrendered the regalia, leaving the cities almost complete self-government. They in turn recognized the imperial sovereignty and swore allegiance. It was a decided triumph for the Lombard communes. So far as the pope was concerned, however, the results of the struggle were indecisive. Frederick had been forced to abandon his anti-pope and to recognize Alexander; but he had retained control of the church in Germany, and neither emperor nor pope had surrendered his claims to supremacy.

Last years of Frederick. Having failed in Italy, Frederick was free to concentrate his attention on Germany, where only one serious problem arose to mar his declining years. A breach in his long friendship with Henry the Lion revived the old Welf-Hohenstaufen feud. Henry had been building up a strong feudal state in Bavaria and Saxony and in the Slavic lands north and east of the Elbe. Unlike the emperor, he was much interested in the rising commercial towns and founded the fortunes of Lübeck and Munich. His government was enlightened, but it bore heavily on the lesser nobles. These brought charges of oppression against him in the imperial courts in 1179. Frederick, who had been estranged from his cousin for a number of reasons, summoned him to appear to answer the charges. Henry refused. After a year he was outlawed on a charge of treason and his fiefs were confiscated. Of all his vast possessions he was allowed to keep only Brunswick and some other allodial lands in the north. His duchies of Saxony and Bavaria were partitioned, split up into smaller units. This marks the end of the preponderant importance of the great duchies, and the rise in their place of a number of smaller principalities. What remained of the duchy of Bavaria was given to Otto of Wittelsbach, whose descendants held it until very recent times. Frederick's reign was brought to a close by the Third Crusade. Like so many of his contemporaries the aged emperor was fascinated by the hope of recovering the Holy Land, and in 1189

he set out with a large army. The story of the crusade will be told elsewhere. The gallant old fighter did not live to meet the Moslems, but perished in the icy waters of a stream in Asia Minor.

Henry VI. During his brief reign, Henry VI (1190–97), Frederick's unprepossessing son, revived his family's feud with the papacy and achieved a remarkable, though brief, success. Cruel and treacherous, Henry had none of the personal charm that had made his father so popular, but he had qualities of astuteness, learning, and determination that made up for the lack. With him the struggle for supremacy enters a new phase. The emperor's goal was now the political isolation of the pope in central Italy. Northern Italy had been won over by the grant of practical independence to the Lombard cities. Having married the heiress to the kingdom of Sicily, Henry also possessed a claim to all of southern Italy below the Papal States, although he was unable to overcome the resistance of the Sicilian nobles until 1194. Then, however, he was in a strong strategic position. The papacy was completely surrounded by lands in his possession. Henry then proceeded to establish his own vassals in the Papal States, reducing the land subject to the pope to the duchy of Rome. Hohenstaufen power was growing steadily in Italy when it was suddenly destroyed by the premature death of the emperor, not yet thirty-three years old.

3. Triumph of the Papacy

Innocent III. Seldom has history seen a more abrupt and thorough reversal of fortune than that which followed the sudden death of Henry VI. While rival candidates were disputing for the imperial crown, the papacy came into the hands of the strongest of all medieval popes, Innocent III (1198–1216). His pontificate marks the highest point of actual power ever exercised by the papacy. Trained as a jurist in the schools of Bologna and Paris, Innocent was thoroughly versed in canon law and ecclesiastical tradition. He was but thirty-seven years old, unusually young for a pope, and in the full prime of his vigor. For eighteen years he ruled the nations of western Christendom as the successor of St. Peter, to whom God had given authority, "not only over the universal church but also over the whole world." Never before had the papal claims to sovereignty over church and secular governments alike been stated with such absolute conviction. Yet Innocent did not regard himself as an innovator. He based his position on the time-honored theory of the papacy, embodied in tradition and canon law, which had been studied so carefully during the twelfth century. His position was different from that of Gregory VII by the measure of the legal and institutional growth of the church in the century and a quarter that lay between them. In claiming a potentially unlimited universal sovereignty, he felt that he was merely asserting the recognized rights of the papacy. He did not, it is true, claim direct authority over secular government in all cases. But he did assert a spiritual authority which might incidentally include secular authority, since it was his duty to judge of the sins of all Christians, including rulers, and any act that had a moral significance (as what human act does not?) came within his jurisdiction.

As a universal sovereign, Innocent's interests were many and various. He followed them all with inexhaustible energy. His interference in the affairs of France and England, his instigation of the Fourth Crusade and the Albigensian Crusade, his work for the suppression of heresy and for the reform and reorganization of the church will be dealt with in later chapters. Here we shall consider only his activity with regard to the empire and Italy.

Philip of Swabia and Otto IV.   Innocent had been pope only a few weeks when a majority of the German nobles elected as emperor Philip, Duke of Swabia, the younger son of Frederick Barbarossa. They had passed over Henry's son Frederick, who had inherited the kingdom of Sicily, on the ground of his extreme youth. Not all the nobles, however, agreed to the election of another Hohenstaufen. In western Saxony and the lower Rhineland there was still a strong Welf faction. In July, 1198, they gathered to elect Otto of Brunswick, the younger son of Henry the Lion. The rival emperors, who were the protagonists in this revival of the old Welf-Hohenstaufen feud, were of about the same age — in the early twenties — but of very different character. Philip was a gentle, amiable soul, always popular, but not a great statesman or soldier. Perhaps he was too fine for success in a rough age. Otto, on the other hand,

had little natural refinement. A contemporary writer described him as a reckless soldier, "roaring like a lion's whelp, incited by the desire for plunder, eager for the battle." He was, however, even less a statesman than his rival. Philip had the advantage of being supported by the large majority of the German princes, while Otto was forced to depend on Cologne and his own Welf lands.

Innocent's policy.   Innocent III had taken immediate advantage of the opportunity offered by the paralysis of imperial government during the civil war to build up a strong political position for the papacy in Italy. As leader of an anti-imperial party, he ousted the German representatives of the emperor from the Papal States and Tuscany. Late in 1198, Queen Constance of Sicily died and left him as guardian to her infant son Frederick. The pope now dominated central and southern Italy. To retain his power there, he had only to prevent the re-establishment of a strong imperial government. For three years he refused to recognize either Philip or Otto, while at the same time asserting his right to decide the issue by conferring the crown on the most suitable candidate. At last, in 1201, he declared openly for Otto IV, after securing from him an admission of his right to decide the election and a full renunciation of all imperial claims to the Papal States, which were now defined at the most extreme limits ever claimed, including Tuscany. Otto was the weaker candidate, and hence the less dangerous. He was also a Welf, traditionally friendly to the papacy. Moreover, Innocent considered it vitally important for the papacy to break the Hohenstaufen bond which tied Sicily to the empire. Despite the pope's aid, however, Otto could make little progress. By 1207 his cause was lost and he fled to England. Innocent was bitterly disappointed, but forced to make the best of a bad situation. In 1208 he recognized Philip of Swabia as emperor, just before that unlucky ruler was murdered.

Innocent and Frederick II.   With Philip dead, Otto easily made good his claims. The country was tired of civil war. In 1209 he was crowned at Rome. Here he renewed his guaranty of the Papal States and made further concessions to the pope, including the practical surrender of imperial control over the German church. But promises meant little to Otto.

Within a few months he had adopted the Hohenstaufen imperial policy and was threatening the independence of the Papal States. In 1210 and again the following year, Innocent excommunicated him and freed his subjects from their allegiance. The result was a Hohenstaufen rebellion in Germany in favor of the young Frederick of Sicily, son of Henry VI, who was now of age. In December, 1211, he was elected by the rebels, with the pope's blessing. Innocent had been forced to support Frederick, much against his liking, by the lack of any other available candidate to use against the perfidious Otto. With two claimants once more to the imperial crown, civil war continued till 1214, when Otto was disastrously defeated by Philip Augustus of France on the field of Bouvines.[1]

Frederick II. Once rid of his rival, Frederick II restored peace in Germany by making concessions to the princes and to the church, and in the year 1220 he returned to Italy, the land he had always considered his real home, there to stage the last act of the Hohenstaufen drama. It is difficult to estimate the character of this last great member of a great family, so contradictory and even hysterical are some of the judgments passed on him both by his contemporaries and by later writers. His enemies of the papal party saw in him an arch-heretic and a monster of depravity, while his admirers hailed him as "the wonder of the world." Even modern scholars have been moved to superlatives in describing him. Some have referred to him as "the first modern king," and one, writing in the *Cambridge Medieval History*, has asserted that, "among the rulers in the centuries between Charlemagne and Napoleon he has no equal." Certainly there was genius in this descendant of German emperors and Norman kings. Brought up among the intrigues and plots of a turbulent court, he had learned to trust no one but himself. He had learned all the uses of deceit and had acquired a self-confidence based on a fairly just assurance of his own mental superiority to those about him. Sicily, where he passed his youth, was a cosmopolitan country, made up of mixed Italian, Norman, Greek, and Moslem peoples, including every possible shade of social and religious opinion. As a product of that varied society,

[1] See below, page 200.

Frederick had developed a keen, skeptical mind, with little religious or moral conviction, but with an enthusiastic interest in literature, science, and philosophy, and a sanely enlightened appreciation of the needs of his kingdom.

Government of Sicily. Whenever he was free to do so, Frederick devoted his attention to his Sicilian kingdom, and it was there that his genius as a ruler showed itself most clearly. His first care was to recover the royal domains, which had been lost during his youth. He then took stringent measures to re-establish absolute government, building up a system of administration by royal officers who would be superior to the feudal nobles. He reorganized the royal courts and councils, recruiting his ministers from men of common birth who had been trained in law, rather than from the nobility. In 1231 he issued a new legal code, based on the principles of Roman law, to supersede the tangle of feudal laws and local customs which had prevailed hitherto. He also reformed the system of taxation so as greatly to increase his income. This bore heavily on the people, but was more than compensated for by his intelligent encouragement of industry, commerce, and agriculture. Frederick also did much to raise the intellectual level of Sicily. He founded the University of Naples, and his liberal patronage of writers and scholars made his court the intellectual center of the West. Under his rule, despotic though it was, Sicily became the most prosperous and civilized country in Europe.

The papacy and the Lombards. As a true Hohenstaufen, however, Frederick could not concentrate all his attention on Sicily. He seems to have cared little for Germany, which during most of his reign he left in the hands of his son Henry, but he was determined to keep Sicily and the empire together, and to unite Italy, if possible, under his rule. This brought him into conflict with the two ancient enemies of his house, the papacy and the Lombard cities. The latter were still, as in the days of Barbarossa, independent, disorderly, and constantly at war with one another. Like his grandfather, Frederick II felt it necessary to enforce order upon them through imperial authority. But despite their mutual jealousies, they could still unite to defend their freedom, and the emperor's first attempts to rule them were met by the formation of a new Lombard

League in 1226. Again the pope joined the Lombards in opposition to the emperor. The grounds of disagreement, however, were not quite the same as they had been in the previous century. Innocent III had triumphantly vindicated the papal claims to universal sovereignty, and the emperor had practically lost control of the German church. The issue of supremacy was still present, but the struggle was in reality more for territorial rule in Italy. Despite his promises, Frederick was threatening the pope's control of the Papal States, while the pope, for his part, could still assert his feudal overlordship over Sicily. The pope had a weapon against Frederick in the latter's rash vow, made in 1215, to go on a crusade. Pope Gregory IX (1227–41) demanded the fulfillment of the vow immediately after his election. Frederick agreed to sail in that year, but, falling sick at sea, he turned back. Gregory thereupon excommunicated him. In 1228, the emperor did finally go on the crusade and by diplomatic negotiations won Jerusalem, but still without mollifying the pope, since he had undertaken the holy war while under the ban of excommunication and had, moreover, treated peacefully with the infidel sultan. It was not till after another year of warfare that pope and emperor signed a peace treaty in 1230, which kept an uneasy truce for eight years.

The conflict revived.   Meanwhile, Frederick continued with varying success his attempts to suppress the Lombard cities. In 1235, he was called to Germany to put down a rebellion led by his son Henry. Returning with German troops, he announced his intention of establishing his authority over the whole of Italy. By 1238, the pope was openly allied with the Lombard League, and in March of the following year he again excommunicated the emperor. From that time on, Gregory and his successor Innocent IV (1243–54) were the relentless leaders of the opposition to Frederick. Both were canonists, fighting for the rights of the church, which they defined more absolutely and with greater claims to secular power than even Innocent III had done. The war dragged on indecisively until the death of Frederick in 1250 brought final ruin to the imperial cause.

Great interregnum.   The papacy still continued in implacable enmity to Frederick's descendants, while the empire fell to pieces. Pope after pope carried on a ruthless war to stamp out "the viper brood of the Hohenstaufen." For four years Frederick's second son, Conrad IV, last emperor of the Hohenstaufen line, continued the struggle, but after his death Sicily was separated from the empire. In 1265 the French-born Pope Clement IV called in a powerful French prince, Charles, Count of Anjou, younger brother of Louis IX, to win the kingdom of Sicily from Frederick's natural son Manfred. The following year Manfred was defeated and slain. Two years later, the last Hohenstaufen, Frederick's grandson Conradin, was captured and executed. In Germany, meanwhile, the imperial government had completely collapsed. While Frederick II was busy in Italy, the nobles had successfully asserted their independence. Rebellion after rebellion had marked the last years of his reign, and when, the year after his death, his son Conrad IV left to carry on the war in Italy, the country was in a state of complete anarchy. After the death of Conrad IV in 1254, there was no generally recognized emperor for nineteen years, until the election of Rudolf of Hapsburg in 1273. This period is called "the Great Interregnum." During those stormy years the German nobles acquired an independence that they were never again to surrender to any emperor.

Results of the struggle.   The papacy had at last triumphed in the long and bitter struggle with the emperors — at least to the extent of temporarily destroying the empire, and leaving it permanently weakened. In these two centuries of conflict, the popes had also built up a great international sovereignty, with sweeping claims to spiritual and secular authority, and with a territorial state in central Italy under their immediate rule. At the same time, the struggle had prevented the development of a strong centralized government, or even of national unity, in either Germany or Italy. Centuries were to pass before either became a national state. But the papal victory was not as permanent as it seemed. For, while the popes were fighting with the emperors, the kings of France and England had been steadily increasing their power and were gradually building centralized territorial states out of feudal chaos. In the Later Middle Ages, the popes were to find these national monarchs more dangerous enemies than the emperors had been.

16

The Growth of the Monarchies

in France and England

DURING THE PERIOD which we have called the High Middle Ages, the society of western Europe was still organized according to the feudal pattern. Nationalism and national states, as we know them, had not yet evolved. Most men were conscious primarily of the loyalty they owed to their local feudal lord. Yet they had also much in common with all the peoples of Catholic Europe — a common social system and a universal church. Medieval society, then, was at once more local and more international than that of modern times. In the last chapter we saw how the results of the long struggle between the emperors and the popes helped to prolong this condition, on the one hand by establishing the popes as undisputed rulers of an international church with claims to secular powers, and on the other by destroying the central government in Germany and Italy. In this chapter we shall see how in the other two great countries of the West, France and England, the reverse development was taking place during the same period. There the monarchs, less troubled by the conflicting claims of the papacy, were slowly centralizing the loose feudal government and were laying the foundations for future national states.

1. French Kings Increase Their Prestige (1060–1180)

Weakness of the Capetian monarchy. By the middle of the eleventh century the royal house of Capet was almost eclipsed in the midst of its great vassals. The king's actual power was limited almost entirely to the royal domain, the Île de France, a narrow strip of territory running north and south from Paris. From this land he drew his chief financial and military support. Even there, however, his authority was none too great, for rebellious barons defied him from behind their castle walls or issued forth to prey upon the peasants or passing merchants and clergy. Outside the domain, the lords of great fiefs like Normandy, Champagne, Anjou, Burgundy, Toulouse, or Aquitaine, though recognizing the king as their overlord, were practically independent, each ruling his own county or duchy as a feudal sovereign.[1] The king had less real power than many of these vassals, but he had one great advantage over them. He was their overlord and he was

[1] See above, pages 168–69, and map, page 196.

also the consecrated king. At the time this meant little, but it might be made to mean more. The first step in the rise of the monarchy would be to exercise both royal and feudal rights as far as possible so as to raise the prestige of the king. The next step would be to use that prestige to expand the royal domain, and then to use the power thus gained to assert control over the outlying fiefs. In accomplishing this, the kings could usually count upon the support of the clergy, who were more closely attached to the monarchy than were the lay nobles.

Philip I.   The long reign of Philip I (1060–1108) marks the first slight advance in the power of the monarchy. A practical if rather ignoble king, Philip succeeded in adding several small fiefs to the royal domain, and he suppressed at least some of the unruly barons of the Île de France. He also succeeded in maintaining control over his ecclesiastical vassals. The investiture controversy did not cause as serious trouble in France as it did in Germany and was settled by a compromise in 1107. The king gave up the formal investiture of bishops and abbots, but retained control over ecclesiastical elections. Thereafter, the French kings were usually in close alliance with the papacy, but kept a firm hand on the French church. The support of both was often of great advantage to them.

Louis VI asserts royal authority.   Philip's son, Louis VI (1108–37), called "the Fat" for obvious reasons, carried on the Capetian program with far greater success than had his father. It was he who really laid the foundations of royal power: first, by suppressing the barons of the Île de France and establishing a secure position for the monarchy there, and second, by vigorously asserting the right of the king to enforce justice throughout the kingdom. Despite the growing weight of flesh, which even his tall and powerful frame carried with difficulty in his later years, Louis was constantly on the move. A king who took his duties seriously had no time for leisure in that violent age, and Louis had all the qualities needed by a medieval monarch. He was a born soldier and a just and conscientious judge. He never thought of interfering with the feudal rights of his vassals, but he did consider it his duty as king and overlord to see that feudal laws

were obeyed and justice guaranteed to all. Year after year, this "ironclad judge" heaved his great weight into the saddle and rode forth to defend the clergy, the weak, and the oppressed. His life was one long battle against feudal tyranny and rebellion, filled with sieges of castles and hand-to-hand fighting, in which the king himself, in his egg-shaped steel helmet and chain mail, swung as lusty a sword as any knight in his army. He left the monarchy with greatly increased prestige and a new moral ascendancy over the feudal nobles.

The Anglo-Norman menace.   The greatest danger to the French monarchy in this century came from the union after 1066 of Normandy with England, and against this coalition Louis was able to do no more than hold his own. Henry I of England, the younger son of William the Conqueror, though in theory his vassal for Normandy, was a much more powerful ruler than Louis. Both his kingdom and his duchy were better organized than France, and besides he had strong allies. His nephew, Theobald, Count of Champagne, whose fiefs bordered the Île de France on both the east and west, aided him in any action against the French king. The Emperor Henry V, too, was his son-in-law, and on one occasion formed an alliance with him against France. This danger was averted by an unprecedented rising of the French nobles in support of their king, but until the death of Henry I in 1135 the situation was always tense.

Louis VII, early years.   With the death of Louis the Fat, the rise of the monarchy was checked, though not entirely stopped. Louis VII (1137–80) was less wise, less decisive in action, and certainly less fortunate than his father. At the very beginning of his reign, he added greatly to the territory of the royal domain by marrying Eleanor, heiress to the duchy of Aquitaine. However, this was not so great a gain as it might seem, and it proved to be only temporary. Aquitaine and its dependencies formed a huge fief, but its nobles were so independent that it did not add very much to the king's resources. During his first years as king, Louis showed more energy than later, but it was sadly misdirected. After a long and useless feud with Theobald of Champagne, he left France to take part in the ill-starred Second Crusade. After his return in 1149, he settled down more seriously to the business of ruling;

but by that time the Anglo-Norman menace had taken a new and more dangerous form through alliance with the house of Anjou.

Rise of the Angevin house.   Seven years before his death, Henry I, who had no surviving son to succeed him, had married his daughter Matilda, the widow of the Emperor Henry V, to Count Geoffrey of Anjou and Maine. He hoped in this way to provide an heir who would not only succeed to the English throne, but would also unite to Normandy the two neighboring counties of Anjou and Maine. When Henry I died, however, his grandson, Henry, later nicknamed "Plantagenet," was too young to take the throne, and the English nobles gave the crown instead to Henry's nephew, Stephen of Blois. In the following years, Geoffrey of Anjou conquered Normandy without serious opposition from either of the weak monarchs, Stephen and Louis VII. When Geoffrey died in 1151, his son, Henry Plantagenet, was eighteen years old, and already a keen and vigorous statesman. The following year, Louis VII, who was always swayed more by personal emotions than by motives of policy,

divorced his flighty southern wife, Eleanor of Aquitaine. Henry married her almost immediately, thus adding Aquitaine to his already formidable collection of fiefs. The acquisition of Eleanor's inheritance meant more to Henry than it had to Louis, since it bordered on his Angevin domain, forming with it a solid block. Including as it did the counties of Poitou, Guienne, and Gascony, it stretched down the western coast of France from the Loire to the Pyrenees, and in its central section eastward across France to the Rhône. In 1154, the Plantagenet became King of England as Henry II, and four years later acquired Brittany. He was now lord of more than half of France and much more powerful than his overlord Louis VII.[1] For his part, Louis had weakly allowed this dangerous collection of fiefs to take place without effective opposition, and later, when he realized the seriousness of the menace, his attempts to lessen Henry's power were feeble and irresolute. Henry remained the practically independent ruler of the lands he had acquired.

[1] See map below.

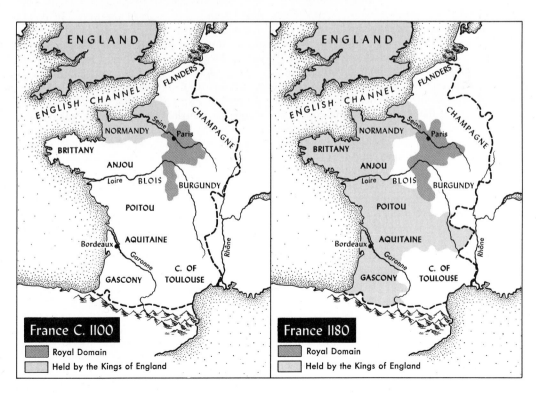

France C. 1100
Royal Domain
Held by the Kings of England

France 1180
Royal Domain
Held by the Kings of England

Growth of royal prestige. In the rest of his kingdom, however, Louis was more successful. He carried on his father's work of defending the oppressed and dispensing justice. He frequently answered appeals for justice against feudal law-breakers outside the royal domain and summoned even the more powerful vassals to answer charges in his court. All who desired peace and order were on the king's side against the nobles. The clergy supported him strongly, and in 1159 Pope Alexander III, who had been driven out of Italy by Frederick Barbarossa, appealed to him for protection. Thus, despite the danger from Anjou, Louis added considerably to the moral authority of the monarchy in France and to its influence in foreign countries.

Royal administration. Much of this success was due to the work of the king's ministers. Louis VI had instituted a policy, which his son continued, of entrusting royal business to clerics or to men of low birth rather than to the great nobles who had earlier filled the offices of the king's household. These men, chosen for their wisdom, training, and ability, were not only more efficient than the ruder nobles, but were devoted to the king's interests, since they had no power of their own independent of the king and had no family ambitions to serve. Abbot Suger of St. Denis, who served father and son faithfully from about 1130 till his death in 1151, was typical of this class. Honest, sane, and tactful, this bald-headed little man gave direction to the warlike vigor of Louis VI and saved the kingdom from disaster in the early years of Louis VII. During the king's absence on the Second Crusade, it was Suger who prevented the feudal nobles from asserting complete independence. Save for this change in the character of the ministers, the royal administration had developed very little since the early days of the monarchy. The king still drew his chief income from the royal domain, and his direct government was limited to it. Beyond the domain, he had only the feudal jurisdiction of an overlord. His court was composed of household officers, who were his personal advisers, and on special occasions the vassals-in-chief who owed him feudal service. Whether as king or as overlord, his government was purely personal and there was very little system about it. His ministers were merely people whom he had chosen to assist him, and their duties were not clearly defined. It was only in the next century, when the royal domain was greatly expanded, that a more regular system of administration began to evolve.

2. English Kings Organize a Royal Government (1066–1189)

Norman feudalism in England. The position of the English kings at the beginning of this period contrasted strongly with that of the kings of France. At the time when Philip I was unable to exercise any authority outside the Île de France, and none too much there, William the Conqueror was master of all England. He had the tremendous advantage that the whole country was his by right of conquest. He kept a large amount of land himself, and the rest he allotted to the Norman barons who had helped him in the conquest. This land was granted out in fiefs to vassals, who held it directly from the king as tenants-in-chief, giving in return a stipulated amount of military service. This military service was provided for by re-granting part of the land to knights, who thus became subvassals of the king. In theory this is the continental system of military feudalism. But in practice the new Norman feudalism in England was far better organized, and the king retained far more control, than anywhere on the Continent. The land had been given by the king to the barons, not merely in theory as confirmation of their hereditary possession of land won by their ancestors as in France, but in actual fact. Moreover, most fiefs were composed of pieces of land scattered in various parts of the kingdom. No single baron was strong enough to defy the king successfully. William collected all feudal dues to the last penny, and there was also some sort of national taxation. This, added to the income from the extensive royal estates, guaranteed the financial independence and stability of the king's government. Finally, William and his successors insisted on the principle that the vassals who held land from the barons owed their first loyalty to the king rather than to their immediate lords. From the first, Norman feudalism in England was a fairly centralized system.

Administration. William I had his full share of the peculiar Norman genius for organization and for adapting all available means

Dover Castle guarded the English port lying closest to France, only 21 miles away across the English Channel. The great square keep, with walls from 17 to 21 feet thick and rising to a height of 83 feet, was built by Henry II in the years 1181–87.

to his own ends. He retained the old Anglo-Saxon system of the shires and shire courts, but to this system he added other elements brought over from the Continent. The most important of these new institutions were the itinerant ministers from the royal court (somewhat like the old Carolingian *missi*) and the sworn inquest or jury (so called from the French *juré,* because composed of men who had sworn to tell the truth). Both of these institutions were used to good effect in collecting information for the famous Domesday Book in 1086, that amazing survey of the land and chattels of the kingdom, compiled for the purpose of making sure of full payment of feudal dues and royal taxes. Ministers from the royal court, mostly educated clergymen, were sent out with writs empowering them to summon a group of freemen from each community, who were to testify under oath as to the exact wealth of each estate. In later times, these itinerant "justices," as personal representatives of the king, and the sworn jury were to be used extensively for all sorts of administrative purposes, and also for the prosecution of justice.

William I and the church. Along with his other reforms, the Conqueror undertook a thorough reorganization of the English church. The Hildebrandine reform movement was at its height, and William, always a pious man, was thoroughly in sympathy with the aims of the reformers, so long as they did not lessen his authority. With the aid of his friend Lanfranc, whom he made Archbishop of Canterbury, the king enforced discipline upon the lax Saxon clergy. He replaced nearly all the bishops and abbots by new men who had been trained in the stricter tradition of the Continent. He took steps to enforce the celibacy of the clergy and to do away with simony. William also set up special ecclesiastical courts, where the clergy could be tried by their superior officers. Nevertheless, he would not accede to all the demands of Gregory VII. He clung to his right of investing the bishops and abbots, who were among his most important vassals; but Gregory was not inclined to make an issue of the matter in England as he had done in Germany. The pope was interested above all else in reform, and so long as William was using his control of the church to such good purpose, Gregory did not feel it necessary to interfere.

Royal administration under Henry I. For thirteen years after the Conqueror's death, his son William Rufus (1087–1100) proved that royal power might be dangerous in the hands of a tyrannical king. However, his reign was not long enough to cause permanent damage. He died unlamented, shot by an arrow while hunting in the New Forest, and the crown

Medieval
England

passed to his younger brother, Henry I (1100–35). Henry was a hard, cool-headed, systematic man, of the true Norman breed, with a strongly legal bent of mind and a passion for order and justice. His primary motive, no doubt, was to strengthen his own power, but he did so in ways that benefited the whole kingdom. Traveling justices, sent out from his court, investigated complaints of feudal oppression, examined the conduct of the sheriffs, and heard numbers of judicial cases, which the king claimed fell within his jurisdiction as breaches of the "king's peace." Henry was perhaps too much interested in his continental possessions for the good of England — he spent more than half his reign in Normandy — but he chose able ministers to carry on his work during his absence. The central government was regularly handled by the king, or his representative, and the king's court, called the *curia regis*. This was normally composed of a fairly small group of ministers and any of the barons whom the king chose to summon. On special occasions all the king's vassals-in-chief might be summoned to it to form the "Great Council." It was only natural that out of this shifting court the specialized task of looking after the royal finances should be given to a more or less permanent group of experienced men, who received the taxes, audited the sheriffs' accounts, and noted expenditures. These men came to be known, from the chequered table at which they sat to reckon their accounts, as the lords of the exchequer. The court of the exchequer was the first of several such courts, which later grew out of the shifting and formless *curia regis*. Like his father, Henry I kept a firm hand on the English church, but now the abolition of lay investiture had become the primary point of papal policy. The question was finally settled in 1107, as in France, by a compromise wherein the king gave up nothing but the formal investiture with the ring and staff.

Anarchy under Stephen. Henry's strong rule was followed by two dreary decades of anarchy and civil war under his nephew, Stephen (1135–54), of whom one contemporary chronicler writes, "he was a mild man, and soft, and good, and did no justice." Henry's daughter Matilda asserted her claim to the crown, while the nobles and great church officers took advantage of the civil war to throw off all royal control. It was a good day for England when young Henry Plantagenet of Anjou restored the hard but just government of Henry I and the Conqueror.

Henry II a great administrator. "Know" We have seen already how Henry II (1154–89) acquired his great feudal dominion in France before he became King of England at the age of twenty-one. Though he continued to spend much of his time in his continental fiefs, it was his work in England that justified his reputation as one of the greatest of medieval rulers. Henry's energy was remarkable, even in a family noted for that quality. His superabundant vitality wore down the ministers who were forced to keep pace with him. He was constantly active, traveling from end to end of his domains, a terror to evil-doers, for despite his violent temper he had all his grandfather's love of order and justice. Every part of England knew the short sturdy figure of the homely red-headed king, the powerful set of the shoulders, and the bow legs, warped from a lifetime in the saddle. He kept in personal touch with the sheriffs whenever possible, and by developing the powers of the exchequer brought them under closer control by the central government. The anarchy of Stephen's reign had made a reassertion of royal authority very necessary. Though he added very little that was actually new to the system of administration, he developed the machinery of government until he had established a permanent centralized system that would survive the neglect or mismanagement of weaker kings.

Royal courts. Henry II had inherited the legal mind of that "lion of justice," Henry I, and his most permanent contributions to English institutions were in the field of judicial and legal procedure. He greatly extended the jurisdiction of the royal courts by adding to the list of cases that were recognized as "pleas of the crown" or breaches of the king's peace, and by throwing open his courts to all freemen in civil suits regarding the possession of land, while at the same time he used the system of itinerant justices in a much more systematic way than before, so as to make royal courts easily available in all parts of the country. The regular use of these traveling justices led to the transference of a large number of cases from the local feudal or shire courts to the royal courts. Royal justice was surer and more fair than that in the local courts and so became more popular. It should also be noted that the king had good financial reasons for doing everything in his power to extend the jurisdiction of his courts, since fines, payments for writs, and so forth were an important part of the king's income. At the same time, the royal courts did much to raise the king's prestige and to unify the kingdom, for the king's justices were gradually developing a system of common law for the whole country, which would eventually take the place of varying local customs. No parallel to this development could be found anywhere on the Continent.

The jury. Perhaps the most important of Henry's innovations was the regular use of the jury as part of the machinery of justice in the royal courts. This was an evolution from the sworn inquest used by earlier Norman kings and now put to a new judicial use. In Henry's time the jury was used chiefly for the accusation or indictment of criminals. Freemen in each locality were summoned by the king's justices and were forced to tell, under oath, if they knew of any criminals in their neighborhood. Criminals thus accused were summoned to the king's courts for trial, no matter who would otherwise have had jurisdiction over them. A further use of the jury, which in some degree foreshadows the later development of the trial jury, was the "assize," a trial in a royal court to settle disputes over the possession of land, in which the jury not only gave evidence, but also rendered a verdict on the basis of their previous knowledge of the circumstances.

The quarrel with Becket. Henry's desire to extend the jurisdiction of royal courts wherever possible caused his one serious conflict with the church, when he tried to encroach on the jurisdiction of the ecclesiastical courts and canon law. We have already noted[1] the great growth of canon law in the twelfth century and the increasingly domineering attitude of the church toward secular governments. Some conflict between the church and a king so absolute and legal-minded as Henry II was almost bound to occur, though the pope himself was too busy with his fight against Frederick

Barbarossa to press the issue in England. Henry claimed that "criminous clercs" (clergymen who had committed crimes), after being convicted in an ecclesiastical court, should be degraded and turned over to royal officers to be punished just as though they were laymen. He also objected strongly to the appealing of cases to the papal court at Rome. In 1162, he secured the election of his most trusted minister, Thomas Becket, to the archbishopric of Canterbury, in the hope that he would be a pliant tool. Henry was disappointed. Now that he was head of the church in England, Becket became the most violent opponent of royal encroachment. He denounced the Constitutions of Clarendon — a statement drawn up by the king in 1164 of the restrictions to be placed on ecclesiastical courts, and papal interference in England — and for six years the quarrel dragged on. It was ended only when Becket was murdured before the altar of his cathedral

The murder of Becket before the altar of the cathedral at Canterbury, as illustrated in a manuscript now in the British Museum.

at Canterbury, by four knights who had apparently taken too literally some things said by the king in one of his towering rages. Becket was considered a martyr and people began to make pilgrimages to his tomb, as they were still doing two hundred years later when Chaucer described such a pilgrimage in the *Canterbury Tales*. The king was forced to do public penance and to withdraw the constitutions so far as they affected the punishment of "criminous clercs" and the appeals to Rome.

Last years. Henry's last years were saddened and embittered by the perennial quarrels and rebellions of his four sons. The old king could rule successfully everywhere but in his own family. Two of his sons died before he did, and at the time of his own death, the other two, Richard and John, were in rebellion against him.

3. *French Kings Expand the Royal Domain (1180–1270)*

Philip Augustus. Let us turn again to the history of France with the reign of Philip II (1180–1223), surnamed Augustus, who opened a new era in the history of the French monarchy by greatly expanding the royal domain at the expense of the English kings. The French kings had already acquired considerable moral authority. It was time to give that authority a solid backing, based on real power drawn from a wide domain under the king's immediate government. Philip was well suited to carry out that task, and fortune favored him. He had a far more decided character than his good-natured father, Louis VII, and, though he lacked the reckless chivalrous spirit of his grandfather, he had other qualities that were equally useful to a king in his difficult position. Sane, clear-headed, and unscrupulous, he kept his eye fixed firmly on his most important objective and seized every opportunity to forward his schemes. He was a politician and a statesman, rather than a feudal warrior. In the first years of his reign, while he was still very young, he suppressed the rebellion of a powerful coalition of nobles, and gained some territory. Then by asserting an hereditary claim to Vermandois and a claim through his first wife to her fief of Artois, he paved the way for further expansion of the royal domain to the north. By steady pressure he gradually added to it until his lands stretched north in a solid block to the English Channel, including the ports of Boulogne and Calais.

Philip takes Angevin fiefs. Philip's greatest ambition was to take over the fiefs held by the King of England, which at the beginning of his reign were many times the size of his own domain. He was largely responsible for stirring up the sons of Henry II to rebellion, but on the old king's death he had to make peace, as both he and Richard I (1189-99) had sworn to go on the Third Crusade. They went together, but soon quarreled, and Philip returned to urge John to rebellion and to begin the conquest of Normandy. Richard was captured by the Emperor Henry VI on his way home and did not return till 1194. Once back, however, the soldier-king soon won back his land, but was killed while besieging a castle in Aquitaine. With John (1199–1216) king of England, Philip's chances were much better. At first he supported the claims of Arthur, the son of John's deceased elder brother, Geoffrey, to the Angevin inheritance. Then, in 1202, he declared that John had forfeited his French fiefs as a contumacious vassal. John was generally unpopular and became much more so when the rumor was circulated that he had murdered the young Arthur. Philip met with little opposition from John's French vassals. By 1205, he had taken possession of Normandy, Anjou, Maine, Touraine, and part of Poitou, and had conferred Brittany on a friendly noble. These were the richest and best organized of the Angevin domains. John was left with only the southern part, the disorderly and half-independent territories of Aquitaine, Gascony, and part of Poitou.

Philip and Innocent III. Like so many of his contemporaries, Philip came into conflict with the claims of Innocent III to supremacy over secular rulers, but on one occasion only was he forced to submit, and then on a moral issue where he was clearly in the wrong. In 1193, Philip had married the Princess Ingeborg, sister of Canute VI of Denmark. Almost at once, for reasons which he himself apparently could not understand, he took a profound dislike to her and repudiated the marriage. Three years later, he married again, though the

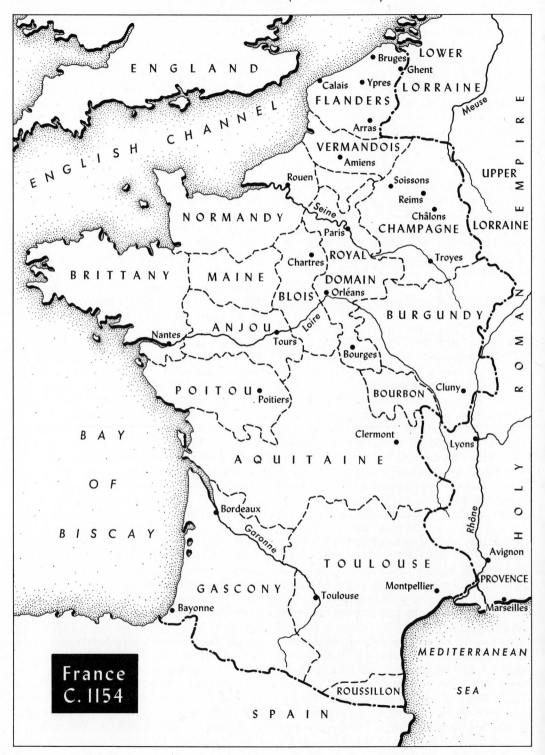

France
C. 1154

pope had not recognized the annulment of his previous marriage. As soon as he became pope, Innocent took up the question with his usual determination and commanded Philip to take back Ingeborg as his lawful wife. In 1200, he enforced his command by placing an interdict on all France except the Angevin fiefs, which were recognized as belonging more to the King of England than to Philip. An interdict meant the suspension of all normal church services in the country. The pressure of public opinion forced Philip to submit and take back Ingeborg. For the rest, Philip refused to allow Innocent to dictate his policies. He persisted in the conquest of John's French lands despite the strong opposition of the pope. Later he was occasionally allied with the pope against John or the Emperor Otto of Brunswick, but for reasons of his own. Not the least of Philip's services to the French monarchy was his insistence that the pope had no right to interfere in purely French affairs.

Albigensian Crusade. It was typical of Philip's attitude toward the papacy that he refused to waste his strength by taking part in the crusade which Innocent had organized against the Albigenses of southern France in 1207,[1] although he was later to profit by it. Knights and barons from all parts of Europe joined this crusade against the heretics. After years of fighting and bloody massacres, which destroyed the glorious culture of the rich southern land and left it desolate, the leader of the crusaders, a Norman baron named Simon de Montfort, succeeded in taking over nearly all of Languedoc from the Count of Toulouse. In the last year of Philip's reign, Simon's son, Amaury de Montfort, unable to defend his lands, offered them to the king. Meanwhile, Philip had been gradually extending his domain south into Auvergne and Aquitaine.

Louis VIII. The work of Louis VIII (1223–26) during his brief reign was merely a continuation of his father's expansion of the royal domain. He made a triumphal march into Aquitaine and turned what was left of the Albigensian Crusade into a royal conquest of Languedoc. He died before his task was completed, but he had accomplished so much that his son, Louis IX, was able quite easily to add

Languedoc and Poitou to the king's domain, leaving the King of England only Gascony and part of Aquitaine.

Louis IX. Louis IX (1226–70) was only twelve years old when his father's death made him King of France. His mother, Blanche of Castile, ruled as regent till he came of age, and continued to have a great deal of influence until her death in 1252. The early years of his reign were troubled by occasional rebellions of the great nobles, who feared the rising power of the monarchy, and by feeble attempts on the part of Henry III of England to recover the lost fiefs. After 1243, however, he had no further trouble with either. For the rest of his reign, he kept France at peace and strove to make peace wherever possible in Christendom. Few kings have been as popular as Louis IX, and it is safe to say that no other king ever impressed his subjects so strongly with his essential goodness. He was popularly regarded as a saint during his lifetime, and the church officially conferred upon him the title of St. Louis shortly after his death. His mother, who was a sternly pious woman, may have been responsible for some of his strong religious devotion and strict sense of duty. He spent much time in prayer, fasting, and ascetic practices. Yet he was no pious recluse, shutting himself away from the world. Despite his saintliness, he was a very practical ruler, and did his duty as king with never-failing energy, though constantly troubled by bad health. He had also a great deal of personal charm. In every way St. Louis, indeed, was the perfect representative of the ideals of his age — the chivalrous knight, the just ruler, and the pious saint. He was true to the ideals of his age, too, in his fanatical religious intolerance. He persecuted heretics with the greatest severity, and he would sacrifice anything to wage war against the infidel.

His crusades. Louis's greatest ambition was to win back the Holy Land from the Moslems. His two expeditions mark the last gasp of the real crusading ardor. His first crusade lasted from 1248 to 1254. It began with a disastrous campaign against the Sultan of Egypt, in which Louis himself was captured and nearly died. He was a fearless fighter, despite his weak physique, but he was not a good general. The second crusade came sixteen years later and Louis's part in it was cut short by his death.

[1] See below, page 247.

Somewhat battered but still full of personality, the statue of Louis IX stands in the north transept of the cathedral of Reims.

Louis IX and the monarchy. During his long and peaceful reign, Louis was able to consolidate the gains made by the monarchy in the preceding century, win the affection and loyalty of the people, and strengthen the system of royal government. When he died, the way was open for the evolution of a more truly national monarchy of the modern type. Louis himself, however, still clung to the old feudal conceptions of government. His administrative and judicial reforms were limited to the royal domain, and when he interfered in the government of the fiefs outside, he did so in accordance with feudal law and custom. He even gave new life to feudalism by granting Artois, Poitou, Anjou, and other fiefs to his brothers as *appanages,* thus separating them from the royal domain and diminishing its size. Yet he felt more strongly than any of his predecessors that his consecration as king gave him special sacred rights and duties. He never hesitated to assert his will in what he considered a just cause. In many ways Louis IX was one of the founders of absolute monarchy in France.

Judicial reforms. As might have been expected from his character, Louis was greatly interested in the enforcing of order and justice. He tried to secure equal justice for rich and poor in his courts, and he himself frequently acted as a judge. He did away with trial by combat, which he considered barbarous, and abolished the old custom whereby the defendant in a trial might challenge his judge to combat if he considered the sentence unjust. Deprived of this right, the defendant's only alternative was to appeal to the royal court to rehear the case, which added considerably to the king's power and prestige. Louis also prohibited private warfare among the nobles, but even he could not stamp out that most cherished right of the nobility.

Royal administration. During the thirteenth century a system of royal administration was gradually taking shape in France, along lines somewhat similar to the development in England the century before. Philip Augustus had done a great deal to systematize the government of the royal domain, by dividing it into administrative districts under royal officers, called bailiffs (in the north) or seneschals (in the south). These royal officers had great powers, which they sometimes abused. Louis IX tried to supervise their activities more closely by sending out representatives, somewhat in the manner of the English traveling justices. The king's court or *curia regis,* that vague body which aided the king in the central government, was also developing along more systematic lines during this period. There was a *chambre des comptes* (though not so named till 1309), corresponding roughly to the English exchequer, and at least the beginning of a distinct court of appeal, which later developed into the permanent *Parlement* of Paris. These specialized courts were not yet composed of a definite or permanent set of ministers, but were merely a part of the *curia regis,* sitting to hear the bailiff's reports or to try cases. Still, there were some more or less permanent members of each, trained men who began to form the nucleus of a professional class of ministers and judges.

Thirteenth-century France. During the thirteenth century, France enjoyed greater prosperity than she had ever known before. Commerce and industry were flourishing and were causing a great growth of town life. In the towns, a new class of independent "burghers," who were neither noble nor villein, were beginning to form an important part of society. During the twelfth century, many of the towns had gained independence from their local feudal lord; before the end of the thirteenth, most of them had come under the direct jurisdiction of the king. The burghers were usually inclined to favor a strong monarchy, because they needed security and order for their business. This was also a period of great educational and cultural advance, fostered by the increasing prosperity. The University of Paris was the center of philosophical and theological learning for all Europe. French lawyers were eagerly studying Roman law, and were drawing from it arguments in favor of absolute monarchy. The vigorous literature in the French language, begun in the previous century, continued to develop in this period. Local dialects were beginning to give way before a common French language. True, local differences were still strong, even within the king's domain. The north and the south still spoke dialects so different that they could scarcely understand one another. Men from Toulouse were foreigners in Paris. Normans were still Normans before they were Frenchmen. Nevertheless, men in all parts of France were beginning to think of themselves as Frenchmen, and to take some pride in the fact.

4. The English Constitution Develops Despite Weak Kings (1189–1272)

We must turn now to see what was happening in England, during the period when Philip Augustus and St. Louis were building up the French monarchy, partly at the expense of English kings. There, despite a series of absentee, unjust, or weak kings, the system of central government, which had been so strongly organized by the great Norman and Angevin kings of the past century, continued to develop steadily. England was a far more united state than France, and when the barons rebelled against a bad king, it was not to establish their own independence, but to force the king to rule justly and according to law. In this age of weak rulers, the English people rebelled against absolutism and laid the foundations of the English Constitution.

Richard I. Richard I (1189–99), the "Lion-hearted," who succeeded his great father, Henry II, on the English throne, was an absentee king. He spent only a few months of his ten-year reign in England. The career of this irresponsible knight-errant belongs more to the history of the Third Crusade or of France than to that of his own kingdom. The royal government, however, under the justiciar Hubert Walter, who was also Archbishop of Canterbury, continued to function as efficiently as if the king had been present, though the justiciar had often a hard time raising the large sums of money demanded by the king for his campaigns. Many towns took advantage of the king's need and purchased charters giving them greater freedom of self-government. The Great Council (the full meeting of the barons in the *curia regis*) also took advantage of the king's absence to assert a little more authority. Otherwise, the strong system of royal administration left by Henry II continued with very little change.

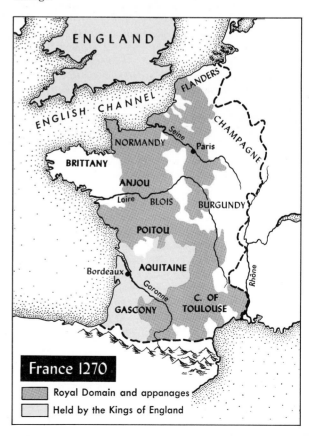

France 1270

Royal Domain and appanages

Held by the Kings of England

John and Innocent III. The royal government was put to a much more serious test under Richard's younger brother John (1199–1216), whose reign was marked by constant oppression, injustice, and failure. John did not entirely lack the ability shown by so many members of his family, but his energy was fitful and spasmodic. He was avaricious, as indeed others of his family had been, but he had neither Richard's romantic charm nor Henry's love of justice to balance it. On the contrary, he seemed to have a special genius for making enemies, and he was apparently lacking in any moral sense or appreciation of the moral sense of others. It was his misfortune, too, to be pitted against powerful adversaries and to be placed in difficult situations, which his own folly usually made worse. The first disaster of his reign was the loss of most of his continental fiefs to Philip Augustus, as has already been noted. Immediately thereafter, he rushed into an unnecessary quarrel with the powerful Pope Innocent III, who up to that time had been very favorable to him and had supported him against Philip. The occasion of the quarrel was a dispute over the election of an Archbishop of Canterbury to fill the place of Hubert Walter, who had died in 1205. Two candidates were elected, one secretly by the canons of the cathedral, the other openly by the clergy, but under the command of the king. Innocent set both aside and gave the post to Stephen Langton, an able and learned English cardinal. John refused to accept him. The pope applied pressure by laying an interdict on England in 1208, and followed it up the next year by excommunicating the king. John retaliated by taking over the lands of the church, thus alienating the English clergy. The nobles were also becoming discontented under his oppressive government and excessive taxation, and there were threats of rebellion. Finally, in 1213, when Philip Augustus prepared to invade England in his own and the pope's interest, John was forced to submit. He not only accepted Stephen Langton, but did homage to the pope for his kingdom, which he agreed to hold as a fief from the papacy.

Magna Carta. John's submission to the pope did not end the discontent in England. In 1214 he joined the Emperor Otto of Brunswick in a war against Philip Augustus, who was supporting Frederick II in his bid for the imperial crown. John hoped that he would be able to recover some of his lost lands while Philip was occupied with Otto. After Otto was defeated at Bouvines, however, John was unable to stand alone against the French king and returned empty-handed to England to find the nation united against him. The barons, who were the fighting force of the kingdom, took the initiative, actively supported by the clergy and the citizens of London. In June, 1215, they forced John to set his seal to the famous Magna Carta or Great Charter. The importance of

The copy of Magna Carta shown below is the re-issue of 1225, now the official version for legal purposes. The only surviving version of the original charter with seal attached is too badly burned to be useful for reproduction.

that historic document was much greater for later times than for its own day. Throughout the next century, until Parliament was definitely established, every despotic act of the king was protested as a breach of the Great Charter, and when, in the seventeenth century, the Stuart kings strove to revive absolute government, the parliamentary opposition cited Magna Carta as the original guaranty of liberty, fair trial, and representative government to all Englishmen. This was, of course, a misreading of what was in reality a feudal agreement. In actual fact, the charter was merely a promise that the king would observe the law in dealing with his vassals, though some vague phrases mention the rights of all free men. The demands of the barons, tempered by the sage advice of Stephen Langton, were moderate and conservative. They asked no more than that the king should observe the law in exercising the royal powers built up by Henry II, and that he should govern justly. Perhaps the greatest significance of the charter was the implication that the law was above the king, and that the barons, as representatives of the whole nation, had the right to force the king to obey it.

Louis invades England.   John had no intention of observing the terms of the charter. Innocent III, as his overlord, refused to recognize it and absolved him from his oath. The barons, however, were determined. They rebelled again and offered the crown to Prince Louis of France, the later Louis VIII, whose wife, Blanche of Castile, was a granddaughter of Henry II. Louis accepted the offer, against the opposition of the pope, but with the secret support of his father. His invasion of England was cut short by the death of John in 1216, the same year that saw the end of Innocent's great reign.

Misgovernment under Henry III.   The opposition of the rebellious barons had been directed against John personally. After his death it was not difficult to reconcile them to his young son, Henry III. The regents, who ruled in the name of the infant king, reissued the charter and promised better government. Conditions in England were fairly normal again, when Henry came of age in 1227 and began to misgovern the country on his own authority. Henry's personal reign runs very closely contemporary with

that of Louis IX. Like Louis, Henry was very pious, but there the resemblance ends, and even his piety was of a very different sort from that of the saintly French king, having little beneficial effect on his character. He was childish, vain, easily influenced by his favorites, but weakly stubborn at the wrong times. He was always hopelessly extravagant, a collector of objects of art and a great builder of churches and palaces. His brilliant but unbalanced imagination conceived magnificent and expensive foreign policies that were impossible of fulfillment. Two characteristics of his government especially aroused the resentment of the English people, aside from the constant burden of royal taxation. These were, first, the large number of important offices he gave to foreign favorites from Poitou or Provence, who were always dishonest and usually incompetent, and second, the supine manner in which he permitted the popes to tax the English clergy and to give the richest offices in the English church to papal favorites, usually Italians. This was the period when the popes were carrying on their last desperate struggle against Frederick II and his descendants. As a result they needed more money than ever before. Only the king could protect the clergy and people from papal exactions, and he was too pious to protest, as even St. Louis would have done.

Attempts to check royal absolutism.   Henry's insane foreign policy — including a promise to aid the pope in crushing the Hohenstaufens, and to pay all the expenses of the war, in return for the recognition of his second son, Edmund, as King of Sicily — and defeats in Scotland and Wales finally aroused the barons to definite action to control the king's irresponsible government. The Provisions of Oxford, which the king was forced to accept in 1258, handed the real powers of government over to a small group of the greater barons. This provisional government failed because it gave too much power to a small feudal group who did not represent the nation. The opposition party then tried to put into effect a much more sweeping reform under the leadership of Simon de Montfort, a younger son of that Simon who had led the Albigensian Crusade. He had come to England years earlier, had been made Earl of Leicester, had married the king's sister, and had become thoroughly English in his sympathies.

After defeating the royalist army at Lewes, Montfort controlled the government for a year (1264–65), until he in turn was defeated and killed. During that time he summoned a meeting of the Great Council to approve his administration. To it were summoned, not only two knights from each shire, which had been done before, but also two citizens from each chartered town. Aside from the representation given to the towns, this "parliament" was not a great innovation. The name was already in common use for similar meetings of the Great Council. Nor did it accomplish much for the present. De Montfort's experiment failed because he tried to force changes too rapidly. However, it did bear fruit in the next reign; for Edward I had learned that it was easier to govern with the cooperation of the people's representatives than against the opposition of the nation.

Thirteenth-century England. England in the thirteenth century was politically a much more closely united state than France. But in one respect the nation was still divided. The upper class were still cut off from the rest by their Norman blood, and still spoke French. Even they, however, were much more English than in the previous century. The loss of the Norman and Angevin lands had separated them from their kinsfolk on the Continent. Throughout the thirteenth century they were rapidly becoming more insular; their French language was losing its purity and was beginning to mix a little with the native Anglo-Saxon of the great majority of Englishmen; and they were as jealous of foreigners as though they themselves had been indigenous to the country. The royal courts, which continued to function well despite the weakness of Henry III, were gradually building up a common law for the whole land — and it was a law more English than French. Norman barons and Saxon burghers united to oppose royal tyranny. The rise of the towns, most of which had bought charters of self-government from Richard, John, or Henry III, gave the Saxon element in the nation a new importance. For in England, as in France, this was an age of prosperity and rapidly increasing commerce, industry, and town life. Everything indicated that when this transitional period was over, there would emerge a nation in which Norman and Saxon elements were fused into something which might be regarded as characteristically English.

"The Christian exults in the death of a pagan,
because Christ is glorified." • Saint Bernard
of Clairvaux (1090–1153)

17

The Crusades and the Expansion of Catholic Europe

So FAR, in dealing with the High Middle Ages, we have concentrated our attention on the great European countries, Germany, Italy, France, and England, and on the growing power of the universal church. We have mentioned only incidentally those infidel or heathen countries, Moslem or Slav, which lay in a menacing ring about Christian Europe to the south, east, and north. For centuries the great Moslem states had dominated the Mediterranean, firmly implanted in Spain, Sicily, North Africa, and the Middle East. But with the beginning of the eleventh century, the tide began to turn. Islam had lost its political unity, and the Moslems' aggressive driving force had begun to decline. On the other hand, Christian Europe was emerging from the dark ages. Its people were gaining a new strength and energy. It was their turn now to be the aggressors. During the eleventh century, Italian merchants broke the Moslem domination of the Mediterranean and opened up regular trade with the Middle East; the Moslems were driven out of Sicily, and the long warfare against them in Spain was begun. Then, at the end of the century, the pope summoned the people of Christendom to carry the war boldly into the enemy's territory in the East, and to recover Jerusalem and the Holy Land from the infidel. This expedition was the first and most successful of a long series of crusades which occupied much of the attention of the western peoples for two centuries. Generation after generation, iron-clad nobles left their quarrels with the king or their neighbors to ride eastward against the infidel; far-sighted Italian merchants plied a busy trade between the homeland and the Christian outposts in Syria; and popes gave reality to their claims of universal supremacy by organizing the fighting forces of Europe in a holy war. Meanwhile, in Europe Christian knights were carrying on steady warfare against the Moslems in Spain and against the Slavs to the north and east, and were gradually expanding the frontiers of Christendom.

1. The First Three Crusades (1095–1192)

Moslems and Christians. The Abbasid caliphs, who had once ruled a great Mohammedan empire from Bagdad, had lost their power long before the crusaders came to the East.[1] In the middle of the eleventh century, the Seljuk Turks took over what remained of their empire, though continuing to recognize the nominal authority of the caliphs as religious leaders. The Turks gave new strength to the Moslem state and made it a greater menace to Christendom. Driving westward, they took Syria from the caliphs of Cairo and most of Asia Minor

[1] See above, pages 126–128.

203

from the Byzantine Empire. Since the tenth century, great numbers of western pilgrims had traveled to the Holy Land to visit the scenes of Christ's life and death, to worship at the Holy Sepulcher, and to do penance for their sins by the cost, toil, and danger of the long voyage. Such pilgrims had been welcomed and treated well by the tolerant Fatimite caliphs; but after Jerusalem was captured by the Turks in 1071, the pilgrimage became more hazardous. Thereafter the returning pilgrims brought tales of Turkish atrocities, which were probably exaggerated, and told of the defilement of the holy places. Europe, then, was already aware of the Turk and in a mood to be easily aroused, when the Byzantine emperor, Alexius Comnenus, appealed to the pope for aid against the infidel who had been threatening Constantinople. The time seemed ripe for a counterattack. Three years before, in 1092, the death of the Turkish sultan had thrown the whole Turkish Empire into civil war and anarchy. Asia Minor and Syria were left under independent and antagonistic princes.

The sculptured effigy of St. Bernard, the great preacher who instigated the Second Crusade, is from his tomb at Clairvaux.

Urban II preaches the crusade.   Pope Urban II gave enthusiastic response to the emperor's appeal. Indeed, it is possible that he may have taken up the idea of a crusade on his own initiative, without urging from the East. Certainly he planned to do more than merely send aid to Alexius. A great council of churchmen and nobles was summoned to meet at Clermont in France. There Urban issued a stirring call to arms. In a masterly speech, he played upon every emotion of his hearers, holding out every possible inducement to those who would join the expedition — remission of sins, protection of their land till their return, and the hope of plunder. He was answered by shouts of "God wills it!" Most of those present at once donned the cloth cross which signified that they were pledged to the crusade. Preachers, of whom Peter the Hermit was the most famous, traveled through France and other parts of Europe, carrying the message and arousing great enthusiasm everywhere.

Motives of the pope.   The pope's reasons for urging the crusade are clear enough. The papacy had gained greatly in prestige since the accession of Gregory VII. Save in Germany, where Henry IV was still in violent opposition, the pope's claims to universal supremacy were generally recognized. By placing himself at the head of a great international movement like the crusade, Urban demonstrated that he, not the emperor, was the real leader of Christendom. There was also a more powerful motive. Urban, like most of the popes after him, sincerely wished to expand the church of which he was the ruler, and to make it as nearly as possible a world church.

Motives of the crusaders.   But why should rough feudal barons, knights, and even merchants and peasants have been stirred by the pope's call to take part in such a perilous undertaking? No single answer to that question can be adequate. In any great popular movement of the kind, many mixed motives must work together. The prime motive was, of course, religious. The Cluniac and papal reform movements had done much to stimulate popular piety. It was an age of violence, but also of strong religious feeling, with a decided bent toward asceticism. To the medieval man, the life of the monk was the only truly religious life. He was deeply conscious of sin; he feared eternal damnation; and he felt the necessity of doing some act of voluntary suffering as atonement for his sins. Great numbers of men, to whom the regular life of the monk was impossible, did penance for their sins by going on pilgrimage to holy places, even as far as Jerusalem. The crusades were in essence super-pilgrimages. But the religious appeal went farther than that. The feudal warrior's conception of loyalty was simple. A man fought for his lord against his enemies. And how could a man show his devotion to God better — or more congenially to his natural tastes — than by fighting for Him against His enemies, the infidels who had defiled Christ's sepulcher? The crusader believed that God had called him to arms through His representative, the pope, and he answered gladly. All the adventurous spirit and love of fighting, that was so characteristic of the medieval knight, urged him on to a glorious enterprise where fighting was no sin. Besides, feudal Europe was becoming somewhat overcrowded. There were landless knights, and younger sons who were short of land. In the rich East, of which they knew little but rumor, there were tempting opportunities for plunder and land to be had for the taking. It must not be forgotten that, from the practical point of view, the crusades were expeditions for the conquest of Syria. As for the Italian merchants, who constantly aided the crusaders, their interests were obvious. They wanted to establish safe trading posts in the Middle East under Christian governments. The Emperor Alexius had hoped that an expedition from the West might aid him in recovering Asia Minor. The crusaders had much larger plans.

The leaders. None of the great rulers of Europe — the Emperor Henry IV, Philip I of France, or William Rufus of England — was sufficiently at peace with the church or his own nobles to take part in the crusade. The leadership, then, was left to a group of great barons, chiefly from France and the lands bordering closely upon it. The royal domain was represented by Philip's brother, Hugh of Vermandois, central France by the wealthy Count Stephen of Blois, whose son later became King of England, and southern France by Count Raymond of Toulouse. From the Rhineland came Godfrey of Bouillon, Duke of Lower Lorraine, together with his brother, Baldwin. The

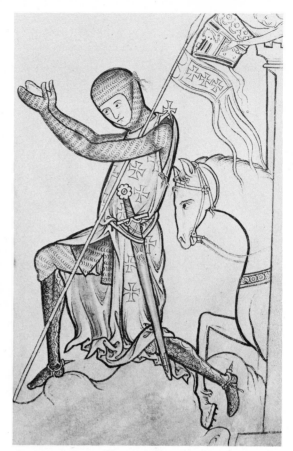

A crusading knight, identified as such by the crosses on his surcoat and pennon, is here pictured in a miniature from a thirteenth-century psalter in the British Museum.

knights of Normandy, to whom expeditions of this kind were second nature, followed Duke Robert, the reckless son of the Conqueror; while Bohemond, the son of Robert Guiscard, and his kinsman Tancred led a formidable band of Normans of the same adventurous breed from Sicily and southern Italy. These last were a valuable addition to the crusade, not only because of their character, but because they had already had experience in fighting the infidel and knew something of the Moslem world.

The First Crusade. Time was needed for preparation, so by mutual agreement the crusaders delayed their start till the late summer of 1096, though some disorganized bands had already preceded them. They traveled by different routes, arriving in Constantinople during the following winter. The Emperor Alexius,

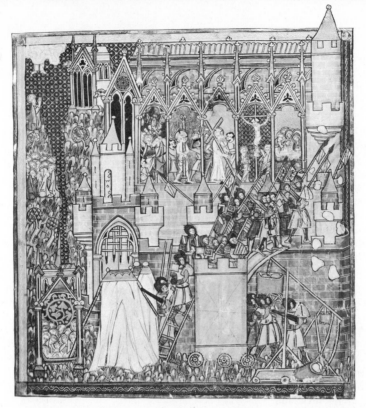

The crusaders storm into Jerusalem. This miniature from a manuscript in the Bibliothèque Nationale shows how the crusaders actually gained entry into the city. Having pushed a tall tower on wheels close to the wall, they lowered a drawbridge to the top of the wall and so crossed over into the city. In the right foreground is a catapult capable of throwing large stones.

who was rather alarmed at the size of the army, persuaded the leaders to take an oath of allegiance to him, on the understanding that they would hand over to him any land conquered or hold it as his vassals. It is impossible to do more than guess at the size of the crusading army, but a recent authority estimates it at between 4,200 and 4,500 cavalry and possibly 30,000 infantry. From Constantinople, the crusaders passed over into Asia Minor. There they captured Nicaea. Moving on, they left the city, together with most of Asia Minor, in the emperor's hands, thus accomplishing for him about as much as he could have hoped from their aid. Their next objective was Antioch, the most important town in northern Syria. On their way, they swung farther east through Armenia, where the friendly Christian population aided them in taking the Turkish strongholds. There Godfrey's brother Baldwin remained behind to found the county of Edessa. The siege of Antioch occupied all the winter of 1097–98. When at last, after great hardship, the crusaders broke into the city, they were themselves besieged by a Turkish army. They were in a desperate position, but their courage was revived by the miraculous discovery of the Holy Lance, or what they believed to be the lance that had pierced Christ's side on the cross. Heartened by this sign, they sallied out and defeated the Turkish army. Quarrels among the leaders and a dispute as to whether they should hand Antioch over to the emperor delayed them for some months. Finally, as Alexius failed to appear, they left Bohemond in possession of Antioch and moved on down the coast. They met with no strong opposition, for the inhabitants of the country were accustomed to conquest and cared little who ruled them. When they arrived before Jerusalem in the summer of 1099, they found that it had been taken from the Turks by an Egyptian force and was not strongly garrisoned. The taking of the city was followed by scenes of pious joy and bloodshed. "The celebration in the church of the Holy Sepulcher, where men wept together in joy and grief, and the merciless slaughter of the inhabitants, well expressed, in combination, the spirit of the crusade."

The kingdom of Jerusalem. After the capture of Jerusalem, many of the crusaders returned home, feeling that they had accomplished their immediate purpose. The remainder stayed to spread their conquests and to

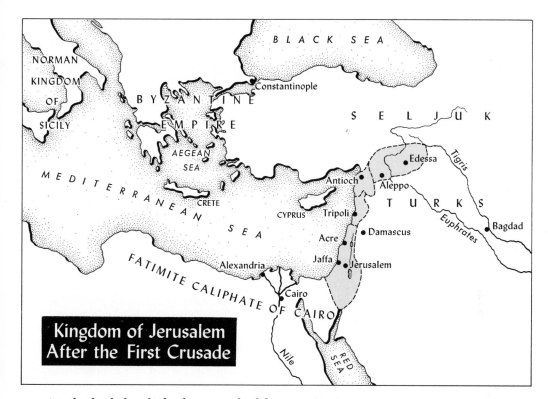

Kingdom of Jerusalem After the First Crusade

Map labels: NORMAN KINGDOM OF SICILY, BYZANTINE EMPIRE, BLACK SEA, Constantinople, SELJUK, AEGEAN SEA, MEDITERRANEAN SEA, CRETE, CYPRUS, Edessa, Antioch, Aleppo, Tripoli, TURKS, Tigris, Euphrates, Bagdad, Acre, Damascus, Jaffa, Jerusalem, Alexandria, FATIMITE CALIPHATE OF CAIRO, Cairo, Nile, RED SEA

organize the land they had taken as a feudal state. The first ruler chosen by the barons, Godfrey of Bouillon, refused the royal title, preferring that of "Defender of the Holy Sepulcher." His brother Baldwin, however, who succeeded him in 1100, took the title "King of Jerusalem." The work of conquest continued for a quarter of a century, greatly aided by fleets from the Italian commercial cities and by a constant stream of fighting pilgrims from the West. The result was the Latin kingdom of Jerusalem, an artificially constructed feudal state, stretching from the southern end of Palestine all along the Syrian coast and thence to the northeast. It was divided into four large units — the kingdom of Jerusalem proper (the royal domain), and three great fiefs: the county of Tripoli, founded by Raymond of Toulouse, the principality of Antioch, founded by Bohemond and Tancred, and the county of Edessa, founded by Baldwin I. The lords of these great fiefs recognized the king as their overlord, but were practically independent sovereigns. Within the royal domain and the three large fiefs, there were lesser baronies and knights' holdings, granted to vassals in return for military service, according to feudal cus-

tom. In the coast towns, merchants from Venice, Genoa, and Pisa built permanent trading posts and were given special privileges. The original inhabitants, including numbers of Jews and Christians who had kept their faith through centuries of Moslem domination, still made up the bulk of the population. The crusaders who settled in the kingdom of Jerusalem were never more than a small minority. They made themselves at home in the new land, gradually adopting the clothing and many of the customs of the natives as being more suited to the climate, which was so different from that they had known in the West.

The Second Crusade. The kingdom of Jerusalem was essentially weak. It was little more than a narrow coastal plain, open to attack all along the flank. Moreover, it was weakened by the rivalries and jealousies of the great lords, of the merchants from the different Italian cities, and of the two great orders of crusading knights, the Hospitalers and Templars, which had acquired a great deal of land since they were founded in the early days of the conquest. There was always feeling, too, between the older settlers and the new arrivals from the West. All that saved the crusaders was an equal lack of unity among their Moslem neighbors. The latter, however, were slowly uniting. In 1144, they reconquered Edessa without much difficulty. News of this disaster led to the organization of the Second Crusade. Moved by the preaching of St. Bernard of Clairvaux, Louis VII of France and the Hohenstaufen emperor, Conrad III, led large armies to the East in 1147, where they accomplished little or nothing. Their failure was due largely to the jealousy and bad faith of the Europeans in Syria whom they had come to aid.

Saladin takes Jerusalem.   The suicidal divisions among the resident Christians multiplied during the next generation, while on the other side the Turkish leader Saladin was uniting both Egyptian and Syrian Moslems under his rule. In 1187, he overran Palestine, took Jerusalem, and occupied all of the kingdom proper, leaving the Latins only the county of Tripoli and the principality of Antioch.

The Third Crusade.   The fall of Jerusalem, after nearly a century of Christian rule, shocked Europe and aroused new enthusiasm for a crusade. This time the three greatest rulers of Christendom took the cross and led their countrymen to the East. The aged emperor, Frederick Barbarossa, was the first to start. He was drowned while crossing a mountain stream in Asia Minor, and most of his followers returned home. The kings of France and England, Philip Augustus and Richard the Lion-hearted, arrived later. It was not until 1191 that the latter, who had stopped on the way to conquer the island of Cyprus, joined the crusaders who were besieging the city of Acre on the coast of Palestine. Philip and Richard were of very different character and were natural enemies. Quarrels soon broke out between them, nearly paralyzing the effectiveness of the crusading army. One of the chroniclers of the period asserted that "the two kings and peoples did less together than they would have done apart." Philip returned home soon after the fall of Acre, leaving Richard to carry on the war against Saladin. Innumerable romances have been woven about the campaigns of these two warriors. Both were courageous and both could be magnanimous, but Saladin showed himself the more civilized of the two. Richard won a place for himself in both Christian and Moslem legend by his reckless daring,

but was unable to capture Jerusalem. In August, 1192, he concluded a truce with Saladin, whereby the Christians gained a strip of the Palestine coast from Acre to Ascalon and the right of free entry for pilgrims going to Jerusalem.

2. Later Crusades

The Fourth Crusade.   The thirteenth century, which opened with the great pontificate of Innocent III, might have been expected to produce some successful crusades. There were a good many crusades, but they were all rather inglorious affairs, and the very first one, inaugurated by Innocent himself, was shamefully diverted from its purpose. Germany at the beginning of the century was preoccupied by the civil war between the rival emperors. The knights who gathered at Venice in 1202, therefore, were mostly French. They had bargained with the Venetians for transportation, but were unable to raise the stipulated price. After much discussion they arrived at a compromise. They would pay for their passage by capturing for the Venetians the rival trading city of Zara, across the Adriatic. Europe was shocked by the use of a crusading army against a Christian city and some of the crusaders refused to serve. But worse was still to come. Zara was taken, but the Venetians drove a hard bargain and the crusaders were still short of funds. The Doge of Venice, who seems to have been the evil genius of the crusade, again tempted the crusaders by pointing out the rich plunder to be had from the sack of Constantinople, provided an excuse could be found for attacking it. The excuse was presented by a pretender to the throne of the Byzantine Empire, who promised the French knights everything they asked if they would aid him. Accordingly, they moved on to Constantinople, captured the city, and looted it amid scenes of wanton violence. Then, when the new emperor was unable to fulfill his promises, they ousted him in turn, and elected one of their own number, Baldwin of Flanders, as emperor. Venice was given special trading privileges and a good deal of territory along the coast and in the islands, as her share of the plunder. The Latin Empire of Constantinople lasted till 1261, when it was retaken by the Byzantine emperor, who still held Asia Minor. That half-century greatly weakened the Eastern Empire.

Later crusades. Intermittent crusades continued through the greater part of the thirteenth century, but they accomplished little. Innocent III, who had been bitterly disappointed by the results of the Fourth Crusade, organized another just before his death. It started in 1217, led by the King of Hungary. The crusaders marched through Syria to Egypt, where they took Damietta, only to lose it two years later. The next crusade was that of the Emperor Frederick II in 1228. As has already been told, he gained Jerusalem by peaceful negotiations rather than by warfare. Other crusades followed, the most important of which were the two, mentioned in the last chapter, led by the saintly French king, Louis IX. His first crusade met with disaster in Egypt. The second, in 1270, was crippled by the death of St. Louis in Tunis, after which Prince Edward of England, who had accompanied him, went on to Syria, but accomplished nothing. It was the last serious crusade.

End of the Latin states in Syria. What was left of the Latin states in Syria dragged on a precarious existence until the last decade of the thirteenth century, but they were pitifully weak. The internal quarrels, factions, and jealousies that had proved so dangerous to them in the twelfth century were now multiplied. It was clear that they could not defend themselves for long without aid from the West — and the extent of that aid was steadily decreasing. By 1291, the last of the Latin possessions in Syria had been wiped out. The Latin kingdom of Jerusalem had come to an end, after an existence of nearly two centuries. As wars of conquest, the crusades had achieved no permanent results; but they had served a great purpose by checking for a long time the westward advance of the Turks.

Waning of the crusading spirit. The failure to hold the lands won in the East was due not only to the weakness and folly of the Europeans in Syria, but also to the gradual decline and final disappearance of the crusading spirit among the western peoples. The repeated calls

A crusaders' castle, known as Krak des Chevaliers, an outpost held by the Knights of St. John of Jerusalem in the twelfth century, still dominates the barren Syrian landscape.

issued by the thirteenth-century popes for new crusades to defend or rescue the Holy Land were answered with ever-diminishing enthusiasm. Expeditions against the Moslems in Spain, the Albigensian heretics in southern France, or the heathen Slavs in Prussia gave the European knights a more convenient opportunity for fulfilling their crusading vows than did the long voyage to Syria. More important than this, however, was the general feeling of disillusionment about the crusades. The diversion of the Fourth Crusade against the Greek Christians of Constantinople, and the uniform failure of the later expeditions, did much to dampen popular zeal. Tales told by the returning crusaders of the selfishness and dissensions of the Christians in Syria had the same effect. Popes and sovereigns, too, had often misused the crusading enthusiasm of the people, raising funds for crusades that were never begun. For more than a generation, the popes who followed Innocent III were more interested in their struggle with the Hohenstaufen emperors in Sicily than in the war against Islam, and preached crusade after crusade against them. Finally, and this is perhaps the most fundamental reason for the decline of the crusading spirit, the peoples of the West were developing new interests that absorbed all their attention. Military feudalism was declining before the rising power of the monarchies and of the commercial middle class. In a thousand imponderable ways, the spirit of Europe was changing. The crusades fitted into the peculiar civilization of the High Middle Ages. As that age passed, the crusades died with it, though pious people dreamed of reviving them for two centuries longer.

Effect of the crusades on Europe. The crusades undoubtedly acted as a stimulus to the awakening economic, social, and cultural life of western Europe. They run parallel in time to a period of intellectual ferment and expanding social energy. But to what extent were the crusades a cause, and not themselves merely an outgrowth, of the rising civilization of the Middle Ages? That is a question to which many answers have been given. It is difficult to specify any single development that would not have taken place in some degree without the crusades. The Italian cities, and through them the other towns of Europe, certainly

benefited directly by the trade with the Christian states in Syria and by the carrying of pilgrims and crusaders to and from the Holy Land. But trade with the Middle East had begun before the crusades, and would inevitably have increased without their help, though not perhaps so rapidly. Europe in this period borrowed largely from the science, philosophy, luxuries, and general culture of the Moslem world. But the most direct contact between Christendom and Islam came through Spain and Sicily rather than the East. The medieval popes undoubtedly gained in prestige from their leadership of such great international enterprises as the crusades. But their supremacy was won on other grounds. Almost the only results for the papacy that can be traced directly to the crusading movement were the institution of the clerical tithe, a direct papal tax levied on all the clergy, and the sale of indulgences. Both of these methods of raising money were continued by later popes after the crusades, which were the original excuse for them, had ceased. The monarchies in France and England probably gained something from the diversion of the fighting energy of the feudal nobles to a distant field. But the rise of the monarchies was due far more to other causes.

Nevertheless, despite all possible qualifications, and even though its effects may have been more in the nature of a stimulus to developments that would have taken place anyway rather than of an original cause, a movement that involved so many people over a period of two centuries must have made a strong impression on the life of the age. The effects of travel depend entirely on the mental equipment and powers of observation of those who travel, and many who made that perilous journey probably learned little or nothing from it. Still, some among the many crusaders and pilgrims must have returned with a broader mental horizon and with new ideas. Aside from what they may have learned from the infidel, knights from all parts of Europe met together and learned the customs of one another's countries. The manners and customs of chivalry became more universal and more highly formalized. The romantic adventures of the crusaders were retold in song and story, giving rise to a new popular literature for the knightly class. Above all, the crusades shook up a fairly settled society and made it less provincial.

3. *The Expansion of Catholic Europe*

While the crusaders were carrying Christianity into the distant lands of the eastern Mediterranean, other Christian soldiers were waging a more permanently successful war against heathen and infidels within Europe itself. Christianity had already spread widely through missionary activity in the lands bordering the Holy Roman Empire to the east and north, and we will pause to note these additions to Catholic Christendom before turning to the armed conquests made by the crusaders.

Bohemia, Poland, and Hungary. The conversion of the Slavs of Bohemia — the modern Czechoslovakia — was begun as early as the ninth century by Byzantine missionaries. But the Bohemians, unlike the Russian Slavs, did not remain in the Greek Orthodox faith. They turned instead to the Roman Church. After the middle of the tenth century, when the German emperor, Otto the Great, forced the Czechs to recognize him as their overlord, Bohemia faced definitely westward. It became a fief of the empire, though it always preserved a separate government of its own, and its duke, who after 1158 bore the title of king, had greater power over his people than had any other of the emperor's vassals. Poland, the other great Slavic country to the east of the empire, was not converted to Christianity until the second half of the tenth century, and then through the work of Roman Catholic missionaries. Unlike Bohemia, Poland did not become a permanent part of the Holy Roman Empire, though it did remain within the Roman Church. It covered a large territory, but seldom enjoyed strong government and was always open to attack from its powerful neighbors. Hungary, the eastern neighbor of the empire to the south of Poland, was still later in receiving Christianity. There were many Slavs in Hungary, but the dominant race were the Magyars, a nomadic people who, like so many others, had drifted into Europe from western Asia. After ravaging Germany for years, they were defeated by Otto the Great in 955 and forced to settle down. Nearly half a century later, they were converted and brought into the Roman Church by their king, St. Stephen. During the thirteenth century, Poland and Hungary formed an invaluable bulwark for western Christendom against the attack of the fierce Mongols, who swept out of Asia across eastern Europe and founded the vast empire called the Golden Horde, which for long dominated Russia.

Conversion of Scandinavia. It was not till the eleventh century that Christianity was firmly established in the Scandinavian lands to the north of western Europe. The Danes were the first to be converted by Catholic missionaries, but there were many heathen still left there at the time when King Canute (1017–35) ruled a great empire that included England and Norway as well as his own country. Norway soon followed and finally Sweden, though not without stubborn resistance from the devotees of the old heathen gods.

Expansion to the northeast. Very different from this process of conversion was the expansion of Christendom to the northeast of the empire during the period of the crusades. Through most of the twelfth century the Germans of Saxony, Holstein, and the North Mark carried on a war of conquest against the heathen Slavs who dwelt to the south of the Baltic, between the rivers Elbe and Oder. It was a war of conquest and extermination. As German authority moved eastward to the Oder, the land was resettled by German colonists, while adventurous German traders established new trading cities all along the Baltic coast. Much of the final success of the struggle was due to the leadership of Henry the Lion, Duke of Saxony and head of the Welf party.[1] Meanwhile, farther east in Pomerania, between the Oder and the Vistula, the Poles had extended Christianity to the Baltic by similarly forceful means. But the Prussians, a wild and warlike people of Letto-Lithuanian stock who occupied the territory between Poland and the Baltic beyond the Vistula, were still heathen and were a constant menace to the Poles. Early in the thirteenth century, the Poles appealed to the crusading order of Teutonic Knights, who had

[1] See above, page 183.

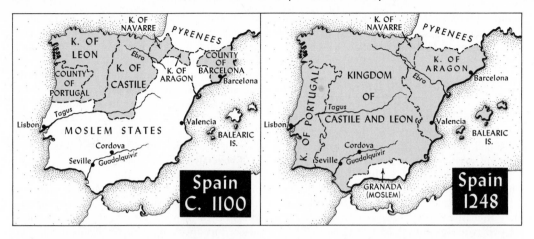

already done good work in the Holy Land, to aid them against the heathen Prussians. They were promised whatever land they could conquer and the donation was ratified by the emperor. The knights began their campaign in 1230, and thereafter pressed the crusade, as they considered it, so strongly that by 1283 they were masters of Prussia. They thus founded a German state on the eastern Baltic, cut off from the empire only by the strip of Polish Pomerania.[1]

Christian conquests in Spain.   Still greater interest attaches to the expansion of Christendom by the conquest of the highly civilized Moslem country in Spain. The collapse of the caliphate of Cordova in 1034, due to internal dissensions, provided a good opportunity for the little Christian kingdoms in the north to expand at the expense of the Moors, as the Moslems in Spain were called. For more than two centuries they continued the struggle with varying success, often aided by crusaders from France and other parts of Europe. In the end, the Christians were almost completely successful in their perpetual crusade. By 1248, only the little kingdom of Granada in the south re-

[1] See map, page 268.

mained in Moorish hands. The rest of Spain was divided amongst four Christian kingdoms. Castile, to which Leon had been permanently united since 1230, was the largest, occupying most of the central and western part of the peninsula. Aragon, the next largest, occupied a triangle, of which one side extended along the Pyrenees from the east and the second stretched down the eastern coast below Valencia. The kings of Aragon, who had become vassals of the papacy in the days of Innocent III, also ruled the Balearic Islands and some territory in southern France, and in 1282 they acquired the island of Sicily after the Sicilians had rebelled against their recent conqueror, Charles of Anjou. In between Castile and Aragon on the northern border was the little kingdom of Navarre, which had been unable to expand because surrounded by its two powerful neighbors. Finally, in the southwest was the newly founded kingdom of Portugal. Spain's period of stress was now past, and she was prepared to take her place in the main current of European history. In the fifteenth century, the union of Castile and Aragon and the extinction of Granada gave her unity and strength and made her one of the great powers of the West.

18

Feudal Society — The Peasants and the Nobles

IN THE preceding chapters, we have traced the main outline of the political events in the feudal kingdoms during the High Middle Ages. It is now time to investigate the manner of life of the men who made up feudal society during this period. For the lives of human beings are the essential material of history, and it is as important to know something of the daily life of the undistinguished individuals who form the great mass of society as it is to follow the careers of famous men or to study the institutions of the age. In Chapter 13 feudalism and the manorial system were described as forms of political, social, and economic organization. Both feudalism and the manorial system took shape in the relatively moneyless economy of the Early Middle Ages. They still continued to form the framework of the social structure during the High Middle Ages, though not without changes resulting from the growth of money economy which followed the commercial revival. With increasing prosperity, the lot of the peasants was gradually improved, while the nobles were enabled to develop a more refined and courtly mode of life and to raise their standard of living. In the High Middle Ages the culture and the social ideals characteristic of the feudal nobility reached their fullest development. In this chapter, we shall try to show how the two great classes of feudal society — the peasants and the nobles — lived during these two centuries, and some-

thing also of what they thought. Although the peasants did not hold fiefs and so, in the strict sense of the word, were not feudal, in a society dominated by feudalism they formed a part of feudal society, much as industrial workers in capitalist countries today may be said to form part of a capitalist society. We will leave to the next two chapters the townsmen and the clergy, who, though living in the midst of feudalism, had yet a separate life and special interests of their own.

1. General Conditions of Medieval Life

Lack of security. The life of the average man in the Middle Ages was short and uncertain. He was a constant prey to disease, to the malign forces of nature, and, above all, to the avarice and brutality of his fellow men. Except in England, where the monarchy was usually strong enough to prevent the worst disorders, there was little security for life or property. Elsewhere, the central government was seldom strong enough to give protection to the people outside the largest cities or the immediate royal domain. The feudal nobles, whose duty it was to protect those dependent upon them, were often too earnestly engaged in pursuing their own interests to bother with police duty or justice — or were themselves a

213

menace to the defenseless. Robbers and brigands infested the roads and made travel dangerous for all but numerous and well-armed parties. Avaricious nobles, too, rode down from their hilltop castles to rob the merchants, pilgrims, and priests who passed upon the highway, or to hold them for ransom. Not content with that, they often fell upon the villages of the defenseless peasants or upon the outlying monasteries, where there was always a chance for plunder. In time of peace, the nobles were often little better than brigands. In time of war, they were usually worse.

Hazards from war.   Warfare, private and public, was indeed still the curse of feudal society, although conditions in this respect were not so bad as they had been in the ninth and tenth centuries. Everywhere on the Continent the nobles had the right to wage private warfare on their neighbors, and they exercised that right freely. The petty campaigns arising from private quarrels were, of course, smaller in scope than the national wars, but they were far more numerous and, in the long run, did much more damage. There were few great battles, but there were innumerable skirmishes and frightful destruction of the lives and property of noncombatants. It was the peasants and to a lesser extent the monks and the inhabitants of the smaller towns who suffered most from medieval warfare. The chief aim of the fighting noble was to weaken and impoverish his enemy by destroying the productivity of his land and, second to that, to acquire plunder. Consequently, he ravaged his enemy's fields, destroyed the standing crops, burned the villages after carrying off the cattle and anything else of value, and massacred or held for ransom the peasants, who were themselves valuable property and the chief source of his enemy's income. St. Peter Damian summed up the situation when he wrote that, whenever two nobles quarrel, "the poor man's thatch goes up in flame." The following description of feudal warfare from the *chanson des Lorrains* is abundantly confirmed by less poetic documents:

They start to march. The scouts and the incendiaries lead; after them come the foragers who are to gather the spoils and carry them in the great baggage train. The tumult begins. The peasants, having just come out of the fields,

turn back, uttering loud cries; the shepherds gather their flocks and drive them towards the neighboring woods in the hope of saving them. The incendiaries set the villages on fire, and the foragers visit and sack them; the distracted inhabitants are burnt or led apart with their hands tied to be held for ransom. Everywhere alarm bells ring, fear spreads from side to side and becomes general. On all sides one sees helmets shining, pennons floating and horsemen covering the plain. Here hands are laid on money; there cattle, donkeys and flocks are seized. The smoke spreads, the flames rise, the peasants and the shepherds in consternation flee in all directions.

And after the campaign "windmills no longer turn, chimneys no longer smoke, the cocks have ceased their crowing and the dogs their barking, . . . briars and thorns grow where villages stood of old." This is what war might mean to the peasants. And in many parts of Europe, war was almost the normal state of society.

Flood and famine.   Nor was war the only hazard of life in the Middle Ages. The medieval man was far more at the mercy of the elements than we are today. Floods often did terrible damage, sometimes wiping out whole towns or villages. Even today, there are occasional disastrous floods; but in that age they were far more numerous and more deadly, for there were no means of controlling them or of bringing relief to the victims. More terrible than the floods were the famines that usually followed them, or that resulted from other adverse weather conditions. Medieval methods of agriculture were crude and unscientific. Too much rain or too little, unseasonable heat or cold, an unusual number of insect pests, or any of the other natural hazards of farming, which today can be combated by scientific means, might destroy the peasant's whole crop. In the eleventh century, the French chronicles record forty-eight famine years. By the end of the twelfth century, methods of agriculture had improved, but there were still eleven famines in France during the reign of Philip Augustus. There were also countless local famines; for roads were so bad that it was difficult to transport food even a short distance to places where local weather conditions, floods, or the depredations of a campaign had destroyed the crops.

Famine did not mean mere shortage of food for the peasant and poor townsman; it frequently meant death by starvation. The year 1197 saw terrible famines in France. A chronicler of Liége wrote that even the rich suffered great privation, and "as for the poor, they died of hunger."

Disease. Epidemic diseases often accompanied famines, spreading like wildfire among the people weakened by starvation. Even in good years epidemics were common. The crowded towns, with their narrow, filthy streets and complete lack of sanitation, were perfect breeding places for disease, nor were the country villages much better. The chronicles of the period are filled with records of the "plague" or "pest." These were generic names for diseases which the people had not sufficient knowledge to describe more accurately. They lacked, too, any scientific knowledge of preventive or curative measures. Harsh experience had taught them that many diseases were contagious, though they did not know why. People often fled from a plague-stricken town, but as they knew nothing about disinfection, they might easily carry the disease with them and spread it through the countryside. Aside from epidemics, the death toll from other diseases or from injuries, which today can be prevented or cured by medical or surgical science, was terribly high. Simple infection of wounds alone led to countless unnecessary deaths, and infant mortality was appalling.

Superstition. One should not imagine, however, that the medieval man took no steps to combat the evils that befell him, but his methods were not those approved by modern science. He believed that all disasters, whether caused by the weather, insects, or disease, were of supernatural origin, a divine punishment for his sins or the malign work of the devil and other evil spirits. His method of coping with disaster was everywhere the same —an attempt to obtain divine aid by public prayers, penance, processions, and supplications to the saints who were noted for their healing powers or who were recognized as the special protectors of the district. When his fields suffered from insect plagues, the helpless peasant turned for aid to the church, and, if he were in good standing with the local clergy, received its full cooperation; for the priest, though somewhat better educated, was as superstitious as the peasant. A solemn anathema issued by the Bishop of Troyes against the "locusts and caterpillars and other such animals that have laid waste the vineyards" of his diocese shows the church giving spiritual aid to the peasants on a large scale. Indeed, the "excommunication of caterpillars" was not uncommon.

When the church failed him, the peasant often turned to ancient superstitions of pagan origin, that had lasted on through centuries of Christianity, sometimes vaguely colored by Christian forms. Magic incantations, witchcraft, and sorcery held a powerful appeal for medieval men, despite the efforts of the church to eradicate them. But this magic was not always invoked to aid men. Often it was used as a threat, for there was black magic as well as white. Thus, to the normal fears of a hazardous life were added superstitious terrors — fear of malign spirits, of old women who were believed to have sold their souls to the devil and who could bewitch children or put a plague on the cattle, or of the "evil eye" which still terrifies the Italian peasants. Yet the church provided strong counter-charms — the sign of the cross or a *pater noster* — and those who were able to make a pilgrimage to the shrine of a famous saint or to touch the casket containing a relic of his body felt well armed against the powers of darkness.

Progress. We must not, however, draw too dark a picture of the life of the Middle Ages. Despite ignorance, poverty, and the dread disasters of flood, famine, pestilence, and war, there was a great deal of stirring and vigorous life. The population of Europe was steadily increasing; the lower classes were gaining greater freedom; and, as we shall see in the next chapter, in the growing towns a new free class was re-creating wealth through the revival of commerce and industry. The thirteenth century, indeed, witnessed a remarkable expansion of economic activity in both city and country. Finally, the High Middle Ages was a period of great progress in education, literature, philosophy, art, and music. But we must turn now from the general conditions of life in the Middle Ages to those that especially affected the peasants, who bore the full brunt of the hazards of medieval life and were only slowly affected by the progress of that period.

2. The Peasants

An inferior social class.   The lines dividing the social classes in the Middle Ages were far more clearly drawn than they are today. Between the two great classes of common and noble there stood a wide gulf that was rarely crossed. All the instincts of medieval men, and especially of the ruling classes, were opposed to change of any kind in the social system. Custom and tradition had the force of law and were supported by the religious teachings of the age. The generally accepted theory of society, as propounded by generations of theologians, recognized three great classes, each of which had a definite function to perform for the good of the whole social body. These were, first, the clergy, whose duty was to pray and to care for the salvation of their fellow men; second, the nobles, whose duty was to fight in defense of the helpless and to keep order; and finally, the peasants and artisans, whose function was to work and to provide the necessities of life for the whole of society, as well as luxuries for the upper classes. These functions were not always faithfully performed, except perhaps by the workers who had little choice in the matter, but the distinction between the classes was not merely a theory. It was based on a clear recognition of existing conditions, and from that very fact was believed to have the sanction of the Divine Will. For it would be blasphemy to maintain that society could be so constituted unless God had so intended it. The duty of the peasant, then, was clear to all. He was to work and to make no rebellion against his lot. The following pious statement from a contemporary chronicle expresses the opinion of noble and cleric alike: "God forbid that the peasants, whose proper lot is daily toil, should abandon themselves to sloth and indolently spend their time in laughter and idle merriment." And toil, unfortunately, carried with it a stigma of social inferiority, for in the early feudal ages almost all the workers on the land were to some extent unfree, and even after they obtained personal freedom, their class bore the stamp of servile origin.

Attitude of the nobles.   The free-born, fighting noble, therefore, had nothing but contempt for the servile, laboring peasant. He was necessary to the comfort and prosperity of his master, but as an individual person he scarcely existed. He was regarded as distinctly an inferior being. The romantic literature of the period, composed for a noble audience, reflects this attitude. When an individual peasant is mentioned, which is not often, he is described as physically grotesque, stupid, and horribly unclean — as, indeed, he probably was. The peasant who appears in the romance of *Aucassin et Nicolette* may be taken as an example:

As Aucassin rode along an old grass-grown road, he raised his eyes and saw in the way a great fellow, wondrously hideous and foul to behold. He had a shock of hair blacker than coal-dust, and more than a hand-breadth between the eyes, and thick cheeks with a huge flat nose and great wide nostrils, and blubber-lips redder than roast flesh, and great hideous teeth. He was clad in hosen and shoes of cowhide, bound round with linden-bast up to his knee; he was wrapped in a thread-bare cloak and leaned on a great knotted staff. . . .

Exploitation of the peasants.   It is not surprising to find that the nobles exploited the peasants. There were, of course, good lords who felt responsible for the security of their peasants and acted justly according to their lights, as well as bad lords who squeezed every possible penny from them. But even the best of lords demanded full payment of the heavy manorial dues from their own peasants and were utterly merciless to the peasants belonging to their enemies. "All that the peasant amasses in a year by stubborn work, the knight, the noble, devours in an hour." So wrote Jacques de Vitry, with no more than the customary exaggeration of the moralist. The greatest of medieval popes, Innocent III, gave similar testimony in his *De Contemptu Mundi.*

The serf serves; he is terrified with threats, wearied with *corvées* [forced labor], afflicted with blows, despoiled of his possessions; for, if he possess nought, he is compelled to earn; and if he possess anything, he is compelled to have it not; the lord's fault is the serf's punishment; the serf's fault is the lord's excuse for preying on him. . . .

The peasants often suffered, too, from the rapacity and dishonesty of the lord's officers. Under a careless lord, the bailiff who acted as his agent, the forester whose duty was to see that the peasants did not cut more than their share of wood or poach the lord's game, and the other petty officials of the manor had a good deal of power, which they frequently abused to extort money from the peasants. These manorial officials themselves sprang from the peasant class, but opportunities for advancement were so few that the desire to take full advantage of such as did arise usually outweighed any fellow-feeling they might have retained for their old neighbors.

The church and the peasants. The clergy were not far behind the nobles in exploiting the peasants. True, they did not rob and kill, as the nobles did in time of war, and they did much to aid the peasants by checking the lawlessness of feudal warfare. But they were one of the two privileged classes whom it was the duty of the peasants to support, and they clung tenaciously to their rights. The parish priests were often merciless in collecting their tithes, and seldom hesitated to use the dread threat of excommunication to force payment. Moreover, the church held a great deal of land, and ecclesiastical lords, in general, were no more lenient with their peasants than were the lay nobles. Indeed, modern research has shown that customary dues were retained with less amelioration and that serfdom lasted longer on monastic estates than elsewhere.

The peasant's work. The daily life of the peasant was a monotonous round of unremitting toil, broken only by the religious holidays prescribed by the church. These were fairly numerous, but as a rule only the most important were observed — and those somewhat unwillingly, for every hour of work was valuable to men whose margin of subsistence was as narrow as that of the average peasant. The working day began at dawn and did not end till dark. Often the best part of the day had to be spent working on the lord's land. Plowing, cultivating, and reaping, caring for the oxen and cattle, hedging, ditching, and carrying produce to market — these filled the day of the ordinary peasant. Others had special tasks which occupied most of their time, like the shepherd,

Peasant life in winter is illustrated in a miniature by the brothers Limbourg in the Book of Hours *of the Duke of Berry (1409– 16). This scene of a village in the snow represents the month of February.*

cowherd, swineherd, hayward, and so forth. Women and children worked with the men in the fields at the reaping or any other task within their strength.

Tools. The peasant's tools were crude and simple. Even the plow, which was too expensive for the poorer peasant to own by himself, was a clumsy affair made of wood, though some had iron at the point. The usual substitute for a harrow was a thorn tree weighted down by logs. An inventory of a peasant's tools in the year 1301 mentions only "a hoe, spade, axe, billhook, two yokes for carrying buckets and a barrel; total estimated value, 10 *d.*" Wealthier peasants doubtless had more tools, for scythes, sickles, and flails were used, but the custom of communal labor probably relieved the individual peasant from the necessity of himself owning all the tools needed for the year's work.

Houses and clothing.   The peasant's house was merely a rough wooden hut, with a thatched roof. It was a squalid and filthy dwelling. In it we would find what one modern historian has characterized as "poverty unadorned." There was no chimney. Cooking was done out-of-doors in the summer. In the winter, when a fire had to be lighted in the house, the smoke escaped, if at all, by the door, and must have nearly suffocated the inhabitants. Few of the peasants had ovens. They sent their bread up to the manor house to be baked in the great oven there. Even those who had ovens of their own had to pay the customary fee for the use of the lord's oven. Sometimes the hut would contain a rough bed, where all the family slept. More often there was merely a pile of straw, alive with vermin, in one corner. Geese and hens wandered freely about the house, and the oxen were usually stabled in a lean-to beside it. In summer, the peasant was probably comfortable enough, for his standards were not high, but the winters must have been terrible. We know all too little about what clothing he wore, save that it was mostly hand-made by the women of the family. The description of a peasant, already quoted, from *Aucassin et Nicolette,* will furnish a rough idea of his dress. It was almost certainly inadequate protection against the cold of a northern winter.

Food.   What evidence we have as to the ordinary food of the peasant illustrates better than anything else the extent of his poverty. Modern farmers, however destitute, have usually enough to eat. The medieval farmer, on the other hand, ate poorly even in good years, and starved in years of famine. Meat of any kind was apparently a rare luxury. A fifteenth-century writer described the food of the peasant thus: "They feed on brown bread, oatmeal porridge or boiled peas; they drink water or whey." In some places the thirteenth-century peasant was probably better off, but all the evidence shows that the same foods — porridge and black bread made of rye or oatmeal, simple vegetables, cheese and whey, with perhaps an occasional egg — were the staples of diet. Beer

was available at times, but not by any means universally. Of course, on feast days the peasant was sometimes admitted to the lower hall of the manor house, where he would gorge himself on richer food at the lord's expense.

Diversions.   The peasant's toilsome life was not entirely unrelieved by color or diversion, though there was little enough. On the great religious holidays, when he was forbidden to work, he might have some share in the excitement that attended the celebrations of his betters. He might be admitted to the feast at the castle or be allowed to watch the knights disporting themselves at the tournament. If he were fortunate enough to be sent with produce to a nearby town during a fair, he might watch the jugglers and tumblers or listen to some wandering minstrel, or have his pocket picked while he gaped openmouthed at the antics of a performing bear. On Sundays and holidays, too, he might join in the dance on the village green or engage in a rough — often very rough — game of football. Frequent prohibitions of dancing and football appear in the records of the period, especially on monastic estates. The following entry in the records of a fourteenth-century monastic manor court may suggest the reason: "From the aforesaid John, John, William, and Robert the servant of Thomas Butler, because they played at ball, through which grievous contention and contumely arose between the lord prior's tenants, as was found by the twelve jurymen, of the penalty elsewhere prescribed, 20 *s.*"

<u>**Morals and religion.**</u>   According to contemporary writers, the peasant's material destitution was matched by an equal spiritual poverty. He was totally uneducated; his morals were often little better than animal; and his religion was grossly material and more than half superstition. Ecclesiastical writers railed against the peasant for his indifference to religion — he neglected the saints' days; he sometimes worked on Sundays; he showed small respect for the parish priest; and he was unwilling to pay the tithe. They described him as avaricious, quarrelsome, dishonest, suspicious, and sullen. Considering his life of grinding poverty, toil, oppression, and terror, it would be surprising if he were not.

Gradual improvement.   Unhappy as the peasants' lot was, it was not as bad at the end of the thirteenth century as it had been two centuries before. The rise of new markets in the growing towns, the opening-up of new land, the increase in general prosperity and the reintroduction of money economy[1] gave the peasants an opportunity to improve their conditions. In many places they acquired personal freedom, and their services to the lord were commuted to fixed money payments. And almost everywhere the lord's free right to exploit his peasants was being restricted.

3. The Nobles

Warlike character. The feudal noble was before all else a soldier. Fighting was the function assigned to his social class by the theorists of the Middle Ages. It was his duty and also his privilege. Everywhere on the Continent the nobles clung to their right to wage private war on their neighbors; and they guarded as jealously their exclusive right to wear the heavy armor of the mounted knight, which made them the effective fighting force of the Middle Ages. Foot soldiers played their part in feudal warfare, probably a larger part than the records show, but they were generally disregarded and despised. The mounted noble trampled even those of his own side under foot when they got in his way, and neither the chronicles nor the romances paid them much attention. To understand the life and character of the medi-

[1] See below, pages 239–240.

eval noble, one must keep in mind this essential fact, that he was raised from his youth to a life of battle, plunder, and pillage. In the last analysis, his political power and his privileged position in society depended on his war-horse, his heavy armor, and his military training.

The noble's castle. They depended only slightly less on the strength of his fortified castle. So long as it stood, his position was secure. He could defy the king or his overlord, or sally out lightheartedly to wage private war on his neighbors. If the war went against him, he could retire behind the safe protection of his castle walls, pull up the drawbridge, and wait till the opposing army was forced to give up the siege. His crops might be destroyed, and those of his peasants who could not get into the castle might be massacred or taken prisoner; but that was merely an economic loss that could be made up by a plundering expedition at some more favorable time. The castle was essentially a fort, but it was also the noble's home in time of peace as in war. It was the scene, therefore, of every aspect of the noble's life.

Description of a castle. The site of the castle was chosen for its defensibility rather than for convenience or ease of access. A hilltop, a rocky promontory, an island, or any similar position would provide a suitable site. We will take as a typical example a baronial castle of the reign of Philip Augustus, set in the acute angle where two rivers join, such as

Château Gaillard, built by Richard I of England in 1198, stands on a precipitous cliff 300 feet above the river Seine guarding the borders of Normandy. Although now a ruin, its strength is still apparent.

is so vividly described by William Stearns Davis in his delightful book *Life on a Medieval Barony*. The castle was open to attack only from the landward side. Approaching from that direction, the enemy would have to overcome a series of cunningly contrived obstacles, which could easily hold off any but a very large and well-equipped army, with plenty of time on its hands. And such armies were rare, for it was difficult to hold feudal vassals to more than forty days' military service in one season. First, they would meet a palisade of sharpened wooden stakes, the "barbican," running across the front of the castle from one river-bank to the other. Between it and the castle was a large open court, the "lists" where horses were exercised and tournaments held. The barbican was designed to be merely a momentary check to allow the garrison time to prepare its defenses. The first serious obstacle was the moat at the foot of the castle wall. It was some twenty feet wide and filled with water. It was spanned by a drawbridge, which could be raised at the first sign of danger. Above it towered the wall of the castle, twelve feet thick or more, from which round towers jutted out so that archers could maintain a cross-fire on anyone who might succeed in

crossing the moat. In the center of the wall was the great gate. It was protected by a heavy iron grille, called a "portcullis," fitted into grooves in the masonry and dropped down from above. The heavy oaken gate, reinforced with wrought-iron bands, was in itself no mean obstacle, even without the portcullis. If the enemy succeeded in battering it down, they would find themselves in a narrow, low-arched passage, where there was little room for fighting and where numbers were no advantage. But suppose the besiegers won through. They were still only in the outer courtyard of the castle and would be subjected to a withering fire from the encircling walls. This court was the "bailey" where in normal times the servants and animals lived and where the daily work of the castle was done. The inner court was protected by still higher and more formidable walls and towers. Within it was the palace, in itself a fortress, where the baron lived. And beyond it, in the extreme point of the angle between the rivers, stood the ancient "keep." This was the oldest part of the castle. It was a great stone tower, the last resort of the beleaguered garrison.

Life in the castle. Compared to the ingenuity expended on making the castle an impregnable fortress, relatively little thought was given to making it a comfortable habitation. The living quarters in a baronial castle of the better sort, such as we have been describing, were a great improvement over the old keep and were more luxurious than the small castles of the lesser nobility, but they were still dark, damp, and inconvenient. The windows in the outer walls were mere arrow-slits set deep in the masonry. They let in very little light, but a good deal of wind, for they were without glass. There was little privacy in the castle. It was crowded with servants, men-at-arms, and transient guests, and there were very few rooms. The great vaulted hall was the center of the social life of the castle. There the lord

Dinner in a noble house, the illustration for the month of January from the Book of Hours *of the Duke of Berry, points up the contrast between the life of the nobles and that of the peasants, depicted for the month of February on page 217.*

and his family and their noble guests ate at a table set on a raised dais at one end, while the less important folk sat at long tables stretching down the hall. There, too, after the evening meal a wandering minstrel might sing or recite one of the interminable epic poems of medieval chivalry. When the lord had retired, those who had no other place to sleep spread their cloaks on a table or on a pile of straw on the floor. In winter a great fire was lighted in the huge stone fireplace, but the hall must have been cold and drafty when one got beyond the range of its heat. The floor was flagged with stone and covered with rushes, which must have become rather foul by spring. Hunting dogs wandered about freely and gnawed the bones thrown to them by the diners.

Diversions. Besides eating and drinking, the castle offered few diversions in time of peace. Of course, the lord and his lady found some occupation in looking after the business of the estate and in overseeing the work of the servants. Still, they were left with a good deal of time on their hands. In fine weather, hunting with hounds or hawks was the favorite amusement of both sexes. The nobles loved the chase second only to war, and guarded it as their exclusive privilege. Peasants who poached the lord's game were harshly dealt with. Then, too, the young noble would spend much of his time in practicing the use of arms, and on special occasions there would be tournaments, of which more will be said hereafter. In winter, the noble inhabitants of the castle enjoyed a variety of indoor games, most of which have a strangely modern sound. Chess was very popular, as were also checkers, backgammon, and various dice games. But reading, which fills so many hours for the modern man of leisure, was literally a closed book to most of the medieval nobility. Small wonder that the noble, as he sat listening to the wind howling about the castle walls, longed for spring and hoped that when it came there would be a good war, with plenty of excitement and plunder. Sometimes, the arrival of company broke the monotony. Any noble visitor, whether friend or stranger, was eagerly welcomed and entertained with lavish hospitality, no matter how large a retinue he might have accompanying him.

King John at a stag hunt, from an early fourteenth-century manuscript. Hunting was the favorite sport of nobles throughout the Middle Ages.

The noble's finances. We may ask where the baron found the money to pay for all this picturesque, if somewhat comfortless, magnificence — the great castle, the host of servants, the horses and hounds, the tournaments, the open-handed hospitality, and the ruinous expenses of war. Achille Luchaire gives us part of the answer:

In order to keep up this style of life, it was necessary to oppress subjects cruelly and take much booty from the enemy. Even so, one could not make both ends meet. And it is one of the striking and characteristic traits of feudal life that the noble, great and small, appears to be constantly in need of money, poor, on the watch for financial expedients, always indebted, and a prey of usurers of all kinds.

The growing prosperity which followed the revival of commerce and city life did, however, raise the standard of living of the landholding class generally. The nobles of the twelfth and thirteenth centuries had more money to spend than had their ancestors in the earlier period, when the produce of the land could seldom be turned into cash. But, unfortunately for their solvency, there were also more things on which to spend money; for the merchants and skilled artisans from the cities could now furnish them with goods which in the Early Middle Ages had been unobtainable luxuries, but which, when made available, soon became necessities. Thus the expenses of noble life seemed always to rise more rapidly than income. Economy was, in any case, never a characteristic noble virtue. Rapacious greed for money was common enough among the nobles, who sought to recoup their failing finances by grinding their peasants, by extorting tolls from passing merchants, by pillaging the lands of their enemies, or by outright robbery, but what money they gained they spent recklessly in conspicuous consumption.

The noble lady. Hitherto, we have said little about the lady of the castle. She was not, in contemporary opinion, as important as her husband or sons, yet her position was steadily improving throughout the High Middle Ages. Feudal society was becoming more civilized, and in the more cultured courts of the higher nobility, at least, the feminine influence was strongly felt. The lady of the castle had, indeed, great responsibilities. When her husband was absent, she took command, and if the castle were besieged, she would manage the defense, often as bravely and skillfully as her lord could have done. Under ordinary circumstances she was responsible for the work of the female servants, overseeing the spinning, weaving, embroidering, and sewing. She was also the hostess, and mingled freely with the knightly visitors to the castle. She had a good deal of social freedom, but in the most important event of her life she had no voice. The feudal lady had no initiative in the choice of a husband. That was made for her by her relatives or her overlord. Feudal marriages were always marriages of convenience, involving the transfer of land or the union of two noble houses. If the lady had no brothers she would inherit her father's fief, and it was vitally important to the overlord to see that the fief, and incidentally the heiress, were given to someone who would make a suitable vassal. Or if she were not the sole heiress she would at least carry a dowry of money or land to her husband. This was far more important than any romantic consideration. The noble lady was far from enjoying equal rights with the men of her class in practical matters; but, in

The statue of the Lady Uta in Naumburg Cathedral is one of the finest pieces of medieval sculpture and a vivid reminder that the Middle Ages could boast their share of feminine beauty.

compensation, she benefited to some degree at least from the idealization of women that sprang from the ideals of chivalry, which were slowly transforming the barbarous noble warrior into the knight and were giving him some of the manners and ideals of a gentleman.

4. *Chivalry and the Knights*

Meaning of chivalry. Every noble, if he could afford it and if he did not enter the church, was made a knight as soon as he came of age. He was then recognized as a member of that great international society of fighting gentlemen, the Order of Chivalry. The word chivalry, as applied to the Middle Ages, is often loosely used with a variety of connotations, but always in reference to the heavy-armed and mounted knights called in France *chevaliers* and in Germany *Ritter,* both words meaning originally horsemen. The word is sometimes used, as above, to denote an international order with fairly definite customs and rules, or again in referring to a band of soldiers of that class, as "the chivalry of France." More commonly today, it is used to refer to ideals of honor, gallantry, and loyalty that were supposed to belong exclusively to men of the knightly class. Chivalry as an order, and to a lesser extent as an ideal, throve in the environment provided by feudalism. It reached its highest development in the twelfth and thirteenth centuries, fading gradually thereafter as it fell out of harmony with changing social conditions and became increasingly artificial. For practical purposes, nobility of birth and knighthood were almost inseparable, since men of common birth seldom attained that honor and nearly all nobles did, but a noble was not born a knight. No matter what his rank, he could achieve knighthood only after a long period of training and after he had come of age to bear the full responsibilities of a feudal warrior.

Education of the knight. The education of the future knight was begun at an early age. When he was still a child, he was sent to the castle of his father's overlord, or some other friendly nobleman, to be "nourished," that is, cared for and trained in all the arts of knighthood. For the first few years, his education would be in the hands of the lady of the castle, whom he served as a page, and who taught him polite manners and the social arts that were already becoming known by the name of "courtesy." At fourteen or thereabouts, he began the really essential part of his training — the handling of arms. He then became one of the squires of the lord who had undertaken to

nourish him. He accompanied his lord everywhere, serving him at meals and when he rose in the morning or retired at night, keeping his weapons and armor polished and in good repair, and riding with him on the hunt. He also followed his lord when he rode to war; carried his shield, helmet, and spear; and led the great war-horse, which was not mounted till the time came to charge. If his lord were thrown from his horse in a battle or tournament, he was expected to rescue him and help him back into the saddle. He was not, however, expected to take part in the fighting, except in an emergency. Meanwhile, his lord was giving him constant training in all the arts of war and was teaching him the duties of a feudal lord. At the age of twenty or twenty-one, after years of this practical education, the young squire was considered ready for knighthood.

Ceremony of knighting. Except on the rare occasion when a squire was dubbed a knight on the field of battle as a reward for signal bravery, the ceremony of conferring knighthood was reserved for one of the great religious holidays or some other special occasion which would help attract throngs of guests and provide an additional excuse for elaborate feasts. The young knight must be started on his career with all due magnificence, and any penurious counting of the cost would shame him. Providing for the knighting of his son was, indeed, one of the most ruinous expenses in the feudal lord's budget, even though a contribution toward it was one of the regular feudal aids to be paid by all his vassals. Some lords were unable to afford it, so that their sons were forced to remain squires indefinitely. The church had its part in the ceremony, though not so large a one in the High as in the Later Middle Ages. After a ceremonial bath the youth spent the whole night in vigil before the altar of the chapel. In the morning he heard Mass; his sword was blessed by the priest; and he was charged to be true to his religion, to aid the church, and to defend the oppressed. He was then clad in new armor, while one of his relatives buckled on his great sword and golden spurs. After that came the really essential part of the ceremony, the "accolade," a blow on the neck delivered by one of the important guests, usually the lord who had nourished him, though in theory any knight might bestow the accolade. Finally, the young knight mounted his horse and ran the "quintain," driving his spear at full gallop against a shield or hauberk fastened to a post. The ceremony was now complete. The young knight was emancipated, recognized as an adult no longer under paternal authority, and entitled to a share in the family estates sufficient to support him.

Tournaments. After the ceremony of knighting, there would be feasting and in all probability a tournament, for no great celebration was considered complete without one. Tournaments were highly valued by medieval knights, not only as their favorite sport, but also as a training school. Even seasoned knights must have constant practice to keep their hand in. The tournament was usually divided into two parts. On the first day, pairs of knights "jousted" together, riding toward each other

at full speed and shattering their lances, if they were lucky, against the other's shield. The knight who was hurled from the saddle or whose lance did not break fairly was declared the loser, and his horse and armor were forfeited to the winner. The next day, there was a general *mêlée* between two groups of knights, which in almost every way resembled a real battle. Knights were wounded, unhorsed, taken prisoner, and sometimes trampled to death. The prisoners were held for ransom as in actual combat. The money to be won from the ransom of prisoners, horses, and armor was one of the attractions of this hazardous sport. But, if some knights made money, others lost it, and all of them flung their money about recklessly in gifts or *largesse* to heralds, minstrels, and servants. The whole tone of the tournament was one of picturesque and careless magnificence — and few of the onlookers ever gave a thought to the poor peasants whose labor made it all possible.

Armor and weapons. Whether in the tournament or in actual battle, the knight's success and safety depended a good deal on the quality of his weapons and armor. Accordingly he took great care in their selection, and was willing to mortgage his patrimony, if necessary, to secure the best. Many a noble thought more of his heavy and finely tempered sword than he did of his wife. In addition to the sword, a knight would carry a lance for the charge, a mace or battle-axe for fighting at close quarters, and a dagger, called a "misericorde," to put a hopelessly wounded enemy out of his agony. The armor of a twelfth-century knight was made up of a cone-shaped steel helmet, a shield, and a hauberk. This last was a loose cloak of linked mail, covering the whole body from the helmet to the knees. Toward the end of the thirteenth century partial plate armor and helmets with closed visors came into use. The full plate armor, so often shown in modern illustrations of knightly scenes, did not appear until the Later Middle Ages.

Ladies watch a tournament in this scene from the Manesse manuscript. The victorious knight is the noble minnesinger, Walther von Klingen, who proved his devotion to his lady, probably the central figure here, by valiant deeds as well as by lyric verses.

Knightly virtues. The knight occupied a privileged position in society, but he had also greater responsibilities than had the commoner. He was expected to maintain a higher standard of conduct along certain lines, and to make some effort to conform to the ideals of chivalry as they were slowly taking shape. Courage, loyalty, and liberality were his prime virtues. He was also expected to cherish his honor more dearly than his life. Just what the knight meant by honor is a little difficult to define, save that he should do nothing that would bring disgrace on himself, his family, or his class, according to the current standards of the age. He must not take unfair advantage of his equals, act meanly in any way, or break his oath; but he could grind down his peasants, run hopelessly into debt, or cheat tradesmen. The laws of chivalry, too, did something, if not much, to limit the brutality of feudal warfare. In this the church helped a good deal. Indeed, in building up the ideal of the Christian knight, as exemplified by the crusading orders or by a St. Louis, the church did much to soften and refine the barbarous character of the medieval warrior.

Chivalric love. But the refinement of chivalry was due, in all probability, more to the ladies than to the church. It was their growing influence in noble society that imposed "courtesy," the manners of the court, on the knights. The twelfth and thirteenth centuries witnessed the first flowering of chivalric love. Gallantry took its place beside the more primitive virtues in the knight's code. Feudal marriage, with the fief as the first consideration, left little room for romantic sentiment between man and wife. But any knight might swear devotion to a noble dame, wear her colors in the tournament and fight in her honor without giving offense, provided he followed the conventions and maintained his devotion on a spiritual plane. The highest idealization of women, combined with a practical recognition of their inferior position in the general scheme of society, was characteristic of medieval chivalry. It found expression in, and was in turn encouraged by, the romantic literature of the age.

The troubadours. In the High Middle Ages, all serious writing was still done in Latin, but there was also a growing popular literature in the language of the people. Mostly it was intended for a noble audience and reflected their manners. In southern France, courtesy and the cult of chivalric love made their appearance earlier than in the rude northern lands. There, in the twelfth century, the "troubadours," wandering poets many of whom were knights of noble birth, composed and sang delightful little love lyrics for the delectation of the most cultured society in Europe. Though limited in scope, their lyrics treated courtly love with delicate subtlety, combining intricate rhyme and graceful meter. This southern poetry reached its fullest development at the end of the twelfth century, before so much of the culture of Provence was destroyed by the terrible devastation that accompanied the Albigensian Crusade, but it continued to exert a stimulating influence on later generations. Dante and Petrarch later drew upon it for inspiration, as did also the northern French song writers of the fourteenth and fifteenth centuries. A similar type of lyric poetry also flourished during the High Middle Ages in the courtly circles of Germany, where the "minnesinger," like the Provençal troubadour, sang of his eternal love for the high-born lady to whom he had pledged his devotion. No finer lyric poetry, indeed, was written during this period than that of the noble Bavarian minnesinger, Walther von der Vogelweide (c. 1170–c. 1230).

Chansons and romances. Meanwhile, in northern France, and spreading from there to England and Germany, a different kind of literature was appearing. There the warlike *chansons de geste* were recited by professional *jongleurs* or ministrels for the amusement of the rough feudal barons. These long epic poems dealt with semi-historical characters, centering in the court of Charlemagne. Some seventy or eighty *chansons* made up what is known as the "Charlemagne cycle." In actual fact, there was little historical truth in them. Their value to the historian lies in the description of customs which were purely contemporary to the authors. In the *chansons,* Charlemagne and his peers act in every respect like twelfth-century nobles. The earliest and finest of the *chansons, the Chanson de Roland,* composed before the end of the eleventh century, is a grand martial poem based on Charlemagne's invasion of Moslem Spain and the massacre of

Walther von der Vogelweide as portrayed in the Manesse manuscript, a thirteenth-century work that contains a priceless collection of minnesinger poetry accompanied by imaginary portraits of the authors.

his rearguard in the pass of Roncesvalles. The spirit of these epics was purely feudal. They dealt with battle, feudal loyalty and rebellion, and hatred of the infidel. But the north, too, was falling under the influence of courtesy, and this softer sentiment found expression in the "romances of adventure," centering in the court of the mythical King Arthur of Britain. Here, in verse and prose, we have tales of knights-errant who fought bravely and often, but from devotion to their ladies or to rescue distressed damsels from ogres and magicians, rather than for the simpler feudal reasons that motivated the heroes of the *chansons*. The legends of the knights of Arthur's Round Table are still the common property of all European literatures. Many of these romances were the work of accomplished poets, like Chrétien de Troyes, who composed the romance of *Perceval* in the reign of Louis VII. The same story appeared again, in a more perfect literary form, from the pen of the German Wolfram von Eschenbach. The romance of *Tristan and Iseult,* perhaps the finest of them all, also appeared in French as well as in the German of Gottfried von Strassburg. Sir Thomas Malory later translated many of the romances into vigorous English prose. There were also other cycles of romances, dealing with the Homeric story of the siege of Troy or the adventures of Alexander the Great, as well as the more historical tales arising from the crusades.

All this contemporary literature is immensely valuable to the historian. But it is easy, and dangerous, if one thinks only of the troubadour lyrics or the romances, to idealize the medieval knight unduly. Their influence, after all, was limited to a fairly small circle in the greater courts. And one must not forget the grim brutality of the *chansons*. Respect for women was a sentiment more often expressed in words than actions, and religion could check only the worst excesses. It might inspire the noble to go on a crusade, to leave lands to the church, or to free his serfs in a fit of deathbed repentance, but it could do little to modify his essentially warlike character. Despite everything that the church, the ladies, or the ideals of chivalry could do, the majority of lords loved only war and pillage.

19

The Cities and the Middle Class —

Commerce and Industry

THE CENTURIES of the High Middle Ages, which saw generations of crusaders ride east to the Holy Land, and in which chivalry and feudalism reached their most perfect development, witnessed also the beginning of one of the greatest economic and social revolutions in the history of Europe. This revolution was brought about by the revival of commerce and industry and the resulting growth of cities and of an urban middle class. The burghers, as the members of the new middle class were called because they lived in walled towns or *burgs,* did not fit neatly into the scheme of feudal society. They were neither servile workers of the soil nor noble-born warriors. They were something new — free men, though of common birth, who made an independent living by trade and industry, using money as the means of exchange, and who banded together for mutual protection in more or less self-governing associations. Their numbers were still small, compared to the great number of peasants. The fighting nobles looked down on them as base-born upstarts. The church regarded them with a suspicious eye, as men given over to worldly concerns that were dangerous to the soul. But they had the Midas touch. They could produce wealth, and through the power of money they were destined eventually to destroy the old feudal society based on hereditary land tenure and to create in its place a new society

based on wealth. In those small and crowded cities, rather than in the rockbound castles of the nobles, lay the seeds of modern society.

1. The Medieval City

External appearance. The medieval city must have presented a picturesque appearance to the wandering merchant who plodded down the dusty road leading to the city gate. First he would see the high encircling wall of heavy stone, surrounded by a moat and surmounted by towers very like those of a baronial castle; for strongly fortified walls were as necessary to the security of the townsfolk as they were to the feudal lord. At sunset the great gates would be closed, and if the merchant were too late, he would have to stay out till dawn. Beyond the wall, he would see a tumbled mass of roofs, sloping at every imaginable angle, and crowned with chimney pots in which storks built their nests. Here and there would arise thin spires of parish churches, and in the center, if it were an episcopal city, the tall cathedral tower would shoot up high above the surrounding roofs, dominating the whole town.

The streets. Once through the gate, the visitor would find himself in one of the main thoroughfares of the city, which led to the market place and thence on through the city to the opposite gate. This would be one of the widest

227

Medieval towns, like the fortified city of Carcassonne above, needed defensive walls. The addition of a second wall in the last half of the thirteenth century, outside that already existing, and the strengthening of the inner wall by every known artifice of military architecture made Carcassonne one of the most heavily fortified cities in France.

streets, though still narrow according to modern standards, probably not more than fifteen or twenty feet from house to house. The other streets were mere alleys, few of them even ten feet wide. They twisted about aimlessly in a crooked maze, as though they had been laid out purely by chance — as indeed they had. The streets were necessarily narrow, because every available inch of space in the city must be utilized. The walls hemmed the city in and prevented normal expansion. Moreover, they had been built around as small a space as possible, in order to make them easily defensible and to save labor and expense. Hence the amazing congestion of population within any medieval city. The streets were usually unpaved, though the main streets in a large city might have a rough paving of cobblestones. There were no means of draining them, so that most of the year they were ankle-deep in mire. They were also befouled by the accumulation of garbage and refuse thrown out of the houses. Medieval ideas of sanitation were, to say the least, primitive. As there was seldom any sewage system, and no garbage collection, the task of clearing away the refuse was left to the pigs who wandered freely through the streets. Small wonder that infectious diseases often swept through the city, decimating the population. All in all, the sordid reality of the streets must

have been in strong contrast to the picturesque appearance of the city from without.

Houses. The streets were made more narrow, dark, and airless than they need have been by the efforts of the burghers to make use of as much space as possible for their houses and shops. The houses were often four or five stories high, and each successive story jutted out beyond the one below, so that the eaves of the houses across the street almost met. If the house belonged to a merchant or artisan — and most houses in the city did — the ground floor would be occupied by a shop, with a horizontal shutter across the front, which in the daytime was let down into the street to form a counter for the display of wares. The houses were built mostly of wood with thatched roofs, and were very inflammable. By the thirteenth century, the wealthier burghers were beginning to build stone outer walls and to use tile for the roofs as a protection against fire. Even so, fires were frequent and, once started, often swept over large parts of the city, for there was no way of fighting the flames except by a bucket line from the nearest well. The city of Rouen was burned six times in the first quarter of the thirteenth century.

Churches. Churches abounded in every quarter of the city, for the burghers were pious folk. The great cathedral in the center of the city was the pride of the pious and patriotic burgher's heart. It was a magnificent building built of solid stone and adorned with intricate carvings, high-arched stained-glass windows, and soaring towers. The cathedrals of the "Gothic" type were the artistic masterpieces of the Middle Ages, never since surpassed for sheer architectural beauty. Within the cathedral there was peace and a dim religious light, in strong contrast to the noise and bustle of the market place outside. The only open space in the city was the square in front of the cathedral or the largest church. There the town market was held, and there the people congregated for all public ceremonies, so that the great church was the center of the life of the city.

The city at night. The busy life of the crowded city was limited to the daylight hours. At sunset the shops were closed and barred. A little later, the great bells of the cathedral rank the "curfew" as a signal to cover all fires, and the city settled down to quiet and darkness. There were no street lights and seldom was there even a light in the houses. When there was a full moon, a little light might filter down between the overhanging eaves, but it could make little impression on the inky blackness of the street below. No honest man traveled the street at night, save on important and unusual business. Then he would take as many armed servants with him as possible, for the streets of any medieval city were dangerous after dark.

The city by day. But if the nights were quiet, the days were filled with bustling activity. The whole city wakened at dawn. Shops were opened and business was begun with the first full daylight. The medieval city was not cursed with the heavy traffic of the modern city, but the narrow streets were none the less crowded and filled with active life. Merchants did their business practically on the street. Peddlers added to the confusion with the raucous cries characteristic of their trade through the centuries. In the market place and at street corners, jugglers and fortune-tellers gathered a crowd about them and collected a few pennies. To the peasant lad, raised in the quiet monotony of a rural manor, the life of the city seemed intense and exciting. Then, as now, the thirst for a more varied life as well as for greater opportunities led young men to leave their country homes to seek their fortunes in the city.

Size of cities. Important as were the cities in the civilization of the High Middle Ages, they were still very small in comparison to their modern counterparts. The total area within the walls of medieval London was less than a square mile. And although by the end of the thirteenth century the more prosperous cities had grown enormously since the Early Middle Ages and were becoming seriously overcrowded, their population was still small by modern standards. Medieval population statistics are generally unreliable, but there is good reason to believe that even by the beginning of the fourteenth century none of the great Italian cities had more than 100,000 inhabitants. London had about 40,000, but no other English city had more than a quarter of that number. Ghent and Bruges, the two largest cities in the Netherlands, had between 40,000 and 50,000. No German city was as large as these; Cologne, the largest, had something over 30,000. Some historians have credited Paris with the rather unbelievable figure of 200,000; certainly it was the largest city in France. The great majority of the cities in all parts of western Europe were in reality no more than small market towns of 1,000 or 2,000 inhabitants.

2. The Revival of Commerce and the Rise of the Cities

Trade in the early Middle Ages. But how had this thriving urban life come into existence in the High Middle Ages, after centuries during which cities had almost disappeared? What was the force that had given new life to old cities and created new ones? The answer is, undoubtedly, trade. Roman civilization, which had been largely urban, had depended on a wide-flung commerce. But Roman trade declined with the break-up of the empire, and the cities declined with it. Only in the part of the Eastern Empire that survived about the great commercial city of Constantinople did it continue to flourish. In the West there were too many forces working against it. First, the barbarian invasions from the north took their toll. Then, in the seventh and early eighth centuries, the westward thrust of the conquering Moslems cut off the Christian lands of the West from the Mediterranean, and hence from all contact with world trade. A century later, the pirate bands of Northmen threw western Europe into chaos and blocked the seacoast to west and north. Throughout the eighth, ninth, and tenth centuries, western Europe was practically land-locked. Only a little trade, born by adventurous Syrian or Italian merchants or by Northmen who alternated trade with piracy, trickled through to the interior. Lacking the stimulus of foreign goods, even local trade declined to the vanishing point. Each manor produced what it needed and, in turn, consumed its own pro-ducts. Under such circumstances, cities served no useful purpose and consequently died of inanition. Where they survived, it was with population sadly diminished, as centers of epis-copal or civil administration or as fortified strongholds. In short, cities disappeared when trade was cut off. They appeared again when trade was revived in the eleventh and twelfth centuries.

Revival of international trade. European commerce revived by re-establishing contact with the outside world. The first impetus came from Italy, where Venice and the Greek cities of the south had never lost contact altogether with the Byzantine Empire. When, in the eleventh century, Christendom began to take the offensive against Islam, their trade with the Middle East increased rapidly. Finally, the First Crusade, at the end of the century, com-pleted the opening-up of the Mediterranean to European traders. The ports of the Levant and the islands were now in Christian hands, and there was a clear road to the East. Venice, cut off from the mainland by her lagoons and forced to make her living from the sea, took the lead in the mercantile revival. She was the trading city *par excellence,* the Queen of the Adriatic, the wealthiest city in the West. But before the end of the eleventh century, Genoa and Pisa, on the other side of the peninsula, were already formidable rivals. Like Venice, they acquired trading posts in the newly con-quered kingdom of Jerusalem. Meanwhile, in the north the ports of Flanders, fortunately situated on the deep estuaries where the Rhine, the Scheldt, and the Meuse flow into the North Sea, were becoming the focal centers of a simi-lar revival of international trade. The original agents here were the far-wandering Northmen, who, after destroying the commerce of the western seas by piracy, restored it again when

they turned to legitimate trade. Their long boats plied the coasts of the Baltic, the North Sea, and the Atlantic and called at English ports. This trade naturally centered upon Flanders, for there the wine and other products of the interior could be exchanged for wool from England or wax, furs, and amber from the Baltic.

Trade spreads inland. From these two focal centers trade spread gradually inland. During the eleventh century, commercial relations with Venice, Genoa, and Pisa gave a great stimulus to the growing towns of the Lombard plain and Tuscany. By the beginning of the twelfth cen-tury, the commercial revival had spread to the ports of southern France and Christian Spain. From there and across the Alpine passes from Lombardy, merchants followed roads and rivers into France and Germany, until they met the northern merchants coming down the rivers from the Flemish coast. For a long time, the plain of Champagne, halfway between Italy and Flanders, was the meeting place for mer-chants of all lands. The penetration of trade into the interior went on slowly, but before the end of the twelfth century all the main trade routes had been opened up, and mer-chants traveled constantly to all parts of Chris-tian Europe.

Traveling merchants. Medieval commerce was conducted largely by itinerant merchants, who carried their wares with them on long journeys. It was a hazardous life, but the profits, when fortune smiled on them, were pro-portionately large. When they traveled by sea, they were exposed to the attacks of pirates or commercial rivals and to the ever-present danger of shipwreck. The medieval mariner knew too little about navigation to venture far from shore, and his ship was too unwieldy to make much headway against a strong wind. There was always danger, therefore, of being blown onto a lee shore. Inland trade was equally hazardous. Few governments were strong enough to guarantee security of life or property to the traveler. The roads were in-fested by robbers and by the impoverished knights and barons who felt that the merchant was their legitimate prey. Whenever possible, merchants traveled together in caravans for mutual protection or joined with bands of pil-grims. Sometimes, too, a merchant would attach himself to the armed retinue of a powerful lord traveling in the same direction.

Roads and tolls. Aside from the dangers from human violence, the state of the roads made inland travel extremely hazardous. Whenever he could, the merchant preferred to travel by river, but often he had to take to the road. Then there was nothing for it but to load his goods on pack animals — horses or mules — or in rude carts, pray to St. Christopher, and hope for the best. Even the best roads were merely rough dirt tracks, deeply scored by ruts and pitted with sinkholes. In rainy weather the carts sank axle-deep in the mud or bogged down completely. Bridges were in equally bad condition. Sometimes they were swept away by floods and not replaced for years. Frequently they were quite unsafe for heavy traffic. Sporadic attempts were made by kings, nobles, monasteries, or religious associations to repair roads and bridges, but with little permanent result. The responsibilities of government were too thoroughly divided under the feudal system to make any consistent or widespread program of public works possible. What legislation there was worked more often to the disadvantage than to the advantage of the merchant, for at every bridge and ferry and on every road he was forced to pay a burdensome toll to the local lord for their upkeep — usually without

visible results. In winter merchant travel practically ceased. At any time it was very hazardous for the lone merchant. As a result, trade fell into definite periods, when at one place or another it was concentrated at fairs to which merchants flocked in large bands.

Fairs. Throughout the High Middle Ages, annual fairs were the most important element in interregional trade. Without them, the exchange of foreign goods would have been greatly restricted, if not impossible. In the twelfth century, the fairs of Champagne were the meeting place of merchants from all parts of Christendom, but there were innumerable others in every country of Europe. Fairs were normally held in cities, but they were usually under higher authority than the municipal government, being controlled by the king, or by a bishop or abbot or great feudal lord, who guaranteed "the peace of the fair." The ordinary government of the city was temporarily set aside, and the exclusive monopoly on trade enjoyed by the merchants of the city — which, as we shall see, greatly hindered the trading of foreign merchants at other times — was broken for the time being. While the fair lasted, any merchant who paid his toll and the rent for his booth could trade freely and securely. He set up his booth in the market square or in the open fields outside the city, exchanged goods

This miniature from a manuscript of the Chroniques de Hainaut, 1448, *shows stone masons completing a bridge while other workers clear the trees ahead of them for the continuation of the road.*

with other merchants from distant lands, or sold his wares to the local tradesmen and smaller merchants or to the burghers of the city and the nobles of the surrounding countryside. When the fair was over, the foreign merchants packed their goods and set out in groups once more to face the perils of the highway in the direction of another fair. Commerce under medieval conditions was necessarily periodic. The fair was the perfect setting for it.

Merchant law. Not the least of the advantages which attracted foreign merchants to the fairs was the guaranty of speedy justice. Ordinarily, the mills of justice ground slowly in the Middle Ages, and they did not grind so very fine. Moreover, each city had its own laws and customs which strangers could not be expected to know. Above everything else, the traveling merchant needed the protection of dependable courts, of law with which he was familiar, and of speedy trials so that his departure for other parts might not be delayed. All these he found in the jurisdiction of the lord of the fair and in the special merchant courts, called in England "pie powder" courts, a corruption of the French *pied poudreux,* from the dusty-footed merchants who frequented them. These courts met "from hour to hour" during the fair, as they were needed. The law meted out was not local or royal law, but a common commercial law, the "law merchant" recognized in all parts of Europe. This body of mercantile law had grown up by custom from the needs of the traveling merchants. It remained largely unwritten, and varied but little from one country to another. Its special field was suits for payment of debts, fulfillment of contracts, and other civil cases arising from trade.

Commerce creates cities. The revival of commerce necessarily led to a renaissance of city life. In the first place, the traveling merchants could not be always on the road. They needed a permanent base for their operations, and that base must be at some place where they could form an association with others of their kind for mutual protection against the dangers of a lawless society that provided little security for the trader. In the second place, foreign trade stimulated local trade and broke up the isolated production and consumption economy of the manor. By introducing foreign

This effigy of Henry II of England is from his tomb in Fontrévault Abbey, Normandy. By suppressing crime and restoring order, this powerful king did much to stimulate the growth of English commerce.

goods and skillfully manufactured articles, the traveling merchant created a demand for commodities that could not be obtained on the manor; and this demand remained to some extent constant throughout the year. At any rate, it could not be entirely satisfied by the annual or semi-annual fairs. There was, then, an opportunity for resident merchants to ply their trade all the year round; and these, like their traveling confrères, sought association with their fellows and so added to the growing nucleus of the town. Finally, commerce created skilled industry. Someone had to make the clothes, weapons, armor, and so forth that the merchant sold to satisfy the demand for more skillfully made goods than could be produced by manorial workmen. So skilled artisans appeared, and they, too, congregated in places where opportunities for trade and protection had already gathered groups of merchants. Indeed, the artisan was often himself a local merchant and vice versa. Here, then, we have the nucleus of a town. As it grew, it became less dependent on the surrounding country and provided a growing market in itself for its own products. But it always depended on trade.

That cities followed trade is clearly shown by a glance at the economic map of Europe.[1] All along the trade routes — at seaports, on the rivers, and at crossroads towns sprang up. To trace the rise of the cities, one has only to trace the main channels of trade and follow their spread throughout Europe.

City origins.   This still leaves the problem, and one much disputed, as to just how any individual city originated and why in any particular place. Very little evidence has survived as to the early history of the towns, and local conditions must have varied widely. In general, however, the most reasonable explanation is that merchants and artisans congregated under the protection of any fortified place which was so geographically situated as to be favorable to trade. Many old Roman cities, which, thanks to the Roman genius for commerce, were usually situated on natural trade routes, had survived as centers of an episcopal diocese. They were walled and the prestige of the bishop made them relatively secure. There were also fortified *burgs,* built as centers of military and civil administration, like the "five boroughs" founded by the Danes in England to hold the conquered population in subjection. Feudal castles and monasteries, too, offered protection. Around the walls of any of these that were favorably situated for trade, merchants and artisans congregated. In time of danger, they could retreat within the walls. They made up the population of a new *burg,* and it was to them that the term burghers was applied. The new *burg* was in time also encircled by a wall. As it grew, it gradually engulfed the original fortification, whose walls were usually destroyed as no longer necessary. The burghers were originally under the jurisdiction of the lord whose protection they sought. Such jurisdiction carried with it many onerous feudal restrictions and services, which often interfered with freedom of trade. Everywhere, therefore, we find the townsfolk working together to secure greater freedom and a larger share of self-government. In the next section we shall see how the full-grown city was governed and what was the status of the burgher class when the cities were well established.

[1] See map, page 299.

3. *The Burghers and City Government*

The burghers.   The burghers formed a new social class, and they had to work out for themselves a new social status, new laws and customs, a new system of government, and new methods of regulating business. They had to experiment, for there was no precedent to guide them. Sometimes the experiments led to disaster. In any case they produced a wide variety of custom, depending on local conditions. Nevertheless, in main outline the status of the burghers and the internal government of the cities were fairly uniform in all parts of Europe, for they arose naturally from the needs of a mercantile and industrial community, which were much the same everywhere. Everywhere the burghers acquired personal freedom, and this was the essential point in determining their social status as a privileged class. Many of the merchants who founded the early towns must have been free from the beginning, though they probably sprang from villein or servile stock. Having in some way escaped from the ancestral manor or the jurisdiction of their lord, they were free because no man knew whence they came and no lord could claim them as his own. At first, however, there were also serfs and villeins of the local lord in the town, but before long these apparently gained the same freedom as their lordless neighbors. Once the new cities were firmly established, personal freedom was recognized as the right of all permanent dwellers within the walls. If a serf could escape from his manor and live for a year and a day in a city, he could not be reclaimed by his late lord. Next to freedom from hereditary servitude, the burghers needed freedom as individuals from the annoyances of manorial jurisdiction and laws, which, having been designed for farm workers, were not adapted to the needs of commerce and industry; and, finally, they needed enough self-government to enable them to regulate their own economic life. But such freedom was seldom won without cost or struggle, and only a few cities acquired full independence.

Struggle for self-government.   The struggle began in northern Italy. We have already seen[1] how the Lombard cities fought for freedom against their bishops and the emperors for a century and a half, until they had forced even the powerful Frederick Barbarossa to recognize their right to self-government as practically independent city-republics. Nowhere else did the cities obtain such complete independence, though the great Flemish cities came close to it, and in Germany a few of the largest acquired the status of free imperial cities, subject only to the nominal authority of the emperor. In most places the burghers were content with less. They were willing to acknowledge the political authority of the king or their lord and to pay taxes. All they asked was that their obligations be defined and limited, that the town as a corporation and not individuals should be held responsible for them, and that, within the town, the burghers should be left as free as possible to manage their own affairs. Often these concessions were obtained peacefully by the purchase of a charter from the king or one of the great lords. This was particularly true in England and on the royal domain and the great fiefs in France. As a rule, the nobles, save for a few rulers of great fiefs like the counts of Champagne, were less favorably disposed toward the cities than were the kings. But they were often forced by poverty to sell charters, and they were gradually discovering that free cities were likely to be more prosperous and could pay them more taxes than those whose freedom of action was hampered by feudal restrictions. In France, many lords founded new towns on their estates, offering very liberal terms to attract settlers, in order to augment their income from the prospective taxes. The towns that had grown up under the jurisdiction of a bishop or abbot had the greatest difficulty in securing freedom. Here there was no opportunity to take advantage of the weakness of a minor or of a careless or absent lord; nor was the church so likely to be in pressing need of money. Besides, bishops who might have been personally willing to grant concessions were loath to do so, lest they seem to be surrendering traditional rights of the church which had been entrusted to them. When the burghers could not secure concessions peacefully by purchase, they were prepared to fight for them. A number of towns

[1] See above, pages 181–183, and map, page 176.

in France formed "communes" during the twelfth century; organized their own government; and wrested recognition of their freedom from their lord, whether bishop, abbot, or noble. Later, in the thirteenth century, most of them came under royal government and lost much of the independence enjoyed earlier, but they still retained a fair measure of self-government.

City government. The government of the typical medieval city was in the hands of a council and a number of executive officers or magistrates (they went by a variety of names), who were nearly always burghers of the city and were chosen by their fellow burghers freely or in collaboration with the lord. Their principal duty was to levy and collect taxes. There were usually direct taxes on income and indirect taxes on the sale of goods. From the money raised in this way, the city government maintained the defenses and public works and the cost of government, and paid whatever taxes the city owed to the king or its lord. The growing political power of the cities and their influence with the monarchy depended largely on this ability to raise money taxes, which had no parallel in the feudal system. The city had also its own system of civil and criminal law and its own courts and judges. City laws and judicial procedure were usually much more enlightened than the ancient customs still enforced in the feudal courts. At least, they were better suited to the needs of men who made their living from commerce and industry. The right to take part in the government of the city was seldom open to all inhabitants. It was limited normally to men of property who were legally recognized as burghers, a privilege which they defended jealously against outsiders and the poorer classes. In some places a small oligarchy of the wealthiest burghers succeeded in gaining control of the government and shutting out the rest.

Markets. Among the duties of the city magistrates were the supervision of the town market and the collection of market tolls, which formed an important part of the city's revenues. Nearly every city had the legal right to hold a market, though they often had to pay dearly for it. In thirteenth-century France, and earlier in England, the kings asserted their exclusive right to issue charters granting that privilege. The markets must not be confused with the fairs. The former were purely municipal institutions for local trade, held for one day only, once or twice a week. Here the peasants from the countryside displayed their produce for sale to the burghers. In some places, in order to augment the tolls, even the merchants of the city were forced to close their shops and sell in the market during market days.

Control of trade. It was not only in the markets that the municipal government supervised the city's trade. Since it was their duty to protect the interests of the whole body of citizens, the magistrates felt justified in exercising a minute control of all business within the city. Perhaps because the city existed in the midst of a hostile environment, wherein the citizens were forced to depend upon one another for aid, the medieval burgher felt that the interests of the individual should be subordinated to the welfare of the whole community. He had, therefore, no objection to a paternalistic government which set prices, supervised methods of manufacture, determined the quality of goods, regulated wages and hours of labor, and prevented any individual from taking unfair advantage of his fellow citizens. The purpose of medieval economic legislation was to guarantee to the worker or seller a fair living and to protect the consumer against fraud or undue cost. Often the city government delegated the actual supervision to the guilds, of which more later, but the final responsibility remained with the magistrates.

Medieval economic theory. The medieval man had no confidence in the economic law of supply and demand as the source of prices, nor in the principle that free competition is the greatest stimulus to trade. If he thought of them at all, he considered them immoral. Instead, he believed that for every commodity there was a "just price," which should be the same in time of shortage as in time of plenty. This just price was set by custom, based on the normal price of raw materials, plus the "reasonable" profit necessary to permit the workers and the merchants to live in the style recognized by public opinion as suitable to their status. The church had a good deal to do with evolving and enforcing this theory, but secular authorities accepted it implicitly as the basis for all legislation regarding price. The statute books of every city were filled with laws designed to enforce the sale of goods at "just" or

A tailor, working in his shop open to the street, as depicted in a fourteenth-century Italian manuscript.

"reasonable" prices, and the guilds, too, did their share. Of course this legislation did not always accomplish its purpose. The principle of the just price was too vague, and the severe penalties constantly re-enacted against "engrossing, forestalling, and regrating" — three kindred methods of cornering the market and withholding goods until the demand had raised the price — show that not all medieval businessmen allowed moral theories to interfere with their desire for gain. The condemnation of "usury" — that is, the taking of interest for money lent — arose from a similar principle. It was believed that money was not an active force, and that to exact a price for its use was to take unfair advantage of the needs of one's fellows. But this was even less observed than the theory of the just price. Despite everything that the church and secular governments could do, money continued to be lent at interest thinly disguised.

Corporate exclusiveness. The efforts of the city government to supervise trade in the interests of the whole community were limited strictly to the city itself. The burghers formed a very exclusive body. They had no interest whatsoever in the prosperity of the nation at large or, indeed, of anyone outside the magic circle of the walls. The merchants of the city were assured a monopoly of its trade, and the monopoly was broken only when it was to their own advantage to do so. This exclusiveness had, as its reverse side, a very strong feeling of corporate responsibility and mutual interdependence among the burghers of the city. They called on one another for aid, shared in one another's bargains, and were responsible for one another's debts. If a merchant defaulted on payment of a debt contracted abroad, the creditor might legally seize the goods of any other merchant from the debtor's city. The medieval city was an independent economic unit, whose citizens were banded together in a close fraternity, presenting a united front to all outsiders. And within the city, the merchants and artisans were ordinarily, though not always, organized in still more closely knit and exclusive associations, known as guilds, through which, as a rule, the city government exercised its control of business.

4. *The Merchant and Craft Guilds*

The merchant guilds. A merchant guild was founded quite early in the history of most cities. It was mentioned in the original charters of many of them. Indeed, the guild was often largely responsible for the success of the city's struggle for a charter. The merchant guild was an association, in which membership was compulsory, of all the burghers of the city who made their living by selling goods, including, in its early days at any rate, the artisans who made goods and sold them directly to the consumer. No one who was not a member of the guild could buy or sell at retail within the city, though foreign merchants might be permitted to sell to the guildsmen or buy from them at wholesale, on payment of a toll, since it was to the advantage of the local merchants to secure raw materials from abroad or to dispose of their surplus stock. A strong bond of fellowship and corporate responsibility existed among the members of the guild. They were pledged to mutual aid in time of need, and every effort was made to guarantee equality of opportunity and to prevent unfair competition. Acting as a corporation, the guild often bought wholesale cargoes of raw materials or goods, at a lower cost than any individual could have procured them, and reallotted them to the members at the purchase price. Finally, the guild regulated prices, the quality of goods, wages, and hours of labor.

Relation to city government. These manifold duties of the merchant guild were in many respects the same as those of the city government. There was, indeed, so close a connection between the two that it was often difficult

Wine merchants offer the year's vintage for sale in a sixteenth-century calendar for the month of October. The huge crane used to hoist the wine casks is operated by men on a treadmill.

to distinguish between them. The guildsmen were the most active burghers and frequently controlled the government of the city. Often the same men served as city and guild officers. But the city government had always wider powers and was superior to the guild, which merely administered the economic side of government and exercised a monopoly of trade. In the course of time, as the merchant guilds began to decline, their powers were taken over in many places by the city administration. The twelfth century was the period of greatest power for the merchant guilds. When industry became more highly specialized, their place was largely taken by the various craft guilds. The merchant guilds or companies, which reappear in the Later Middle Ages, were of a different character, dealing usually with some particular line of trade.

Craft guilds. The craft guilds were essentially industrial, but they had also a mercantile character. They were composed of artisans of a given trade or craft, who manufactured or prepared goods and sold them, usually directly to the consumer. The type of work which each guild could undertake was strictly defined. In the larger cities, where there were a great many craft guilds, they were very highly specialized. For example, there might be two separate guilds for the making of men's and women's shoes. In smaller places, on the other hand, several allied crafts might be lumped together. Each guild exercised a monopoly of its particular trade in the city. The right to sell their goods must have been transferred to them in some way from the merchant guild which had exercised a blanket monopoly on all selling. The history of the relation between the two types of guild is very obscure and no doubt varied from place to place. In general, it seems that the monopoly and other powers of the merchant guild were parceled out to the craft guilds, and that the merchant guild either continued as a vague aggregate of all guilds or merged with the city government.

Apprentices. The craft guilds were exclusive bodies, limited to the skilled trades, and one could become a member only after a long period of thorough training. The first step in the making of a guildsman was the apprenticeship. Apprentices usually began their training quite early, at ten or twelve years of age. The

lad's parents would enter into a contract with a master of the craft — that is, a full-fledged member of the guild — to undertake their son's training. In most cases they paid him a small fee. The apprentice then went to live in the master's house. He was expected to do whatever work he could. In return he received full instruction in all the arts of the craft and also his food, clothing, and lodging. Later, as he became a valuable worker rather than a liability to the master, he might receive a small wage. The bond between apprentice and master was very close. The latter acted as a foster-father and exercised a father's authority. The apprentice, however, was not entirely at the master's mercy. The guild supervised the training of apprentices and protected their rights. It fixed the length of the period of training, which varied in various guilds from two or three to ten or twelve years, depending on the amount of skill required for the craft. The average was perhaps about seven years. The guild also limited the number of apprentices, usually to two or three, whom any one master might take. This was done partly to ensure the proper care and training of the apprentices, partly to prevent any master from gaining an advantage over his fellows by the employment of a large number of cheap workers, and also to cut down competition by limiting the number of men trained in the craft.

Journeymen. When the apprentice had completed his period of training satisfactorily, he was promoted to the status of journeyman or day laborer (so called from the French word *journée*, meaning a day). He was now a free worker, paid by the day, and could hire with any master who wanted his services. During the next few years, he was expected to acquire more experience and skill and to save enough money to set himself up in a shop of his own. The next step was to apply for full membership in the guild. He must then undergo a strict examination at the hands of the masters, and might be called upon to submit a sample of his work, his "masterpiece," together with proof of good character and religious orthodoxy. If he passed this test, he was received into the guild as a master.

Masters. The master was at once a worker, employer, and retail merchant. In the little shop on the ground floor of his house, in full

To become a master in a craft guild, a workman normally had to prove his skill. In this picture from a fourteenth-century Florentine manuscript, a carpenter and a mason are being judged by the consul of the guild of workers in wood and stone.

view of those who passed on the street, he manufactured his goods with his own hands, supervised the work of his journeymen and apprentices, and displayed his products for sale. No permanent class distinction cut him off from his employees, since they themselves expected to become masters in the course of time. He was not a capitalist in any real sense of the word, since the restriction imposed by the guild on the price and quality of his goods and the number of men whom he could employ prevented him from making more than a decent living for himself. These restrictions were, in part, self-imposed, for the master was a full member of the guild and had his share in choosing its officers and in making its rules. But if those rules prevented him from rising above his fellows, they also protected him from the competition of others who might try to do the same.

Purpose of the craft guilds. In this we find the chief purpose of the craft guilds. They were designed to limit competition and to keep any member from doing anything that would be to the disadvantage of the rest. At the same time, they exercised a local monopoly and protected their members from outside competition. The sense of social solidarity and corporate responsibility, the conviction that the interests of the individual should be subordinated to the good of the whole community, which we have already noted as characteristic of the medieval cities, was felt very intensely within the guilds. Hence all the minute regulation of industry. The craft guilds fixed prices, regulated wages and hours of labor, and demanded a fixed standard of quality in the goods produced. These regulations were strictly enforced by the guild officers, who regularly inspected the shops of the masters. So far as was humanly possible, each guild member was guaranteed equality of opportunity. He was given a share in the wholesale purchases of raw materials made by the guild. No other master could tempt his workers away from him. Indeed, in many guilds, the other masters were forced to lend him workers in case of special need. A regulation of one of the London guilds shows this spirit of cooperation: "And if anyone of the trade shall have work in his house that he cannot complete, or if for want of assistance such work shall be in danger of being lost, those of the said trade shall aid him that so the said work be not lost." But the guild regulations did more than protect the guild members; they also protected the consumer, and assured him sound workmanship and fair value. The city government, which held the final authority, would see to that, though the guildsmen themselves took a pride in their craft and realized that it was to their advantage to have a reputation for selling sound goods at a just price.

Aside from their economic functions, the craft guilds had a distinct social purpose in caring for their members in time of adversity. They were friendly societies. If a guildsman fell ill or through any other mischance was poverty-stricken, he was cared for from the guild funds. When he died, the guild paid the expenses of his funeral and, if necessary, undertook the support of his widow and children. All the social life of the city centered in the guilds. The great feasts in the guildhall relieved the monotony of daily toil and drew the guild members closer together. The guilds had also certain religious functions. They took part in religious celebrations and processions and often supported a chapel or shrine. And almost everywhere they guarded against heresy among their members.

Advantages and disadvantages. The guild system offered many advantages to the medieval worker and consumer, but there were also disadvantages which became more apparent as the economic life of Europe assumed larger proportions and as the need for protective associations became less acute. The system maintained a high standard of quality in the goods produced, guaranteed honest value to the purchaser, and at the same time ensured to the guildsman a fair living, with little chance, it is true, of becoming wealthy, but also with little chance of being ruined. On the other hand, the minute supervision of work and the innumerable regulations tended to check individual enterprise and to retard invention or progress of any kind. Even the social solidarity of the guild was not an unmixed blessing to society. The guildsmen helped each other, but they were intensely jealous of other guilds which infringed on their monopoly, and they suppressed ruthlessly all competition from those who were not members. One modern historian has compared the guild in a vivid metaphor to a feudal castle, which protected but imprisoned those it sheltered and which might easily degenerate into an instrument of tyranny over those outside. The guilds, however, were not alone responsible for the exclusiveness and the close regulation of local trade and industry, which were characteristic of the economic policy of the medieval cities. There were cities in which no formal guild organization existed or where guilds developed only in the Later Middle Ages; but in these cities wages, prices, the quality of goods, and so forth, were as closely regulated by the city government as they were in the towns where regulation could be carried out through the guilds. There were also a great many market towns so small that there were not enough craftsmen to make a guild organization practicable.

Beginnings of capitalism. The forms of commercial and industrial organization that were most characteristic of the High Middle Ages represent a pre-capitalist type of economy, even though it was one in which money was becoming an essential factor as a medium of exchange. Limited markets and the city or guild regulations, which checked competition and prevented the local shopkeepers and craftsmen from expanding their business, made it impossible for the majority of medieval burghers to make more than a decent living from their labors. Even the traveling merchants, who were less easily controlled by city ordinances, seldom made large enough fortunes to be considered capitalists. But among the latter, especially in Italy where the importation of luxuries from the East offered unusual opportunities for profit, there were some who were already accumulating capital far beyond the needs of subsistence and who were beginning to think of profits as something to be reinvested in a constantly expanding business. Among such merchants the use of credit and other techniques of capitalism were well established before the end of the thirteenth century. But business enterprise that in volume and method can be regarded as capitalistic was still exceptional. We will, therefore, leave the discussion of early capitalism till we come to the Later Middle Ages, when it became more common.[1]

5. Influence of the Cities on European Civilization

The growth of the cities and the rise of the burgher class with its active economic life, in the midst of feudal society and yet apart from it, were bound to have tremendous effects on every aspect of European civilization.

Money economy. In the first place, they created a new kind of wealth. In the earlier feudal ages, when nearly all wealth sprang directly from the cultivation of the soil, there was very little money in circulation. It was not needed to any large extent, for feudal dues were mostly paid in services or produce, and trade was carried on largely by barter, that is, by the direct exchange of goods on a local scale. What money did exist was usually hoarded. The revival of commerce and industry made great

[1] See below, Chapter 24.

changes in this respect. Money once more circulated freely wherever merchants bought or sold. Because they were the centers of trade, a large part of the money in circulation flowed to the cities. In its possession lay the power of the new burgher class. Their use of it revolutionized the social and political as well as the economic life of Europe.

The peasants. The burghers were not consciously interested in the fate of their peasant neighbors. Yet unwittingly they helped them obtain better conditions and greater freedom. The burghers did not as a rule produce their own food, but they had money to buy it. They provided the peasants with a constantly growing market for their produce outside the narrow confines of the manor. This made it worth while for the peasants to increase the production of their crops and enabled them to amass a little money, with which they might purchase freedom or concessions from their lord. It also encouraged the lords to clear wasteland and place it under cultivation. During the two centuries of the High Middle Ages the amount of land under cultivation in western Europe was almost doubled. In order to attract workers to the new land, the lords were forced to offer very liberal terms, including more or less complete freedom. This in turn reacted favorably on the status of the peasants on the old estates. There, many lords had to make concessions, which often took the form of emancipation and the commutation of personal services into cash payments, in order to keep their peasants from running away to seek a better living or greater freedom on new land or in the cities. This was, of course, a gradual process and not uniform everywhere. But by the end of the Middle Ages, in all the most civilized parts of Europe, a fair measure of the personal freedom and the money economy of the towns had spread to the rural manors.

The nobles. The nobles gained much, but eventually lost more, from the rise of the cities. They shared in the growing prosperity that followed the revival of urban life; but there was a limit to the amount of money they could raise from the sale of produce from the demesne land. Those who commuted the labor services of their peasants or rented parts of the demesne for cash might increase their immediate income, but they could not increase it much further

thereafter, since such bargains tended to become fixed by custom at the initial rate. Meanwhile, as we have already noted, the standard of living of the nobles was, as a rule, rising more rapidly than their income, so that they were more or less chronically short of funds. In still other ways, many of which did not become apparent until the Later Middle Ages, the expansion of money economy weakened the position of the nobles. So long as tenure of land and the unpaid services of dependents represented the principal form of wealth, the nobles' position was secure; but in the long run they could not compete with the new forms of moneyed wealth arising in the cities.

The monarchy. The new money economy not only tended to weaken the independent power of the feudal nobles; it also tended to strengthen the power of central government. It was the factor which more than anything else enabled kings to recover the control of the army, the legal jurisdiction, and the effective authority which in the Early Middle Ages they had been forced to abandon to their feudal vassals. Taxation was essential to strong government, but adequate taxation was impossible until money had begun to circulate freely. Even then, the feudal system made small provision for regular taxation, and the monarchs found the readiest source of taxation in the cities. The burghers, for their part, needed a strong central government to protect trade and preserve order, and were willing to pay for it. They were in no small degree responsible for the eventual rise of the monarchies and the decline of feudalism.

Culture. The influence of the cities on medieval culture is less easy to appraise than their effect on social and economic conditions. The burghers were hard-working businessmen, and for long they were not particularly interested in art, literature, or philosophy. Yet they felt the need for education and, as some of them acquired wealth and leisure, they began to develop a secular culture that was characteristically their own. It was in the cities that the brilliant culture of the Renaissance arose, and in the meantime the burghers had done more than any other class to stimulate that growth of material prosperity without which the great cultural advances of the High Middle Ages would have been impossible.

> "Law is a regulation in accord with reason, issued by a lawful superior for the common good." • Saint Thomas Aquinas (1225–74), *Summa Theologica*

20

The Church, Religion, and Culture

ONE CANNOT read far in the history of the High Middle Ages without realizing something of the vast importance of religion and the church in the daily life of men. The medieval man lived in constant and intimate contact with the supernatural. He believed that the world was the physical center of the universe, and that God had created the whole mighty structure in order that the earth might serve as the stage on which men played their brief mortal drama, until death should furnish the cue for their final exit. The central theme of this human drama was the struggle between divine grace and the evil wiles of the devil for the souls of men. And, after that last mortal exit, began the new and grander drama of eternity, with the scene shifted to heaven or hell according as the individual man had played his part on earth. Every act of the drama was played under the direction of a host of spirits, good or evil, saints or devils, who did not hesitate to use all the forces of nature to protect or destroy men, to lead them to salvation or tempt them to perdition. The struggle was a close one, and the end of each man's drama was uncertain. There were bad men as well as good — and in abundance — but all were religious in the sense that they believed in the reality of the drama and strove, so far as their character permitted, to foil the devil and win for themselves a happy ending.

But if the drama of human salvation was controlled ultimately by supernatural powers, it had also its earthly directors, men to whom God had entrusted the care of souls. These were the clergy, one of the three classes into which society was divided. It was their function to help men secure salvation. This function was so vitally important to all men that the clergy, who exercised it, had acquired greater powers than were possessed by any merely worldly government, and these powers were vested in the church. For the priest who cared for men's souls did not stand alone. He was a member of a great international institution, which was in itself a kind of state, superimposed on all secular states and having an administrative system, laws, property, and taxes of its own. The pope was the ruler of this state; the clergy were its officers; and the laymen in all Christian countries of western Europe — the Greek Orthodox peoples of the East stood apart from it — were its subjects.

1. The Church as an Institution

The papacy. In earlier chapters we have shown how the organization of the church first took shape and how the Bishop of Rome became its recognized head in the days of the declining Roman Empire, and, later, how the church became involved in the feudal system, while the popes fell for a time under the domination of the emperors. Finally, we have told the story of the long and successful struggle of the popes, from Gregory VII to Innocent III, to establish

241

their supremacy over secular rulers. At the same time the popes were working with equal success to enforce their authority over all the clergy and to centralize still further the administration of the church. The bishops who were royal officers and feudal barons as well as ministers of the church, presented the most serious problem. The popes, however, gradually succeeded in strengthening their control over the bishops, while at the same time they decreased the bishops' independent authority by encouraging the lesser clergy to appeal from their jurisdiction to the papal court. During the twelfth and thirteenth centuries, more settled conditions enabled the popes to keep in closer touch with the clergy in distant lands than had been possible in the Early Middle Ages. The growth of money economy also encouraged centralization by making it possible for the popes to finance a larger staff of administrative officers.

The curia and the cardinals. As the administration of the church became more highly centralized, a tremendous mass of business was referred to Rome, which the pope could not deal with single-handed. He was assisted by a host of subordinate officers and clerks, who made up the papal *curia* or court. He had also an advisory council in the college of cardinals. The cardinals were appointed for life by the pope and ranked second only to him in the ecclesiastical hierarchy. Their importance depended largely on their exclusive right to elect the popes, which had been guaranteed to them by the decree of Nicholas II in 1059.

The bishops. Outside of Rome, the principal administrative officers were the bishops, each of whom was the head of the church in his diocese. The diocese was the most important territorial unit for church administration. A number of dioceses grouped together formed a province and the bishop of the principal diocese of the province was called an archbishop. He outranked his brother bishops and had some vague authority over them, but his relation to them was that of a chief among his equals. In the Early Middle Ages, the bishops had been almost independent rulers of the clergy in their dioceses. By the thirteenth century, they had lost a good deal of that independent power to the pope. However, they had still to attend to all the business of the diocese, to supervise the

morals of the clergy, to administer the sacraments of ordination and confirmation, and to preside over the ecclesiastical courts, though, of course, some of their executive duties could be delegated to archdeacons or other subordinate officers. They had also important secular duties to perform as feudal lords or royal ministers. They were frequently summoned to the royal court or to accompany the king on a military campaign. Still, arduous though its duties were, the episcopal office carried with it great wealth and power, and it was eagerly sought by ambitious men. Most of the bishops were nobly born, and many of them had undoubtedly entered the church from motives of ambition rather than piety. There were bishops who took their religious duties seriously and whose life was an example to the people, but there were also others whose manner of living could scarcely be distinguished from that of the lay nobles.

The canons. In the principal city of each diocese there was a cathedral, which was the bishop's church. Here there was a "chapter" of canons, who were responsible for the conduct of the services. The cathedral canons bore much the same relation to the bishops that the cardinals did to the pope. They assisted him in the administration, acted as an advisory council, and had the sole right, according to canon law, of electing a new bishop, though their choice was, in practice, frequently dictated by the king or some other feudal superior. At the head of each chapter there was a dean, elected by the canons. By the thirteenth century the cathedral chapters had acquired a good deal of land, which, with the support of the popes, made them fairly independent of their bishops. With each canon's "prebend" or office went the income from a definite piece of land. As a result, the prebends were often sought by young nobles who had no particular religious interests. The popes were forced to issue frequent edicts, usually in vain, ordering canons to remain in residence and to attend to their duties. As a measure of reform some chapters were organized on a monastic basis with a rule of communal life.

Parish priests. The smallest unit of ecclesiastical administration was the parish, and it was the parish priest who came most directly in contact with the people. In country districts the parish was usually identical with the village or manor. The parish church was endowed with land, a share in the cultivated fields of the manor. The priest drew his income from this land and also from offerings and the tithe. The last, which had originally been a free offering for any religious purpose, had become a definite tax on the income of all parishioners, enforceable by law. However, the priest was not permitted to keep all or even the largest part of his income. Part of it went to the bishop in various forms of ecclesiastical tax and part to the "patron" of the church. The latter was usually the lord of the manor whose ancestors had originally endowed the church with its land. In the feudal age the parish church, like almost everything else, had become feudalized. The church, with its lands and tithe, was a "benefice" or "living" which the patron bestowed upon the priest, while retaining a share of the church's income for himself. The patronage of a church was, therefore, a lucrative property and, where the patron was a lay lord, it might be passed on by inheritance or alienated by sale or gift. The patron had, in addition, the right of "presenting" or nominating the priest, though the presentation must be confirmed by the bishop of the diocese. This naturally produced many abuses. Lay patrons often gave the living to favorites or sold it to the highest bidder, with little regard for the suitability of the candidate for his office. Of course, many churches were on ecclesiastical estates, where the patron was a bishop or abbot, from whom greater care for the spiritual character of the appointee might be expected. Also, in many cases, the patronage of churches was given or sold by pious laymen to a bishop, a monastery, or a cathedral chapter. But clerical patronage also led to abuses. The clerical patron — bishop, abbot, or dean — might hold the office of priest for himself and appoint a "vicar" as a substitute, who did all the work and received only a small proportion of the income for himself.

Character of the priests. Under such circumstances, a high standard of character and training could scarcely be expected, especially among the priests or vicars of the poorer country parishes. They were recruited mostly from the peasant class and were poorly educated, if not actually illiterate. Both secular writers and reforming preachers agree in condemning priests for carelessness and immorality, or at least for conduct unbecoming their sacred office, and the records of episcopal visitations furnish more concrete evidence of the failings of many of the clergy. We read that some neglected the church services or absented themselves entirely and hired an unfit substitute. Others misused their power in order to extort money from their parishioners, defrauded the church, or engaged in secular businesses such as money-lending. Priests could no longer marry, but there can be no doubt that the law of celibacy was frequently violated. When specific charges are omitted, the writers accuse them of being more worldly than religious, as well they may have been, considering the manner in which many of them obtained their position. "Our priests," writes a contemporary preacher, "immersed in material things, disturb themselves little about those of the spirit. They differ from laymen in dress, not at heart; in appearance, not in reality. They belie by their deeds what they preach from the pulpit. Tonsure, garb, and speech give them the superficial varnish of piety; underneath the sheep's clothing are concealed hypocrites and ravening wolves." We must beware, however, of taking the strictures of the reforming preachers too literally, for they were likely to take for granted the numerous priests who did their duty faithfully and to generalize from the most notorious examples.

Ecclesiastical courts. Aside from all its other activities, the church had wide judicial powers. These were exercised in the episcopal courts, which administered ecclesiastical or canon law rather than the civil law of the secular courts. The bishops claimed jurisdiction over all persons who in any way could be classed as clergy, including students and deacons who had not been ordained priests, as well as over widows, orphans, and crusaders who were regarded as wards of the church. They also claimed a variety of cases, not involving the clergy, in which the dispute was of a moral or religious nature. In this latter class fell all cases concerning marriage, business deals sanctioned by an oath, and testaments witnessed by a priest, as well as offenses against religion, such as violation of church property, heresy, and blasphemy. The sentences prescribed in criminal cases by canon law, which always avoided the shedding of blood, were notoriously lighter than those of the civil courts. Hence, despite the opposition of secular governments, the episcopal courts were sought by all who could claim "benefit of clergy." Fines were the most common punishments inflicted, with the result that the courts furnished a considerable part of the bishop's revenues. This fact also goes far to explain the opposition of the kings, especially in France and England, to the transference of cases from the royal to the ecclesiastical courts. They were still more opposed — and in this they had the support of the bishops — to the growing custom of appealing cases from the local church courts to the papal *curia* at Rome. The appeals to Rome not only took a good deal of money out of the country; they also removed important cases from the jurisdiction of the bishops, whom the kings could more or less control, to a distant and independent court.

Papal revenue. By the thirteenth century the popes had so far succeeded in the centralization of authority that they were able to draw a large income from the clergy of all parts of Roman Christendom. It was not till the Later Middle Ages, however, with the further expansion of money economy, that the popes worked out fully the various methods of adding to their revenue. We will leave the subject, therefore, for further discussion in Chapter 24.

2. The Sacraments, Popular Religion, and Heresy

The preceding outline shows the church as a great human institution, a spiritual state, separate from and superior to the lay world, which it taxed and governed with legal authority. But how did it acquire and maintain its authority? What did religion mean to the ordinary layman? And was there no revolt? These are significant questions and must be answered in some fashion if we are to understand the religion of the Middle Ages.

Heaven and hell. A partial answer to these questions can be stated briefly. To the medieval man, religion and the universal church, with its sacramental powers, were inseparable. He could not conceive of one apart from the other. The pope was the Vicar of Christ, the representative of God on earth, and to him and his subordinate officers God had entrusted the salvation of mankind. Could any man defy such authority with eternity at stake? Even the most thoughtless man lived under the shadow of eternity. Before him lay the awe-inspiring alternative of heaven or hell, and of these two he thought more often and more vividly of the latter. He could scarcely imagine the bliss of heaven, but hell was a place of eternal physical torment as real to him as was the land of a neighboring county. Indeed, a Norman peasant had probably a clearer mental picture of the topography, climate, and general living conditions of hell than of those of Burgundy or Aquitaine. And he believed that no man, because of the original sin inherited from Adam and the sins which he himself would inevitably commit, could by his own unaided efforts win salvation and avoid damnation. He must depend on divine grace, which was channeled to man through the sacraments of the church. The fear of hell was somewhat softened by the development of the doctrine of purgatory, which was an intermediate state between heaven and hell, where those who were not hopelessly damned but were not yet ready for heaven might spend after death an indeterminate period of further penance and purgation through suffering. But even purgatory could not be reached without the aid of the sacraments.

Sacraments. The doctrine of the sacraments had developed slowly since the early days of Christianity. It was not fully developed till the twelfth century. There were seven sacraments in all. That of baptism, administered as soon as possible after birth, cleansed the child of original sin and signified his entry into the church. Without it there could be no hope of salvation. The sacrament of confirmation, administered by a bishop, came later, during adolescence, and marked the communicant's conscious acceptance of the faith, thus confirming his baptism. Extreme unction was the final sacrament, the last rite performed for a dying man to prepare his soul for eternity. These three, in the normal course of events, were administered to every man and woman once. The other two universal sacraments were more frequent. The sacrament of penance, following confession and proof of repentance, washed away the guilt of sin and left only the necessity of doing some act of penance in this world or in purgatory to prepare the soul for heaven. Finally, and most important of all, the Eucharist, administered generally during the service of the Mass, was received as the body and blood of the Savior and admitted the communicant to a share in the saving grace resulting from Christ's supreme sacrifice. The two remaining sacraments, marriage and ordination, were administered to laymen and clergy respectively. Each was considered indissoluble, the former so long as both parties lived, the latter for life, though under certain conditions the bond of marriage might be broken by a special dispensation from the church.

Power of the clergy. The power of the clergy and the authority of the church rested securely on the sacramental system. For, with the exception of baptism, which in an emergency could be administered by any Christian, only a priest, who had himself received the sacrament of ordination from a bishop, could administer the sacraments. The clergy, in other words, held a monopoly that guaranteed their position. They alone could purvey to the people the precious gift of salvation. The wealth, political influence, and legal authority of the church followed naturally on that fact. Disobedience or rebellion could be met by excommunication, which cut the offending person off from membership in the church, and hence, unless the ban were lifted, from all hope of salvation. Moreover, the priest was kept in close touch with his parishioners through the confession which must precede the sacrament of penance. He thus gained an intimate knowledge of their affairs and could wield a great influence over their lives.

Popular religion. The important part played by the sacraments in the scheme of salvation tended to make them appear to the popular mind as the only essential factor in religion. The average man of the Middle Ages, illiterate and not too far removed from barbarism, was no theologian. He might easily fail to grasp the spiritual significance of the sacraments and come to view the actual ceremonies as a sort of mechanical process sufficient to secure his entry into heaven. Despite the warnings of devout churchmen, people came to regard the

The Romanesque façade of the cathedral of Angoulême has the rounded arches, the heavy walls, and the massive weight characteristic of Romanesque architecture.

formal acts of the sacraments as having a supernatural power in themselves. This tendency on the part of simple folk to reduce spiritual concepts to material terms was characteristic of all aspects of popular religion. Uneducated men, whose minds were not trained to think in abstract terms, demanded physical symbols that they could see and touch, and often they forgot that the symbol was not itself the reality.

Saints and devils. The veneration of saints and the popular belief in the constant participation of saints and devils in the events of daily life arose in part from this natural mental process. God seemed far removed from human affairs and Christ was too often pictured as a stern judge. Men felt the need of some more human and understandable figures to act as intermediaries between man and God. This role was admirably filled by the Virgin Mary and the saints, who had been human and might still retain human characteristics or at least have sympathy with human frailties. From the veneration of the saints came much of the warmth, color, and simple piety of medieval religion, but it also led to a good deal of materialistic superstition. The activity of the saints was not limited to keeping men from temptation or enabling them to escape punishment for their sins. They also came to the assistance of men in purely material ways, curing their sickness, protecting their crops, finding lost articles, and performing a host of beneficent services for those who sought their aid. To people who believed that the universe was governed by supernatural rather than natural laws, there was no inconsistency in such supernatural interference in the ordinary sequence of cause and effect. It was a natural consequence of a literal or material interpretation of the eternal conflict between good and evil forces in the universe, which was the essential plot of the divine drama. For there were innumerable demons or devils as well as saints, and these were quite as active. They tempted men into sin; ruined their crops by storm or insect pests; afflicted them with sickness; struck church steeples with lightning; or, more ingenious in their rage against the church, caused the choir to doze or the priest to stutter during Mass.

Relics and pilgrimages. Veneration of the saints was also extended to include the relics of their mortal existence — their bodies as well as their clothing and personal belongings. These relics of famous men would at any time have a sentimental value, such as today we should give to the pen used by Shakespeare, and would be eagerly sought by collectors. But the relics of the saints meant much more than that, for they shared the miraculous powers of the saints themselves. To touch them was enough to heal one's illness or to keep one from harm. The bones of one of the major saints were worth more than a king's ransom, and pilgrims came from far places to seek aid or comfort at the shrine that housed them. Pilgrimages, too, were often undertaken as a full or partial performance of penance prescribed by the church. All through the medieval centuries, bands of pilgrims might be met daily on any of the main roads of Europe.

Heretics. The great majority of medieval men undoubtedly accepted the authority and teaching of the church without question, and could not think of religion apart from it. But there were some heretics who rebelled, and their numbers increased during the twelfth century until they had become a serious menace to the church. We know less than we should like to know about the opinions of medieval heretics, since we are forced to rely mostly on accounts written by their orthodox opponents. It is clear, however, that, though different groups held quite different opinions, all the more popular heresies can be accounted for by the same general causes. They were due, in one way or another, to the failure of the church to provide satisfactory spiritual inspiration, and were motivated by dissatisfaction with the mechanical nature of the sacramental system and, still more, with the character, wealth, and power of the clergy. They were nearly all anti-sacramentarian and anti-clerical.

Albigenses and Waldenses. The two most important heretical sects, the Albigenses and the Waldenses, flourished chiefly in southern France, though they spread also into neighboring countries. The former, who were also called Cathari, were the most numerous and made their appearance as early as the eleventh century. Their central doctrine seems to have been a very literal and rather morbid identification of everything physical or material with the forces of evil in the universe. This led to the rejection of all material symbols of religion — sacraments, crosses, relics, or images — and an extreme asceticism, at least among the inner circle of the "perfected," who were sworn to abstain from marrying, owning property, eating flesh, or shedding blood. The ordinary "believers," who made up the greater part of the sect, were allowed greater freedom. The Waldenses seem to have been much more normal and their doctrines were closer to true Christianity. Except in the south of France, where they were included in the mass persecution of the Albigenses, they were not rigorously pursued by the church, and remnants of them survived for centuries in Piedmont, Germany, Bohemia, Hungary, and even in orthodox Spain. Their founder was a rich merchant of Lyons, Peter Waldo, who about the year 1170 gave away his property to the poor and began preaching in an effort to recall men to the simple doctrine of Christ as found in the Gospels. Neither he nor his followers had at first any thought of heresy, but their vigorous condemnation of the wealth and worldliness of the clergy soon led to their being condemned by the church. Forbidden to preach, they were forced to separate themselves from the church and to justify their position by the claim that any good Christian had the right to preach and that the sacraments were not necessary to salvation. Their protest against the clerical monopoly was never entirely forgotten. It undoubtedly did something, though how much is uncertain, to prepare the way for Wyclif, Huss, and Luther.

Albigensian Crusade. Throughout the twelfth century the church had made fitful efforts to suppress heretics, but it was Innocent III who first devoted the full authority of the papacy to the task of destroying these enemies of the faith. In 1207, he summoned the chivalry of Europe to take part in a crusade against the Albigenses. The story of that crusade, which was led by Simon de Montfort, has been recounted briefly in Chapter 16. The northern knights laid waste the rich lands of southern France and slaughtered thousands. They struck a mortal blow to the flourishing culture of Languedoc and Provence as well as to heresy, but the latter at least would soon have revived had the work of the crusaders not been followed by the preaching of the newly founded orders of friars and by the steady persecution of heresy carried on by the papal Inquisition or Holy Office, now for the first time firmly established. Inquisitorial procedure — that is, the searching out and trying of heretics — was not new. It had been a regular part of the bishops' judicial duties. But the bishops were busy men and often none too zealous. In 1233, therefore, Pope Gregory IX gave a permanent commission, later more fully developed, to regular inquisitors who were to set up special courts, though still in formal cooperation with the bishops, for the discovery and trial of heretics. The methods of the Inquisition — the secrecy of the trials, the refusal to divulge the names of the accusers so that the accused might answer them, the full and accurate records kept by the court, and the use of torture to extort confessions — inspired

dread wherever the institution was established, and in the long run succeeded in stamping out most open heresy. The sentences imposed ranged from public penance to life imprisonment. Stubborn heretics, however, who refused to recant, or those who later relapsed into heresy, were turned over to the secular government to be burned at the stake.

3. *The Monks and Friars*

The monks and nuns. Aside from the laymen and the "secular" clergy, there were large numbers of monks and nuns who lived apart from the world in accordance with the monastic rule. The rule followed by most of them was still that of St. Benedict, or a variation upon it, and the monastic ideal had changed very little since the early days of monasticism.[1] The monks and nuns were often called simply "religious," for their way of life was considered the most truly Christian, more likely to win salvation than that of either layman or secular priest. Those of the male religious who were clerics or in orders were also classified as "regular" clergy, i.e., living by a monastic rule (*regula*). The very popularity of the monastic life led to the relaxation of discipline in many monasteries or to the observance of the letter rather than the spirit of the rule. Many men and women entered the monastery or the convent for reasons that had little to do with religion — and not all of them willingly. Sons and daughters of noble families who could not be provided for from the family estates were sometimes relegated to the cloister. Weaklings who could not hold their own in a violent society, and men who sought only leisure and security found in it a refuge. Ambitious youngsters saw in it an opportunity for advancement; for the monasteries possessed wide lands and the abbot was a feudal lord with a large income and great political power. It is not surprising, then, to find many monks who lived in luxurious idleness or who left their monasteries on every possible pretext to renew contact with the world they had forsworn, so that contemporary preachers complained that one could not go anywhere without stumbling over a monk. Even had they wished, the abbots

[1] See above, pages 94–96.

and monks could not have remained cut off from the world. They were often better educated than the laymen, and kings and lords used them constantly as ministers, messengers, or negotiators. Even St. Bernard had to spend most of his life outside his beloved walls.

Monastic reforms. Yet, despite the worldliness of many monks and the tendency both in the monastery and outside to an easy acceptance of the forms of religion, there were still many earnestly religious people in the Middle Ages to whom the monastic ideal made a strong appeal and who strove to put it into practice. In one monastery after another the rule was for a time rigidly enforced or was made still more stringent, until the fame of the monastery spread abroad and brought a shower of pious gifts. Eventually the reformed monasteries would become wealthy and lax. The enthusiasm for reform would die down and they would settle back into the ordinary routine. Several of the reformed monasteries founded numbers of branch houses or priories, thus forming a "congregation" under the rule of the abbot of the home monastery. The results of the reform were in this way spread over a large territory. The great Congregation of Cluny included more than two thousand houses by the middle of the twelfth century. Like most of the congregations, Cluny was exempt from episcopal control and subject only to the pope. Its influence on the general reform of the church and the establishment of papal supremacy has already been noted.[1] As its prestige declined,

[1] See above, pages 175–177.

its place of leadership was taken by the Cistercian Congregation, founded at Cîteaux in 1098. The latter owed much of its fame to St. Bernard, who wielded a greater spiritual influence than any other man during the first half of the twelfth century. Among the other reformed congregations the most important was the Premonstratensian order of regular canons, founded at Prémontré in 1120, who followed the Augustinian rule.

The friars. The monastic reforms raised the spiritual level of the monks, temporarily at any rate, but they could have no more than an indirect influence on the people outside the monasteries. The monks were hampered by the rule, strongly enforced in the reformed monasteries, which bound them to their houses. In order to win heretics back to the faith and to give spiritual inspiration to the people at large, what was evidently needed were the services of men who combined the unworldly devotion of the ideal monk with the ability to move freely among the people and to preach directly to them. It was in answer to this need that the two great orders of friars (brothers) were created in the early years of the thirteenth century. The Franciscans and Dominicans were a new kind of monk. Strictly speaking, they were not monks at all, for they did not live in monasteries, but wandered freely among the people getting their living by begging, whence they were called the mendicant orders.

St. Francis. St. Francis of Assisi (1181 or 1182–1226), who founded the Friars Minor or Franciscans, was one of the most lovable of the medieval saints. His father was a rich

A procession of Dominican friars as it appears in a manuscript illuminated by Jean Pucelle in Paris in the 1320's.

Italian merchant, but Francis, with his romantic temperament, cared little for business. In his youth he lived a gay, irresponsible existence, loving poetry and gallant gestures. His conversion from this frivolous life came suddenly, when he was still in his early twenties. With characteristic wholeheartedness, he gave what money he had, including some of his father's, to repair a ruined chapel; cut himself off from his businesslike family; and set out in absolute poverty to preach to the poor, confident that the necessities of life would be provided. In his new way of life, Francis lost none of his joyous spirit, his love of poetry and nature, or the personal charm that had always attracted men to him. He adopted poverty gaily, not as a penance but as a liberation from the ties that bind men to earth. He soon acquired followers and, in 1210, secured the verbal sanction of Innocent III for this nucleus of an order. Thereafter the brothers grew rapidly in numbers and were given a complete rule, which was confirmed by Pope Honorius III in 1223. Before long, the gray-cloaked friars were familiar figures on every highway and in every crowded slum of western Europe. They were a universal order, exempt from the authority of the bishops. Their general was subject only to the pope. As they became more popular, the ideals of the friars began to change. They accepted gifts of houses and furniture, despite the rule of poverty on which St. Francis had insisted so strongly, and their high standard of character gradually declined. A few, however, clung to the spirit of the rule, with the result that after a long and bitter controversy the order was finally divided.

St. Dominic. St. Dominic (1170–1221), the founder of the order of Preaching Friars named after him, was a native of Castile. He was well-educated and became a canon and later a subprior of the Augustinian order. In 1205, he accompanied his bishop on a mission into southern France. There he was shocked by the amount of heresy he found and soon began to preach in an effort to win back heretics to the orthodox faith. For the next eleven years he continued his preaching, though often in danger from the violence aroused by the Albigensian Crusade. Like St. Francis, he gathered a group of followers about him. He

The Christ-like Saint Francis of Assisi inspired some of the finest religious art of the early Renaissance. This portrait by Cimabue (c. 1240–c. 1302) is a detail from a large fresco in the Franciscan church at Assisi.

received papal recognition for his order in 1216, though the final rule was not drawn up till four years later. St. Dominic was a man of admirable character, gentle and kindly and absolutely fearless; but he lacked the rare spiritual charm of the Italian saint, and his main purpose was the more limited one of converting heretics rather than giving spiritual inspiration to the orthodox, who often needed it quite as badly. He, too, insisted on the vow of poverty, but he valued it not as an end in itself, as St. Francis did, but because it would increase the prestige and influence of the preaching brothers. When poverty seemed a disadvantage rather than an asset, the Dominicans departed from the rule without the conflict which tore the Franciscan order on that point. Friars from both orders were frequently entrusted with the conduct of the Inquisition, but it was naturally the Dominicans who gave most time to the grim task of suppressing heresy, from which came the name of *Domini canes* ("the hounds of God") often applied to them.

Influence of the friars. During the first century after their foundation the mendicant orders exercised a tremendous influence that fully justified their unrivaled popularity. They converted thousands of heretics and gave new life and fervor to popular religion everywhere. The friars were given full power to hear confessions, independent of the local clergy who had so often proved unfit for their duties, and they were remarkably successful in restoring frequency of confession. In the Later Middle Ages, however, when the character of the orders had begun to decline, their confessional power frequently led to abuse, and the parish priests complained that they were both lax and avaricious, granting easy absolution in return for gifts. But the influence of the friars was not confined to popular religion. They did great services also to the cause of learning. The Dominicans were from the first devoted to education, as befitted an order created for the combating of heretical opinion. Albertus Magnus and Thomas Aquinas, who were largely responsible for shaping the scholastic philosophy which sought to base the articles of faith on a firm foundation of reason, were both Dominicans. Nor were the Franciscans far behind, though St. Francis had warned them against too much education. The names of St. Bonaventura, Alexander of Hales, Roger Bacon, Duns Scotus, and William of Occam bear witness that the Friars Minor were fully equal to their rivals in learning.

4. *The Revival of Learning and the Universities*

The revival of learning. During the High Middle Ages, in every field of human endeavor, the peoples of the West emerged from the darker ages into the full light of medieval civilization. The great revival of learning, which took place during that period, was the intellectual counterpart of the economic and social energy that produced the new trade and town life, of the religious force that built the great structure of the medieval church, and of the tendency toward social stability that was gradually imposing order upon feudal chaos. The inspiration for the new learning came largely from the Greek and Moslem East, partly through the crusades, partly through Italy, but still more from Moslem Spain. The scientific and philosophical works of Aristotle, the writings of the ancient Greek mathematicians and physicians, usually from the translations and commentaries made by Arabic scholars, were now eagerly studied. The bare bones of the *trivium* and *quadrivium* (the elements of grammar, rhetoric, and logic, and of arithmetic, astronomy, geometry, and music respectively), which had made up the sum of early medieval education, paled into insignificance before this mass of new material. The old monastery and cathedral schools were no longer adequate to cope with the demands of this enlarged curriculum. They gave way gradually before the rising universities.

Rise of the universities. The twelfth century was the period in which the earliest universities took shape. By the end of the century those of Bologna, Paris, Montpellier, and Oxford, at least, were well established. We do not know just when to date their beginnings, for they simply grew, evolving slowly from the need for protection of students and teachers and from the natural tendency of men with common interests to organize themselves and to form institutions. The official charters granted by king and pope in the early years of the thirteenth century were merely the recognition of an accomplished fact. The University of Paris served as a model for all northern universities, including Oxford, which owed its origin to the recall of English students from Paris about 1167; Cambridge, founded by a migration from Oxford in 1209; and the German universities which sprang up in the fourteenth and fifteenth centuries. Early in the twelfth century, Paris became a famous center of learning, drawing students and teachers from all parts of Europe. The fame of the brilliant young philosopher, Peter Abelard, attracted hundreds of students, and after his departure the theologian, Peter Lombard, and scores of other teachers maintained the reputation of the city. Originally, these teachers had given private courses independently. But for a variety of reasons this proved unsatisfactory to both students and teachers. Some form of organization was obviously necessary.

Organization. The formation of a university as a guild of teachers and students was

A university lecture, as depicted by the fifteenth-century painter, Lorenzo de Voltolino, shows Henricus de Allemania lecturing on ethics to a more or less attentive class.

the logical solution of the problem. In order to prevent unqualified men from teaching, the chancellor of the cathedral was empowered to grant licenses to those who had passed a satisfactory examination, which, of course, necessitated the fixing of a curriculum of studies so that the candidates would know on what material they were to be examined. Those who were granted licenses were called masters of arts and formed the governing body of the university, the faculty of arts. Following the analogy of the guild, the students may be considered as the apprentices, and the bachelors as the journeymen with a limited license who were permitted to teach in certain elementary courses. The master's degree was accepted as a guaranty of proficiency, sought by all, even though all did not intend to use it for active teaching. After becoming a master of arts, if the student wished specialized training in one of the professions, he might pursue a further course of study leading to the degree of doctor and admittance to the faculties of theology, medicine, or law. The University of Bologna, famous for its law school, was organized somewhat differently, for there the governing body was the society or university of students, who had first organized for mutual protection against teachers and townspeople alike. The faculties were there subordinate to the students. Most

of the southern universities followed this model rather than that of Paris.

Privileges. The universities were essentially clerical institutions. Both teachers and students were classed as clerics, and so were exempt from ordinary civil jurisdiction. The charter granted to the University of Paris by Philip Augustus in 1200 recognized this exemption from the jurisdiction of royal or municipal courts. Further independence of local authority was acquired shortly after by papal edict. The university, as a corporation, was freed from the jurisdiction of the bishop, and disciplinary powers were vested in the faculty, subject only to the pope. The same arrangement was also made in regard to the other universities, thus giving them a remarkable degree of corporate independence.

Student life. The jurisdictional authority of the university was important, for the students were a riotous lot at times. The medieval university provided no organized sports or student activities to serve as an outlet for youthful energy and high spirits, and it was an age when men resorted easily to physical violence. Despite all prohibitions, many a student carried a knife concealed under his gown, and used it on the slightest provocation. Contemporary preachers raised their hands in horror at the drunkenness, violence, and immorality of the students, all the more because they were legally clerics; and the student poems and songs, which celebrate the less respectable joys of life in charming but unclassical Latin, bear out the indictment. Undoubtedly the medieval students were more undisciplined than those of modern times, but otherwise they were very much like students in all ages. In the letters and records that have survived, we can find all the recognizable types — students rich and poor, diligent and lazy, those who were earnestly laying the foundations of a career, and those who were merely enjoying a vacation from home. Letters written home for more funds to meet unexpected expenses, none too well itemized, were evidently as common then as now. So were letters from parents complaining that their sons were wasting their time and their parents' hard-earned money in irresponsible pleasures.

Method of instruction.   The medieval university had very little of the physical equipment that seems so important in its modern counterpart. In the twelfth and thirteenth centuries it had no buildings, except an occasional residential college for poor students, no laboratories, no library, and even no regular classrooms. A staff of teachers was all that the university possessed. Classes were held in a room in the professor's house or in a hired hall. In Paris, the students sat on the floor, which was covered with straw, while the professor lectured from a platform with a desk to hold his notes. The classes were long, beginning often at daybreak, and the rooms must have been cold and uncomfortable. The sole method of instruction was the lecture, based on a definite textbook. Medieval scholars had great respect for authoritative books, of which there were still relatively few, and the business of the professor was to explain and comment on the authorities in his field. Books were scarce and expensive, since all had to be copied by hand. Few students could afford to own their texts, though they could often rent them. As a rule, however, the method of lecturing made the possession of texts by all the students unnecessary. Taking the text passage by passage, the professor read it slowly so that the students could copy it verbatim. He then expounded it sentence by sentence, drawing upon his knowledge of the subject for every possible ray of light that could be shed upon its meaning. At the end of the course, the student's notes, if he were diligent, would comprise a complete copy of the text with the lecturer's gloss or explanation.

The arts faculty.   The course in the faculty of arts leading to the M.A. degree, normally a six-year course with the bachelor's degree somewhere along the way, was the essential part of the university curriculum. It was taken by all students, including those who intended to enter the higher faculties later. The *trivium* and *quadrivium* still formed the framework of the curriculum, but the proportion of emphasis had shifted. By far the most time was given to the former, and of the three subjects included in it (grammar, rhetoric, and logic), logic far outstripped the rest. In the first half of the twelfth century, there had been a considerable revival of interest in classical Latin literature; but the introduction of Aristotle's *Logic* at about the same time and of his *Metaphysics* in the early years of the thirteenth century turned the attention of scholars more and more to logic and philosophy, while grammar and rhetoric sank back into second place. They became merely a means to the end of teaching Latin, the language in which all texts were written and all lectures delivered. The Latin of the medieval universities was strictly utilitarian. It was used to convey information and hence remained a living tongue, changing and adapting itself to fit the needs of the age in a way that would have been impossible had it remained bound to classical precedent. Logic and philosophy were also used for practical purposes, furnishing a method of study that could be applied to theology, medicine, law, and science. They were the universal tools of the medieval scholar, who was more given to close, hard reasoning from authoritative texts and to metaphysical speculation than to experiment or to observation of natural phenomena.

Theology.   Theology was the "Queen of the Sciences" in the Middle Ages, for it was the science that explained religion and showed men the way to salvation. Its development in this period was for the most part the work of men who were teachers in the universities, hence called "schoolmen" or "scholastic" theologians. The majority of them were connected with the University of Paris, which far outstripped all other schools in this field. Three problems especially interested the scholastic theologians. One was the problem of conflicting authorities, for all theological speculation was founded upon close study of unquestioned authorities, of which the Bible was the chief, with the works of the Fathers and the decrees of the church ranking a close second. That these authorities did not always agree was brought forcibly to the attention of the theologians in the first half of the twelfth century by that rash and brilliant young teacher, Peter Abelard (1079–1142), who is now remembered chiefly for the story of his tragic love of Heloise. His arrangement of conflicting authorities in direct opposition to each other in a work boldly entitled *Sic et Non* ("Yes and No") challenged the logical subtlety of the schoolmen to bring them into harmony. Among the scholars who undertook that task, the most successful was Peter Lombard, whose *Sentences* became the standard textbook of theology.

Reason and revelation. A second and more fundamentally important problem arose from

This idealized fifteenth-century portrait of St. Thomas Aquinas was painted by the Florentine artist Fra Angelico.

the introduction of ancient Greek philosophy, with Moslem commentaries, into the world of medieval Christian thought. It not only furnished the schoolmen with a quantity of pre-Christian metaphysical speculation; it also inspired them to put their trust in natural reason guided by logic. At the same time, however, they were in possession of a body of divinely revealed truth, which reason might strive to understand, but must never challenge. When employed in the service of the faith, logic and philosophy might be valuable allies of theology; but when pursued for their own sake, they might become subtly subversive forces. For many of the early schoolmen, the problem of reconciling reason with revelation was solved by the formula, borrowed from Augustine and restated by St. Anselm of Canterbury in the late eleventh century: "I do not seek to know in order that I may believe, but I believe in order that I may know." This was no denial of the potency of reason. It merely asserted that reason can achieve valid results only when informed by revealed truth. The recovery of the complete works of Aristotle, together with the commentaries of the great Arabic philosopher, Averroës, in the thirteenth century, made it more difficult for many schoolmen to maintain this position. Deeply impressed by the logical coherence of Aristotle's philosophy, which they regarded as the supreme achievement of natural reason, the Christian followers of Averroës were forced to assume that Aristotle's conclusions might be true in philosophy but, where they conflicted with Christian dogma, untrue in theology. The conflict between reason and revelation could thus be solved only by keeping philosophy and theology in separate airtight compartments. It was to meet this danger, without falling back upon the Augustinian formula, that St. Thomas Aquinas (1225–74) undertook in his great *Summa Theologica* to construct a comprehensive synthesis of philosophy and theology. Reason and faith were for Aquinas merely different ways of reaching truth. There can be no conflict between them since there can be but one truth, for all truth comes from God. Reason, aided by Aristotelian logic and metaphysic, he would employ as far as it would go, leaving to faith in revealed truth only such matters as were beyond the reach of reason.

The Gothic façade of the west front of Reims Cathedral has the pointed arches, the soaring verticality, and the abundant sculptural decoration of the high Gothic.

Thus he held that the existence of God and the immortality of the soul, for example, could be proved by natural reason, but that such doctrines as the Incarnation of Christ and the Atonement were susceptible to proof only through revelation.

Realism and Nominalism. The controversy concerning the relation of reason to revelation was inseparably bound up with a third problem, that of the reality of "universals," which divided medieval schoolmen and was of basic importance to scholastic thought. The problem, put in its simplest form, is whether absolute reality is to be found in individual things or only in the general conceptions or ideas, the "universals," which have existed from the beginning of time as "forms" in the mind of God. The philosophers who took the latter position under the influence of Plato and the Neoplatonists were called Realists. For them the idea of man, for example, is an ultimate reality. It is a "universal" which existed before there were individual men and exists eternally apart

from men. Individual men are but imperfect reflections of the universal reality. The opposing or Nominalist school, on the contrary, held that only the individual thing is real and that the "universals" are merely names given to groups of individual things which are sufficiently similar so that for purposes of convenience they can be classified under one term. Between these extreme points of view there was room for compromise. Abelard held that both the individual and the universal had absolute reality. Aquinas, too, held a modified Realism, closer to Aristotle than to Plato. He argued that the "universals" possess eternal reality, but that they also exist *in* individuals as their "essence." It was by assuming the reality of "essences" as "universals" that Aquinas was able to bring all material and immaterial beings, natural and supernatural, into a great chain of being stretching upward from inanimate nature to God. Only through some form of Realism could reason deal with transcendental or supernatural beings as knowable and so offer rational proof of the articles of religious faith. Realism also furnished a valuable support to the authority of the church by placing the emphasis on the church as an eternal, ideal entity rather than upon the individual and fallible human beings who compose its membership. The fourteenth century brought a reaction toward Nominalism under the influence of Duns Scotus (d. 1308) and the more extreme teaching of William of Occam (d.c. 1349). Believing that the human mind can grasp only the reality of particular things, Occam rejected the possibility of proving the truths of religion by reason. In the field of theology, then, the triumph of Nominalism in the fourteenth and fifteenth centuries destroyed that system of thought which made possible the logical proof of those things which the Christian believes, and threw men back upon faith, thus preparing the way for the ideas of Luther and the Protestant Reformation. In a wider field the Nominalist mode of thinking was a step toward the modern preoccupation with individual things, to the historians' interest in individual men and events, to the political liberals' emphasis upon the individual citizen rather than the state as an ideal whole, and to the scientists' interest in concrete things as they individually behave.

Natural science. Despite the experimental work of Roger Bacon and others at Oxford in the thirteenth century and of some of the Paris Nominalists in the fourteenth century, the medieval schoolmen made no such contribution to the natural sciences as they did to philosophy and theology. The ways of thinking characteristic of medieval scholasticism were suited to abstract speculation rather than to observation of concrete things or to the construction of scientific hypotheses of the modern sort. The schoolmen absorbed the ancient Greek sciences contained in the works of Aristotle, Ptolemy, and others, together with the additions and comments made by Arabic scholars, but they added little of their own. Natural science was not their major interest, and they tended to consider it, when they considered it at all, within a theological and metaphysical frame of reference. Their habitual reverence for authoritative texts led them to accept the errors as well as the useful knowledge contained in

the works of the ancient scientists, and their training led them to depend too exclusively on deductive logic. As philosophers they were interested in abstracting the essences of things rather than in measuring their physical properties, and this tendency was reinforced by the influence of Aristotelian physics, which explained the action of natural phenomena by the qualities or "dispositions" supposed to be inherent in them. One of the first prerequisites to the founding of modern science, as we shall see in Chapter 36, was, indeed, the rejection of Aristotle's "qualitative" physics.

Medicine. Medicine, like the other natural sciences, suffered from a method of study which was admirably suited to theology or philosophy, but not to sciences which have to deal with concrete physical things. The works of the ancient Greek physicians, Galen and Hippocrates, and the commentaries of such famous Arabic doctors as Avicenna, were accepted as authorities. From them the medieval physicians drew logical conclusions that were often totally erroneous because not checked by practical observation. They were also led astray by the Greek theory that disease was caused by a lack of balance between the four "humors" of which the fluid parts of the body were composed. There was much superstition, too, in medieval medical theory. Nevertheless, advances were made, and there was probably more genuinely scientific thought in the schools of medicine than elsewhere in the medieval universities. The oldest medical school was that at Salerno, where Arabic influence was strong, but in the thirteenth century it was surpassed by Bologna, Padua, Montpellier, and Paris.

Law. The logical method was much better suited to the study of law. Feudal law, with its infinite variations in practice, was largely ignored and the schools concentrated on a close study of Roman civil law, as embodied in the Justinian Code, and the canon law based on Gratian's *Decretum,* compiled about the middle of the twelfth century. Here the medieval scholars were dealing with authorities and principles, a field well suited to the method of logical deduction in which they excelled. The results of their work were of immense value both to the kings, who were trying to build up a system of royal law to take the place of feudal custom, and to the church, whose authority they placed on a firm legal foundation. The law schools attracted large numbers of students, since a degree in canon or civil law or, better still, in both, opened the way to a lucrative career.

5. Religious Art and Music

In an age when religion was so powerful a factor in everyday life, and when the church so largely dominated society, it is not surprising that the art which best expressed the emotions and aspirations of the people should be religious art. Not that all medieval art was

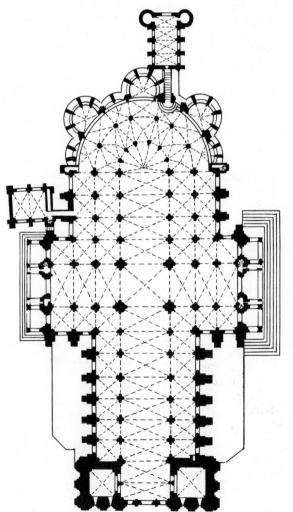

religious, but religion did inspire the finest products of artistic genius because it appealed so strongly to the artist's imagination, and also because religious art was encouraged and financed by the most powerful institution of the age, the church. This is particularly true of architecture, the most highly perfected art of the Middle Ages, to which all the other arts were subordinated. There were magnificent castles and elaborate guildhalls, but none of them can compare for richness of beauty with the cathedrals.

The Gothic cathedrals.   During the twelfth and thirteenth centuries, the gradual evolution of the Gothic style of architecture out of the older Romanesque brought about a radical revolution in the construction of churches and cathedrals and produced the finest examples of medieval architecture. The characteristic feature of Romanesque architecture was the use of round arches and vaults, which necessitated very heavy walls to carry the weight of the roof or forced the substitution of wooden roofs for stone. The pointed arches, which were characteristic of the Gothic style, were not only stronger but also carried the weight more directly downward, with less lateral thrust. What made the Gothic cathedral a masterpiece of engineering was not, however, simply the use of the pointed arch and vault but the combination of these with pillars and buttresses to form a skeleton framework which took the weight of the roof off the walls. As a result almost all the wall space could be used for great decorative windows. As the ground plan of Chartres cathedral on this page shows, the skeleton of a Gothic cathedral consists of an outer row of piers supported by buttresses and a corresponding row of pillars separated from the outer piers by an aisle running down each side of the building. Each group of four piers or pillars formed a quadrangular unit roofed by a groined vault which rose in a triangular wedge from each of the four sides to meet at a point in

In this ground plan of the cathedral of Chartres, the dotted lines represent the ribs supporting the vaults of the quadrangular units of which the cathedral was composed. The vaults running down the center of the nave and the transepts are much higher than those of the side aisles.

the center. This vault rested on ribs of stone, which formed pointed arches on all four sides of the quadrangle, with two transverse ribs springing from each angle and meeting in the center. These ribs carried the weight of the vault down to the pillars and piers. In the interior of the building, the lateral thrust of each set of ribs was compensated for by the lateral thrust of the adjoining groups, while the thrust against the outside piers was taken by the buttresses. The whole structure was thus a living complex of thrusts and counter-thrusts, held in an equilibrium so perfectly balanced that most of the cathedrals which have not suffered the ravages of war still stand after seven or eight hundred years.

Sculpture and painting. Sculpture as an independent art scarcely existed in the Middle Ages, but it was highly developed none the less, being employed in lavish fashion for the decoration of cathedrals and churches. Painting was also used for the same purpose, though not so extensively, for in the Gothic cathedrals the stained-glass windows occupied most of the clear wall space and themselves furnished color and picture. The purpose of both painter and sculptor was to edify and instruct an illiterate people, as well as to add to the beauty of the building. Their work was often cramped by tradition and conventionalized by the necessity of fitting it into the architect's plans. During the twelfth and thirteenth centuries, however, the Gothic sculptors, especially in northern France, were working away from the stiff formalism that had characterized the earlier medieval styles. Their figures stood more freely in space and were hence more fully rounded. Draperies hanging in long graceful folds still hid the human figure, but there was a great advance in the direction of naturalism, which made the statues of the saints seem very real and human. In this respect the painters lagged behind, for they had not yet learned to give their figures the illusion of roundness and depth or to place them in perspective.

Liturgy. It was not only through the beauty of line and color, carved stone, and stained

The nave of Amiens Cathedral, built during the mid-thirteenth century, is typically high Gothic. Note the ribbed vaults of the nave and the pillars, set between pointed arches, which separate the nave from the side aisles.

The view of the great Gothic cathedral of Notre Dame in Paris from the east shows the flying buttresses which prop the upper walls of the choir and apse.

glass, that the cathedral expressed and satisfied the artistic instincts of medieval people. It was also the scene of the colorful services of the church, the drama of the Mass, accompanied by the soaring music and verbal beauty of the Latin liturgy. The prayers, chants, and hymns of the Latin service satisfied the universal human craving for music and poetry, and combined it with religious emotion. Medieval Latin poetry reached its highest expression in the hymns, which were introduced into the liturgy of the Mass or were composed for the daily offices or special festivals of the church. During the Early Middle Ages the poetic form

of the Latin hymns had become less and less classical, as the quantitative meter characteristic of classical verse was gradually replaced by an accented meter. Finally — a still more radical break with classical tradition — rhyme was introduced under the influence of the contemporary vernacular Romance poetry. Before the end of the eleventh century this evolution was complete. The great hymns of the following period were all written in rhymed stanzas with a vigorous accented rhythm, which was admirably suited to musical setting.

Church music.   What music we know from the Early Middle Ages was church music, and the most important musical developments of the High Middle Ages arose also in the service of the church. It is true that there was secular music throughout the medieval period, for men have always danced and have always sung of liquor, love, or fights, but this secular music was not written and preserved until the coming of the troubadours in the twelfth century. The history of medieval music presents a great many technical problems and, despite the labors of recent musicologists, many points still remain obscure. Certain it is, however, that music played a large part in medieval life and was, perhaps, of all the arts the closest to the hearts of the people. Here we can do no more than note certain main lines of development. The predominant type of church music during the Early Middle Ages was plain chant. It is also called Gregorian from the tradition which ascribed its codification and universal adoption to Pope Gregory the Great. Gregorian music consisted of a vocal setting of the church liturgy for solo and choir. It can best be described as a single-line melody, and since it was primarily a musical setting of biblical prose it had no regular or measured rhythm. Like Christianity itself, it came originally from the Middle East, but it spread wherever Christianity spread because it became an integral part of the church service, and the authority of the church enforced liturgical uniformity as it did doctrinal orthodoxy.

The Virgin of the North Portal from the cathedral of Notre Dame in Paris, a fine thirteenth-century statue, represents the Virgin as a young matron.

Rise of polyphony. The free, soaring melodies of the Gregorian chant were well suited to the expression of religious exaltation, but as a musical style it was too alien and too restricted to satisfy permanently the musical taste of western Europe. The most important development in medieval music was the gradual evolution out of the Gregorian of polyphonic or many-voiced music with a growing tendency toward measured rhythms. As early as the ninth century the first step in the direction of polyphony was taken by adding to the Gregorian melody a parallel voice, which followed it note for note at the interval of a fourth or a fifth. This simple variant, which seems to show an incipient desire for harmony, was called organum. In the following centuries further embellishments were added with a third voice and with voices moving in freer relation to one another, until by the middle of the twelfth century composers had abandoned Gregorian and its simpler variants and were striking out on new lines, creating increasingly free and complex musical patterns. The break with the Gregorian tradition, however, was not yet complete. Gregorian melodies were still used as a base, called the *cantus firmus,* but so stretched out as to have lost their melodic character. Above this base additional lines of freely composed music were added in more rapid meters and with usually a different verbal text in each voice. Though still a long way from modern harmonic construction, this music was moving steadily toward measured time under the necessity of keeping the independently composed lines together. Before the end of the thirteenth century the new polyphonic music had reached a degree of complexity that threatened to defeat its musical as well as its religious purpose, and church authorities began to look askance at its more extreme manifestations. It was still in the experimental stage, but one marked by immense vitality. Like the

The figure of Christ, from the doorway of the south transept of the cathedral of Chartres, is a fine example of Gothic sculpture of the early thirteenth century.

Gothic cathedrals in which it grew, for it was born in Northern France and Flanders in the same era as Gothic architecture, medieval polyphony was an elaborate structure of moving parts held together by the balance of tensions leading down to a buttressed base.

SECTION E

THE LATER MIDDLE AGES AND

Verrocchio's equestrian statue of the *condottiere*, Bartolomeo
Colleoni, was commissioned by the Venetian Senate.
It stands by the church of Santi Giovanni e Paolo in Venice.

HE RENAISSANCE (c. 1270–c. 1520)

No accurate dates can ever be assigned to the beginning or end of a period in the development of history, save for purposes of convenience and with the understanding that the dates chosen are purely arbitrary. Since dates are convenient, however, and having allowed for every sort of qualification and mental reservation, we have taken the year 1270 as marking the end of the High Middle Ages. That year saw the last crusade and the death of that very medieval saint-king, Louis IX, with whom passed the predominantly feudal monarchy in France. Two years later, Edward I of England began the reign that was to found Parliament and to mark the longest step yet taken toward fashioning a centralized monarchical state out of medieval feudalism. And in 1273 the shattered Holy Roman Empire was revived in the weakened form characteristic of its later history with the election of the first emperor of the house of Hapsburg. Europe was now about to enter upon an unsettled period of social, political, economic, and intellectual change, marked by the steady decay of medieval institutions and medieval culture. During the following two and a half centuries, feudalism, the guild system of commerce and industry, the universal authority of the papacy, and the scholastic methods of thought and education declined, while in their place arose institutions and ways of thinking of a new and distinctly modern character. When this period of the Later Middle Ages was over, Europe stood on the threshold of the modern age. Centralized territorial states had replaced the local autonomy of feudal lords and burgher city governments, and had also broken up the unity of Christendom. Man's knowledge of the world had been greatly expanded by daring explorations to the distant East and the unknown West; and man's curiosity regarding himself and the world he lived in had been stimulated by the intellectual ferment of that age which in the history of culture is generally known as the Renaissance.

21

Germany and Eastern Europe

THE LONG struggle between the emperors and the popes, with the accompanying feud between the houses of Welf and Hohenstaufen in Germany and the Guelf and Ghibelline parties in Italy, had left the Holy Roman Empire a shattered wreck at the end of the High Middle Ages. After the death of the last Hohenstaufen emperor, Conrad IV, in 1254, there was no generally recognized emperor for nineteen years, though several foreigners claimed the empty title. The empire seemed about to dissolve; but in 1273, the period of the "Interregnum" was brought to an end by the election of a German emperor, and the empire continued to survive, though in a greatly weakened state. Italy was no longer a part of the empire except in theory. Few of the emperors during the Later Middle Ages attempted to exercise authority over the independent Italian city-states. Even in Germany the imperial power could not be revived in any effective way. It had become a land of semi-independent principalities and city-states, in which the emperors enjoyed more prestige than power. Leagues of districts and cities, like the Swiss Confederation and the Hanseatic League, organized in mutual defense against the forces of anarchy about them and learned to depend on their cooperative strength rather than on the emperor for protection. Meanwhile, to the east of the empire, Poland was expanding into a large, though fundamentally weak, territorial state; fierce Tartars swept out of central Asia across Russia, and retired after two centuries, leaving the princes of Moscow to form the beginnings of the modern Russian state; and from the southeast the Ottoman Turks carried the crescent of Islam from Asia Minor into the Balkans, destroying the Byzantine Empire on their way.

1. The Empire Survives in a State of Disintegration

Rudolf of Hapsburg. The German princes had made good use of the opportunities provided by the Interregnum to establish their independence, and this they intended to keep. Nevertheless, they felt the need of a ruler who would be strong enough to suppress the worst confusion and lawlessness, though not strong enough to interfere in the government of their own states. The tradition of the empire was still strong. Only an emperor could complete the formal structure of the feudal state and give a semblance of legality to the princes' authority. There was still enough German national feeling, too, to make them insist that the emperor should be a German. They therefore agreed on the election of Count Rudolf of Hapsburg (1273–91), who seemed to meet all the requirements to perfection. His family was an ancient and honorable one, with large estates on the northwestern slopes of the Alps, but it was not one of the great princely houses. He himself was popular, a fine, upstanding figure of a man, with a reputation for amiability and knightly valor. On the whole, Rudolf made a very satisfactory emperor. He used his prestige wisely to put down lawlessness and to reestablish peace wherever possible by diplomatic negotiations. At the same time, he made no attempt to interfere with the rights of the princes, and he sold privileges freely to both princes and cities. Only one thing alarmed the electors. Rudolf was bent on acquiring land and power for his family. He seized the German fiefs of King Ottokar II of Bohemia, who had refused to recognize his election, and from them granted Austria, Styria, and Carniola to his own son Albert, thus founding in southeastern Germany a strong domain, which the Hapsburgs were to keep until the present century.

Emperors from different families. Rudolf's success had shown that the imperial title still meant something, if not very much. It had also warned the electors not to leave the crown in one family, lest it become too powerful. Passing over Rudolf's son, Duke Albert of Austria, they chose Adolf of Nassau (1292–98), a Rhenish count who was willing to promise anything the electors demanded as the price of the crown. He failed to keep his promises, however, and before long the disappointed Duke Albert was able to stir up a rebellion among the discontented princes. Adolf was defeated and slain, and the Hapsburg duke was elected in his place. Albert spent his reign (1298–1308) in an attempt to strengthen the authority of the crown, but was assassinated by a member of his own family before he could accomplish anything definite. Again the electors turned from the powerful Hapsburg family. This time they offered the crown to Count Henry of Luxemburg, whose lands lay in the half-French, half-German country to the west of the Rhine. Henry VII (1308–13) had many of the qualities that should go to make a ruler. He had also a high conception of the imperial dignity, and it was this that caused his downfall. The desire to be crowned at Rome and to reassert imperial authority in Italy, which had lured so many medieval emperors to destruction, led him to purchase temporary peace in Germany by scattering privileges among the princes and to embark on an expedition across the Alps. In Italy he was hailed with delight by many, including the great poet Dante, who hoped that he would be able to end the struggle between the Guelf and Ghibelline parties and restore peace. He himself became involved in the party feud, however, and died after three years of fruitless strife.

Rudolf of Hapsburg, the founder of the fortunes of the house of Hapsburg, was a man of great dignity and commanding presence. The portrait comes from a tapestry in the Royal Court Museum in Vienna.

His only solid accomplishment had been the winning of Bohemia for his son John before leaving Germany. This accession of territory to the house of Luxemburg proved again the value of the imperial title. Both Frederick of Hapsburg, the son of the late Emperor Albert, and Louis, Duke of Bavaria, made a bid for it. The result was a disputed election, a civil war, and the final triumph of the latter candidate. During his long reign, Louis IV, "the Bavarian" (1314–47), concentrated his attention on adding to the lands held by his family, the Wittelsbachs. He won for them Brandenburg, the Tyrol, and four provinces of the Netherlands. Except for a long-drawn-out struggle with the popes, which will be discussed later,[1] this was the most important event of his reign. Much of this territory was later lost, but the Wittelsbachs clung to the rule of Bavaria until the revolution that followed the First World War.

Weakness of imperial authority. During all this time, the passing of the imperial crown from family to family with each generation prevented the emperors from taking any consistent steps to strengthen their authority outside their family domains, or even from developing any strong desire to do so. Any move in that direction would have met with strong opposition and would have had to be carried out at the emperor's own expense; for neither princes nor cities could be forced to pay taxes or furnish military service with any regularity. No emperor could afford to undertake seriously such a colossal task, especially as the crown, with whatever increased authority he could give it, would in all probability pass to some other family at his death. Had the monarchy been hereditary, as in France and England, there would have been a much stronger incentive to make its power effective. As it was, the chief value of the imperial title was the right it gave the emperors to regrant "escheated fiefs," that is, fiefs that had reverted to the crown through lack of heirs. The emperors used this right to add to their own domain. The crown, in short, was regarded principally as a good investment for the family of the emperor.

Charles IV. After the death of Louis the Bavarian, the imperial title was given back to the house of Luxemburg, where it remained with one short break for nearly a century. But neither Charles IV (1347–78) nor his sons did anything to strengthen the imperial power in Germany. They were not really German and were not much interested in Germany. Charles had inherited the kingdom of Bohemia from his father, King John, the brilliant, erratic son of Emperor Henry VII, and he was always ready to sacrifice the empire to the interests of his family and his kingdom. A later emperor once called him "the arch-father of Bohemia and arch-stepfather of the empire." The former title, at least, he earned by his wise and conscientious rule of Bohemia. He kept peace and order there; reformed the judicial and administrative system; founded the University of Prague; and in general made Bohemia one of the greatest of the imperial states.

Golden Bull. With unusual realism, Charles IV recognized the futility of trying to establish an effective monarchy in Germany. All that could be done, he thought, was to take steps to prevent further disintegration. He had no confidence in the Diet of the empire as an institution of government. This body, which was a meeting of all the princes as vassals of the emperor, was always hopelessly divided and had shown itself to be quite powerless. Charles turned instead to the electors who, he hoped, might cooperate to prevent war and keep order if their own position was sufficiently secure. With this in mind, he published the Golden Bull at the Diet of 1356. The bull carefully defined the method of election and the personnel of the electors so as to prevent further disputes over the imperial title, such as had so often split Germany into warring factions in the past. There were to be seven electors only, including three ecclesiastical princes (the Archbishops of Mainz, Cologne, and Trier) and four secular princes (the Count Palatine of the Rhine, the Margrave of Brandenburg, the Duke of Saxony, and the King of Bohemia). The rest of the bull was taken up with provisions for protecting the power of the electors. They were to have full sovereign power within their states; their territories were not to be divided for any reason; those of the secular electors were to be inherited according to the rule of primogeniture; and the title was to remain attached to the territory. The Golden

[1] See below, page 290.

The Golden Bull determined the status of the Electors of the Empire. The whole document was originally fastened together by a silk cord and seal.

Bull was the nearest approach to a written constitution the empire ever had, and it was immensely important for the later history of Germany. It prevented many possible civil wars over elections, and it checked the breaking-up of the larger states through divided inheritance, since other princes soon followed the example of the electors in adopting the rule of primogeniture. The electors, of course, gained most from the bull. They became practically independent sovereigns, ruling well-defined territorial states as allies rather than subjects of the emperor.

Later Luxemburg emperors. Under the sons of Charles IV the imperial power declined still further. The elder of the two, Wenceslas (1378–1400), was indolent and habitually intoxicated. He had difficulty in maintaining his position in Bohemia, while in Germany he neglected his duties so scandalously that the electors finally deposed him and chose in his place Rupert, Count Palatine of the Rhine (1400–10). Wenceslas was still ruling Bohemia when Rupert died, but the electors again rejected him and gave the imperial crown to his younger brother Sigismund (1410–37), who had been King of Hungary since 1387. More interested in Hungary than in the empire, Sigismund made only occasional brief visits to Germany. Except at the Council of Constance,[1] where he used his great diplomatic ability to help restore peace to the church, he did nothing to justify his election. It was at Constance, incidentally, in the year 1415, that Sigismund gave the Mark of Brandenburg with its electoral title to Frederick of Hohenzollern, whose descendants were in time to make it the nucleus of the Prussian Kingdom and finally of the modern German Empire.

The crown passes to the Hapsburgs. The election of Albert II (1438–39) and Frederick III (1440–93) of Hapsburg in succession restored the imperial crown to the house of Hapsburg, where it remained as long as the empire lasted. The change, however, brought no improvement in imperial authority. The policy of the Hapsburgs was an entirely selfish one. They were interested primarily in their own family fortunes.

State of Germany. The empire was by this time little more than a geographical expression or, as one contemporary writer put it, the shadow of a great name. Germany had lost all national unity, but this was to some extent compensated for by the growing power of the rulers of territorial states like Austria, Bavaria,

[1] See below, page 294.

Hesse, and the electoral principalities. In these we find the development of strong centralized government and, in some cases, of representative institutions, very similar to that which was taking place during the Later Middle Ages in France and England. The Estates or *Landtage* of Bavaria and Bohemia in particular acquired a share in the government comparable to that of the Estates General in France. Outside these greater principalities, however, all was hopeless confusion. There were a number of ecclesiastical states, ruled by archbishops, bishops, or abbots, and innumerable small territories under the jurisdiction of independent barons or free knights of the empire, who recognized no superior except the emperor. There were also some sixty free imperial cities, which were independent city-states, save for the emperor's nominal authority. In this tangled mass of petty independent jurisdictions there was no power strong enough to enforce law and order or to give protection to life and property. Conditions were bad enough in the large states and within the walls of the imperial cities. Outside these, the most frightful state of lawlessness prevailed.

2. *The Swiss Confederation and the Hanseatic League*

Despite the disintegration of the empire and the general lawlessness and frequent petty wars that resulted, Germany was on the whole more prosperous than ever during the centuries of the Later Middle Ages. Commerce and industry flourished in the cities. The failure of the central government was undoubtedly a great handicap, but the people of the empire did not accept a state of anarchy with spineless resignation. Many parts of the empire were forming independent states or associations. We have already noted the development of the larger territorial states. Where these did not exist, leagues of knights, districts, or cities were formed for mutual defense.

Swiss Confederation. The Swiss Confederation, out of which has grown the modern state of Switzerland, originated in a league of three small rural districts or cantons in the Alpine valleys about the Lake of Lucerne. The league was formed for mutual defense against

the exactions of their feudal overlords of the house of Hapsburg. The three cantons, Schwyz, Uri, and Unterwalden, occupied a mountain district no more than thirty-five miles square, but they were important because they commanded the great trade route to Italy through the St. Gotthard Pass. In 1315, they won a brilliant victory at Morgarten, where they caught an army led against them by Leopold of Hapsburg in a narrow pass and almost wiped it out, killing between fifteen hundred and two thousand of the pick of Hapsburg chivalry. Thereafter, they remained practically independent states under the empire. Neighboring cities and cantons, envying them their freedom, soon joined the confederation. By the middle of the fourteenth century, there were eight members, Zug, Glarus, Lucerne, Zurich, and Berne having been added to the original three. By 1513, the number had been increased to thirteen, including the prosperous Rhine city of Basel, while the territories around the frontier in almost all directions had either been reduced to subjection or brought into a friendly alliance with the confederation.

Its character. A passionate love of freedom and independence was the outstanding characteristic of the Swiss people. It was at once the strength and the weakness of the confederation. The cantons would stand together in sturdy defiance of all outside authority; but within the league each canton guarded its independent rights just as jealously. Each had its own separate government, though all sent representatives to a general Diet where matters of foreign policy or general interest were discussed. The laws of the Diet, however, could be enforced only through the governments of the cantons. There was always a good deal of friction and jealousy among the cantons, arising from differences in character and interests. Most of the cantons were German, but those to the southwest with their dependencies were French-speaking, while most of the subject or allied districts to the south were Italian. Moreover, the "Forest Cantons" which had originally formed the confederation were entirely rural, while several of the later additions, like Zurich, Berne, and Basel, centered around busy commercial and industrial cities. Through their wealth, these latter tended to dominate the confederation, thus arousing the jealousy of the

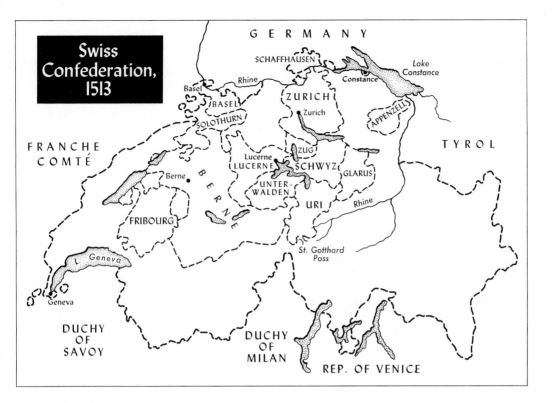

Forest Cantons which never forgot that the Swiss owed the origins of their freedom to the hardy mountaineers who defended the Alpine passes against the might of the Hapsburg.

Growth of the Hansa. While the Swiss were forming a confederation for mutual defense on the southern borders of Germany, the rich merchant cities of the north were joining in a still more powerful association to protect their commercial interests. The land along the southern shores of the Baltic had been acquired from the Slavs and settled by Germans only recently, during the twelfth and thirteenth centuries. Here the emperor's authority had never been strong, and with the decline of the empire it ceased to function altogether. The merchants in the new German cities of this district, as well as those in the hopelessly disorganized northwestern section of old Germany, were forced to depend on their own efforts to ensure their safety when traveling and to secure trading rights abroad. Only by working together and pooling their resources could they maintain a fleet large enough to suppress the pirates who swarmed in the Baltic and the North Sea, or bring sufficient pressure to bear on foreign

states to make them grant favorable commercial treaties. From this necessity grew the league of North German cities, generally known as the Hansa or Hanseatic League. The first step in the association had been taken by the cities of Hamburg and Lübeck about the middle of the thirteenth century. Other cities joined them in rapid succession. By the end of the century, the Hansa had secured trading privileges of a very favorable kind in London, Bruges, Bergen, and Novgorod. These cities remained the chief foreign markets for North German trade in England, the Netherlands, Norway, and Russia respectively.

Organization of the league. The formal organization of the Hanseatic League, however, was not completed till the middle of the fourteenth century. Even then it was no more than a vague and loosely defined confederation of cities, some seventy in all, though the number is uncertain owing to frequent desertions and realliances. The member-cities were grouped under four general territorial divisions: those of the eastern Baltic, the western Baltic, northwestern Germany, and the lower Rhine. In these districts the cities of Danzig, Lübeck,

Brunswick, and Cologne were recognized as holding a position of rather vague leadership. On important occasions, representatives from all the cities met together to decide questions of foreign policy or to make trade regulations. Despite its loose organization, the league was strong enough to play a very important part in the politics both of northern Germany and of the Scandinavian countries, and to keep an almost complete monopoly of the Baltic trade.[1]

Teutonic Knights.   The history of the Hanseatic League is closely bound up with that of the order of Teutonic Knights. It was these crusading warriors who had made possible the expansion of German colonies and trade to the eastern Baltic by their conquest of Prussia from its heathen inhabitants in the thirteenth century.[2] The knights encouraged German peasants, nobles, and burghers to migrate to their newly conquered territory. Numbers of new German cities sprang up along the coast and

[1] See below, pages 304–305.
[2] See above, pages 211–212.

the river-banks. Danzig, Marienburg, Königsberg, and a score of others became flourishing commercial centers. They formed one of the "quarters" of the Hansa, and the league could always count on the knights as allies in its wars with the other Baltic powers. The decline of the order in the fifteenth century was thus a serious blow to the league. By that time, too great prosperity had begun to undermine the discipline and religious character that had made the knights so effective an organization during their period of conquest. In 1410, the Poles invaded the territory of the knights and defeated them disastrously at the battle of Tannenberg. The order retained its land for another half-century, but in a weakened and impoverished condition. A second and more disastrous war with Poland ended in the Peace of Thorn, 1466. The western part of Prussia was annexed to Poland and the Grand Master of the order had to do homage for the remainder of his territory as vassal of the Polish king.

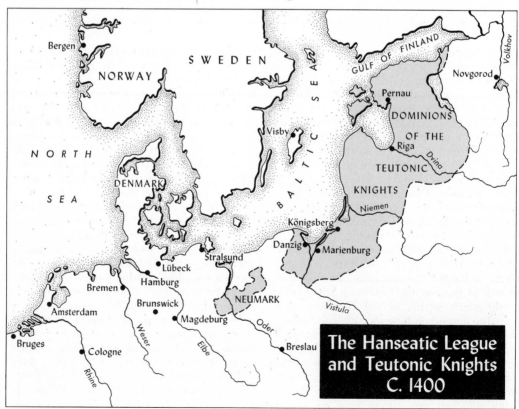

The Hanseatic League and Teutonic Knights C. 1400

The Scandinavian countries. Relations with the three Scandinavian countries, Denmark, Norway, and Sweden, also formed an important part of the history of the Hanseatic League. Since the break-up of the Danish empire of King Canute in the eleventh century, the Scandinavian countries had taken no active part in European affairs and were in general rather more backward than their southern neighbors. In the fourteenth century, Denmark was the most active of the three, and an attempt on the part of its king to encroach on Hanseatic trade led to a war with the league that lasted from 1361 to 1370. The league was finally successful. By the Treaty of Stralsund, the Hansa was given complete freedom of trade in Danish territory. For a generation the league dominated Scandinavian politics as well as trade, but toward the end of the fourteenth century its influence was endangered by the union, first of Denmark and Norway and finally of Sweden also under one ruler in the Union of Kalmar, 1397. The union, which lasted till the end of the Middle Ages, was never a very strong coalition, but it was a standing menace to the Hanseatic monopoly of northern trade. In the sixteenth century, Sweden gradually acquired a dominating position in the eastern Baltic.

3. Eastern Europe

Expansion of Poland. Let us turn now to a brief survey of the history of eastern Europe during the Later Middle Ages. Throughout most of the fourteenth century, the Slavic kingdom of Poland, which was the empire's largest eastern neighbor, was engaged in a long conflict, in alliance with the Teutonic Knights, against the heathen Lithuanians, whose territory stretched along the eastern frontier of Poland from the Baltic to the Black Sea. In 1386 this situation changed abruptly. By the marriage of a Polish princess to Jagiello of Lithuania and the election of the latter as King of Poland, the two states were united and Lithuania formally adopted Christianity. The territory of Poland was thus more than doubled and she acquired an outlet to the sea both to the north and the south. The new power of the combined countries was turned immediately against the Teutonic Knights, who, with the conversion of the Lithuanians, had

no further religious reason for their existence. We have already noted the defeat of the order and the acquisition by Poland of western Prussia in 1466. Poland was now one of the largest territorial states in Europe; but it was never able to make full use of its potential power. It lacked unity and stability. In old Poland the cities had been largely Germanized, while the country districts had remained Slavic, and in the new acquisitions the population was a mixture of Lithuanian and Russian Slav having little in common with the Poles. Moreover, the elective monarchy and the selfish independence of the Polish nobles prevented the development of a strong central government. Anarchical feudalism lasted in Poland long after it had died out in the western states.

Tartar conquest of Russia. Beyond Poland in eastern Europe the Slavs of Russia labored under the yoke of their Tartar masters. All through the Middle Ages the Russians had faced east rather than west. Since their conversion to Christianity in the tenth century, they had been members of the Greek Orthodox Church. They looked to Constantinople for leadership in religion and culture as well as for trade. The great principality of Kiev which ruled most of Russia in the early eleventh century, though Scandinavian in origin, was distinctly Byzantine in civilization. Even after it broke up into a number of minor principalities, the Greek Church and Byzantine-Russian culture continued to give some national unity to the Russian people. Then came the Tartars. They were of much the same race as the Huns and other Asian peoples who had invaded Europe from time to time since the fourth century. Under the leadership of their great khan, Jenghis, the Tartar nomads conquered a vast empire in the first quarter of the thirteenth century, which included all of central Asia, China, and southern Asia as far as the Himalayas. Later, the grandson of Jenghis Khan, Batu, led his conquering horsemen west through Russia, laying waste the country as he went. By 1242, he was raiding Poland and eastern Germany, until he was recalled by the death of the great khan, the son of Jenghis. In the division of the Mongol Empire which followed, Batu was left the western section, including most of Russia, where he founded the khanate of the Golden Horde. Meanwhile,

The features of Sultan Mohammed II, the conqueror of Constantinople, are best known from the portrait by the Venetian artist, Gentile Bellini, now in the National Gallery, London.

the Tartars had also invaded the Moslem world, sweeping across Persia as far as Bagdad. For some two hundred and forty years, the Tartars of the Golden Horde continued to rule Russia. They had caused tremendous destruction of life and property during their first wild invasion, but thereafter they did not interfere seriously in the life of the people except to collect taxes with an iron hand.

Rise of Moscow. During the period of Tartar rule, the Russian princes governed the people under the suzerainty of the khan, and even the task of collecting taxes was delegated to native princes. It was this fact that accounts for the rising power of the principality of Moscow. In 1328 a prince of the Muscovite family was commissioned by the khan to collect the tribute. His descendants retained the commission and used the authority delegated to them by the khan to build up the power of their family. Moscow became the center of Russian culture and, after the fall of Constantinople, of the Orthodox Church. Meanwhile, the Muscovite princes were expanding their territory at the expense of the cities and lesser princes about them. In 1478, Prince Ivan III

(1462–1505) conquered Novgorod, the great commercial city which had never been subdued by the Tartars and which had maintained a prosperous trade with the West through the merchants of the Hansa. Two years later, Ivan declared his independence of the khan and threw off the Tartar yoke. The Golden Horde had been declining in power for a long time and gave up its hold on central Russia almost without a struggle, leaving it to the rule of the Prince of Moscow, who thus formed the beginnings of the modern Russian state.

Turks invade Europe. While the Tartar power was fading in Russia, eastern Europe was being menaced from the south by the advance of still another nation of Asiatic origin. The Ottoman Turks were originally nomads who, like the Seljuk Turks of an earlier time, had drifted westward from central Asia and had adopted Islam. By the middle of the fourteenth century, they had conquered the provinces of the Byzantine Empire in Asia Minor, and in 1354 they crossed the Hellespont to gain their first foothold in Europe on the Gallipoli peninsula. Once established in Europe, the Turks spread their conquests through the Balkan states until only the city of Constantinople remained under the rule of the emperors. Surrounded by Turkish armies, the ancient capital of the empire maintained a prolonged and gallant defense, but its situation was hopeless. At last in 1453 it fell, and the last remnant of the Byzantine Empire ceased to exist. As a fitting symbol of the end of an epoch, the conquering sultan, Mohammed II, converted Justinian's great church of Sancta Sophia into a mosque. The mass of the Christian population perforce settled down under Turkish rule, but a few of the wealthier classes fled to Italy, carrying with them as their most precious possessions Greek manuscripts, which served to stimulate the growth of Greek studies there. The event was not, however, as decisive for the development of Renaissance humanism as historians used to think, for in fact the revival of classical Greek was already well begun in Italy before the arrival of the refugees.

Further expansion. Having taken the Byzantine capital the Turks were free to turn their undivided attention to further expansion. They completed their conquest of Greece, Bosnia, Serbia, and Albania, and invaded Hungary.

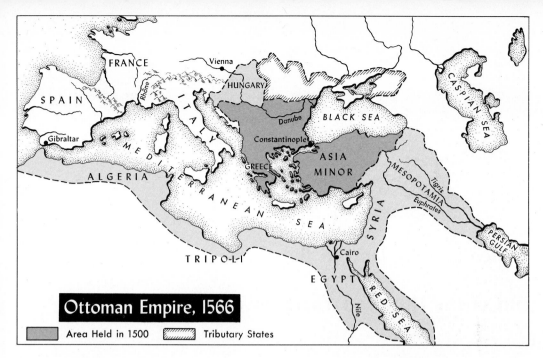

Ottoman Empire, 1566

Area Held in 1500   Tributary States

There they were checked for a time by the resistance of the Hungarians under the leadership of their kings, John Hunyadi and Matthias Corvinus. In the early years of the sixteenth century, however, the Turks finally broke the Hungarian resistance and took over the greater part of the kingdom. From there they went on to threaten Austria and by 1529 were hammering at the gates of Vienna. That marked their furthest advance to the west on the European mainland; but in the meantime the Ottoman power was also expanding to the south and east at the expense of other Moslem states in Asia and Africa. During the reign of Selim I (1512–20) the Turks conquered Mesopotamia, Syria, and Egypt, and under his successor Suleiman I (1520–66) they spread their conquests along the North African coast from Egypt to the Atlantic. Europe in the sixteenth century was thus faced by a new Moslem state almost as large as that of the Abbasid caliphs.

The Turkish state. The Turkish state was different from those of Christian Europe, not only in its religion, but also in the whole character of its government. It was an absolute autocracy, in which the sultan exercised unlimited power. It was unique, too, in that its administrative staff and the most effective part of its army — the élite corps known as the janizaries — were composed of slaves, mostly recruited from the conquered Christian popula-

tion, forcibly converted to Islam, and carefully trained for their specific duties. Training and discipline lent an efficiency to these servants of an autocratic government unequaled in Europe; but, at the same time, it was an unhealthy system, and in the long run it undermined the power of the state, so that after the sixteenth century it began to decline.

The European reaction. The fall of Constantinople was a shock to Christian Europe comparable to the Moslem conquest of Jerusalem in the twelfth century. And, as on that occasion, pope after pope summoned the princes of western Europe to lead a crusade. But the time when the nations of Christendom could sink their quarrels in a common effort against the infidel was long since past. Only the countries immediately attacked put up any effective resistance. From 1463 to 1479 the Venetian Republic fought desperately to check the growth of Ottoman power in the eastern Mediterranean, but in the end the Republic was forced to make peace, surrendering her colonies in the Aegean, but retaining trading rights in the Ottoman dominions and a privileged trading post in Constantinople. Austria, too, resisted and finally repelled the Turkish advance. The other European countries, however, paid no more than lip service to the common cause, and before long were treating the Turkish state as an equal European power.

22

France and England to the

End of the Hundred Years' War

IN THE last years of the thirteenth century, both France and England were about to enter on a period of gradual transition from medieval to modern states. In France feudalism was still strong, but the Capetian kings had expanded the royal domain till it included more than half the kingdom, and the monarchy was already a real power in the land. In England the royal government was much farther advanced, though feudal barons still strove to control it. In both countries the first step in the transition was marked by the realization that the military and financial methods of feudalism were no longer adequate to meet the needs of the central government. The kings of France and England were forced to levy extra-feudal taxes that were national in scope, and to this end they summoned to their courts for aid and counsel representatives of their humbler subjects who were not their immediate vassals. The feudal Great Council thus evolved into the French Estates General and the English Parliament. These institutions had barely begun to take shape before both countries were plunged into the long and bloody struggle known as the Hundred Years' War. The war dragged on its weary way, laying waste the richest land in France for generations and to a lesser degree draining the resources of England, but in the end leaving both well on the road to a hard-won national unity. In France the monarchy emerged triumphant and uncontrolled. In England, on the other hand, Parliament had profited skillfully from the king's need for money to carry on the war. The foundations of constitutional government were so firmly planted that they could outlast the disturbances of royal family feuds and the absolutism of Tudor and Stuart kings.

1. Consolidation of Royal Government in France (1270–1328)

Philip III. Philip III (1270–85) inherited from his saintly father, Louis IX, a large royal domain and an authority that even the most powerful of his vassals had been forced to respect. To both of these legacies Philip added considerably during his otherwise rather inglorious reign. By reversion and marriage he expanded the royal domain to include the counties of Toulouse, Poitou, and Champagne, not to mention numerous other small additions acquired on one pretext or another. Under him, too, and thanks in all probability more to the incessant activity of his ministers than to his own efforts, the royal government developed steadily in efficiency and practical power.

Philip IV and his ministers. With the reign of Philip IV (1285–1314), called the Fair, we enter definitely on the transitional period in the history of the French monarchy. The time was now ripe for the king to assert his position as king rather than as mere feudal overlord, and for him to adopt what may well be called a national policy both at home and abroad. This Philip the Fair did with momentous results; but how much of the credit or blame should be awarded to the king himself is still a matter much debated by historians. There seems good reason to believe that the real driving force behind the royal government came less from the king than from his ministers. These men were professional administrators; unlike the great vassals and prelates who had filled the councils of the early feudal kings, they were of comparatively humble birth. They had been trained in the royal court and depended entirely on the king for their position. Hence they were devoted to the king's interests. Most of them were lawyers, well versed in Roman law and impregnated with its monarchical principles. They were cool-headed, sagacious, and unscrupulous enemies of feudalism, the papacy, or any other power that infringed on the king's rights. In the midst of their vigorous activity we can only dimly discern the enigmatic figure of the king.

Foreign policy.   Philip's assertion of royal authority throughout France soon brought him into conflict with his two most independent vassals, Edward I, King of England, who held the fiefs of Guienne and Gascony in southwestern France as a legacy from his Angevin ancestors, and the Count of Flanders, whose fief to the north included rich commercial and industrial cities closely connected by trade with England. War with Edward broke out in 1294. After four years of fighting, both parties agreed to a truce which was finally confirmed by a peace treaty five years later. The Count of Flanders, however, who had joined Edward in the war, was not included in the truce. Left to himself, he was forced to submit, and his rich county was added to the French king's domain. Philip's success in this direction was brief. In 1302, the Flemish burghers rose in revolt, massacred French residents, and almost annihilated a French army sent against them at Courtrai. Three years of bitter fighting followed before Philip restored peace by giving Flanders back to its count at the price of a heavy indemnity. Meanwhile, Philip's diplomats had been pressing French claims along the eastern frontier and bit by bit adding imperial lands to France. The most important acquisition in this direction was the Free County of Burgundy (Franche Comté) which Philip acquired through the marriage of his eldest son to the count's heiress. Finally, and not least important of his foreign policies, Philip strongly opposed the interference of Pope Boniface VIII in French affairs, with far-reaching results that will be recounted in the next chapter.

Templars crushed.   His expensive wars with England and Flanders left Philip in great need of money, and his victory over the papacy opened up at least one way of recouping his losses. The religious order of Knights Templars was a tempting prey, for the Templars had grown enormously rich in land and money. They had become great bankers and had lent large sums to the king. Moreover, since the conclusion of the crusades, they had no longer any valid reason for existence. Philip, therefore, set about cold-bloodedly to accomplish their ruin, with a view to canceling his debts and confiscating their wealth. Their trial, begun in 1307, continued for five years. The knights were arrested and forced under torture to confess to the most horrible charges of immorality and blasphemy. A widespread propaganda accompanied the prosecution, all the more effective because of the secrecy that had always shrouded the life of the order. The final act in this judicial farce was the abolition of the order in 1312 by Pope Clement V, who was completely under the thumb of the French king. Their lands were to be given to the Knights Hospitalers, but in France, at least, it was the king who profited.

Origin of the Estates General.   As the government of Philip the Fair was more nearly national than that of any of his predecessors, it is not surprising to find him breaking with feudal precedent and making a bid for popular support by summoning representatives of the burgher middle class as well as his feudal vassals and the clergy to give consent to his decisions on matters of national importance. The Estates General, as the new assembly of all three classes or estates came to be called, was summoned only at times of crisis, such as the struggle with Boniface VIII in 1302, which motivated the first summons, or the attack on the Templars in 1308, or when unusual taxes were needed. The last was, indeed, the most important reason for the innovation. The greatly increased expenses of the royal government, particularly in time of war, could no longer be met out of the regular income from the royal domain and feudal dues, or even by such extraordinary measures as the debasement of the coinage or the confiscation of property belonging to Jews, Templars, or Lombard bankers. New taxes on all classes were necessary; and these could be collected more easily if the people at large had given their consent through their representatives, even though it were only a matter of form and royal officers still found it necessary to haggle over details of collection with feudal magnates or with smaller regional assemblies. French kings had long been accustomed to summoning their vassals-in-chief, lay and ecclesiastical, to their court to give aid and counsel. What makes Philip's action a new departure was the extension of that summons to representatives of the towns — that is, to the commons who were his subjects rather than his feudal vassals — to meet with the Great Council.

A general tendency. Though a new departure for the French monarchy, the summoning of the Estates General was not an isolated instance of appeal by a ruling prince for support from representatives of the rising urban middle class, whose possession of money made them an increasingly important group from the point of view of a financially embarrassed prince. Other states, including England, the Spanish kingdoms, the Empire, and the territorial principalities of Germany, were following the same procedure at this time. Moreover, in France itself the great feudatories, the half-independent vassals outside the royal domain, were doing the same thing in summoning the estates of their own territories. The Estates General was so named to distinguish it from the local or feudal estates, some of which maintained their separate existence for centuries.

Organization of the Estates. The Estates General did not acquire its name or full organization at once, but with repeated meetings the new body gradually took shape. For consultation the assembly split up into three bodies, each made up of the representatives of one of the estates of the realm, the clergy, the nobles, and the commons respectively. The last-named, the

"Third Estate," was composed mainly of representatives elected in various ways by the burghers of the chartered towns. Later, at times, the election was extended to include the country districts as well. But as most of the land was owned by the nobles, the only commons who were important enough to be represented on most occasions were the city middle class. The function of the estates was not to initiate legislation or to control the government. Their duty was to consent to whatever the king proposed, though they might present lists of grievances in the hope that the king would take steps to redress them. The new institution was a means of bringing the royal government into closer contact with the most important classes in the state. That it failed to serve this purpose as effectively as it might have done was due to the fact that the king was still not strong enough to weld the estates into a really national assembly. After the time of Philip the Fair the Estates General seldom met as a single body representing the whole kingdom. Usually the estates of Languedoc and those of northern France met separately and some meetings included still smaller areas. On the other hand, the resulting weakness of the estates prevented them in the long run from exercising an effective control of royal government and so left the road open to the development of royal absolutism.

House of Valois. After the death of Philip the Fair, his three sons followed him on the throne in rapid and uneventful succession. All three died without male heirs, thus breaking the long-continued succession from father to son since the time of Hugh Capet. The crown then passed to a nephew of Philip the Fair, Philip of Valois, who took the title Philip VI (1328–50). From this time till the accession of the Bourbon kings at the end of the sixteenth century, the ruling dynasty in France was known as the house of Valois.

2. Growth of Constitutional Government in England (1272–1327)

Edward I. The history of France under Philip the Fair finds in many respects a close parallel in that of England under Edward I (1272–1307), Philip's contemporary and natural enemy. There, too, the king consolidated the royal government, and appealed to popular support by summoning representatives of the commons to his council. In England, however, thanks to the constructive work of the Angevin kings in the twelfth century and of the royal ministers in the thirteenth, there was already a much more closely united state than in France; feudalism was not so decentralized, and the king's authority was more nearly universal and more effective. It needed only the work of a wise and strong king to complete the first step in welding England into a strong constitutional state. And for such a purpose Edward I was ideally qualified. His appearance and character were well suited to catch the popular imagination and to make him a national hero. He was tall and well built, a good soldier and at least every other inch a gentleman. He had, moreover, a sound legal mind and a genius for organization. Before he came to the throne he had had a good deal of experience as the most active force in the government under his feeble father Henry III. Historians have hailed him, not only as the conqueror of Wales, but, more important, as a great legislator and organizer, the English Justinian and the father of the English Parliament.

Conquest of Wales.   Edward's ambition to make England a strong and united state led naturally to attempts to bring all parts of the island under his rule. The mountainous districts of Wales had never been fully conquered by either Saxon or Norman. There the Welsh clansmen maintained their own Celtic language and customs and fought bitterly for the freedom they prized more highly than either settled government or economic prosperity. Norman barons, called the Marcher Lords because it was their duty to defend the march or border, had gradually encroached on the Welsh valleys until less than half of Wales was left under the native prince, and even he was in theory the vassal of the English king. Early in Edward's reign, however, the Welsh prince, Llewellyn, gave the king an excuse for conquest by throwing off his allegiance. Edward's first campaign in 1277 was successful; but it was easier to conquer the Welsh than to hold them in subjection. In 1282, the king had to reconquer Llewellyn and his rebellious mountaineers. This time he reorganized the principality, dividing it into shires of the English type, directly under the royal government. Later, he

made his eldest son titular Prince of Wales, which title has normally been conferred upon the heir to the English throne down to the present time. There were other rebellions and much discontent among the patriotic Welsh for generations, but Edward had succeeded in making Wales a permanent part of the English state, to the eventual benefit of both peoples.

Wars with Scotland and France.   With Wales conquered, Scotland remained the only part of the island outside Edward's rule. Here he had to deal with a feudal kingdom, less advanced but otherwise not greatly different from his own. The settled Lowlands, at least, were closely akin to England, containing a strong intermixture of Saxon, Danish, and Norman blood and having already adopted Saxon-Norman speech and customs. A disputed succession to the Scottish throne gave Edward his first opportunity to interfere in the northern kingdom. Despite the distraction of his war with the French king, Edward marched north and conquered Scotland in 1296. But he had reckoned without the independent spirit of the Scottish people who soon rose in rebellion against their foreign master under the leadership of the knightly William Wallace. A second conquest, accomplished in 1305, after years of campaigning, lasted no longer. The Scots rose again under a new claimant to the throne, Robert Bruce, and Edward died before he could reach Scotland to crush the new rebellion. In neither Scotland nor France had he any returns to show for his expenditure of men and money. Indeed, so far as Scotland was concerned, all that he had accomplished was to arouse in the Scottish people a lasting hatred of England and to drive them into a practically permanent alliance with France.

Royal administration and courts.   The reputation of Edward I as a great statesman rests more securely on his contribution to the formation of English governmental institutions than on his conquest of Wales or his brief successes in Scotland. Institutions that had been vague and fluid took definite shape under his hands. In the interest of good government and the unity of the state, he undertook the task of making the royal administration more efficient and of centralizing authority under the crown at the expense of the barons, who might still be dangerous if their wings were not clipped. Depending on middle-class ministers, trained by long service for their duties, and on the new and important class of professional lawyers, he built up a well-ordered machine of government and justice entirely responsible to the king. The *curia regis* was now fairly clearly divided into special courts with well-defined functions — the exchequer for dealing with financial matters, the courts of common pleas and the king's bench for trying civil and criminal cases respectively, and the king's council, which not only assisted the king in the general business of government, but also took cognizance of all cases that did not fall under the jurisdiction of the special courts. There was little about this system that was absolutely new, but its more definite and efficient organization added greatly to its effectiveness as an instrument of government for the whole state. All England was beginning to look to the king and his courts for government and justice.

Common law.   Edward was more than a great administrator. He was also the first great English legislator. Under him the English common law — that is, the law used in the king's courts and hence common to the whole country — was given the form which it was to keep with very little change for centuries. This law had been created by custom rather than legislation. Hitherto, the work of the king's courts had been confined to interpreting it by judicial decisions. Now the king began to legislate. Working with his council, Edward I issued statute after statute, supplementing or altering the common law so as to give it definite form and to bring it into touch with contemporary needs. No single thing, perhaps, has done more to make England a unified state than the development of the common law. It was the king's law and the law of the whole kingdom; before it feudal and local customs faded away.

Origins of Parliament.   Last, but not least, of Edward's contributions to the building of English institutions was his establishment of Parliament, including representatives from the middle class of town and country, as a regular part of the state government. Here, as with the king's council, courts, and law, his work consisted not so much in creating something

absolutely new as in combining and giving a more definite and permanent form to earlier institutions. Neither Parliament nor representation was new in Edward's reign; but the two had never been combined on a national scale, or at least not with sufficient frequency to give the new institution which resulted from the combination a permanent status, for the parliamentary experiment of Simon de Montfort in 1265 had failed and other summonses of representatives had been only partial and irregular. As in the case of the Estates General, the origin of the Parliament as a consulting body and royal court is to be found in the Great Council of the king's vassals-in-chief, though in England it had been much more frequently summoned and was better organized than in France. By the thirteenth century, it was regularly composed of the most important lay and ecclesiastical barons of the kingdom. To this assembly were now added representatives from the middle class, but unlike the Third Estate in France they included knights from the country as well as burghers from the towns. For the origins of this type of representation we must look to a uniquely English institution, the shire courts, to which for generations representative knights and burghers had been summoned to give information for administrative and judicial purposes, to serve on presentment juries and even to pass judgment. They were summoned because they knew local conditions and customs. When Edward I summoned two knights from each shire and two burghers from each chartered town to meet with the Great Council, he was, from one point of view, merely centralizing the representation in the shire courts into one for the whole kingdom, while from another point of view he was extending the Great Council to include representatives of his subjects throughout the state as well as his great vassals.

Purpose and organization.   Edward began the summons of representatives early in his reign. Owing to his numerous wars and the increased scope of his government, the king was no longer able to meet his expenses from the customary taxes and feudal and judicial dues. He realized that new taxes, which must fall heavily on the burghers and small landowners, would be much more easily collected if those classes, through their representatives, had given their consent. The representatives of the commons, as they were called, were not yet an essential part of Parliament, but after 1297 it was recognized that their presence was necessary when any non-feudal taxes were proclaimed. Taxation, however, was not the only purpose of Parliament. It was also a court for the redress of grievances that fell outside the jurisdiction of the common-law courts. By including the representatives, the king opened the way for petitions of grievances from the middle class, which it was the duty of Parliament to redress. Finally, and this is perhaps the most important motive for summoning the commons, Edward desired a broader and more national basis for his government than was provided by the barons alone. The knights of the shire and the burghers could furnish invaluable information regarding local conditions, and on returning home they could explain the acts of the government to their neighbors. Under Edward I, Parliament was not yet organized in the form we know. When the representatives were present, they stood at the foot of the hall and took no part in the proceedings, save to give consent or to express an opinion when asked. However, they were already forming the habit of consulting separately as to what decision they would give, and were thus paving the way for the formation of a separate House of Commons.

Edward II.   Under Edward II (1307–27), the first Edward's amiable but shiftless son, Parliament was still more firmly established. It took advantage of the king's weakness to assert a measure of independence that would have been impossible under Edward I. The custom of calling the commons to consent to taxation continued regularly until it had acquired a firm basis of precedent. For the rest, the reign of Edward II was an unfortunate one. After the defeat of his badly managed army by the Scots at Bannockburn in 1314, he gave up all hope of renewing the conquest of Scotland. His incompetent rule gave the barons an opportunity to reassert the influence they had lost under the strong hand of his father. After a long-drawn-out opposition, the barons broke into open rebellion in 1327 and deposed the king in favor of his young son, Edward III, who ruled England for the next fifty years.

3. France and the Hundred Years' War

Edward III and Philip VI had each ruled about a decade when England and France were plunged into a war that lasted intermittently through the greater part of the reigns of five kings in each country. During all that time, the war exercised a powerful effect on the development of both countries, but as it was fought entirely on French soil it had a much more immediate effect on the internal history of France than on that of England. We shall trace its course, therefore, primarily in its relation to French history. The war has been rather inaccurately named by historians the Hundred Years' War. It was in reality either more or less than that, since from beginning to end it covered more than a century, though there were less than a hundred years of actual fighting.

Causes of the war.   The war might also be considered merely a continuation of the age-old conflict between the French kings and their too-powerful English vassals. Philip Augustus had taken over most of the French fiefs of the English-Angevin house at the opening of the thirteenth century. His successors had encroached still further so that at his accession Edward III held only a part of Aquitaine and Gascony in southwestern France and Ponthieu in the north, as vassal of the French crown. But the French monarchy had meanwhile grown too strong to tolerate the possession of French land by a foreign king, while, for their part, the English kings, who were beginning to think in national rather than feudal terms, found their position as vassals increasingly humiliating. The situation was becoming an impossible one, fraught with irritation for both monarchs. It was made still more difficult by the English interest in Flemish trade and the possibilty of an English alliance with the Flemish burghers whose prosperity depended upon the importation of English wool to feed their weaving industry. The long-standing alliance between France and Scotland, which was always hostile to England, also added to the international tension. This situation had led to war in the time of Philip the Fair and Edward I. The causes of the war under

Philip VI and Edward III were much the same, save that now the English king had an hereditary claim to the French crown, through his mother who was a daughter of Philip the Fair. This claim he was prepared to press, once war seemed inevitable, as a justification of his position and as a means of winning over the Flemish cities.

First phase of the war.   The first phase of the war was marked by steady misfortune for France. Philip VI was hampered by a rebellion in Flanders and a civil war in Brittany over the succession to the duchy. Moreover, the French army was not so effectively organized as the English, which was now a disciplined and paid royal army rather than a mere feudal levy, and neither Philip nor his successor John II (1350–64) was a match for his opponent in military skill. The first hostilities ended with the destruction of the French fleet by English and Flemish ships off Sluys in 1340, followed by a five-year truce.

Crécy.   The next disaster came in 1346. Edward III had landed an army of some ten thousand men in Normandy, had marched up the Seine almost to Paris, and had then turned north, pillaging the country as he went. The French army, which far outnumbered Edward's forces, finally closed with him on the famous field of Crécy (1346). There the heavily armored but undisciplined French knights charged in vain against the dismounted English men-at-arms, while the English archers with their magnificently effective long bows spread death in their ranks. For the first time in a great battle, the modern method of combined missile and infantry fighting had triumphed over the medieval heavy armed cavalry. This fact made Crécy a sign and a portent, though its significance was not fully realized for some time to come. The battle ended in a rout, and Edward went on his way to besiege and capture Calais. A truce in 1347 ended hostilities again till 1355.

Poitiers.   When the war was resumed, the Black Prince, Edward's brilliant son, began a similar pillaging march through French territory, this time from the direction of Gascony. John II, who was now King of France, hurried south with a large army and met the English at Poitiers (1356). The battle was another

triumph for the English archers. The chivalrous but incompetent King John was outgeneraled by the Black Prince, his knights were mowed down, and he himself was taken prisoner. After four more years of fighting, France was at the end of her resources. There was no choice but to make peace on the best terms obtainable. The treaty was arranged at Brétigny in 1360. The English king was given full possession, free of all feudal obligations, of Calais and Ponthieu in the north and of Aquitaine and Gascony as they had been in the reign of Henry III. Moreover, the French were to pay an enormous ransom for the release of King John. It was still not all paid when John died in 1364.

Jacquerie.   The first period of the war left France in a frightfully weakened condition. The defeat of the French armies at Crécy and Poitiers was as nothing compared to the constant devastation of the whole northern and western part of France. On their pillaging raids, the English army systematically laid waste the country along the line of march. Nor was that the worst; for both armies, lacking a commissariat, had to live off the country in time of truce as well as in war, and the companies of mercenary soldiers kept up an uninterrupted career of plunder, leaving a trail of ruined crops, burned dwellings and the corpses of noncombatants to mark their passing. War in the fourteenth century still retained this characteristic of feudal warfare, that there was more plundering than fighting and that it was the peasant and townsman who suffered most. To this general suffering was added a burden of taxation such as France had never before known. Again and again the king called the Estates General to secure their consent to the taxes needed to finance the war. But the people were sullen and discontented, and the estates were growing bolder. The estates called by Philip VI in the year of Crécy and the following year refused to consent and demanded reforms in the government. After Poitiers they threatened what amounted to revolution. Led by a Parisian merchant, Étienne Marcel, and backed by the armed citizens of Paris, the estates of northern France demanded and for a time secured practical control of the government, which was then in the hands of the Dauphin Charles. At this point

This representation of Bertrand du Guesclin, the Breton knight who was given command of the French army by Charles V, may not be a realistic portrait, but it does illustrate the kind of plate armor worn at the time.

the situation was complicated by that desperate and tragic rising of the peasants known as the Jacquerie from the name "Jacques" commonly applied to the peasant. Goaded to desperation by their sufferings, the peasants gathered in bands in 1358, murdered their lords wherever they could find them, and burned their châteaux. The revolt, however, was hopeless. The prince, with the aid of the terrified nobles, crushed the poorly armed peasants and massacred some twenty thousand of them. With them fell Marcel, whose opposition to the prince had been vaguely connected with the Jacquerie and had never had really national support. The Estates General had overreached itself and had lost its best opportunity to become a necessary and permanent part of French government.

Success under Charles V. When Charles V (1364–80) became king, he was prepared to profit by the lessons he had learned when acting as regent during his father's imprison-

ment. He at once began the reconstruction of government finances and the reorganization of the army with a success that won for him the title Charles the Wise. He called the Estates General, which he had reason to distrust, as seldom as possible, and when he did so he was able to secure permanent taxes which made future meetings less necessary. These taxes fell chiefly on the commons, and so were readily voted by the first two estates who formed a majority of the assembly. For the collection of the new taxes, he organized an administrative machinery that lasted for centuries. The army was put on a more regular footing, with knights and archers enrolled in companies and paid by the king. After five years of preparation, Charles was ready to reopen the war. He himself took no part in the fighting, since he was more a scholar and statesman than a warrior. Instead, he entrusted the command of the army to the capable and popular Breton knight, Bertrand du Guesclin. For the first time, the French enjoyed the advantage of superior generalship over the English. Du Guesclin may have been, as commonly reported, the ugliest man in Brittany, but he was certainly a great soldier with years of practical experience behind him. Avoiding pitched battles, he occupied, bit by bit, nearly all the territory ceded to Edward at Brétigny. On the other side, Edward III was drifting into second childhood and the Black Prince's health was failing. After the truce in 1375, the English retained only Calais and a narrow strip of coast in the south between Bayonne and Bordeaux. The next year the Black Prince died, to be followed in 1377 by his father. A renewal of the war was cut short three years later by the death of both Charles V and du Guesclin.

Charles VI and civil war. For the next thirty-five years the war languished, with frequent truces and one fairly definite peace in 1396. The English kings whose reigns fall in this period, Richard II and Henry IV, had too many domestic troubles to pay much attention to a foreign war. But France was unable to take advantage of the opportunity, for she, too, was weakened by misgovernment and distracted by civil strife. Charles VI (1380–1422) began his reign as a child, with his selfish uncles in charge of the government. Of these, Philip, Duke of Burgundy, was the most important, and the most unscrupulous. In 1388, the young king came of age and began a brief period of good government and reform with the aid of his father's old ministers. But this fortunate period was brought to an end within four years by the first of those violent fits of insanity which rendered Charles permanently incapable of controlling the government. For some time thereafter the Duke of Burgundy and the king's younger brother, Louis of Orléans, rivaled each other in exploiting the royal government in their own interests. The rivalry between Burgundy and Orléans became still more intense when, in 1404, Philip of Burgundy died and was succeeded by his crafty son, John the Fearless. John had inherited a large territory, which included Flanders and Brabant as well as Burgundy, and hoped

Charles VII, the French monarch whom Joan of Arc helped to make king, as portrayed by Fouquet in later years when events more or less justified the superscription, "The Very Victorious King of France."

through control of the French government to build up a practically independent state between France and Germany. As Louis was the chief obstacle to his plans, he had him assassinated in 1407. Opposition to John continued, however, under the leadership of Louis's kinsman the Count of Armagnac. By 1411, the two factions, Burgundian and Armagnac, had come to blows in open civil war.

The war renewed. After a good deal of fighting, the Armagnacs had gained temporary possession of the mad king and the government, when the new King of England, Henry V, decided to take advantage of the situation and reopen the war with France. Having secured the neutrality of John of Burgundy, Henry landed an army near the mouth of the Seine in 1415 and advanced into Picardy. The French army, led by the Armagnac princes, met him at Agincourt. The French greatly outnumbered the English force; but again, as at Crécy and Poitiers, the superior discipline and tactics of the small English army gave it an overwhelming victory. Henry then undertook the systematic conquest of Normandy, while the Duke of Burgundy seized Paris and the king. The Dauphin Charles now headed the Armagnac party. He was trying to reach an agreement with John of Burgundy in 1419 when the latter was murdered by some Armagnac enthusiasts. Peace between the two parties was now impossible. Philip, the new Duke of Burgundy, promptly formed an alliance with Henry V. He signed a treaty in the name of the king, whereby the dauphin was disinherited; Henry was to marry the daughter of Charles VI; act as regent till the king's death; and thereafter inherit the French crown. Henry, however, died a few months before Charles VI, leaving to his infant son, Henry VI, a claim to the throne of France and actual possession of the northern half of the country.

Joan of Arc. South of the Loire, the Armagnacs still fought on under the leadership of the dauphin, who now took the title Charles VII (1422–61), though he had not yet been officially crowned, and there was a widespread rumor that he was illegitimate. He was not a man of forceful character, but he had a few able and devoted followers and managed to hold his own fairly well against the Duke of Bedford,

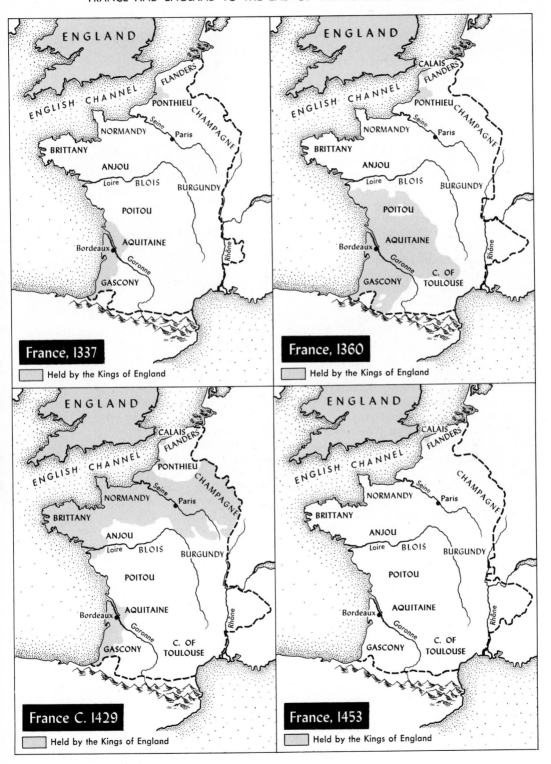

France, 1337
☐ Held by the Kings of England

France, 1360
☐ Held by the Kings of England

France C. 1429
☐ Held by the Kings of England

France, 1453
☐ Held by the Kings of England

who acted as regent for Henry VI in France. By 1429, however, his position was becoming precarious, when the appearance of that remarkable young woman, Joan of Arc, at his court inspired Charles and his supporters with new confidence and energy. The story of the peasant girl of Domremy who believed, and made others believe, that God had chosen her to save France and win the crown for its rightful king is well known. For a year she led the French army, raising the siege of Orléans and cutting a path for the king to Reims, in whose ancient cathedral he was crowned and consecrated after the manner of his ancestors. It was a triumph quickly followed by tragedy. In May, 1430, "The Maid" was captured by the Burgundians who sold her to the English. After months of imprisonment, she was tried on charges of heresy and witchcraft, and finally burned at the stake. But she had not died in vain. She had given new spirit to the army and the king, though he let her die without raising a hand to save her, and she had aroused a patriotic fervor among Frenchmen that has never since died out. The war lasted two decades longer. It was a period of slow but steady success for French arms. The king made peace with Burgundy in 1435 and repelled the English step by step. The tactics of his general, Dunois, were much the same as those employed by du Guesclin, and equally successful. By 1453, only Calais was left in English hands and the Hundred Years' War was over.

Results of the war. France had suffered terribly during the long conflict, but she emerged from it a united state with a new national consciousness. The attempts of both the Estates General and the great princes to control the government had failed. The way was now clear for the establishment of absolute monarchical rule.

4. England from Edward III to Henry VI (1327–1461)

Much of England's history during the Hundred Years' War has already been told through tracing the fortunes of her armies in France. We must turn now to a brief survey of the

This portrait of Edward III in his old age is from the bronze effigy in Westminster Abbey. It was made, probably by John Orchard, on the king's death in 1377.

political events and the social and constitutional developments in the country itself during this period.

Edward III and Richard II. The reign of Edward III (1327–77) was a period of success and popularity for the king in his vigorous youth and middle age, followed by failure and popular discontent in his premature and undignified senility. While he still retained his strength of mind, Edward was absorbed heart and soul in the war with France, and was prepared to sacrifice royal rights and prerogatives to Parliament and to give the people good government in order to secure the financial support necessary to military success. He was always a good politician as well as a brilliant general. When his powers began to fail, his son, the Black Prince, for a time took his place as a national hero. But, unfortunately, he too fell a prey to premature illness and death, leaving his unscrupulous younger brother, John of Gaunt, to act as regent for the old king and later for the prince's infant son, Richard II (1377–99). During the twelve years of Richard's minority, Parliament took advantage of the weakness of royal government to press its claims more strongly than ever, and after the king came of age he was forced for a time to accept a constitutional regime. Richard, however, was arrogant, hot-headed, and foolish, determined to exercise an absolute authority that was no longer practicable. A brief attempt to rule without Parliament led to a revolution. Richard was forced to abdicate in favor of Henry of Lancaster, son of John of Gaunt.

The Lancastrian kings. Henry IV (1399–1413) owed his crown to Parliament. He was not the next heir to the throne, and so could not claim it by direct descent. Moreover, the fall of Richard II had demonstrated the folly of ignoring Parliament. Under the Lancastrian kings, therefore, that body developed a larger share in government than ever before. The greater part of the reign of Henry IV was spent in suppressing rebellions and in making good his claim to rule. His efforts were eventually successful. He left the power of his house so firmly established that his son Henry V (1413–22) was able to renew the French war with startling success and to threaten the power of Parliament. But at the height of his career, Henry V died and the royal government was again weakened by a regency for an infant king. Even when Henry VI (1422–61) grew up, the government remained weak, for he proved to be an utterly incompent ruler. The country was torn by the strife of baronial factions and disturbed by the lawless violence of returned soldiers who were maintained by wealthy lords. Parliament took a larger share in government than ever, but it was too often dominated by noble cliques. Meanwhile, the war with France was lost and before the end of Henry's reign England was thrown into the chaos of civil war.

England and the war. The effect of the Hundred Years' War on England, socially and constitutionally, was in many respects different from its effect on France. The English people had not suffered so much. Despite high taxes,

the war was popular with all classes, for all had a stake in it. It was always Frenchmen who were plundered and Englishmen who profited, a situation well calculated to arouse patriotic enthusiasm. The greater part of the English army was composed of yeoman archers, drawn from the non-noble class. They were paid by the king and they brought home with them their share of plunder as well as their just share in the glory of Crécy, Poitiers, and Agincourt. Englishmen did not have to be nobles to take pride in English victories or to profit from them. The commons, too, in so far as they were represented in Parliament, took advantage of the financial needs of the government much more wisely than did their French contemporaries. In one respect only did England suffer directly from the war. During its last years and after it was over, the country was flooded with restless and lawless soldiers, who were a constant source of violence and

The coronation of Richard II as depicted on the left wing of the Wilton Diptych shows the kneeling monarch with his patron saints in the background. This fine panel painting, executed by an unknown artist about 1395, is now in the National Gallery, London.

This graphic representation of a mass burial during the Black Death in 1349, from a French miniature in Brussels, suggests the appalling loss of life from the great plague.

who provided the manpower for the Wars of the Roses.[1]

Black Death and Peasants' Revolt. The war was not the only factor in the social development of England in this period. By the beginning of the fourteenth century, it was clear that the rise of money economy was slowly breaking up the old manorial economy which had dominated medieval agrarian society. Villeins were beginning to secure the commutation of their personal services to money payments, and were in some places securing personal freedom. In the second half of the century this process was greatly accelerated, due in part to a great international disaster. In the years 1348–50, the whole of western Europe was swept by an epidemic of plague known as the Black Death, which may have been brought from the East by merchant ships. The toll of deaths was terribly high, reputedly a third of the total population. Moreover, recurrences of the plague in 1361, 1368 and at intervals thereafter, though with diminished force, retarded recovery for decades. All countries suffered, but in England, which was more ready for change, the result was a social revolution. There were not enough villeins left to till the fields. Wages rose to unprecedented heights. Many villeins seized the opportunity to bargain for freedom with their lords or ran away in search of free employment elsewhere. For years the government strove with little success to fix wages at the old levels. The chief result was a growing discontent, aggravated by an increasing burden of royal taxation, that finally found expression in the Peasants' Revolt of 1381. The revolt failed, but strong economic forces were working on the villeins' side[2] and their emancipation went slowly but steadily on. By the end of the fifteenth century, they had practically all obtained freedom and had become tenant farmers, or hired farm laborers. or had drifted off to seek work in the cities.

[1] See below, pages 341–342.

[2] See below, pages 307–308.

Administration and justice. Meanwhile, the steady evolution of the English constitution continued. A new court, the chancery, was established to take over the civil cases referred to the king's council from the common-law courts. These cases were mostly outside the scope of common law. The court of chancery provided a solution by applying the principle of equity. An equally significant innovation was made in the administration of local justice during the reign of Edward III. In every county prominent knights or landowners were given power to judge minor criminal cases. They were called justices of the peace. Being men of respectable social position who were thoroughly acquainted with conditions in their neighborhood, their judgments were usually respected and in accord with local opinion. For centuries they remained a very important part of English judicial machinery.

Development of Parliament. The most important constitutional development of this period, however, was the gradual evolution of Parliament from the rather vague body founded by Edward I to something like its modern form, and the firm establishment of its position as a permanent and necessary part of government. We have already seen how Parliament as a whole took advantage of the kings' financial needs to increase its powers. The Commons made especially good use of the kings' need for money to carry on the war. They had learned to bargain. Before giving consent to taxes they would present petitions for the redress of grievances, and often these petitions were made into statutes by the king and were given the force of law. The Commons were thus acquiring the practical ability to initiate legislation. Parliament, and particularly the House of Commons, had still a long way to go before reaching its present position, but all the essential ingredients were present before the end of the Hundred Years' War. Later kings might dictate to Parliament or try to override it, but none could afford to ignore it.

Contrast with Estates General. In this respect the history of the English Parliament is in strong contrast to that of the French Estates General, which never succeeded in becoming an essential part of the government, but, on

The Peasants' Revolt of 1381 as depicted in a fifteenth-century Flemish miniature.

the contrary, was called less and less frequently after the middle of the fourteenth century and eventually almost ceased to exist. One fundamental difference between the two institutions lay in the earlier centralization of government in England while both countries were still largely feudal. The English kings were strong enough to compel the barons from all parts of the country to attend the Great Council even before it evolved into Parliament. In France, on the other hand, the great lords from outside the domain remained strong enough to ignore the king's summons almost to the end of the feudal era. From the very beginning then, the English Parliament was more truly national in scope than the estates. There was an equally fundamental difference also in the composition of the English House of Commons and the French Third Estate. The latter was composed almost entirely of representatives of the urban middle class, who had no interest in the country districts and nothing in common, socially or in economic interest, with the nobles and clergy in the other two estates. The English Commons, on the other hand, included landowning knights from the shires as well as burghers, and these knights had much the same social and economic interests as the members of the House of Lords. Indeed, many of the knights who came up from the shires were related to the lords by family ties, for in England, unlike any continental country, the younger sons of the barons were excluded from the family inheritance and lost their status as nobles. Together with the numerous knights who held only one or two manors, but who would have been classed as nobles on the Continent, they formed the peculiarly English class of gentry who, in society and in the House of Commons, formed a connecting link between the lords and the merchant middle class. From the social point of view, then, the English Parliament was more truly representative than the Estates General, and the two English houses could work together to influence the monarchy as the three estates never could.

The end of the Hundred Years' War found both England and France on the verge of becoming united monarchical states. Both countries had yet to pass through a brief period of civil war (the Wars of the Roses in England and the war with Burgundy in France), but when that was finished, in each country the king became the direct ruler of the whole state by virtue of his royal title rather than as a feudal lord. In England, however, the king still had to rule by constitutional means through Parliament, whereas in France, once the great nobles had been suppressed, the king was left absolute and uncontrolled. The story of these last developments we shall leave to a later time.[1]

---

[1] See below, pages 379–380.

23

The Decline of the Papacy in the Later

Middle Ages

THE GREAT AGE of the medieval papacy fell
within the two centuries after the accession of
Gregory VII. During that time, successive
popes built up for the Roman See a spiritual
monarchy over all western Christendom, a
hegemony based on canon law, on a highly
centralized administrative system, and on
claims, often put into practice, to supremacy
over secular rulers. At the end of that period
they succeeded in destroying the power of the
emperors, whose opposition had been the most
serious obstacle in the way of their triumphal
march. It was apparently a decisive victory,
but the papacy was to pay dearly for it. The
last phase of the struggle with the Hohenstaufens had revolved around the temporal rule
of the popes over the States of the Church in
central Italy, to maintain which they had taxed
the church heavily and had even preached
crusades against the emperors. Their devotion
to this worldly cause, which was of little general interest to Christendom, lost for the popes
much of the sympathy and respect of both
people and clergy in other lands. And it was
on their hold over the hearts and minds of the
people, rather than on the theories of canon
law, that the popes must depend for the ultimate support of their power. Moreover, the
defeat of the emperors had not removed all
opposition to papal supremacy. The rising
territorial monarchies in France and England
were to prove more dangerous opponents than
the emperors had ever been. By the end of
the thirteenth century, the time had passed
when any pope could exercise authority over
French and English kings as Innocent III had
done. When Boniface VIII tried to do so,
stating his claims to supremacy more strongly
than even Innocent had done, he failed disastrously. From that moment the power of the
popes began to decline. Their prestige continued to wane through the seventy years of
subjection to French influence at Avignon,
through the disgraceful rivalries of the Great
Schism and the opposition of the councils that
followed, until, by the middle of the fifteenth
century, the pope was little more than an Italian prince who was also the administrative
head of the church.

1. Boniface VIII and Philip the Fair

Boniface VIII. When Boniface VIII (1294–
1303) ascended the throne of St. Peter, he
had no reason to believe that the prestige of
the papacy had been in any way impaired.
There had been no strong pope to put its
power to the test since the end of the war with

The aged pontiff, Pope Boniface VIII, with two cardinals beside him, from a painting by Giotto in the basilica of St. John Lateran in Rome.

the emperors, and possibly no one could gauge the subtle changes in popular opinion that had taken place in the interim. The character of the new pope was certain to make his pontificate a crucial one in the history of the church. He was already in his late seventies and had behind him a lifetime of political and diplomatic activity. He had been one of the most vigorous and capable of the cardinals, but his great capacities were offset by equally great failings of character. He was arrogant, ruthless, and immensely vain, and he showed little evidence of deep moral or religious conviction. His policies seem to have been motivated more by personal and family pride than by devotion to the welfare of the church. The early years of his reign were spent in crushing the powerful Roman family of Colonna in the interest of his own less powerful house, the Gaetani. At the same time, his love of power drove him on to an uncompromising assertion of all those claims to universal supremacy with which his

long training in canon law had made him thoroughly familiar.

Clericis laicos. His conception of papal authority soon brought Boniface into conflict with the kings of France and England. The first crisis arose from the much-disputed question of the relation of the clergy and church property to the state. In 1296, Philip IV (the Fair) and Edward I were at war and both demanded subsidies from their clergy to help meet the unusual expenses. They argued that the clergy, as subjects of the state, should contribute to the defense of the realm in return for the protection afforded them by the royal government. The pope, on the other hand, asserted that no secular ruler had the right to tax churchmen or church property. That right could be exercised only by the pope as ruler of the church. This view Boniface expressed in a famous bull, called *Clericis laicos* from the first two words of the text. The bull forbade the clergy of any country to pay subsidies of any kind to secular rulers without the pope's consent. Philip promptly replied by forbidding the exportation of money from the country, ostensibly as a war measure, but with the effect of cutting off the papal income from the French church. Edward also took vigorous action, which amounted to the outlawing of the English clergy who refused to pay the subsidies. Faced by this decided opposition, and finding that the clergy would not support him strongly against their king, Boniface was forced to withdraw the bull.

The jubilee of 1300. The pope, however, soon recovered confidence. The crushing of the Colonna in 1298 made his position at Rome secure, and in 1300 he celebrated the first jubilee year. Immense crowds of pilgrims — their number has been reckoned as high as two million — flocked to Rome to take advantage of the special indulgences and spiritual benefits promised to all who came to the Holy City and contributed to the papal coffers. The success of the jubilee gave Boniface economic independence and an exaggerated confidence in the loyalty of the people to the church. He was ready again to assert his authority over his royal opponents.

Conflict with Philip. It was the King of France who bore the brunt of the second conflict with the haughty pope. The immediate cause of the quarrel this time was the question of clerical exemption from civil jurisdiction. Philip the Fair had condemned the Bishop of Pamiers in Languedoc, apparently on ample grounds, for treason and other serious crimes and asked the pope to degrade him from his office prior to the execution of his sentence. As might have been expected, Boniface refused to recognize the right of a secular court to try an ecclesiastic. In December, 1301, he called the case to Rome for a new trial, and at the same time issued two bulls, one renewing the prohibitions of *Clericis laicos,* the other taking Philip to task for misgovernment. Feeling that the independence of his government was at stake, Philip decided to make an unprecedented appeal for popular support. In April, 1302, he called the first Estates General and stated his own side of the case to them, with the result that all three estates, including the clergy, addressed letters of protest to Rome.

Unam sanctam. This opposition merely spurred Boniface on to a more extreme statement of his authority, extending the controversy into the wider field of the supremacy of church over state. The bull *Unam sanctam,* published in November, 1302, contained the most absolute statement of supremacy over secular rulers ever issued by any pope. Most of the arguments were not new, but the whole tenor of the bull was without precedent in its uncompromising force. It concluded with the flat statement that "for every human creature it is absolutely necessary for salvation to be subject to the Roman Pontiff." The bull was followed by an ultimatum to Philip demanding his complete submission under threat of excommunication.

The fall of Boniface. The pope had gone too far. Feeling that submission was impossible, Philip decided to take the offensive as the only alternative left him. He called an assembly of the barons and higher clergy of France, before which his ministers accused Boniface of heresy, simony, and a host of other crimes. Meanwhile, his chief minister, Guillaume de Nogaret, was dispatched to Italy to arrest the pope and bring him back to answer the accusations of the king before a general council. On his arrival in Italy, Nogaret discovered that the unsuspecting pope had gone

to the little mountain town of Anagni to escape the summer heat. There the French minister followed him, accompanied by an armed band which had been raised by the pope's bitter enemy, Sciarra Colonna. They had little difficulty in breaking into the town and seizing Boniface, whom they found deserted by his court, but arrayed in all the dignity of his pontifical robes. They did not hold him long, for the people of the countryside rallied to his rescue and freed him, but the damage was already done. The aged pope died within the month as a result of shock and chagrin. And with him died the medieval papacy.

2. *Waning Prestige of the Popes at Avignon*

Babylonian Captivity. For two years after the death of Boniface VIII, the outcome of his struggle with the French monarchy remained in some doubt. The next pope elected lived for only a few months, and in the long interregnum that followed, Philip the Fair was able to bring sufficient pressure to bear on the cardinals to force the election of a French pope, who took the name Clement V (1305–14). The papacy was now brought definitely under the influence of the French king. Clement was in France at the time of his election, and Philip used every possible means to keep him there. The disturbed condition of Italy, torn by the strife of the Guelf and Ghibelline factions, offered an excuse to the pope for not taking up his residence in Rome. Instead, after four years of wandering about France, he set up the papal capital at Avignon. There the popes remained for nearly seventy years. The city was not actually in French territory — it was in Provence, then a fief of the Angevin king of Naples — but it was just on the border of France and well within the sphere of French influence. The popes were doubtless safer there than in Rome, but it was mainly French interest that kept them from returning to their proper home in the ancient capital of western Christendom. Clement's acquiescence in crushing the Templars at the request of Philip the Fair, and in other matters, demonstrated the importance to the French kings of keeping the popes at Avignon. And the popes, being

French themselves, were willing enough to stay. Twenty-five of the twenty-eight cardinals appointed by Clement V were French, thus ensuring the election of another French pope — and so it went through seven successive reigns. To other nations it seemed that the rulers of the church were being held captive under the domination of France, whence the name "the Babylonian Captivity of the Church" generally applied to this period in papal history.

John XXII and Louis IV. French influence on papal policy was especially evident in the relations of the Avignonese popes with other European powers. During the first half of the fourteenth century, it was the settled policy of the French kings to keep the Holy Roman Empire weak and divided, in the hope that they might be able to expand their domain eastward at the expense of the imperial lands in the Rhône and Rhine valleys. To this policy Clement's successor, John XXII (1316–34), lent his hearty support, the more willingly because he was eager to restore papal authority in Italy and wanted no imperial interference there. He therefore did nothing to help settle the disputed election between Louis of Bavaria and Frederick of Hapsburg which had caused a civil war in Germany.[1] Even after Louis won a decisive victory in 1322, John refused to recognize him and ordered him to cease acting as emperor until he had received papal confirmation. When Louis refused to admit the pope's right to confirm or reject a successful candidate for the imperial crown, John excommunicated him. The quarrel dragged on, keeping Germany in a state of unrest, until the death of Louis IV in 1347. John's successors would have been willing to make peace, but were prevented by fear of the French king. Meanwhile, in 1338 the German Diet proclaimed the principle that the emperor's election was valid without the consent of the pope. Later this principle was confirmed by the Golden Bull of 1356. The popes thus lost one of the rights which supported their claim to supremacy over the emperors, a right which their medieval predecessors had asserted vigorously and had used on more than one occasion as a pretext for interfering in imperial affairs.

[1] See above, page 264.

Critics of the papacy. The controversy with Louis the Bavarian had other unfortunate results for the papacy, since it served to focus attention on the problem of papal authority and furnished the occasion for damaging attacks on the whole theory of papal supremacy. Louis had found useful allies in the Spiritual Franciscans, a branch of the Franciscan order which had been condemned by John XXII for their assertion of the doctrine of the absolute poverty of Christ and the apostles. Among these was the great English Nominalist philosopher, William of Occam, whose learning and skill in debate had won for him the title of "Invincible Doctor." His intellectual weapons Occam now turned upon the papacy in a rapid fire of devastating criticism. He denied the papal claims to temporal sovereignty and even set limits to the pope's spiritual authority. His arguments were based largely on the authority of the Bible, which should be interpreted, not only by the pope and the clergy, but by "the discretion and counsel of the wisest men," a rather vague phrase that seems to foreshadow the theory of the supremacy of a council over the pope.

Defensor pacis. In the field of political theory, an even more forceful assault on papal supremacy was delivered by two secular writers, Marsiglio of Padua and John of Jandun, who published the *Defensor pacis* in 1324. In this significant book the authors developed theories so far in advance of their age that its full influence was felt only in later generations. Arguing that in both state and church the sovereign power rests with the people and is only delegated to rulers so long as they fulfill their function by ruling wisely, the authors assert that the papacy is a human institution without authority save that given it by the Christian people. The pope's supremacy over the clergy is a mere presidency created for administrative convenience. All important questions of faith should be referred to the superior authority of a general council representing the Christian community. The pope has no right to "coercive jurisdiction" which belongs only to the state, and it is the pope's claim to this that disturbs the peace of Christendom. In opposing him, the emperor is acting as "the defender of the peace." Further, the clergy, save for their spiritual duties of teaching, preaching, and administering the sacraments, are not essentially different from other Christian citizens. In temporal matters they should be subject to the government of the state.

Papal finance. The daring propositions of the *Defensor pacis* were too extreme to gain wide support at once. In the meantime the popes at Avignon successfully carried on the work of their predecessors in centralizing the administration of the church and in using their control of the clergy to increase their income. The popes now needed more money than ever before, for they had lost most of their revenues from the States of the Church in Italy and they had to expend large sums for the building of a new capital at Avignon with a magnificence and luxury that would uphold their prestige in Christendom. To meet ever-increasing demands, therefore, the Avignonese popes systematized and perfected all the established methods of taxation and invented some new ones. The financial genius of John XXII, especially, was responsible for the extension of many old practices and for some important innovations. The clerical tithe, one tenth of the net income from ecclesiastical benefices, levied originally for the purpose of a crusade, now became a regular tax payable to the papacy. John XXII also claimed the "annates" — that is, the first year's income from the benefices of the more important clergy — as well as the revenues from all benefices during a vacancy. Even the "procurations," which were the fees paid to bishops to meet the expenses of visits of inspection in their dioceses, now went to the papacy, with the result that visitations practically ceased in many places. Finally, the popes at Avignon secured the right, despite the canonical rules regarding election, to name the holders of many of the most important ecclesiastical offices in Christendom as well as a large number of the lesser ones. And these offices were seldom given away without some substantial return, not to mention the innumerable fees paid by the clergy for the confirmation of their offices. Never had the ancient evil of simony[1] flourished so openly at the papal court.

[1] See above, page 177.

Opposition in England. The heavy weight of papal taxation aroused grave discontent in the countries outside of France. In England it led to open opposition on the part of the government, for the English kings, who were at war with France, felt an especially keen resentment at seeing so much English money going to a French pope. Edward III even went so far as to protest that "the successor of the apostles was commissioned to lead the Lord's sheep to pasture, not to fleece them." Papal "provisions" or appointments to English benefices were particularly unpopular because the offices were so often given to officials at the papal *curia* or other foreigners. In 1351, Edward III had Parliament pass the Statute of Provisors making this practice illegal. Two years later he sought to curtail papal interference in England still further by issuing the Statute of Praemunire, which made the appealing of cases from the local ecclesiastical courts to the papal court illegal without the king's consent. In the long run, however, the statutes had little effect, save to force the popes to share some of the spoils with the king.

Popular discontent. More serious, however, than the opposition of state governments was the popular discontent aroused by the demoralization of the clergy which resulted from the financial and administrative policies of the Avignonese popes. It is unsafe to accept at their face value all the denunciations of the morals and manners of the clergy made by both secular writers and reforming preachers; yet the evidence of a decline in the moral and spiritual standards of the church during the period of the Babylonian Captivity is too strong to be altogether denied. It could not well be otherwise. Appeals to Avignon from episcopal jurisdiction, the cessation of episcopal visitations, and the absence of foreign incumbents from their posts all tended to disrupt ecclesiastical discipline. Moreover, the whole body of the clergy suffered from the demoralizing effects of simony. Bishops or priests who had purchased their offices were likely to regard them as an investment and to be more interested in making them pay than in performing their spiritual duties. There were undoubtedly many earnest and conscientious priests, like the poor parson of the *Canterbury Tales*. But that Chaucer considered him an exception to the general rule is shown by his description of the other clerics who rode with that cheerful company on the road to Canterbury. One need not read far in the literature of the fourteenth century to find sweeping criticisms of the wealth, worldliness, and immorality of the clergy and plentiful signs of a general lack of respect for them.

Return to Rome. As time went on it became increasingly clear that the papacy was losing both popularity and prestige, and that this was due in part to the continued residence of the popes at Avignon, which had become a symbol of all the papal abuses of the age. A French pope could not command the loyalty of other nations as could a pope living at Rome, the traditional capital of the universal church. The Italians especially resented the absence of the popes from Italy, since it cut them off from their accustomed share in the profits of the papacy. Rome had built its entire economic life about the papal *curia*. Deprived of it, the city was left desolate and poverty-stricken, dominated by quarreling noble factions, while the States of the Church were in a constant turmoil and threatened to escape entirely from papal control. Yet this very situation made the return to Rome difficult and dangerous. A brief visit to Rome made by Pope Urban V in 1367 ended in disillusionment. Ten years passed and a new pope was elected before the project was renewed. At last, in 1377, Pope Gregory XI decided to make the long-deferred move, lest Rome and the States of the Church should be lost beyond recovery. He was welcomed with delirious joy by the Roman populace.

3. *The Great Schism, Heresy, and the Councils*

Beginning of schism. All who were most sincerely interested in the welfare of the church had welcomed the end of the Captivity and the return of the papacy to Rome. No one could have foreseen that the death of Gregory early in 1378 would plunge the church into a situation infinitely worse than anything that had gone before. The papal

court was scarcely settled in Rome before a new pope had to be elected. The majority of the cardinals, who were French and homesick for Avignon, undoubtedly wanted another French pope. The Roman people, on the other hand, were determined at all costs to keep the papacy now that they had recovered it and clamored wildly for a Roman pope, or at least an Italian. The election was held in the midst of scenes of mob violence that terrified the cardinals. They hastily chose an Italian, who took the name Urban VI (1378–89). He was a Neapolitan who had risen to the rank of archbishop through the favor of some of the French cardinals at Avignon. But if the cardinals hoped that he would be grateful to them and amenable to their control, they were bitterly disappointed. From the first he treated them with a brutal contempt that led some observers to suspect his sanity. Finding their position intolerable, the cardinals withdrew from Rome and held a new conclave. They declared that the election of Urban was invalid because it had taken place under threat of violence. In his place they elected a French cardinal, Clement VII (1378–94). The new pope with his cardinals then returned to Avignon. In Rome, meanwhile, Urban denounced and excommunicated Clement and the rebellious cardinals, and appointed twenty-eight new cardinals of his own. There were now two popes and two colleges of cardinals, and the people of Christendom were faced by the problem of deciding whether the pope at Rome or the pope at Avignon was the true successor of St. Peter. The church was split from top to bottom and the schism was not to be healed for nearly forty years.

Effects of the schism. The question of the validity of the election of Urban VI or Clement VII was one that might honestly puzzle any impartial observer. The various states of Europe, however, made the choice of adherence to one or other of the rival popes mostly on political grounds. Italy, with the exception of Naples which was traditionally connected with Avignon, rallied to the Roman pope. France, naturally enough, recognized Clement. National enmities or alliances dictated the position of the other powers. Scotland, Spain, and those of the German princes who were friendly to France adhered to Clement, while England, Flanders, Portugal, the Empire, and the Scandinavian countries gave their obedience to Urban. The schism had disastrous effects both on the prestige of the papacy and on the spiritual health of the entire church. The rival popes thundered against one another, each denying the other any claim to authority, so that conscientious men did not know which way to turn. Rival claimants fought over ecclesiastical offices and the clergy everywhere were demoralized. Moreover, both popes were in desperate need of money, since each could draw revenues only from the part of the church that adhered to him. As a result, all the financial abuses of the Captivity were multiplied, with correspondingly evil effects. Popular discontent was redoubled and criticism of the clergy and the papacy became bolder. In England and Bohemia, demands for reform crystallized into heresy.

Wyclif. The leader of this movement in England was John Wyclif, a distinguished scholar and professor at Oxford. His first protests against papal supremacy and the wealth of the clergy, published in 1375, won for him the friendship of John of Gaunt, who was already acting as regent for the aged Edward III. They also called forth an official condemnation from Gregory XI in 1377. The scandal of the papal schism, which occurred in the next year, urged Wyclif to a more fundamental and far-reaching attack on the whole ecclesiastical system of his day. Like the later Protestant reformers, whose doctrines he foreshadowed in many respects, Wyclif appealed to the authority of the Bible against that of canon law or the customs and dogmas of the medieval church. He felt that the ills of the church, most of which sprang from the wealth and temporal power of the clergy, could be cured only by a return to the simpler life and teaching of the early Christians. It was the duty of the state to disendow the clergy when they failed to use their wealth for spiritual ends. Wyclif's theories regarding the equality of all Christians and the superiority of the state over the church in temporal matters are somewhat reminiscent of the *Defensor pacis,* but on theological grounds he went farther than Marsiglio had done. Still relying on the

authority of the Bible, he denied the validity of pilgrimages, the veneration of saints, and the power of the clergy to grant absolution for sins, and even attacked the fundamental doctrine of the material presence of Christ's body in the sacrament of the Eucharist. His doubts regarding the sacramental power of the priests, especially those who were living in sin, struck at the very heart of the church's power over the lay world. In this direction, however, he was traveling too fast for the thought of his age. It was only the weakness of the papacy and the doubtful support of John of Gaunt that enabled him, after he had been expelled from Oxford, to pass his last years in peace as a parish priest at Lutterworth. He died in 1384. His followers, who were called Lollards, preached his doctrines throughout England for some years until they were stamped out as dangerous heretics by Henry IV. But Wyclif's trenchant criticism of the church could never be wholly suppressed. Many of his ideas were to be asserted again at a more favorable time by the Protestant reformers of the sixteenth century, and in the meantime his teaching had spread to the distant land of Bohemia, where it received an enthusiastic welcome.

Huss and the Bohemian heresy. The movement for the reform of the Bohemian church in the early years of the fifteenth century was not entirely due to the influence of Wyclif. For some time before they learned of him, reforming preachers had been protesting against the wealth and immorality of the Bohemian clergy, who seem to have been unusually corrupt. It was Wyclif's teaching, however, that provided the great Bohemian reformer, John Huss, with the weapons he needed to gain popular support for his attack on the church. Like Wyclif, Huss was a scholar and professor — he taught at the University of Prague — but he was less a theologian and more a conscious nationalist than the English reformer. To his moral indignation against the corruption of the church was added a strong patriotic feeling against the German clergy who had secured most of the important posts in the Bohemian church. It was this combination that made him so popular among the native Bohemians and so dangerous an opponent of the papacy and the empire. In 1414, Huss was summoned to appear before the general council called by Emperor Sigismund at Constance to answer charges of heresy. He was tried and condemned, and after refusing to recant was burned at the stake in July, 1415. The emperor had treacherously repudiated the safe-conduct he had given him. The burning of Huss made it impossible to reconcile the Bohemian rebels to the church. The Hussites formed a separate sect, fiercely loyal to the memory of their martyred national hero. Their resistance ended only after years of furious fighting, and then only by a compromise on the part of the church.

Attempts to end schism. The growth of heresy in England and Bohemia demonstrated in the most forcible fashion the disastrous results of the schism of the papacy. But even without that object lesson, the evils of the schism were so apparent that both laymen and clergy in all parts of Christendom realized that it must be brought to an end, lest the whole structure of the universal church be destroyed. The popes themselves and the cardinals on both sides loudly proclaimed their eagerness

The Emperor Sigismund, who summoned the Council of Constance, is here portrayed by a contemporary artist.

to end the schism, but none was willing to make the first move or to sacrifice his position. Even the death of the original schismatic popes did not bring about reconciliation, for new popes were elected to fill their respective places. Under such circumstances, the only hope of decisive action seemed to lie in a general council which could coerce the popes. The arguments of the *Defensor pacis* for the superior jurisdiction of a general council were at last beginning to bear fruit. But who was to call a council if the popes would not? There lay the difficulty.

Council of Pisa. Eventually a group of cardinals from both "obediences" met and took upon themselves the responsibility of summoning a general council to meet at Pisa in 1409. Despite the doubtful legality of the council, an imposing array of churchmen attended. The first act of the council was to depose the two reigning popes, the Roman Gregory XII and his rival Benedict XIII. The cardinals present then proceeded to elect a new pope who took the name Alexander V. The latter, however, died within a few months and was replaced by Cardinal Baldassare Cossa as John XXIII. He was an able but unscrupulous man who had risen to prominence by methods more worthy of an Italian despot than of a churchman. Meanwhile, Gregory and Benedict had refused to accept their deposition and had been able to find some support in the conflicting interests of the European states. The council had merely made matters worse. Instead of two popes there were now three. *Ecce reductio ad absurdum.*

The Council of Constance. This impossible situation lasted for five years. It was the Emperor Sigismund who found the only possible solution by asserting his right as Roman emperor to call a council of the church as the great Constantine had done at Nicaea. The new council, attended by representatives from all parts of the Roman Church, assembled at Constance in 1414. After much negotiation the three popes were deposed or forced to abdicate, and in 1417 a Roman cardinal of the Colonna family was elected as Martin V

John Huss being burned at the stake as depicted in a contemporary German chronicle.

(1417–31). The schism was ended and the papacy was restored to Rome. In dealing with other pressing problems, however, the council was less successful. We have already noted that the burning of John Huss failed to check the Hussite heresy. The attempts of the council to reform the abuses in the church, which had arisen during the period of the Captivity and the schism, were almost equally fruitless. It did, however, issue two very important decrees, one asserting the superiority of a general council over the pope, the other providing for the calling of future councils at frequent intervals.

The conciliar movement fails. In this conciliar theory, the Council of Constance had left a legacy dangerous to the authority of future popes, but on the whole its action had strengthened rather than weakened the papacy, at least in so far as it had restored the pope to Rome and left him without rivals. Martin V and his successor Eugenius IV (1431–47) were able to establish themselves in a position of fair political security in the Papal States, to regain some measure of control over the clergy, and, in the long run, to withstand the menace of conciliar authority. In this they were aided by the political weakness of the greater European states. The council scheduled to meet in 1423 was so poorly attended that the pope had no difficulty in dissolving it before anything could be accomplished.

Council of Basel. The second council, however, which met at Basel in the first year of the pontificate of Eugenius, presented a more serious opposition. The necessity of ending the Hussite wars called forth a large attendance, and the success of the council in arranging a compromise that reconciled all but the most extreme Hussites to the church gave it considerable prestige. The council, moreover, was determined to effect a sweeping reform of the church "in head and members," beginning with the papacy. After long opposition, Eugenius attempted to bring the council under his control by transferring it to Ferrara; but as most of the council ignored the papal summons and remained at Basel, the council that met at Ferrara and then at Florence in 1438–39 was really a new one. The Council of Ferrara-Florence occupied itself mainly with an attempt, briefly successful, to reunite the Roman Catholic and Greek Orthodox churches. Its only lasting result was to stimulate the study of Greek at Florence through the influence of the learned Greek delegates. Meanwhile, the remnants of the Basel Council had elected an anti-pope, Felix V. For ten years the council and its pope continued the struggle with Rome, but the selfish intrigues and political bickerings of its members gradually destroyed its prestige, while Eugenius succeeded in coming to terms with most of the European powers. At last, in 1449, Felix resigned his empty title and the Council of Basel allowed itself to be dissolved. The conciliar movement had failed; its theories were discredited; and thereby the popes were left without constitutional checks within the church.

Pragmatic Sanction of Bourges.   Martin V and Eugenius IV had done much to restore the papal authority, but the popes were still far from possessing the powers they had had before the fall of Boniface VIII. Never again could they exercise effective supremacy over secular rulers, and even within the church their control was limited by the practical power of the great state governments. This was particularly true in France where, in 1438, King Charles VII had published a law known as the Pragmatic Sanction of Bourges which set definite limits to papal interference in ecclesiastical elections, papal taxation, and appeals to Rome. In short, it established a sort of national church under the control of the French monarchy. The governments of England and Germany took less radical action, but were moving in the same direction, and later the Spanish monarchy gained almost complete supervision of the church in Spain.

Decline of papal prestige.   The century and a half between the bull *Unam sanctam* and the dissolution of the Council of Basel had, indeed, witnessed a terrible decline in papal prestige, even though some considerable recovery of papal power had been made after the Council of Constance. The financial exactions of the popes at Avignon and the scandal of the Great Schism, the political theories of Occam and the *Defensor pacis,* the sweeping criticisms of the church launched by Wyclf and Huss, the conciliar movement and the growing power of the national monarchies had all contributed to the destruction of papal authority, and the fifteenth-century popes, who were more interested in establishing a temporal state in Italy than in giving religious leadership to Christendom, could not win back what had been lost.

"In the name of God and of profit." • Motto
inscribed on the ledgers of an Italian merchant
of the fourteenth century

24

Medieval Economy in Transition

DURING the fourteenth and fifteenth centuries,
European economy passed through the decisive
stage in the transition from medieval to modern forms. The preceding period had witnessed a remarkable expansion of commerce,
industry, and agriculture, but that expansion
had been confined to characteristically medieval institutions, of which the most typical
were the merchant and craft guilds and the
manor. Before the end of the thirteenth century, however, the continued growth of money
economy had begun to break down the traditional patterns of economic life. In the following centuries, modern forms of commercial,
industrial, and agricultural organization gradually took shape amid the wreckage of the
medieval. The transition was accompanied by
severe economic crises, depressions, and social
unrest. The incalculable tragedy of the Black
Death (1348–50), which reduced the population of western Europe by as much as a third,
was a shock from which both rural and urban
society recovered but slowly. The resulting
disruption of European economy, however, did
not check the growth of new forms of economic organization. Indeed, in many ways it
stimulated their development. Competition for
shrinking markets forced merchants, bankers,
and industrial entrepreneurs to perfect the
techniques of capitalism, while the labor shortage resulting from the Black Death was at
least one factor in the disintegration of the
manorial system.

1. The Growth of Capitalism in Italian Commerce, Industry, and Banking

Italian commerce. Thanks to her fortunate
geographical position in the midst of the Mediterranean Sea, Italy was the first country to
profit by the great commercial revival that began in the eleventh century and continued
through the High Middle Ages. Adventurous
traders from Venice, Genoa, and Pisa long
monopolized the trade between the eastern
Mediterranean lands and western Europe, exchanging western textiles, metals, and other
goods for the products of skilled Byzantine and
Moslem industry or the still more priceless
goods brought by caravan from the fabulous
East. Much of this trade dealt with articles
that were of very high value in proportion to
their bulk and weight, so that a single boatload
might carry a fortune. Eastern spices, silk,
cotton, sugar, and dye stuffs were all high-
priced commodities since they could not be
produced in Europe. There were risks involved in trade with distant lands, but the
profits were proportionately high. Since no
one could estimate the "just price" of foreign
commodities, the Italian merchants were free
to charge what the traffic would bear.

Growth of capital. The position of the
Italians as middlemen between the East and
the West thus presented unusual opportunities

for the accumulation of capital far beyond the merchants' needs for living expenses, capital that could be reinvested in larger enterprises with a view to still larger profits. Many Italian merchants had accumulated great fortunes long before the end of the thirteenth century. They had also begun to work out the basic techniques of commercial capitalism, and, above all, they had begun to regard the reinvestment of their profits in larger enterprises as the major aim of business. It is this point of view that differentiates the modern capitalist most clearly from the typical medieval tradesman who looked upon his business principally as a means of making a decent living. It was a point of view possible as yet only for merchants trading on a large scale with distant lands. Until the beginning of the modern age, the retail merchants, shopkeepers, and craftsmen who served the local market continued to function within the normal medieval pattern.[1]

The sedentary merchant.   The essential element in the growth of Italian capitalism during the Later Middle Ages was not so much the continued expansion of the volume of trade as the further development of capitalist forms of business organization and the perfecting of techniques for the handling of credit, exchange, and large-scale enterprises. This development was accelerated by the fact that shipping and travel were becoming less hazardous, while competition was becoming more intense. The age of great risks and proportionately high profits was passing. The successful merchants of the fourteenth and fifteenth centuries were forced to substitute close calculation and rational organization for the adventurous opportunism of the first period of expansion. One of the important factors that helped to speed up this change in business practice around the year 1300 was the introduction by the Venetians and Genoese of large galleys for carrying valuable freight. These galleys were seaworthy even in the open ocean, and since they carried both oars and sails, they did not have to wait for a favorable wind to work in and out of port. Moreover, since they usually sailed in fleets and carried large crews, they could repel any piratical attack. From the

beginning of the fourteenth century, galley fleets sailed regularly from Italy to England and Flanders, thereby establishing direct contact with the focal point of northern trade and by-passing the Champagne fairs. They also sailed regularly from Italy to Egypt, Syria, and Constantinople. With relatively safe and regular transportation thus established to both the Middle East and the West, the Italian merchants gradually ceased to travel with their goods, finding it more economical to stay at home in their counting-houses and direct through correspondence the activity of partners or agents abroad. The traveling merchant, so characteristic of medieval trade, was thus replaced in Italy by the sedentary merchant, the prototype of the modern businessman. And like the modern businessman, the Italian merchant of the Later Middle Ages extended the scope of his enterprise by doing much of his business on credit, and by pooling his capital with that of other merchants in various forms of partnership or corporate organization.

Partnerships and firms.   The temporary partnership was one of the commonest devices by which the sedentary merchant extended his activities and divided his risks. Such partnerships enabled him to engage in a wider variety of enterprises than would have been possible on his own capital or credit alone. He thus avoided the danger of entrusting all his eggs to one basket. The normal partnership of this kind consisted of a small group of silent partners, who contributed only their capital, and an active partner who acted as manager and traveled with the goods. At the conclusion of the venture, which was usually a single voyage, the profits would be divided, the active partner being given a fixed share for his services, while the silent partners received shares in proportion to their investments. Though still common, this form of partnership became less frequent toward the end of the fourteenth century as means of communication became more dependable and many merchants preferred to deal directly by correspondence with resident agents in foreign parts. A merchant could thus carry on a variegated business in many parts of the world with greater continuity than the temporary partnerships could permit. The form of organization, however, which offered the maximum advantages of continuity

---

[1] For discussion of typical medieval commerce and industry see above, Chapter 19.

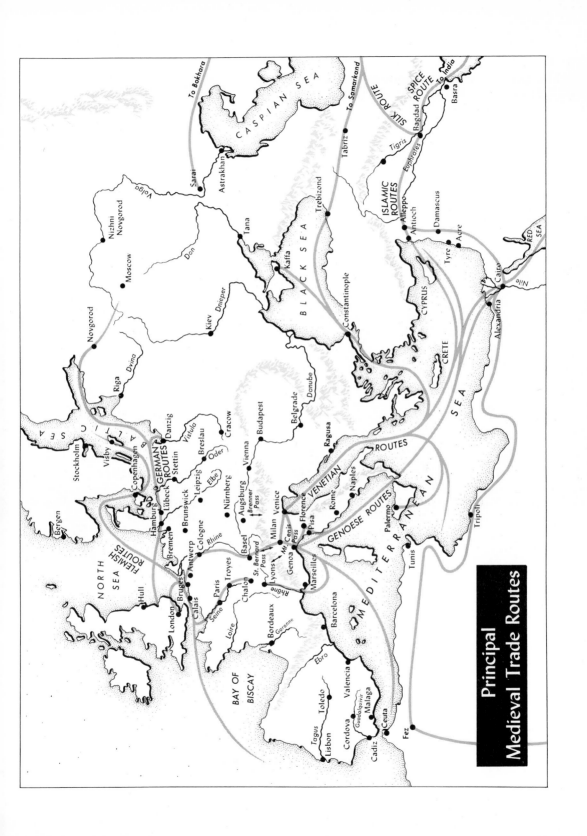

To Bokhara

CASPIAN SEA

SPICE ROUTE

To Samarkand

To India

Bagdad

Basra

SILK ROUTE

Sarai

Astrakhan

Volga

Tabriz

Tigris

Euphrates

ISLAMIC ROUTES

Nizhni Novgorod

Tana

Trebizond

Aleppo

Antioch

Damascus

RED SEA

Moscow

Don

Kaffa

Acre

Tyre

Nile

Cairo

Dnieper

Kiev

BLACK SEA

Constantinople

Alexandria

CYPRUS

Novgorod

CRETE

Riga

Dvina

Danube

M E D I T E R R A N E A N   S E A

BALTIC SEA

Stockholm

Visby

Danzig

Cracow

Budapest

Belgrade

Ragusa

ROUTES

Copenhagen

Stettin

Vistula

Breslau

Vienna

VENETIAN

Naples

GERMAN ROUTES

Lübeck

Oder

Leipzig

Elbe

Nürnberg

Augsburg

Brenner Pass

Milan

Venice

Florence

Rome

Bergen

Hamburg

Bremen

Brunswick

Cologne

Rhine

Basel

St. Bernard Pass

Mt. Cenis Pass

Genoa

Pisa

GENOESE ROUTES

Palermo

NORTH SEA

FLEMISH ROUTES

Antwerp

Bruges

Troyes

Chalon

Lyons

Marseilles

Tripoli

Hull

London

Calais

Paris

Seine

Rhône

Tunis

Loire

Bordeaux

Garonne

Barcelona

BAY OF BISCAY

Ebro

Valencia

Tagus

Toledo

Cordova

Guadalquivir

Malaga

Ceuta

Fez

Lisbon

Cadiz

Principal Medieval Trade Routes

and large operating capital was the family firm. Most of the large operations in international commerce and finance were, in fact, carried on by organizations of this type, consisting of the members of a family group who pooled their resources and worked under the direction of the head of the family. The firm might include relatives by marriage as well as trusted employees who were not actually members of the family. Though acting under the direction of the home office, junior partners frequently took up residence as agents or set up branch offices in the foreign countries with which the firm traded.

Credit, banking, and exchange. Such firms, although essentially commercial, were also active in money-lending, banking, and handling foreign exchange, where a large international organization, reserves of capital, and a well-established reputation were needed. Since a good deal of the business of this period was conducted on borrowed capital, commercial firms and individual merchants were able to keep their surplus capital employed by lending it at interest. The church's prohibition of usury, as lending at interest was called, was still in effect, but there were numerous ways of circumventing it. The doctrine of usury had developed in the pre-capitalist period when there were few opportunities for the profitable investment of money. The theologians who formulated the doctrine, therefore, were not thinking of money borrowed for the purpose of making money. They were thinking chiefly of consumer loans and regarded the charging of high rates of interest for such loans as immoral exploitation of the needs of one's fellow men. With the growth of capitalism this situation changed, but the condemnation of usury was too deeply imbedded in canon law to be abandoned. Merchants who needed borrowed capital, however, found ways of circumventing the letter of the law, and money-lending flourished at interest thinly disguised. In addition to commercial loans, the large firms frequently lent money to kings, princes, popes, and prelates. These were usually large loans, and they often brought in return commercial or other privileges as well as high rates of interest. They might, however, prove hazardous. Two Florentine firms, the Bardi and the Peruzzi, who between them had lent Edward III of England a million and a half gold florins, were forced into bankruptcy when the king repudiated his debts. Most of the firms with foreign branches or associates were also engaged in the profitable business of transferring money from place to place by means of bills of exchange. It was frequently necessary for merchants or governments to convey money quickly and safely to distant countries. They could accomplish this by purchasing a bill of exchange from a banker who had international connections. The bill operated very much like a modern bank draft. The money would be transferred on the banker's books without any actual shipment of coinage, the banker meanwhile making a profit through his expert knowledge of the rates of exchange between countries using different systems of coinage. The Italians, with their far-flung network of branch offices and agencies and their vast experience, were able to hold a virtual monopoly of this lucrative business until almost the end of the fifteenth century.

Bookkeeping. The growing complexity of commercial and financial dealings necessitated much more systematic and accurate bookkeeping than had been needed in the early days of the revival of trade. The sedentary entrepreneurs could not keep their accounts in their heads, as could the traveling merchants or the shopkeepers whose stock in trade was within the reach of their eyes. Credit operations could not be left entirely to the memory and good faith of the parties involved. Above all, partnerships and firms had to keep accurate account of the investment of each member and his share in the profit or loss. The new forms of business thus demanded an ever larger amount of paper work. One Italian merchant left at his death in 1410 some 500 ledgers and more than 150,000 commercial letters of various sorts. During the fourteenth century double-entry bookkeeping gradually replaced single entry and in the following century became standard practice among Italian merchants. The double entry, under debit and credit, applying the basic principle of all modern accounting, served not only to simplify bookkeeping, but also to point directly to profit or loss on each enterprise and so to encourage more careful calculation of risks.

Capital in industry. Opportunities for the investment of capital in industry were considerably more limited than in commerce or finance, since the greater part of industrial production was still carried on by master craftsmen who manufactured goods on a small scale and sold them at retail across the counters of their shops. In a few large industries, however, where the raw material was imported and the bulk of the finished product exported for sale abroad, the merchants who handled the import-export business found it profitable to assume control of the industry, and thus became industrial employers and entrepreneurs. The most important of these were the cloth-weaving industries, not only because of their size, but also because so many different kinds of labor were involved that no one craftsman could complete the process. It was therefore more economical for the merchant who owned the raw material to put it out to a series of workers and pay them wages for their labor. In this way the flourishing woolen and silk-weaving industries of Florence, Lucca, Siena, Genoa, Venice, and other Italian cities had by the beginning of the fourteenth century fallen entirely under the control of merchant capitalists.

The woolen industry in Florence. Florentine wool-weaving furnishes the most notable example during this period of a large capitalist-controlled industry. It grew rapidly once the opening of a sea-route to England enabled the Florentine merchants to import directly the fine English wool which was regarded as essential for the making of cloth of the highest quality. By 1338, according to Giovanni Villani, the Florentine historian who was himself a wool merchant, there were two hundred woolen-cloth manufacturing firms in Florence and some thirty thousand workers, or about one-third of the population of the city. The manufacturers were organized in a special merchant guild, the *Arte di Lana* or wool guild, which completely controlled the industry. The division of labor and the variety of skills involved in the production of fine cloth forced the development of a highly complex form of industrial organization. The raw wool had first to be beaten, washed, and carded in the merchant's warehouse. It had then to be put out to spinners, mostly women who worked in their own homes, to be spun into thread. The thread was then put out to weavers, most of whom also worked at home. From the weavers, the cloth passed in turn to fullers, dyers, stretchers, shearers, finishers, and other

workers with special skills. Throughout the process the merchant employer retained ownership of the material and paid wages, usually by the piece, to the whole series of workers. The Florentine wool guild thus differed essentially from the craft guilds, in which independent artisans completed the manufacture of their product from beginning to end and sold it at retail. The members of the *Arte di Lana* were not master craftsmen, but rather merchant employers, while the workers were not members of the guild, but "subjects" under the guild's authority. The powerful guild could always gain the support of the city government in enforcing its regulations and in preventing the workers from forming any sort of organization to strike for higher wages or better working conditions. The workers, who at the best of times lived on the barest margin of subsistence, seethed with impotent fury against the combination of economic and political power that held them down, and at least once, in 1378, they rose in a wild and briefly successful revolt. The rising of the Ciompi, as the wool workers were called, was, however, doomed to failure from the start and was savagely suppressed.

Social effects of capitalism. Before concluding this discussion of the rise of capitalism in Italy we should note some of the ways in which capitalism affected the social and cultural developments of the age, not only in Italy, but also somewhat later in the other European countries, as they in turn experienced the rise of a capitalist economy. First of all, the growth of capitalist business concentrated wealth in the form of money and credit in the hands of a relatively small class of entrepreneurs. It raised them far above the urban middle class of small merchants, shopkeepers and craftsmen, not only in wealth, but also in social position and political power. The great merchant-banking family of the Medici, for example, rose in the fifteenth century to be rulers of Florence. At the other end of the social scale, industrial capitalism created a new class of propertyless wage-earners, akin to the modern industrial proletariat, who had none of the privileges or security that the medieval guild system guaranteed to the craftsmen. By making it possible for men with inherited wealth to invest their money without themselves participating actively in business, the

"The Banker and His Wife" by the Flemish painter Quentin Matsys is a typical example of Netherlandish art.

growth of capitalist forms of business organization also created a leisured class, the members of which were free to devote themselves to the learned professions, to the cultivation and patronage of literature and the arts, or simply to the enjoyment of life. To this leisured class the Renaissance owed much of its brilliant culture, and it owed an especial debt to those whose great fortunes made it possible for them to patronize and support scholars, poets, musicians, and artists.

2. The Growth of Capitalism in Northern Commerce and Industry

In the countries to the north of the Alps, capitalism developed later and more slowly than in Italy. In general the wealth of the northern countries was drawn largely from agriculture. Most northern cities were essentially market towns, serving the needs of the landholding classes of the surrounding countryside. Small-scale production and sale for a local market could be carried on through guild organization and city regulation much as it had been in the preceding centuries. True, some signs of capitalism were beginning to appear even within the retail guilds, especially in the larger cities. During the long recession

which followed the Black Death, the masters in many guilds set up barriers against the entry of journeymen, other than their own sons or sons-in-law, into mastership so as to avoid undue competition for what remained of the market. Later, when the recovery began and the market was once more expanding, these restrictions were retained, the masters thus taking advantage of their monopoly to expand their individual businesses. As a result, an increasing number of journeymen were forced to remain permanently in the wage-earning class, while the masters became small merchant employers. This, however, represented no more than a kind of semi-capitalism. For the growth of a more genuine capitalism we must consider chiefly those places where there was a large-scale distant trade or where there were large export industries.

The Netherlands: commerce. Throughout the Later Middle Ages, the Netherlands were the focal point to and from which flowed the main lines of northern trade. In the ports of Bruges and Antwerp, spices purchased in Cairo might be exchanged for furs brought from Novgorod, and Rhine wines could be exchanged for English tin. These ports formed the northwestern terminus of the trade carried by Italian galleys from the Mediterranean, and also the southwestern terminus of the trade carried from Scandinavia, North Germany, and Russia by merchants from the cities of the Hanseatic League. They were thus the connecting link in a semicircular trade route that ran from the Levant to the eastern Baltic. They were also the principal outlets for the river-borne trade of northern France and the Rhineland, and to them went the bulk of England's foreign commerce. This international trade brought great wealth to the Netherland cities, but in the Later Middle Ages the merchants of the Netherlands took relatively little part in the carrying trade that radiated from their ports. Instead they conducted a profitable business as brokers or agents for the foreign merchants. This form of business brought prosperity to a fairly large merchant class, but did not as a rule create large fortunes. Even the business of handling foreign exchange, which made Bruges one of the great financial centers of Europe, was left largely to the Italian colony, composed of members of the great Italian banking firms.

Industry. The solid prosperity of the Netherland cities depended even more on industry than on commerce or finance. All through the Middle Ages the Flemish cities, especially Bruges, Ghent, and Ypres, maintained a large wool-weaving industry based on the use of imported English wool. At the beginning of the fourteenth century the Flemish wool workers revolted and gained the right to organize independent guilds to protect their interests. They also secured some share in the city governments. But no political agitation or economic legislation could give the workers economic independence. By its very nature, a large textile industry was doomed to control by merchant employers who put out the wool to be worked up, and paid wages to the workers. Though somewhat better off than the Florentine proletariat, the Flemish wool workers remained in a state of social unrest, and launched violent revolts at intervals throughout the fourteenth century. Toward the end of the century their economic situation was made more desperate by increasing unemployment. The growth of a weaving industry in England, which absorbed more and more of the English wool, caused a decline in the great Flemish industry and finally, in the fifteenth century, reduced it to ruin. Its place

was taken, however, by new textile industries in both Flanders and Brabant, including the making of fine linen cloth, laces, tapestries, and carpets. These new industries, in which no established guilds existed to protect the workers, were organized along completely capitalist lines, being wholly controlled by merchant industrialists. They throve particularly in the towns and cities that had not been great industrial centers in the Middle Ages and so had not the firmly established tradition of economic regulation that existed in old cities like Bruges and Ypres.

England: the wool trade. The economy of England and that of the Netherlands were for centuries closely related because of the paramount importance to both countries of the wool trade. Wool was essential to the old Flemish industry and it was by far the most important of England's export products. It was also an invaluable source of revenue for the government. From the time of Edward I, the English kings placed a heavy tax on exported wool, about one-third of its value, thereby gaining a large part of the cash income needed for war and the expenses of government. As a means of facilitating the collection of the tax, the English kings designated a city in the Netherlands as a "staple" or compulsory market to which all English wool must be exported, thus focusing trade and making it easier to control. They also granted a perpetual monopoly of the wool trade to a company of merchants known as the Merchants of the Staple. This was a "regulated company," that is, an organization of merchants, each of whom traded independently on his own capital, but whose dealings were regulated by the officers of the company. This regulation was regarded as necessary in order to limit the supply, thus keeping the price of wool at the staple high enough to cover the tax.

The cloth industry. An unforeseen result of the staple system was to encourage the growth of a weaving industry in England, since it enabled English manufacturers, who did not have to buy taxed wool, to undersell their Flemish competitors. By the mid-fifteenth century, cloth had almost entirely replaced wool as an export product, and before the end of the century a new regulated company, known as the Company of Merchant Adventurers, was formed to handle the cloth trade with the Netherlands. The growing weaving industry in England was from the beginning controlled by merchant capitalists, but it differed in many ways from the continental industries. Since wool was not an imported product, but was grown in many parts of the country, the industry was widely scattered. There were no great weaving cities in England in this period. Wool dealers bought up wool locally and put it out to spinners and weavers in the small towns or villages in the neighborhood. Though the total volume of cloth manufactured in England in the fifteenth century surpassed the production of either Flanders or Italy, the conditions under which the English industry operated prevented the growth of large individual enterprises. The wool manufacturers enjoyed a solid prosperity, mute evidence of which can still be seen in the magnificent churches they built in what are now mere country villages. But they did not as a rule make large fortunes or become financiers. Moreover, most of them did not themselves take part in the export trade, but rather sold their cloth in London or other ports to merchants who made a second profit by selling it abroad.

The London companies.   During this period the foreign trade of England was concentrated increasingly in the city of London. Though a good deal of it was still handled by foreigners, especially Italians and the German merchants from the Hanseatic cities, the greater part had been taken over by English merchants well before the end of the fifteenth century. These merchants imported wine from Gascony and a great variety of manufactured goods from the Netherlands; in return they exported wool, cloth, tin, iron, and pewter utensils. Medieval London was a guild-ridden city and membership in a guild was essential for the conduct of business. With the growth of foreign trade abroad, however, the character of the greater guilds began to change. Wholesale merchants were no longer restricted to dealing in the goods from which their guild took its name. The vintners still handled most of the wine trade, the fishmongers still specialized more or less in fish, the grocers in spices and drugs, and the mercers in silk, fine fabrics, and other luxury imports. But members of any of these guilds might import or export any goods that

promised a profit, and they all dealt in cloth. Meanwhile, within the merchant guilds a clear distinction was growing up between the wholesalers, who practiced all the techniques of capitalist enterprise, and the small retail shopkeepers. Before the end of the fifteenth century the wholesalers had formed separate organizations within a dozen or so of the more important guilds. These were known as "livery companies" because their members wore a special and expensive costume or livery on public occasions. Thanks to their wealth and corporate organization, the "merchants of the livery" were able to control the policies of the guild and reduce the poorer shopkeepers to subjection.

Hanseatic commerce.   A somewhat similar combination of individual capitalist enterprise with corporate regulation, though on a larger scale, was to be found among the North German merchants of the Hanseatic League. The rise of this great league of cities as a political and economic force, which dominated northern commerce for more than two centuries, has already been noted in Chapter 21.[1] The main axis of Hanseatic trade ran northeast from Bruges and London, in both of which cities the Hansards had their own independently organized communities, through the North Sea and the Baltic to Novgorod in Russia, with side branches into Scandinavia and North Germany. Eastbound, the big Hansard sailing ships carried cloth, metal wares, wine, spices, and manufactured goods of various sorts. On the return trip they carried raw materials from the north: timber, pitch, tar, grain, furs, wax, and, most valuable of all, the dried herring which fed a large part of Europe during Lent and on the days of abstinence prescribed by the church. Acting as middlemen in this trade between distant places, the merchants of such centrally located cities as Hamburg and Lübeck worked out forms of business organization and methods of handling capital similar in many respects to those adopted by the Italians under much the same circumstances. The typical Hanseatic businessman was a sedentary merchant, who directed the activity of junior partners or agents abroad from his home office, organized partnerships and firms, operated on credit and kept account

[1] See above, pages 267–268.

books. The Hansards, however, were much less free from regulation than were the Italians. The League maintained strict discipline and regulated all the activities of its members. Hanseatic capitalism, moreover, was less complex than the Italian, since it depended exclusively on commerce and was not extended to include industry or very much in the way of banking or finance.

South German capitalists. Toward the end of the fifteenth century a more extensive and complex form of capitalist enterprise developed in Augsburg, Nürnberg, and other South German cities, largely as a result of a boom in copper and silver mining in the neighboring mountain country. During the Middle Ages, small independent miners had exhausted the veins of ore that could be reached easily from the surface, and after the middle of the fourteenth century production had fallen off. What was needed to revive it was the investment of sufficient capital to pay for the labor required to sink deep shafts and for the machinery to keep them drained and in working condition. This capital was furnished in the second half of the fifteenth century by commercial family firms, which had grown prosperous from the trade that flowed through Augsburg along the overland route from Venice north to Leipzig and the Baltic ports. Once the copper and silver mines had been put into profitable production, the next step was to organize and control the smelting and metal-working industries and the sale of the finished products. All the various branches of the metal industries thus tended to come under the control of a few great firms of merchant industrialists, while miners and metal-workers tended to lose their independence and sink to the position of a wage-earning proletariat. Interest in mining also involved these firms in state finance. The German princes, including the Hapsburg emperors, claimed certain "regalian" rights over all mines situated on their lands. These were profitable rights, and the princes, who were perennially in need of ready cash, were frequently willing to turn them over to financiers as security for loans. The great firms with mining interests were thus forced to become money-lenders on a large scale to the German princes, and from there went on to banking and finance operations on an international

This picture of St. Joseph at work as a carpenter was painted by the Master of Flémalle, one of the great founders of fifteenth-century Flemish painting. A finely detailed view of the city can be seen through the window of the shop.

scale comparable to those of the great Italian houses.

The Fuggers. Of the dozen or so great South German firms which rose to international prominence in the last years of the fifteenth and the beginning of the sixteenth century, the Fuggers were the most famous, though two other Augsburg firms, the Welsers and the Hochstetters, controlled enterprises

Jacob Fugger the Rich with his bookkeeper appears in a painting done by the bookkeeper, Matthäus Schwartz, himself, in 1516. The cabinet in the background bears the names of the cities where branch-offices of the great Augsburg firm were located.

almost as large and widespread. The great period of Augsburg finance coincided fairly closely with the lifetime of Jacob Fugger the Rich (1459–1525), under whose direction the family became the wealthiest in Europe, with a capital of some two million gold gulden. Driven by an insatiable thirst for profit, Jacob expanded the area of the firm's activity, opening branches in Venice, Rome, Lisbon, Antwerp, Lyons, and other centers, and dealing in commodities of all kinds, in international exchange, and in public and private loans. In 1519 he lent Charles V the half million gold florins that enabled him to bribe the Electors and win the imperial title. For a time

after the death of Jacob the Rich, the Fuggers and other Augsburg firms continued to prosper, but then a decline set in and most of them ended in bankruptcy. The influx of silver from the New World broke the boom in South German mining, and too many of the loans made to kings and princes were never repaid.

Capital and government. Aside from lending money to royal governments, the new capitalists found many ways in which service to kings could be profitable. In the Later Middle Ages, the rulers of the consolidated territorial states were using every means to increase their revenues by taxation, but the expenses of war and government and the cost of maintaining a splendid court were also rising. Government, in short, was becoming a big business, and neither kings nor nobles had the training to handle complex financial problems with any degree of efficiency. It was natural, then, that rulers should turn for aid to the merchants and bankers whose success in business was a guarantee of their financial ability. And it was perhaps equally natural that many of the businessmen who became finance ministers of the crown should take advantage of their position to increase their own private fortunes by means that would not stand too close investigation. Aside from pure graft, there were fortunes to be made from army contracts, from purchasing supplies for the court, from farming taxes and from numerous other more or less legitimate uses of political influence. The spectacular career of Jacques Coeur (1395–1456), the wealthiest merchant of fifteenth-century France, furnishes a classic example of the opportunities — and risks — that royal service might offer an aspiring financier. Coeur had already made a great fortune by a wide variety of investments in Mediterranean commerce, copper and silver mining, money-lending, and banking before he became for fifteen years master of the mint and royal treasurer to Charles VII. In this position his fortune increased notably, but eventually he fell from royal favor, having perhaps lent the king too much money. He was condemned on a number of charges, for which there was apparently little foundation, and imprisoned. His wealth was confiscated by the king, who thus rid himself of his largest creditor, wiped out his debt, and filled his treasury in one shady transaction.

3. *The Break-up of the Manorial System*

The manorial system, as described in Chapter 13,[1] took shape during the Early Middle Ages, at a time when there was little regular commerce, when city life had almost disappeared, and money had ceased to circulate freely. The manor was therefore designed to be as far as possible a self-sufficient economic unit, and to operate without money-rents or wages. These basic conditions, which had brought the manor into existence, began to change, however, when the revival of commerce in the eleventh century led to the restoration of city markets and money economy. In the following centuries the manor gradually ceased to be a self-sufficient unit isolated from the world about it. Both the peasants and the lords' agents sold produce in the city markets, so that money entered the manorial system and gradually changed its internal organization. The change, however, was so slow as to be almost imperceptible, for the peasants were inherently conservative and loath to alter their ways. Their communal life was bound by custom, its rhythm set by the slow progression of the seasons. The manorial structure thus outlived the conditions that had made it necessary. There were many signs of its disintegration in the twelfth and thirteenth centuries, but it was not until the Later Middle Ages that it changed so fundamentally as to be no longer recognizable.

Demesne farming abandoned. The demesne was the heart of the early medieval manor. This was the land the lord reserved for his own use, and from his point of view the whole system existed primarily as a means of securing unpaid labor for it. When city markets emerged, the demesne became important as a source of cash income as well as of food, and in some places during the twelfth and thirteenth centuries there was something like a boom in demesne farming. To make the demesne pay, however, required careful management, and few feudal lords were good managers, even when they were at home, which was seldom. Actual management of the

[1] See above, pages 154–157.

demesne was, as a rule, left to a bailiff who could not always be trusted. Under these circumstances many lords found it convenient to lease out parts of the demesne to tenants in return for a cash rent. This process, already begun in the thirteenth century, was greatly accelerated in the fourteenth, especially after the Black Death, when the shortage of labor made demesne farming more difficult. Wages rose sharply in the second half of the century, and it became almost impossible to keep peasants who still owed labor services from running away in search of free land or better conditions elsewhere. Within a century after the Black Death, demesne farming had almost entirely disappeared in England and in many parts of the Continent, and the lord of the manor had become simply a landlord, living on the rents paid by his tenants. When this happened, one of the essential elements of the manorial system had disappeared.

Labor services commuted. The gradual abandonment of demesne farming was accompanied by the commutation of the labor services —week work and boon work — which the unfree peasants owed their lord as payment for the use of the land they held in the common fields. While the population was growing fairly rapidly, as it was in the thirteenth century, some lords found it profitable to commute labor services to money payments and use the money to hire poor landless peasants, who would work full time and for low wages. This may have been a good bargain for the lords at the time, but later, when labor was scarce and wages high, they would have been better off if they had retained the services owed them. By then, however, it was very difficult, if not impossible, to reclaim labor services that had been commuted, and difficult enough to enforce those that were still owed. Commutation, then, was one of the reasons why demesne farming was abandoned in the years following the Black Death. On the other hand, when lords ceased to farm part of the demesne their need for labor services decreased proportionately and the only sensible course was to commute them to money payments. It is clear that both processes were at work and contributed to the disruption of the old system, but it is not always clear which was cause and which effect.

Serfs emancipated. When the labor services owed by an unfree tenant were thus commuted, he had taken a long step in the direction of obtaining his freedom. Not only was he relieved of the most onerous and degrading duties resulting from his servile status, but thereafter it was much less important to his lord to keep him in bondage. The lord could still require from his serfs or villeins the payment of heriot or merchet and other servile dues,[1] but once he had lost his claim on their labor he could more easily be persuaded to sell them their freedom for a lump sum or for an addition to the rent they owed him for their land. In this way serfdom disappeared in England, except for occasional rare instances, before the end of the fifteenth century, and though there were still serfs in France and Germany, they were no more than a small minority. The advantages of freedom, however, were often more spiritual than material. The emancipated serf was not necessarily richer, and he was often less secure. But freedom was a boon that could not be measured in economic terms.

Peasant conditions. On the whole, the economic condition of the peasants, as well as their legal status, seems to have been improving during these last centuries of the Middle Ages. The labor shortage that followed the Black Death put the peasant in a strong bargaining position. The commutation of services to fixed payments also worked to the peasants' ultimate advantage because of a persistent decline in the value of money, due to debasement of the coinage in most of the European countries. Peasants, therefore, who owed fixed payments rather than labor services were actually paying less and less rent for their land. But improvement in the peasants' lot was neither steady nor uniform. In a transitional period of this kind it was inevitable that while some profited others should suffer. Perhaps the most significant result of the break-up of the manorial structure was that the more fortunate or more enterprising peasants were able to increase their holdings and become prosperous farmers, while those less fortunate or less able lost their land and sank to the position of hired laborers. Certain it is that the dislocation of the old system created a great deal of social unrest, as much among those who were impatient because improvement was so slow as among those who actually suffered from the changing conditions. The Peasants' Revolt of 1381 in England was but one of many similar expressions of agrarian unrest during these centuries.

Landlords impoverished. The system of fixed rents paid in coinage of declining value, which worked to the advantage of the peasants, was naturally to the disadvantage of the landlords. Eventually many of them would find ways of adjusting the balance in their favor, but during these transitional centuries the landholding class in general was becoming increasingly impoverished. The disintegration of the manor also weakened the social position of the lords by cutting the ties that bound their people to them. There was a vast difference between the position of the medieval lord of the manor, who was monarch of all he surveyed, and the mere landlord, who lived off the rents his agents collected. Moreover, once the manor had ceased to be a closely knit unit, impoverished lords were frequently tempted to sell or mortgage their land and their rights bit by bit. And the purchaser, more often than not, was a wealthy burgher who welcomed the opportunity to rise in the social scale by becoming a country gentleman.

---

[1] See above, page 157.

"Greeting: — It is possible that some word of me may have come to you, though even this is doubtful, since an insignificant and obscure name will scarcely penetrate far in either time or space." • Francesco Petrarch (1304–74), Letter to Posterity

25

The Age of the Renaissance in Italy

In the two and a half centuries between the last of the crusades and the beginning of the Lutheran Reformation, there occurred a profound, if gradual, transformation in the character of European civilization. It was an age of transition in which medieval institutions were slowly crumbling and characteristically medieval ways of thinking were losing their force, while at the same time evidences of modern society and modern culture began to make their appearance, at first in partial form, but, as time passed, with ever-increasing completeness. In Italy, the land of wealth and cities, this change began earlier and progressed with greater rapidity than in the more thoroughly feudalized lands north of the Alps. Moreover, in that land of golden opportunities, of political unrest and swiftly shifting fortunes, the break-up of medieval civilization seemed to give a new and stimulating freedom to the human spirit, so that the age of transition became also an age of great intellectual activity. New vistas opened up before the eager curiosity and limitless ambition of men who were shaking themselves free from the bondage of ecclesiastical authority and corporate society. They awoke to a new appreciation of the glories of the mortal world they lived in, with its unbounded possibilities for wealth, power, artistic pleasure, and intellectual satisfaction for those who had the will to seize them. Finally, on this rich soil, provided by the awakened genius of the Italian people, fell the seeds of antique culture, to bring forth such

plentiful fruit that for centuries men thought of that age as a *renaissance* or rebirth of the civilization of ancient Rome and Greece. But the culture of the Italian Renaissance (we may as well keep the word, since it has been hallowed by centuries of use) did not owe its existence primarily to the revival of antiquity, though it was influenced by it. Its roots were fixed firmly in the Middle Ages; but the conditions of its growth were changing, and the fruit was not always the same. So far as it can be defined, the age of the Renaissance was an age of chaotic change, in which there was much that was still medieval, much that was recognizably modern, and much also that was peculiar to itself. It bridged the gap between the High Middle Ages and modern times, but it was also a cultural period in its own right, filled with a great political, social, and intellectual ferment.

1. Renaissance Society

Urban society. The society of the Italian Renaissance was essentially urban, for, to a degree unparalleled elsewhere in Europe, Italy was a land of cities, and her wealth was founded upon an urban rather than an agricultural economy. We have already noted in the preceding chapter the way in which the geographical position of Italy made her the commercial center of medieval Europe. Under the impulse of the commercial revival, cities had sprung up quickly during the High Middle Ages in Lombardy, Tuscany, and the States of the Church. Early in their history they had formed communal governments, and during the twelfth and thirteenth centuries they took advantage of the long quarrel between the emperors and the popes to secure freedom from imperial control. Before the beginning of the Renaissance most of the cities of central and northern Italy were already practically independent city-states, dominating the country districts around them. They thus became the centers of political and social as well as economic life for the whole land. The feudal nobles could not resist their attraction. Leaving their isolated rural castles, they moved into the cities and became the neighbors of the non-noble burghers. In this urban society, in which all classes were represented, medieval class distinctions inevitably became less pronounced. Birth still meant a great deal, but wealth or political power might mean more; and where these were lacking, literary, artistic, or any other outstanding ability was sufficient to gain an entry into the homes of the noble or the rich.

The secular spirit.   The changes in society brought about by wealth and city life were reflected by equally significant changes in the interests and mental attitude of at least the wealthy and leisured classes. The methods of capitalism demanded literacy of all who engaged in business, while the wealth it produced enabled an increasingly large number of laymen to secure a good education. To a far greater extent than had been possible in the Middle Ages, laymen participated actively in literature and learning, and their worldly interests added to the secular content of Renaissance culture. At the same time, the busy life of the cities, the new possibilities for the enjoyment of life and for the satisfaction of aesthetic tastes or intellectual curiosity, provided by luxury, wealth, and leisure, all tended to thrust thoughts of religion and of the future world farther into the background of men's minds. The growing disrespect for the papacy and the organized church, due to the scandals of the Babylonian Captivity and the schism, also did something to heighten this tendency. But more important than these in breaking the dominating force of religion were the manifold distractions and worldly interests inseparable from the society of the age. The men of the Renaissance, however, were seldom really irreligious. Few if any were atheists or even

unorthodox. Perhaps they had merely fallen into that "forgetfulness of God in time of prosperity" against which medieval preachers were wont to warn their flocks. Certainly the world and the flesh had no terrors for this generation, even though they might still fear the devil. This is what is meant by the "secular spirit" of the Renaissance men who threw themselves heart and soul into the full enjoyment and eager exploration of the world about them.

Individualism.   In this vital urban society men awoke to a new consciousness of themselves as individuals. Of the modern characteristics that were making their appearance in this chaotic age of transition, few are more significant or more difficult to define than the individualism that so many historians have noted as a contrast to the corporate or class consciousness of medieval society. Men, of course, have always known that they were individuals. But in the stratified society of the Middle Ages, where social status depended on membership in a closed corporation, whether guild, monastery, or manor, or on rank in the feudal system, men were inevitably more conscious of their ordained place in the scheme of things than of their own individual personalities. As the medieval social structure began to crumble, however, careers were thrown open to talent. In the rapidly shifting politics of the Italian cities, nobility of birth was not essential to power; the new capitalistic methods of business enabled some men to accumulate wealth far beyond their fellows; and the generous partonage of art raised low-born artists high above the level of the ordinary artisan. There seemed no limit to what any man might accomplish, aided only by fortune and his own ability. In the new secular spirit, too, men found a double incentive for the full development of their individual powers. Immortal fame in this world came to seem more important than immortal life in the next; and the eager enjoyment of all that this world had to offer stimulated men to the development of all sides of their personalities, so as to wring the maximum of experience or pleasure out of life.

The ideal of the complete personality.   This new realization of individual potentialities brought to life a new social ideal — that of the well-rounded personality — to take the place of the medieval ideal of the man who perfectly represented the qualities of his class or group. It was an ideal that found practical expression in the amazing versatility that characterized so many Italians in the fifteenth century. Statesmen like Cosimo and Lorenzo de' Medici, the bankers who ruled Florence, soldier-despots like Duke Federigo of Urbino, and businessmen like the Florentine Palla Strozzi were also scholars and cultured patrons of the arts, while innumerable examples might be cited of artists who practiced painting, sculpture, and architecture with equal facility and still found time for the pursuit of scholarship and philosophy. And this versatility of interest was not limited to men of unusual genius. The average man of culture now sought consciously to acquire at least an adequate familiarity with all branches of human activity so as to develop his personality to its fullest extent. In the schools conducted by Guarino (1374–1460) at Ferrara and Vittorino da Feltre (1378–1446) at Mantua, the practice of arms and all forms of athletics, music, and courtly manners, as well as a thorough training in the arts and classical literature, were included among the things that a gentleman should know. The Renaissance, indeed, produced a new standard for the gentleman or courtier. As Baldassare Castiglione (1478–1529), himself a paragon of courtiers, tells us in his charming *Book of the Courtier,* the man who would make his way successfully into the highest ranks of society must now be not merely, or necessarily, nobly born, though that is an advantage, nor a great warrior, though he should be skilled in arms, but a fully developed personality, an amateur of all arts and all branches of learning and a master of some, possessing, above all, grace, tact, good manners, and personal charm. The contrast between the boisterous and often brutal manners of a Richard the Lion-hearted and the wide education and sensitive *finesse* of a Castiglione marks the development from the medieval to the modern ideal of a gentleman.

Violent contrasts. So far, as seems inevitable in dealing with the Renaissance, we have dwelt chiefly on the highlights of the age, the signs of progress and the evidences of modern tendencies. But there were also deep shadows, and the evolution away from medieval conditions was not always a progress toward higher standards. The age of the Renaissance in Italy was above all an age of confusion and con-

Baldassare Castiglione, the cultivated gentleman whose Book of the Courtier *set a pattern for the courtly society of the Renaissance, is portrayed here in a painting by Raphael.*

trast in politics, in religion, in morality, and in individual characters. Medieval and modern characteristics existed side by side in the same society or the same person, producing violent contradictions and startling incongruities. As the fifteenth century drew to a close, the people of Florence, who for years had followed the leadership of Lorenzo de' Medici, most cultured and worldly of statesmen, fell suddenly under the spell of the ascetic monk, Savonarola (1452–98), only to react again in a short time and burn their former idol. The despots, who ruled by force and cunning, recognized the binding power of no law, human or divine. The eager development of all man's faculties meant only too often the development of the baser as well as the higher instincts. Princes like the Visconti of Milan might combine inhuman cruelty with the most delicate appreciation of art, and artists like Benvenuto Cellini (1500–1570) might be little better than thugs in their private lives. The most enlightened and rational of Italian statesmen guided their policies by the auguries of charlatan astrologers. In every court in Italy the veneer of refined and learned society covered dark stains of immorality, and lavish magnificence paraded the streets of every city in glaring contrast to the most wretched poverty.

All that has been said about the Renaissance did not, of course, occur at once, nor would it all be true of any one time. The age of the Renaissance evolved slowly and was constantly changing. In the remainder of this chapter, we shall trace the historical developments of the age in politics, literature, music, and art in an attempt to place the whole in its proper historical perspective.

2. Evolution of the Italian States to 1494

Italy in the fourteenth century.   The Italian Renaissance was born in the midst of political chaos. The history of Italy in the fourteenth century is the history of confusion thrice confounded. As a nation in the political sense, Italy did not yet exist. Only in the southern kingdom of Naples was there any political unity. The rest of the peninsula was divided into a host of petty city-states, which had acquired almost complete independence from the overlordship of emperor or pope. Each of these states was torn by hostile factions and was frequently at war with its neighbors. The traditional feud between the Guelf and Ghibelline parties gives some slight coherence to Italian politics in this century, but that ancient quarrel had lost almost all of its original meaning in the tangle of local interests and antagonisms. Cities fought each other for control of trade routes or merely to destroy commercial rivals; country districts rebelled against domination by the cities; and within the cities classes and parties fought for control of the government, and mercenary soldiers fished happily in the troubled waters.

Rise of the despots.   In the midst of this confusion, two general tendencies may be observed: first, the destruction of republican governments at the hands of despots, and second, the expansion of the larger city-states at the expense of the less powerful ones. The first of these, indeed, was well under way at the beginning of the fourteenth century. Nearly all the cities of northern and central Italy had begun their independent career as republican communes dominated more or less by an upper class of mixed merchant and noble families. Toward the end of the thirteenth century, the power of this old ruling class was challenged by the newly rich capitalists and also by the middle class of craftsmen and shopkeepers, so that class warfare and frequent revolutions threatened to destroy the internal peace and order that were essential to the prosperity of business. The only possible solution of the problem seemed to be the government of the city by a dictator or despot, who would be strong enough to keep order and who would impose peace at the cost of political liberty. Some few states, like Venice and Florence, escaped actual despotism, but they were scarcely more democratic, since their government was controlled by a small group of wealthy families. The manner in which the despots acquired their absolute power differed, of course, from place to place. Some turned a temporary authority, legally delegated to them as officers of the state, into an extra-legal power; others were mercenary soldiers or local feudal lords who seized the government by force of arms; while still others used their wealth to gain control of the republican governmental machine.

Character of the despots.   The despots, like men of any other class, differed widely in character, but certain characteristics were common to almost all of them. They were mostly men of unusual ability and force of character, for only so could they have risen to power without the support of legal or constitutional claims. They regarded themselves as above the law, and having broken with all traditional forms of government, they were free to reorganize the state to make it serve their own wealth and power. They had, indeed, something of the calculating spirit which characterized the new capitalist entrepreneurs. They were often ruthless, cruel, and treacherous, because they had to rule by force and through fear. Nevertheless, they frequently gave their cities a wiser and more stable government than these had enjoyed under the old republican communes. As Machiavelli pointed out in his justly celebrated handbook for despots, *The Prince* (1513), it was to the interest of the despot himself to maintain the prosperity of the city he ruled, and no despot could rule for long

SWISS CONFEDERATION

DUCHY
DUCHY OF
OF Milan
Padua
Turin Pavia Venice
SAVOY MILAN M. OF
MANTUA Po
SALUZZO D. OF
FERRARA
GENOA D. OF MODENA Ravenna
Genoa Bologna
REP. OF LUCCA REP. OF Rimini
Florence
Pisa Arno FLORENCE Urbino
Siena STATES Assisi
REP. OF
SIENA OF THE

VENETIAN REPUBLIC

DALMATIA

ADRIATIC SEA

CORSICA
(TO GENOA) CHURCH
Tiber Rome

THE KINGDOM
OF
Naples
Salerno Bari
KINGDOM NAPLES
OF SARDINIA

Palermo

KINGDOM OF
SICILY

Italy, C. 1494

unless he did so. Most of the despots were intelligent enough to realize that they must win the respect, and, in some measure, the gratitude, of their people. It was this desire, as well as genuine love of culture, that caused so many of them to gather poets, scholars, and artists to their courts by the promise of generous rewards. No small part of the artistic and literary glory of the Renaissance was due to their liberal and remarkably discriminating patronage.

Condottieri. Still the despots could neither have won nor held their power had not the people of Italy generally lost the ability or desire to fight in defense of their liberties. The responsible citizens were too busy with profitable business to waste time in military training, and no republican party government, nor for that matter any despot, could afford to take the risk of revolution involved in arming the lesser populace. The Italian states, therefore, were forced to depend on mercenary soldiers from outside for defense against foreign enemies and to keep down rebellion among discontented citizens or the disaffected subjects of the conquered towns and country. These mercenary soldiers were organized in large bands under their own leaders, called *condottieri,* who sold the services of the whole band to the highest bidder. For the *condottieri* war was a business enterprise, and they conducted it solely for the sake of profit. They did not care for whom they fought or why, so long as they were paid. Their chief interest was to keep the war going as long as possible, for peace meant unemployment. In the main they seem to have been fairly good soldiers, though Machiavelli criticized them severely, but their methods were behind the times. The temporary nature of their employment made it impossible for the *condottieri* to train large bands of infantry. They had to depend largely on cavalry although the terrain of Italy is for the most part unsuited to cavalry tactics. They resorted, therefore, to endless marches and countermarches, maneuvering for position, and they were always more dangerous to noncombatants than to one another. It was a vicious system, and not the least of its evils was that it left Italy without any really adequate defense against foreign invaders from the great territorial states of Europe.

This bust of Niccolò Machiavelli gives a vivid impression of the great Florentine political theorist; it is also a fine example of sculpture in terra cotta.

Expansion of states. The second general tendency in the history of Italy during this period — the expansion of the greater states at the expense of the less powerful ones — began later than the rise of the despots and was not completed till the fifteenth century. But by 1454, the year in which the Peace of Lodi ended the long conflict between Venice and Milan, it had progressed so far that only five great states and some three or four lesser ones remained of the scores that had dotted the map of Italy at the beginning of the Renaissance. The five great states were the duchy of Milan, the republics of Venice and Florence, the States of the Church, and the kingdom of Naples. Of the lesser states, the republics of Siena and Lucca still maintained their independence in southern Tuscany, as did the marquisate of Mantua and the duchies of Ferrara and Modena, both in the hands of the Este family. In the States of the Church, too, there were still some practically independent little city-states, ruled for the most part by despots, but they were soon to be suppressed by the popes Alexander VI and Julius II.

An attempt to trace the history of each of the original Italian states would be neither possible in the space at our command nor particularly profitable. We will limit our attention, therefore, to the development of those great states which survived.

Milan. All through the Middle Ages, Milan had been the wealthiest and most powerful of the numerous cities in the rich Lombard plain which commands the Alpine passes to northern Europe. In the twelfth century it led the Lombard League in the struggle for independence from imperial control. Like its neighbors, however, Milan lost its freedom to a despotic ruler at the dawn of the Renaissance. In 1311, Matteo Visconti, head of a Ghibelline family already powerful in the city, established a lasting dictatorship with the approval of the Emperor Henry VII, who gave him the title of Imperial Vicar. He also began the expansion of the city-state by the conquest of several neighboring towns. The great period of Milanese expansion, however, did not begin till the reign of Giangaleazzo Visconti (1378–1402). This cunning and unscrupulous despot succeeded in conquering nearly the whole of Lombardy and seriously threatened Tuscany and the States of the Church. He also won international recognition for his family by purchasing from the Emperor Wenceslas the title of Duke of Milan (1395) and by marrying his daughter Valentina to Louis of Orléans, the son of Charles V of France. After the death of Giangaleazzo, much of his newly conquered territory was lost; and during the next half-century his sons, Giovanni Maria (1402–12) and Filippo Maria (1412–47), had to wage an almost constant war against Venice and its allies to defend what was left of their heritage. When Filippo Maria died, his duchy included only the western half of Lombardy. He was the last Visconti duke, having left no heirs except an illegitimate daughter who had married the vigorous, common-born *condottiere,* Francesco Sforza. The citizens of Milan took advantage of the situation to re-establish republican government, but they had lost the ability to rule themselves and within three years Sforza had made himself Duke of Milan (1450–66). Four years later he made peace with Venice, and from then on almost to the last year of the century the house of Sforza ruled Milan in comparative peace, making it one of the richest states in Italy, as well as a center of art and learning to which men of genius resorted gladly.

Venice. To the east of Lombardy the great merchant city of Venice, built out over her lagoons, commanded the Adriatic Sea. Since the first revival of medieval commerce, Venice had been one of the richest cities in Europe. Her geographical position made her the natural middleman in the trade between the eastern Mediterranean and western Europe, while the lagoons which cut her off from the mainland gave her a security that enabled her to stand aloof from the tangled feuds of Italian politics. Moreover, unlike the other Italian republics, Venice had evolved a stable system of government that prevented revolutions and party strife. Since the thirteenth century the mass of the people had been excluded entirely from the government, which was monopolized by an oligarchy of wealthy families. From these the doge (a life president) was elected, as were also the grand council, the senate, and the powerful Council of Ten, who, after 1310, kept check on the doge and senate. This political stability enabled Venice to recover from a desperate struggle with her trade rival, Genoa, in the fourteenth century, whereas Genoa was left so badly shaken that it fell under the domination, first of France, then of Milan. The beginning of the fifteenth century marks a decided turning point in the history of the republic. Alarmed by the Visconti conquest of Lombardy, the Venetians determined to abandon their aloof position among their lagoons and to acquire territory on the mainland that would protect the city from its too powerful neighbor, and would keep open the routes to the Alpine passes which were so necessary to Venetian commerce. After conquering Padua, famous for its ancient university, in 1405, the republic's forces moved on into Visconti territory. The long war which followed was fought chiefly by mercenaries, and the superior wealth of the merchant city was the deciding factor. When the final peace treaty was signed at Lodi with the new Sforza Duke of Milan in 1454, Venice ruled a mainland state in eastern Lombardy and around the head of the Adriatic as large as, or larger than, that of its rival Milan.

Florence. On the western coast of Italy, to the south of Lombardy, lies the district of Tuscany, bounded on the east and south by the

Lorenzo de' Medici, called "the Magnificent," poet, patron, and uncrowned prince of Florence, was one of the most striking figures of the Renaissance. This terra cotta bust, by Verrocchio, is now in the National Gallery, Washington.

States of the Church. All this territory, except Siena and Lucca, was gradually brought under the rule of the expanding republic of Florence, which conquered even the great mercantile city of Pisa in 1406. Florence had grown tremendously rich from its woolen and other industries. It was also one of the greatest banking centers of Europe and was, besides, the recognized leader of Italy in all branches of culture. But despite their unusually high level of intelligence and the amazingly large number of men of genius to be found among them, the people of Florence had never succeeded in working out a sound republican constitution. All through the fourteenth century and the first part of the fifteenth, the city was a prey to frequent revolutions or party feuds and was dominated most of the time by a small group of wealthy families. This system caused so much disturbance and injustice that in 1434 the majority of the Florentine people accepted without protest the control of their government by Cosimo de' Medici, the head of a great banking family which was to rule the city for the next sixty years. Florence remained

a republic in form, but Cosimo and his successors were in reality its despotic rulers, though they held no official title and merely controlled the republican machinery from behind the scenes, rather after the fashion of a modern American municipal boss. On the death of Cosimo after thirty years of wise government that won him the title of *Pater Patriae* (father of his country), he was followed by his son Piero (1464–69). Under Piero's rather uncertain guidance the power of the Medici seemed to be slipping, but it was fully restored by his brilliant son Lorenzo "the Magnificent" (1469–92). With Lorenzo the prestige of the Medici name reached its highest point. He was a man of complex character and versatile genius, at once poet, patron of art and learning, statesman and diplomat. It was in no small measure due to his diplomatic skill that Italy was kept in a state of relative peace during his lifetime. His son Piero, however, proved unfit to carry on the family tradition. His weakness in dealing with the French invasion of 1494 roused the Florentine people to drive the Medici out of the city, though they were to return later.

The States of the Church. The States of the Church stretched clear across central Italy and included the Romagna, which extended up the eastern coast beyond Ravenna. This large territory was in theory ruled by the pope, but during the Babylonian Captivity and the schism petty despots had set up practically independent governments in nearly every city except Rome, and even there the popes were none too secure. After the schism was ended by the Council of Constance (1417), the fifteenth-century popes had to face the problem of bringing these independent lords to obedience, no easy task since most of them were professional *condottieri*. Greater progress might have been made had not some of the popes been more eager to replace these despots by members of their own families than to subject them to papal rule. Engrossed in these family and political interests, the Renaissance popes became more and more worldly until there was little to distinguish them from the other Italian princes. They formed diplomatic alliances, made and broke treaties, and hired armies of mercenaries for wars of conquest or defense. Like the other princes, too, they kept up a luxurious court and spent huge sums of money on magnificent buildings and in the patronage of artists and scholars. Nicholas V (1447–55), who founded the Vatican Library, and Pius II (1458–64) were enthusiastic devotees of the revived classical literature. The latter, indeed, had gained an international reputation as a classical scholar under his own name of Aeneas Silvius before he became pope, though afterward he did rather repent his devotion to pagan letters. His successor, Paul II (1464–71), had reasonably sound ideals, though he was unable to put them very successfully into practice; but the three following pontificates showed a steady decline in papal morality. Sixtus IV (1471–84) and Innocent VIII (1484–92) had no interest beyond the advancement of their numerous nephews and children, and at the end of the century the infamous Borgia pope, Alexander VI (1492–1503), reduced the papacy to the lowest depths of degradation. The reign of the Borgia, however, did much to strengthen the States of the Church politically. Alexander's vigorous son Cesare Borgia at last succeeded in reducing the greater part of the States to obedience, thus enabling the warlike Julius II (1503–13) to complete the task and build up a strong secular state. Under the latter pope and his successor, the Medicean Leo X (1513–21), the golden age of the artistic Renaissance cast over Rome a sunset light shortly to be followed by gathering shadows.

Naples. All of Italy south of the States of the Church was included in the kingdom of Naples, to which at times the kingdom of Sicily was united. Its history during the age of the Renaissance consists almost entirely of dynastic struggles between the different branches of the French family of Anjou, descendants of that Charles of Anjou who had won the kingdom from the last of the Hohenstaufens in 1266, and the royal house of Aragon, which had acquired Sicily in 1282 and finally, in 1435, succeeded in gaining the kingdom of Naples as well. Here feudalism still survived as an active force, and the intellectual

movements of the time made little impression save as importations at the royal court.

Italy on the eve of the invasions. For a full generation before the beginning of the foreign invasions in 1494,[1] Italy was kept in a more or less peaceful condition by the establishment of a balance of power among the five great states. Diplomatic relations shifted from time to time, but for the most part Milan, Florence, and Naples formed a loose alliance to hold the balance against Venice and the papacy. This alliance was cemented by a series of marriages between the Sforza family and the Aragonese house of Naples, and depended also on the friendship of both with the diplomatic Lorenzo de' Medici. Even the small, though warlike, states of Ferrara, ruled by the family of Este, and Mantua, ruled by the Gonzagas, were drawn into the circle of family marriages. This system, however, could do no more than keep a temporary and uneasy peace within Italy. It offered no basis for union against a foreign enemy. The way for the invasion of ·Italy by

[1] See below, pages 344–346.

In this fresco by Melozzo da Forlì, Pope Sixtus IV is appointing the humanist Platina (kneeling figure) librarian of the Vatican. The standing figures represent four of the pope's too numerous nephews. The second from the right is Cardinal Giuliano delle Rovere, the future Pope Julius II.

Cesare Borgia, the son of Alexander VI, was admired by Machiavelli for the ruthless efficiency with which he reduced the Papal States to order. The portrait is by an unknown Venetian painter.

France and the other great European powers was paved by the suspicion and antagonism with which the Italian states regarded one another and by their complete lack of Italian patriotism.

3. The Literary Renaissance

We have already noted in passing that the age of the Renaissance was characterized not only by economic, social, and political changes — the growth of capitalism, the development of urban society, and the rise of despotic states — but also by a great intellectual and artistic activity along new lines, which expressed, or resulted from, the other changes in Italian society.

Beginnings of Italian literature. One of the earliest developments of the new age was the creation of an Italian literature, which gave to Italy a national language that served as a bond of unity never realized in the political field. Some signs of this development may be observed in the last years of the High Middle Ages, in the adaptation to Italian uses of forms taken from the lyric poetry of southern France, and in the synthetic "court language" fostered by Frederick II in Sicily. But the close relation between spoken Italian and

the Latin that was the general literary medium, as well as the great variety of dialects represented in the numerous Italian states, had prevented the growth of a universal Italian literary tongue. Literary Italian was largely the creation of three fourteenth-century writers who were at least sufficiently typical of their age to abandon old traditions and, confident in their own creative genius, to strike out new paths for themselves.

Dante, Petrarch, Boccaccio. Dante, Petrarch, and Boccaccio, these three were the triumvirate who first formed the literary language of modern Italy. All three were Florentine by descent, although the first two were exiles, and they used the Tuscan dialect as the basis of their literary language. In other respects, however, they were very dissimilar, and the differences in their character are typical of the gradual drift away from medieval modes of thought. The first and greatest of the three, Dante Alighieri (1265–1321), seems to belong more to the Middle Ages than to the Renaissance. The idealized love poetry of his *Vita Nuova* is nearer to the troubadour tradition of medieval Provence than to the worldly loves of the Renaissance poets. Above all, his greatest work, the magnificent *Divine Comedy*, presents, in its breathtaking voyage through Hell, Purgatory, and Paradise, a panoramic survey of all medieval thought. Yet he is not purely medieval. His characters are not merely personified types in the manner common to medieval writers, but are individual personalities. In his confident individualism, indeed, he foreshadows the coming age, and, despite his interest in religion and philosophy, he was a layman, a member of that secular, urban society that was to fashion the new world.

The second of the triumvirate, Francesco Petrarca or Petrarch (1304–74), was considerably less medieval. His introspective absorption in his own personality, his longing for immortal fame and the intensely human quality of his lyric poems addressed to Laura, together with his passionate interest in classical antiquity, mark him as a true man of the Renaissance, though his occasional religious reactions and ascetic impulses show that he is not entirely removed from the Middle Ages. His influence on the shaping of Italian poetry, especially the sonnet and brief *canzoniere,* is second only to Dante's whose use of the Tuscan dialect he reinforced and purified.

The chief contribution of Giovanni Boccaccio (1313–75) was the shaping of an Italian prose style. Lacking the depth of character and spiritual insight of his two great fellow citizens, this amiable and worldly Florentine burgher was perhaps more typical of his city and his age than either of them. He observed the surface of life with keen enjoyment and described it with a clarity that made the stories of his *Decameron* models for later novelists.

The revival of antiquity. The rapid development of Italian literature was cut short with the death of Petrarch and Boccaccio and it was not revived again till the second half of the fifteenth century. The new language could not compete with the amazing revival of interest in the classic literature of ancient Rome. Even Petrarch and Boccaccio were far more interested in their Latin than in their Italian writings, and for two full generations after their death it thrust the "vulgar" tongue completely into the background. The relation between the "revival of antiquity" and the Renaissance has not always been clearly understood. It seems certain, however, that the former was the result rather than the cause of the economic, social, and psychological changes that we have already noted as characteristic of this age, though in turn it influenced and altered their development. The Latin classics were not a discovery of the Renaissance. Many of them were in common use, though chiefly as models of grammatical construction, throughout the Middle Ages. But the deep chasm which separated medieval life and medieval ideals and modes of thought from those of pagan antiquity made any real understanding of the ancient writers almost impossible. In the fourteenth and fifteenth centuries, however, there was growing up in Italy a society, essentially urban, secular, and based on wealth, which was not far removed from the civilization of ancient times, though it was not yet nearly so perfectly formed. It is not surprising, then, that Italians of this age should discover a new meaning in the classics. In these pre-Christian writings

Botticelli's delightful representation of the birth of Venus, who, according to one Greek myth, was born out of the sea, illustrates the preoccupation of the Renaissance with classical pagan antiquity.

they found a culture that seemed to embody everything for which they were blindly groping. They applied themselves, therefore, with devout enthusiasm to the study and imitation of antiquity, inspired by the conviction that the road to progress lay in a return to the glorious past that had preceded what they considered the Gothic barbarism of the Middle Ages.

Humanists.   The men who devoted their lives to the study of the classics were called humanists, i.e., those who sought to acquire *humanitas*. This word was used, in the sense made familiar by Cicero, of the mental cultivation which befits a man, particularly as expressed in refined literary form. To the men of the Renaissance it inevitably meant, by implication, a philosophy of life and one in strong contrast to the preoccupation with the things of the spirit and the future world that had played so large a part in the learned writings of the Middle Ages. It both expressed and strengthened the secular tendencies of the new age. The humanists remained Christian in faith, some of them devoutly so; but few of them escaped the influence for better or for worse of pagan philosophy and morals.

Restoration of classical Latin.   The humanists were indefatigable workers. They were driven by their reverence for antiquity to undertake the double task of restoring the works of classical authors to their original form, while at the same time perfecting their own knowledge of classical Latin style, including the details of correct spelling, inflection, syntax, scansion, and so forth, which had been almost forgotten during the Middle Ages. The only copies of the ancient authors they could find were the work of medieval scribes who were often careless and ignorant of the niceties of grammatical construction. Every manuscript was filled with errors. The humanists had, therefore, to learn the rules of classical grammar from the study of imperfect manuscripts and then to apply that knowledge as they acquired it to the correction of the errors. This could be accomplished only by constant and painstaking comparison of all the manuscripts available.

Search for manuscripts.   This led to a frantic search for old manuscripts. Petrarch led the hunt and inspired his friend Boccaccio and others to take it up. Monastery libraries were ransacked and every new fragment was hailed with delirious enthusiasm. Often the searchers found that they were too late, for many old monastic foundations had degenerated and their libraries had been allowed to moulder from neglect. Boccaccio tells us how he sat down and wept amidst the wreckage of priceless manuscripts in St. Benedict's old monastery at Monte Cassino. For three generations and more the search continued. Fortunes were spent and emissaries sent to the farthest corners of Europe. One of the most fortunate of the discoverers was the Florentine humanist Poggio Bracciolini (1380–1459), who for forty years was attached to the papal court and made good use of the embassies on which he was sent to hunt manuscripts in the countries north of the Alps. Merchants, princes, and popes shared the scholars' enthusiasm and spent vast sums in collecting libraries. It was they, too, who rewarded with generous patronage the humanists who wrote in the newly recovered classical style.

The revival of Greek.   The revival of ancient Greek literature in Italy came later than that of classical Latin. The knowledge of Greek had died out almost completely in the West and it was hard to find instructors who could teach even the rudiments of the language. The beginning of the revival may be dated from 1397, when a competent Greek scholar from Constantinople, Manuel Chrysoloras, was persuaded to come to Florence to teach. He stayed only three years, though he had been given the most flattering reception, but he had done enough to give the Italian humanists a start. Thereafter they studied Greek almost as enthusiastically as the ancient Latin. The ecumenical council of Florence in 1438–39, which brought a host of Greek scholars to that city, gave a further impetus to Greek studies. A few years later, in 1453, the conquest of Constantinople by the Turks drove great numbers of Byzantine refugees to seek a living in Italy by teaching or by copying and translating Greek manuscripts. The humanists of Italy eagerly absorbed all the Greek classics, but they reserved their greatest enthusiasm for the philosophy of Plato, now made available for the first time in its original form. Cosimo de' Medici found time in the midst of his manifold duties to found a Platonic

At the dawn of the Renaissance Giotto made the first revolutionary stride away from the two-dimensional character of medieval painting toward a more realistic representation of figures and space. Free from unessential detail, his figures have a rounded solidity and stand so that one feels one could walk around them.

9 *Adoration of the Magi, by Giotto, fresco in the Scrovegni Chapel, Padua, 1305. (Scala)*

By the first half of the fifteenth century, both northern and Italian painters had mastered the problems of modelling and perspective, but with very different styles, as illustrated by the two Annunciations on this page. The infinitely minute detail of the Flemish van der Weyden contrasts with the uncluttered clarity of the Italian Fra Angelico, and reminds us that northern panel painting grew out of the illuminator's miniature art. The humility and apparent poverty of Fra Angelico's Mary also reflects the special quality of his personal piety.

10 *Annunciation, by Roger van der Weyden, c. 1435. Louvre, Paris. (Réunion des Musées Nationaux)*

11 *Annunciation, by Fra Angelico, fresco from San Marco, Florence, c. 1440 (?). (Scala)*

While some Italian painters at the beginning of the fifteenth century still showed the influence of the "International Gothic Style" which had grown up during the preceding century, the youthful Masaccio returned to the more simple and solidly constructed figures of Giotto, but with a far more expert handling of proportion, perspective, and space, and a freer use of expressive gestures. In the mid-fifteenth century Piero della Francesca carried on that tradition, thus forming a link from Giotto through Masaccio to Michelangelo.

12 *The Resurrection, by Piero della Francesca, fresco in the Palazzo Communale, Borgo San Sepolcro, c. 1463. (Scala)*

13 *The Tribute Money, by Masaccio, fresco in the Brancacci Chapel, Santa Maria del Carmine, Florence, c. 1427. (Scala)*

14 *Madonna of the Canon van der Paele, by Jan van Eyck, c. 1435 (?). Musées Communaux, Bruges.*

The three madonnas on this page illustrate once more the difference between northern and Italian styles. Jan van Eyck's madonna enthroned, with a realistic portrait of the donor, is typically Flemish, while the madonnas of Raphael and Leonardo da Vinci, in their harmonious composition and classic purity, belong to the Italian High Renaissance.

15 *Sistine Madonna, by Raphael, c. 1513. Staatliche Kunstsammlungen, Dresden.*

16 *St. Anne with Madonna and Child, by Leonardo da Vinci, c. 1516. Louvre, Paris. (Réunion des Musées Nationaux)*

Academy in Florence. There, in the later years of the fifteenth century, the learned Ficino (1433–99) and the brilliant Pico della Mirandola (1463–94) taught a synthesis of Platonic philosophy and Christian theology that was to have a profound influence on the humanists of northern Europe.

The critical spirit.   Absorbed as they were in restoring the works of the ancient Latin and Greek authors and in perfecting their own classical style, the Italian humanists were more deeply concerned with the problems of philology and correct literary form than with original thought. A good deal of what they wrote was scarcely more than an exercise in style and a rehashing of ideas drawn from classical sources. In the words of one rather unfriendly critic, "having nothing to say, they said it interminably." Yet they did perform a service of immense and lasting importance to modern civilization by making the body of ancient literature fully available; and, as a by-product of their philological studies, they developed an independent critical spirit which could be carried over into other fields. They were often as prone to accept without question the validity of anything found in the ancient writers as their medieval predecessors had been to accept the authority of the Bible, the Fathers, and Aristotle. But the change from one authority to another had given them a new point of view, and the training they received in comparing, correcting, and restoring the manuscript copies of the classics had furnished them with a sound critical method. This method of literary and historical criticism, detached from reverence for religious authority, was used by the Roman humanist Lorenzo Valla (1405?–57) to good effect in proving that the "Donation of Constantine," on which the papacy had based a large part of its claims to secular power, was a ninth- or tenth-century forgery. The Christian humanists of the north were later to use the same critical spirit in a much more far-reaching attack on medieval religious institutions.

The revival of Italian poetry.   Toward the end of the fifteenth century, the Italian literary world began to lose the exclusive preoccupation with the classics which had characterized it for more than a hundred years. By that time the major part of the humanists' task had been accomplished. The writers of the late fifteenth century, having learned good classical Latin and Greek in childhood, could afford to take it somewhat for granted and were free to return to their national language, which had been but little used for literary purposes since the days of Dante, Petrarch, and Boccaccio. Lorenzo de' Medici encouraged the revival of the vernacular and himself set the example by writing Italian verse. Under his influence the scholar-poet Angelo Poliziano (1454–94) wrote polished poems in Italian as well as in Latin and Greek. Meanwhile Italian poetry was also being revived at the ducal court of Ferrara, which, under the discriminating patronage of the house of Este, had become one of the most brilliant centers of culture in Italy. Here a romantic interest in medieval chivalry led to a revival of epic poetry in what the members of this aristocratic and sophisticated court conceived to be the manner of the old French *chansons de geste*. Urged on by the Este princesses, Matteo Maria Boiardo (c. 1434–94) retold the story of the *Chanson de Roland* with much romantic modification in an Italian epic entitled *Orlando Innamorato*. It was left unfinished at his death, but Ludovico Ariosto (1474–1533) was persuaded to write a sequel. Ariosto was too much the product of his age to take medieval romance very seriously, but the epic form gave full play to his talent for poetic imagery and fanciful narrative, always touched with irony. His *Orlando Furioso* overshadowed its predecessor and remains one of the masterpieces of Italian literature. In the midst of a busy life as courtier, secretary, and diplomat in the service of the Este family, Ariosto also found time to write many fine Italian lyrics and several comedies which were performed at the court of Ferrara. It was at Ferrara, too, as a protégé of the Este dukes, that Torquato Tasso (1544–95) wrote most of his best poetry. Although he may be considered the last great poet of the Italian Renaissance, Tasso belonged to the period of the Counter-Reformation, and the religious spirit of that age breathes through his epic of the First Crusade, the *Jerusalem Delivered*.

Italian prose.   By the opening of the sixteenth century, Italian was also beginning to hold its own with the ancient languages as a medium for serious prose. Castiglione's *Book*

The Paduan painter, Andrea Mantegna, was fascinated by the costumes and architecture of Roman antiquity and also by the problems of perspective. This fresco, painted about 1455, depicts St. James being led to his execution.

of the Courtier (1518), one of the most widely read books of the sixteenth century, was written in Italian. So also were the works of Niccolò Machiavelli (1469–1527), the shrewd Florentine historian and political theorist, whose name has furnished every European language with a synonym for the cynical sacrifice of moral means to political ends. Like most educated Italians of his generation, Machiavelli was well versed in the classics. His *History of Florence* shows the influence of classical models, and his most thoughtful comments on history and politics were presented in the form of *Discourses* on the first ten books of the great Roman historian, Livy. His original thought, however, was based on his own observation of Italian politics during some fifteen years as a secretary and diplomat in the service of the Florentine Republic. When the Medici returned in 1512, he was driven into exile, and in the following embittered years he wrote his most famous book, *The Prince.* Here he analyzed, with little regard for moral considerations, the methods by which a prince might rule successfully. His maxims, illustrated by references to the ruthless policies of such Renaissance princes as Cesare Borgia, have both shocked and fascinated generations of readers. A few years

later Francesco Guicciardini (1482–1540), another disillusioned Florentine politician, added to the impression that Italian politics were completely divorced from morality by the picture of the troubled years from 1492 to 1534 which he presented in his *History of Italy*. Machiavelli may have felt that his book was justified by the hope that his advice might enable the Medicean prince to whom it was dedicated to unite Italy against her foreign invaders, but no such justification can be found for the cynical realism of Guicciardini. Both men were very widely read, and both were masters of the historian's art as well as of clear-cut Italian prose. Together they have done much to color the modern conception of the Italian Renaissance in somewhat darker tints than the facts altogether warranted.

4. The Artistic Renaissance

The social and intellectual changes that were taking place in Italy during the age of the Renaissance were reflected by changes in spirit and form in the arts as well as in literature, and these were accompanied by a change in the character and status of the artist.

The status of the artist. The medieval artist had been typical of his age. He was a member of a corporation — nearly all medieval artists were guildsmen — and he worked within the traditions and rules of his craft. He was regarded, and regarded himself, as an artisan. He no doubt took an honest pride in his work, but he was scarcely more likely to attach his name to it than a carpenter or an armorer would be. Being practically anonymous, he had little incentive to break away from the traditional methods used by his fellows, nor, probably, was he free to do so. Moreover, the purpose of his art was most often religious, not so much because religion played such a large part in his life as because the church was the wealthiest and most frequent patron of his services. Here, too, the medieval artist was limited by tradition, for the character of religious art had become highly conventionalized and he was not encouraged to make innovations or to copy too closely natural beauty, which was always suspected by the medieval church. Now, in the Late Middle Ages and the Renaissance, the development of a wealthy educated secular society, with a keen interest in art as it portrayed the beauties of this world, gradually changed the status of the artist and the conditions affecting his art. The artist of outstanding genius was in great demand. He might receive from princes, merchants, and bankers rewards far beyond those of the ordinary artisan. His name and the individual character of his work became assets of high value. Working for men who were losing their respect for medieval traditions, the artist was free to strike out along new lines and to develop his individual genius to its fullest extent.

Painting.   Of the major arts, painting was the most characteristic of the Italian Renaissance and was developed to the highest degree of perfection. Here the Italian love of color found its fullest expression. Until almost the end of the period, Florence was the greatest center of painting, as of literature and most of the other arts. There, in the opening years of the fourteenth century, Giotto (1276–1336) took a long stride away from the stiffly formalized technique of earlier religious painting toward a greater naturalism. Throughout the rest of the century his successors were moving steadily in the direction he had indicated, though their work was still primarily religious and they had not yet acquired the technical knowledge or skill required to accomplish their full objective. The fifteenth century was a period of adventurous experimentation and rapid progress in technique. Driven by the desire to copy natural beauty or the outward appearance of their fellow men as accurately as possible, the fifteenth-century artists mastered the laws of perspective and shadow, discovered how to give their figures modeling and depth, and greatly improved the methods of blending colors. Their figures stand freely and easily in three-dimensional space. The art of this period was increasingly devoted to secular subjects, although religious themes still predominated. Portrait painting, the result of that desire to be remembered by posterity which all the great or wealthy men of the Renaissance felt strongly, became for the first time a fashionable form of art. We have not space to mention all the fifteenth-century painters, but it would be unforgivable to ignore the names of three Florentine painters: Masaccio (1402–29?), who in his brief life at the beginning of the century set a standard of technical perfection far ahead of his generation; the Dominican Fra Angelico (1387–1455), who in his many fine frescoes combined realism with a delicate religious sensibility; and Botticelli (1447–1510), whose graceful paintings show most clearly the influence of classical paganism on the thought and art of the age.

The great masters.   After the artists of this age of experimentation and naturalism had worked out the necessary rules of technique, came the golden age of Renaissance painting. Naturalism for its own sake seemed less important to artists who had mastered the means of achieving it. The influence of classical art, too, encouraged them to abandon the indiscriminate reproduction of every detail of the subjects before them and to subordinate the parts of the picture to the harmonious composition of the whole. The generation of the great masters of the High Renaissance spanned the end of the fifteenth century and the beginning of the sixteenth. The first of these was the Florentine Leonardo da Vinci (1452–1519), the most versatile man of his age. He was a master of all the arts, a poet and a musician as well as a practical engineer and an experimental scientist of the first rank. In

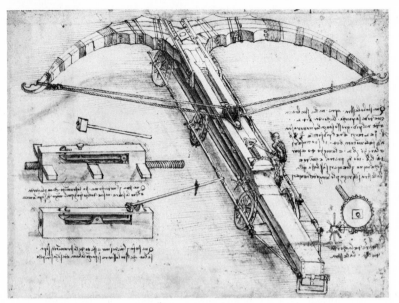

Leonardo da Vinci filled his notebooks with sketches for all sorts of mechanical contrivances. Like many of his other inventions, this enormous crossbow on wheels was never put into effect. The detail at the sides shows the screws and cogwheels to be used in winding it up.

this enigmatic genius there was a driving curiosity that impelled him to discover what lay beneath the surface of things. His Mona Lisa, whose mysterious smile has puzzled and fascinated generations of critics, and the disciples grouped about Christ in the Last Supper are studies in character as well as works of compelling beauty. The work of Raphael (1483–1520) is not so profound, but no one surpassed him in the perfection of his coloring or the serene harmony that pervades all his paintings. Though he died in early middle age, he produced an amazingly large number of finished works, many of them under the patronage of the popes Julius II and Leo X, including the School of Athens and the marvelous Madonna for the Sistine Chapel. It was Julius II, too, who subsidized some of the best work of Michelangelo (1475–1564), having persuaded him to turn from sculpture to painting for the decoration of the Sistine Chapel. The result was a magnificent fresco, covering the whole roof of the chapel, which secures the place of Michelangelo for all time among the master painters. In it, as in everything he did, one can see the tragic driving force, the grandeur of design, and the deep religious emotion that make Michelangelo unique among the artists of the Renaissance.

Sculpture. The development of sculpture followed in most respects the same general lines as did that of painting. In the Middle Ages it had shared the religious and corporate character of the other arts, having been used mainly for the decoration of churches and cathedrals. Beginning with Niccolò Pisano before the end of the thirteenth century, Renaissance sculptors gradually moved away from Gothic conventions toward a more realistic copying of nature. As in painting, the fifteenth century was a period of experimentation and technical progress, influenced to a greater extent than was true of painting by imitation of classical models; for many ancient statues were now being disinterred and studied with keen interest. Sculpture was rapidly securing recognition as an independent art devoted to secular uses and freed from its subordination to religious architecture, though many artists, like Ghiberti (1378–1455), whose bronze gates in bas-relief for the doors of the cathedral baptistery were the wonder of all Florence, still worked on the decoration of churches. The masterly equestrian statue of the *condottiere* Gattamelata by the Florentine Donatello (1386?–1466) is one of the best examples of the new independent and secular type of sculpture. The golden age of sculpture coincides with that of painting, and here again the powerful figure of Michelangelo towers above the other masters. In this, his most natural medium, his best work, including the noble David, the deeply religious Pietà, and the magnificent tombs of the Medici, were done in his native Florence before and after the years spent in the service of Julius II in Rome.

Architecture. The changing conditions and ideals of the Renaissance brought changes in architectural style, often resulting in buildings of great beauty. Yet it is doubtful if the changes mark a clear improvement. Though perhaps better suited to the spirit and needs of their own age, Renaissance architecture lacked the harmony and grandeur of the Gothic cathedrals. In the experimental period of the fifteenth century, individualism ran riot as each architect strove to adapt the antique Roman and medieval Gothic types to contemporary needs, while at the same time expressing his own originality. Of these, Brunelleschi (1377–1446), who built the churches of San Lorenzo and Santo Spirito in Florence, was perhaps most successful; but it remained for the Lombard architect, Bramante (1444–1514), who drew the original plans for St. Peter's Church in Rome, later altered by Michelangelo, to evolve out of the old traditions a really harmonious style.

Music. During the greater part of the fourteenth and fifteenth centuries, Italy contributed much less to music than did northern France and the Netherlands. There were some notable developments in the secular music of court and carnival, and Franciscan piety inspired popular *laude* sung by groups of laymen after their daily work; but the great age of Italian Renaissance music came after the first quarter of the sixteenth century and will be discussed in Chapter 36.

Having reached its golden age, the artistic and intellectual Renaissance did not last long. It faded with the passing of the peculiar social and economic conditions that had produced it. The loss of political liberty through conquest by foreign powers, the loss of intellectual freedom through the action of the Counter-Reformation, and the decline of economic prosperity due to the shifting of trade routes to the west sapped the energy of Italy. But in the meantime the Renaissance had crossed the Alps to exert a great influence on the culture of the north.

The Pietà, now in St. Peter's in Rome, is one of Michelangelo's most beautiful and appealing sculptures. In this youthful work all of Michelangelo's deeply personal religious feeling found expression.

The story of Abraham and Isaac, as depicted by Ghiberti in relief in one of the bronze panels of the doors of the Baptistry in Florence, marks a high point in early Renaissance sculpture.

325

26

The Waning of the Middle Ages

and the Renaissance in the North

THE PERIOD of transition from medieval to modern civilization began later in northern Europe than it did in Italy, and, once begun, it developed more slowly and along somewhat different lines. For, in the north, feudalism was more firmly entrenched behind its moats and castle walls; religion lay closer to the hearts of men far removed from the pagan beauty of the sun-drenched Italian land; and in the quadrangles of Oxford and the dusty halls of the Sorbonne, the ghosts of Thomas Aquinas and Duns Scotus walked undisturbed, long after Italian scholars had deserted them to follow after the still older ghosts of ancient Greece and Rome. But throughout northern Europe the same leaven was at work as had transformed society in the more prosperous south. Here, too, commerce and industry were bringing wealth and with it thriving urban centers and an aggressive, self-confident new middle class, whose energy was to disrupt medieval society. Yet the product of the transformation would not be altogether the same as in Italy, for in the north cities were fewer and farther between, and the new society was to find its focus in the centralized territorial state rather than in the city.

The fifteenth century and the early sixteenth witnessed the gradual disappearance of many medieval characteristics in society, religion, and culture, and the contemporary growth of much that we recognize as modern. The old and the new existed side by side or inextricably interwoven, and the old gave place to the new so slowly that major changes are discernible only through the lengthened perspective of the years. Men of the fifteenth century did not know that the Middle Ages were dying. They knew only that times were not what they had been; that graybearded men bewailed the passing of the good old days, while aggressive youngsters who had studied in Florence or Bologna spoke slightingly of Gothic barbarism; and that there was now something very like contempt mixed with the envy on the face of the stolid burgher as he watched the gaily dressed knights passing the windows of his countinghouse.

1. Decay of Medieval Institutions

Decay of feudalism. In the fifteenth century, feudalism was fading fast. Some of its economic and social forms might survive for three centuries and more, but of its independent existence as a political force there remained only a shadow by the beginning of the sixteenth century. As in Italy, it was the power of money that wrecked the older forms of society. But in the great territorial states of the north, the influence of money was less direct; for there it worked through the growing power of the rulers of the states, and it was the state that absorbed feudalism into itself.

Nobles lose monopoly of fighting. All through the Middle Ages, the political independence of the nobles and their privileged position in society had depended in large part on their exclusive monopoly of the arts of warfare. So long as their castle walls remained a sure defense against all enemies, so long as their expensive weapons and armor, their great war-horses and the skill that comes only from long years of training gave them an indisputable superiority over common men in battle, so long as prince and people must depend on them for the defense of the state, for so long was the position of the nobles at the apex of society secure. But in the fifteenth century the introduction of gunpowder as an effective instrument of battle and siege placed a weapon in the hands of common men, which enabled them to meet the heavily armored knights on relatively even terms. At the same time, the increase in the amount of money available through taxation or loans gave to the rulers of the states a tremendous advantage over the less wealthy nobles in the use of this new and expensive weapon. Income sufficient to pay troops also freed monarchs from the necessity of depending on the services of their feudal vassals for their military force. The kings of great states like England, France, and Spain, and even the princes of smaller territorial states like those of Germany, could now raise and maintain armies, composed largely of common soldiers, against which the nobles were helpless. As early as the fourteenth century, the English kings had used the plebian long bow to good effect and had demonstrated the superiority of a disciplined army over a feudal levy on the fields of Crécy and Poitiers. The use of gunpowder made the state army a universal institution. Unable to ignore or oppose their king, the nobles enlisted in the royal army and took the king's pay. They still fought, such being their nature, but they fought at the bidding of the twin powers of monarchy and money.

Economic decline of the nobles. In yet another way, money — or the lack of it — was working to deprive the nobles of their cherished independence. While the businessmen, who were beginning to discover the profitable uses of capital, and the monarchs, who were acquiring greater powers of taxation, were growing wealthier, the nobles as a general rule were becoming poorer, for the feudal system had never been designed to produce fluid wealth. As we noted in Chapter 24, monetary inflation during this period had the inevitable effect of raising prices, while the income of the nobles, based on hereditary rights and immemorial custom, remained relatively the same. As a general rule the intrusion of money economy into the manorial system worked to the disadvantage of the landlords. To make matters worse, their pride forced them to maintain their social position by an ostentatious display of luxury and pomp that would have been ruinous to men of much larger incomes. Confronted by failing resources and rising expenses, the nobles were forced to seek aid from the royal purse. And the kings were well content to aid them by the gift of pensions, sinecure offices at court, or positions in the army and church, thereby establishing a system of patronage that made the nobles more than ever dependent upon them. The feudal noble, in short, was becoming a royal courtier.

The decline of chivalry. Changing methods of warfare, economic stress, and the growing power of the monarchy, which were thus transforming the life of the noble class, could not but alter the status of the knights and the customs and manners of chivalry; for, as we saw in Chapter 18, chivalry was the most characteristic aspect of the life of the feudal nobility in the High Middle Ages. It was at that time a universal order to which every noble warrior aspired, and it set the standard of conduct for the knight on the field of battle, in the tournament, and among the ladies of the court. This standard continued to be honored, at least by lip service, through the period of the Hundred Years' War; but the sporting attitude of the medieval knight was ill suited to the realities of warfare between royal armies of the new type. Froissart, whose *Chronicles* are the best contemporary account of the first half of the Hundred Years' War, tells a number of stories of chivalrous encounters between opposing knights and of the courtesy of knights to their noble prisoners; but he also shows the same knights haggling over the amount of the ransom to be exacted from their captives. Knights had become mercenary soldiers, for without pay few could afford the heavy plate armor which they now needed to protect them from the deadly long-bow and the new firearms. Even with pay, many impoverished nobles could not afford the extra expenses involved in maintaining the social position of a knight. In the fifteenth century, only a minority of the French nobility or the English gentry became knights, and there were certainly more squires than knights among the men-at-arms who formed the heavily armored cavalry in the royal armies. For practical purposes, the knight was being replaced by the professional soldier; and, with that change, discipline on the field of battle gradually replaced the chivalrous lunacy that had wrecked the French armies at Crécy and Poitiers.

Tournaments and orders of chivalry.   But as chivalry lost its practical value for warfare, it flourished with unprecedented magnificence in tournament and court. Never had the outward trappings of chivalry shone so brilliantly as in these years when it was losing contact with reality. Tournaments became highly formalized and generally harmless combats between richly caparisoned knights, clad from head to foot in plate armor. Their primary function was no longer to train fighting men, but rather to add to the pageantry of royal courts. The new monarchies, indeed, were subordinating chivalry to their own interests and using it as a means of enhancing their own prestige. More and more, kings reserved to themselves the right to confer the honor of knighthood, while at the same time they debased the currency of chivalry by conferring knighthood upon officials, jurists, and financiers who had never lowered a lance in battle. They also struck a blow at the old idea of a universal order of chivalry by creating new national orders. Of these the Order of the Garter, founded by Edward III in 1340, and the magnificent Order of the Golden Fleece, founded by the semi-royal Duke of Burgundy in 1430, were the most famous, but there were many others.

Decay of the universal church.   While other medieval institutions were thus decaying, the universal church, too, was declining in power and prestige. In a great many ways the fourteenth and fifteenth centuries were disastrous ones for the Catholic Church. The papacy, with its wide claims to supremacy over all Catholic Christians, had come into violent conflict with the growing power of the centralized territorial states and had been defeated. National interests had combined with moral disapproval to break the vast authority that the church had wielded during the High Middle Ages. The fourteenth century witnessed the tragedy of Boniface VIII, the Babylonian Captivity, the scandal of the Great Schism, the growth of a strong anti-clerical sentiment, the destructive criticisms of William of Occam and Marsiglio of Padua and the heresies of Wyclif and Huss. The fifteenth century, in turn, opened with the menace to papal authority of the conciliar movement, and when that had passed, the popes were left in an anomalous position as Italian princes whose power over secular governments had vanished and whose control of the church itself was limited by the rulers of the great states.

2. Rise of Centralized Territorial States

From the foregoing summary of the decay of medieval institutions, social, economic, and religious, one fact emerges clearly. While other and older institutions were crumbling, the centralized territorial states — in some cases one may almost call them national states — were rising to ever-greater power and importance, aided by the power of money and supported by the moneyed burgher class whose business interests demanded order and strong government.

Centralization and consolidation.   The decline of political feudalism left the rulers of the territorial states without serious rivals. Economic and social factors had contributed to this result, but from the constitutional point of view it was accomplished by a double process of consolidation of territory and centralization of governmental authority in the hands of more or less absolute princes. The growth of

France as a united monarchical state is the most perfect example of this dual process. There one can see clearly how the kings used both these means to transform an indirect feudal lordship into a direct royal government over the whole state. Generation after generation, they consolidated the territory under their direct rule until every fief in the kingdom had been incorporated into the royal domain. Meanwhile, by constantly enforcing their royal rights so far as they were able, they had gradually acquired the power to deal directly with all the people of the state, not merely with their immediate vassals. During the Hundred Years' War they won the right to tax all their subjects directly, going over the heads of the feudal lords. For a time the Estates General had seemed a possible rival to royal power, but when feudalism collapsed, the estates proved too weak to exercise an effective check on the authority of the king. With variations due to differences in their past history, most of the other states of Europe were undergoing a similar development as the Later Middle Ages drew to a close.

Economic control. The consolidation of the territorial states carried with it the centralization of economic as well as political control. During the Middle Ages commerce and industry had been controlled by the individual cities, because the city government was the only power to which the burghers could look for adequate protection and regulation. As the central government of the state grew strong, it was natural that it should endeavor to regulate the economic life of the whole country, offering protection to merchants both at home and abroad, encouraging new industries, and striving to increase the wealth and power of the state in relation to its neighbors. The rigid regulation of national economy, generally known as "mercantilism," which was characteristic of the early modern period, was as yet, however, in its infancy, and fuller discussion must be left to a later chapter.[1]

National culture. The tendency toward centralization of political and economic life could not but have an effect, quite as important if less tangible, on the culture and sentiments of the people. As the concept of the united

[1] See below, pages 437–439.

state loomed larger before their vision, local traditions and local interests waned. Differences in speech and custom in different parts of the state gradually became less pronounced. In short, the strengthening of the centralized state was accompanied by the growth of a common culture that was national in scope rather than local. The invention of printing in the middle of the fifteenth century, by facilitating the circulation of books in the national tongue, gave a great impetus to the nationalization of culture, but more time than the period we are now considering would be needed to establish it completely. Still, the beginnings of the tendency can already be seen. Cause and effect, however, are not always too clear and there was probably more involved in the growth of national cultures than the mere development of centralized states. The rise of national culture in Italy and Germany, where the whole country was not included in a strong centralized state, is an exception worth noting.

National sentiment. We are on a little firmer ground when we turn to the consideration of the growth of national sentiment or, at least, of a growing feeling of loyalty to the state. In those countries where cultural and political boundaries more or less coincided, the incipient growth of national consciousness clearly followed the development of a strong state. In part, no doubt, it was the natural result of the established fact that the state was now the all-important unit and its ruler the power to whom all men turned for protection and government. That one was a Norman became less important than that one was a Frenchman, in proportion as the feudal government of Normandy was merged with the royal government of France. The great international wars of the fourteenth and fifteenth centuries also played their part in building up national sentiment, for war is always a powerful stimulus to patriotism. Whereas wars in the Middle Ages had been mostly feudal and had tended to strengthen local loyalties, these later wars developed a national character. The Hundred Years' War, with its memories of Crécy, Agincourt, and Joan of Arc, made Frenchmen conscious that they were Frenchmen, and Englishmen conscious that they were not Frenchmen, and therein lay the seeds at least of modern nationalism.

Break-up of the unity of Christendom. So far we have emphasized the triumph of the territorial state over local interests and the resulting expansion of the people's horizon from the narrow confines of the fief or city to the larger circle of the state. But that is only part of the story. Equally important is the contraction of common interest from the larger unity of Catholic Christendom to the smaller one of the indivdual state. For, in the Middle Ages, localism had existed side by side with an internationalism unparalleled in modern times. The two are not mutually exclusive. To the man of narrow local loyalties, all people from outside his little circle are foreigners. It matters little whether they come from his own state or another. Feudalism had recognized no national frontiers. A Norman lord would do homage as cheerfully to an English as to a French king. Trade, too, was as much international as local. Merchants wandered freely from one country to another, attending the open fairs and being judged by the common merchant law. The only exclusive monopoly they encountered was that of the city governments or guilds, and that operated equally against natives of the country. Finally, the church was a great international institution that held all men of Catholic Europe together in the common brotherhood of the Christian faith and in common obedience to its laws. It gave to Europe a common culture, and in the Latin tongue a common language for education and learning. This international unity was broken up by the rise of the centralized states. In so far as the political, economic, and cultural interests of the people were concentrated on the state, they ceased to be international. Even the church was falling under the control of state governments. The state was too powerful to tolerate particular interests within itself or to admit the interference within its borders of any outside power. It is this fact that goes far to explain the breaking away from the ancient church of so many of the northern states during the Protestant Reformation.

3. The New Piety in the North

Germany and the Netherlands. Despite the waning power of the universal church, however, the people of northern Europe were not lacking in piety. Corruption in the church and the failure of its authority were not necessarily accompanied by a decline in popular religion, though that was doubtless often the case. On the contrary, much of the criticism of the clergy, the opposition to the papacy, and the attacks on the sacramental system which we have noted in the fourteenth and fifteenth centuries were inspired by a genuine piety that engendered a sincere moral indignation against manifest abuses, and only incidentally served the interests of the state governments. At the same time there was a powerful movement of awakening piety in Germany and the Netherlands which was to have a strong influence on both the Renaissance and the Reformation in the north. But it was not piety of a kind to strengthen the loyalty of the people to the organized church of their day. This movement originated with a group of religious mystics who, though orthodox sons of the church, cherished ideals that were not altogether in keeping with its contemporary practices, and who strove to transcend, without breaking away from, its mechanical organization.

The mystics. To describe or analyze pure mysticism is almost impossible. There have always been mystics and probably there always will be, but they themselves have never been able to describe their emotions in a way fully comprehensible to the practical mind. Perhaps it will be sufficient to say that, to the mystic, religion is a purely personal aspiration of the individual soul seeking unity and harmony with the divine power. In that ecstatic feeling of unity with God and harmony with His universe the mystic finds his supreme happiness. For our purposes, the important effects of a revival of mysticism at this time are, first, the increase in fervid piety in an age that had begun to take religion for granted, and second, a growing indifference to the sacramental system in an age when that system, though of vital importance to the authority of the church, was becoming formal and mechanical in its operation. The mystics did not doubt the necessity of the sacraments as did the Lollards and some other heretics. But they did place less emphasis upon their importance. The mystics' aims were too personal, too immediate, for them to place much reliance on formalized observances, or to feel the need of a priest to

The brutal realism of Grünewald's "Crucifixion" is characteristic of one strain in the super-charged religious atmosphere of Germany before the Reformation.

act as an intermediary between the individual soul and God.

Mysticism in Germany. The new mysticism began in Germany. Its founder was a German Dominican friar, Master Eckhart (1260–1327), and to him the movement owed its philosophy. Its influence on popular piety, however, came through the work of one of his disciples, Johann Tauler (c. 1300–61), who preached to the common people and gained a wide hearing. Unlike most preachers of the time, he did not represent salvation as the aim and end of religion, but emphasized the love of God as an end in itself. To this end any man, no matter how poor or ignorant, might aspire through simple faith, prayer, and purity of life. This was a kind of mysticism within the comprehension of the masses. Tauler was the leader of a group known as the Friends of God, which did a great deal to raise the standards of German morality and piety. The essence of the mystics' teaching was gathered together toward

the end of the fourteenth century in a little anonymous volume which Luther, who admitted its great influence on his thought, named *The German Theology*.

The Dutch mystics. In the Netherlands, mysticism flowered later and exercised a more direct influence on the thought of the new age. Here as in Germany it produced one great book, the immortal *Imitation of Christ* of Thomas à Kempis, written in the first quarter of the fifteenth century and still popular after more than five hundred years. The doctrine of this most widely read expression of the new piety, or *devotio moderna* as it was called, was very simple: he who would be a true Christian must live as Christ lived, think as he thought, and imitate him in every possible way. It was an ideal with which the church could not quarrel, yet it ignored the elaborate system whereby the clergy were made indispensable to the salvation of men. In the Netherlands, too, the mystics formed a society, known as the

Brethren of the Common Life who devoted themselves to the education of boys. Throughout the fifteenth century, their schools, especially the large school at Deventer in Holland, were important instruments in spreading the new learning of the northern Renaissance, and did much to shape the ideals of many of the most influential humanists.

4. The Renaissance Crosses the Alps

In northern Europe the Middle Ages died more slowly than in Italy. The new economic and social developments appeared later and in less concentrated form than in the crowded urban society of the south. It is not surprising, then, that the literary Renaissance, which was inspired by the revival of the classics to meet the intellectual needs of the new society, did not cross the Alps until a century after Petrarch and Boccaccio had begun to spread the gospel of antiquity in Italy. In these last years of the transitional age, there was a deeper piety and a more profound preoccupation with religon in the northern countries than was common among the more secularly minded Italians. Hence, when the north turned to the classics with new zeal, under the influence of the Italian Renaissance, it was more indifferent to the pagan spirit of the ancient writers. Hu-

manists of the north might revolt against the restrictions and abuses of the medieval church, but they remained Christian, and that not merely in form, but with a deep moral and religious interest as well. They sought in the Latin and Greek classics a more human morality and philosophy than the scholasticism of the Middle Ages had provided, but they did not ignore the Christian past. Like the Italian humanists, they turned for guidance to antiquity, but it was to Christian as well as to classical antiquity, to the Bible and the Fathers of the church, to Jerome and Augustine, not less than to Cicero and Virgil.

Invention of printing. The spread of the new classical learning in the north was greatly aided by the rapidly increasing use of printed books which followed the invention of printing by Johann Gutenberg of Mainz about the year 1447. Part of the technique of printing was known and used before the time of Gutenberg's epoch-making invention. A few short pamphlets or books had been printed by means of wood-cut blocks, the whole contents of a page, usually a picture and a few lines of text, being cut on a single wooden block. But this method was expensive, awkward, and wasteful. The blocks were difficult to make, could be used for only one work, and were soon worn out. The important part of Gutenberg's innovation,

A Florentine printer's shop as shown in an engraving of c. 1570. At the right a workman is screwing down the press, while at the left typesetters are selecting type from the fonts.

which made printing really practicable, was the use of movable metal type. Each letter was cast in a matrix or model. Any number could be cast from the same matrix, thus making the production of type inexpensive and guaranteeing uniformity. The type could then be assembled in any desired order, and after the book was printed could be taken apart or "distributed" and used again and again for other books.

Its effects. The effects of the printing press on the general intellectual development of Europe can scarcely be overestimated. Its immediate result for the spread of humanism in the north was to place the classics and the writings of Christian antiquity at the disposal of all who could read them, at a moderate price, and to afford the humanists themselves a far wider audience than would have been possible before. Hitherto all books had been written by hand and were often inaccurate as well as expensive. Even in Italy manuscripts were scarce and dear. In the north, where there were proportionately fewer wealthy bibliophiles and the distance between libraries was greater, the study of the ancient writings would have presented enormous difficulties. Within a few years after the invention of printing, however, the number of books in existence had increased tremendously and the cost of each would average less than an eighth of that of a manuscript copy. The new technique spread with amazing rapidity to all parts of Europe. Before the end of the fifteenth century, there were more than a thousand printers whose names are still known, and more than thirty thousand editions had been published.

Second generation of humanists. The new learning, as the humanists called the study of the ancient tongues, was introduced into the northern countries during the second half of the fifteenth century, and before the end of the century it had become fully naturalized. The last decade of the fifteenth century and the first two of the sixteenth marked the high tide of northern humanism. These years witnessed the mature labors of the second generation of northern humanists, most of whom had studied in Italy and who had entered into the full inheritance of classical and Christian antiquity. Under its inspiration they strove to reform contemporary education and religious thought and practice. They prepared the way for the Protestant Reformation, only to find many of the reforms for which they had been working overwhelmed in a sea of dogmatic argument and partisan passions.

Christian humanism. These northern humanists had all the reverence for antiquity, and all the scorn for the Middle Ages, that was characteristic of their Italian brethren. Indeed, reaction against medievalism may be taken as the keynote of their thought. The charm and purity of the ancient Latin style made them look with contempt upon the crabbed Latin of the medieval theologians, whose spiritual descendants still ruled in most of the schools and universities. The sane and well-balanced attitude toward life in this world, which they found in the classics, appealed to them more strongly than the one-sided, other-worldly philosophy of the medieval scholastic doctors. But above all, and this was their unique contribution, they found in the Scriptures and the writings of Christian antiquity a simple, vivid religion, which they felt had been distorted by long centuries of involved theological argument and buried beneath the accumulated mass of medieval church tradition. It was their task to restore this early "evangelical" faith in all its purity. To do this they believed that they must first restore and study all the Christian sources, the Bible and the early Fathers of the church, in their original form and in their original language. This necessitated a full scholarly knowledge of Greek and Hebrew as well as of good Latin. All this brought them into violent conflict with the conservative teachers and theologians, who still clung to the medieval traditions in education and theology, who preferred the medieval commentaries to the original texts, and who were ignorant of Greek and Hebrew.

Reuchlin. In Germany, the outstanding leader of the new movement was Johann Reuchlin (1455–1522). He had studied in Italy, and after his return to Germany devoted his life to the study of Hebrew as an aid to the understanding of the Old Testament. As a preliminary step he published the first Hebrew grammar north of the Alps in 1506, a work of great service to the new scholarship. His open opposition to a scheme for the suppression of Hebrew books caused him to be charged with heresy by the inquisitor of Cologne, backed by the Dominican teachers in the university there. The resulting trial, which lasted six years, roused a storm of controversy. It was one of the first cases in which both sides appealed to public opinion through the medium of the printing press. On Reuchlin's side were the humanists, on the other the monks and conservative theologians. In this literary debate, the humanists, equipped with a far superior Latin style, had all the best of it. When argument failed, they resorted to ridicule with devastating effect. One work in particular remains an immortal monument to the wit of the humanists. The _Letters of Obscure Men_, written anonymously by one of the young humanists at the University of Erfurt, is still good reading for its hilarious humor and biting satire. It is composed of a series of letters addressed to one of Reuchlin's principal opponents, presumably from his humble admirers. Written in comically barbarous Latin, the letters exposed the ignorance, superstition, and naïve gullibility of the obscure monks and priests who rallied to the defense of tradition. A supplement, even more bitter, appeared shortly after from the pen of the bellicose German knight and poet, Ulrich von Hutten.

Lefèvre d'Étaples. In France, Jacques Lefèvre d'Étaples (c. 1455–1536) did for the New Testament what Reuchlin was doing for the Old. He, too, had studied in Italy, returning to teach at Paris. The aim of his work was to discover the real meaning of the New Testament text, treating it as a human document, though divinely inspired. His study of the Greek originals brought new light to bear on the teaching of Christ and the apostles, and had a considerable influence on the thought of Luther and other reformers.

Colet and More. The principal figure among the Christian humanists in England was John Colet (d. 1519), dean of St. Paul's Cathedral in London and founder of St. Paul's School. Though not a great scholar, despite his years of study in Italy, he was a man of high character and deeply interested in reforming the thought and practice of the church. His influence directed the activity of a number of writers more learned than himself. Among his friends was St. Thomas More (c. 1478–1535), whose _Utopia,_ published in 1516, presented the humanist's picture of an ideal society, one that has given inspiration to social reformers ever since.

Erasmus. By far the most influential of all the Christian humanists, however, was Desi-

St. Thomas More, the author of the Utopia, _chancellor of Henry VIII, and martyr to his faith, is shown here in a portrait by Holbein._

derius Erasmus of Rotterdam (c. 1469–1536). It was he more than anyone else who formulated and popularized the reform program of Christian humanism. He was born in Holland, educated by the Brethren of the Common Life in their school at Deventer, and entered a monastery at an early age. However, he soon escaped from that narrow environment and thereafter led a wandering existence, living for years in France, England, Italy, Germany, and Switzerland, equally at home wherever there were learned men who could converse with him in the classical Latin that was almost his mother tongue. Until Erasmus was about thirty years of age, the study of the classics absorbed his attention to the exclusion of almost everything else. During these years he acquired a thorough knowledge of classical literature and the easy, graceful Latin style that was to secure him universal recognition as "the Prince of the Humanists." It was not till about the time of his first visit to England in 1499, during which he met John Colet and Thomas More who became his lifelong friends, that he turned seriously to the religious studies that were to occupy the largest share of his attention for the rest of his life.

Greek New Testament. The chief aim of Erasmus's work in the field of religious thought was the restoration of Christianity to its early simplicity as taught by Christ himself and by his disciples. He thought of Christianity as a guiding philosophy for the direction of daily life, rather than as the system of dogmatic beliefs or ecclesiastical practices which the medieval church had all too often made it appear. He described his religious ideal in a significant phrase, "the philosophy of Christ," in which, perhaps, we can trace the influence of the Brethren of the Common Life and the *Imitation of Christ.* This conception of religion made a thorough understanding of the original meaning of the Scriptures vitally necessary. He felt that the Vulgate, as the Latin version of the Bible accepted by the church was called, could not be entirely trusted, since it was a translation to start with and had been recopied, with possible errors, for centuries. Erasmus, therefore, undertook the task of editing the Greek text of the New Testament from the earliest available manuscripts. After years of labor he finally published it, with extensive annotations, in 1516. It was the first time that the New Testament had been printed in its original language. The conservative theologians, who had been accustomed to following the Vulgate as the final authority and many of whom were ignorant of Greek, were profoundly suspicious of the new edition and attacked Erasmus bitterly.

Erasmian reform. Meanwhile, Erasmus was also working busily for the reform of those practices in the church that to him seemed out of harmony with the Christian spirit. This he hoped would be accomplished by the growth of enlightened education and a clearer understanding of the philosophy of Christ, aided in the meantime by common-sense criticism of existing abuses. The best known of his numerous works in this field are the *Praise of Folly* and the *Familiar Colloquies,* wherein he ridiculed the wealth and self-seeking power of the clergy and the monastic orders, as well as practices, such as pilgrimages, fasts, and the veneration of relics, which seemed to him merely external forms, of no value unless in-

spired by a deep inner piety. Erasmus had a devastatingly satirical wit and had early discovered that ridicule can sometimes be a more effective weapon than heavy argument. Because of his command of Latin style, his wit and humor, everything he wrote was widely read. He helped to prepare the way for the Reformation, though he himself refused to be drawn into the conflict that followed it and remained within the church.

5. *The Fine Arts and Music*

Throughout this transitional period, the art of Italy and that of the northern countries developed along partially independent lines, but with each exerting an intermittent influence upon the other. On the whole, northern sculpture and painting moved more slowly away from the medieval spirit and style and seems less clearly to belong to the Renaissance. The northern sculpture of the fourteenth and fifteenth centuries, indeed, seems to represent a late phase of the Gothic rather than a Renaissance style. And though the Flemish painters of the fifteenth century displayed a mastery of naturalistic technique that more than rivals the Italians, their pictures reflect a less radical change in point of view. In music, on the other hand, northern France, England, and

This is one of several portraits of Erasmus of Rotterdam, the prince of the humanists, by Hans Holbein the Younger.

Roger van der Weyden's "Descent from the Cross," painted about 1435, expresses the deeply emotional piety inspired by the devotio moderna.

the Netherlands took the lead and created the Renaissance style that was to sweep western Europe in the sixteenth century.

Illumination in northern France. The great advances in the direction of naturalism and the realistic handling of space made by Giotto and his Italian successors exerted a strong influence on the painting of northern France in the fourteenth century. But, whereas the Italians specialized in large murals or panel paintings, the most characteristic painting of northern France was in miniature and was devoted to the illustration of books. It was, in fact, a continuation of the medieval illuminator's art, an art that had long flourished in the Gothic lands where the architectural style gave little opportunity for mural painting. Medieval illuminated manuscripts had been largely confined to monastery libraries, but in the fourteenth century secular princes and great nobles at the French court began to collect beautiful books much as they collected jewels and gold plate. Under their patronage,

skilled miniaturists, many of them imported from the Netherlands, illustrated both secular and religous books with paintings which gradually lost their function as pure decoration and became independent pictures. The numerous books of private devotion or "Books of Hours" presented an especially favorable opportunity for landscape painting in the calendar-like pictures representing each month of the year. The pictures on pages 217 and 219 and color illustration 7 are taken from the most famous of these, the *Book of Hours* of the Duke of Berry, illustrated by the Limbourg brothers about 1416.

Flemish painting. With the opening of the fifteenth century, the center of northern painting shifted from the Île de France to the Netherlands. The semi-royal court of the Dukes of Burgundy was now resident there, and in the rich Flemish cities artists could also count on the liberal patronage of merchants and financiers, the wealthiest and most cosmopolitan society north of the Alps. Under these favorable circumstances, they adapted the minutely realistic technique of the illuminators to larger panel paintings and developed a degree of sheer technical virtuosity that surpassed the most naturalistic work of the contemporary Italians. A part of this technical advance may be ascribed to the use of oil as a medium for binding pigment, for, though oil painting was not entirely new, Jan van Eyck (c. 1390–1441) was the first painter to exploit its possibilities fully. Nothing but pure personal genius, however, could account for the incredible skill with which Van Eyck built up harmoniously integrated pictures out of an infinite number of minutely accurate details. Whether he portrays the Annunciation or a madonna enthroned, together with a vivid portrait of the donor, the three-dimensional figures stand freely in a fully realized space, dominating the scene despite the wealth of detail that draws the eye away in admiration of the jewel-like perfection of clothing and furniture. If there is anything lacking, it is a sense of life and movement, a sense vividly present in his greatest successor, Roger van der Weyden (1400–1464), whose "Descent from the Cross" is pure drama. There is a more human quality, too, in the appealing portraits and religious scenes of Hans Memling (c. 1430–94), who marks the end of the Flemish school.

German painting. The great era of early Flemish painting had passed its peak before new tendencies began to make their appearance in German art. Here the pioneer genius, who grafted Italian influences on the sturdy stalk of native German tradition, was Albrecht Dürer (1471–1528) of Nürnberg. One of the most versatile of artists as well as one of the most profoundly thoughtful, with something of the wide-ranging scientific curiosity of Da Vinci, Dürer experimented with paintings, drawings, wood-cuts, and engravings and left an immense number of brilliant sketches as well as finished works. Many of these give evidence of the deep concern with moral and religious problems that later led him to enthusiastic acceptance of Luther's doctrine. Many, too, were portraits characterized by a vivid verisimilitude that has seldom been equaled. A generation later Hans Holbein the Younger (1497–1543) of Augsburg followed in Dürer's footsteps as a portrait painter, but without his spiritual depth

"Knight, Death, and the Devil," by Albrecht Dürer, 1513, is a fine example of the art of copper engraving, developed soon after the invention of printing to illustrate books. The subject was apparently suggested by Erasmus' Manual of the Christian Soldier.

or wide range of interest. The series of portraits painted during Holbein's long visit to the court of Henry VIII of England are of special interest to the modern historian. Both Dürer and Holbein came from South German cities where a wealthy patrician class of merchants and financiers maintained close relations with Italy. A more purely German style is evident in the forceful and deeply emotional but also harshly angular painting of Matthias Grünewald (1480–1530), whose home was in a small town near Frankfurt.

Sculpture. In the northern lands where Gothic architecture flourished, sculpture had developed during the High Middle Ages as an inseparable adjunct to the great Gothic buildings, and so firmly rooted was the Gothic style that it continued, though with significant modifications in the direction of greater naturalism

This delicate wooden statue of St. Elizabeth was carved by Tilman Riemenschneider, one of the finest German sculptors of the pre-Reformation period.

and refinement, throughout the fourteenth and fifteenth centuries. A group of Franco-Flemish sculptors working in the Île de France and Burgundy, of whom Claus Sluter (died c. 1406) was the most famous, contributed especially to the growth of realism in French sculpture. A still more striking realism is characteristic of the distinctively German art of wood-carving, which flourished in the late fifteenth and early sixteenth centuries. The figures carved by Tilman Riemenschneider (1468–1531), in their lyric grace, and those of Hans Brüggemann, in their sturdy and highly individualized realism, although little known, rival the best of the French late Gothic sculpture.

Music. The combination of medieval traditions with new techniques and a new sense of artistic form, which characterized so much of the art of the Northern Renaissance, was especially noticeable in music. Throughout the fourteenth and fifteenth centuries, a series of Franco-Flemish composers — Guillaume de Machaut (1300–1377), Guillaume Dufay (1400–1474), and Josquin des Prez (1450–1521), to mention only the most important — took over the medieval polyphonic tradition, refined it, freed it from the shackles imposed by a limited range of rhythms and tonal intervals, combined choral with instrumental music, and composed both secular and sacred music in which the parts were woven into a harmonious whole. That the Renaissance composers were themselves aware of creating something new is demonstrated by the appearance of the term *Ars nova,* "the new art," in the works of the musical theorists around the beginning of the fourteenth century. The composers of this period are no longer anonymous. We know the names of most of them, and they received the social homage due to creative artists. Their works were performed in cathedral and court by highly trained professional musicians. Nor was the cultivation of polyphonic music dependent entirely upon the patronage of the church or the princely courts. In the cities of Italy and the Netherlands groups of burghers formed societies or confraternities for the performance of vocal and instrumental music. It is difficult without being unduly technical to indicate the changes in musical form introduced during this period, for the evolution from medieval traditions was gradual and the transition to modern conceptions of rhythm and tonality was still far from complete. The majority of Renaissance composers still frequently used the medieval device of the *cantus firmus* as a base and erected upon it a structure of independent musical lines related to one another only by the laws of counterpoint.[1] But by the middle of the fifteenth century some at least of the composers were beginning to compose all voices simultaneously so that the relation between them was more closely integrated than was possible when the lines were composed successively. The use of canon or imitation — that is, the repetition of phrases or figures more or less exactly, though at a different pitch, in one voice after another — served in many instances to bind the whole work together in a web of sound.

[1] See above, page 259.

27

The States of Europe at the

Dawn of the Modern Age

IN THE LAST HALF of the fifteenth century and
the first two decades of the sixteenth, the period of transition from the High Middle Ages
to the early modern era was drawing to its
close. The general characteristics of that
change we have already noted. The purpose
of this chapter is to pass in brief review the
history of the principal European states during
these years, so as to show the general structure
of Europe at the beginning of modern times,
before we pass on to the new era that began
with the Protestant Reformation, the foundation of the vast Hapsburg empire of Charles V,
and the long struggle between the rival dynasties of Hapsburg and Valois. In all parts of
Europe we shall find somewhat similar developments taking place. Under strong and more
or less absolute rulers, aided by the support of
the rising middle class, the territory of the
various states was being consolidated and the
authority of the central government was tri-
umphing over the last remnants of feudal independence. At the same time, the territorial
princes were transferring control of industry
and commerce from the cities, which had been
the focal centers of economic life under the
medieval guild system, to the state government, thus laying the foundations of modern
economic nationalism. Strengthened by this
newly won control of the political and economic forces of their states, the monarchs of

Europe also began in these years to seek additions to their territory by conquest, from which
sprang those dynastic wars, alliances and
counter-alliances, so characteristic of European
history in the first centuries of the modern era.
Finally, this period witnessed a significant shift
in the center of gravity of European trade from
the east to the west, due to the discovery of
new lands and new trade routes in the Atlantic.

1. Spain and Portugal

The Spanish peninsula. Nowhere can the
developments listed above be more clearly observed than in the history of Spain, which rose
during this period to the first rank among European states. Hitherto the various kingdoms
of the Spanish peninsula had played a relatively insignificant role in the general history
of Europe. They were cut off from the remainder of the continent by the high barrier of
the Pyrenees and had not yet learned to use
the Atlantic as a highway of commerce to the
Far East and West. Moreover, the Christian
states had had to wage a long war of conquest
to win their land from the Moslems, and they
had since wasted much energy in fighting
among themselves. In the middle of the fifteenth century, the peninsula was still divided
into five separate kingdoms. Of these Castile,
with which Leon had been incorporated, was

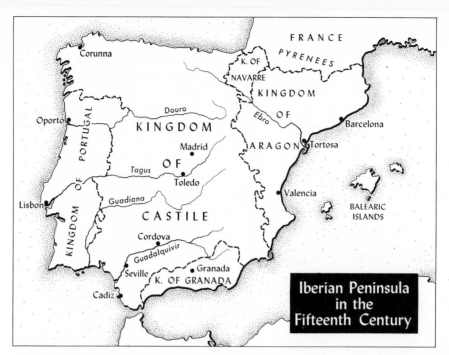

Iberian Peninsula
in the
Fifteenth Century

much the largest. It occupied the whole central plateau and included more than sixty per cent of the entire peninsula. The smaller kingdoms of Aragon and Portugal lay along the coast to east and west respectively. Far to the north, the little kingdom of Navarre straddled the Pyrenees, and in the extreme south the Moslem kingdom of Granada still remained as a reminder that Spain had once belonged to Islam.

Castile and Aragon. The long period of warfare with the Moslems and the gradual expansion by conquest had left a permanent impress on the character of Castile. The Castilian people had grown up a fighting race, rigidly orthodox. Moreover, Castile had acquired its territory bit by bit, and each new acquisition formed a separate unit in the state under the control of half-independent feudal nobles or the orders of crusading knights. As a result, the condition of feudal anarchy common to most countries in the Middle Ages had lasted in Castile till after the middle of the fifteenth century. The power of the crown was also limited to some extent by the Cortes, an assembly representing the upper and middle classes, something like the French Estates General. Castile was mostly an agricultural and pastoral country, none too rich, though its industry and commerce were soon to be stimulated by the opening-up of exclusive markets in the New World, and the importation of

gold and silver from Mexico and Peru would bring it for a time a false prosperity. Aragon had a stronger central government, though there, too, the king was hampered by feudal nobles and the Cortes. Thanks to its position on the eastern coast, it had a more highly developed commerce than had Castile. The acquisition of Sicily in the thirteenth century and the islands of Majorca and Sardinia in the fourteenth by the ruling family of Aragon gave it a considerable share of the Mediterranean trade.

Union of Spain. The foundations of the future greatness of Spain were laid by the union of all the peninsula except Portugal under the rule of Ferdinand of Aragon (1479–1516) and Isabella of Castile (1474–1504), who were married in 1469. When they inherited their respective kingdoms a few years later, the two greatest states in Spain were brought under a united government, though for another generation they remained separate in theory. The combined power of the two monarchs made further conquest possible. In 1492, the year in which Columbus carried the flag of Castile to the New World, they conquered the kingdom of Granada, thus wiping out the last independent Moslem state. Thereafter, Ferdinand launched an ambitious and astute foreign policy, designed to make Spain a power to be reckoned with in European affairs and to add territory to the possessions of his family. For his part in the Italian wars, of which more later, he acquired the kingdom of Naples from the lesser branch of the Aragonese dynasty in 1503, and in 1512 he conquered all of Navarre south of the Pyrenees.

Rise of royal power in Spain.   The reign of Ferdinand and Isabella accomplished not only the territorial consolidation of Spain, but also the centralization of authority in the hands of a strong royal government. This was especially necessary in Castile, where the independence of the feudal nobles had sadly weakened the government and had produced a frightful amount of lawlessness and disorder. The monarchs began by restoring order and security for life and property and went on to strip the feudal nobles and the great crusading orders of their independent powers and to reduce them to subjection to the crown. In this task, Ferdinand and Isabella could count on the support of the common people, who preferred a strong government to feudal anarchy. The monarchs then turned their attention to the reform of the Spanish church, which had been thoroughly feudalized and had become rather lax in discipline. They acquired from Pope Sixtus IV the right to nominate all the higher ecclesiastical officers in Spain and used that right to fill the church with men of high character and unquestioned orthodoxy, who would also be devoted to the crown. As a result, the Spanish church became an instrument for the extension of royal power, and was to be the strongest bulwark of orthodox Catholicism in the religious conflicts of the sixteenth century. The Spanish Inquisition, founded in 1478 under the control of the monarchy, was used to crush all signs of heresy and to root out what elements of Moslem religion remained. The expulsion of Moors and Jews strengthened the religious and racial unity of the country, but was a sad blow to its commerce and industry. Finally, it was Ferdinand and Isabella who began the process of whittling away the authority of the Cortes of Castile and Aragon, now the sole remaining check on the authority of the crown. There were rebellions against Ferdinand's rule in Castile after Isabella's death, but the two monarchs had done their work so well that their successors were able to build up the most absolute monarchy in Europe.

Portugal.   Despite the union and expansion of its powerful neighbors, the little kingdom of Portugal on the western coast still retained its independence. Like the other kingdoms in the peninsula, it had played an unimportant part in European history until nearly the end of the fifteenth century. Then it, too, rose to sudden power, a change due almost entirely to the courageous energy of its great navigators. As we shall see when we come to deal with the explorations and discoveries of this era, Portuguese sailors vied with the Spanish in finding new trade routes through the Atlantic, and, like Spain, Portugal enjoyed a period of great if somewhat illusory prosperity.

2. England

Wars of the Roses.   England had scarcely emerged from the Hundred Years' War (1453) when it was plunged into a long, intermittent civil strife between rival factions in the royal family and the higher nobility. The war had left England a dangerous legacy of disorder. The great nobles had become accustomed to keeping large bands of armed retainers, and accustomed also to violence and bloodshed. Every baron had a following among the knights and gentry of his neighborhood, who wore his livery and would fight for him. He repaid their services by "maintaining" their interests in the law courts or in private quarrels. This custom of "livery and maintenance" frustrated the normal action of justice and restored something like the old condition of feudal anarchy. The weak government of the feeble-minded Henry VI utterly failed to keep order, as it had failed in the war against France. Moreover, the weakness of the king opened the way for quarrels between one faction or another of the baronage who sought to control the government. These factional disputes broke into open civil war in 1455 between the followers of Richard, Duke of York, next heir to the throne after Henry's infant son, and the supporters of the reigning house of Lancaster, though it was not till 1460 that York definitely claimed the throne. He was killed shortly after, but his son continued the struggle and succeeded in winning the crown as Edward IV (1461–83). The Lancastrian party was now in opposition to the king and the fight went on to an accompaniment of treachery and murder. On the death of Edward IV, his brother Richard III (1483–85) seized the crown from his infant nephew Edward V, and added to this fairly normal crime the more shocking one of having the young Edward and his brother murdered. Recent research has raised some doubt as to whether he was in fact guilty of instigating the murder of his nephews, but it was widely believed at the time and was more than the English people could stand, even in that callous age. They deserted Richard and welcomed Henry Tudor, a distant heir to the Lancastrian claims, who made a successful bid for the crown in 1485. These frequent and rather petty civil wars are known collectively as the Wars of the Roses from the white and red roses that, according to tradition, were the badges of the houses of York and Lancaster respectively.

Slaughter of the barons.   The civil wars had affected the majority of the population surprisingly little, save as they interfered with security and good government. The people generally were neutral. No principle of any kind was at stake. It was merely a party fight among the nobles and the royal family. But for that very reason the Wars of the Roses had one very important and lasting influence on the course of English history. They destroyed the old nobility. Each battle thinned the ranks of the old feudal families, and each turn of fortune was followed by executions and the confiscation

of ancient family estates. From this time on, the monarchy was to have little trouble with the barons. Feudalism in England, which had long been dying, had received its death blow.

Henry VII.   A new era in England's history opened in 1485 with the reign of Henry VII, first of the Tudor sovereigns. Having no very sound hereditary claim to the throne, Henry knew that his only hope of keeping it lay in giving the people the kind of government they wanted; and they wanted, above all, peace, security for life and property, and an opportunity to carry on their business under favorable conditions. They were tired of factional strife and the violence of the nobles. In short, they wanted a strong government, devoted to the interests of the people. No one could have been better suited to the task of satisfying those demands than the quiet, self-contained, and hard-headed Tudor. There was nothing very colorful or dramatic about his personality, but he had a thorough understanding of the needs of his country and a remarkable ability to get things done. Under his canny guidance, England's transformation from a medieval to a modern state was well-nigh completed.

Restoration of order.   The most vital problem facing the new Tudor king was the restoration of order. This could be accomplished only by reducing the power of the remaining barons. Henry set about the task with great energy, excluding them from his royal council and using the Court of the Star Chamber, which was the royal council in its judicial capacity, to suppress livery and maintenance, and to punish all attempts on the part of the lords to interfere with the prosecution of justice or to oppress their humbler neighbors. With the Star Chamber court to deal with the great lords, the local courts were left free to punish the lesser criminals. A task of this magnitude takes time, and something was still left to be done by his successors, but when Henry VII died he left England in a reasonably orderly condition, with the royal authority unquestionably supreme in the state.

King Richard III, in this striking portrait in the National Portrait Gallery, London, shows a personality very different from that presented by Shakespeare and even by many historians.

Foreign alliances. Next to order at home, Henry needed peace abroad and recognition of his title by foreign powers. This he secured by obtaining a marriage alliance with Spain, which was rapidly becoming one of the strongest of the European states. The marriage of his son Arthur to Catherine of Aragon, daughter of Ferdinand and Isabella, was a diplomatic triumph. The death of Arthur shortly thereafter threatened to break the bond, but it was renewed by the betrothal of the widowed Catherine to Arthur's younger brother, the future King Henry VIII. The Tudor family thus gained the support of the powerful Spanish dynasty, which was already allied by marriage with the imperial Hapsburgs, who held, among other possessions, the Burgundian Netherlands. Not the least of the benefits accruing from this alliance was that it ensured to English merchants fair treatment in the ports of Spain and the Netherlands.

Encouragement of commerce. Henry VII, indeed, never forgot the interests of the merchants. English commerce, especially the rich trade in wool and woolen goods, had been growing rapidly during the fifteenth century, but with very little help from the central government. A large part of English trade was still handled by foreigners, some of whom, like the Hanseatic merchants, had greater privileges in English ports than the natives themselves. Moreover, lacking strong support from the state, English merchants could not always secure favorable treatment in other countries. Henry undertook to change all this as far as possible. At the beginning of his reign he passed legislation through Parliament designed to give English ships, manned by English sailors, a monopoly of carrying certain types of goods. Wherever possible, he cut down the privileges of foreign traders in England so as to give the advantage to their native competitors, and, where the foreigners still held privileges in England, he sought treaties with their home governments to secure reciprocal privileges for English merchants. The commercial treaties, cemented by family alliances with Spain and Burgundy, opened up great opportunities for English trade. All in all, Henry's economic policies were typically modern. Their chief characteristics — the protection of native trade and industry from foreign competition, the securing of commercial treaties with other states, the transference of economic control from the cities to the state government, and the close alliance between the monarchy and the middle class — were all to be adopted by English governments for the next three centuries.

Accession of Henry VIII. It was a prosperous, orderly state and a strong royal government that Henry VIII inherited in the year 1509. The young king was active and ambitious. Under his rule England was to play a larger part in international affairs and to take the first decisive steps in a religious revolution. Henry VIII looms larger than his less spectacular father on the pages of English history, but it was the elder Henry who laid the foundations of Tudor England.

3. France, Burgundy, and Italy

The successful conclusion of the Hundred Years' War was a triumph for the French monarchy. Charles VII was not the greatest of kings, but he had driven out the English and had saved his country from disintegration. The war had taught the French people that the safety of the country depended on the king alone, for the great nobles had almost ruined France by their selfishness and the Estates General had proved incompetent. The people generally, and especially those of the commercial and industrial middle class, would have welcomed a strong royal government over the whole state; but before there could be such a government, the kings had still to complete the subjugation of the nobility and the consolidation of France by bringing the few remaining half-independent fiefs directly under their control. This task was barely begun by Charles VII. It was left for his son and grandson, Louis XI (1461–83) and Charles VIII (1483–98) to carry it to a successful conclusion.

Louis XI and Charles the Bold. The most powerful and independent of the French fiefs still outstanding was the duchy of Burgundy. Although descended from the French royal family, the Burgundian dukes had by the fifteenth century acquired extensive territories outside of France and had gradually ceased to regard themselves as subjects of the French crown. In addition to their original duchy, they held Franche-Comté, Luxemburg, and the rich counties and duchies that made up the Netherlands. To these possessions Duke Charles the Bold (1467–77) added Alsace and Lorraine. In reality, Charles ruled what was practically a kingdom in that debatable land between France and Germany, reminiscent of the ancient kingdom of Lothair, and it is not surprising that he should desire the title of king. His ambitions inevitably brought him into violent conflict with Louis XI. For a time he seemed to be having the best of it, but he had also aroused the enmity of his warlike neighbors, the Swiss, and it was they who finally brought about his defeat and death. His daughter Mary kept up the struggle with France, aided by her husband Maximilian of Hapsburg, until her death in 1482. Maximilian then made peace with Louis. The duchy of Burgundy was surrendered and was brought directly under the French crown. Alsace and Lorraine were also returned to their former owners, but the rest of the Burgundian states were kept by Philip the Handsome, the son of Mary and Maximilian, to make a formidable addition to the lands of the house of Hapsburg.

Consolidation of France. Meanwhile, Louis XI was using his undoubted talent for diplomacy and intrigue to good effect in subjugating the other semi-independent feudatories of France. The character of this strange, cunning, and unscrupulous man will always be an enigma to historians. He was superstitious, treacherous, and cruel; yet he must be given credit for his invaluable services in making France a united nation. When he died in 1483, the duchy of Brittany was almost the only fief outside the royal domain. Charles VIII was still a boy, though officially of age, when he succeeded to the throne, but fortunately Louis had left his daughter, Anne of Beaujeu, with authority to act as guardian to her young brother until he should grow up. For nine years this princess, whom her wise if somewhat misogynous father had called "the least foolish woman in Europe," practically ruled France. It was her energy that put down the last rebellions of the French nobles and finally, after years of fighting, secured the union of Brittany with the royal domain by the marriage of Charles VIII to Anne, Duchess of Brittany, in 1491. With this acquisition the consolidation of France into a united territorial state was practically complete.

Triumph of monarchy. As in Spain, the territorial consolidation of France was accompanied by the centralization of power in the hands of an absolute monarchy. The nobles were robbed of almost all their political authority and the Estates General was reduced to a negligible position. During and after the war, the French kings had secured the right to levy taxes on their own authority throughout the state. With this financial backing, they could maintain a standing army with which the nobles could not compete. Moreover, they could ensure the subjugation of the nobility by taking them into their pay. The nobles became courtiers and served in the élite companies of heavy cavalry which formed the core of the royal army. In compensation for their lost independence, the nobles retained their social prerogatives and the more substantial privilege of practical immunity from taxation. Only occasionally hereafter, under very weak kings and when the country was torn by religious strife, would the nobles attempt to reassert their independence, and then with no permanent success. Meanwhile, the middle class in France, as elsewhere, profited by the restoration of order and the gradual assumption of economic control by a strong government. At the end of the fifteenth century, France was prosperous and all classes looked to the king as the embodiment of the national state.

France and Italy. Charles VIII had scarcely taken over the government of his newly united kingdom from his wise sister before he began to dream of adding to his glory by wars of conquest. And Italy, rich and cultured, but weakened by its fatal lack of unity, seemed a prize within the easy grasp of the absolute ruler of a great state. Moreover, Charles had inherited the old Angevin claim to the kingdom of Naples, and few monarchs in that age of dynastic greed could bring themselves to ignore such a claim when a favorable opportunity for pressing it was presented. In 1494, France was strong and united, while the political situation in Italy made any united resistance to an invader extremely unlikely. The balance of power in Italy, which depended on the alliance of Milan, Florence, and Naples, had been overturned after the death of Lorenzo de' Medici in 1492.[1] Milan was at this time under the nominal rule of the young Duke Giangaleazzo Sforza, grandson of the *condottiere* Francesco Sforza, who had founded the dynasty in 1454. For many years, however, the real power in the Milanese state had been in the hands of the duke's uncle Ludovico Sforza, called Il Moro, acting as regent. Even after he came of age and married, the duke seemed content to leave control of the state to his powerful uncle; but his wife was more ambitious, and her father, King Alfonso II of Naples, supported her demand that Il Moro turn over the government to the titular duke, and incidentally to his wife and her Neapolitan relatives. Piero de' Medici, forgetting his father's diplomatic policy, supported Alfonso's demands. To protect his usurped authority, Ludovico Sforza then turned to Charles VIII, inviting him to invade Italy and offering to help him in the conquest of Naples. So began for France the long series of futile wars in Italy. For more than half a century, French kings wasted men and money in the vain attempt to conquer and hold a land that had little in common with France, while neglecting to round out their frontiers to the north and east within the natural boundaries of the Rhine and the Alps.

Charles VIII invades Naples. The first French invasion of Italy was little more than a military parade, with some comic-opera effects. Charles VIII crossed the Alps in September, 1494, marched down through the peninsula without encountering serious opposition, and by the early spring of the following year had conquered the whole kingdom of Naples, still without fighting a real battle. However, Naples was easier to win than to hold. The tactlessness and brutality of the French soon made them unpopular in the kingdom, while to the north the other Italian states, belatedly alarmed at the presence of the foreign invader, began to unite. Charles was forced to withdraw from Italy, leaving a garrison in Naples which was easily driven out by Alfonso's son Ferrante in 1496. The only immediate result of the invasion had been the expulsion of the Medici from Florence by the

indignant citizens, when Piero supinely surrendered the outlying Tuscan forts to Charles.

Louis XII invades Italy. Charles's expeditions had shown the ease with which conquests could be won in Italy, and the next French king, Louis XII (1498–1515), had not been a year on the throne before he followed his example. Louis, who was a cousin of the late king, had inherited a claim to Milan through his grandmother Valentina Visconti, Duchess of Orléans. He therefore directed his attack against Milan, which he had isolated by winning over Venice and Pope Alexander VI with promises of aid for their own selfish ambitions. The French army made short work of the Milanese mercenaries. The duchy was conquered and Ludovico Sforza was taken prisoner. Louis then prepared to move against Naples. The major difficulty in that direction was the probable opposition of Ferdinand, King of Aragon and Sicily, who might resent the expulsion of his kinsmen of the lesser branch of the house of Aragon from Naples. Louis avoided this difficulty by inviting Ferdinand to become a partner in the conquest. Naples was again taken without serious opposition, and again the French found it impossible to hold what they had won. Almost immediately the two conquerors quarreled over the division of the spoils. As a result, war broke out between them in 1502, and before the end of the following year the French were driven out and Naples was added to the growing possessions of Spain.

The League of Cambrai. With France holding the duchy of Milan in the north and Spain the kingdom of Naples in the south, the independence of Italy was sadly threatened; but still the other Italian states could not unite against the menace of foreign domination. The next few years were occupied by shifting alliances and cold-blooded land-grabbing on the part of both Italian and foreign states. Venice was the first to suffer. That rich republic had aroused the enmity and greed of the other powers by its unfortunate policy of landward expansion. Both the French king, now Duke of Milan, and Maximilian of Hapsburg, who had been elected emperor in 1493, claimed parts of the Venetian territory, as did also the warlike Pope Julius II (1503–13), whose determined ambition was to recover full

[1] See above, pages 316–317.

control of all land that had ever belonged to the Papal States. These three formed the nucleus of the League of Cambrai (1508), later joined by Ferdinand of Aragon, for the partition of Venice. Most of the fighting was done by the French and papal troops, and with considerable success. The proud republic was on the verge of ruin when Julius II made a separate peace with it in 1510, on condition of receiving the lands that had been taken by Venice from the Romagna.

The Holy League. Having won all he wanted from Venice, the pope then turned against his French allies, who were becoming dangerous neighbors. In 1511, Julius succeeded in breaking up the League of Cambrai and forming a new "Holy League," composed of the papacy, Venice, and Spain, and soon joined by the Swiss, Maximilian, and Ferdinand's son-in-law, Henry VIII of England. Its purpose was to drive the French out of Italy and, incidentally, to distract the attention of France while Ferdinand conquered Spanish Navarre. The French won an initial victory in the bloody battle of Ravenna early in 1512, but before the end of the year the Holy League had achieved its objective. The French were again forced to withdraw from Italy, leaving Milan to Il Moro's son, Maximilian Sforza, under the protection

of the Swiss. Florence was returned to the Medici as punishment for having allied with France.

Francis I reconquers Milan. For a brief period Italy was restored to something like its state prior to the invasions. But in 1515 a new king, Francis I, ascended the throne of France and immediately followed the example of his predecessors in seeking glory beyond the Alps. The young king swept down into Italy with a powerful army, defeated the combined Swiss and Milanese forces at Marignano, and within a few months had reconquered the duchy of Milan. One very important result of this invasion was the Concordat of Bologna, arranged in 1516 between Francis and the new pope, Leo X, whereby the king surrendered the "liberties" of the French church asserted in the Pragmatic Sanction of Bourges (1438), but received in return the right to nominate all the higher clergy in France.

The wars in Italy had by this time lasted more than two decades. Italy had paid dearly for its lack of unity, and France had merely paved the way for a long and costly struggle with the house of Hapsburg, to whose rising fortunes we must now turn our attention.

4. Germany and the House of Hapsburg

Disunion of Germany. Germany in this period presents the one great exception, outside of Italy, to the general rule of territorial and political consolidation and the rise of strong central government. The amalgamation of the German monarchy with the impressive but impractical Holy Roman Empire and the disastrous conflict with the papacy had prevented the formation in either Italy or Germany of a unified state. In the middle of the thirteenth century the empire had seemed on the point of dissolution. It was revived, but with scarcely more than a nominal unity, and it grew no stronger. The emperors had still very little

Raphael's magnificent portrait of Julius II gives a vivid impression of the warlike old pope who completed the recovery of the Papal States. Later this picture was copied almost exactly by Titian.

real authority. They could raise neither adequate revenue nor an effective army outside their own family lands, nor were they strong enough to keep order and enforce justice throughout the empire. The Diet of the empire — the assembly of princes and representatives from the free imperial cities — was equally powerless to secure obedience to its laws. The Emperor Maximilian I did make some attempt to strengthen the central government but accomplished little, for, like the other emperors of this period, he was far more interested in advancing the position of his family than in adding to the imperial authority. This lack of unity in the empire, however, was compensated for to some extent by the consolidation of the larger states within Germany. In these individual states, duchies, margravates, and the like, something like the same tendency toward centralization that we have noted in the monarchical states was taking place. Finally, it must not be forgotten that, despite political and social disorder, Germany was on the whole very prosperous in these years and was undergoing a spiritual and intellectual revival under the influence of the Christian Renaissance.

Hapsburg emperors. The most striking development in German political history during this period, and one that was to have a tremendous influence on the whole history of Europe, was the phenomenal rise of the Austrian house of Hapsburg. After the election of Albert II (1438–39), the imperial title remained in the Hapsburg family generation after generation until it came to be considered almost as an hereditary right. Albert was followed by Frederick III (1440–93) and Maximilian I (1493–1519). It was the latter of these who was chiefly responsible for bringing into the Hapsburg family that vast collection of lands outside of Germany that was to make his grandson, Charles V, the most powerful ruler in Europe in the next generation. Charming, cultured, and impractical, Maximilian played a part, usually pretty ineffective, in every international crisis of that crucial period when the monarchs of France and Spain were consolidating their territories and were turning to the conquest of Italy. Maximilian was the perpetual victim of magnificent and visionary schemes, for which his economic and military

Dürer's portrait of the Emperor Maximilian I, 1518, is the best existing likeness of the emperor who made the Hapsburgs the strongest dynasty in Europe.

resources were ludicrously inadequate. His participation in the Italian wars brought him nothing but grief, while his devotion to his family interests and to foreign projects ruined his chances of building up a strong imperial government in Germany. His only success was due to the skill and good fortune with which he arranged a series of marriage alliances with other dynasties. But that alone was enough to make his house the most powerful in Europe.

Hapsburg marriage alliances. The first of the marriages that was to do more for the Hapsburg family than conquest had ever done took place in 1477, when Maximilian himself married Mary of Burgundy, the daughter and sole heiress of that reckless duke, Charles the Bold, who had just met his death in battle with the Swiss. To this marriage was born a son, Philip the Handsome, who inherited the Burgundian estates, including the Free County of Burgundy (Franche-Comté), Luxemburg, and the rich provinces of the Netherlands, after his mother's early death. In 1496, Philip was married to Joanna, the daughter of Ferdinand and Isabella, under whom the kingdoms of Spain had been united. Within a year this marriage became unexpectedly important because of the death of Joanna's only brother, which left her the heiress to the combined territories of Castile and Aragon. Ten years after

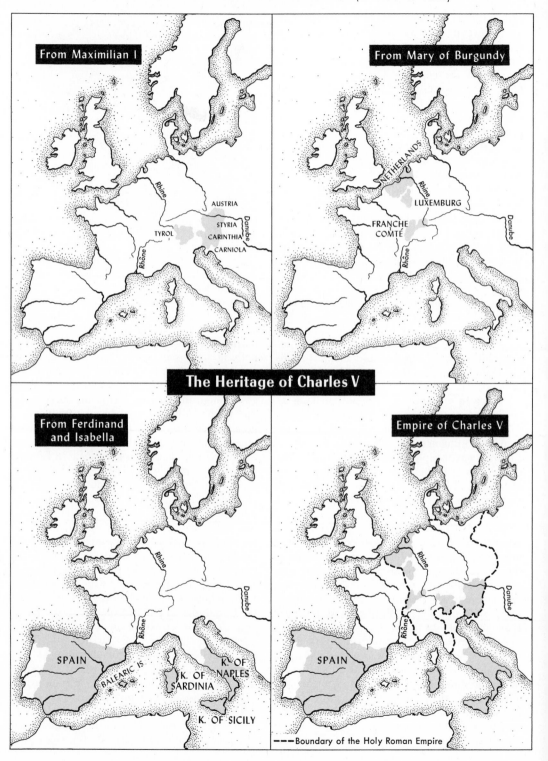

From Maximilian I

AUSTRIA
STYRIA
TYROL
CARINTHIA
CARNIOLA

Rhine
Rhône
Danube

From Mary of Burgundy

NETHERLANDS
LUXEMBURG
FRANCHE COMTÉ

Rhine
Rhône
Danube

The Heritage of Charles V

From Ferdinand and Isabella

SPAIN
BALEARIC IS
K. OF SARDINIA
K. OF NAPLES
K. OF SICILY

Rhine
Rhône
Danube

Empire of Charles V

SPAIN

Rhine
Rhône
Danube

- - - Boundary of the Holy Roman Empire

their marriage, Philip died and his wife Joanna was adjudged insane. The hereditary claims of both were thus left to their six-year-old son Charles, who immediately succeeded to his father's Burgundian states. With the death of his maternal grandfather Ferdinand in 1516, the young Charles also inherited the united kingdom of Spain, plus the Aragonese kingdoms of Sardinia, Sicily, and Naples, and the Castilian claim staked out by Columbus and other explorers to the new world of the Americas. When, in 1519, his paternal grandfather Maximilian died, Charles added to these the hereditary Hapsburg lands in Germany, which included the duchy of Austria and the adjacent duchies of Styria, Carinthia, and Carniola and the county of Tyrol. In that same year he was elected emperor as Charles V, and thereby gained the imperial rights of government, such as they were, over all of Germany and northern Italy. With this vast accumulation of Burgundian, Spanish, Austrian, and imperial lands, Charles V, at the age of nineteen, became the ruler of a larger territory than had been collected under one monarch since the break-up of Charlemagne's empire.[1]

5. *Expansion of the European Horizon by Exploration*

In this last part of the transitional period between the High Middle Ages and the beginnings of modern times, while the states of Europe were consolidating under the impulsion of economic forces to form strongly centralized units, the cupidity and economic rivalry of those states caused an eager search for new trade routes that resulted in a vast expansion of the horizon of Europe. Not only new trade routes but new lands were discovered, and a new world was opened up to European exploitation. The beginning of the modern age in Europe coincides with the beginning of the modern world.

Early geographical knowledge. What knowledge medieval Europe possessed of the world outside its narrow borders it had inherited mostly from ancient Greek geographers. These had been aware that the earth was a sphere,

[1] See map, page 348, and genealogical table in the Appendix.

and Eratosthenes (c. 200 B.C.) had calculated its circumference with remarkable accuracy at about 25,000 miles. Most of this ancient fund of knowledge was transmitted to medieval Europe through the encyclopedic *Geography* of Claudius Ptolemy (c. 150 A.D.), who, incidentally, gave a much smaller calculation of the circumference of the earth — about 18,000 miles — and so inspired explorers with undue optimism. More precise information concerning the outlines of the known world was added by medieval Moslem and Christian navigators and map-makers. In the best medieval maps, Europe, northern Africa, western Asia, and the lands bordering on the Indian Ocean were shown fairly clearly. Much as the medieval navigators had done for the science of geography, however, the first great addition to Western knowledge of the world during the Middle Ages was made by travelers who pressed eastward overland until they reached the rich and populous countries of the distant East.

Marco Polo. Of these the most important were three members of an enterprising Venetian merchant family. In 1271, Niccolò and Matteo Polo, who had already traded in the western portion of the great Tartar Empire that covered all central Asia and eastern Europe, set out on a second expedition to the East. This time they took with them Niccolò's young son Marco, and they did not stop in the western lands of the Golden Horde. Instead, they pressed on through central Asia until they arrived at the court of the Tartar emperor, Kublai Khan, in the Chinese city of Pekin. They were kindly received and were given positions of honor in the Tartar government. Marco, especially, became a favorite of the great khan and was sent on numerous expeditions to almost every part of the Tartar Empire. For seventeen years he remained in the khan's service, visiting lands unknown to Europeans before his time and traveling roads where no European was to follow him until the nineteenth century. At last, wearied of exile, the Polos returned home, traveling this time by water around the eastern and southern coasts of Asia to India and thence by land to the Mediterranean.

The lure of the East. After his return, Marco Polo published his famous memoirs.

The Polo family en route to China, an illustration from the Catalan Atlas *in the Bibliothèque Nationale, Paris. The inscription reads: "This caravan has started from the Empire of Sarra to proceed to Cathay."*

His account of what he had actually seen is amazingly accurate, though to his contemporaries it seemed the wildest exaggeration. Still, if only a part of what "Marco of the millions" recounted was true, there was in the East wealth such as Europe had never dreamed of, and held, moreover, by a people who loved the arts of peace more than war. To Europeans, poor and warlike, Cathay (China) became the promised land of unbelievable wealth, an easy prey if only it could be reached, or at any rate the source of a fabulously rich trade. And aside from Marco Polo's story, the West had already ample evidence of the rich possibilities of trade with the Far East. The trade in pepper, cinnamon, and other spices highly valued in an age when artificial means of preserving food were rare, in silk, precious stones, and other luxury goods, had helped to found the fortunes of Venice, Genoa, and Pisa. But the Italians could not trade directly with the producers of these commodities. The Moslem middlemen, who commanded the land and water routes between India and the Mediterranean, took the lion's share of the profits. The long overland route through central Asia was impractical for regular trade. Was there not some other way of getting to India and China, a direct route by water that would enable Western merchants to sail directly to the source of Eastern wealth?

Search for a new route to the East. It was the hope of finding such a route, either by sailing south around Africa or west to Asia, which was believed to be much less distant than it actually is, that inspired daring Portuguese, Spanish, French, and English seamen of the fifteenth century, and even earlier, to set out on perilous voyages of exploration into the unknown Atlantic. Fear of the Atlantic was ingrained in the minds of European sailors, accustomed as they were only to coasting voyages, though the use of the magnetic compass as a guide in the open sea had long been known, and the *caravels* developed by the Portuguese in the fifteenth century were seaworthy little ships, capable of long ocean voyages. Exploring voyages were, however, expensive as well as hazardous, and for a long time they brought few results. Small wonder that progress was very slow. Had it not been for the authority of the great state governments, backed by the capital and the demands of the merchant class, the age of discovery might have been postponed indefinitely. It is doubtful, indeed, if it could have been achieved by the medieval system of guild and city economy. It was no coincidence that discovery followed the rise of the centralized states and the beginnings of capitalism; nor was it coincidence that the explorations were nearly all sponsored by the states along the Atlantic seaboard. For the people who faced the Atlantic felt the need of a new route to the East more keenly than the Italians, who were on the whole well enough content with their existing monopoly of the Eastern trade, second-hand though it was.

Portuguese sail around Africa. The little kingdom of Portugal, situated at the southwest tip of Europe, took the lead in fifteenth-century exploration of the African coast and of the neighboring islands of the Atlantic. The Portuguese were not the first to set out, but they were the most persistent, thanks in large part to the intelligent direction and unflagging enthusiasm of a prince of the royal family, Henry "the Navigator," who for more than forty years prior to his death in 1460 devoted himself to the encouragement of exploration. Henry's motives were a strange mixture of scientific curiosity, crusading zeal, and national ambition. Some of his ideas, such as his hope of reaching the upper Nile from the western coast by way of the Senegal River and thus outflanking the Moslems in North Africa, proved erroneous. Nevertheless, his explorers achieved important results. Before his death they had founded permanent settlements in the islands of Madeira and the Azores, had set up a regular trade, partly in slaves, with the Guinea coast, and were already pushing farther south. The sure profits of the Guinea trade, however, tended to keep explorers from going farther, and twenty-six years passed before the first Portuguese ship, commanded by Bartolomeo Diaz, rounded the southern extremity of Africa in 1486. The way to India was now open. In 1498 a Portuguese fleet under Vasco da Gama sailed into the Indian harbor of Calicut and established the first direct commercial contact between Europe and the Far East, thereby giving Portugal a monopoly of the rich Eastern trade which she held for nearly a hundred years.[1]

Discovery of America. In the meantime, while the Portuguese were still feeling their way down the African coast, other explorers were following the lure of the East out across the open Atlantic. The ancient error of Ptolemy in underestimating the size of the world was still accepted. A further error, made by Marco Polo, contributed to the belief that the land mass of Europe and Asia extended much farther around the earth than it does; for he put the eastern coast of China thirty degrees of longitude further east than even Ptolemy had done, and Ptolemy had overestimated the size of the land mass from east to west by fifty per cent. There were encouraging legends, too, of islands midway in the Atlantic that would serve as stepping-stones across the sea. Since they knew nothing of the two continents that barred the way (for the discovery of America by the Northmen had been long since forgotten), the explorers who sailed straight west into the Atlantic had every reason to believe

that they were on the shortest and most convenient route to China or India. There was nothing novel in the plans of the Genoese captain, Christopher Columbus, who sailed westward with a charter from the Spanish government in 1492, except his determination to sail straight on till he encountered land, instead of turning back as his predecessors had done to look for the mythical islands of the Atlantic. It was a determination founded upon faith in his mission and an unquenchable optimism. Selecting out of the various estimates made by ancient or medieval geographers those which were most favorable to his purpose, he assumed the distance from the Canary Islands to the east coast of Asia to be less than a third of what it actually is. On that first voyage into the unknown, wind and weather favored the little fleet all the way, and after thirty-three days Columbus sighted land just about where he expected to find it. Having touched the islands of the Greater Antilles, he returned with the assurance that he had found India. Later explorations brought disillusionment. In the next few years, Spanish explorers coasted

This portrait of Christopher Columbus is a copy made in about 1525 of an earlier painting which has been lost. It is considered the closest existing likeness of the great explorer.

[1] For discussion of the Portuguese commercial empire in the East, see below, pages 439–441.

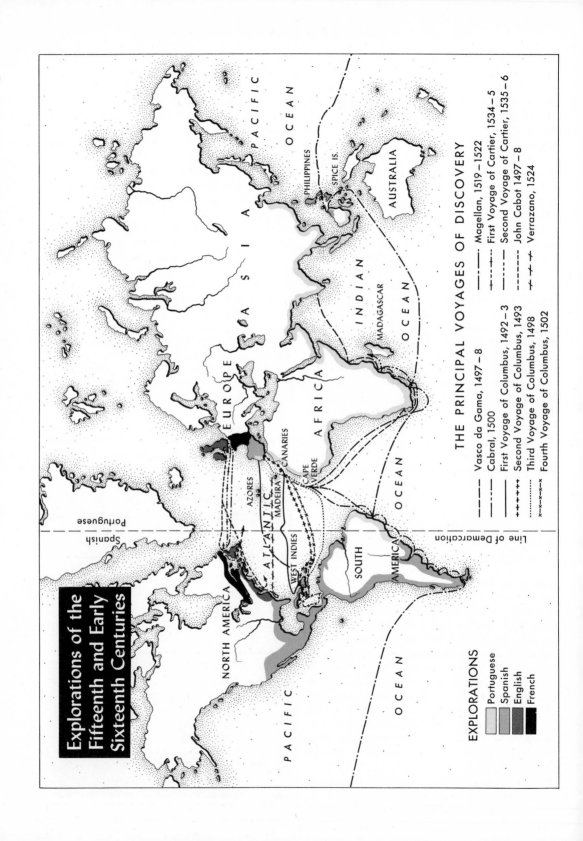

Explorations of the Fifteenth and Early Sixteenth Centuries

THE PRINCIPAL VOYAGES OF DISCOVERY

———— Vasco da Gama, 1497–8	—·—·— Magellan, 1519–1522
—·—·— Cabral, 1500	—+—+— First Voyage of Cartier, 1534–5
++++++ First Voyage of Columbus, 1492–3	—·—·— Second Voyage of Cartier, 1535–6
·········· Second Voyage of Columbus, 1493	———— John Cabot 1497–8
x—x—x— Third Voyage of Columbus, 1498	—+—+— Verrazano, 1524
Fourth Voyage of Columbus, 1502	

EXPLORATIONS

Portuguese
Spanish
English
French

Line of Demarcation

Spanish · Portuguese

PACIFIC OCEAN

ATLANTIC OCEAN

INDIAN OCEAN

EUROPE

ASIA

AFRICA

NORTH AMERICA

SOUTH AMERICA

AUSTRALIA

MADAGASCAR

PHILIPPINES

SPICE IS.

AZORES

MADEIRA

CANARIES

CAPE VERDE

WEST INDIES

the mainland from Florida to Brazil and found it to be an impassable barrier.

Spanish conquests in New World. Despite their disappointment at not reaching the East, the Spanish adventurers settled down to the conquest and exploitation of the lands they had found. This process was accompanied by the most frightful cruelty to the helpless natives. Yet for all their brutal exploitation, the Spaniards found in the islands where they first settled no great or sudden wealth, though the colonies they founded proved permanently valuable. It was not till they reached Mexico that their dream of finding El Dorado was realized. The conquest of the Aztecs of Mexico by Hernando Cortez and a small Spanish force in 1519 brought to light a store of gold and silver such as no European had ever seen before. A few years later, a handful of Spaniards under Francisco Pizarro began the conquest of Peru, where they took from the peaceful Incas quantities of gold and silver that surpassed even the riches of Mexico. Further discussion of the colonial empire founded by Spain in the Americas must, however, be left to Chapter 35.

Circumnavigation of the globe. The Spanish government, meanwhile, had not given up all hope of establishing direct contact with the East and of cutting in on the Portuguese trade with the Spice Islands. Spanish-Portuguese rivalry dates back to the beginning of the discoveries. As early as 1493, Pope Alexander VI had divided the new-found lands into two hemispheres, assigning to Spain all lands lying west of a line drawn three hundred and seventy leagues to the west of the Azores and to Portugal those east of that line.[1] One of the first results of this demarcation was that Portugal claimed Brazil — which was touched on by the Portuguese captain Cabral in 1500 on his way to India — as extending to the east of the line. The division also caused a dispute as to whether the East Indies were in the Eastern or Western Hemisphere. It was to settle this dispute and to find, if possible, a western route to the East that the Spanish government sent out an expedition of five ships in 1519 to sail around South America. The expedition was commanded by a Portuguese noble, Ferdinand

Magellan, who had sailed with his countrymen to the East, but had since entered the service of Spain. It was a long and hazardous voyage, one of the most daring as well as one of the most important of all the explorations. After following the eastern coast of South America to its southern tip, Magellan passed through the dangerous straits that are still called by his name and struck out into the southern Pacific. Three terrible months passed before he sighted inhabited islands, the Ladrones. Magellan himself was killed a little later in a fight with natives of the Philippines, but what was left of his crew went on with their one remaining ship. In September, 1522, their number now reduced to eighteen, they arrived home, the first men to have sailed completely around the world. They had proved that, despite the immense size of the Pacific Ocean, it was possible to sail westward to Asia, but also that it was an impractical route under sixteenth-century conditions. And, incidentally, they had discovered the Philippine Islands and claimed them for Spain.

French and English explorers. The kings of England and France were as eager as their southern neighbors to find a route to the lands of spices and gold, but they had less immediate success. As early as 1497, Henry VII sent out a Genoese captain, called by the English John Cabot, who touched the borders of the New World at Cape Breton and Labrador. Francis I, too, sent out explorers to search for a route to China. Under his orders the Florentine navigator, Giovanni da Verrazano in 1523 probed the coastline of North America from the Chesapeake Bay to Maine, and in two voyages in 1534 and 1535 Jacques Cartier explored the St. Lawrence River as far as the site of Montreal, where he was checked by the impassable Lachine Rapids. In 1541, Francis sent Cartier out once more, this time with instructions to found a colony, but the expedition was a failure and the king lost interest in land that promised little wealth and served only to block the road to the East. The vain search for a northwest passage to China continued throughout the sixteenth century. It was not till the following century, however, that France and England began to utilize the North American land by establishing colonies that were to form the basis of great colonial empires.

[1] See map, page 352.

SECTION F

THE REFORMATION AND THE

Queen Elizabeth I is carried from a
state function by nobles of her court.

WARS OF RELIGION (c. 1520–c. 1660)

In the first two decades of the sixteenth century, the transition from the medieval to the modern world was nearing completion. Feudalism had lost most of its independent political significance and the centralized territorial states were almost full grown. The corporate economic life of the High Middle Ages was disappearing, though the modern form of individualistic capitalism was not yet fully developed. The church still held the allegiance of all western Europe, but it was no longer the dominating institution that it had been in the twelfth or thirteenth century. Even that intellectual and artistic efflorescence that glorified the age of transition and which we call the Renaissance was passing its peak. Europe was again about to enter upon a new era with new problems. As the second decade of the sixteenth century drew to a close, two events signalized the nature of the coming age and revealed the problems that were to concern the people of Europe for the next century and a half. Martin Luther set in motion the forces that were to break up the universal church into warring sects and to make religious controversy the focal center for political rivalries, economic and social discontents, and intellectual activity. And Charles V was elected Emperor of the Holy Roman Empire, thus completing the accumulation of territory which brought the greater part of Europe under the rule of the house of Hapsburg and precipitating a century and a half of dynastic wars. Because of the dominating part played by the religious revolution and religious rivalry, we have called the period from about 1520 to 1660 the age of the Reformation and the Wars of Religion. But it was also an age of frequent dynastic wars; it witnessed the development of modern forms of state government and many modern forms of culture; and it saw the expansion of European commerce throughout the world and the planting of permanent European colonies overseas.

28

The Reformation and the

Founding of the Protestant Churches

EUROPE was a very different place in the early years of the sixteenth century from what it had been in the thirteenth. In the intervening years the most characteristically medieval aspects of European civilization had disappeared or were rapidly disappearing, and modern society had begun to take recognizable shape. Yet one medieval institution, and that the greatest of all, still stood, unchanged in form though considerably shaken and with alarming fissures appearing here and there in its once solid masonry. The real unity of western Christendom had been broken up; yet the Roman Church still maintained its traditional place as the embodiment of all religion in western Europe; the papacy still kept alive its claims to universal sovereignty, and the clergy still exercised their monopoly over the means of salvation. The church, it is true, had changed in some respects since the thirteenth century, but not as a rule in ways that made it a more satisfactory minister to the needs of the new age. Nothing could be more certain in this age of rapid change than that some of the people at least would demand changes in their religious life to fit the changes in their worldly existence. And such changes could not be effected without extensive changes in the church; for in that age religion was in-

separable from the church, just as the church was inseparable from the state and society. The most devout churchmen recognized that a reform of the church was necessary and hoped to bring it about in ways that would leave the outward structure intact. They were too late. Before they could accomplish anything, the explosive forces of the new nationalism, the new ethical and moral interests of the bourgeois class and the new humanistic piety, combined with old grievances against Rome and discontent with the clerical system, were ignited by the fiery preaching of Martin Luther, and the resulting explosion split the unity of the ancient church beyond all hope of rebuilding. What occurred was in reality a religious revolution, and it is this revolution that is generally referred to by historians as the Protestant Reformation, or simply the Reformation.

1. Causes of the Reformation

The immediate acceptance of Luther's revolutionary doctrine by all kinds of people in all parts of northern Europe is sufficient proof that those who welcomed the new movement did so for a wide variety of reasons. No such spontaneous reaction of popular sentiment could have sprung from any single cause or have been inspired by a single motive. We must look for the causes of the Reformation, then, in the economic, political, social, and cultural, as well as religious, background of the age. These various causes have already been mentioned and explained in previous chapters. Here we can give only a brief summary to gather them together and to indicate their bearing on the problem of the Reformation.

Abuses in the church. The most obvious cause of the Reformation was the necessity of reforming abuses in the church, a necessity that had been widely recognized for the past two centuries or more, without much being done about it. The wealth and temporal power of the church; the special jurisdiction of ecclesiastical and papal courts; the appointment of foreign papal favorites to high ecclesiastical offices; the avarice, carelessness, ignorance, and immorality of some of the clergy; the evils of simony and the financial exactions of the papacy — all these served to arouse a strong feeling of discontent with the church as it was, particularly when they bore heavily on the purses of the laity.

Influence of earlier reformers. Still the fact that there were abuses in the church would not in itself have caused such a widespread revolt from the Roman communion as took place in the Reformation. The need for reform was no greater when Luther nailed his theses on the church door at Wittenberg than in the days of William of Occam, Marsiglio, Wyclif, and Huss. Yet these earlier reformers failed, while Luther succeeded. Why? Aside from the fact that Luther provided a more satisfactory theological formula to justify revolt, it is clear that in the meantime conditions had changed so that more people were prepared to break with the church than before. The early critics of the church and the papacy had been voices crying in the wilderness. They had propounded many of the ideas later asserted by Luther, but they had secured only a relatively small following because the time was not yet ripe. They had not labored entirely in vain, however; for, among the factors that prepared the way for the success of the Reformation, the memory of their teaching, never wholly forgotten, must be given a prominent place.

Revolt from the sacramental system. The sacramental system was the rock upon which the early revolts against the authority of the church had foundered. However much men might feel the need of reform, they felt still more keenly the need of those services that only the clergy could perform. When, more than a century after Wyclif and Huss, Luther reasserted their doctrine of the priesthood of all believers, one of the important reasons for his success was that in the meantime certain religious and social developments had combined to make a good many men less ready to admit dependence on the priests and the sacraments for their salvation. In Germany and the Netherlands, the mystics, whom we have already noted,[1] had preached an inner piety, a religion that consisted chiefly of an immediate communion between man and God and left little room for the mediation of a priest. During that time, too, in the cities where the seeds of both the Renaissance and the Reformation found their most fertile soil, the growing education, individualism, and self-reliance of the prosperous middle class tended to make them resent the necessity of depending for their salvation on the ministration of the priests. This tendency to rebel against the church's most fundamental belief was more dangerous to it than any amount of criticism of abuses in the clerical system.

Changing spirit of the age. In other ways the changing spirit of the new age was causing men, especially of the bourgeois class, to lose interest in the beliefs, ideals, and traditions of the medieval church. The medieval ideal of the truly religious life, as embodied in monasticism, had stressed poverty, asceticism, and other-worldliness as among the prime virtues. But with increasing prosperity, money was playing a much more important part in men's lives, and by the beginning of the sixteenth century the age in which St. Francis of Assisi had sung the praises of his Lady Poverty and had enrolled enthusiastic recruits in her service had long since passed. Practical businessmen had begun to think of poverty as a social evil rather than as a saintly virtue. Other-worldliness made small appeal to men absorbed in the business of this world, and asceticism

[1] See above, pages 330–332.

had few charms for the hard-working burgher who looked forward soberly to an old age spent in quiet enjoyment of the results of honest trade. Next to monasticism the strongest force in shaping the spirit as well as the form of the medieval church had been feudalism. And as feudalism lost vitality, the medieval church lost the social atmosphere that had been most congenial to it. To the middle class of city dwellers especially, whose temper was to shape the interests of the new age, the chivalric-feudal spirit of the crusading era, which was also the great age of the medieval church, had very little appeal. St. Louis was no more akin to them than was St. Francis. The elaborate and colorful ritual of the Catholic Church rather jarred on their sober minds. In some vague way, very difficult to express, they felt it to be more suited to the gilded and extravagant society of the feudal nobility than to their own businesslike world. Added to that, of course, was the fact that the church conferred solid benefits upon the great nobles, whose sons became bishops, whereas the economic relations of the bourgeoisie with the church represented an unfavorable balance of trade.

But for the present we are discussing the failing appeal of the ideals of the medieval church, and in that connection one further factor must be noted. The saints themselves were losing something of their appeal to the popular imagination. Not only were the ideals they represented losing conviction, but the number of saints on the calendar had grown too great for the proper observance of saints' days, and their relics had been too freely peddled about the country. Perhaps they had grown too familiar to be given the respect formerly accorded them.

Influence of humanists.   The intellectual basis for the revolt against medievalism in the church was provided by the Christian humanists.[1] Whole-heartedly devoted to the study of antiquity, they had learned to despise medieval traditions as products of "Gothic" barbarism. Erasmus was not the only one of them who ridiculed pilgrimages, the supernatural power of relics, the practices of monasticism, and the temporal power of the papacy, on the ground that these things were not part of

original Christianity. It was the humanist emphasis on the literal study and reinterpretation of the Bible from original sources that gave Luther his most potent weapon. It was a commonplace among the enemies of the Reformation that Erasmus had laid the egg which Luther hatched.

National opposition to Rome.   Among the other causes of the Reformation, the interests of the state governments and the strength of national opposition to papal authority must not be forgotten. Indeed, few if any of the changes that had taken place in the preceding century did more to make the break with Rome politically possible than the development of the centralized territorial states and the growth of national consciousness which we have noted in the last two chapters. As these grew stronger, both prince and people resented more and more keenly the payment of taxes to a pope whom they had come to regard as an Italian prince, the appeal of cases from the national courts to the papal court at Rome, and the interference of a foreign power in their national affairs. This was particularly true in England, Germany, and the Scandinavian countries, where the rulers had not secured such control of the national church before the Reformation as had the kings of France and Spain. The opportunity presented to the kings and princes of these countries to gain complete control of the church in their states, as well as the financial advantages that would result from the stoppage of papal taxation and from the confiscation of church lands, was a strong inducement to them to embrace the Reformation movement. Without the help of the secular governments, it is doubtful if the new churches could have been securely established in many of the northern states.

2. Luther and the Reformation in Germany

Martin Luther.   By the second decade of the sixteenth century, Germany was ready for a religious revolution. All that was needed was a leader who would unite men of varied interests and show them the way. That leader was Martin Luther (1483–1546). In his ringing phrases the inarticulate discontent with things

---

[1] See above, pages 333–335.

as they were and blind gropings for a more satisfactory religious life found expression. And in his doctrine of salvation by faith alone, all who were ready to rebel against the authority of the church found for the first time a justification for revolt that carried conviction to their consciences. Luther did not cause the Reformation; but he gave the signal for its start and shaped its course. So far as any man can, Luther influenced the history of his age.

Early years. Luther's parents were Saxon peasant folk, stern, hard-working, and pious, somewhat better off than the average, for they were able to give their son an excellent education. In 1501, at the age of eighteen, young Martin entered the Saxon university at Erfurt. There, for four years, he studied the Nominalist philosophy that still dominated the old school, but he also read the classics and talked to the enthusiastic group of young humanists who were known as the "Erfurt poets." Having completed his course in the faculty of arts, Martin began the study of law in accordance with the wishes of his practical father. Almost immediately, however, he changed his mind and entered the local monastery of one of the orders of mendicant friars, the Augustinian Eremites. Two years later he was ordained priest, and in 1508 was moved to the house of his order at Wittenberg to teach in the new university recently founded there by the Elector of Saxony, Frederick the Wise. There followed nine years of outwardly peaceful academic activity, during which Luther lectured to students, preached in the castle church, and began to acquire a considerable local reputation. But quiet though they seemed, they were years of mental turmoil for the young friar, until the discovery of the doctrine of faith brought peace to his soul, and, before long, strife to all Christendom.

Justification by faith. Since his entry into the monastery, Luther had been tormented by the fear that nothing he could do would be sufficient to merit salvation. Indeed, it was this fear that caused his sudden decision to become a monk. He had carried with him from the peasant environment of his childhood a conception of God as a stern, unforgiving judge, and he had accepted the current teaching of the church that salvation depended on "good works," which included the sacra-

AETHERNA IPSE SVAE MENTIS SIMVLACHRA LVTHERV EXPRIMIT AT VVLTVS CERA LVCAE OCCIDVOS

Martin Luther from an engraving by Lucas Cranach the Elder. Executed in 1520, it is the earliest of several portraits of Luther by Cranach, who was a close friend of the reformer.

ments, prayer, fasting, and, if one would be sure, the ascetic practices of monasticism. But, though he devoted himself to an excessive asceticism, he still found no assurance that he had merited salvation. His reading of St. Augustine further shook his faith in his own efforts by the suggestion that only those who are predestined to receive divine grace will be saved. And who can know that he is among those chosen? The answer to all his problems came to him suddenly about the year 1515, from the reading of a verse in St. Paul's Epistle to the Romans on which he was lecturing to the university students. It contained the phrase, "The just shall live by faith." He had often read it before, but now he saw in it a new meaning — that man may be justified, i.e., saved, by faith and by faith *alone*. Doubtless only those predestined for salvation would be given faith; but to possess faith, which is the means of salvation, is also to possess the conviction that one will be saved. It took some time for Luther to work out all the logical consequences of his doctrine, for he was not essentially a systematic thinker. Eventually, however, he was forced to the conviction that,

This graphic scene, representing an indulgence seller at work, is from a contemporary woodcut by Jörg Breu the Elder.

if faith alone was needed for salvation, then the good works of the church, fasts, pilgrimages, and even the sacraments, were unnecessary, and that no man was dependent upon the services of pope or priest for his salvation.

Indulgences. With these ideas running through his mind, it was inevitable that Luther should begin to criticize some of the practices of the church arising from the doctrine of good works. As it happened, the question that first aroused him to open protest was that represented by the papal indulgence proclaimed by Pope Leo X to obtain money for the building of St. Peter's Church in Rome. The granting of indulgences had been a common practice in the church for more than two centuries. It was an integral part of the church's scheme of salvation and had become an important source of papal revenue. In theory it was an elaboration of the penitential system, the origins of which date back to the early days of the church. Following confession and proof of contrition, the sinner received absolution for his sins through the sacrament of penance. He was then free from the guilt of sin and the fear of eternal damnation. But he still owed further atonement in the form of penance or punishment in this world and, after death, in purgatory. The first indulgences or remissions of further penance were granted by the popes, acting as the successors of St. Peter, to the crusaders. Later, pilgrimages or other good works were substituted, until in the fourteenth

century the Avignonese popes set the precedent of accepting money payments as constituting the major part of the necessary good works.

The ninety-five theses. To Luther, however, convinced that faith alone could save men from the results of sin, it now seemed clear that indulgences were not only useless but actually harmful, since thereby men were encouraged to put their trust in something that could be of no help to them. He felt bound, therefore, to issue a warning. As the simplest method of securing a hearing, he prepared a list of ninety-five theses or propositions on the subject, and announced his willingness to defend them in public debate. Following the usual academic practice, he posted these theses on the church door where all could read them, and awaited developments. To his surprise the theses aroused a perfect furor of interest. They were soon printed and circulated all over Germany. That they carried conviction to their readers was attested by a sharp decline in the sale of indulgences.

Luther drifts from the church. In 1517, Luther had no thought of breaking away from the ancient church, but the next three years saw him forced step by step farther from it. In order to meet the arguments of the papal legates who were sent to demand that he recant, he had to work out his ideas to their ultimate conclusion. Almost against his will, for he had a natural respect for authority, the Wittenberg friar was forced to realize that his beliefs were contrary to many of those held by the church and that there was no place for him within the Roman communion. He had found in the Bible, however, as he interpreted it, a firm support for his convictions, and resting on that divinely inspired authority he confidently defied the authority of the pope.

The pamphlets of 1520. Leo X was delayed in taking decisive action against Luther by what seemed to him the more important business of the imperial election in 1519. This hotly disputed election worked doubly to the advantage of Luther; for his prince, Frederick the Wise, was able to secure from Charles V, as the price of his support, a promise that the rebellious friar should not be condemned without a hearing before the Imperial Diet. This meant further delay, and Luther used the time to good effect by writing a series of pamphlets with a view to publicizing his beliefs and winning the support of the German people. He was amazingly successful. The *Address to the Christian Nobility of the German Nation on the Improvement of the Christian Estate* was a stirring appeal to German patriotism against the tyranny of Rome. In it he called on the German princes to reform the church and also outlined a comprehensive program. A second pamphlet, *The Liberty of a Christian Man,* explained in popular fashion the practical bearings of his doctrine. These two pamphlets, directed primarily to laymen, were written in forceful German and so reached a far wider audience in Germany than if they had been written in the Latin which was normally used by both scholastics and humanists for serious discussion. He reverted to Latin, however, for a third pamphlet, *The Babylonian Captivity of the Church,* a more scholarly exposition of his views on the sacramental and sacerdotal system, designed to appeal to a more learned audience of clerics trained in theology.

Luther at Worms. When at last the summons came calling Luther to appear before the Diet of the empire at Worms in the spring of

1521, he went with the assurance that he had the sympathy at least of the majority of the German people. He was at the height of his popularity. All who nursed grievances against the church or hoped for reform wished him well, for the split in the church had not yet gone so far that it was necessary to take definite sides. Nevertheless, it took real courage to walk into the lions' den, with the fate of John Huss at Constance as a warning of what might happen. It was a dramatic moment when the Saxon peasant friar faced the assembled dignitaries of state and church and firmly refused to recant. Next day he left Worms. Within a few days he was proclaimed an excommunicated heretic by the church and an outlaw by the empire. But by that time he was safe in the lonely castle of the Wartburg near Eisenach, where he had been conducted by the orders of Frederick the Wise. There he passed a year in enforced leisure, which he put to good use by translating the New Testament into German. The Old Testament he translated later, completing it in 1532. Since his whole

Leo X, the first Medici pope and the cultured son of Lorenzo the Magnificent, made Rome a center of art and letters but did little for the spiritual life of the church. The portrait is by Raphael.

Dürer's portrait of Frederick the Wise of Saxony, the prince whose support saved Luther at a crucial moment in his career, was painted more than twenty years before the Reformation.

program rested on the authority of the Bible as against that of church tradition, it was essential for his success that the Bible should be readily accessible to the people. The importance of his German Bible can scarcely be overestimated. It has often been called the most powerful Reformation tract, and it had almost as much influence on the development of the German language as on German religion. Luther was a master of his native tongue, and his Bible played a part as important in fixing the standard of modern German as Dante's *Divine Comedy* did for modern Italian.

The Lutheran Church. The peaceful interlude in the Wartburg marks a turning point in Luther's career as a reformer. Hitherto he had been a sturdy rebel against church authority and a champion of individual liberty of conscience. He was now to become the organizer of a church of his own and an increasingly conservative defender of established authority. Returning to Wittenberg in the spring of 1522, he began at once the task of reconstruction. His first action was to moderate the extreme changes put into effect by some

of his more radical followers during his absence. He then set about the business of organizing a new church on as conservative a basis as possible. In the Lutheran Church, as it finally took shape, a good deal of the old Catholic doctrine and practice was retained. Nevertheless, there were changes of vital importance. In accordance with Luther's denial of the doctrine of good works and hence of the validity of the sacramental and sacerdotal system, all of the sacraments were abolished except baptism and the Lord's Supper, which are specifically mentioned in the Bible, and even these lost their character as good works. Pilgrimages, fasts, veneration of saints and relics, and the rest of the traditional practices based on the doctrine of good works also went by the board. The clergy, no longer considered as having special sacramental powers, were permitted to marry and live the life of ordinary men. The monastic orders were entirely dissolved. Thus was broken down the barrier that had separated the clergy from the laity and had made them a separate caste with unique privileges. Finally, the church, in everything save questions of belief, was placed directly under the control of the state government. The superintendents, who replaced the former bishops, were practically state officers.

Defection of the humanists. With the definite organization of a separate church, Luther lost the support of many who had sympathized with him before the Diet of Worms. Among these were the majority of the Christian humanists, including their leader, Erasmus. They had favored Luther's early demands for reform within the church, but were repelled by his violence and dogmatism. When the time for a final decision came, they found their loyalty to the ancient church too strong to be broken, especially as Luther's theological doctrine seemed to them no improvement on that of the old church. Erasmus was bitterly disappointed at the ruin of his hopes for a peaceful reform to be accomplished by education and without schism or turmoil, and he found it impossible to accept Luther's denial of man's free will or ability to work out his own salvation. The defection of the humanists was a serious loss to the new church, leaving it more conservative and dogmatic than ever.

The Peasants' War. The Lutheran Church was scarcely begun before it lost the support of another and more numerous class, the majority of the German peasants and poor city workers, who were alienated by Luther's conservative attitude toward the great social revolution which swept across Germany in 1525. The Peasants' War, as it was called, was a general rising of the downtrodden peasants, frequently joined by the discontented working classes in the towns, to demand justice and relief from crushing economic and social burdens. It had been preceded by a long series of similar revolts, extending over the past two hundred years, but becoming increasingly frequent since the turn of the sixteenth century. These earlier risings, however, had been confined to limited districts. What made the present rebellion at once more general and more radical was that the peasants had found, in Luther's assertion that the Bible is the only real authority, a justification for revolt and a program of social reform that would unite the discontented elements of different parts of the country in a common movement. Their dream of restoring the social conditions of evangelical Christianity was impractical, but it gave the necessary religious coloring to their demands. Beginning in Swabia, the revolt spread rapidly through central and southern Germany. For a time the old order seemed seriously threatened. Luther was as much alarmed as the princes at this revolt against established authority. With a singular lack of sympathetic insight, he urged the peasants to remember the Biblical injunction to obey the magistrates. Then, when they refused to listen, he called on the princes to crush and slay the "thievish, murderous hordes of peasants." The lords needed no such encouragement. The revolt was put down with appalling savagery. The peasants and artisans sank back into a hopeless economic slavery and looked no more to Luther for guidance.

Divergence of creeds. Instead, great numbers of them joined one or other of the numerous little sects which now formed as independent groups apart from both the Catholic and Lutheran churches. Luther's example had been more potent than he could have wished, especially now that he was the active head of a triumphant state church. In the days when he was in rebellion against the Catholic Church, he had confidently asserted the right of the individual man to interpret the Bible and religion generally in the light of his own reason and conscience. And though he later denied that right to others in practice, and though the Lutheran Church, like all other Protestant state churches, persecuted dissenting opinion, yet the ultimate sanction of Protestant belief continued to be the reason and conscience of individual men rather than the authority of a universal, apostolic church, as was true with Catholicism. As a result, Protestants in every land continued to assert the right to individual judgment in opposition to the state church, whatever it might be, and to found dissenting sects.

The Anabaptists. In Germany the sectarian revolt took a great variety of forms, with wide divergence between the sects in creed as well as in moral and social teaching. Nevertheless, they all shared a few common characteristics, and since most of them refused to recognize the validity of infant baptism and insisted on rebaptizing their converts, they were generally known as Anabaptists. They were all recruited from the submerged and downtrodden classes; they refused obedience to the state church and sometimes to the state; they founded their doctrine, whatever it might be, on a literal, unhistorical interpretation of the Bible with a view to restoring the simplicity of primitive Christianity; and they were cruelly persecuted everywhere by Catholic and Protestant states alike. Ignorant they may have been, but they were deeply pious and their history is ennobled by an inspiring record of heroic constancy in the face of persecution. Despite every effort of the persecuting state churches, they continued to exist, and their modern descendants are to be found in the Baptist, Mennonite, Moravian and other churches.

Consolidation of Lutheranism. If Lutheranism lost heavily through the defection of the humanists, the peasants, and the proletariat, that loss was compensated for by the adherence of the middle and upper classes in an increasingly large number of the German states and free cities. Within Luther's lifetime, nearly half of Germany officially adopted his church. The princes found in it a valuable support for their governments, while the burghers found in Luther's teaching a moral and ethical ideal as well as an individual spiritual life more in harmony with their character than that provided by the medieval church. The victory of Lutheranism was in part the triumph of the territorial state over the universal church, but it was also the triumph of a new lay-bourgeois ethic over the feudal-clerical-monastic ideals of the Middle Ages. It was not the least important result of the Reformation that the good citizen — the pious layman, who was a good husband and father, honest, hard-working, and thrifty — supplanted the ascetic monk or the crusading knight as the ideal Christian.

Religious war and peace.   The founding of Lutheran state churches inevitably caused grave political complications in Germany. Church and state were too closely united to admit of any degree of religious toleration. The Lutheran princes claimed the right to determine the religion of their states as Catholic rulers did, and when at the emperor's dictation, the Diet of Speyer in 1529 passed a resolution denying that right, the Lutheran princes drew up a formal protest. It was from this that they came to be called Protestant, a name later applied to all non-Catholics. Shortly after this, both Lutheran and Catholic princes formed leagues for mutual protection, and Germany was divided into two armed camps. Charles V was eager to restore religious unity to his empire for political as well as religious reasons, but was too busy elsewhere to bring strong pressure to bear on the heretics until 1546. He then declared war on the Protestant league, only to find that he had delayed too long. Though successful at first, he found that the new religion was too firmly established to be permanently crushed. Finally he was forced to agree to a compromise that left each prince free to make his state either Catholic or Lutheran as he chose. This was the Religious Peace of Augsburg, signed in 1555.[1] It kept an uneasy peace in Germany for the rest of the century.

Lutheranism in Scandinavia.   By this time, Lutheranism had gained nearly the whole northern half of Germany. It had also spread to the Scandinavian lands. The Reformation in Norway, Denmark, and Sweden followed much the same course as in the German states, the rulers taking the lead and establishing national churches directly under the control of the state, though here the episcopal system was retained.

3. *Zwingli and Calvin and the Reformation in Switzerland*

Luther's doctrine seems to have been peculiarly suited to the Teutonic mind. Outside of Germany and Scandinavia, pure Lutheranism never gained any permanent hold, though Luther's influence and example played a large part in the spread of the Reformation to other lands. Except in England where the Anglican Church grew up under a variety of influences, the Protestants in other countries, Switzerland, France, the Netherlands, and Scotland, to name the most important, followed the leadership of Zwingli and Calvin. The Protestant churches founded in these countries were generally known as the "Reformed Churches," to distinguish them from the Lutheran.

Zwingli's early environment.   To the south of Germany, and closely connected with it by bonds of tradition, language, and trade, the thirteen cantons of the Swiss Confederation maintained an independent existence as the freest and most democratic states in Europe.[2] Situated at the heart of Europe, Switzerland was in constant contact with her great neighbors, Germany, France, and Italy. Sturdy Swiss foot soldiers, the finest of their time, fought for pay in the armies of France and Italy, while the merchants of the city cantons grew rich on the trade that flowed through the Alpine passes from Italy to Germany. In the northern cities of Zurich, Basel, and Berne, Christian humanism of the northern type had taken firm root. Erasmus found at Basel a printer for his Greek New Testament and a circle of congenial friends with whom he spent many of the later years of his life. It was in this stimulating intellectual atmosphere that Huldreich Zwingli (1484–1531) grew up and received his education. He entered the priesthood at about the time that Luther was taking his final vows in the monastery at Erfurt; but in the years when the German friar was seeking salvation in agony of soul, the future Swiss reformer was devoting himself to the study of the classics. He was a thorough humanist and Erasmus was his idol. It was due to his influence that Zwingli first turned to the study of

[1] See below, page 378.

[2] See above, pages 266–267.

evangelical Christianity, though for many years his interest in religion was fairly perfunctory.

The Reformation in Zurich.   In 1519, shortly after he had been transferred to the minster church in Zurich, Zwingli experienced a religious conversion. At the same time he began to read Luther's first pamphlets. He immediately became a reformer and preached to such good effect, appealing both to the desire for reform and the patriotic resentment of Roman domination, that he gradually won over the city council and a majority of the people to his views. In 1525 the last Catholic mass was celebrated in Zurich. That event marked the completion of the Reformation in the canton. The "Reformed" religion, which now became the official doctrine of Zurich, was in many respects similar to Lutheranism. The sacramental system, the celibacy of the clergy, monasticism, fasts, and the veneration of saints and relics were abolished. Like Luther, Zwingli founded his teaching on the authority of the Bible, but he interpreted it more freely and with more radical results. The point on which he differed most widely from Luther was in his interpretation of the sacrament of the Lord's Supper, which he considered merely a symbolical commemorative service, whereas Luther, though denying the Catholic doctrine of transubstantiation, insisted on the real presence of the body and blood of Christ in the elements of bread and wine. This distinction foiled all attempts at union between the two branches of Protestantism, but it was not the only difference. Zwingli was less absorbed in theological dogma than Luther. He was a practical reformer with much of the Erasmian conception of religion as a philosophical guide to daily life.

Spread and opposition.   From Zurich the reform spread to the other city cantons and even beyond the borders of Switzerland to Strassburg and other German cities of the upper Rhine. The five forest or rural cantons, however, were more conservative and remained loyal to Rome. In 1529 they united in alliance with Austria to oppose the Reformation. The bitter feeling between the two religious parties soon led to open war, which ended with the defeat of Zurich, left alone to face the Catholic forces, in 1531. The Peace of Cappel, which followed, was moderate, leaving each canton free to determine its own religion, but the Re-

formed Church had suffered a serious loss in the death of Zwingli, who was killed in the final battle. For a time it was left leaderless, until the arrival of Calvin opened the second period of the Swiss Reformation.

Calvin.   John Calvin (1509–64), the new leader who did more than even Zwingli had done to form the spirit of the Reformed Church in Switzerland and the other countries that adopted it, was by birth and training a Frenchman. He was born of moderately well-to-do parents in Picardy and educated at the University of Paris and in the law schools of Orléans and Bourges. At Paris he received a thorough training in the classics, which left him with an excellent Latin style and may have been in part responsible for the skill in handling his native tongue that made him one of the greatest masters of French prose in his century. His legal training was equally important, for to the end of his days his thought on all religious and moral questions retained a strongly legal cast. Shortly after he had completed his studies, Calvin was converted to the new doctrine of the Reformation, through reading the works of Erasmus and Luther. But France at that time was no safe place for heretics and he was forced to flee. He took refuge in the Swiss city of Basel in 1534 and there began his first theological writing.

Calvinism.   Two years later, Calvin published the first edition of his *Institutes of the Christian Religion*. From time to time thereafter he added to it in new editions and also translated it from the original Latin into French. When finished, this work contained a complete summary of that system of theology and morals generally known as Calvinism. More than any other book it was responsible for the spread of Protestantism to the non-Lutheran countries. Its clarity of thought and remorseless logic carried conviction more inescapably than did the mystical fervor of Luther. There was little that was really original in Calvinism, for the fundamental doctrines were Luther's almost without exception, and yet the total effect was very different from Lutheranism. The chief difference, aside from the more logical and consistent development of Calvin's thought, lay in a decided shift in emphasis. Starting with the same belief in man's inability to save himself by good works, Luther

John Calvin, the theologian whose influence on the Protestant Reformation was second only to that of Luther, as portrayed by a contemporary artist.

placed the greatest emphasis on the saving power of faith, whereas Calvin thought much more about the majesty and power of God, who predestines certain souls for salvation and assigns the rest of mankind to hopeless damnation. Calvin's was a sterner doctrine, and its sternness was reflected in his moral teaching and legislation. He considered it the duty of the church and state to make men moral in the strictest legalistic sense. No part of his teaching had a more profound influence on the life of the Calvinist countries than this. The civilization of America to this day shows traces of the Calvinist morality brought over to these shores by the Puritan immigrants who founded the early colonies in New England.

Calvinist morality. In the emphasis on strict morality lay the one apparent logical inconsistency in Calvin's doctrine. Yet if it did not follow logically from his doctrine of predestination, it was psychologically necessary. No serious man — and Calvinism appealed essentially to serious men — contemplating the awful majesty of God and the foreordained alternatives of eternal salvation or damnation,

could remain indifferent to his own fate in eternity. And since no man could be sure that he was of the elect, and since nothing he could do of his own will could change the immutable decree of predestination, the Calvinist lived under the shadow of a terrifying uncertainty. According to all logic, the fact that he could do nothing to change his fate should have made him indifferent to his conduct in this world, but the doctrine of predestination had instead exactly the opposite effect. For it might safely be assumed that those whom God had chosen to be saved would be men who would lead good moral lives. The fact of living a strictly moral life did not prove that one was of the elect, but if one were leading an immoral life it did prove that one was not. Hence there was at least a partial assurance in the former case, and it was a bold man who could spurn even such uncertain comfort. Further, Calvin and his followers tended to take their conceptions of God and of morality more from the Hebraic Old Testament than from the New. To the Calvinist, moral laws were veritably laws, such as Jehovah had handed down to Moses on Mount Sinai, and in enforcing moral laws, including the strict observation of the Hebrew Sabbath, Calvinist rulers and ministers felt that they were carrying out the will of Jehovah. To understand the spiritual atmosphere of any Calvinist country, whether Geneva, Scotland, or New England, one must know the atmosphere of the Old Testament prophets and the Pentateuch.

Reformation in Geneva. The laboratory in which Calvin worked out the practical application of his doctrine was the city of Geneva. It lay in the French-speaking district on the borders of Switzerland and was not yet a fully fledged member of the Swiss Confederation when Calvin first entered it in 1536, though it was closely allied with the Protestant canton of Berne, which was supporting the Genevan citizens in their struggle for freedom from the rule of their bishop and count, both of whom were members of the house of Savoy. The Reformation in Geneva, therefore, began partly as a political expedient, as a means of freeing the city from episcopal control. The chief Protestant preacher, Guillaume Farel, was finding grave difficulties in organizing the Reformed Church among people who were not all converts by conviction. Such was the situation when Calvin came to Geneva for a brief visit and was commanded by Farel in the name of the Lord to stay and help him. For three years Calvin and Farel strove to organize and purify the new church, but aroused so much opposition by their unbending discipline that they were finally driven out. The new church, however, was hopelessly divided without their leadership, and in 1541 the people of Geneva begged Calvin to return on his own terms. For the remainder of his life Calvin was the real ruler of Geneva, though all opposition to him was not crushed until 1555. Under the new constitution, which Calvin helped to form, the government of Geneva was a sort of theocratic republic, with the administration of state and church so closely interwoven that it is difficult to determine which was responsible for the legislation that made Geneva the most moral city in Europe.

Spread of Calvinism. From Switzerland, Calvinism spread to other countries. In some sections of southern Germany it replaced Lutheranism, but mostly its converts were found in countries where the Lutheran reform had gained no strong foothold. The Reformation in France soon became thoroughly Calvinist, and largely through Calvin's influence it gained ground steadily, despite the royal persecution which prevented the organization of Reformed churches till about 1555. The history of the Huguenots, as the French Protestants were called, belongs, however, mostly to the period of the Counter-Reformation and the religious wars in the second half of the sixteenth century. The same holds true for the Calvinist or Reformed churches in the Netherlands, Bohemia, and Scotland.

Democratic tendency of Calvinism. We may note here, however, the influence of the Genevan prototype on the organization of the Calvinist churches in other countries. Without exception the Calvinists opposed control of the church by the state and, as far as possible, avoided a hierarchical church organization through which authority could be imposed from above. They maintained the equality of all ministers and hence opposed any episcopal system. The church in Geneva was not in spirit democratic, having evolved in an aristocratic republic under the despotic will of John

Calvin, but it contained the seeds of democracy, which could bear fruit under more favorable conditions. In most of the countries to which Calvinism spread, the Reformed churches began as persecuted minorities, and the Calvinists were forced into rebellion against the royal government by their belief that they must obey the laws of God rather than those of man. Under these circumstances each congregation organized as a separate unit, choosing its own minister, and only later was a larger national organization formed, a Synod or Presbytery consisting of the ministers and elders of the various congregations. Authority in the Reformed churches thus derived originally from the congregations. The ministers, as the interpreters of God's word, exercised immense moral authority. They examined and ordained new ministers, but the congregations retained the right to select their own minister from those duly ordained. This democratic base of church organization was more firmly established in Presbyterian Scotland than elsewhere, and, as we shall see, it was one of the reasons for the antagonism James I displayed toward the Calvinist Puritans in England. During the course of the seventeenth century, indeed, many English Puritans seceded from the Anglican Church and formed Congregational churches. And since many of the early colonists who settled in America were Puritans, Congregationalists, or Presbyterians, they established the democratic form of church government in the new land, thereby contributing a powerful force to the later development of democratic political government in the colonies which were to become the United States.

4. The Reformation in England Under Henry VIII and Edward VI

In the English Reformation the same causes were present as have been noted in connection with the revolt from Rome in the continental states; but they were present in a very different ratio. National, political, and economic motives played a much more important part in the early stages of the movement in England than did religion. Under Henry VIII, little more was accomplished — or aimed at — than the transference of the political control and the temporalities of the English Church from the pope to the king. The religious Reformation followed the political. It was not till after Henry's death that England became in any real sense Protestant.

Preparation for the break. Henry VIII was as nearly an absolute ruler as any English king ever became, and his will was the determining factor in bringing about the break with Rome at the time when it occurred, yet Henry could never have forced his people to throw off their ancient obedience to the pope had not a great many of them been already prepared to welcome the move. National opposition to papal interference in English affairs had found bold expression from time to time since the fourteenth century, when Parliament had passed the Statutes of Praemunire and Provisors.[1] England had suffered more than most countries from the financial exactions of the papacy and from the appointment of the pope's foreign favorites to high ecclesiastical offices. Moreover, England had been the scene of Wyclif's daring attack on the wealth and temporal power of the clergy, and though his Lollard followers had apparently been crushed, the memory of his teaching had never been entirely forgotten. The Christian humanists, too, had done their share to prepare the way for the Reformation here as on the Continent. John Colet, St. Thomas More, and the rest of Erasmus's circle of English friends, though most of them remained loyal Catholics, had made evangelical Christianity and the idea of a practical reform of church abuses familiar to the educated classes. Finally, Lutheranism had been brought over from Germany by merchants and wandering scholars, aided by the printing press, and was spreading slowly through the urban middle class. When Henry rebelled against papal authority, then, he could count on a considerable amount of popular support.

Early years of Henry VIII. In the early years of Henry VIII, however, there was little to indicate his future role in the history of the English church. Indeed, he was generally considered a strong champion of orthodoxy. In 1521 he published a violent attack on the Lutheran heresy, for which the pope awarded him the title of Defender of the Faith. Besides,

he was too much engrossed in his ambitious foreign policy, in which he was encouraged by his chief minister, Cardinal Wolsey, to pay much attention to the reform of the church at home. And though Henry apparently realized that clerical privileges, ecclesiastical courts, and papal jurisdiction were now the only remaining obstacles in the way of his complete control of his kingdom, Wolsey, who was papal legate in England and hoped to be pope, was always able to distract his attention and stave off any action against the rights of the church. More than once, papal ambassadors warned the pope that if Wolsey fell, the church in England would suffer, and by 1527 Wolsey was slipping. His foreign policy had accomplished nothing except to waste the accumulated treasure of Henry VII and to burden the English taxpayers. Henry was already losing confidence in the cardinal, when the affair of the divorce precipitated Wolsey's ruin and brought on the break with Rome.

The royal divorce. In 1527, Henry had been married to Catherine of Aragon for eighteen years and, but for one daughter, Mary, was still childless. Therein lay the immediate occasion of all the momentous events of the next few years. Henry needed a male heir to preserve the Tudor line and there was apparently no hope from Catherine. The death of all Catherine's sons in infancy began to seem to the king a divine judgment upon him for having broken the Biblical injunction against marrying a deceased brother's wife, for Catherine had previously been married, briefly, to his elder brother Arthur. Henry had secured a papal dispensation at the time of his marriage, but now conscience and inclination running together were sufficient to convince him that the marriage had not been valid. He was eager to marry again and had already chosen as his future wife Anne Boleyn. He therefore instructed Wolsey to secure a divorce, or rather an annulment, from Pope Clement VII. But in 1527 the pope was in no position to take action against Catherine. She was the aunt of Charles V, and Charles was master of Italy. The imperial troops had just sacked Rome and the pope was in their power.[2] Negotiations dragged on until Henry lost all patience. In

---

[1] See above, page 291.

[2] See below, page 373.

1529 he called a Parliament that was to declare the English Church independent of Rome. Wolsey was deprived of his office and the following year was arrested on a charge of treason. Meanwhile, Parliament had begun to pass act after act reducing clerical privileges and papal authority. By 1533 it had so far separated the English Church from Rome that the new Archbishop of Canterbury was able to annul the king's marriage.

The Anglican Church. The next year Parliament took the final step needed to establish the complete independence of the English national church. All relations with the papacy were severed and the king was declared by the Act of Supremacy to be the "supreme head" of the Church of England. This meant that one more kingdom had been lost to the once universal church. It was one more example of the triumph of central government over separate interests, of state over church, of nationalism over the unity of Christendom, that was characteristic of the age. The change was made with very little opposition because the majority were ready for it. Besides, it was a very conservative revolution. Except for the substitution of royal for papal authority, there was no very marked change in the outward organization of the Anglican Church. The most radical change was the gradual dissolution of the monasteries and the confiscation of their lands. Again Parliament willingly lent its authority to the king's will, for the monks had long been unpopular and the confiscation of the monastic lands enriched both the state and the wealthy burghers and gentlemen who purchased them from the king. The sale of the monastic lands at well below their normal price incidentally gave to a considerable number of the most influential classes in England a material incentive to oppose any reconciliation with Rome, which might lead to a restoration of the confiscated lands to the church.

Conservative doctrine. There was even less change in the official doctrine of the church than in its organization. Henry was still a champion of orthodoxy so far as was possible. A few earnest Catholics, like St. Thomas More, were executed for their refusal to accept the king as supreme head of the church, but there were as many martyrs on the other side who suffered because they were too Protestant.

Parliament authorized the use of the English Bible, and some changes were made in religious practice, but Henry was determined to keep the essentials of the Catholic faith. In 1539, as a Catholic reactionary party gained ascendancy at court, Henry passed through Parliament an act defining the faith of the Anglican Church in six articles, all quite Catholic in tone, and this act was enforced by severe persecuting laws. The political break with the Catholic Church, however, inevitably opened the way for criticism of Catholic doctrine and, despite everything that Henry could do, Lutheran and Calvinist opinions were spreading rapidly in England.

The doctrinal Reformation. When Henry VIII died in 1547, he left his throne to his infant son Edward VI (1547–53) and the government to a Council of Regency headed by the Protector Somerset, the young king's maternal uncle. During the next six years a doctrinal Reformation was accomplished to supplement the political and constitutional Reformation of the previous reign. There can be no doubt that Protestants, whether Lutheran or Calvinist, or a compromise between the two, were still in a distinct minority, but they were an influential minority and strongly represented in the Council. The repressive laws of Henry VIII were repealed almost at once. The next step was to prepare an English liturgy and enforce its use by an Act of Uniformity in 1549. This was the first Book of Common Prayer, the work of Archbishop Cranmer, whose grand English cadences still are heard in the services of the Anglican Church. Three years later it was revised so as to make it more acceptable to the extreme Protestants, and at the same time the official creed of the church was defined in the Forty-two Articles of Religion. These were made as vague and general as possible so as to enable those who were almost Catholics, as well as Lutherans and Calvinists, to remain within the church. England was still far from unanimity in religion. All that the government was working for at the moment was a decent outward uniformity, while at the same time favoring a steady drift toward real Protestantism. But the question was still an open one when the premature death of Edward replaced his Protestant government by the Catholic regime of Mary Tudor.

"To God I speak Spanish, to women Italian, to men French, and to my horse — German."
• The Emperor Charles V (1519–56)

29

The States of Europe in the

Age of Charles V

DURING THE period in which the unity of the Catholic Church was broken and the Protestant churches were founded, the rulers of Europe had often other and apparently more important problems to consider than the fate of religion, though that was something that could never be entirely forgotten. The outstanding factor in the relation of the European states to one another in this period was the existence of the vast dynastic empire of Charles V, which threatened the rest of Europe with the menace of Hapsburg domination. We have already seen[1] how this great accumulation of territorial states came to be united under the rule of the young heir to the Hapsburg, Burgundian, and Spanish dynasties, and have noted at the same time the development of strongly centralized states throughout Europe, under rulers who had acquired new national and dynastic ambitions with the acquisition of absolute authority in their own lands. Before the accession of Charles V, national and dynastic rivalry had embroiled the European countries in a greedy struggle for the spoils of Italy. That rivalry now took on a new character. Francis I of France stood pitted against the mighty Hapsburg as his sole rival for the hegemony of Europe. They had too many conflicting interests to remain at peace with each other, and the destruction of either

would have meant the domination of Europe by the victor. The other states, therefore, were drawn into the struggle in the hope of maintaining the balance of power, that is, a state of international equilibrium. Meanwhile, within each territorial state, the rulers continued still further to centralize the government and to develop unhampered sovereign power.

These major themes of European history were repeated in miniature among the German states that made up the Holy Roman Empire. There the ambitions of Charles for centralized control and dynastic aggrandizement met the similar ambitions of the territorial princes. The German princes feared Hapsburg domination as much as did the rulers of the other European states. And in Germany, more than elsewhere, the situation was complicated by the religious revolution and by the constant threat of Turkish aggression from the east. The result here was the establishment of a temporary equilibrium among the German states that matched the larger equilibrium of Europe.

1. The Rivalry of Hapsburg and Valois

Three young monarchs. In 1519, almost all of western Europe — the Scandinavian countries, Switzerland, and parts of Italy were the only exceptions — owed allegiance to one

---

[1] See above, pages 347–349, and map, page 348. See also genealogical table in the Appendix.

or other of three young and ambitious monarchs who for a generation were to remain the principal actors in the international drama.

Charles V (1519–56). The youngest of the three, Charles V, had just been elected emperor of the Holy Roman Empire; but the shadowy imperial sovereignty over Germany represented only a small fraction of his real power. He was already the hereditary ruler of the Hapsburg family lands in and around Austria; of the Burgundian states of Franche-Comté, Luxemburg, and the Netherlands; as well as of the Spanish kingdoms of Castile and Aragon, Sicily, Naples, and Sardinia, and those new lands in the Americas whose store of gold the Castilian *conquistadores* were only beginning to touch. This imposing array of possessions made Charles the most powerful monarch in Europe; yet not so powerful as would appear on the surface, for in actual practice the available strength of his empire was always considerably less than the total strength of its component parts. It was a purely dynastic empire, accumulated by a series of family alliances. It lacked both national and geographical unity. The person of Charles was the only bond holding his scattered dominions together. To utilize the full resources of each in a common policy, or to satisfy their varying interests, would have taxed the genius and energy of a Charlemagne. And the nineteen-year-old ruler who accepted that appalling task was not a brilliant youth. He was not even personally attractive, being of a somewhat stolid nature and having inherited the more unfortunate Hapsburg features. But, as time went on, he proved that he possessed a large measure of sound common sense, industry, patience, and a degree of determination verging on stubbornness. These qualities in the long run served him better than the more brilliant and attractive traits of his rival of the house of Valois.

Francis I (1515–47). Francis I of France was a little older than Charles and had already won military glory by the conquest of Milan. He had a good deal of surface charm and culture; but his character was essentially frivolous, without depth or substance. Had he possessed any of the qualities of greatness, he might have fared very well in his contest with the Hapsburg, for, though he ruled less land,

it was united in one compact national state, over which he had absolute control. Instead, he was vain, inconsequent, absorbed in selfish pleasures, and gifted with a fatal genius for snatching defeat from the jaws of victory.

Henry VIII (1509–47). Between these two monarchs stood the Tudor Henry VIII of England. His aim was to keep the balance between them so even that the influence of England, though a relatively weak state, might become the determining factor in European affairs. It was a sound policy, but Henry got less from it than might have been expected, for both he and his chief minister, Wolsey, too often mistook pointless duplicity for diplomatic skill and he was never prepared to back his promises by determined action.

Emperor Charles V as painted by Titian, one of the great portrait painters of the late Renaissance.

This portrait of King Francis I of France, by Jean Clouet, possibly fails to do justice to the gallant king, who was regarded — at least by his courtiers — as a handsome man.

Causes of the war. It is a commonplace of history that war between Charles V and Francis I was inevitable, and certainly there were enough causes for friction to make peace between them impossible in that age when the personal or family interests of rulers were considered sufficient reason for war. In the first place, France was surrounded by Hapsburg territory,[1] and its king felt it necessary to break the Hapsburg power in self-defense. Then, too, Charles and Francis had conflicting dynastic claims to territory in half a dozen places. In the northeast, Francis held the duchy of Burgundy, which Charles claimed by right of descent from Charles the Bold, while Francis revived an old feudal claim to Charles's Netherland provinces of Flanders and Artois. In the southwest, Francis supported the claims of his kinsman the King of Navarre to the territory annexed by Charles's grandfather Ferdi-

[1] See map, page 375.

nand. Finally, both rulers hoped to dominate Italy. There, Francis held the duchy of Milan, which Charles claimed as a fief of the empire, while Charles ruled the kingdom of Naples, which Francis claimed as heir to the house of Anjou. And as if these various grounds for conflict were not enough, the two young rulers had been rival candidates in the imperial election, which created a strong personal animosity between them.

The war, to the Treaty of Madrid. Of the two, Francis was better prepared for immediate war, since all his resources were concentrated in a single compact state. Charles had pressing problems to meet in Spain as well as in Germany, and he was in desperate need of money. He was fortunate, however, in being able to postpone hostilities until 1521. By that time he had met the Imperial Diet at Worms, had disposed of his family interests in Germany by entrusting the Hapsburg lands there to his brother Ferdinand, and had gained allies, for what they were worth, in Henry VIII and Pope Leo X. The war opened with campaigns on three fronts, in the Netherlands, in Navarre, and in Italy, but throughout the war nearly all the serious fighting was concentrated in the last-named country. For four years the fortunes of war shifted from one side to the other, as did also the alliances of the papacy and the other Italian states. The French lost Lombardy and regained it. In the spring of 1525 their success seemed certain, when the situation was suddenly reversed. In a bloody battle fought before the walls of Pavia, the imperial troops destroyed the French army and captured the French king. It seemed like a decisive victory for Charles, but his resources were too far exhausted for him to take full advantage of it. He did not press the war, but contented himself with keeping Francis a prisoner in Spain until his resistance was so worn down that he would accept the terms dictated to him. By the Treaty of Madrid, January, 1526, Francis solemnly pledged himself to give up the duchy of Burgundy, as well as all claims to the disputed territories in the Netherlands, Navarre, and Italy.

The war, to the Treaty of Cambrai. Despite his solemn oaths and the pledge of his knightly honor, Francis had not the slightest intention of keeping the terms of the treaty. No sooner

was he back in France than he was busy organizing the League of Cognac, composed, with France, of the Italian states: Venice, Florence, the papacy, and Milan, which had been given as an imperial fief by Charles to one of the Sforzas. All of these now became the natural enemies of the victorious emperor through their desire to keep the balance of power in Italy. Henry VIII declared himself favorable to the league, but did not join it. It was an alarming situation for Charles. As usual, he found it hard to raise enough money for foreign war from his scattered possessions and still harder to get the money to Italy. Charles, Duke of Bourbon, a French prince who had deserted France and now commanded the imperial army in northern Italy, found it impossible to keep his troops in order without pay. In 1527 they mutinied and forced Bourbon to lead them to Rome, to collect their own pay from the pillage of the rich papal city. The sack of Rome, which followed, was as brutal and as thorough as any that the eternal city had suffered from the Goths or Vandals. The Spanish soldiers in the emperor's army left a bitter memory of cruelty and greed, while the German mercenaries, mostly Lutheran, took a special delight in deeds of sacrilege. The capture of Rome left Pope Clement VII helplessly in the emperor's power. Neither Rome nor the papacy would ever again enjoy the same wealth or freedom. For them the glory of the Renaissance was over. A new French invasion also marked the year 1527, but again Francis saw hope of victory turned to defeat. By 1529 both sides were ready for peace. The Treaty of Cambrai was in main outline a repetition of that of Madrid, except that Francis was allowed to keep Burgundy, which Charles had learned he would not give up anyway. Like the former treaty, this was to prove no more than a truce.

The war, to 1556. The war dragged on through the remainder of the reign of Charles V, but intermittently. The emperor was left free from time to time to attend to the affairs

King Henry II of France ended the wars in Italy and began the severe persecution of Protestants. The portrait is by Jean Clouet, the most distinguished painter of the French Renaissance.

of his various lands, to stem the tide of Turkish invasion, and to try to crush out the Lutheran heresy that was dividing Germany, but never for long enough to accomplish decisive results. The enmity of the Valois crippled him at every turn. More than once, the French king formed alliances with the Protestant princes of Germany and with the Turks against the emperor. Even the death of Francis I did not end the strife, for his son Henry II (1547–59) carried on the feud. The situation was still very much the same when, in 1556, Charles V voluntarily laid down the heavy scepter he had wielded so long. He left the Hapsburg lands in Germany and the imperial crown to his brother Ferdinand, his western states to his son, Philip II of Spain.

The Treaty of Cateau-Cambrésis. The concluding act of the long rivalry of Hapsburg and Valois is little more than a brief epilogue. In

1559, Philip II and Henry II signed the Treaty of Cateau-Cambrésis, the terms of which settled the questions at issue between the two powers for the remainder of the century. France acquired some small additions of territory along her northeastern border, but in return finally renounced all claims to lands in Italy, the Netherlands, or Spain. This renunciation was in itself a solid gain for France. Her opposition to the encircling power of the Hapsburgs had perhaps been justified, but the men and money expended on the vain attempt to conquer territory in Italy, which could never have become an integral part of France, were wasted. The final abandonment of the Italian dream removed one of the principal causes for war, while the splitting of Charles's empire between his brother and son reduced the fear of Hapsburg domination. A rough equilibrium among the European powers was thus established, which lasted for the most part during the coming half-century of internal religious wars.

2. Charles V and His Empire

Problems of Charles V.   If the contest with the kings of the house of Valois formed the central theme of the reign of Charles V, it must not be forgotten that, along with this foreign problem, Charles had also to deal with a host of problems connected with the internal government of his various states. These states were so scattered and so diverse in nationality, language, economic and cultural interests, and even in religion, that no one consistent policy could be applied to all. No policy, that is, except the traditional policy of the Hapsburgs, which was to capitalize every opportunity for the aggrandizement of the family. Dynastic ambition was not a trait peculiar to the Hapsburgs; it was shared by most European rulers. But Charles could not identify it with national interests as could the kings of France or England. He was born and brought up in the Netherlands, yet his empire was too large for him to subordinate his major policies to Flemish interests. He was always a foreigner in Germany and Italy. In the latter he worked for Hapsburg domination rather than Italian unity, and in the former he allowed the interests of the Austrian Hapsburg states and the

distractions of his dynastic war with France to thwart his efforts to rebuild a united imperial state. So far as Charles did identify himself with any country, it was Spain.

Spain.   In the sixteenth century, Spain was the most powerful state in Europe, with the possible exception of France. It was certainly the strongest of the states ruled by Charles, and it was there that he made his permanent residence, leaving it only when the pressing needs of his other possessions demanded his presence. He became in time a thorough Spaniard and won the loyalty of the Spanish people by convincing them that their country was the center of his empire and that their interests were his. His victories were in fact Spanish victories, won largely with Spanish gold and the incomparable Spanish foot soldiers. Moreover, his rigid Catholic orthodoxy, which tended to alienate him from his northern subjects, was perfectly congenial to the Spaniards, the most orthodox nation in Europe. They fully approved of his bloody conversion, or extermination, of the Moorish population in the southern provinces, though it meant the destruction of the most industrious class in the peninsula. There was here no conflict between church and state, but rather a strong mutual support.

Prosperity of Spain.   In these years the wealth of Spain was a byword in Europe; yet for all its apparent prosperity, the economic strength of Spain was not so secure as it seemed. Before another generation had passed, it was destined to begin a rapid and permanent decline. The truth was that Spain was living on unearned increment, the gold and silver stolen from Mexico and Peru. This sudden wealth stimulated industry and commerce for a time, but in the end it proved a curse — the curse of Midas. There was too much gold. It raised prices to a higher level than in any other country, with the result that Spain bought more than it sold. The most lasting benefits, therefore, went to other countries. The tremendous expense of Charles's foreign wars, too, helped to drain the country of its gold, while bringing no economic return. This wealth lasted about two generations. When it was gone, there was nothing left.

The Netherlands.   Next to Spain, Charles depended most on the wealth of the Netherlands

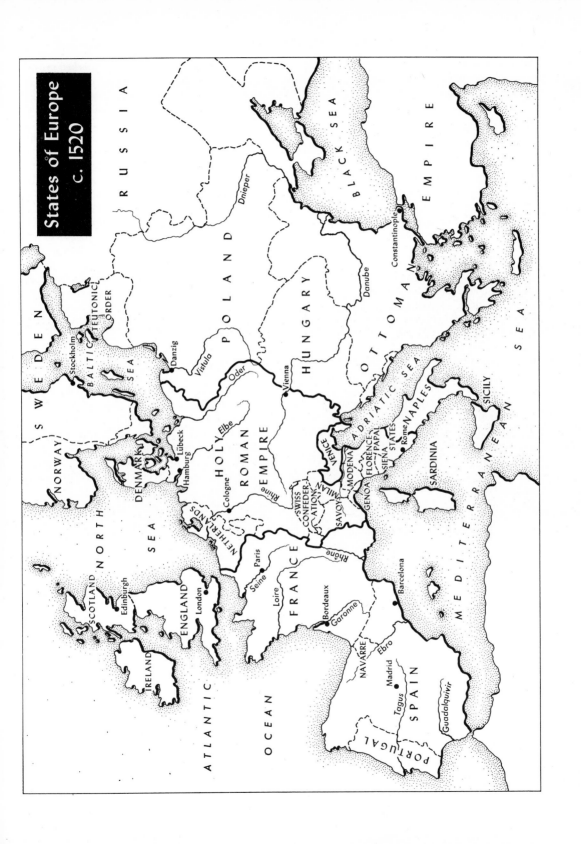

States of Europe
c. 1520

RUSSIA

SWEDEN

NORWAY

BALTIC TEUTONIC ORDER

Stockholm

BALTIC SEA

Danzig

POLAND

Vistula

Oder

Dnieper

BLACK SEA

Constantinople

OTTOMAN EMPIRE

HUNGARY

Danube

Vienna

DENMARK

Lübeck

Hamburg

Elbe

HOLY ROMAN EMPIRE

Cologne

Rhine

NETHERLANDS

SWISS CONFEDERATION

SAVOY

MILAN

VENICE

MODENA

GENOA

FLORENCE

SIENA

PAPAL STATES

Rome

NAPLES

ADRIATIC SEA

SARDINIA

SICILY

MEDITERRANEAN SEA

NORTH SEA

SCOTLAND

Edinburgh

ENGLAND

London

IRELAND

ATLANTIC OCEAN

Paris

Seine

Loire

FRANCE

Bordeaux

Garonne

Rhône

NAVARRE

Ebro

Barcelona

SPAIN

Madrid

Tagus

PORTUGAL

Guadalquivir

and was most at home there. Under his rule the Netherlands prospered, despite heavy taxation, and the frontiers were rounded out by occasional conquests. Except for one serious rebellion at Ghent in 1539, the people remained loyal to their native prince. Nevertheless, there was a growing discontent under the surface, the fruits of which were to be reaped by Charles's son Philip II. There was reason for the suspicion that the emperor was exploiting their resources for his own advantage rather than theirs. The prosperity of the Netherlands was due more to the industry and keen trading sense of the people than to the government, and what advantage accrued to trade from the connection with Spain scarcely compensated for the heavy taxes levied to support Charles's foreign policies, in which the Netherlands had no real interest. Besides, the emperor's attempts to suppress heresy in all his dominions aroused resentment, for, despite persecution that kept them under cover, Lutheran, Anabaptist, and finally Calvinist opinions were gaining many converts.

Italy.   If the Netherlands were still a source of strength to the Spanish monarchy, though destined to be a ruinous expense in the next generation, Italy probably cost more than it was worth to Spain. Here the interests of Charles were purely dynastic. He made no attempt to establish national unity in Italy. All he aimed at was to acquire as much land as possible for his family and so to manage the remaining states as to bring the whole peninsula under Hapsburg domination. And this he accomplished. Milan was conquered, while Florence, Genoa, the papacy, and the smaller Italian states preserved their nominal independence only by subservience to the dominant power.

Germany.   It was in Germany that Charles encountered his most difficult problems and met with the least success. Although it was the ancient home of the Hapsburg family, Charles was always a foreigner in Germany. He spent little time there, and constantly put off dealing with German problems until he had leisure from his more vital interests elsewhere. This, however, was not the only reason for his failure. It is doubtful if the most German of emperors could have revived the outworn Holy Roman Empire at this late date, or have preserved in it more than a formal unity. True,

there had been of recent years a marked growth of German national sentiment, which Charles might have used if he had identified himself strongly with German nationality; but class jealousies, the independence of free cities and imperial knights, the territorial sovereignty of the princes, and, in addition, the new religious differences were centrifugal forces stronger than any feeling of national unity.

The council of regency.   At his first Imperial Diet in 1521, Charles took steps to meet the two most important problems of the empire, the reform of imperial government and the suppression of the Lutheran heresy. In neither was he successful. The solution of the former problem was attempted through the creation of a council of regency, which would rule during the emperor's absence, and which he and the electors hoped would hold the empire together. After Charles left, however, the council proved powerless to act in any important matter. It had no adequate military or financial power, and even the princes on the council ignored its decisions. It was completely discredited by its failure to suppress the rebellion of the Rhineland knights, led by Franz von Sickingen, in 1522, and the Peasants' Revolt three years later, both of which were put down by the independent action of the princes most concerned. These two rebellions prove how strong was the social discontent among all classes, a discontent having its roots in the economic readjustment of the new age but given additional impetus by the first impact of Luther's revolutionary teaching.

The Protestant party.   The emperor's legislation against Luther had no more effect than had the attempt to reform the imperial constitution, and largely for the same reason. The imperial authority was not strong enough, especially with Charles engrossed in affairs elsewhere, to coerce the princes or the governments of the free cities. During his long absence no serious effort was made to enforce the Edict of Worms. The Lutherans were left free to organize their church wherever they had the support of the local government. Even when Charles finally returned to Germany in 1530, after concluding a temporary peace with Francis I, he was unable to give his full attention for long to the growing Protestant menace. After an attempt at reconciliation had failed, the emperor gave the heretics six months in which to return to the church, after which, he declared, he would suppress them by force. But before Charles could put his threat into effect, he was forced to temporize by the necessity of gaining all the support he could get against the Turks, and the opportunity for decisive action was lost.

The Turkish menace. For more than a century, Christian Europe had lived in fear of the Ottoman Turks, who in 1453 had completed the conquest of what remained of the Byzantine Empire by the capture of Constantinople. During the succeeding generations their conquests had continued at the expense of both their Christian and their Moslem neighbors.[1] Their armies seemed invincible. At the time when Charles V was elected emperor, they held all of southeastern Europe, and before long the West was shocked by the news of a further Turkish advance up the Danube, under the command of the new Sultan, Suleiman II, "the Magnificent" (1520–66). In 1526 his army defeated the Hungarians and killed their brave king on the field of Mohács. In 1529 the Turks laid siege to Vienna, but were driven back; and now, in 1532, they were advancing on Austria again.

Ferdinand and the Turks. Hitherto, Charles's brother Ferdinand, to whom he had entrusted the German Hapsburg lands, had borne the brunt of the defense against the Turks. On the death of his brother-in-law, King Louis II of Hungary and Bohemia, at Mohács, Ferdinand had been elected king of both countries. His attempts to defend his newly acquired kingdoms as well as his hereditary Austrian lands kept Ferdinand too busy to take any action against the Lutherans. The new Turkish advance of 1532 forced both Charles and Ferdinand to come to terms with the heretics. Charles dropped his plans for crushing Protestantism for the time being and came to his brother's aid, driving back the Turks and recovering part of Hungary. The demands of his other possessions, however, prevented Charles from following up his victory. Before the end of 1532 he was on his way back to Spain via Italy. Ferdinand was again left to carry on the struggle alone, which he did without much success. Finally, in 1547, he and the emperor secured a precarious peace by

recognizing the Turkish possession of the greater part of Hungary.

The League of Schmalkalden. Meanwhile, with Charles once more absent from Germany and absorbed in other interests, Protestantism spread rapidly, while the Protestant party formed a defensive organization against the time of the emperor's return. As early as 1531, when there still seemed a chance of immediate action by the emperor, the chief Protestant states — principalities and free cities — had joined together in the League of Schmalkalden for mutual defense. As other princes were converted to Lutheranism, they too joined the league. Though often weakened by the petty jealousies of the princes, the league made a formidable force. More than once the kings of France and England sought alliance with it against the emperor. With each year it became increasingly clear that Charles must return and crush the league, or all hope of restoring the political as well as religious unity of the empire would be lost. But, what with campaigns against the Algerian pirates in the Mediterranean, wars with France and the Turks, a rebellion in the Netherlands, and other troubles, fourteen years passed before Charles was once more free to take up the task he had abandoned in 1532. By that time, about half of Germany was Protestant, including four of the seven electors.

Schmalkaldic War. Nevertheless, when Charles at last opened war on the League of Schmalkalden in 1546, he had fair prospects of success. His army was smaller than that of the league, but it contained a large number of those Spanish foot soldiers who had proved themselves to be the finest fighting material in Europe, and it was commanded by the able and ruthless Duke of Alva. His chief advantage, however, lay in the lack of unity among the leaders of the league and in their equally fatal lack of military strategy. As the chief Protestant princes separated to protect their own lands, the emperor attacked them singly and forced one after another to submit. Charles then set about the suppression of Protestantism in the states of the vanquished princes. The next five years proved that it was easier to defeat the princes than to reconvert their people. They had been Lutheran too long to give up their religion at the command of even a victorious emperor. In 1552, the Protestant

[1] See map, page 271.

princes rebelled, aided by an alliance with Henry II of France. Three years more of anarchy at last persuaded the emperor to give up all hope of crushing Lutheranism in Germany, and to make peace.

Religious Peace of Augsburg.   The final settlement of the religious strife in Germany, at least for the sixteenth century, was arranged at the Diet of Augsburg of 1555. It is called the Religious Peace of Augsburg. It kept Germany free from further religious war for more than sixty years; but there were terms in the compromise that maintained a constant tension between the Protestant and Catholic parties and promised serious trouble at some future date. That promise was fulfilled in the following century in the frightful devastation of the Thirty Years' War.[1] Four major principles laid down by this treaty are worth remember-

[1] See Chapter 34.

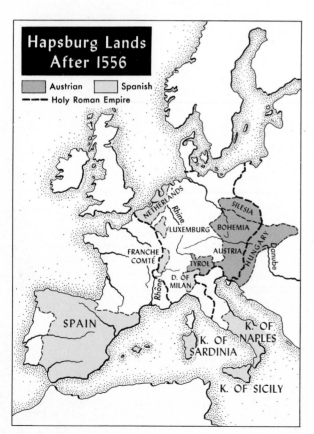

Hapsburg Lands
After 1556

Austrian   Spanish
— — — Holy Roman Empire

NETHERLANDS
Rhine
LUXEMBURG   BOHEMIA   SILESIA
FRANCHE   AUSTRIA   HUNGARY
COMTÉ   TYROL   Danube
Rhone   D. OF
MILAN
SPAIN
K. OF
SARDINIA   K. OF NAPLES
K. OF SICILY

ing: (1) The princes of the various German states and the governments of the free cities were to be free to choose between the Lutheran and Catholic faiths. The princes were to have the right to enforce the religion of their choice upon their subjects, but the free cities on the Lutheran side could not expel a Catholic minority. This principle, which made the religion of the state that of its ruler, is generally known by the phrase *cujus regio ejus religio.* (2) This principle was to apply only to Lutheran and Catholic governments. It did not extend to Calvinists, though their number was increasing. (3) An "ecclesiastical reservation" made an exception of ecclesiastical princes (archbishops, bishops, and abbots), who ruled territorial states. In case any of these should become Lutheran, he was to surrender his state, which would remain under the control of the church; but Lutheran subjects of such princes were not to be forced to give up their religion. (4) Protestant states were to retain whatever church property they had confiscated prior to 1552. The Peace of Augsburg marks a definite stage in the disintegration of the empire, not only because it determined that Germany should remain divided between two religions, but because it recognized the sovereign authority of the princes in the important matter of religious control. It was a victory for the princes in their struggle for independence as much as for the cause of Protestantism.

Abdication of Charles V.   The Religious Peace was followed shortly by the abdication of Charles V. His dealings with his German empire had been generally unfortunate. He was embittered by one more failure at the end. He could not persuade the electors to accept his son Philip as his successor. He was forced, therefore, to split his inheritance. He surrendered the German Hapsburg lands to his brother Ferdinand, who had ruled them since 1521, and with them went the imperial crown. The remainder of his possessions, the Burgundian and Spanish inheritance, he left to his son Philip II. The abdication was completed in 1556. The weary emperor then retired to a Spanish monastery, where he died three years later. He was not an old man, but he had carried a tremendous burden of responsibility almost from childhood.

3. *The Monarchy in France and England*

Royal power in France. The kings of France who were the contemporaries of Charles V were rather less successful than he in foreign affairs, but, on the other hand, they had less trouble with the internal government of their state. We have already noted the triumph of the French monarchy over the nobles and the estates who might have checked its power. When Francis I came to the French throne, he took over a practically absolute government, and the royal power had grown still stronger when he handed it on to Henry II. It had been strengthened by one more generation of tradition, a generation in which the royal rights had been repeatedly asserted and stated in legal form by the school of legists who were trained in Roman law at the University of Toulouse. The treason of the Duke of Bourbon was the only indication that the great nobles who were related to the royal family might again be a menace to the crown; for the present, at least, the nobility were obedient courtiers and soldiers in the king's pay.

Taxation and finance. Francis I and Henry II were often hard pressed for money to carry on their foreign wars. What income the government had, however, was entirely at the disposal of the king, and with reasonable care it should have been sufficient, though the expense of a standing army was considerable. The French army was strong in artillery and cavalry, having the fighting nobility to call on for the latter arm, but it was always weak in native infantry. For this wing of the service, the king had usually to depend in part on Swiss and German mercenaries, who were willing to fight under any flag so long as they were paid. In addition to the army, a good deal of money was spent in pensioning nobles and on the expenses of a luxurious court. The largest part of the royal income came from the *taille,* a direct tax, the amount of which the king could increase at will. Extraordinary expenses were often met by the sale of offices, many of them unnecessary ones created solely for the purpose of sale. This, of course, created a financial burden on the government for the future. On the whole, the financial system was awkward and wasteful. Later, during the Wars of Religion, its inadequacy came near ruining the monarchy.

King and church. The royal finances and royal authority were both strengthened by the power which Francis I acquired over the church in France. The terms of the Concordat of Bologna (1516) left the king with almost complete control of appointments to the higher ecclesiastical offices in the country. He used this power freely to reward the loyalty of the nobles and also to pay the diplomats and ministers who served him, thus relieving the royal treasury of a considerable drain. A further extension of royal power over the church came in 1539, when the king transferred jurisdiction over the great majority of cases from the ecclesiastical courts to the royal courts. The fact that the king had already acquired all the control of the national church and its wealth that he desired was one of the most important factors in deciding the fate of the Reformation in France. Had it been otherwise, Francis might easily have followed the example of other northern rulers in breaking with Rome. As it was, he remained strictly orthodox and persecuted heresy whenever he was on good terms with the pope, though neither he nor his son scrupled to ally themselves with the Protestant princes of Germany. Henry II was much more severe than his father in the persecution of French heretics, and, indeed, had more to work on, for despite persecution the Calvinist faith was spreading rapidly in France.

Tudor absolutism. Across the Channel from France, Henry VIII inherited a government that was almost as absolute as that of the Valois kings, and, like Francis I, he handed it on to his son still further strengthened. England was now a full-grown national state. Most of the old medieval institutions still lived on in form, but the substance of their power had been transferred to the crown. The central government controlled commerce and industry, once the duty of the towns and guilds; it had taken over the full administration of justice, either through the royal courts or through the justices of the peace, who were the unpaid servants of the crown; and during the reign of Henry VIII the king also took over the supreme government of the English Church, thus completing his sovereignty over

Holbein's portrait of King Henry VIII shows the king in later life, but still an arrogant and dominating figure.

all institutions and all individuals in the state. Before this all-powerful monarchy, the old feudal nobility faded into insignificance. They were excluded from the king's council, which was the chief instrument of the central government, in favor of middle-class men or the new nobility created by the crown, men trained in legal and administrative service and wholly devoted to the king. At the same time, their local jurisdiction was superseded by that of the justices of the peace, who were recruited from the country gentry.

King and Parliament.   But if Tudor government was absolute, it was also popular, and scrupulously constitutional. Parliament never died out in England as the Estates General was dying out in France. Under Henry VIII, Parliament might seem little more than a subservient tool in the hands of the king; but it

was a tool that he used constantly and kept in good condition. All Henry's major policies, for example his radical change in the government of the church and his dissolution of the monasteries, were carried out by act of Parliament. Henry VIII was, indeed, a master in the art of handling Parliament. Under his skillful guidance it became a dependable support to the royal authority by giving a legal coloring to the king's acts, rather than a check upon him. Yet all Henry's skill in avoiding the appearance of tyranny would have been useless had not the majority of his policies been genuinely popular, at least with the burghers and country gentlemen from whom the House of Commons was recruited. The success of the great Tudor monarchs, Henry VII, Henry VIII, and Elizabeth I, depended in large part on the fact that they understood their people, that their policies were thoroughly English, and that they never forgot the economic interests of the gentry and the middle class.

Tudor finance.   The task of carrying on an absolute government in England was made easier by the fact that it was relatively inexpensive. High taxation would soon have destroyed the popularity of the government. But the kings of England in the sixteenth century were freed from many of the expenses that burdened the royal treasury, and hence the people, elsewhere. There were not so many greedy nobles to pension as in France, and for some time Henry was able to take care of his favorites by means of the confiscated monastic lands. The administration of local justice cost nothing, being carried out by the unpaid justices of the peace. And, the greatest saving of all, the English kings did not need to maintain a standing army, as did the continental rulers whose borders were always open to invasion. Though Henry VIII was frequently drawn into continental complications, the number of English troops employed on the Continent was never large. Instead of building up a strong permanent army, Henry devoted his attention to the more important, but less expensive, task of creating a royal navy.

"St. Dominic did this; I, too, will do it. St. Francis did this; therefore I will do it." •
St. Ignatius Loyola (1491–1556)

30

The Catholic or Counter-Reformation

FOR HALF A CENTURY after Luther nailed his theses on the church door at Wittenberg, the Protestant Reformation continued to spread, until the very existence of the Roman Catholic Church seemed threatened. At the end of that half-century, one or other of the three great Protestant churches was firmly established, with the active support of the state, in the three Scandinavian kingdoms, in about half of Germany and Switzerland, and in England and Scotland; Calvinism was in open rebellion against a Catholic monarch in the Netherlands and was fighting on fairly even terms in France; while the Catholic states of Germany, as well as Poland, Bohemia, and Hungary, were honeycombed with the Protestant heresy, and signs of it had been seen even in Italy, the home of the Roman Church. Then the tide turned. Within the next generation, the Catholic Church recovered much of the ground lost in Germany and the neighboring countries to the east, and made secure its permanent hold on the Latin nations to the south. This dramatic reversal was the work of the Catholic Reformation or Counter-Reformation, as it has been variously called, depending largely on the writer's point of view.

Historians have long debated whether the reformation of the Catholic Church in the sixteenth century was a spontaneous movement, springing from the desire of the Catholic peoples who were emerging from the age of the Renaissance for a deeper piety and a reform of ecclesiastical morals, or whether its inspiration was the necessity of rallying all the forces of the church against the growing menace of Protestantism by the revival of a more vital Catholic piety, by the strict definition and teaching of orthodox doctrine, and by the removal of those abuses that were so largely responsible for the defection of the north. The truth seems to be that it was both. That its origin was partly spontaneous is shown by the frequent and widespread demands for reform in the days before Luther was heard from, and in the following years before Lutheranism had become a serious danger to the church. A reform of clerical morality and a revival of piety within the church, a true Catholic reformation, would undoubtedly have taken place without the stimulus of the Protestant Reformation. But, lacking that stimulus, the Catholic Reformation would have followed a very different course from that which it actually took. As the Protestant menace increased, the efforts of the Catholic reformers were turned more and more toward the combating of heresy, so that in its mature form the Catholic Reformation was in very large part a counter-reform. The activity of the Council of Trent, the repressive measures of the Inquisition and the Index, and the work of the Jesuits, which

"The Burial of Count Orgaz" by El Greco, 1586, combines the gloomy formality of the Spanish court with the religious aspiration of the Counter-Reformation.

were the chief agencies of the reformation, were directed principally to the defense of the church against heresy and to the recovery of those who were lost to it.

1. The Early Catholic Reformation

The Spanish reform. The spontaneous Catholic Reformation won its first and most complete success in Spain, and it was the Spanish spirit that dominated the movement later as it drifted into the Counter-Reformation. The state of religion in the Spanish peninsula at the end of the Later Middle Ages was in many respects unique. The long crusade against the Moslems had tended to identify the defense of the orthodox faith with the growing sentiment of national patriotism, so that there was not a country in Europe where

heresy was regarded with greater abhorrence. Spain had been less affected by the Renaissance revolt against medievalism and by those social changes that together helped to deaden the piety of Italy and to prepare the peoples of the north for new religious ideals and beliefs. The spirit of Spain was unquestioningly orthodox, and its piety of a type wholly in keeping with the ideals of medieval Christianity. Moreover, the monarchy had won control of the Spanish church and the interests of state and church were closely identified. Everything, therefore, favored the purely orthodox reformation begun by Cardinal Ximenes in the closing years of the fifteenth century with the full support of the monarchy. The result was a marked improvement in the morals and educational standards of the clergy, which in turn led to a strong revival of piety among the people under their care. But the Spanish reform had also its darker side of persecution and intolerance. The Inquisition was introduced into Spain in a new and more effective form, to crush by force and terror all deviation of opinion from the strict lines of medieval orthodoxy.

Catholic reformers in Italy. In Italy, too, during the early decades of the sixteenth century, Catholic reformers were working earnestly to revitalize the spiritual life of church and people; but their efforts were isolated and did not meet with the immediate success achieved by the reform in Spain. Indeed, in this late and rather decadent period of the Renaissance, Italy presented no very hopeful field for either clerical reform or religious revival. The great mass of the people were orthodox enough, but superstitious rather than pious; and in Italy, more than anywhere else, the papal *curia* was a perpetual stumbling block to reform. Most of the abuses in the church had a financial reason for their existence and to remove them would cause a sharp decrease in the revenues of the pope and of the members of his court. Hence the vested interests at Rome were opposed to reform. At the same time, Italy had received too many material benefits from the Italian papacy to rebel against it, as the northern states did, and there was no state government strong or independent enough to take the initiative in reform, as was done in Spain. Nevertheless, there were in Italy many earnest and devout men, some of them holding high offices in the church, who were sincerely interested in reform. All were united in their hope of a Catholic reformation; but as time went on they drifted into two fairly distinct groups, separated by divergent ideas as to the policy to be pursued in regard to Protestantism. The one group, best represented by the Venetian humanist and statesman, Contarini, hoped for reconciliation with Protestant reformers on the basis of practical reform and a liberal interpretation of Catholic doctrine; the other, typified by the Neapolitan Bishop Caraffa, were equally eager for reform, but with no change or compromise in doctrine or usage, and favored the suppression of heresy by the means that had proved so successful in Spain.

Revival of religious orders. Meanwhile, though efforts for practical reform were thwarted by lack of papal cooperation, considerable progress was made in the revival of religion among the masses of the people. Much of the credit for this work was due to new or revived religious orders of which the most influential was the Capuchin order, founded in 1526 as a reformed branch of the Franciscans. The spirit of the new order was medieval rather than modern; its inspiration was a return to the ideals of St. Francis. Like the early Franciscans, the Capuchins devoted themselves to preaching a simple piety among the poverty-stricken masses, and no group did more to gain popular support for the early Catholic Reformation than these kindly enthusiasts, whose pointed hoods soon became familiar sights in every market place. Good work, too, was done by the new Theatine order, founded by Bishop Caraffa in 1524 with the object of reforming the secular priesthood. It was composed of priests who had taken monastic vows, and it had a wholesome influence on the clergy in all parts of Italy.

The papacy takes up reform. With the accession of Pope Paul III (1534–49), following the death of the harassed and vacillating Clement VII, the Catholic reformers at last began to receive some cooperation from the papacy. Several of the most distinguished leaders of the reform party, including Contarini and Caraffa, were made cardinals, and a committee of cardinals was appointed to investigate conditions in the church. The report which they submitted showed so many abuses in the papal *curia* and throughout the government of the church that it was thought wise to suppress it, lest it give aid and comfort to the heretics. A beginning, however, was made in the reform of the *curia,* but as the energy of the aged pope declined, his zeal for reform also diminished and the results were disappointing. Still, the pontificate of Paul III marks an important turning point in the history of the church, the end of the Renaissance papacy and the beginning of the Counter-Reformation.

Failure of conciliation. In the early years of Paul's reign, the liberal reformers, led by Cardinal Contarini, seemed to be in the ascendancy at Rome. They were prepared to make some compromise with the spirit of the new age, as represented by both the Renaissance and the Reformation, and they still hoped to re-establish the unity of the Catholic Church by reconciliation of the Protestants. That accomplished, a general Catholic Reformation, free from the distractions of partisan strife and dogmatic controversies, would be possible. It was the policy proposed at the beginning by Erasmus, and it was doomed to failure now as then. Contarini and his friends failed to realize the fundamental nature of the differences separating the new churches from the old. They had, however, powerful support in Charles ·V, who was determined to restore religious unity to Germany and would have been glad to do so by peaceful means. In 1541, a serious effort was made to establish a mutual understanding at a religious colloquy held at Regensburg. Contarini was the chief representative of the Catholic Church, and the liberal and conciliatory Melanchthon the principal spokesman for the Protestants. Thanks to Contarini's tactful diplomacy, both sides made surprisingly liberal concessions, yet they failed to come to any agreement on the fundamental question of the sacraments. The net result of the colloquy was to prove the impossibility of reconciliation even under the most favorable circumstances. The party of conciliation was discredited and quickly lost influence.

Opening of the Counter-Reformation. Its place was taken by the conservative reformers under the leadership of Cardinal Caraffa. This meant that hereafter the Catholic Reformation in Italy would follow the Spanish model and would become more and more a Counter-Reformation, directed against the growth of Protestantism. For more than a decade Spain had dominated Italian politics; from this time on the spirit of Spain was to dominate Italian religion as well. The reform of practical abuses in the church and the revival of popular Catholic piety continued, but they were coupled with strict orthodoxy and stern repression of all deviating opinion.

2. Loyola and the Society of Jesus

Of the various agencies through which the Counter-Reformation was brought about, possibly none had a wider influence in retaining the loyalty of those who were still members of the Roman Church, or in winning back those who had deserted it, than the devoted preachers and skillful teachers who made up the Society of Jesus. In the Jesuits, as they were popularly called, the most powerful missionary organization the world has ever seen was placed at the disposal of the papacy.

Ignatius Loyola. In the year when Martin Luther faced the Emperor Charles V at the Diet of Worms, the man who was to organize the church's best defense against Luther's teaching was fighting as an officer of Charles's army in the besieged city of Pampeluna in northern Spain. He was a noble from the Spanish Basque province of Guipuzcoa, one Don Iñigo Lopez de Recalde de Loyola, better known to history as Ignatius Loyola (1491–1556). He was wounded before the city was taken, and in the months of anguish that followed, his whole attitude toward life was changed. He determined to abandon his career as a soldier of the Spanish king for that of a soldier of Christ. Hereafter he would fight only with the weapons of the spirit, and would strive to emulate the deeds of the medieval saints, as in his earlier days he had imitated the heroes of chivalric romance. When he had recovered, except for a slight lameness that lasted through life, he set out on his new career with characteristic enthusiasm. As he himself tells us, he had still much to learn about the religious life. Some three years passed before he gave up his hermit life and extravagant self-denial and determined to devote his life to aiding the salvation of his fellow men. He realized that for this purpose he would need more education, especially in theology. He therefore set about the difficult task for a man of his years of learning Latin, which was a prerequisite to study in any university. In 1528, he matriculated in the University of Paris, where he remained for the next seven years, studying patiently and meanwhile gathering about him a group of disciples to aid him in his major purpose.

The Spiritual Exercises. If Loyola never became a great scholar, he had other qualities that made men who were more learned than himself follow his leadership. Aside from his absolute sincerity, unswerving determination, and those indefinable gifts of personality that any leader of men must possess, Loyola's most valuable asset was his uncanny insight into the workings of the human mind. This was abundantly proved by his Spiritual Exercises,

This portrait of St. Ignatius Loyola by Sanchez Coello catches something of the dedicated spirit that characterized the founder of the Jesuit order.

the book that helped to win his first followers and that later maintained the character of his order. Based on a detailed, introspective study of his own experience in the early days of his conversion, it gives directions for a period of intensive contemplation, lasting normally about four weeks, and designed to produce in the participant those soul-shaking emotional experiences that Loyola himself had undergone over a much longer time. The *Exercises* left an indelible impression on the minds of those who passed through the course faithfully, and transformed them into devoted and obedient soldiers of the church.

Founding of the Society. Such was the training of the little group of companions who gathered about Loyola at Paris. There were six of them when, in 1534, they took an oath to go to Jerusalem, as soon as their studies were completed, there to do missionary work among the Moslems, or, if that proved impossible, to go to Rome and place their services at the disposal of the pope. The six had been carefully selected. They were all men of unusual character, ability, or learning. Among them was the Basque noble, Francis Xavier, who was to become the most famous of the Jesuit missionaries, and the Spaniards, Lainez and Salmeron,

who later exercised a decisive influence at the Council of Trent. In 1537, the companions, with three more added, met again in Venice, but, finding the road to Jerusalem blocked by the Turkish war, took the alternative course of going to Rome. The next two years were spent preaching and teaching in various parts of Italy. This experience showed them the crying need for work such as they were doing, and they determined to organize as a permanent order. After some delay, they received papal confirmation of their plan from Pope Paul III in 1540. The following year Loyola was elected first general of the order. The new order was called the Society of Jesus, but a more accurate translation of the Latin *Societas* would make it the "Company of Jesus," for Loyola intended the word to be used in the military sense. They were to be a company of spiritual soldiers, fighting under the banner of Jesus. During the next ten years, the rapidly growing society received many extensions of privilege from the pope, and these, together with a more complete draft of the constitution, were confirmed by a bull of Pope Julius III in 1550.

Its purpose. The purpose of the society was set forth clearly in the constitution, which Loyola finally completed just before his death, and in the bull of 1550. The best brief statement is in the latter: "The company is founded to employ itself entirely in the defense of the holy Catholic faith." In particular, that meant the defense of the church by helping to retain the allegiance of her people, by adding to her membership through the conversion of the heathen, and by winning back as many as possible of those who had been lost to the various Protestant sects. The order was not founded specifically for the combating of heresy, but that became one of its chief duties. The method to be employed by its members was fourfold: first, to educate the young in orthodox schools; second, to win influence with the doubtful through their services as confessors; third, to carry on missionary preaching in heathen or heretical lands; and fourth, to acquire diplomatic influence in international affairs by serving in the courts of nobles and princes. Unlike the earlier monastic orders, the society was not founded primarily for the salvation of its own members, though that was taken for granted, but to accomplish a definite purpose. For that reason, the keynotes of the constitution were efficiency and obedience. The spirit of the Jesuits was the spirit of their founder, and Loyola was a Spaniard and a soldier. As a Spaniard he was unshakably loyal to the orthodox faith and to the traditional practices and authority of the organized church, whose head was the pope. As a soldier he never questioned the orders or policies of his superior officer, in this case the pope, and he expected equally unquestioning obedience from those under his command. In the *Spiritual Exercises* he had insisted on the necessity of mental obedience to the church, "always defending her teaching and never opposing it," and in the constitution he stressed above all else the necessity of absolute obedience, first to the pope and second to the general and other superiors of the order.

Organization.   Loyola's emphasis on efficiency, which followed naturally from his conviction that the order was intended primarily to accomplish a definite purpose, was reflected in the military organization of the society and in the rules for the selection of new members. Novices were to be carefully chosen, with due regard to those qualities, such as good appearance, pleasing personality, intelligence, suitable character, and good social standing, that would make them most useful. Before becoming a full-fledged member of the society, the young man had to pass through a long period of spiritual training and education, during which he might be dismissed at any time. He was then assigned to one of the several different classes into which the society was divided, according to his ability or experience. All members took the customary monastic vows of poverty, chastity, and obedience, but there was an inner circle of the most experienced members who took an additional vow of special obedience to the papacy. From these "Professed of Four Vows" the executive officers were chosen. At the head of the whole order stood the general, elected for life, with absolute authority over all members. Under him were the provincials and a descending hierarchy of inferior officers, very much like that of a modern army. The Jesuits were a mobile as well as a disciplined body. Any member could be dispatched at a moment's notice to whatever field seemed most in need of his services. As a further innovation in the interests of efficiency, Loyola freed his order from those restrictions of dress, ascetic practice, regular hours, etc., which were common in the monastic orders, but which might interfere with the duties of missionary preachers and teachers.

Growth of the society and its work.   The society thus formed grew with amazing rapidity and soon spread to every country of Europe as well as to the heathen lands beyond the seas. At the death of Loyola there were twelve provinces and some fifteen hundred members. Preaching and hearing confessions made up the largest part of their work, but their service as educators was perhaps more important. Jesuit schools and colleges soon sprang up in every Catholic country, and were regarded as among the most efficient of their age. The opportunity provided by their schools to shape the thought of the younger generation, in addition to their work as preachers and confessors, enabled the Jesuits to exert a great influence on the people, the results of which were amply demonstrated in the success of the Counter-Reformation. In later centuries they were frequently charged with working more for the formal adherence of the masses of the people to the church than for their spiritual betterment, and their methods were subjected to a good deal of criticism. The emphasis on efficiency had its dangerous side. But in their early days, at least, the people saw in them only the most unselfish and devoted as well as the most effective servants of the church.

3. *The Council of Trent* (1545–63)

The Jesuits had barely begun their work when the rulers of the church took steps to strengthen its defenses against Protestant heresy by the calling of a general council, which was to determine the character of the Counter-Reformation. It met in the imperial city of Trent, just north of the Italian border, in three separate periods. The first period, 1545–47, fell in the reign of Paul III, the second, 1551–52, in that of Julius III, and the last, 1562–63, in the reign of Pius IV.

Problems involved.   From the very beginning of the Lutheran movement, there had been frequent demands for a general council.

At first Luther and his followers had appealed from the authority of the pope to that of a general council, and later the Catholic reformers who hoped for reconciliation, as well as the Emperor Charles V, took up the cry. They were joined by the Spanish bishops and the conservative reformers of Italy, who agreed that a council was necessary for reform, but who were violently opposed to any policy of doctrinal compromise or reconciliation. In addition, all opponents of papal authority in the church worked for a council. The popes, however, were very loath to call one, for they had unhappy memories of the councils of Constance and Basel, and feared that the chief result would be an attempt to limit their authority. When Paul III finally agreed to summon a council, he did so as the result of a policy that few of those who demanded it would entirely approve. Since the failure of conciliation at Regensburg, the pope and the Counter-Reformation party, who were now in the ascendancy at Rome, had determined on a new policy, which was to recognize the loss of the Protestants as a whole as irremediable, and to concentrate on the defense of what remained, with the hope of winning back individual heretics wherever possible. This was to be done by an authoritative definition of Catholic doctrine on all disputed points, so as to clarify the differences between the old and the new churches; by active repression of heretical opinion in all Catholic countries; and by reform of those practical abuses that left the church open to reproach. This policy appealed to the Spanish churchmen, but not to the majority in France and Germany, who still hoped for some compromise with the new ideas; and even the Spanish reformers were opposed on one very important point. They had little hope of the papacy reforming itself and felt that reform should be carried out by the council, whereas the papal party felt that this part of the task should be left to the authority of the pope.

The council. With all these divergent ideas as to the work the council was to do, it is not surprising that its meetings were stormy, or

that there were such long gaps between them. The political interests and animosities of the various states helped to complicate the situation still further. On the whole, however, the papal party was able to carry through its policy. At the very beginning, the pope secured a working control of the council by obtaining a decision that only bishops and heads of religious orders, who were present in person, should have the right to vote. This enabled him to maintain a loyal Italian majority, for Trent was close to Italy and the prelates from more distant countries were usually prevented by wars, expense, or other inconveniences from attending in large numbers. Still, the papal control was never very secure, and the papal legates were forced to compromise on the matter of reform, permitting its discussion, but on the condition that the definition of doctrine should be taken up at the same time. As a matter of fact, most of the time of the council was occupied with the latter question. All through the council, the Jesuits Lainez and

One of El Greco's most effective portraits is that of Fray Felix Hortensio Paravicino, a Dominican friar.

"The Ecstasy of St. Theresa" by Gianlorenzo Bernini expresses the mystical element in the Counter-Reformation in a characteristically Baroque style.

tagonistic churches with irreconcilable differences in belief, the Roman Catholic Church was given a coherent and authoritative statement of orthodox faith which was to prove a powerful instrument for the preservation of unity. The lines of demarcation between Protestantism and Catholicism were sharply drawn. Almost every one of the doctrinal decrees of Trent was designed to meet some Protestant dogma. Among the most important was the decree defining authority. Luther, Calvin, the Anabaptists, and other Protestants had appealed to the sole authority of the Bible against that of the church and the papacy. This was the authoritative foundation for Luther's fundamental doctrine of salvation by faith alone as well as for the general Protestant attack on the sacramental system, the secular power of the papacy and the clergy, monasticism, the veneration of saints, and the other practices of the church which had grown up in post-Biblical times and hence were not mentioned in the Bible. Forced to meet this argument, the council decided that the Bible and the tradition of the church were of equal authority, and that both could be interpreted only by the church, which in practice meant by the pope as head of the church. In addition, the traditional Latin translation of the Bible, the Vulgate, was declared to be the only authoritative version. This adherence to tradition as the best weapon against the innovators was the keynote of all the major doctrinal decrees of the council. By establishing the authority of tradition, however, the Council of Trent bound the modern Catholic Church to medieval precedent and made any later change in either doctrine or practice extremely difficult. Still, the very insistence on tradition had its value, for it gave to the Roman Church the prestige and authority of unbroken continuity with the past, which the newer Protestant churches necessarily lacked.

Reform decrees. The work of practical reform, so far as it was actually accomplished by the council, was of secondary importance. Still, it did outline a comprehensive program of reform abolishing the worst abuses and making provision for better discipline and higher educational standards among the clergy. The practical execution of these decrees, however, was beyond the power of the council,

Salmeron exerted a great influence on the members and were often instrumental in winning them over to agreement with the wishes of the papal party. During the last session, the diplomatic pope, Pius IV, took pains to secure the agreement of the great Catholic monarchs before submitting his projects to the council, and so won his way through what seemed an almost impossible situation. The final triumph of the papal authority was assured when the council in its closing session voted to present all its decrees to the pope for confirmation.

Definition of doctrine. The most important result of the Council of Trent was the final definition of Catholic doctrine. At a time when all religious opinion was in a state of flux, and when Protestantism was splitting up into an-which ceased to exist as soon as its work was done. It had to be left to the executive authority of the pope and his successors. Fortunately, the majority of the later popes proved worthy of the trust. The Catholic Church never again suffered from the lax discipline or worldly-minded leadership that had left it so open to criticism during the period of the Renaissance.

4. The Counter-Reformation in Action

Reforming popes. With the conclusion of the Council of Trent, all the forces of the Counter-Reformation swung into action, under the leadership of reforming popes. Without the support of papal authority, which was strengthened rather than otherwise by the council, no permanent success would have been possible. Even before the end of the council, the papacy had been responsible for a good deal of reform, in the reign of Paul III and still more under Paul IV (1555–59), who as Cardinal Caraffa had for years been the leader of the conservative Catholic reformers. After Trent, the spirit of the Counter-Reformation ruled at Rome. During the remainder of the sixteenth century, two popes in particular, Pius V (1566–72) and Sixtus V (1585–90), were zealous exponents of clerical morality and rigid orthodoxy. Under Pius, the Catholic Church took on new vigor, crushed out all opposition in the lands it controlled, and began a remarkable period of reconquest. Catholicism was no longer on the defensive. It was carrying the war into the enemy's country. Under Sixtus, as the power of Spain declined, the papacy took its place once more as the leader of the Catholic world, though no longer with the secular power that had hampered rather than helped its spiritual authority in earlier times.

Inquisition and Index. In the Latin countries of Italy and Spain, where the Counter-Reformation triumphed most completely, the work of reform was accompanied by savage re-pression of heresy. The Inquisition, which was the chief agent of repression, was not a new institution. It had been used with terrible effect against the heretics of southern France in the thirteenth century. In the closing years of the fifteenth century, it was revived and given new and more effective powers in Spain. Then, in 1542, when the Counter-Reformation first gained headway at Rome, Cardinal Caraffa persuaded Pope Paul III to reorganize the papal Inquisition in Italy on the Spanish model. Throughout the remainder of the Counter-Reformation period, the Holy Office, as the Inquisition was officially named, with its secret trials and its power to turn over condemned heretics to the secular government to be burned at the stake, maintained a reign of terror, completely successful in stamping out all open signs of heresy in Italy and Spain. North of the Alps and the Pyrenees it never gained a firm foothold, though Philip II at one time tried to introduce it into the Netherlands. A second and almost equally important agent

The Grand Inquisitor, Don Fernando Niño de Guevara, looks out sternly from a portrait by El Greco.

for the suppression of unorthodox opinion was the Index of Prohibited Books, an elaborate system of censorship of the press, designed to prevent the publication or circulation of any book that might suggest to the people ideas derogatory to the church or to orthodox belief. One of the immediate results of the Council of Trent was the publication of the Tridentine Index, which superseded earlier lists, and was enforced wherever the cooperation of the civil government could be obtained. Later, a permanent Congregation of the Index was instituted by Pius V to keep the work up to date. The effect of this rigid control of the press in molding the thought of the Spanish and Italian people can scarcely be overestimated.

Intolerance on both sides.   It is only fair to note that the persecution of heresy and the censorship of heretical books were by no means confined to the Catholic Church. Tolerance of varying opinions in matters of religion was a virtue that found few champions in the sixteenth century. To both Protestant and Catholic theologians, the heretic who endangered men's souls was a deadly enemy of mankind. Moreover, in every country, church and state were so closely united that a dissenting religious sect was likely to become a seditious political party, and the persecution of heresy by the state often appeared as the punishment of treason or sedition. Nevertheless, the persecution of heretics was never as thorough or as savagely enforced in the Protestant countries as it was in Italy and Spain, for in none of them was there a separate institution, with the terrible powers of the Inquisition, dedicated to that purpose.

The Jesuits.   However successful the negative measures of suppression might be in stamping out heresy in Catholic lands, they would never have accomplished the real revival of Catholic piety, much less the reconquest of doubtful or openly Protestant lands, which took place during the Counter-Reformation. For this, aside from the work of the Council of Trent and the reforming popes, credit must be given to the Jesuits. Their methods were positive and constructive. They preached, heard confessions, and taught, reviving the piety of the indifferent, directing the consciences of the penitent, and instilling orthodox beliefs and devotion to the church into the minds of the young in their formative years. And they went out as missionaries to the lands that were drifting toward Protestantism. Some of their most effective work was done in Germany where, under the leadership of Peter Canisius, they brought about a revival of Catholic education and piety in the states whose rulers were still Catholic, but whose people were on the verge of heresy.

Results.   By the end of the sixteenth century, the Counter-Reformation, like the Protestant Reformation, had spent its aggressive force. By that time the religious map of Europe was fairly definitely fixed. In each country the church, whether Protestant or Catholic, had become closely identified with the political governmental interests of the state, and could count on them for permanent support when the wave of religious enthusiasm died down. France had emerged from the Wars of Religion with a recognized Protestant minority, but with Catholicism assured as the national faith. Poland had been won back from Protestantism, and Germany was evenly balanced between the two opposing creeds, with little chance of further conquest by either.

31

The States of Europe in the

Age of Philip II

FOR MORE than forty years, from 1556 to 1598, Philip II of Spain occupied a place in European affairs scarcely less influential than that so long held by his father, Charles V. The first half-dozen years of Philip's reign marked the opening of a new era in the history of most of the states of Europe. The scenes shifted and new figures replaced the old on the European stage. In France, the death of Henry II left the government in the hands of his widow, Catherine de' Medici, and her weakling sons; in England, the last of the Tudors, Elizabeth I, began her long and prosperous reign; and in Scotland the ill-fated Mary Stuart took over the government in the midst of a religious revolution. Nor were the changes of these momentous years merely changes in the cast of characters in the European drama. The strife of Lutheran and Catholic in Germany had just been settled by the Religious Peace of Augsburg; in the next few years, Protestantism was permanently established in England and Scotland; the Netherlands were drifting fast toward open revolt against Spain; France gave up her claims to Italy, thus ending the long Hapsburg-Valois wars; the French Huguenots opened the Wars of Religion that were to devastate France with civil strife for more than a generation; and in 1562 the leaders of the Catholic Church met in the final session of the Council of Trent.

These years set the stage for the history of Europe during the remainder of the sixteenth century. In many respects the age of Philip II (1556–98) was very different from that of Charles V. Both the Renaissance and the Reformation had passed their peak, and other problems engaged the attention of the European peoples. The action is often confusing, the motives tangled and difficult to follow. But two or three main threads, often interwoven, run through the history of the whole period. They are: the Spanish-Catholic policy of Philip II, the driving force of the Counter-Reformation, and the rising commercial interests of England and the Netherlands.

1. Spain Under Philip II

Policy of Philip II. The son of Charles V, who inherited the crown of Spain with its dependencies in the Netherlands, Italy, and the Americas, clung throughout his life to a consistent policy and to the conviction that it was God's purpose for the people of Europe. That policy may be briefly stated. It was, in the first place, to enforce absolute government and strict conformity to the Catholic faith in all his dominions; second, to use the unified force thus established to make Spain the dominating power in Europe; and, finally, to use this Spanish hegemony as God's instrument for the restoration of religious unity to western Christendom under the Roman Catholic Church. In essence it was the dream of Charles V in his later years, but narrowed and intensified in his son by the shearing away of the German half of the Hapsburg empire, by Philip's Spanish upbringing, and by the influence of the Counter-Reformation, which made Philip a more bigoted Catholic than his father had ever been. In short, where Charles had been a cosmopolitan emperor, to whom his family interests meant more than any country, Philip was a Spanish king, a Spaniard born and with a Spaniard's narrow patriotism, rigid orthodoxy, and relentless hatred of heresy. Philip's problems were made simpler than his father's by the loss of the German lands, but he had still a baffling variety of tasks to demand his constant attention, and, as in his father's case, his efforts were hampered at every turn by the utter inadequacy of the financial means at his disposal.

Character. He was hampered, too, by fatal inadequacies in his own character and ability. Philip had a very strong sense of duty, and he was an indefatigable worker. But, in an absolute ruler, industry may be nearer a vice than a virtue, when it is the product of a narrow, plodding mind, without understanding of men and lit by no spark of imagination. Philip's conscientious attention to every detail of government too often led to fatal delays. His best-intentioned efforts were often misdirected. His was the strength and weakness of the monomaniac. The conviction that his cause was the cause of God and Spain, and he himself the chosen instrument of God's will, held his spirit firm through countless trials, but it also closed his heart to mercy and his mind to counsel.

Religious persecution. Philip was successful in carrying out the first part of his policy, at least in Spain. There the enforcement of universal orthodoxy was relatively easy, for the majority of the Spanish people were as stanch Catholics and as intolerant of heresy as Philip himself. The Inquisition had done its work well in the past half-century. Still there were alarming signs of heresy here and there in the last years of Charles V. Philip's first act, therefore, on his return to Spain in 1559, was to stimulate the Inquisition to renewed activity. The fires of the *auto-da-fé,* that terrible ceremony in which heretics were burned to death, spread across Spain. The persecution was thorough and effective. Even the suspicion of

Titian's portrait of King Philip II of Spain suggests the cold and enigmatic character of the Spanish king, which made him respected by many but loved by few.

heresy was eradicated and it did not make its appearance again. There was still, however, in southern Spain one large group of very doubtful Catholics, the Moriscos of Granada. They were not heretics in the ordinary sense of the word, but descendants of the Islamic Moors who had been forcibly converted by Charles V. Philip had good reason to believe that their professed Christianity was no more than skin deep. Determined to crush out all signs of Moslem faith or practice, he instituted a series of repressive measures that finally goaded the Moriscos to a desperate rebellion. The revolt was put down with frightful thoroughness. The helpless Moriscos were massacred or transported into servitude in Castile. Granada, which had been the richest agricultural land and the most prosperous center of industry in Spain, was left a barren waste.

Absolute government. Religious unity was closely bound up in Philip's mind with the establishment of his own absolute authority in

Spain. Each would help the other and both were necessary in order to place the full resources of the country at the disposal of his greater purpose. The way had been prepared for him. He had only to carry on the work of Charles V in weakening the already feeble constitutional powers of the Cortes and in excluding the nobles from an active share in the civil government. His chief contribution was the development of a highly centralized bureaucratic administration, in which most of the offices were held by men of low birth who would be entirely dependent upon him. He himself was the center of the whole system, supervising the work of all departments, often to the most petty details.

Taxation and commerce.   So far, Philip succeeded in putting his policy into effect. But it did not have the desired result of making Spain a greater nation. On the contrary, both the country and the government grew steadily poorer, and when Philip died the fabulous wealth of Spain was fading to a memory. From the beginning, indeed, Philip was in constant financial straits. The ambitious foreign policies of Charles V had already reduced the government to the verge of bankruptcy, and Philip was forced to meet expenses almost as great from diminishing resources. Italy had never contributed much to the royal treasury, and the Netherlands on which his father had depended so heavily were in revolt during most of Philip's reign, thus making them a source of expense rather than of income. The whole burden, therefore, fell upon Spain. But, even from this source, the amount that could be collected steadily decreased, as stupid economic legislation and a misguided system of taxation aggravated the decline of Spanish prosperity. The net result of Philip's financial policy was to kill the goose that laid the golden egg. The *alcabala,* a tax of ten per cent on every sale of goods, to mention but one of many burdensome taxes, was in itself enough to strangle the commerce of Spain and starve her industry, and to these were added innumerable hampering regulations and prohibitions, which in the end gave most of Spain's trade to the English or Dutch and drained the country of its gold and silver.

Results in Spain.   The results of Philip's unwise policy in Spain were not at once discernible. Thanks to the conquered wealth of the New World and to the apparent strength acquired through union with the great Hapsburg empire, Spain had become the most powerful of the European nations during the reign of Charles V. For a long time after his death, she was able to maintain the appearance of greatness and an undiminished prestige, but under Philip the reality of Spanish power was crumbling. Two important successes, however, helped to hide this fact. In 1571, the Spanish fleet administered a decisive defeat to the Turks at Lepanto, and in 1580, Philip succeeded in making good an hereditary claim to the kingdom of Portugal, thereby uniting the whole peninsula under his rule and adding the great Portuguese colonial empire to that of Spain. Nevertheless, in summing up the results of Philip's government of Spain through nearly half a century, one must note more failure than success. He left his country impoverished, his people orthodox and proud, but unindustrious. Spain still seemed greater than it was, but before long internal decay would destroy its prestige.

Failure abroad.   Meanwhile, Philip's attempts to carry out that part of his policy which concerned the rest of Europe did not meet with even the partial success he achieved in Spain. The Netherlands rebelled against his autocratic Spanish-Catholic government, and the northern provinces broke away to form an independent Protestant state. Henry IV foiled his efforts to crush out Protestantism in France and to dominate the French government in alliance with the Catholic party. Finally, his hopes of restoring England to the Catholic Church and of gaining control of Spain's most dangerous commercial rival led only to the supreme disaster of the Armada.

2. The Revolt in the Netherlands

Philip and the Netherlands.   In almost every respect, the Netherlands were very different from Spain and they could not be made to accept the same policies or methods of government. It was one of the tragedies of Philip's reign that he never fully understood or became reconciled to that fact. The sovereignty of the seventeen provinces that made up the Netherlands was his by hereditary right, but there

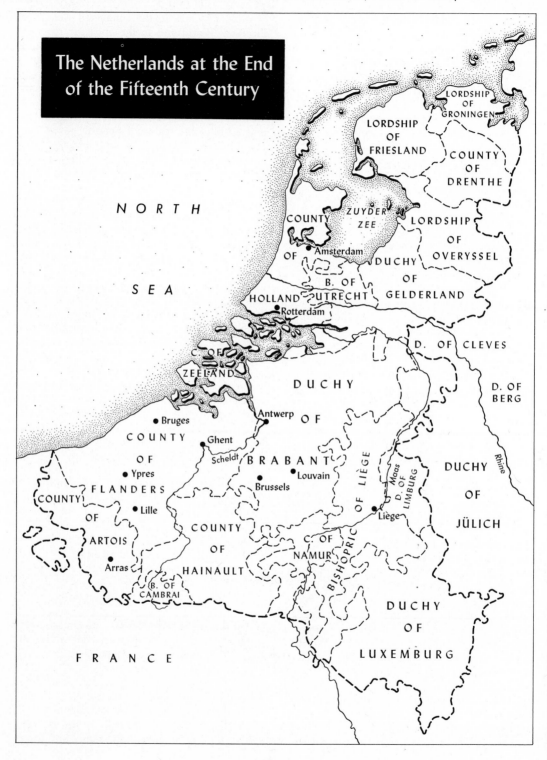

The Netherlands at the End of the Fifteenth Century

LORDSHIP OF GRONINGEN

LORDSHIP OF FRIESLAND

COUNTY OF DRENTHE

NORTH

ZUYDER ZEE

COUNTY

LORDSHIP OF OVERYSSEL

OF   ● Amsterdam

SEA   DUCHY

OF

B. OF   GELDERLAND

HOLLAND ● UTRECHT

● Rotterdam

D. OF CLEVES

C. OF   D. OF BERG

ZEELAND

DUCHY

Antwerp   OF

● Bruges   COUNTY   ● Ghent

OF   Scheldt   BRABANT

● Ypres   ● Louvain

FLANDERS   Brussels   DUCHY

COUNTY   D. OF LIMBURG   OF

● Lille   JÜLICH

OF   COUNTY   ● Liège

ARTOIS   OF   C. OF

● Arras   HAINAULT   NAMUR   BISHOPRIC OF LIÈGE

B. OF CAMBRAI

DUCHY

OF

FRANCE   LUXEMBURG

Maas

Rhine

was no other political bond to hold them together, and each province had its own cherished institutions and ancient privileges. Even national and linguistic unity were lacking; for the northern provinces were predominantly Germanic and Dutch-speaking, while the southern were more nearly French in tradition and language. Situated at the commercial crossroads of northwestern Europe, the Netherlands were the home of a vigorous commercial and industrial people, prosperous and independent. Their position left them open to all the cultural and religious influences of the age and, despite persecution, many had adopted one or other of the current Protestant faiths. Lutheranism and Anabaptism had been the first to make an impression, but at the time when Philip began to rule, Calvinism was spreading rapidly in the northern provinces. The government of a people who were so divided, yet so prosperous and independent, would require a good deal of tact and understanding. Charles V, himself a native of the Netherlands and their own prince, had possessed those qualities in sufficient degree to retain their loyalty, though there was a good deal of discontent in his later years. Philip had neither tact nor understanding — and he was a foreigner.

Causes of the revolt. The causes of the revolt were inherent in the character of Philip and his Netherland subjects and in the irreconcilable opposition between his general policies and their economic, political, and religious interests. From the beginning they distrusted him as a foreigner who did not speak their language and had no sympathy with their point of view. Philip was, indeed, a Spaniard first and last. He regarded the Netherlands as satellites of Spain, to be used for Spanish interests. Economic grievances soon gave point to their resentment of this attitude. Philip was in desperate financial straits. He was forced to begin his reign by increasing the burden of taxation, already high enough under Charles V, and most of the money wrung from the Netherlanders was spent in Spain. Still worse, he strove to restrict their commerce so as to give the advantage to Spanish merchants. Political grievances fed their resentment still further, as Philip tried to force upon the Netherlands a centralized, absolute government like that of Spain, regardless of the ancient constitutional

rights and traditional privileges of the separate provinces. Finally, Philip's determination to crush out heresy in all his dominions permanently alienated the growing number of Protestants, while his arbitrary reorganization of the church government (including the creation of a number of new bishoprics) aroused the opposition of many Catholics. Philip's rigid Catholic policy was not the sole cause of the revolt, but, once the revolt had begun, it was the factor that made impossible any reconciliation of the provinces that were predominantly Protestant.

Beginning of the revolt. Despite these various causes of discontent, the first ten years of Philip's reign passed before there were any signs of open rebellion. Following his father's abdication, Philip remained in the Netherlands until 1559, when he returned to Spain, never to visit his northern possessions again. From that time on, he left the government of the distant provinces to a series of regents, of whom the first was his half-sister, Margaret of Parma. He always insisted, however, on a vexatiously detailed supervision of the regent's activity from his cabinet in Madrid. So far as he gave independent authority to anyone, it was to his chief minister in the Netherlands, Cardinal Granvelle, who became so unpopular that Philip was forced to recall him in 1564. The power of this minister, who was not a native of the Netherlands, was especially resented by the great nobles, who were accustomed to being consulted in affairs of state. The most important of these, Prince William of Orange, had been shown high favor by Charles V, but now found himself neglected. He was not, however, responsible for the first outbreak of the revolt, though he was later to be its greatest leader. In 1565, a group of young hotheads from the lesser nobility, together with some of the wealthy burghers, organized to protest against the arbitrary government, the foreign ministers, and the Inquisition. The following year, some two hundred and fifty of them gathered to present a formal petition to the regent. They accomplished nothing, but the incident is memorable because it was then that the rebels acquired the name of "Beggars," applied to them in derision by one of the regent's councilors and carried by them in defiant pride throughout the revolt. The protest of

Of this portrait of William of Orange at the age of forty-eight, his biographer, C. V. Wedgwood, says: "Looking at Adrian Key's portrait, it is easy to understand why the ordinary people called him 'Father' openly and came to him with their troubles."

the nobles was followed by wild anti-Catholic riots and image-breaking on the part of the Protestant proletariat, and Philip began to lay plans for crushing the independence of his turbulent and heretical subjects. In 1567, William of Orange resigned his offices and retired to his German estates in Nassau to organize resistance; the first army of the Beggars was defeated by government troops; and Philip sent a Spanish army to the Netherlands.

Alva's reign of terror. The arrival of ten thousand veteran troops under the Duke of Alva, who now replaced Margaret as regent, opened one of the darkest and most blood-stained pages in European history. Philip had ordered Alva to crush all opposition both to the government and to the Catholic faith, and he could scarcely have found a more perfect instrument for his purpose than this hardened campaigner, who shared to the full his blind Spanish patriotism and hatred of heresy. For six years (1567–73) Alva raged through the land, imprisoning, executing, and confiscating the property of those who were suspected of either rebellion or heresy. Even the greatest nobles were not spared. The gallant Lamoral of Egmont and the Count of Hoorn were among the first to fall. In addition, Alva levied crushing taxes (including the Spanish *alcabala* or ten per cent tax on sales), which almost ruined the commercial and industrial prosperity of the Netherlands beyond repair. All this was not accomplished without opposition, but the people of the Netherlands were cowed by fear, and the duke's Spanish veterans easily defeated the German and French mercenaries recruited by William of Orange. The only success of the rebels was won on the sea. From 1569 on, the "Sea Beggars," lawless privateers who hated Spaniards and Catholics as much as they loved fighting and plunder, preyed on Spanish shipping along the Atlantic coast. At first they had operated from friendly English ports, but in 1572 they acquired a base on the coast of Holland by capturing the harbor of Brill. This first success on land encouraged other towns in Holland and Zeeland to rebel. In July, the Estates of Holland proclaimed William of Orange their stadholder, and despite frightful sieges and massacres, the northern provinces never again submitted entirely to Spanish authority. Even Philip could see that the reign of terror had borne its logical fruit in bitter hatred of Spain, and in 1573 he recalled Alva, replacing him by the more pacific Don Luis Requesens.

William unites the provinces. Throughout these bloody years, William of Nassau, Prince of Orange, was the heart and soul of the rebellion. He was a German by birth and his title was derived from a principality in southern France, but he had large estates in the Netherlands and became a Netherlander at heart. He was a tolerant man who hated religious persecution, and after the beginning of the revolt he threw in his lot with the Protestant minority. It was his grim determination, his refusal to accept defeat, and his patient and skillful diplomacy that kept the spark of rebellion alive during the darkest years. A discreet capacity for keeping his own counsel was one of his outstanding gifts, whence the name William the Silent by which he is best known in the annals of his adopted country. His constancy was rewarded by success in the years following the removal of Alva. Sternly refusing all conciliatory offers short of complete religious freedom and restoration of the old political rights, he kept up the fight, meanwhile uniting the northern provinces under his leadership and working to win the cooperation of the south. This latter object he achieved in 1576 after the Spanish troops, who had been left unpaid and leaderless by the death of Requesens, mutinied and perpetrated the horrible massacre known as the "Spanish Fury" at Antwerp. Goaded by this final outrage, the Estates General of the southern provinces signed the Pacification of Ghent, a treaty with Holland and Zeeland to stand together against the Spanish tyranny.

Final split. The union, however, did not last long. The common hatred of Spain was offset by too many differences between north and south. They did not speak the same language, and the aristocratic governing class of the industrial southern provinces had little in common with the democratic commercial states of the north. The chief barrier between them, however, was the difference in religion. The years of persecution had driven the most stubborn Protestants from the south to the more easily defended and rebellious northern provinces, which were now fanatically anti-Catholic, while the south was left fairly free from Protestantism. It would therefore not be difficult for an astute diplomat to stir up dissension between the provinces, and this was the aim of Alexander Farnese, Duke of Parma, who arrived with a new Spanish army to take over the regency in 1578. The famous Parma, already renowned as a soldier but equally skilled as a diplomat, was not long in getting results. Early in 1579, a group of the southern provinces signed the Treaty of Arras, forming a league for the protection of the Catholic faith. This was immediately answered by the Union of Utrecht, in which the northern provinces banded together to resist religious persecution and Spanish rule "with life, blood, and goods." These two treaties mark the final split between north and south. In the following years, Parma conquered or cajoled the remaining rebels in the south and restored the ruined land to the Spanish crown and the Catholic Church, while the little Protestant states in the north struggled on to maintain their independence and to form the Dutch Republic.

The Dutch Republic. Philip never became reconciled to the loss of the most prosperous part of his Netherland possessions. William the Silent was kept busy defending his country against Parma's armies and trying in vain to get substantial aid from France. After the assassination of William in 1584 the danger increased. There was no strong central government in the new republic, and each of the provinces claimed independent sovereign powers. Aid from England helped them over the difficult period of the next four years until events elsewhere relieved the pressure. Parma's attention was distracted, first by Philip's plans for the invasion of England, then by wars with the French Huguenots and later with France itself. Meanwhile, two new leaders appeared who united the provinces and shepherded them through two decades of war to final security. Jan van Oldenbarneveldt gave wise direction to affairs of state, while Maurice of Nassau, the brilliant son of William the Silent, became stadholder of the various provinces and led the Dutch army to victory after victory. A truce in 1609 practically ended the war, but Spain did not formally recognize the existence of the Dutch Republic as an independent state until 1648. Meanwhile, the Dutch had prospered mightily. Their seaborne commerce had not been wrecked by the revolt as had the industry of the southern provinces, and, though the long war with Spain was expensive, their expanding commerce more than made up the loss. Despite its small size, the Dutch Republic was now one of the greatest commercial powers in Europe with trade extending from the West Indies to the Far East. Together with England, it fell heir to the commercial supremacy that was slipping from the hands of Spain.

3. *The Wars of Religion in France*

The Treaty of Cateau-Cambrésis and the death of Henry II, both in the year 1559, ended an epoch in French history — that of the long foreign wars against the encircling Hapsburg power and for the domination of

Italy. For the next forty years, French history centered on new problems, as foreign wars gave place to the civil Wars of Religion.

French Protestantism (to 1559). The Reformation came to France as an importation from Germany and Switzerland, though the way had been prepared by some of the earlier French humanists. From the first it had to make its way against the opposition of the monarchy, for the French kings had already acquired all the control of the church in France that they needed and regarded heresy as a menace to national unity. In the early years Francis I was fairly tolerant, but as Lutheranism gained ground, he commenced an intermittent persecution, which became more severe and constant in the last decade of his reign. Under Henry II the persecution became still more severe. Nevertheless, Protestantism continued to spread, finding many converts among the burghers, gentry, and nobility, and took on a more aggressive character. The secret of this new energy was the influence of John Calvin and the shift among French Protestants from Lutheranism to Calvinism. Calvin was himself a Frenchman and a master of French prose. He maintained a personal supervision of the struggling Protestant communities from his stronghold on the eastern frontier, and gave them the benefit of his genius for organization. Moreover, as we have already noted, the Calvinist form of church organization was especially well adapted to the formation of a church in opposition to a hostile state government. In the year 1559, which saw the death of Henry II, the first French Protestant Synod met secretly in the king's own city of Paris to work out a national organization for the Reformed Church in France.

Rival noble families. The next step in the development of French Protestantism followed almost immediately. It became a political party, headed by a group of great nobles who were held together by family ties. Under the absolute monarchy of Francis I and Henry II, the majority of nobles were little more than courtiers and soldiers. Nevertheless, there were a few great nobles, divided into two family groups, both more or less closely related to royalty, who exercised great influence at court. Under the feeble rule of Henry's sons, they became rivals for the control of the govern-ment, and, as one group was Protestant, though of fairly recent conversion, the other extremely Catholic, their rivalry became an integral part of the religious struggle. On the Protestant side were the two foremost princes of the blood, Anthony of Bourbon, King of Navarre by virtue of his marriage to the heiress Jeanne d'Albret, and his brother Louis of Condé. Allied to them by marriage was the able and deeply religious Gaspard de Coligny, Admiral of France, who, together with his two brilliant brothers, gave the soundest leadership to the Protestant party. On the other side, the family of Guise headed the ultra-Catholic opposition to heresy. They were a younger branch of the ruling house of Lorraine and were closely connected by marriage with the royal families of France and Scotland. Duke Francis of Guise, the head of the family, had acquired a great military reputation and considerable popularity in the recent wars with Spain; two of his brothers were cardinals and royal ministers; his sister Mary was Regent of Scotland as widow of James V and mother of the young queen, Mary Stuart, who now became Queen of France as the wife of Henry II's eldest son, Francis II (1559–60).

The Guise ascendancy. As Francis II was still too young to rule, though he had passed the legal age of majority, the government fell naturally into the hands of the queen's uncles, the brothers Guise. They at once made use of the known Calvinist leanings of their rivals, the Bourbon-Coligny group, to drive them from court, thus forcing them into opposition as avowed leaders of French Protestantism. During the next year, the Guises redoubled the religious persecution, filling the prisons and keeping the executioners busy, while in self-defense the Protestants were forced to organize as a political-religious party. It was at about this time that the Protestants in France came to be known as Huguenots. They were drifting rapidly toward rebellion when the Guise ascendancy ended for a time with the death of Francis II, after only a year's reign.

Catherine de' Medici. The crown now passed to Henry's second son Charles IX (1560–74), who was still a child. His mother, Catherine de' Medici, promptly seized control of the royal government as regent. Hitherto this daughter of the famous Florentine family

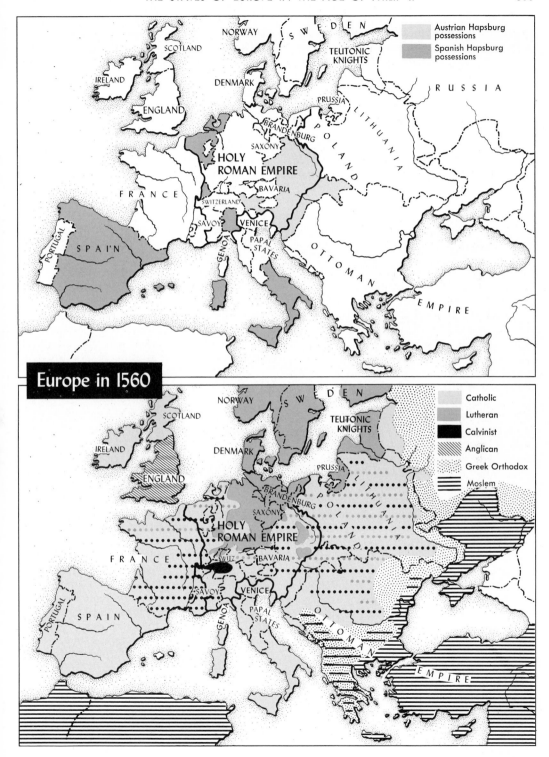

Austrian Hapsburg possessions
Spanish Hapsburg possessions

NORWAY
SWEDEN
SCOTLAND
TEUTONIC KNIGHTS
IRELAND
DENMARK
RUSSIA
ENGLAND
PRUSSIA
LITHUANIA
BRANDENBURG
POLAND
SAXONY
HOLY ROMAN EMPIRE
FRANCE
BAVARIA
SWITZERLAND
SAVOY
VENICE
PORTUGAL
SPAIN
GENOA
PAPAL STATES
OTTOMAN
EMPIRE

Europe in 1560

Catholic
Lutheran
Calvinist
Anglican
Greek Orthodox
Moslem

NORWAY
SWEDEN
SCOTLAND
TEUTONIC KNIGHTS
IRELAND
DENMARK
ENGLAND
PRUSSIA
BRANDENBURG
LITHUANIA
SAXONY
POLAND
HOLY ROMAN EMPIRE
FRANCE
BAVARIA
SWITZ
SAVOY
VENICE
PORTUGAL
SPAIN
GENOA
PAPAL STATES
OTTOMAN
EMPIRE

had played a secondary role as the wife of Henry II and mother of the late king, but from this time on she was to be a principal actor in the hectic French drama. For a quarter of a century she directed the government of her remaining sons, and wielded whatever power was left to the French crown. Through it all she clung to a consistent policy, though it was one that had every appearance of inconsistency. Her aim was simply to maintain control of the government for herself and her sons and to keep the kingdom at peace so far as possible. To do that, she played off Guise against Bourbon, extreme Catholic against Huguenot, and strove whenever possible to build up a center party of moderate Catholics who would be loyal to the crown and would help to keep the peace.

Protestant aggression.   Catherine's first action was to stop the persecution of the Protestants and to issue an edict granting them a limited freedom of worship. If Catherine hoped that this would keep the peace or conciliate the Huguenots, she was mistaken. Calvinism had gained steadily and became increasingly militant under the weight of persecution. When the pressure was lifted, it spread with startling rapidity and remained as militant as ever. The Protestants were never more than a small minority of the population of France, perhaps not more than ten per cent, but their strength was far greater than their numbers would indicate. They were recruited chiefly from the most energetic and influential classes — the industrial and commercial townsmen and the fighting gentry from the country, to whom were added a few great nobles. They were characterized by a high morality and earnestness of purpose that made them in every way a respectable as well as formidable group. Filled with hope, they were now determined to win full freedom at all costs. Catherine's moderate edict failed to satisfy them. At the same time, it aroused strong opposition from the extreme Catholics. Fanaticism on both sides flared to fever heat. Catholics and Protestants alike rioted and desecrated each other's churches in every corner of France. In 1562, the Duke of Guise, placing himself at the head of a group of Catholic nobles, seized control of the government and forced Catherine to recall the edict of toleration. But the Protestants had

gone too far to submit. They took arms to defend their faith and opened the Wars of Religion.

First Wars of Religion.   France now entered on a decade of alternate civil war and uneasy peace. Despite their great inferiority in numbers and frequent defeats the Huguenots held their own by virtue of able leadership and unshakable determination. The murder of Francis of Guise in 1563 weakened the Catholic party, and in the following years nearly all the original leaders on both sides fell, leaving Coligny the outstanding figure in France. Meanwhile, Catherine pursued her vacillating course, alternating persecution with toleration, and striving to restore peace and keep control of the government. In the years 1570–72, she seemed about to obtain her objective. She arranged a peace treaty, granting a fair amount of freedom to Protestants in places where they were in the majority; summoned Coligny to court; and planned to win over the Huguenot leaders by marrying her daughter Margaret to young Henry of Bourbon, who had succeeded his father Anthony as King of Navarre and would in time become the natural leader of the Huguenots.

Massacre of St. Bartholomew.   As usual, however, Catherine had failed to reckon with the fanatical passions on both sides, which indeed she could never understand. The Huguenots were still unsatisfied and the Catholics were developing a strong opposition under Duke Henry of Guise, the son of the old Catholic leader. Moreover, Catherine began to fear the influence of Coligny with the king, now of age, whom he was trying to persuade to help the Protestant rebels in the Netherlands and to seize the opportunity provided by the revolt to annex the French-speaking provinces. Peace seemed as far away as ever, and Catherine decided to throw in her lot again with the Guises. She persuaded herself that the admiral and the few remaining Huguenot leaders were the principal obstacles to peace, and that if they could be removed, the Huguenot resistance would collapse. Their presence in Paris for the wedding of Henry and Margaret provided the opportunity, and on St. Bartholomew's Eve, 1572, Catherine and the Guises laid the plans that led to the terrible massacre of the following day. They had probably intended no more than the murder of Coligny and the other chiefs, which Henry of Guise supervised himself, but, as news of the killing spread, the fanatical Paris mob rose to take a hand, and before morning some two thousand Protestants had been slain. Similar massacres in other cities soon accounted for thousands more.

The Catholic reaction. Despite the loss of their leaders, the Huguenots still fought on, although it was clear that they had passed the peak of their power and were losing ground. Their numbers had been cut down by war and massacre and it was only in the south and west of France that they were strong enough to hold their own. Protestantism was no longer spreading. On the contrary, a strong Catholic reaction had set in under the influence of the Counter-Reformation and the activity of the Jesuits. Moreover, the whole country had suffered terribly from the wars, and the ruined people not unnaturally blamed the stubborn Protestants. The royal government was almost bankrupt, and Henry III (1574–89), who succeeded his brother Charles IX two years after the massacre, was too feeble to control the situation. In 1576, the extreme Catholic party, headed by Henry of Guise, took matters into their own hands and formed the Catholic League for the suppression of Protestantism. During the next few years, the league gained a wide following and also the assurance of support from Philip II.

War of the Three Henrys. The death of Catherine de' Medici's fourth son, the Duke of Alençon, the last of the Valois line, brought about a crisis and precipitated the final struggle. Henry III was in feeble health and had no sons, and the nearest heir to the throne was now the Protestant Bourbon prince, Henry of Navarre, who for some years had been the most active leader of the Huguenots. Rather than accept him, the league was prepared to go to any lengths. In 1585, the leaguers signed a treaty with Philip of Spain in open defiance of their king. The war that followed is called the War of the Three Henrys. Lacking resources or the strength to use what he had, Henry III was caught between the league, led by Henry of Guise, and the Huguenots who followed Henry of Navarre. At first the unfortunate king submitted to the dictation of the league, then in a burst of futile energy he

strove to free himself by the assassination of Duke Henry. Vengeance followed within the year. In 1589, he was himself assassinated by a fanatical leaguer, and Henry of Navarre proclaimed himself King of France as Henry IV (1589–1610).

Settlement under Henry IV. The death of Henry III did not at once end the wars, for his successor had still to overcome the opposition of the league and of Spain. His religion was the chief obstacle in his path to the throne. Except for that, the French people would have accepted him willingly enough, for they were weary of war. After four years more of fighting, Henry IV finally realized that the obstacle was insurmountable. He submitted and formally adopted the Catholic faith. After that he had little trouble in reconciling the leaders of the league, though he had still to fight a war with Spain, for Philip II was loath to give up his dream of dominating France through the Catholic party. The war ended on terms favorable to France in 1598, the last year of Philip's reign. In the same year, Henry provided a settlement of the religious problem for France, which in main outline was to last for nearly a century. By the Edict of Nantes, he guaranteed freedom of conscience and full political rights to all Protestants. The Wars of Religion were ended. Protestantism in France had secured a legal status, but its great days were over. During the next century it faded slowly, as the interests of the age shifted. Meanwhile, with peace restored at home and abroad, Henry IV was free to turn his attention to the reconstruction of his shattered kingdom. But that is a story that must be left for another chapter.

4. England Under Elizabeth I

Catholic interlude: Mary. Before Protestantism was finally established in England, there was a brief Catholic interlude. When the young King Edward VI died, the fate of religion in England was still far from certain. The English Reformation had begun as a political and national revolt against Rome, supported by economic motives, rather than as a primarily religious movement. The people had acquiesced in Henry's establishment of a national Anglican Church, but neither king nor people had changed their doctrinal beliefs in any very marked degree. True, Protestant teaching of the various types emanating from Germany and Switzerland gained many converts, especially in the influential commercial class and among the gentry of the south, and under Edward doctrinal Protestantism made rapid progress. Still, there is reason to believe that when Edward's eldest sister Mary Tudor, the daughter of Henry VIII and Catherine of Aragon, came to the throne in 1553, the greater number of Englishmen were either still Catholic or were sufficiently indifferent to accept either church as the government should decide. The proof is that Mary, herself a devout Catholic, was able to restore Catholicism as the official religion with the aid of Parliament and to reunite the English Church to the Roman. There was no rebellion, and the Catholic restoration might have been successful but for two things. In 1554, Mary married Philip II of Spain and joined Spain in a close alliance that reduced England to the position of a Spanish satellite. And she persecuted Protestants with a harshness that won for her the name of Bloody Mary. The Spanish alliance, coupled with the persecution and the restoration of papal authority, aroused national resentment in England and hatred of Spain and the papacy. When Mary died, most Englishmen were formally Catholic, but Catholicism had become more unpopular. The issue was still to be decided.

Elizabethan settlement. The crucial decision was made by a young woman of twenty-five, Elizabeth I (1558–1603), Anne Boleyn's daughter, and the last of the Tudors. The new queen had been raised as a Protestant, but she was no fanatic. What she wanted was a national church, free from Rome and subject only to the royal authority, Protestant in character, but liberal enough so that all but the most stubborn extremists might conform. She procured it by act of Parliament in 1559. In the matter of church government, Elizabeth followed the example set by her father. An Act of Supremacy re-established the Anglican Church under the supreme authority of the crown, with the old episcopal system otherwise unchanged. This was followed by an Act of Uniformity, which prescribed the use of a Book of Common Prayer, modeled on that of Edward VI, as the only legal form of worship.

Since this portrait of Mary Tudor is by Antonio Moro, a Flemish painter justly celebrated for lifelike portraits, we can be sure that Mary Tudor looked much like this.

Having secured the outward uniformity that was so essential for political reasons, Elizabeth was prepared to leave a good deal of leeway in matters of doctrine. The creed as stated in the Prayer Book and the later Thirty-Nine Articles was predominantly Protestant, but the phrasing at crucial points was vague enough so that the more moderate Catholics, who did not hold strongly to the papal obedience, might attend the national church without too great a shock to their consciences, while almost all Protestants, whether they had taken their opinions from Wittenberg or Geneva, could interpret it to suit their own convictions. The Elizabethan settlement of the church was a characteristically English compromise and amazingly permanent. Elizabeth reigned long enough to see it firmly established and it has lasted in its main outlines down to our own time. Divergent parties soon arose and later many dissenters seceded, but in Elizabeth's time, at least, the great majority of Englishmen remained within the church. Only the more radical Protestant sects and the extreme Catholics remained stubbornly aloof. They were punished and harassed by fines, but were not persecuted so severely as to arouse public sympathy for them.

England and Scotland. The peaceful and permanent establishment of a Protestant church in England was closely bound up with the conversion of Scotland to Protestantism just at the time when Elizabeth was beginning her reign. The coincidence was of vital importance to both countries. United by a common religious interest, England and Scotland were both able to withstand the threat of domination by the great Catholic states of the Continent, Spain and France respectively.

Reformation in Scotland. Scotland was still a very backward country, almost medieval in its social and political structure. Its church was dominated by lawless nobles, was disproportionately wealthy for a poverty-stricken country, and was probably the most corrupt in Europe. It was an easy target for the attacks of the Protestant reformers. Moreover, the latter had patriotic national sentiment on their side. The Scottish people were growing restless under the rule of the French regent, Mary of Guise, while their queen, her daughter Mary Stuart, was living at the French court and in 1558 married the heir to the throne of France. They resented the treatment of Scotland as a dependency of France, and as the Guises were ultra-Catholic, Catholicism came to be associated in the popular mind with French domination. All the materials for a conflagration were present. All that was needed to set the land ablaze was the fiery preaching of John Knox, who had imbibed Calvinism at the source during a period of exile in Geneva. In 1557, a congregation of Scottish nobles signed the first Covenant for the defense of the Protestant faith. Two years later, Scotland was in armed rebellion against the French Catholic regent, and in 1560 Elizabeth sent aid to the rebels to help them drive out the French troops. That action was decisive. It secured the triumph of Protestantism in Scotland and ended the long-standing enmity between the two British countries.

Mary and the Presbyterians. When Mary Stuart came to rule her Scottish kingdom in 1561, she found the Calvinist Presbyterian Church already firmly established. The fact that the Reformation had come to Scotland in the form of Calvinism and in opposition to the government made the religious situation in Scotland very different from that in England. The Presbyterian Church was founded as the result of a revolution that swept away the old episcopal system. As was characteristic of Calvinist churches everywhere, its organization was essentially democratic, with the final authority vested in the congregations and their elders and ministers. Such a church could not be controlled by the state, but, on the contrary, could bring powerful pressure to bear on the government. This Mary Stuart soon found to her cost. Through seven years of folly and romantic adventure she fought the power of the church, only to be beaten by it. At last she fled from the country to take refuge in England, leaving her infant son, James VI, to be brought up by Presbyterian divines.

Anglo-Spanish rivalry. If Protestant England gained a new ally in Protestant Scotland, she also acquired a new enemy in Catholic Spain. Philip II could never be reconciled to the loss of England both to the Catholic Church and to the Spanish sphere of influence; and the hostility between the two countries was further aggravated by a growing commercial rivalry. English commerce and industry were expanding rapidly in Elizabeth's reign,[1] and English merchants were beginning to carry on a profitable trade with the Spanish colonists in the New World, despite everything the Spanish government could do to exclude them. The fact that open trade with the Spanish colonies was denied to them forced the English merchants to become armed smugglers and pirates, and incidentally made England a militant sea power. For years before there was formal war between England and Spain, merchant-privateers like Drake and Hawkins plundered the Spanish Main, captured treasure ships, and perfected a new technique of naval warfare. Religion added bitterness to the commercial rivalry. The English merchants were mostly Protestant, and they took a double satisfaction in every blow struck against the commercial monopoly of Catholic Spain.

[1] See below, page 445.

Protestant sea power. Nor were they the only Protestant seamen who combined profit with religious satisfaction in daring assaults on Spanish commerce. By an odd coincidence, the sea power of both the Netherlands and France was almost entirely in Protestant hands, that of the rebellious Dutch and Huguenots respectively, who held the best of the Atlantic ports and issued forth to prey on the shipping of Spain. From the North Sea to the Caribbean, militant Protestantism rode the seas and harassed the great Catholic state, whose land armies were still regarded as invincible. It was the English privateers, the Huguenots, and the Sea Beggars of Holland, who, by strangling Spanish trade and cutting Spain off from the Netherlands, made possible the success of the Dutch revolt. Or, if that were not enough, the aid, official and otherwise, sent from England to the Protestant rebels in the Netherlands may be considered a decisive factor. Small wonder that Philip II finally determined

to crush the island kingdom which had become the chief menace to his cherished plans for the aggrandizement of Spain and the restoration of Catholicism to Europe.

The war with Spain. It is more surprising that he did not attack England earlier, when, indeed, he would have had a better chance of success. But there were a number of good reasons for his delay. At first he had hopes of restoring the ascendancy over England, which he had lost on the death of Mary, by marrying Elizabeth, or by playing upon the queen's fear that France would press the claims of Mary Stuart. And Elizabeth's astute diplomacy maintained the delusion as long as possible. Then the Netherlands revolted and Philip put off war with England until he should have regained control of his northern possessions. He lacked the sea power to land an army in England, so long as the English could count on the aid of Dutch and Huguenot privateers, and with every passing year the English themselves became more formidable opponents on the sea. Philip accordingly turned to conspiracy with English Catholics to rid himself of Elizabeth and to restore Catholicism in England by replacing the Protestant ruler with the Catholic Mary Stuart. The weak point in Elizabeth's position was that she was the last of the direct line of Tudors, that her legitimacy was disputed by all good Catholics, who had never recognized the validity of Henry's divorce from Catherine and marriage to Anne Boleyn, and that Mary Stuart, as great-granddaughter of Henry VII, was the next claimant to the throne. For years Elizabeth's life was in constant danger from Spanish-Catholic plots, which, incidentally, served to arouse in patriotic Englishmen an undying hatred of Catholic Spain. So long as Mary Stuart lived, neither English independence nor Protestantism was safe. Elizabeth protected the unhappy queen as long as she could, but at last, in 1587, she submitted to the popular demand and ordered

One of the few portraits of Queen Elizabeth I probably painted from life, this picture gives a striking impression of the firm character of the queen who gave her name to one of England's most glorious ages. It was painted about 1575 by an unknown artist and is now in the National Portrait Gallery, London.

Fireships, carried by wind and tide, broke up the formation of the Spanish fleet and enabled the English to engage the scattered ships at a crucial moment in their battle with the Armada.

her execution for treason. There was now nothing to delay Philip any longer. He declared open war immediately. It lasted until after the end of Elizabeth's reign.

The Spanish Armada. Though the war dragged on for years, its fate was settled at the very beginning by the dramatic defeat of Philip's great Armada in 1588. He had strained the financial resources of Spain to the utmost in order to build a fleet great enough to crush the English navy and transport an invading army to England. But more than money is needed to build an effective navy. Philip listened too little to the advice of experienced sailors, and entrusted the command to landsmen and soldiers. From beginning to end, the history of the Armada is a story of short-sighted stupidity and hopeless bungling. No account was taken of the new technique of naval warfare, based on the use of heavy cannon in light, handy ships, which had been worked out by Drake, Hawkins, and other privateers and introduced into the small but efficient English navy. The story of how the towering galleons of the "invincible" Armada were destroyed by the winds and waters of the English Channel, ably assisted by the men and guns of the English navy, is too well known to need recounting. The destruction of the Armada marked a definite stage in the decline of Spain's power, while for England it was the start of a great era of ascendancy on the sea.

32

The Establishment of Absolute

Monarchy in France

THE SIXTEENTH century, which had opened with such brilliant promise for France, drew to its close in the midst of disillusionment and disaster. When the century began, France had seemed about to enter upon a new and glorious epoch of national strength. The monarchy had apparently won at last its long fight for centralized government and national unity against the independent feudal nobility; and the dream of extending French power across the Alps into the fabulous land of Italy seemed already an accomplished fact. But sixty years of foreign wars ended with the abandonment of the costly Italian dream; and a further generation of civil Wars of Religion left France distracted and desolate, powerless in foreign affairs and internally divided, with her people impoverished and her government bankrupt, and with the ancient specter of feudal independence once more raising its head to mock an impotent monarchy. Just as the century ended, however, there were signs of renewed hope. Henry of Bourbon, King of Navarre, had become King Henry IV of France, and under his strong hand, peace, unity, and order were restored to the troubled land. Once secure upon his throne, Henry devoted himself to the task of reconstructing his shattered country and restoring the power and prestige of the monarchy

at home and abroad. Many of the results of his work were wasted in the years following his death, but the task of strengthening the state was taken up again by Richelieu and by Mazarin to such good effect that when the young King Louis XIV took over the personal government of his kingdom in 1661, he found France the foremost power in Europe and himself an absolute monarch, whose authority was questioned by neither noble nor commoner.

1. Henry IV Reconstructs France

Edict of Nantes (1598). Though Henry IV had inherited the royal title in 1589,[1] five years of fighting passed before he was officially crowned, and it was not till 1596 that he received the submission of the last of the Catholic League. Meanwhile, he had been forced into war with Philip II of Spain, and peace at home was very uncertain while the real issue of the Wars of Religion was still unsettled. Born soldier though he was, Henry was eager to restore peace, so that his country might have an opportunity to recover from the devastating turmoil of the preceding generation. In 1598, he brought the war with Spain to an end by

[1] See above, page 401.

the Treaty of Vervins, and in the same year he issued the epoch-making Edict of Nantes, which accomplished the still more important objective of securing internal peace for France by a fair settlement of the vexatious religious problem. Henry had become a Catholic for reasons of state, because he was to be the ruler of a country that was predominantly Catholic, but he had not forgotten his old Huguenot followers. The Edict of Nantes granted them complete freedom of conscience, the right of public worship in all places where it already existed and in a number of other specified places, and the right to hold any public office. As a temporary guaranty that these rights would be respected, the Huguenots were also given the privilege of governing and garrisoning some two hundred cities, mostly in southern and western France. This was a dangerous concession and caused trouble later, but the establishment of religious toleration was wise and just. That part of the edict remained in force for nearly a century. It reunited the kingdom and made France the one country in Europe where men of two different religions could dwell together in peace and equal citizenship.

Henry's task. With the restoration of peace at home and abroad, Henry IV was free at last to take up his colossal task of reconstructing France, restoring the power of the monarchy, and rehabilitating French prestige in Europe. It was a task that might well have daunted a lesser man, for it involved every aspect of government. In the first place, the government must be rescued from bankruptcy and its finances put on a firm footing. Next, the people must be helped to recover their lost prosperity. Then the authority of the central government must be strengthened and the nobles reduced to obedience. And finally, the king must use all the power of the revived state, with the aid of skillful diplomacy, to teach the other powers of Europe that France was still a nation to be reckoned with.

Henry and Sully. For the carrying-out of this great task, no king in French history was better suited by nature than Henry IV, or, perhaps it would be fairer to say, than Henry IV aided by that most careful, energetic, and honest of French ministers, the Duke of Sully. The restoration of France was the product of the cordial collaboration of these two men of very different character. They had been friends and companions in arms from their youth up. During the troubled years of the Wars of Religion, Henry had learned to depend on Sully, then Marquis of Rosny, for those compensating qualities which he himself lacked. They were both good soldiers, though Sully fought with a cold Calvinist fury that was in marked contrast to the king's reckless, swaggering gallantry, but it was in the council rather than on the field of battle that Sully proved his worth. For Henry needed someone to check his tendency to extravagance. He was genial, friendly, endowed with the personal magnetism and understanding of men's characters which are essential to a leader, but also inclined to be profligate. His best qualities of mind were clear intelligence, sound common sense, and the kind of constructive imagination that is needed to shape the general policies of a state. In short, Henry was a popular king and a wise statesman, but he had not the qualities that make an administrator. And France needed an administrator. Henry realized that need and knew that in Sully he had the man to meet it.

Royal finance. Sully's most immediate and pressing problem was to free the government from its apparently hopeless financial embarrassment. Years of foreign and civil wars, the weakness of the last Valois kings, and the confusion, inefficiency, extravagance, and corruption that pervaded every branch of the financial administration had combined to bring the state to the verge of bankruptcy. The people were crushed by heavy and inequitable taxes; yet the royal income was utterly inadequate to meet current expenses. In part this was the result of a vicious financial system inherited from the Middle Ages. A badly organized multitude of officials and a criminally careless system of bookkeeping made waste and corruption almost unavoidable. Moreover, the method of levying taxes was unjust and terribly wasteful. The *taille*, a personal and property tax, which represented the largest part of the royal income, was paid almost entirely by the poorer classes, since nobles and clergy were exempt and the wealthy bourgeoisie could often escape their just share. In order to raise money quickly, this and other taxes were "farmed out"

After fighting his way to the throne, Henry IV restored peace and stability to France after the long civil strife of the Wars of Religion.

to private persons or corporations in return for a lump sum. The tax "farmers" then collected as much as they could — usually far more than they had paid the government — from the defenseless people. It has been reckoned that under a weak administration not more than twenty-five per cent of the taxes paid by the people ever reached the royal treasury. Sully made no serious effort to reform this vicious system, but he did try to ensure its being honestly administered. He imposed a reasonable amount of order upon the administration, insisted on a strict accounting for all income and expenditure, did away with a number of useless offices, forced dishonest officials to disgorge, and saw to it that the money collected in taxes did not disappear on its way to the treasury. By such measures, Sully was able to decrease the *taille,* while at the same time increasing the royal revenue, and by cutting

down waste and extravagance he was able to provide plenty of money for all the legitimate expenses of government, including the cost of building up a strong army and financing public works and other measures for promoting general prosperity. By the end of Henry's reign, Sully had paid off nearly a third of the national debt, and had accumulated a substantial surplus for use in any emergency.

Economic recovery. In his preoccupation with the finances of the royal government, however, Sully did not forget that the wealth of the state depends in the long run on the prosperity of its citizens. Careful though he was to keep down royal expenses, he spent money freely on the improvement of roads, bridges, canals, and harbors, thus stimulating the economic life of the state by providing safe and convenient means of communication. He was also greatly interested in the promotion of agriculture, which he believed to be the true basis of national prosperity. With characteristic energy he undertook the draining of marshes, the reclaiming of wastelands, and the resettling of districts deserted during the late civil wars. In addition, he opened up a foreign market for the farmers by removing the prohibition on the exportation of grain. To all this the king gave his hearty support, and also added some important innovations of his own. Henry, indeed, was a sounder economist than Sully, and took an active interest in both industry and commerce, which his minister tended to ignore. It was the king who introduced the silk industry into France, stimulated other industries by subsidies and monopolies, made favorable commercial treaties with Spain and England, and founded the French colonial empire by sending out the first colonists to New France, the Canada of the future. And, most important of all, Henry gave to France a dozen years of peace and security, which was all a naturally industrious people needed to work out their own economic salvation. When Henry's reign ended, there was still much poverty in the country, but the general economic condition was vastly improved, and France had taken a long step in the direction of national recovery.

Subjection of the nobles. Meanwhile, Henry had to deal with other than economic problems. Equally important was the task of restoring the authority of the crown, on which the security of the state depended. The civil wars, which had come near to ruining the monarchy, had given a new lease on life to political feudalism. The great nobles had recovered a part of their old independence, and they were always a destructive and disorganizing force in the life of the nation, unless kept well in hand by a strong king. In his struggle for the crown, Henry had been forced to buy off the great nobles of the Catholic League, but once his position was secure he taught them that he was their master. More than once discontented nobles rebelled, but the rebellions were easily crushed. The mass of the people, and especially the solid middle class, were unshakably loyal to the king who had given them peace, security, and a chance to prosper. With their backing, Henry built up as strong a monarchy as France had yet seen. His government was an intelligent, unoppressive absolutism, and that was the best that France could hope for under the circumstances. France had no institutions capable of building up a constitutional monarchy, and the civil wars had proved that the only alternative to absolutism was anarchy.

Foreign policy. Much of Henry's energy, too, was taken up with foreign affairs. He saw the issues clearly and pushed every advantage, so that the growth of France's prestige abroad kept pace with her internal recovery. The king's foreign policy may be summarized in a very few words. His main objective was to free France from the menace of the encircling Hapsburg powers, by weakening Spain and Austria in any possible way. The Hapsburg states were not as strong as they had been, but France still lay wide open to invasion from four different directions. To the south, Spain held Roussillon on the French side of the Pyrenees; to the north, she held Flanders, and to the east, Franche-Comté, both divided from France by indefensible frontiers; and to the southeast, Savoy, friendly to the Hapsburgs, opened the way to invaders from northern Italy. With her enemies inside her only geographical defenses, France would never be safe while the Hapsburgs remained strong enough for aggressive action. While giving his country time to draw its breath and recover its strength, Henry devoted himself to diplo-

macy. He won the alliance of the Duke of Savoy, thus blocking the road from Hapsburg Italy; and in Germany he succeeded in mobilizing a group of Protestant princes in opposition to the Hapsburg emperor. Meanwhile, he was building up a national army and waiting for the right moment to strike a more forcible blow.

Cleves-Jülich succession. When the moment came, Henry rushed to war with his old enthusiasm, but death stopped him before he could accomplish anything. The cause of the war was the death, in 1609, of the Duke of Cleves, Jülich, and Berg, three small but strategically important states on the lower Rhine, near the borders of France. There were two claimants to the succession, both Lutherans, though the people were Catholic. The Emperor Rudolf promptly sent an Austrian army to occupy the duchies, pending the settlement of the succession. Henry naturally considered this act a menace to France. He mobilized his troops at once and rallied his Protestant allies in Germany and Holland. It was to have been a general war against the Hapsburgs in both Germany and Spain. Everything was ready and Henry was about to join his army in the field when an assassin struck him down as he rode through the streets of Paris. The king's death paralyzed the French government. France withdrew from the war and the anti-Hapsburg alliance disintegrated. Without French aid and Henry's energetic leadership his Protestant allies could not hope to carry on the war.

2. *Richelieu and Mazarin Establish Absolute Monarchy*

Interlude of disorder: the regency. With the death of Henry IV, the character of French government changed abruptly for the worse. Fourteen years passed before France found again, in Richelieu, a strong hand to guide her destiny. Those years form an interlude of waste, misgovernment, rebellion, and a shiftless foreign policy, during which the best results of Henry's reign were frittered away. For the first half of that period (1610–17), France was ruled by a stupid and irresponsible woman, Henry's widow, Marie de' Medici, acting as regent for their young son Louis XIII, and by her worthless Italian favorites. The queen had no understanding of her late husband's policies. She reversed almost every one of them, with disastrous results. She discharged Sully and the rest of Henry's ministers; she wasted the money he had saved and allowed the administration to lapse back into its old state of inefficiency and corruption; she permitted the great nobles to rebel and bought them off, instead of crushing them by force; and, finally, she reversed Henry's anti-Hapsburg policy and sought an alliance with Spain, the alliance to be cemented by the marriage of Louis XIII to the Spanish infanta.

Louis XIII.   Meanwhile, the young king was growing up, disregarded by his mother and humiliated by her all-powerful favorite, the Italian adventurer, Concini, who had become chief minister of the kingdom. In his loneliness, Louis turned for friendship and counsel to his royal falconer, who accompanied him on the hunting expeditions that were his favorite pastime. With this rather obscure gentleman he planned the overthrow of his mother's arrogant minister. The plot was put into effect in 1617. Concini was killed and the queen-

mother was banished from the court. The king then took over the government in his own right, with the former falconer, now Duke of Luynes, as his chief minister. The change, however, did not bring any marked improvement in government, for Luynes was a fool and the king was young and inexperienced. So the interlude of disorder continued until 1624, when Louis handed over the government to the capable hands of Cardinal Richelieu, who remained his chief minister almost to the end of his reign.

Richelieu.   For eighteen years (1624–42) Richelieu was master of France. He dominated every branch of the government and shaped the policies of the state. Yet he could not have done so without the steady support of the king. Louis gave him complete authority because he was convinced that Richelieu was the most capable man in France. That Richelieu overshadowed the king does not prove that the latter was a weakling, for no weakling could have backed the terrible cardinal with such stubborn determination against the hatred of the royal family and the whole court. For Richelieu was never popular. Indeed, Louis himself never really liked his awe-inspiring minister, but he trusted him and approved his policies. Throughout his ministry, Richelieu devoted himself with fanatical energy to the accomplishment of two main objectives: first, the unification of the whole state under the absolute authority of the crown, and second, the raising of France to a dominating position among the nations of Europe. It was part of the policy of Henry IV, but only part; for Richelieu, though utterly devoted to the crown and the state, cared nothing for the welfare of the French people. He never realized, as Henry did, that the strength of the state depends on the prosperity of its people. He was prepared to sacrifice their interests ruthlessly to what he believed to be the good of the state.

Richelieu and the nobles.   That lack of human interest and understanding kept Richelieu from being a really great statesman, but in one respect at least his ruthlessness was justified.

Marie de' Medici, the Italian wife of Henry IV, was a silly woman, but she had the kind of face that Rubens loved to paint. The portrait is now in the Prado Museum in Madrid.

A stern hand was needed to control the great nobles, for under the weak rule of the regent and the young king they had resumed their old lawless ways. They must be crushed if the king was to be really king. In his devotion to the ideal of absolute monarchy, therefore, Richelieu became the avowed enemy of the nobles and no name or title was great enough to save a traitor from the executioner's block. He had spies everywhere, and one conspiracy after another ended in a series of executions before it could become a menace to the state.

Suppression of the Huguenots. The same motives determined Richelieu to crush the political power of the Huguenots. He was not a religious fanatic and did not believe in the practical utility of persecution, but the Huguenot party was a menace to the king's authority and to the unity of the kingdom. The Edict of Nantes had left them in armed possession of a number of walled towns and with a religious-political organization of their own. Moreover, they were prepared to use their privileged position to make a bid for further independence. They had rebelled once in 1621, before Richelieu came into power, and he had been minister for only a year when they rebelled again. This time he had to make peace, for the government was not yet strong enough to crush them, but he was working busily so that when the next opportunity occurred he would be ready to take decisive action. He had not long to wait. In 1627, the irresponsible interference of Charles I of England on the side of the Huguenots precipitated another rebellion. The war lasted for two years, with most of the action centering around the siege of the strongly fortified seaport of La Rochelle. It held out for a year, but, when it fell, the Huguenot resistance soon crumbled. In 1629, the rebels submitted, giving up all their fortified strongholds and the last of their special military and political privileges. Richelieu had accomplished his purpose, and having done so, he wisely refrained from religious persecution. The main body of the Edict of Nantes, which guaranteed the Huguenots freedom of conscience and equal citizenship with Catholics, was left intact. Shorn of their political organization, but otherwise untouched, the French Protestants settled down to become loyal and useful members of the state.

Cardinal Richelieu, the chief minister of Louis XIII, was for eighteen years the real ruler of France. This portrait in the National Portrait Gallery is by Philippe de Champaigne.

Foreign policy. Having now nothing to fear from the Huguenots, and not much from the great nobles, Richelieu was free to turn his attention to the aggrandizement of France on the international stage. His foreign policy was a revival, *in toto*, of that of Henry IV. His aim was to win security for France and a possible expansion of territory by weakening the Hapsburgs. He was the natural ally of all enemies of Austria and Spain, and would aid them with money or arms as the occasion demanded. To this end he devoted the largest part of his energy in the later years of his ministry. That story, however, belongs more properly to a later chapter dealing with the Thirty Years' War, in which he played a conspicuous part.

Administration. At the end of his life, Richelieu might well look back upon his career of service to the state with satisfaction. He had accomplished everything he really cared about. He had raised French prestige abroad; he had crushed all dangerous opposition to the monarchy at home; and he had built up a strongly centralized government. Yet Richelieu's administration was far from being an entirely successful one, and nothing shows the limitation of vision which kept him from being a really great statesman more clearly than his inability to realize the extent of his failure. His successes had been won at too great a cost to the state, and he left France miserable and impoverished. The people were ground down by the excessive taxes raised to pay for his foreign wars; commerce and industry languished; and even the government was drifting perilously close to financial ruin.

Intendants.   In one respect at least, Richelieu did attempt to reform the unwieldy administrative system. He sent out royal officials, called "intendants," with arbitrary powers to take over many of the duties of the noble governors of the provinces and the other traditional local officials. This reform was in keeping with his general policy of centralizing the government of the state under the king's council and strengthening the authority of the crown at the expense of such feudal institutions as still survived. The intendants were usually

well-trained, middle-class men, on whose loyalty the king could rely more securely than on that of the great nobles. Though not as systematically established under Richelieu as they came to be later, the intendants already formed the basis of a governmental bureaucracy that would be of great service in holding the country together in any political crisis.

Mazarin and Louis XIV.   The structure of central government which Richelieu had created was put to a severe test in the years following his death. For the king died within a few months after his minister (May, 1643), and the crown was left to a four-year-old child, Louis XIV, with his mother, Anne of Austria, acting as regent. Such a situation almost inevitably spelled trouble, but Richelieu had bequeathed to the young king, with the centralized administration, an able minister to act as his successor, and together they saw the royal government through a troubled period of foreign war and rebellion at home to eventual triumph. The new minister was an Italian who had been for years in Richelieu's service, the Cardinal Mazarin. Until his death, early in 1661, he remained chief minister of France, and in that time, he carried out most of Richelieu's policies to their final conclusion. Supple and conciliatory, where Richelieu was hard and ruthless, the Italian cardinal had not the awe-inspiring personality of his predecessor, but he was intelligent and he walked faithfully in the path set by his former master.

The Fronde.   That path led him safely through the early years of the regency and to the conclusion of the Thirty Years' War in 1648. But Mazarin was an even worse financial administrator than Richelieu. The expenses of the war grew heavier by accumulation, and with each year the burden of taxation became more intolerable to the people. Moreover, the great nobles who had hated and feared Richelieu hated his successor also, but did not fear him so much. In 1648, a group of the great nobles, in uneasy alliance with the citizens of Paris, took advantage of the economic discontent to break into open rebellion. This was the first of the two rebellions

Cardinal Mazarin, an Italian, succeeded Richelieu as chief minister of France. Philippe de Champaigne painted the portrait.

that are collectively known as the Fronde. It was quickly ended by a compromise. The trouble, however, was not ended. The next year the rebellion was renewed on a broader scale. For two years (1650–52) it threatened the hated minister and the whole system of absolute royal government. The danger would have been greater if the rebels had been united in their interests or had had the backing of strong popular support. But the Fronde was not really a constitutional struggle. The princes who led it were irresponsible, motivated by nothing more than the desire to ruin the cardinal and weaken the royal government to their own selfish advantage. The solid middle-class adherents of the Fronde were soon disillusioned, leaving the nobles and the mob to go their own reckless way until the rebellion crumbled. The futile activity of the Fronde was in reality the death flurry of political feudalism in France. Never again would the nobles take arms against their king. It left the monarchy stronger than ever, for it reinforced the conviction of the French people that the only hope for peace and security lay in the absolute authority of the king. One of the tasks begun by Henry IV and carried on by Richelieu was finished at last.

Triumph of France and the king. Another, however, still occupied Mazarin's attention. Although the Thirty Years' War had ended in 1648, France was still at war with Hapsburg Spain. Mazarin carried on the war with fair ability against a weakening enemy, and at last brought it to a successful conclusion with the Peace of the Pyrenees in 1659, whereby France acquired Roussillon and some other important bits of territory along her frontiers, in addition to that awarded her at Westphalia.[1] Mazarin had now not long to live, but he had the satisfaction of knowing that he had completed Richelieu's work. France was indisputably the first power in Europe; the Hapsburg states were tottering; and the young King Louis XIV, who was soon to take over the government into his own hands, would find himself the unquestioned master of his kingdom. If the French people still groaned under an insupportable burden of taxation; if the administrative system was still wasteful and inefficient; if the government was still not far from bankruptcy, that could not be helped. Richelieu's dream, if only a part of that of Henry IV and Sully, had been fulfilled.

[1] See below, page 432.

33

The Decline of the Monarchy in England

WHILE in France the first two Bourbon kings and their ministers were busy restoring the unity of the country after prolonged civil religious wars and were building a firm structure of absolute monarchy, across the Channel in England events were following an almost exactly opposite course. There, the first two Stuart kings were effectively, if unconsciously, destroying absolute monarchy and were driving a united nation, which had grown strong and prosperous during years of internal peace and firm government, to disunity and the final outbreak of civil religious wars. The end of the sixteenth century saw England approaching the close of one of the most glorious periods of her history, the reign of Queen Elizabeth I. This last representative of the house of Tudor had guided England through troubled waters to confidence and security. She had defended England's independence against the aggressive power of Spain, and English Protestantism against the driving force of the Counter-Reformation. She left to her Stuart successors a country that was prosperous, loyal to the crown, and with a strong national consciousness that had found expression in a magnificent national literature. Yet it was a country that would need very careful handling if the Stuart kings were to continue the absolute government established by the Tudors. The story of the next half-century is the story of

their utter failure to carry on the Tudor tradition. In that crucial half-century, absolute monarchy was broken, never to be restored, and Parliament won for itself a permanent place in the government of England.

1. The Legacy of the Tudors

Tudor absolutism. The age of the Tudors came to an end in 1603 with the death of Queen Elizabeth. The crown then passed to the house of Stuart with the accession of James I. But if the reign of the Tudors was over, the results of their rule remained as a legacy to their Stuart kinsmen. One important part of that legacy was a tradition of absolute government. It was, however, absolutism of an unusual kind, dependent on conditions that were peculiar to England. The Tudors were satisfied with the practical exercise of royal power. They did not insist on defining their authority, nor did they put forward sweeping claims to unrestricted rule. On the contrary, they were scrupulously careful to cloak their absolute power in a decent covering of constitutional legality. Both Henry VIII and Elizabeth, whose reigns between them covered most of the sixteenth century, took great pains to secure the consent of Parliament for their most autocratic acts. This, in truth, had not been difficult, for their policies were for the most part

414

popular with the majority of Englishmen; the people felt the need of a strong government in a time of general insecurity; and both Henry and his brilliant daughter were masters of the art of persuading the people's representatives in Parliament that what they wanted was for the best interests of the state.

Parliament. Under this system of legal absolutism, Parliament, though it lost the habit of independent initiative, was actually consolidating its position. In practice, an act of Parliament was little more than the official seal affixed to the expression of the royal will; but the fact that the king's authority was repeatedly expressed by means of an act of Parliament built up a tradition which Parliament might use against the king, if the two ever came into conflict. In short, the Tudors kept alive a subservient Parliament to give legal or constitutional sanction to the acts of their absolute government; and as a result of that policy they left, as part of their legacy to the Stuarts, a constitutional body which was not yet conscious of its power, but which might become a menace to the authority of less popular rulers.

Tudor society. The potential power of Parliament depended largely on the peculiar structure of English society, and was increased by certain changes that took place under the strong and peaceful government of the Tudor monarchs. Following the destruction of the greater part of the old feudal nobility in the Wars of the Roses, Henry VII was able to rid England of the last remnant of independent feudalism. In time, the Tudors created a new peerage to take the place of the old; but England no longer had anything that could be called a noble class, such as existed in every country on the Continent. Only those few peers who sat in the House of Lords were legally recognized as noble. All the rest of the landowning aristocracy, including the younger sons of the peerage, were classed as gentlemen (or collectively as the gentry), and were represented in the House of Commons. These country gentlemen were roughly of the same social class as the lords, though with many gradations of social importance; yet they were not cut off by any impassable barrier from the professional or commercial burghers of the cities, for younger sons of the gentry often enough sought their fortunes as apprentices in

the business houses of the towns or entered the professions, and many a country gentleman owed his estate to some wool-trading ancestor whose daughter had married into a county family. It was from this class of the gentry that the great majority of the members of the House of Commons were chosen, whether as representatives of the rural shires or of the towns. The English Parliament, then, was a body which represented all the influential classes in the state, and it was not split by any strong division of class interest between nobles and commons or between country and city.

National sentiment. There was a latent menace to absolute monarchy in such a Parliament, but during the Tudor period it remained steadfastly loyal to the crown. England in the sixteenth century developed a strong national consciousness and an aggressive patriotism, as it rose from a position of insecurity and comparative insignificance in European affairs to confidence and power. And that national patriotism came to be more and more closely associated with loyalty to the ruling house. The struggle against the combined forces of the Counter-Reformation and Spain during Elizabeth's long reign contributed more than anything else to this mingled feeling of patriotism and loyalty. The reverse side of English national consciousness was hatred of Spain and the papacy; for the conspiracies of Philip II to place the Catholic Mary Stuart on the English throne, and his later attempt to invade England with the avowed intention of restoring the Catholic Church there, united Catholicism with the threat of Spanish domination in the minds of the English people, just as it made Protestantism synonymous with English independence and reinforced their loyalty to Elizabeth, who stood as the defender of both. After the victory over Philip's great Armada, Englishmen felt a new pride in their country, and were obscurely conscious that that pride included the queen and the Protestant religion.

National security. But if the victory over Catholic Spain made Englishmen more patriotic and more loyal to the queen, it also made them feel less keenly the need of a strong monarchy. England had at last won a sense of security to which it had long been a stranger. Protestantism and English independence were

This view of the House of Commons in 1625 comes from a print in the Manuscript Room of the British Museum.

now safe. There was no longer any serious threat of foreign invasion or internal division. And to this feeling of national security was added a growing sense of personal security among the well-to-do classes of country and city, as a result of years of orderly government and an increasing national prosperity. Thus, the last of the Tudors left a country in which the influential classes were patriotic and loyal, but also more secure and hence more independent.

The national church. Elizabeth also bequeathed to her successors a national church, subordinate to the crown. The Elizabethan settlement of the religious issues that troubled the sixteenth century was achieved without provoking civil war or armed rebellion. It separated the Anglican Church permanently from the Roman Catholic and furnished it with a uniform ritual, embodied in the Book of Common Prayer, and with a rather loosely stated Protestant creed. It succeeded in winning the adherence of the majority of Englishmen by allowing considerable latitude for variations of opinion, but it failed to establish real religious unity. Aside from the Catholics, who remained outside the new church, there were divergent groups within the church itself, and the opposition between these became stronger

as the opinions of each group crystallized. Not the least of the problems with which Elizabeth's successors would have to deal was that of maintaining the unity of the national church.

2. *Decline of the Monarchy* (1603–40)

James I. The man who fell heir to the Tudor legacy was Elizabeth's distant cousin, James Stuart (1603–25), the son of the unhappy Mary Queen of Scots. Since infancy he had held the title of James VI of Scotland, and now in middle age he became also James I of England, thus uniting at last the two kingdoms of Britain. Few kings have entered upon the government of a country with better intentions than James, and few have ruled with more disastrous results. His character, ideas, and training made him singularly unsuited to the task of carrying on the Tudor tradition. Education he had in plenty. No more learned man ever sat on the throne of England. But his education was of a pedantic kind, and he was much given to theories of "kingcraft" that had very little relation to reality. He had plenty of experience in government, too, but it was in the government of a country still partly medieval and certainly very different from England. For all his learning, he was hopelessly ignorant of the peculiar laws, traditions, and sentiments of the English people, or even of the fact that they had any. And if he never came to understand the temperament of the English people, he was equally unfortunate in his judgment of individual men. By a kind of fatality, he surrounded himself with friends who were either rogues or fools, and, because of the strong human affections that made him a lovable man, if an untrustworthy king, he allowed his worthless favorites to administer the government as they chose. James was not in any way a bad man. He was merely miscast for his royal role. But it is from such miscasting that historical tragedies are made.

Divine right of kings. The new king's most cherished theory was that of the "divine right of kings." That kings received their authority directly from God and that to oppose their will was to fly in the face of Providence was an idea already familiar on the Continent. It appealed to James because of its theoretical completeness, and also because his sad experience with turbulent barons and stubborn Calvinist ministers in Scotland had persuaded him of the value of an absolute government which drew its sanction from some more stable source than popular consent. This theory he brought with him to England, and he never came to realize how antagonistic it was to the English tradition. Where the Tudors had ruled in fact, but had carefully preserved legal and constitutional forms, and had been satisfied with an authority that was all the more real for being undefined, James insisted on the extreme definition of his rights, and even when he was forced to make concessions in practice, he spoiled the effect by blatant assertions of his superiority to the law and to the will of the people as represented in Parliament.

Puritans. The first three years of James's reign decided the fate of the Stuart monarchy, for in those years the new king committed himself to definite policies on all the most perplexing problems of government. One of his first actions was to announce a decided policy of opposition to the Puritans. It is difficult to say exactly what is meant by Puritanism, for the term has been very loosely used. It covers a variety of types and a variety of opinions on doctrine and church government. The Puritans whom James first met on his way down from Scotland were not the Puritans who later founded New England, nor yet those who made up Cromwell's godly cavalry. As yet, the term Puritan signified only the more extreme Protestants, more or less Calvinist in theology, who wished to "purify" the church of the remnants of Catholic ritual and practice that still remained as part of the Elizabethan settlement of the Church of England. That settlement had been essentially a compromise, and so long as the terms were not too rigidly defined, both "High Church" Anglicans, with a leaning toward ritual, and Puritans, who wished a simpler service, remained peacefully within the church. The Puritans, however, were anxious to have their position made more secure, and hence presented a petition to the new king asking recognition of their right to a modified service. James argued with the Puritan clergy, for he could never resist an argument, and in the end lost his temper. The real reason for his opposition was that he suspected them of wanting to adopt a democratic form of church government like that of the Presbyterian Church in Scotland, which had already caused him so much trouble. James realized that absolute government would be impossible unless the state church were ruled from the top through the bishops. To destroy the episcopacy would be to strike a death blow to absolute monarchy. Shouting his famous epigram, "No bishop, no king," James swore that he would make the Puritans conform or would "harry them out of the land." James's bark was always worse than his bite, and very little active persecution followed. But he had made permanent enemies of a constantly growing number of stern and pious men, most of whom belonged to the influential classes of city burghers or country gentry. They could not as yet be called a party, but they formed the backbone of the opposition to all the king's unpopular policies.

Catholics. While James thus alienated the left wing of Protestantism, he was equally unfortunate in his dealings with the Catholics, who stood at the opposite end of the religious spectrum. True to his large ideas of kingcraft, he at first treated the Catholics leniently, in the hope of uniting all religions under his beneficent rule. But when the fines levied on those who did not attend the Anglican Church were lifted, so many stayed away that he became alarmed and re-enforced them. Embittered by this betrayal of their trust, a group of extreme Catholics hatched a plot to blow up the Parliament buildings at a time when the king, his council, and the whole Parliament would be assembled in November, 1605. This was the famous Gunpowder Plot. It was discovered in time, however, and its chief result was to renew in the minds of English Protestants the fear and hatred of Catholicism which had existed before the defeat of the Armada. James might have utilized that feeling, but instead he turned it against himself by seeking an alliance with Spain.

Foreign policy. In foreign policy, James looked to find a perfect field for the exercise of kingcraft. His theories were often sound, but they seldom worked out successfully, and about all he accomplished was the further exasperation of his already discontented subjects. His first move, the ending of the war with Spain in 1604, though entirely justified, was unpopular with the Protestant merchant class who had been carrying on an illicit trade with the Spanish colonies. The opposition to this move, however, was nothing to the sullen fury aroused by his negotiations, pursued from 1619 to 1623, for the marriage of his son Charles to the daughter of the King of Spain. These were the years when Spain was actively aiding the Austrian Hapsburg emperor in crushing Protestantism in Germany.[1] Protestant England looked on appalled as the king deserted the German Protestants in their hour of need, stopped the persecution of Catholics in England, and worked to give England a Spanish Catholic queen, who might, in time, give England a half-Spanish and possibly Catholic king. Religious and national sentiment united in violent opposition. The negotiations failed, and young Charles returned from Spain, still a Protestant and a bachelor, to the great relief of the people. But the damage was done.

James and Parliament. The general discontent with the king's foreign and domestic policies found a means of expression in Parliament. The time had come when that body, so long subservient to the Tudors, was no longer content to accept the dictates of a less popular ruler. The Commons was filled with men from just those classes that were most decidedly opposed to the government on religious, national, and commercial grounds. A great majority of the members were Puritans, or at least strongly Protestant, and, though most of them were of the gentry, a large number held borough seats and represented the city merchants who regarded Spain as a commercial rival as well as a religious and national enemy. Independent, practical, and often austerely pious men, they openly resented the extravagance of the royal government, the incompetence of the king's favorites, and the evil reputation of the court. To make matters worse, James showed no tact in dealing with them, and, from the first, alienated Parliament by disregard for its traditional privileges. When he lectured his first Parliament on the subject of the divine right, the startled Commons replied with a unanimous expression of dissent. Hitherto they had not troubled themselves greatly about the definition of their authority, but now they began a careful study of English history, gathering together, and occasionally distorting, every precedent that would strengthen their position. The king's extravagance gave them their best weapon. Lavish in his gifts to friends and surrounded by careless and corrupt ministers, James was unable to live within the independent royal revenue. Additional taxation was generally regarded as subject to the consent of Parliament. At any rate, the Commons now asserted that right, and threatened to hold up appropriations unless the king would redress their grievances. Time and again, James dismissed a stubborn Parliament, only to be forced to call another. The struggle was still going on when James died and left a sadly discredited monarchy to his son.

Charles I. Perhaps it was not yet too late to undo the damage of James's reign, but Charles I (1625–49) did nothing to heal the breach between king and people. He heartily subscribed to his father's theories of divine right; he continued to govern through the ministry of worthless favorites; and he was even more strongly opposed than his father had been

[1] See below, pages 427–431.

This triple portrait of Charles I of England was painted by Van Dyck to serve as a guide for the Italian sculptor Bernini.

to Puritanism. Charles was a dignified, cultured, and kindly man, loyal to his friends, but woefully lacking in the kind of imagination that is essential to a statesman. Though brought up in England, he had no more understanding of the English people than had the Scottish James, and he had much less understanding of the Scots, whom he was also called upon to rule.

Petition of Right. The events of the early years of Charles's reign ended all hope of cooperation between king and Parliament. The Duke of Buckingham, favorite of both James I and Charles, was the power behind the throne until he was assassinated in 1628. The new king could scarcely have made a more injudicious choice than to entrust the government to this brilliant but unstable man. Under his reckless guidance, England careered into a hopeless war with Spain, the impolitic marriage of Charles to the Catholic sister of Louis XIII of France, and a brief war with France that could end only in humiliation for England. The war with Spain and that in aid of the Huguenots against the French king should have won the support of Parliament; but the utter incompetence of Buckingham served only to enrage the Commons, while the French marriage aroused all the old fear of Catholicism. Parliament, therefore, refused supplies and threatened to impeach Buckingham. The king dismissed one Parliament after another with

nothing accomplished, and finally tried the experiment of raising money for the war by forced loans. In 1628, however, Charles was forced to call Parliament again, and as the price of its cooperation in raising taxes, he accepted the Petition of Right. This petition, one of the cornerstones of British freedom, was a clear statement of the illegality of the exercise of absolute power on four crucial points: martial law, the billeting of soldiers on the civilian population, arbitrary taxation, and arbitrary imprisonment. The first two were a protest against the means used by the king to support an army without funds, a protest inspired in part by fear lest the army be used to coerce the people. The second two points were designed to protect the right of Parliament to control such taxes as were not a recognized part of the royal prerogative, and to protect individual citizens from arrest and imprisonment by the king for political reasons. These provisions, if respected, would have made absolute government impossible. Charles accepted them; then broke them; and when Parliament in protest again refused supplies, he determined to rule without it.

Experiment in absolutism. For eleven years, from 1629 to 1640, Charles tried the experiment of personal government without calling Parliament. To the king, it seemed the only possible alternative. If he could not rule with

Parliament — and he could not without abandoning his principles — he would rule without it. He recognized in part what that decision meant. He would have to give up all thought of a vigorous foreign policy for lack of funds, and would have to strain to the utmost every legal means of taxation within the royal power. What he did not realize was that such a policy was doomed to failure. Had Charles possessed a strong army, he might have coerced the whole population into the payment of unparliamentary taxes. Lacking that, he chose rather to distort the laws, laying a heavy burden of taxes on the relatively small but very influential class of propertied gentry and burghers who fell within the scope of royal taxes. This policy aroused a deep resentment among just those people whom he could least afford to offend, while at the same time it did not bring in enough money to maintain an army with which to meet a rebellion. One factor, however, worked in the king's favor. So long as he could avoid calling Parliament, the general discontent had no means of expression. Without leadership, the English people, unused to rebellion, were sullenly but helplessly passive.

Laud and the church. So they might have remained if Charles had not, in addition to economic and political oppression, trespassed upon their freedom of conscience. He gave a free hand to Archbishop Laud, the most thorough exponent of High Church Anglicanism, to enforce conformity to the strictest form of Anglican ritual and practice. Laud's plan was to smother Puritanism by preventing every possible means of expression. He expelled from their churches all clergy suspected of Puritan leanings; he censored the press; and he used the authority of the government to suppress all meetings for religious purposes outside the established church. Under this steady pressure, the gap between Puritan and High Churchmen widened and became a more conscious antagonism. Religious doctrines and political theories became curiously involved, as men of many different types silently ranged themselves in opposition to king and church. Puritanism now represented a complex of ideas, sentiments, and resentments, held · in varying proportion. The men who sat sullenly

George Villiers, Duke of Buckingham, the handsome and brilliant but irresponsible courtier who charmed both James and Charles, from a pencil drawing by Rubens.

through the prescribed services of the Anglican Church, and muttered threats against the government as they returned home to read their Bibles in privacy, were characterized by some or all of the following — by a Calvinist belief in predestination; by a strict morality that showed itself in stern simplicity of life and disapproval of Sunday games; by a growing hatred of ritualistic church services, of all bishops and of Laud's hand-picked clergy; and by an equally strong hatred of royal despotism.

Revolt in Scotland. It was Scotland that gave the signal for rebellion and provided the opportunity. In 1637, Laud and the king determined to extend the enforcement of the Anglican service to Scotland, to replace the traditional Presbyterian form. This was sheer madness, as James I, who knew his stubborn Scots even if he never learned to know his Englishmen, might have told them. More accustomed to the ways of rebellion than their law-abiding English neighbors, the Lowland Scots rose as one man, and swore to a Covenant to defend their religion. Charles then marched north with a meager army to force them to obedience, only to find a nation in arms awaiting the attack with a godly fervor. Lacking money, and with his people heartily out of sympathy with his plans, Charles could not raise anything like an adequate army. The two "Bishops' Wars" of 1639 and 1640 were no more than futile demonstrations. The king was forced to make a humiliating peace with his northern subjects and to promise them a large indemnity as the price of the withdrawal of the Scottish army from England.

The Long Parliament. Absolutism without adequate financial resources had failed. In October, 1640, Charles summoned a Parliament to raise money to pay the indemnity and to reëstablish the royal finances on a firmer basis. This was the Long Parliament, which lasted through years of opposition, civil war, and the experiment of the Commonwealth. It provided the long-awaited opportunity to organize opposition to the king.

3. The Civil War and Cromwell
(1640–60)

Parliament curbs absolutism. The members of the new Parliament were almost unanimous in their determination to curb the absolute powers of the monarchy. Led by John Pym, a Puritan gentleman of great ability, the Commons at once launched an attack on Laud and the Earl of Strafford, the two chief ministers of the king. Laud was sent to the Tower, while Strafford, more dangerous because more powerful, was condemned to death by an act of attainder. Parliament then proceeded by one act after another to strip the king of the powers that had made absolute rule possible. Provision was made for regular meetings of Parliament. The arbitrary and more or less extra-legal courts of Star Chamber and high commission were abolished, as were also those taxes which kings hitherto had been able to collect without consent of Parliament. In the course of a few months, this determined Parliament destroyed absolutism in England forever. For when the monarchy was restored in 1660, it was the limited monarchy left by these acts of 1640–41.

Division of parties. So far, Parliament had been nearly unanimous. The Puritan majority, however, were not content to stop there. They went on to a "root and branch" attack on the episcopal system in the church and to claim for Parliament powers over the army and the executive authority that would have made Parliament as absolute as the king had ever been. Divisions now began to appear in the ranks of the Commons. Many men who had joined heartily in the acts to curb royal absolutism hesitated at proposals to transfer full authority from king to Parliament, contrary to constitutional precedent. And the same men, though willing enough to check the power of Laud's High Church bishops, suspected as they were of leaning toward Catholic practice, balked stubbornly at Puritan proposals to do away with the Prayer Book, endeared to them by years of familiarity. Parliament was dividing on religious and political grounds, with Puritans and Parliamentarians on one side, moderate Anglicans and rather reluctant Royalists on the other. At last in 1642 the crisis came, and men in Parliament and in the nation had to make a definite choice. In January, Charles made a frustrated attempt to arrest five members of Parliament who were recognized as the leaders of the opposition. In self-defense, the Commons took unconstitutional measures to raise an army. The king fled to Oxford, and with him went the Royalist minority in the Commons and a majority of the Lords. There was now open war between king and Parliament, or what was left of it.

Cavalier and Roundhead. All through the summer of 1642 the opposing sides were mustering their forces. In the long run, only a minority of the population took an active part, but they were the influential minority. The great mass of agricultural laborers remained neutral, except when pressed into the infantry on one side or the other. The volunteers were yeoman farmers, gentlemen, and the industrial and commercial classes of the towns. The line between Royalist and Parliamentarian, however, represented no clear class division. Yeomen and gentlemen fought on both sides, and,

The plain, stern face of Oliver Cromwell, shown here in a portrait by Sir Peter Lely, was well suited to the commander of the New Model Army and the ruler of the Puritan Commonwealth.

though London and the seaports were the strongholds of Parliament, there were Royalists in every city and a majority in some. In general the Royalists were stronger in the north and west, while Parliament could count on a majority in the eastern and midland counties. But even this geographical alignment was only partially valid. It was not a war of sections any more than it was a war of classes. In the final analysis it was a war of opposing political and religious principles or sentiments. The ancient feeling of loyalty to the crown was the force that rallied men about the royal banner. Some of those who found that they could not desert the king in the face of a call to arms were Puritans, but most of them were Anglicans, Catholics, or men to whom religion was not a dominating passion. Among them were enough of the hard-drinking, hard-riding gentry to give the whole Royalist party the name of Cavaliers. On the other side were men in whom the memory of royal oppression was stronger than the sentiment of loyalty. For the most part they were Puritans, for it was the Puritans who had suffered most under the recent absolutism, and the stern determination to win religious freedom was one of the few sentiments strong enough to make Englishmen take up arms against their king. Yet not all Parliamentarians were Puritans, and not all Puritans were of the strict type painted by popular fancy. There were enough of the latter, however, to win for their party the name of Roundheads, from their refusal to wear the flowing curled hair affected by their less austere opponents.

Civil war. The war lasted four years (1642–46). It was a strange, scrambled affair, with much aimless marching about. Only the Royalists had a definite strategy in the plan to converge on the city of London and capture it, which, however, never succeeded. The Parliamentarians had the advantage of holding the great seaports and controlling the wealthiest cities, so that they could draw supplies from abroad and could pay for superior equipment. The navy, too, was on their side, and Scotland was their ally. In the long run, though, the deciding factor was the New Model Army, recruited from among the most extreme Protestants and organized by the only real military genius whom the war produced, Oliver Cromwell. Well armed, well drilled, and kept under a strict military and moral discipline, the New Model formed the shock troops of the Parliamentary army. Cromwell's "Ironside" cavalry proved their disciplined worth against Prince Rupert's wild Cavaliers at Marston Moor in 1644. By the end of the war the New Model included about a fourth of the Parliamentary forces, and by far the most effective part.

Independents vs. Presbyterians. With the surrender of the king in 1646, Parliament faced the difficult problem of arranging a permanent settlement. One question was what to do with the king. Few men were prepared to abolish monarchy. But could Charles be trusted to maintain a constitutional authority, limited by Parliament? And while Charles foiled all negotiations by his bewildering inconsistencies and double-dealing, another vital problem rose to the surface. As the price of the Scottish alliance, Parliament in 1645 had agreed to make Presbyterianism the state religion of England. It was a compromise that satisfied most Puritans, for some kind of state church was needed, though few were really Presbyterian in the Scottish sense. It did not, however, satisfy the New Model Army. This grim organization had been recruited from among the most extreme Protestants, men whose individualistic love of religious freedom made them oppose any state-controlled church. They were the Independents, differing among themselves in theological views, but united in the conviction that each congregation must be free to determine its own religion. Now, the Presbyterian Parliament, flushed with victory, made two serious mistakes. It persecuted Anglicans, on the one hand, thus embittering the defeated Royalists, and, forgetting who had won the war, it also passed persecuting acts against the Independents and proposed to disband the New Model without its back pay. The result was a second brief civil war, with Royalists, Parliamentary Presbyterians, and Scots in a curious alliance against the Independents. The latter, led by Cromwell, were again victorious. And, not to be cheated of the fruits of victory, the army chiefs now took control. In December, 1648, they forcibly purged Parliament of its Presbyterian members, leaving only a small minority who could be trusted to do what the army wished. Two months later, this "Rump Parliament" abolished the House of Lords.

Execution of Charles. The Independent army was in the saddle, and in no temporizing mood. Parliament had betrayed their hopes of religious freedom, and they could not trust the king. All hope of a peaceful, amicable settlement that would preserve the things they had fought for seemed lost. They were riding the tiger, and there was nothing to do but go on. Cromwell was now the undisputed leader of the army and what remained of Parliament. He had labored patiently to preserve a constitutional monarchy, but was now convinced that that was no longer possible. With grim courage, he accepted the logic of the situation and instituted the trial of the king. Charles Stuart met his death with dignity, while England staggered under the shock, and men who had fought against him united with those who had rallied round his banner to hail him as a martyr. The execution of the king wiped out the memory of his oppressive government and made the great majority of Englishmen Royalists at last. England was a republic now, but a republic ruled by a small minority of armed men who could not count on popular support.

Commonwealth and Protectorate. During the next eleven years (1649–60), England passed from one experimental form of government to another. The first was the Commonwealth, a republic governed by a Council chosen by the Rump, as the remnant of the Long Parliament was called which still held the legislative authority. This was changed in 1653 by the forcible dissolution of the Rump, and a new constitution was substituted, making England a Protectorate, with Cromwell as Lord Protector and a carefully selected Parliament to hold the legislative authority. Even the most carefully chosen Parliament, however, could not cooperate with the army chiefs, and further changes followed, making Cromwell king in all but name. Whatever the form of constitution, in actual fact England was ruled by Oliver Cromwell with the backing of the army. It was not the kind of government that anyone wanted, perhaps least of all Cromwell. But it was apparently the only form of government possible at the time; the only form that could save the country from anarchy or further civil war. England was not yet ready to restore the Stuart monarchy, and there was still too much division of opinion to permit of a true republic. The rule of Cromwell and the army provided a working government, which, however, dared not permit a freely elected Parliament. Such a government could not last long; but under the capable guidance of Cromwell it lasted long enough to give England time to recover from the civil war and to restore her prosperity and her prestige abroad.

Cromwell's foreign policy. The internal government of England under Cromwell was peaceful and orderly, but the warlike spirit of the Puritan army had plenty of opportunity to express itself in relation to Ireland, Scotland, and the neighboring states on the Continent. During the period of the Commonwealth, Cromwell had to crush strong opposition in both Ireland and Scotland. In the former, the Catholic majority rose in support of the Stuart heir, the future Charles II. The Puritan army invaded Ireland and put down the Catholic rising with a barbarous cruelty such as they had never shown in dealing with their Protestant enemies. To this day, the "curse of Cromwell" holds an unforgettable place in the memory of the Irish people. In Scotland, where the opposition was Presbyterian rather than Catholic, Cromwell was much more merciful. After defeating the Scots, he left them with a settlement that was eminently fair, though unpopular because it was forced upon them by the English and also because Cromwell insisted on toleration of the other Protestant sects. Having restored peace to the British Isles, the militant Commonwealth turned to war with the Netherlands, the chief commercial rival of England. More than any other group in the population, the new government represented the commercial class. Cromwell zealously fostered their interests, reviving trade with the colonies and striving by a new navigation act to build up England's carrying trade at the expense of the Dutch. The war with the Netherlands proved that England had not lost her mastery of sea warfare and left her once more mistress of the narrow seas. Later, Cromwell, as Protector, launched another naval war against Spain for similar commercial reasons and with equal success. Before his death in 1658, he had made England a ranking power again among the nations of Europe.

The Stuart Restoration. On the whole, Cromwell accomplished a great deal, and much that was of permanent value, for many of his economic policies were carried on by the restored Stuart monarchy. Yet his government grew steadily more unpopular. Englishmen who had fought against the king had not fought to substitute a military despotism for the ancient monarchy. The new government had not given the people political freedom, and, though Cromwell guaranteed a large measure of religious toleration to all save Catholics and Anglicans, the Puritan government instituted a moral oppression as irksome as the religious oppression of Charles. Under the pressure of what would today be called blue laws, enforced by the army, many a former Puritan turned Cavalier and many a former Parliamentarian turned Royalist. When the death of Cromwell left the Protectorate to his feeble son, the nation was very nearly unanimous in its opinion that only one course lay before it — to restore the Stuart monarchy in the person of Charles II, with adequate guaranties that the powers of Parliament, as fixed by the acts of 1640–41, would be respected. This decision was put into effect without further civil war, thanks to the intervention of General Monk, now in command of the army, who used his power to secure a freely elected Parliament, which invited Charles II to return. In 1660, the new king was welcomed home with delirious demonstrations of joy. England had a legitimate king again; but he would not be an absolute ruler, nor would any king in the future successfully revive the claims of the first two Stuarts. The Anglican Church, too, was restored and for a time persecuted dissenters; but the principle of religious freedom was not lost and was soon to come into its own, at least so far as dissenting Protestants were concerned.

34

The Thirty Years' War

THE FIRST half of the seventeenth century witnessed the last and greatest of the religious wars, a war that for thirty years (1618–48) devastated Germany and involved, before it was over, nearly every state in Europe. For more than half a century before the war began, the Religious Peace of Augsburg (1555) had served to maintain an uneasy peace between the Protestant and Catholic forces in Germany. But conditions had changed since 1555, and with the opening years of the seventeenth century it became increasingly apparent that the settlement could not last much longer. The revived energy of Catholicism under the impetus of the Counter-Reformation, the rising power of militant Calvinism, the territorial greed and jealous independence of the German princes, the dynastic ambitions of the house of Hapsburg in both its branches, and the national interests of France, Sweden, and other European powers all tended to increase the tension and to produce a situation that menaced the peace of Europe. In these years, Germany was a vast powder magazine, which any chance spark might ignite. For there were more than religious problems involved. Political and economic motives played their part in the war from the first, and, as the war continued, religious issues sank into comparative insignificance before the greed and mutual hatred of territorial states and ruling dynasties. When the war was over, Germany lay prostrate; the Holy Roman Empire had been reduced to an empty shell; and out of the final settlement emerged the modern state system of Europe.

1. The Background of the War

Counter-Reformation in Germany. The years following the Religious Peace of Augsburg marked the high tide of Protestantism in Germany. For a time the momentum gained by the Lutheran Reformation in its early days carried it on to further conquests, especially in northern Germany. But as the century drew on, the tide turned. The Catholic Church in the period of the Counter-Reformation gained a new and aggressive energy and began to recover some of the lost ground. In every German state where the prince was still Catholic, the Jesuits set up their efficient schools and exerted a steady, tactful influence on both the people and their princes. One Catholic prince after another seconded their efforts by energetically enforcing the principle of the religious peace which gave the prince the right to dictate the religion of his subjects. Thus large sections of southern Germany, including Bavaria, the Austrian Hapsburg lands, and the ecclesiastical states of the Rhineland, were purged of their numerous Protestant population and became almost unanimously Catholic. By the beginning of the seventeenth century, German Catholicism had developed a decidedly militant spirit, and had found two powerful

425

During the Thirty Years' War, pike and musket were the normal weapons of the infantry. In the hands of well-drilled troops they were effective weapons against a cavalry attack.

and devoted champions in the young Maximilian, Duke of Bavaria, and his contemporary, Ferdinand of Styria, cousin and heir of the Hapsburg emperor.

Calvinism in Germany. In contrast to this Catholic revival, Lutheranism seemed to be sinking into a state of passive apathy. All that was positive and aggressive in the Protestant faith was now concentrated in the growing Calvinism which had established itself in several of the upper Rhineland states and in Bohemia, and had won over the Elector Palatine and the Elector of Brandenburg. The stern faith of Calvin provided the moral force needed to meet the revived energy of Catholicism, but the growth of Calvinism in Germany weakened rather than strengthened the Protestant cause, for Lutheran and Calvinist were divided by an antagonism almost as deep as that which separated Protestant and Catholic.

Defects of the Peace of Augsburg. The growth of Calvinism, indeed, was one of the principal factors that tended to nullify the settlement arranged by the Religious Peace of Augsburg. In 1555, Calvinism had not yet become a power to be reckoned with in Germany, and the Calvinists had been excluded from the

terms of the peace.[1] Thus, unlike their Lutheran neighbors, they had no legal status. But even the Lutherans were no longer fully protected by the religious peace. It had recognized the right of the Lutheran princes to hold those church lands which they had confiscated prior to 1552. A good deal of church land, however, was secularized (i.e., taken over by the Lutheran lay governments) after that date. So long as Protestantism was in the ascendant, no effective protest could be made, but as the Catholic forces gained new strength, they asserted that these lands were not included in the peace and still belonged to the church. A similar problem arose from the interpretation of that part of the peace known as the ecclesiastical reservation. According to this clause, ecclesiastical princes (bishops or abbots ruling territorial states) who became Protestant were to give up their land, which was to be retained by the church. This provision, however, had been violated on numerous occasions, and most of the bishoprics in northern Germany, as well as many smaller ecclesiastical principalities, had become secular Protestant lands.

Armed leagues. The growing feeling of insecurity among the Protestant princes led in 1608 to the formation of an armed league, the Evangelical Union, under the leadership of the Calvinist Elector Palatine. It was largely a Calvinist league, for they were in the most serious danger, but some Lutherans were included, though the sequel was to show how little they were prepared to sacrifice for their Calvinist allies. The following year, the challenge of the union was met by the formation of a Catholic League led by Maximilian of Bavaria. The Protestant and Catholic forces in Germany were now ranged in hostile armed camps. Peace was maintained only by the even balance of power. Should any circumstance upset that balance, war would be inevitable.

Position of the Hapsburgs. This intricate adjustment of forces in Germany was further complicated by the rather anomalous position of the Hapsburg emperors. Though they were all orthodox Catholics, the emperors whose reigns occupied the time between the abdication of Charles V and the outbreak of the

[1] See above, page 378.

Thirty Years' War, were not aggressive champions of Catholicism. Their interests were confined in large measure to the aggrandizement of their hereditary family lands, which included, besides Austria and the other Hapsburg territories in southern Germany, the kingdoms of Bohemia and Hungary. In addition, of course, they held such vague authority over the entire Holy Roman Empire as still adhered to the imperial title. The princes of Germany, however, both Catholic and Protestant, had already gained a good deal of independence, and desired more. This fact tended to prevent any wholehearted cooperation between the emperors and the other Catholic princes. Indeed, the emperor was pointedly left out of the Catholic League. The league might join with him in a common effort against the Protestants, but the princes of the league would be careful to see that the imperial authority was not strengthened by a victory over the Protestant princes. In the long run, the only support on which the Hapsburg emperors could count without question, outside of their own territory, was that of the Spanish branch of the family. Always intensely conscious of their dynastic solidarity, the Austrian and Spanish branches of the house of Hapsburg, though divided since the abdication of Charles V, had maintained a very close relationship, reinforced by frequent intermarriages. Any German war involving the Austrian Hapsburgs, therefore, would certainly also involve Spain. And Spain, though greatly weakened through internal decay, was still to all outward appearances the greatest power in Europe.

Bohemia. As it happened, the Hapsburgs were involved in the coming war, and that from the very beginning, for the spark that ignited the conflagration was the revolt of the Bohemian Calvinists against their Hapsburg ruler. The rebellion was motivated by a mixture of national and religious aspirations. Nowhere in Europe was national consciousness stronger than in this Slavic land, where a Czech population had for centuries been ruled by German kings; and heresy was ingrained in this people, whose ancestors two centuries before had defied the might of Catholic Christendom in memory of the martyred John Huss. Under the feeble rule of the emperors, Rudolph II (1576–1612) and Matthias (1612–19),

the Bohemian Protestants, the most aggressive of whom were Calvinists, had gained a measure of religious freedom. Their rights were guaranteed by a royal charter, but they depended in reality upon the weakness and tolerance of the emperor. This fact explains the consternation of the Bohemians when, in 1617, the childless Matthias designated as his heir his cousin Ferdinand of Styria, notoriously the most fanatical opponent of Protestantism in Germany. To make matters more alarming, Matthias forced the Bohemian Diet to accept Ferdinand as their hereditary king, in violation of the ancient tradition that the Bohemian crown was elective. Seeing both their religious and national freedom endangered, the Czech nobles determined to strike without delay, before Ferdinand could consolidate his power.

2. The Thirty Years' War (1618–48)

Periods of the war. The story of the thirty years of warfare, which opened with the Czech-Calvinist rising in Bohemia, is a rather complicated one, but it is made somewhat easier to follow by the fact that it falls readily into four major periods: (1) the Bohemian revolt, beginning in 1618; (2) the Danish intervention, beginning in 1625; (3) the Swedish intervention, beginning in 1630; (4) the French intervention, beginning in 1635 and lasting till the end of the war.

Bohemian revolt. The Bohemian revolt was begun with a dramatic gesture of defiance. Determined to commit their fellow countrymen irrevocably to rebellion, a group of Czech noblemen entered the royal palace at Prague and heaved the emperor's representatives bodily out of a window, from which they fell, with considerable loss of dignity, but with no fatal injury, into the moat below. There was now no turning back. The Bohemians organized an army, though with characteristic irresponsibility the nobles refused to contribute the money necessary to make it really effective, while on the other side Ferdinand began to mobilize his forces. He could count on a certain amount of support from Spain, the pope, and the Catholic League, and early in 1619 the opportune death of the aged Matthias gave him the additional prestige of the imperial title as Ferdinand II (1619–37). Still he might have been left practically alone to deal with his rebellious subjects if the Bohemians themselves had not called in outside aid and turned the rebellion into a general religious war. In the summer of 1619, the Bohemian Diet elected Frederick, the Calvinist Elector Palatine, king of Bohemia, and that rash young prince accepted the dangerous honor. The choice of Frederick had been inspired largely by the hope that he would be able to secure aid from his father-in-law, James I of England, as well as from the other Protestant princes of Germany. But James, who was engaged in negotiations for a marriage alliance with Spain, contented himself with giving good advice, and the Lutheran princes had no desire to risk a war for the sake of Calvinism and the elector's territorial ambitions. On the other hand, the union of the Calvinist Palatinate with Bohemia threatened to upset the delicate balance between the religions, and drove Maximilian of Bavaria and the Catholic League to the assistance of the emperor. The campaign in Bohemia was brief and decisive. The combined army of the emperor and the league, commanded by Maximilian's veteran general, Tilly, routed the undisciplined Bohemians outside of Prague in the fall of 1620, and the unfortunate Frederick fled the country.

Catholic triumph.   The net result of this first stage of the war was a triumph for militant Catholicism. Ferdinand proceeded to stamp out Protestantism in Bohemia with ruthless severity. The lands of the rebels were confiscated and a relentless persecution forced the Protestant populace either to give up their religion or to emigrate. Meanwhile, a similar fate befell Frederick's native County Palatine on the Rhine. Sincere Catholic though he was, Maximilian of Bavaria was not above demanding a high price for his services to his church. The emperor was forced to turn over to him Frederick's electoral title and with it his lands. The conquest of the Palatinate kept the war going till 1623, and the fear and indignation aroused among the Protestant princes by this high-handed act, coupled as it was with a threat to the rest of German Protestantism by swinging the balance of power to the Catholic

side, ensured the continuation of the war on a still broader basis through foreign intervention.

Danish intervention.   For the present, German Protestantism seemed to have collapsed into a state of helpless passivity. But aid was soon forthcoming from outside Germany. England had broken off the marriage negotiations with Spain, and young Charles was eager to revenge his humiliation. The Dutch, too, were willing to cooperate in any Protestant alliance that would enable them to fight Spain. Finally, with the promise of aid from England and Holland, Christian IV of Denmark was ready to invade Germany and join hands with the Lutheran princes in a war against the emperor and the Catholic League. Christian's motives were partly religious, for he was a Lutheran; but in rather greater degree he was moved by the hope of winning territory and by the necessity of protecting certain secularized church lands already in the possession of his family. The Protestant princes of Germany, too, had lands as well as their religion to protect. The time seemed ripe for intervention as the Danes marched into northern Germany in 1625.

Wallenstein.   Meanwhile, the Emperor Ferdinand, unwilling to trust entirely to the army of the league and too impoverished to raise an adequate army himself, had turned for assistance to one of the most remarkable adventurers in the history of Germany, the enigmatic Wallenstein. This obscure Bohemian noble had fought his way to power, wealth, and titles by sheer ability and the driving force of an unscrupulous ambition. Born a Protestant, he had become a nominal Catholic, but was unencumbered by any religious loyalties. By skillful profiteering in confiscated lands after the Bohemian revolt, he had accumulated a colossal fortune, and he now offered to raise an army at no expense to the emperor, provided he were given a free hand to support it by plunder and to repay himself in conquered territory. His great military reputation, backed by promises of good pay and plunder, brought soldiers of fortune flocking to his banner from every country in Europe and representing every variety of religious creed. He had an army of over fifty thousand men when he marched north to cooperate with Tilly and the army of the league. Together they were too strong for Christian, who had found small support from his allies.

Van Dyck's portrait of Wallenstein gives a vivid impression of the great mercenary general. He is holding a marshal's baton.

The Danes were defeated at Lutter in 1626 and slowly withdrew from Germany. The Catholic-imperial forces were left in control of northern Germany, and Wallenstein proceeded to establish what amounted to an independent sovereignty in captured territory along the Baltic coast. It is not clear just what were the plans of this inscrutable genius; but he seems to have offered Ferdinand a military despotism, based on religious toleration, that would make Germany a united state under an absolute Hapsburg monarchy. The emperor, however, was too irresolute, perhaps too suspicious of his powerful general, and certainly too strongly Catholic to accept such a proposal. He listened instead to the urging of the Catholic League that he use his victory for the Catholic cause.

Edict of Restitution. The league had not forgotten the confiscated church lands nor the secularized bishoprics and abbacies. If the lost ecclesiastical states could be won back to the control of the church, the provision of the religious peace which empowered a prince to dictate the religion of his people would enable Catholic bishops or abbots to stamp out Protestantism in some of the richest cities and territories in northern Germany. It seemed too good an opportunity to be ignored, and in 1629 Ferdinand issued the Edict of Restitution, commanding the restoration to the church of all ecclesiastical lands secularized since the Peace of Augsburg. The edict was a fatal blow to peace, for it aroused Protestant feeling from passive resignation to bitter resentment and ensured the continuation of the war, just at the time when the Treaty of Lübeck with Denmark seemed about to end it. To have carried out the edict would have meant taking from princes and people land and religious freedom which they had held securely for two or three generations. It would have meant the end of Protestant territorial supremacy in northern Germany. Further, the enforcement of the edict depended largely on Wallenstein and his personal army, for it could be put into effect only by a powerful army and by methods of brute force. And Wallenstein, who disapproved of the edict because it meant the ruin of his larger plans, was fast drifting into open antagonism to the league. Ferdinand would have to choose between the two. He had, in fact, already chosen. In 1630 he submitted to the demands of the league and dismissed his great general.

Swedish intervention. When Ferdinand thus gave up the only armed force strong enough to enforce his rash policy, a new champion of the Protestant cause had already landed in Germany. The decision of Gustavus Adolphus, King of Sweden (1611–32), to take up the cause of his fellow Lutherans in Germany opened the third period of the war, that of the Swedish intervention. The motives of Gustavus, like those of most of the participants in the war so far, were a mixture of religious partisanship and territorial greed, save that with this hero-king, "the Lion of the North," religion was a more sincere motive than with most, and his territorial ambitions were but part of a long campaign to make his country secure and a power in the north. Ever since his accession, at the age of seventeen, to the throne of a beleaguered, impoverished, and divided kingdom, Gustavus had fought to consolidate his state and to win for it that supremacy in the Baltic upon which its economic

This painting by Diego Velasquez celebrates the surrender of the Dutch town of Breda to the Spanish forces during the Thirty Years' War.

and political life depended. His reign was from the beginning a perpetual war — war with Denmark, 1611–13, war with Russia, 1614–17, and war with Poland, 1617–29. As a result of each, he had won additional territory on the Baltic coast and a more complete control of the Baltic trade. Now all that he needed was a foothold in northern Germany to make the Baltic indeed a "Swedish lake." For years he had been watching the course of the war in Germany and biding his time. In 1630, he decided that the time for intervention had come. He was free from the threat of war elsewhere; the collapse of German Protestantism demanded instant action; and he had the promise of financial aid from France, whose cardinal-minister Richelieu was willing to forget religious differences in his eagerness to aid anyone who would indirectly serve France by weakening the Hapsburgs.

Protestant successes. The Protestant deliverer received at first a cold welcome from the Lutherans whom he had come to defend. They had been overawed by the power of the emperor and the league and they were suspicious of the foreigner. The Electors of Brandenburg and Saxony maintained a stubborn neu-

trality, while the city of Magdeburg, which had declared for Gustavus, was captured and cruelly sacked because the Elector of Brandenburg would not permit the Swedish king to cross his territory to its relief. Not till Gustavus had invaded Brandenburg and ranged his guns before the walls of Berlin did the elector finally consent to join forces with him. The imperialists under Tilly then tried to win over the Elector of Saxony by a similar show of force, but with the opposite result. The cautious elector was finally aroused to opposition and joined Gustavus with a force of some eighteen thousand men. Thus reinforced, the Swedish king fell upon the Catholic imperial army at Breitenfeld, not far from Leipzig, in September, 1631. The Saxon contingent proved worthless, but the Swedish army, which Gustavus had reorganized along entirely new lines, justified its reputation as the most formidable military machine in Europe. Outmaneuvered and outfought, Tilly retired with the shattered remnants of his army, while Gustavus proceeded on a triumphal march through the Rhineland into Bavaria, where Tilly was again defeated, and this time the old Bavarian general was left dead on the field. The Swedish king now dominated Germany, and the balance of power swung high in favor of Protestantism. In desperation the emperor turned again to Wallenstein. For months Gustavus and Wallenstein fenced carefully, but at last, in November, 1632, the two great generals met in a desperate battle at Lützen. The result was a victory for the Swedes; but it was a victory more disastrous than any defeat, for it cost them the life of their king. With his death the Swedish-Protestant cause lost direction and cohesion. Only Gustavus could have reaped the fruits of his brilliant victories.

Peace of Prague. For a time, however, the momentum of victory carried the Swedes on to further conquest under the guidance of the Chancellor Oxenstjerna, who acted for the young Queen Christina. But they were weakened by heavy losses and by the defection of the Elector of Saxony, who refused to cooperate any longer, though he continued the war as an independent party. Meanwhile, Wallenstein was leisurely refitting his army in Bohemia and refusing to take decisive action. Perhaps he was plotting treason. Ferdinand, at any rate, decided, now that the greatest peril was past, to rid himself finally of his dangerous general. In 1634, Wallenstein was assassinated by some of his own soldiers. In the same year the Swedes were defeated at Nördlingen by an imperial army. The tide was turning against them and they soon lost a large part of their conquered territory. The emperor was quick to take advantage of this favorable turn to make peace with Saxony and the other German Protestant states, for both sides were tired of the war, and the emperor's own resources were nearly exhausted. According to the terms of the Peace of Prague (1635), all disputed ecclesiastical lands were to be restored to those holding them in 1627. This amounted to a revocation of the Edict of Restitution. With the signing of the Peace of Prague, the religious phase of the war ended. And the war itself might have ended, had France been willing to permit it.

Richelieu's foreign policy. The religious significance of the war had always been a matter of secondary importance to Cardinal Richelieu. Heir to the foreign policy of Henry IV, the cardinal's aims were clear and simple, however complex the methods he might see fit to use. He could never forget that France was still surrounded by Hapsburg territory. To make his country secure and powerful, the Hapsburg states must be reduced to impotence, and France must win defensible frontiers on the Rhine and the Pyrenees. So long as other powers — the German princes, Holland, England, Denmark, or Sweden — were engaged in the process of wearing down the resistance of Spain and Austria, Richelieu was content to wait, offering no more than diplomatic and financial aid to the enemies of the Hapsburg dynasty. After the Peace of Prague, however, the war seemed about to end with the Hapsburg power still not completely crushed. The Swedes were not included in the treaty, but they could not continue long alone. It was time for France to intervene with all her strength.

French intervention. With the active intervention of France in 1635, the war broadened to truly European dimensions. Before declaring war on Spain and Austria, Richelieu had formed an alliance with the Swedes, the Dutch, who were to attack the Spanish Netherlands, and Savoy, which opened the gates to northern Italy. German princes were again involved in the war on one side or the other. For thirteen years the war continued, with few notable battles but extensive devastation of the occupied territory. Although there was fighting along the Pyrenees, in northern Italy, and in the Netherlands, it was still Germany that suffered most from the ravages of native and foreign armies. During the early stages of their intervention, the French met with small success. In the course of time, however, the undrained wealth and reserve energy of France began to tell against the already exhausted Hapsburg states. The French army became more efficient with experience and gained the additional advantage of able leadership when the command was given to two young generals, Condé and Turenne, of whom the former was responsible for the decisive defeat of the Spanish army at Rocroi in 1643. Richelieu had died before this brilliant victory, but his successor Mazarin carried on the war with equal energy. As the war drew on, the French and Swedish armies joined forces, invaded Bavaria and closed in on the home territory of the emperor. Meanwhile, peace negotiations had begun.

They dragged on interminably, but at last the terms were agreed upon and the Thirty Years' War ended in the Peace of Westphalia.

3. The Peace of Westphalia and the Peace of the Pyrenees

Peace of Westphalia.   The Peace of Westphalia (1648) was the work of the first great European peace conference. It marks the end of the era of religious strife and the beginning of the new era of dynastic and national wars for economic or territorial aggrandizement. In its adjustment of territorial boundaries and in the recognition of the sovereignty of states hitherto considered subject to the empire, it laid the foundations for the modern state system of Europe. Until the Napoleonic era, most of the further territorial changes were considered merely readjustments of the settlement of Westphalia.

Territorial compensations.   The victors in the long struggle demanded, and received, additions of territory as compensation for their efforts. (1) France, the laborer come late to the vineyard, profited most, receiving the strategically important bishoprics of Metz, Toul, and Verdun, and the "sovereignty" of Alsace except for the free city of Strassburg, thus making a notable advance toward the Rhine. (2) Sweden obtained western Pomerania and some neighboring territory on the Baltic, as well as the bishopric of Bremen on the North Sea. (3) Brandenburg received, in return for the surrender of western Pomerania, three secularized bishoprics and the succession to the archbishopric of Magdeburg, and was confirmed in the possession of eastern Pomerania. (4) The problem of the Palatinate was solved by dividing it between the Duke of Bavaria and the son of the late Elector Palatine, both to hold an electoral title.

Political provisions.   The peace also recognized certain important changes in the political status of the powers involved. (1) The Holy Roman Empire, though continuing to exist as a formal entity, was practically dissolved, since each prince in Germany was recognized as a sovereign power, free to make peace or war and to govern his own state independently. As a result, the authority of the imperial Hapsburgs was limited more than ever to their own hereditary lands, and their policy became more and more a purely Austrian one. (2) France and Sweden acquired, with lands in the empire, the right to vote in the Imperial Diet. (3) The accomplished fact of the independence of Holland and Switzerland was formally confirmed, and they entered the state system of Europe as free and independent powers.

Religious settlement.   The religious issues of the war, almost forgotten, were settled in the simplest possible way by recognizing the facts of the existing situation. (1) Secularized church lands were to remain in the possession of those holding them in 1624. (2) The Calvinists were admitted to the privileges of the Religious Peace of Augsburg with the right, accorded to Lutheran and Catholic princes, to determine legally the religion of their states. The Peace of Westphalia did not establish religious toleration, but Germany was too impoverished for any prince to risk the loss of subjects by enforcing religious uniformity.

Effects of the war.   The most important results of the war, however, were not of a kind that could be summarized in the terms of a peace treaty. For three decades the Four Horsemen of the Apocalypse had ridden through all the rich land of Germany, scattering death, disease, and destruction in their wake. Pitched battles were few and unimportant compared to the loss of life from famine, disease, and the brutality of marauding soldiers. The armies on both sides plundered, burned, tortured, and killed, without regard to the supposed friendship or enmity of the helpless people. Such statistics as can be procured reveal that the total population in Germany and Bohemia was reduced to about two-thirds of what it had been. The relative loss of property may have been still greater.

France and Spain.   For Spain, too, the war was disastrous. She had been drained of her vitality and was to suffer still more, for she was not included in the Peace of Westphalia. She had already lost Portugal, which had taken advantage of the war to assert her independence, and had lost Roussillon to the French. Nevertheless, Philip IV still hoped to recoup some of his losses, and Mazarin was loath to make peace till he had completed the ruin of France's most dangerous enemy. The war between France and Spain, therefore, continued. At first it seemed certain that nothing could

"The Massacre of the Innocents," as painted in 1563 by Pieter Brueghel the Elder, is a realistic picture of the sack of a contemporary village. Such scenes must have occurred very frequently in the following century during the Thirty Years' War.

save Spain from a crushing defeat that would leave her shorn of her most valued possessions. She was saved just in time by the outbreak of the Fronde in France. That futile rebellion of the French nobles distracted Mazarin's attention, and when it was over France was too weak to carry on the war alone. In 1657, Mazarin made an incongruous alliance with the Protestant regicide, Cromwell. Thus reinforced, France had again the advantage over her enfeebled enemy. In 1659, Philip IV was forced to accept a peace, which was humiliating enough, but not as bad as it might have been if France had been able to push home her first successes.

Peace of the Pyrenees. The Peace of the Pyrenees ended the long struggle between the rival dynasties of France and Spain. It ended also the last vestige of Spain's claim to ascendancy in Europe and transferred that claim to France. By the treaty, France acquired Roussillon, which meant the winning of the Pyrenees as a southern frontier, and the county of

Artois from the Spanish Netherlands. The peace was sealed by the marriage of the young king, Louis XIV, to Maria Theresa, the daughter of Philip IV. With the conclusion of this treaty, Mazarin could die content, for the greater part of the task begun by Henry IV and carried on by Richelieu was now complete.

Treaty of Oliva. The treaties of Westphalia and the Pyrenees restored peace to the greater part of Europe. But in the north war clouds still hung over the Baltic, where Frederick William of Brandenburg was exploiting the old enmity between Sweden and Poland with the aim of securing a free title to East Prussia. Even the warlike Baltic powers, however, were weary of war and in 1660 the intervention of England, Holland, and other great states was enough to bring the northern struggle to a close. Brandenburg, Sweden, and Poland signed the Treaty of Oliva recognizing Frederick William's free sovereignty in East Prussia, and all Europe was at peace for the first time in more than a generation.

35

The Commercial Revolution

and Overseas Expansion

THE PERIOD which witnessed the Reformation, the Counter-Reformation, the wars of religion, and the formation of the modern state system witnessed also a vast expansion of European economic activity. In the century and a half after 1520, the European nations reaped the first fruits of the great age of exploration and discovery and embarked upon the career of economic and colonial expansion which has since then spread European civilization throughout the world. European adventurers, merchants, and missionaries invaded the distant East and the unknown lands of the West, looting, trading, colonizing, and introducing Christianity to primitive peoples together with the more dubious blessings of an acquisitive civilization. In these years, too, capitalism, the early growth of which was discussed in Chapter 24, spread until it encompassed the greater part of economic life. The pioneering period of capitalism was past; few new forms of business organization or new techniques for handling capital were devised; but the change in rate of growth was so great as to be almost revolutionary. When we consider the overseas expansion of European trade, the vastly increased variety and volume of goods transported, and the resulting increase in the wealth of nations, the term "commercial revolution," which some historians have applied to this period, seems not unjustified.

1. Economic Expansion and the Growth of Capitalism

Expansion overseas. The expansion of European commerce overseas greatly accelerated the growth of capitalism. It increased still further the volume of production and exchange, which had been growing steadily since the middle of the fifteenth century. The overseas trade extended over far longer routes than any known to the late medieval Italians. And, as we have seen, distant trade had always offered unusual opportunities for capitalist exploitation. Large sums of money were required to finance voyages to India or the New World, and the returns might be long delayed. The immense profits which might accrue from this worldwide trade were thus available only to individuals or corporate groups who could afford to invest large sums of capital and leave it tied up over a considerable period of time. Despite the fact that the early explorations were financed and directed by state governments which claimed a share of the profits, it was capital that made the new trade possible and it was the capitalists who, in the final analysis, profited most.

The price revolution. The discovery of the Americas produced an incalculably stimulating effect upon the European economic system entirely aside from the general expansion of the market which it brought about. The growth and smooth functioning of capitalist business demanded an adequate supply of coinage, even though much business was done on credit, and though the techniques by which monetary exchange was carried out on paper were constantly improving. The flood of gold and silver, which for more than a century poured into Europe from Mexico, Peru, and other parts of the New World, met this demand to an unprecedented degree. It made possible larger accumulations of money; it lubricated the wheels of business; and it caused a steady rise in prices to the advantage of the entrepreneur. Some 200 tons of gold and 18,000 tons of silver entered Spain by official count in the years between 1520 and 1660, and thence spread throughout Europe, since much of Spain's new wealth was used to maintain armies abroad or to purchase goods from countries with more advanced industries. Prices rose everywhere as the increased supply lowered the value of money, doubling or trebling before the end of the sixteenth century. This rapid upward trend added to the profits of the merchants by widening the differential between the prices at which they bought and sold. It also added to the profits of industrial entrepreneurs by enabling them to employ cheaper labor, since wages did not rise as rapidly as prices. For the same reason, of course, it bore heavily on the industrial proletariat and tended to broaden the already widening gap between the employing and the working classes. The drastic price rise was also disastrous to many noble landlords, who drew their principal income from fixed rents.

Trade shifts to the Atlantic. A further result of the opening-up of new ocean trade routes, and one of epoch-making importance, was a decisive shift in the center of gravity of European trade from the Mediterranean to the Atlantic. And with the resultant economic growth of Spain, Portugal, England, Holland, and France came the economic decline of Italy, the country which for centuries had led the rest of Europe in the accumulation of wealth and the development of capitalism. From the beginning, Italy's pre-eminence had been founded upon her monopoly of the rich trade in Eastern luxuries, and to that trade the Por-

tuguese discovery of an all-water route to India struck a fatal blow. Italy's industries and her trade with the lands bordering the Mediterranean still continued, but in a diminishing degree, for both suffered from growing French, Dutch, and English competition. Inherited wealth and inherited skill also enabled the Italians to hold for a long time an important though no longer dominant position in international finance. But Italian capitalism was no longer a dynamic force.

The Antwerp Bourse. For a time in the sixteenth century, before Antwerp was ruined by the revolt of the Netherlands against Spanish rule, it took the place of the Italian cities as the leading center of European commercial and financial capitalism. It also took the place of Bruges as the principal port of the Netherlands. To Antwerp came Portuguese, Spanish, Hanseatic, Dutch, and English merchants, and the agents of the great banking houses of Italy and South Germany. To Antwerp, too, came royal ministers seeking loans for their governments. Unrestricted trade in commodities in this free port soon led to equally unrestricted trade in foreign exchange, in the discounting of bills of sale, in the future sale of commodities, in private bonds and public debts. From 1485, the Antwerp Bourse or Exchange was open daily and was used by the merchants of all nations for the exchange of goods. It was also the scene of frantic speculation. Here anyone with a little spare capital could take a flutter on the market, and there were always plausible promoters to sell shares in the blue sky to the unwary. Antwerp was the first great money market and its Bourse the first great exchange of the modern world. But her day of glory was short. It ended with the sack of the city by Spanish troops in 1576 and the closing of her harbor by the Dutch shortly thereafter. In the seventeenth century, the Antwerp money market was dispersed among rival cities, notably Amsterdam, London, and Lyons.

Organization of capital. As the hectic story of the Antwerp Bourse indicates, the techniques of capitalism were developing rapidly among the nations bordering the North Atlantic. But few of the prevailing methods of organizing large enterprises were new. Partnerships and family firms were still the most common forms of commercial association.

This view of Antwerp harbor in 1520 is one of the drawings made by Albrecht Dürer during a trip through the Netherlands in 1520–21. He made numerous sketches and also kept a diary as a record of his travels.

Much of the Spanish trade with the colonies, for which the royal government provided regulation and control, was carried on by means of temporary partnerships, like those developed earlier in Italy.[1] Regulated companies operating under royal charter, like the Merchant Adventurers who monopolized the trade between England and the Continent, still furnished merchants engaged in international trade within Europe with a larger form of association and the protection and regulation they required.

Joint-stock companies. For transoceanic trade, however, where it was necessary to equip fleets for long voyages, to treat on distant shores with native potentates, to build forts, to fight for trade against pirates or competitors, or to sink capital for long periods in planting colonies, the regulated companies in which each merchant traded on his own capital proved inadequate. In Spain and Portugal, the monarchy took over the supervision of trade and colonization, but elsewhere the need for large and continuous operations was met by the formation of joint-stock companies. These companies had almost all the characteristics of a modern corporation, though they also resembled the regulated companies in having been granted a monopoly and a semi-official status by the national government. They were formed by selling shares to a large number of investors, and these shares, once the company

was formed, could be bought and sold in the open market. They thus represented a new kind of transferable property. Although most of the shareholders were probably merchants, anyone with money to invest could buy shares, with the result that members of the gentry, the nobility, and the professional classes were drawn into the sphere of capitalist activity. As in a modern corporation, the management was left to elected or appointed officers, who might not themselves be large shareholders. The great joint-stock companies, as has been suggested, were organized for overseas commerce and colonization; but it was a form of organization that could be adapted to many purposes, and it was frequently used to float large industrial undertakings, such as mining, where a long-term investment was required.

Capital in agriculture. The impact of capital upon agriculture and landholding came later and was much less decisive than in commerce or industry. The medieval manorial system, it is true, had disintegrated more or less completely before the end of the fifteenth century, to be replaced by a system of cash rents and wages.[2] But this triumph of money economy scarcely spelled capitalism. Noble landholders were unaccustomed to thinking of their land simply as an investment from which to make a profit. Many such landlords, however, were being forced by the combination of

[1] See above, pages 298–300.

[2] See above, pages 307–308.

fixed rents and rising prices to sell their land to wealthy burghers who felt that a landed estate would help them to move up in the social scale, and these brought to the land something of the attitude of the capitalist businessman, an attitude that spread gradually to the older landholding families. In many places landlords forced tenants to accept short-term leases, thus making it possible to increase the rent at frequent intervals. In England, too, many landlords found it profitable to enclose land that had been farmed by their tenants and turn it over to sheep grazing. This might bring the landlord a larger cash return, but it was disastrous for the tenants who were evicted from their holdings.

2. Capital and the State: Mercantilism

Capital and the state. The evolution of capitalism coincided fairly closely in time with the rise of central government in national or territorial states, and the two movements were in many ways closely related. Money furnished the sinews of royal government; money in ever-increasing quantities was needed to pay the cost of an army and navy and of an administrative and judicial system; money was needed, too, for the bribes, pensions, and sinecures that turned feudal vassals into royal courtiers and for the maintenance of a court to enhance the king's prestige. In the last analysis, it was money that enabled kings and princes to assert their authority throughout their states and to hold their own in the international struggle for power. The cost of warfare was rising steadily during the period of religious and dynastic wars, as armies became larger and equipment more expensive, and warfare was a normal condition during a large part of this period. The ability of governments to meet these growing demands depended to a certain extent on the growth of capitalism, since its methods of business not only increased the total amount of taxable wealth in the state, but also concentrated wealth in readily taxable form. Moreover, when taxation proved insufficient and governments were forced to borrow, the capitalist financiers were their sole resort. The rulers of Europe soon realized the

extent to which their own power, or that of the state, depended on the prosperity of the capitalist businessmen, and with that realization they began consciously to promote the interests of capital.

Before discussing the conscious promotion of business by the state, however, let us note some of the ways in which the rise of territorial states unconsciously favored the growth of capital. We have already explained how the development of central governments aided the accumulation of large fortunes among those financiers who, like Jacques Coeur, were called into royal service as finance ministers. Moreover, the supplying of goods for the state armies and the royal courts furnished some of the most profitable opportunities for the investment of capital in large-scale commercial transactions. More important than any of these factors, however, was the greater security and order which strong centralized governments alone could enforce. So, if the rulers of the European states realized their need of a prosperous business class, the capitalist merchants and manufacturers realized as clearly their need of a strong state government.

The state an economic unit. This close relation between the new type of state and the new type of business inevitably tended to make the territorial or national state the most important unit in economic life, just as the city had been in the High Middle Ages. Medieval merchants and artisans had looked to the city government for protection, and it in turn had regulated their activity, either directly or through the agency of the guilds, in the interest of the whole city community. All trade outside the city was in a sense foreign trade, and was intermunicipal in character. Now, with broader economic interests to consider, the capitalist merchants and manufacturers began to look to the state for protection, and the state government in turn regulated trade and industry for the good of the whole state.

Mercantilism. The economic policy adopted by the European states when they took over the regulation of business was in many respects similar to that of the medieval cities, except that it was carried out on a much larger scale. The activity of the individual was still controlled, though not so rigidly, for the good of the whole community. This national economic policy is generally known as "mercantilism." It was developed to its fullest extent in the seventeenth and eighteenth centuries, but it was also generally practiced in the sixteenth century and signs of it were apparent at an even earlier date. Mercantilism consists essentially in the regulation of industry and commerce by the state government, with a view to making the state more prosperous and hence more powerful in relation to neighboring states. One of the primary aims of mercantilist policy, though by no means the only one, was the accumulation in the state of as large a supply of money — i.e., gold and silver — as possible. Actual money played a much more important part in the conduct of business then than now. Moreover, in the days before the credit system became so highly developed as to enable states to float large national debts, money was very necessary to pay the expenses of the growing national armies on which the safety of the state depended. And the amount of money that the government could collect in taxes depended more or less on the amount in existence in the state. The government, therefore, regulated trade whenever possible, so as to encourage exports and limit imports. This was called maintaining a favorable balance of trade, for if a country sold more than it bought, more money would come into the state than would leave it. Another aim, closely allied to the first, was to increase the wealth of the state by founding colonies, as Spain and Portugal did in the sixteenth century and England, France, and Holland in the seventeenth, and to exploit them in the interest of the mother country. The mercantilist state always endeavored to maintain an exclusive monopoly of trade with its colonies, exchanging manufactured goods for raw materials of greater potential value. Since war was an ever-present possibility in the mercantilist age, the preparation for war was a regular part of every government's economic policy. This explains why some states, like France, frequently forbade the exportation of grain, so that the country would not be dependent on its neighbors for food in case of war. It was also one of the reasons why maritime states, like England, promoted the shipbuilding and fishing industries and issued navigation acts to encourage native shipping, thus building up a merchant marine manned by trained seamen which could serve as a naval reserve.

Monopolies. If the purpose of state economic legislation was in many ways like that of the medieval cities, the theory which justified it was still more clearly a legacy from the Middle Ages. Merchants still thought in terms of a "well-regulated trade" rather than of unrestricted enterprise. The right to trade was still not regarded as the natural right of every resident; it was rather a privilege to be granted by the government as it saw fit. From this it followed naturally that the government which granted the right to trade had full power also to regulate the method of trade. Every sixteenth-century state government exercised that power in a variety of ways, but nowhere was the theory of privilege and control demonstrated more clearly than in the granting of monopolies to companies or groups of merchants for some specific type of trade. Sometimes a state would grant a monopoly to foreign merchants when it needed the goods that only they could supply, or in order to secure reciprocal advantages for its own merchants in foreign countries. More commonly, however, the monopolies were granted to organizations of native merchants. Such were the monopolies given by the governments of England, France, and Holland to the companies that opened up trade with the Far East, or the earlier monopoly of exporting English cloth to the Netherlands granted to the Company of Merchant Adventurers. These monopolies served the double purpose of excluding foreigners from the trade and of encouraging the most effective native trading organizations by freeing them from both native and foreign competition. In addition, the government often profited directly by retaining for itself shares in the monopolistic companies.

Regulation of industry. In regulating industry, the mercantilist governments followed the same principles as those which motivated their commercial legislation. Indeed, the two cannot be separated. Realizing that the wealth of a state depended in large part on its productive power, the best rulers in the mercantilist age made every effort to stimulate manufacturing, especially of those goods that could be exported in order to maintain a favorable balance of trade or that might be useful to the state in time of war. With this in mind they granted monopolies and even subsidies to those companies, guilds, or localities that seemed best fitted to produce needed goods. Whenever possible they strove to introduce and foster new industries that would make the state more independent of other countries. Thus, in the late sixteenth century the silk industry was introduced into France with government aid, and the glass industry was founded with royal monopolies in both France (1551) and England (1567). Government regulation and aid, however, did not always serve their intended purpose, and not infrequently industries were more hampered than helped by the well-meaning efforts of a paternalistic state.

Labor and poor relief.   When the state took upon itself the task of controlling the economic life of its citizens, it was forced also to assume the responsibility for adjusting those social problems that arose from the working-out of economic conditions. This was a relatively new problem for state governments, but before the end of the sixteenth century state legislation designed to fix wages and regulate conditions of labor was fairly common. Such legislation was usually much more favorable to the capitalist employers, who could bring pressure to bear on the government, than to the unorganized laborers, yet the interests of the latter and of the unemployed were not entirely neglected. The Elizabethan Poor Laws and the famous Statute of Apprentices (1563) are but examples of numerous state laws that were intended, in part at least, to protect the laborers and care for the poor.

3. Portugal and Spain Overseas

The discovery of new trade routes and new lands overseas stimulated the development in the mercantilist states of a national economic policy that would exploit the new-found opportunities to the utmost. The profits to be gained from trade and plunder had furnished the original incentive to exploration, though missionary zeal for the conversion of the heathen lent a touch of idealism to a movement which badly needed it. All the early explorers were inspired by the hope of finding a direct sea route to the source of those Eastern luxuries that had made the fortune of medieval Italy. Christopher Columbus died still clinging to the belief that he had found the shortest way to the Indies, but other Spanish explorers were soon disillusioned. The opportunity to found colonies in lands thinly populated by primitive peoples seemed a poor substitute for trade with the fabulous East; and until the gold and silver of the American mainland was discovered, it was clear that the Portuguese had chosen the better part.

India.   When the Portuguese finally concluded the long series of explorations which led them around the southern tip of Africa to India, they found a vast subcontinent, densely populated, the heir to a civilization more ancient than that of the Europeans, but politically divided and constantly torn by internal strife. The century preceding the arrival of the Portuguese was filled with the utmost political confusion, with no power strong enough to enforce order. The caste system which prevailed among the Hindus also divided the population by imposing impassable social barriers between the classes, so that even where the Hindu religion was dominant it brought no real unity. And, since the thirteenth century, Islam, introduced by Turkish conquerors, had spread widely in the north, thus injecting an element of religious antagonism which has kept the people of India divided to the present time. India, then, was incapable of presenting a united front to the acquisitive Europeans seeking to monopolize trade in Indian waters. Nor were the Indian people a match for the Westerners in naval or military technique.

The Malabar Coast.   The western or Malabar coast of India, where Vasco da Gama made his first landfall near Calicut in 1498, was peculiarly well suited to serve as a base of operations for Portuguese expansion in the East. A mountain range, the Western Ghats, cuts off this portion of the coast from the interior, leaving a narrow strip of territory at that time ruled by a number of petty warring princes. The mountain slopes produced great quantities of pepper, one of the most valuable commodities for sale in European markets; but what was more important, it was in the Malabar ports that the Arab merchants for centuries had picked up the spices, gems, ivory, Indian cottons, and Chinese silks which they carried through the Red Sea or the Persian Gulf and thence overland to the Mediterranean. The Portuguese soon realized that in these ports, which served as centers of exchange between the farther East and the West, they could seize the heart of the Eastern trade. Taking advantage of the mutual jealousy of the local princes, they gained allies and secured the right to establish fortified posts at strategic points along the coast. From these bases they maintained a permanent fleet and waged a war of extermination on the Moslem merchants who traded westward. The flimsy Arab craft, built only to sail before the periodic monsoon winds, crumbled under the fire of Portuguese cannon, and after a large Egyptian fleet had been destroyed in 1509 without the loss of a single Portuguese ship, the Moslem traders withdrew from the Indian Ocean. The same year, the great Portuguese viceroy, Alfonso de Albuquerque, seized Ormuz, the port which commanded entrance to the Persian Gulf, and in 1510 he gained possession of the city of Goa on the Malabar coast, a magnificent harbor which for centuries remained the capital of the Portuguese empire in the East.

The Spice Islands. Complete domination of the trade west from Malabar was, however, but the first step in the fulfilment of Albuquerque's dream of conquest. The next step was to move on eastward and to plant strategic naval bases in the Malay Archipelago and the Moluccas, thus completing control of the spice trade to its source. Here, too, the Portuguese were fortunate in finding populations ruled by petty princes, none of whom were strong enough to resist them. From these Far Eastern bases, the Portuguese were able to establish more or less direct trade with China and even to open contact with the distant island kingdom of Japan. In the islands, as on the Indian mainland, the Portuguese made no attempt to conquer or colonize on a large scale. What they sought was a trade monopoly, and for that they needed only the bases from which to control the commerce of the eastern seas. Trade in the most valuable commodities such as pepper, cloves, nutmeg, mace, Chinese silk, and lacquer were reserved as a royal monopoly to be handled exclusively by authorized Portuguese ships. Native merchants were permitted to trade in other types of goods, but only under Portuguese licence, and any ship sailing without an official pass was liable to be seized.

The Portuguese empire. The purely commercial and maritime character of the Portuguese empire in the East accounts in part for its rapid rise and almost equally rapid decline. It was a mushroom growth which struck no deep roots. A small country like Portugal, though blessed with a breed of hardy seamen, could not hope to colonize densely populated lands where the climate was unfriendly to Europeans. Moreover, the monopolistic policy of the Portuguese government prevented the free enterprise that might have developed a more vigorous economic life in the Portuguese settlements. The Eastern trade, indeed, was regulated primarily for the profit of the royal government. It brought wealth to the monarchy and to the capitalist firms to which the government farmed out portions of its monopoly. It also brought wealth to numerous noble officials who used their position to line their pockets in more or less legitimate ways; but for the few who found wealth, there were countless more who found in the Indies nothing but disease and death. The Portuguese government in the East was an autocratic bureaucracy, which in time became hopelessly corrupt. The authority of the viceroy in Goa, who was appointed for a three-year term by the home government, was in theory absolute, but in practice was limited by the difficulty of keeping in touch with scattered posts separated by hundreds of miles of water.

Its decline. The arrival of Dutch and English interlopers in the East at the end of the sixteenth century struck a death blow to the Portuguese empire there, but long before their arrival it was visibly declining and showed alarming signs of internal rot. The appalling mortality on shipboard and in tropical harbors was draining Portugal of its manpower, and the quality of the emigrants was deteriorating. Moreover, those who had come out early had nearly all married native women, and their descendants lost much of their national character and loyalty. In one respect only did the Portuguese settlements retain their original character. Thanks to the activity of the clergy and the favor shown the church by the royal government, the Portuguese in the East remained strongly Catholic and most of the native inhabitants of their settlements were converted to Christianity. Missionary activity also gained numerous converts throughout the East, though they could not have comprised more than a small minority of the vast population. Despite the ties of blood and religion which they had established with the native peoples, however, the Portuguese hold on their Eastern possessions was always precarious. Their empire was an artificial creation and depended on support from home. And Portugal itself was a declining power. At home as abroad, a small upper class reaped the profits of empire, while the mass of the people gained little advantage. The royal government, which monopolized and regulated the Eastern trade, was satisfied with the quick profit which came from importing oriental wares. It permitted merchants from other countries to buy these goods in Lisbon and gain the secondary profit that came from distributing them throughout Europe. Most of the goods sent back to the East in trade were also produced in more highly industrialized countries, so that the domestic industry and trade of Portugal were not greatly stimulated.

Portuguese Brazil.   Absorbed in its Eastern venture, the Portuguese government for a long time ignored the land in the Western Hemisphere claimed for it by Cabral in 1500. More than thirty years passed before any attempt was made to colonize Brazil, and at first the colony grew slowly. Eventually, however, the profits from mining, sugar plantations, and lumber attracted more immigrants, and Brazil became a prosperous colony. After the sixteenth century it was by far the most important Portuguese possession overseas, and it has remained an active center of Portuguese culture to the present day.

Spain in the Americas.   The colonial empire which Spain was meanwhile building in the New World also grew slowly from an unpromising start. No profitable trade could be carried on with the primitive tribes of the Caribbean islands. Even the Aztecs and the Incas on the mainland had nothing much to offer but their accumulated stores of gold and silver, and these the *conquistadores* cleaned out in one colossal act of robbery with violence. Thereafter, Spanish trade with the newly discovered lands depended on the founding of

colonies to exploit the natural resources of the land, its mineral wealth, and its people. Force of circumstance thus determined that, whereas the Portuguese empire in the East was purely commercial and maritime, the Spanish empire in the West was necessarily colonial and required as a first step territorial conquest and the enslavement of the native population. The Spanish empire overseas did, however, resemble the Portuguese in that it was the work of adventurers seeking easy wealth rather than of immigrants looking for land to cultivate by their own labor, and also that it was throughout its career subject to the autocratic royal government of the mother country.

Colonial expansion.   After the conquest of Montezuma's Aztec empire by Cortez in 1521, the interest of the Spaniards shifted from the islands to the mainland. Profitable plantations of sugar and tobacco, worked mostly by Negro slaves imported from Africa, still continued in Hispaniola and the other islands, but their importance was overshadowed by the greater opportunities offered by the larger and more varied areas of the mainland. There the search for gold and silver was the principal incentive

This highly ornate Portuguese Madonna is an example of what happened to European art when transplanted to the immensely rich colonies in the New World.

Hernando Cortez, the conqueror of Mexico is shown here dressed in ceremonial armor. His coat of arms is in the upper left-hand corner.

to further exploration and conquest, an incentive constantly renewed by the discovery of new and fabulously rich deposits in Mexico, Peru, Venezuela, and almost the whole length of the Andean range. Well before the end of the sixteenth century, Spanish colonists had acquired a relatively firm hold on Mexico and Central America, on almost the entire coastline of South America except Brazil, and on the southern fringe of what is now the United States from Florida to California.

Character of the colonies. Much of this vast territory was but sparsely occupied by Spanish immigrants. Mexico City, Lima, and three or four of the principal ports became large cities and centers of transplanted Spanish culture. But elsewhere the Spaniards were a thinly-spread ruling class, who lived by exploiting the native population. European colonies in tropical or semi-tropical lands have seldom been as thickly settled by immigrants as have those in temperate climates. Europeans find it difficult to work in tropical climates. The Spaniards who came seeking easy

wealth, at any rate, showed no inclination to work so long as they could force the natives or the imported African slaves to do it for them. Moreover, most tropical lands produce only a few marketable crops, such as sugar, cotton, tobacco, and indigo, which can be grown profitably on large plantations with cheap labor, but which offer little inducement to small independent farmers. Mining, which produced most of the wealth of the New World in the sixteenth century, also lent itself to exploitation by large firms working with forced native labor. Royal policy furthered this tendency by conferring land in large blocks, together with the native population, on noble adventurers or royal favorites. The normal pattern of society in Spanish America became, and long remained, one of concentrated wealth contrasted with extreme poverty, of arrogant exercise of economic and political power on the one hand and servile subjection on the other — with little gradation between.

Colonial government. The problem of governing such distant and widely scattered colonies was one for which there was no precedent, and the Spanish government solved it in the only way that seemed natural to an absolute monarchy in the mercantilist age. All the lands claimed by Spanish explorers were legally possessions of the Castilian crown. Its authority was represented by a viceroy, whose power was almost unlimited except for the orders, often very detailed, which he received from the home government. As the colonies expanded, a more complex administrative organization evolved. By the middle of the sixteenth century the Spanish possessions were divided into two great viceroyalties, that of New Spain which included Mexico, Central America, Venezuela, and the islands, and that of Peru, which constituted the Spanish territories in South America. These great divisions were further subdivided into provinces called *audiencias,* and these in turn into smaller governorships, the whole system thus forming an administrative hierarchy not unlike that of the ancient Roman Empire. Final authority in all matters, however, remained with the home government, and was exercised through the all-powerful Council of the Indies, which wrestled resolutely, though often misguidedly, with the problem of governing distant lands and strange peoples to the profit of the crown and the greater glory of God.

The church in America. The strong religious feeling of the Spanish people and their rulers ensured that the propagation of the faith would be a major concern of the government in the New World. Nowhere else in Europe were church and state so closely bound together in mutual support as they were in Spain, and that close relation was transplanted to the colonies. Having assumed responsibility for the religious welfare of its new possessions, the Spanish monarchy claimed authority over the colonial church in everything except doctrine. The church in Spanish America thus assumed the character of a national church, subject more directly to the Council of the Indies than to the papal *curia*. It proved to be one of the most powerful supports of the royal government in the colonies, and in return was richly endowed with large landed estates, complete with native labor.

Economic policy. Genuine as the missionary zeal of the Spanish monarchs undoubtedly was, it did not preclude a lively interest on their part in the profit that might accrue to the crown from possessions in the New World. In accordance with the prevailing mercantilist theory, the royal government was primarily interested in the importation of gold and silver bullion, on which, incidentally, it claimed a royalty of twenty per cent. Mercantilist theory also prescribed close governmental regulation of trade and the exclusion of all foreigners. The colonies were to serve the double purpose of supplying the mother country with raw materials and of furnishing a market for the products of Spanish industry. The work of directing the colonial economy to achieve these ends was carried out by the *Casa de Contratación* (House of Trade) in Seville, under the supervision of the Council of the Indies. The time required to communicate with the colonial authorities made its task extraordinarily difficult, and many of its regulations, however well intentioned, did more harm than good. In the second half of the sixteenth century, Dutch and English privateers, who found the bullion carried by the Spanish fleets irresistibly attractive, created further difficulties, as did also the regrettable tendency of the colonists to carry on illegal but untaxed trade with foreign interlopers. After 1562 an attempt was made to meet these hazards by limiting all trade with the colonies to one great fleet a year.

Decline of Spain. The wealth drawn from the New World made Spain for a century the most powerful state in Europe, but, as was true also of Portugal, an empire founded on battle, murder, and sudden wealth brought no lasting prosperity. The price revolution, noted earlier in this chapter, affected Spain earlier than other countries and placed Spanish industries at a disadvantage in competition with other states where prices were lower. The heavy taxes and rigid regulations imposed by the royal government cramped commercial and industrial activity both at home and in the colonies. Foreign wars drained the wealth of the state and left the government bankrupt. By the end of the sixteenth century, Spain was fast declining, both economically and as a power in European politics, although her colonial empire lasted for another two centuries. The mark she left on the Americas, however, was a permanent one. In language, religion, and culture, the American lands to the south of the United States have remained for the most part fundamentally Spanish.

4. Dutch, English, and French Commerce and Colonies

The northern passage. The countries along the Atlantic seaboard to the north of Spain and Portugal began their overseas expansion later than did the two great pioneering nations. Though exploration of the eastern coast of North America was begun by John Cabot in 1497, the northern countries showed little interest in the bleak and forbidding land which barred the way to the Far East. Instead, almost to the end of the sixteenth century, English, French, and Dutch explorers concentrated their attention on the search for a northern passage to the East, only to be frustrated again and again by the impassable Arctic ice. The hope of finding a northwest passage died with Henry Hudson in 1610, but before then it had become apparent that Portugal and Spain controlled the only trade routes or colonies that offered large and easy profits. Around the turn of the century the Dutch and

"The Seven Provinces," flagship of the Dutch fleet, is an example of the kind of warship that gave strong support to Dutch merchants in their struggle for a share in both the Western and the Far Eastern trade during the seventeenth century.

the English, both at war with Spain and therefore with Portugal which had fallen to Philip II in 1580, determined to break the Portuguese monopoly and invade her Eastern preserves by the southern route. And in the following years the English, Dutch, and French governments at last sent out colonists to make what they could of the unpromising lands in North America not claimed by Spain.

Dutch commerce. The newly founded Dutch Republic was peculiarly well equipped to challenge Portuguese and Spanish maritime power. Since the fifteenth century, when the Dutch began to exploit the herring fisheries of the North Sea, their sea-borne trade had grown tremendously. They had taken much of the Baltic and Scandinavian trade from the cities of the Hanseatic League; they had opened commerce with the Mediterranean; their ships carried much of the coastwise trade of France; and they had become the principal distributors of the oriental wares brought to Lisbon by the Portuguese. They had also developed a great shipbuilding industry. Ships that were the most efficient and economical in the world to operate; a breed of hardy sailors and a vigorous class of bourgeois merchants; the international finance concentrated in Amsterdam; and a government wholly devoted to promoting commerce; these factors combined to make the new republic a commercial power capable of challenging any European rival.

Dutch in the East. The Dutch Republic had scarcely been born when the union of Portugal with Spain under Philip II closed Lisbon to Dutch merchants. The latter realized that they would now have to go to the source if they were to keep their Eastern trade, and in that venture patriotism and piety reinforced the lure of gain. In 1595 a joint-stock company sent the first Dutch fleet around Africa to the Spice Islands, and in succeeding years other companies followed its example. A more concerted effort, however, was needed to break the long-established hold of the Portuguese on the island trade, and so in 1602 the rival Dutch companies were merged under governmental authority to form the Dutch East India Company, a giant joint-stock company with a capital of more than six million florins. The policy of the Dutch company differed in two respects from that of the earlier Portuguese invaders of the East. The Dutch did not attempt to control all trade in Eastern waters as the Portuguese did from their bases on the Malabar coast. They concentrated on monopolizing the spice trade, and, after destroying the Portuguese fleets and driving them from the islands, they set about gaining political as well as economic control of the Malay Archipelago and the Moluccas, thus establishing a territorial rather than a purely commercial empire. They also established trading posts on the Indian mainland, which with the collapse of Portuguese power was thrown open to European trade. From these posts they were eventually driven by English competition, but so firmly established was their empire in the East Indies that it remained under their rule until the twentieth century.

Dutch in the West. Despite their commitments in the East, the Dutch did not fail to take part in the contest for commerce and colonies in the West which opened anew with the seventeenth century. In 1621 the Dutch West India Company was founded with a monopoly similar to that of its eastern predecessor. Under its direction a Dutch colony was established in the Hudson Valley, which had been discovered and claimed for the Dutch by Henry Hudson in 1609. The Dutch settlements, however, were scarcely more than fur-trading posts, and in 1664 the colony fell into the hands of the English. The real interests of the company lay further south where it fought, raided, and smuggled among the Spanish and Portuguese colonies. It captured Curaçao and some other islands and gained a foothold in Guiana on the South American mainland. These possessions served as bases for trade, but were otherwise of no great importance.

Economic growth of England. While Dutch commerce was rising, England too was experiencing a remarkable economic expansion. Under Elizabeth and the Stuarts, England was already well launched on the career of industrial growth that in the nineteenth century made her the workshop of the world. Woolen cloth weaving was still her principal industry, but mining and metal working were developing rapidly under the stimulus of new techniques and large capital investments. It was this solid base of industrial production that eventually gave her an advantage over the Dutch in the competition for world trade. In the meantime, English sea-borne commerce, though it was growing rapidly, still lagged behind the Dutch. English merchants were the first to make extensive use of joint-stock companies, backed by royal charter, as a means of opening up new and distant trade areas. The Muscovy Company, founded in 1555, financed explorations of the northeast passage and established a trading post at Archangel in northern Russia. The Eastland Company (1579) penetrated the Baltic Sea in competition with the Hansards and the Dutch, and the Levant Company (1581) opened up trade with the eastern Mediterranean. Temporary joint-stocks also financed the ventures of Sir Francis Drake and other privateers who hunted through all the Spanish waters and worked out the methods of naval warfare that would enable them to "singe the King of Spain's beard."

English in India. The most important of all the English joint-stocks, however, was the East India Company, founded in 1600 for much the same reasons as inspired the contemporary venture of their fellow-Protestants in Holland. Open war with Spain had broken out in 1587, and as a result the English merchants had been excluded from their profitable trade with Lisbon. The new company was founded to trade directly with the East. It was not at the beginning a permanent joint-stock and it had at first nothing like the financial backing of its Dutch rival. After some years of conflict it was forced to abandon the Spice Islands, which remained a Dutch preserve, and to concentrate its attention on the trade with the Indian mainland. There the company gained a firm foothold and, in the period after 1660, fought successfully against Dutch and French competitors, subdued native states, and laid the foundations for the British Empire in India.

English in America. The first sixty years of the seventeenth century were years of promise rather than achievement for England in the West as well as in the East. Beginning with the Virginia Colony planted at Jamestown in 1607, joint-stock companies or noble proprietors who had been granted a charter by the crown planted a series of colonies on

The picture above is the earliest known view of New Amsterdam, the Dutch settlement later conquered by the English and renamed New York. The skyline of lower Manhattan has changed considerably since then.

the inhospitable eastern coast of North America from New England to the Carolinas. Other, and for the moment more profitable, colonies were also established in the West Indian islands, Bermuda, and the Bahamas. The English colonies on the mainland were very different in character from the tropical settlements of the Spaniards. The English found no gold or silver; the native population was sparse and warlike and could not be enslaved; the land produced no profitable export crop until the Virginia colony began to cultivate tobacco successfully; and there was little hope of profitable trade until the colonists themselves became sufficiently numerous to furnish a market. The one advantage the English colonies possessed was that they drew immigrants in large numbers. The climate was suitable for European settlers, and the political and religious conflicts that disturbed England in the seventeenth century drove numbers of people to seek refuge and religious freedom in the New World. The English government did not attempt to impose uniformity on the scattered settlements, and the rise of parliamentary government in mid-century was favorable to the growth of self-government in the colonies. The survival of the colonies during the early years of hardship, their later expansion inland, and the steady growth of their prosperity were due to the colonists themselves rather than to the efforts of a paternalistic government.

French in Canada. The French colony founded in Canada at about the same time as the earliest English settlements in America, on the other hand, was from the beginning inspired and directed by the royal government in accordance with mercantilist principles. During most of the sixteenth century, the French kings were too deeply absorbed in foreign and civil wars to pay much attention to colonization. The early explorations of the St. Lawrence by Verrazano in 1524 and Jacques Cartier in 1534 and 1540 led to no permanent settlements. But once the Wars of Religion were over, Henry IV and, in the next generation, Cardinal Richelieu moved to stake out an imperial claim in North America. In 1608 Samuel Champlain founded the first permanent French settlement in the New World at Quebec. In the following years fur-traders and missionaries pushed exploration far inland along the river systems and the Great Lakes, and forts were established at strategic points. The French colony nevertheless grew very slowly. Richelieu's policy of barring the Huguenots from emigration to the new colony prevented it from becoming a refuge for religious dissenters, and the rigors of the northern winter discouraged permanent settlement. When in 1626 the cardinal founded the Company of the Hundred Associates to exploit the Canadian fur trade, the charter demanded that it bring out colonists, but few came. In 1660 the French population in Canada numbered only about 2,500, and most of these were traders, soldiers, or missionaries. After that date, the colony received a new stimulus from the vigorous mercantilist policy of Colbert, the great finance minister of Louis XIV. An autocratic government like that of the home country was established and constructed a circle of forts to contain the growing English colonies and to fight them for control of the vast inland area which no adequate French immigration was forthcoming to colonize. But the struggle for possession of North America, as well as the conflict between France and England for control of the trade with India, falls outside the chronological limits of this chapter. This aspect of European expansion will be treated in Part Two.

36

The Culture of the Early Modern Period

THE PERIOD which opened with Luther's protest, the coronation of Charles V, and the first circumnavigation of the globe, and which closed with the death of Cromwell and Mazarin and the end of the wars of religion, was a productive one in all fields of literature, art, and music. It was also a period of remarkably vigorous growth in the natural sciences. Indeed, it witnessed the most significant phase in the development of the scientific thought which, more than any other intellectual trait, distinguishes modern from medieval civilization. In all these fields, the end of the sixteenth century marked a change in style or a shift in emphasis, so that for purposes of discussion a division in the period may be made at about that point. The years 1520 to 1600 represent what may be called the late Renaissance, although they encompassed almost the whole of the literary Renaissance in France and England. The first half of the seventeenth century initiated the period commonly designated in histories of art and music, and sometimes also in histories of literature, by the term Baroque. These distinctions do not apply very aptly to the history of science, but even there the turn of the century marks the point at which modern methods may be said to have fully emerged.

1. Language and Literature

Decline of humanism. By 1520 Erasmus, the prince of the humanists, had passed the peak of his career, and the great revival of antiquity which he personified was on the wane. The classics were long to remain the foundation of all liberal education, and Latin would still serve for centuries as the international language of scholars and scientists; but writers who aimed to reach the general public were turning decisively to their national languages. The great expansion of the reading public, which resulted from the invention of printing and the spread of education among the upper and middle classes, was partly responsible for this change. Although most educated people could read some Latin, many found it easier to read their native language. Writers in both poetry and prose were also discovering that they could express themselves with greater freedom and originality in their mother tongue. Latin had been throughout the Middle Ages a living language adaptable to the needs of schoolmen, lawyers, chroniclers, and hymn writers. But after the humanists had revived classical standards and made them the only acceptable norms, Latin ceased to grow. It was the supreme irony of the humanists' achievement that the rebirth of antiquity which they brought about ended in Latin and Greek becoming dead languages.

Influence of the classics. The classics did, however, continue to exert a profound influence on the evolution of European thought and literature. Until the Romantic movement in the early nineteenth century broke the spell, they may, indeed, be said to have set the tone for the greater part of modern literary culture. From them poets, dramatists, and prose writers gained a sense of form that had been largely lacking in medieval writing. Study of the ancient authors, too, opened up areas of secular knowledge and of human experience which greatly broadened the scope of literature, and in this period numerous translations made the contents of the classics available even to those who could not read them in their original form. They thus served not only as models but as a constant source of inspiration to writers in every European language. It was the lasting service of the humanists to our civilization that they preserved and made fully available to the modern world its ancient heritage.

The modern languages.   During this period the major European languages were becoming national in scope and were crystallizing in the form they have retained with minor changes till the present time. In this respect, as in so many others, Italy was far ahead of the rest of Europe. There, thanks to the combined genius of Dante, Petrarch, Boccaccio, and other Florentine writers, a national literary language was founded in the fourteenth century, based on the Tuscan dialect. In much the same way, two centuries later, the publication of Luther's translation of the Bible made his Saxon dialect the literary language of Germany. In France the problem, common to all European countries, of creating a national literary language was complicated by the fact that there were not only innumerable local dialects, but also two distinct languages, the *langue d'oïl,* spoken in the north, and the *langue d'oc,* spoken in the south. But, unlike either Italy or Germany, France had by the sixteenth century become a strongly centralized state, and the influence of the royal court and of the capital was strong enough to make the French spoken in the Paris region the national literary language. The situation in England was similarly complicated by the existence of two distinct languages in the Middle Ages, the Norman French, spoken by the aristocracy, and the Anglo-Saxon, spoken by the mass of the people. These two languages began to merge only toward the end of the fourteenth century, and then only in the London area. Chaucer, who was London-born, can be read today with much less difficulty than can his west-country contemporary, William Langland. However, it was not till the sixteenth century that the language of London

and the court became national in scope and fixed in its modern form. No one need stumble over the poetry of Wyatt and Surrey, who wrote in the reign of Henry VIII, and the speech of Shakespeare's contemporaries seems strange to us only in its poetic vigor.

French literary Renaissance.   French historians are generally agreed that the literary Renaissance in their country began in the early sixteenth century and that the inspiration came largely from Italy. The Italian wars, which began in 1494, drew large numbers of the French aristocracy to Italy, and a taste for Italian culture was part of the booty they brought back across the Alps. Under Francis I, the French court became a center for the dissemination of Italian influences in art, literature, and learning. The humanists' enthusiasm for the ancient classics was itself largely an importation from Italy; together with the example of the Italian writers who had been trained in the classical tradition, it exerted a powerful influence on the shaping of French literature. There was, however, no clear or immediate break with the native literary tradition inherited from the Later Middle Ages. The classical and Italian influences did not become dominant until the middle of the sixteenth century, when a brilliant constellation of young poets, known as the Pléiade, undertook somewhat self-consciously to refine French poetry by imitating the Latin and Greek classics and the works of the Italian poets. But, while proclaiming the poverty of the French language and literature and the necessity of drawing upon the antique sources to enrich them, the Pléiade stoutly defended the suitability of their native tongue as a medium for exalted poetry. This twofold program was enunciated in 1549 by Joachim du Bellay in the *Defense and Illustration of the French Language,* the word "illustration" here being used in the sense of praise or making illustrious. The work of the Pléiade in theory and practice marked the first important step in the formation of the classical French style which reached its fullest development in the age of Louis XIV. Most of the group were but mediocre poets, too closely bound by imitation of classical models, but two of them at least, Pierre de Ronsard (1534–85) and Joachim du Bellay (1522?–60), wrote poems of imperishable beauty.

Michelangelo was primarily a sculptor, and his paintings show the sculptor's vision. His idealized figures, as three-dimensional and strongly modelled as statues, have an inherent energy that reflects his own powerful personality.

17 *God Creating Adam, by Michelangelo Buonarroti, fresco on ceiling of the Sistine Chapel, Vatican, 1508—10.*

Titian, the "Grand Old Man" of Venetian painting, was contemporary with Michelangelo — born about two years later, he outlived him by a decade — but he differed from the great sculptor-painter in almost every respect. Paint was his natural medium, as it was with most Venetians, and he built up his pictures, many of them portraits, out of light and color without clear outline. The self-portrait at the right shows him in extreme old age, but still clear-eyed and master of his art.

18 *Self-Portrait, by Titian, c. 1565. Museo Nacional del Prado, Madrid.*

As the classical art of the High Renaissance was passing, a younger generation of painters began to strive for exaggerated effects by elongating their figures or by emphasizing the dramatic tension of the scene. These painters are commonly called "mannerists." This term fits Parmigianino better than it does Tintoretto, although there is a touch of mannerism in Tintoretto's departure from the classical norm of balanced harmony.

19 *Madonna of the Long Neck, by Parmagianino, c. 1535. Uffizi, Florence. (Scala)*

20 *Presentation of the Virgin, by Tintoretto, c. 1552. Madonna dell'Orto, Venice. (Scala)*

21 *Abduction of the Daughters of Leucippus, by Peter Paul Rubens, c. 1619. Alte Pinakothek, Munich. (Joachim Blanel)*

The seventeenth century introduced the era of Baroque art, exemplified here by the Italian-trained Fleming, Peter Paul Rubens, whose grandiose designs, lush figures in swirling motion, and "painterly" style are typically Baroque.

Bourgeois Holland in the seventeenth century was little touched by the Italianate Baroque. Here Rembrandt van Rijn, the most profoundly penetrating painter of his age, created out of shadow and light pictures that pierce below the surface of things to bare the spiritual essence of his subjects. Here, too, Jan Vermeer of Delft painted intimate scenes in exquisite detail and with a subtly graded tonal range of color. In their tranquillity, his pictures seem the very opposite of Rembrandt's, yet they have a depth of their own.

22 Jeremiah Mourning the Destruction of Jerusalem, by Rembrandt van Rijn, 1630. Rijksmuseum, Amsterdam.

23 Soldier and Laughing Girl, by Jan Vermeer, c. 1657. Copyright the Frick Collection, New York.

Rabelais and Montaigne. The two greatest prose writers of the sixteenth century were also profoundly influenced by their study of classical antiquity, but it is the secular, broadly humane spirit of the ancient authors that is evident in their work, rather than the imitation of classical forms. The genius of both, indeed, was far too original and independent to admit of their imitating anyone, even the ancients whom they revered. François Rabelais (1490–1531) belongs to the generation of the humanists, but there is no classical restraint in his rambling and ebullient stories of *Gargantua* and *Pantagruel.* He was a teller of tall tales, but beneath the exaggeration and lusty humor of his work there was also a serious substratum of philosophical thought, a declaration of man's right to full enjoyment of the pleasures of mind and body in this pleasant world. Michel de Montaigne (1533–92) belonged to the troubled era of the Wars of Religion. That age of violent passions, however, had not made him a partisan. On the contrary, the conflict of dogmatic beliefs had suggested to his reasonable mind that neither side of the argument was in possession of the whole truth. With calm curiosity, he examined one after another of the problems that vexed his age, and, having examined them from all sides in his thoughtful *Essays,* left them illuminated but still unsolved. He was at once the heir to the inquiring critical spirit of the Renaissance and the father of modern rationalism.

The Précieux and the Academy. The first half of the seventeenth century is more notable for the refinement of the French language than for the production of great French literature. Two generations of uninspired poets and second-rate prose writers devoted themselves to a laborious study of the rules of grammar and to precision and refinement in the use of words. This devotion to form won for them the name of *Précieux.* The vigorous writers of the classical age of Louis XIV, who have overshadowed them, owed the excellence of the language they used in no small degree to the men who had worked so hard to perfect it. The age of Richelieu also provided French literature with a permanent tribunal of literary taste consecrated to the standardization of the language, in the French Academy which was founded by the cardinal in 1635.

English literary Renaissance. In England, as in France, classical and Italian models exerted a stimulating influence on the literary Renaissance, which began in the reign of Henry VIII and reached its full bloom in that of Queen Elizabeth. And here, too, the court and the capital set the tone. A flood of lyric poetry runs through the sixteenth century from Sir Thomas Wyatt (1503–42) and Henry Howard, Earl of Surrey (1516–47), to Sir Philip Sidney (1554–86) and Michael Drayton (1563–1631). In no other country did the sixteenth century produce so many first-rate poets or such a volume of memorable verse. Despite all classical and foreign influences, the poetry of the Tudor age was thoroughly English, much less consciously imitative than that of contemporaneous French writers. Edmund

The old Swan Theater, as sketched by a Dutch visitor to London. It was in theaters like this that the plays of Shakespeare and the other great Elizabethan dramatists were performed.

Spenser (1552–99), whose great epic *The Faerie Queene* sang the praises of Elizabeth, had obviously taken Ariosto and Tasso as models, but his work, filled with strong national sentiment, has a vital originality that frees it from the curse of imitation. Nowhere, however, were the vigor and originality of Elizabethan England so clearly evident as in the work of the dramatists, for this was the period in which the English theater was born and in one generation reached heights never since surpassed. The towering figure of William Shakespeare (1564–1616) has dwarfed his lesser contemporaries, but we must not forget that he was but one of a brilliant group, which included Christopher Marlowe (1564–93) and Ben Jonson (1573–1637) and which even without Shakespeare would have made this a great age in the history of English drama.

The early Stuart period.   After the passing of the great Elizabethans, the English drama declined, but the tradition of lyric poetry continued, though with less exuberant vitality. The growth of Puritanism was inimical to the theater, and the increasing religious and political tension which culminated in the Civil War cast a shadow over the literature of the early Stuart period. The mature poetry of John Donne (1573–1631) gives evidence of a serious preoccupation with religious problems,

and in mid-century John Milton (1608–74) wrote in *Paradise Lost* a religious epic worthy of being ranked with Dante's *Divine Comedy*. There were also in these years, it is true, Cavalier poets whose lyrics are as light as anything produced at the court of Elizabeth, but the prevailing tone of Puritanism was not decisively broken until the Stuart Restoration in 1660.

Spain's "Golden Age."   For Spain, as for England, the last part of the sixteenth century and the first decades of the seventeenth were a period of immense literary productivity. It is often called the Golden Age of Spanish literature. In dramatic writing, indeed, Spain surpassed England in quantity, though not in quality, for she produced no Shakespeare. Lope de Vega (1562–1635), the most prolific of the Spanish dramatists, depicted every aspect of contemporary life in his innumerable plays, of which some 450 have been printed. But despite the grace and dramatic invention that endeared him to Spanish theater-goers, he has been little read outside of Spain. Miguel de Cervantes (1547–1616) also wrote plays, but his fame does not rest on them. It is as the author of one book, the story of *Don Quixote de la Mancha,* which Macaulay called "incomparably the best novel ever written," that Cervantes takes his place among the few great

The sixteenth-century French library pictured here represents one aspect of the great revival of literature that occurred in the sixteenth and early seventeenth centuries.

writers who are not for an age but for all time. Wherever Western civilization has spread, men have read the adventures of the gentle, chivalrous, and fantastically muddle-headed knight of La Mancha, and have coined the term "quixotic" to designate a misguided but not unadmirable strife for lofty ideals.

2. Art and Music

The declining Renaissance. By the end of the 1520's the age of the High Renaissance was passing, although the indestructible Michelangelo lived on until 1564, dying at the age of eighty-nine, and in the North both Hans Holbein the Younger and Lucas Cranach lived well into the Reformation period. With the passing of the great Renaissance masters, the creative energy of Italian art seemed for a time exhausted. Lesser artists imitated the technique of Michelangelo without the vitalizing force of his genius. In the North, too, imitation of Italian models made the second half of the sixteenth century a period of rather uninspired art, except for the landscapes and peasant scenes painted by Pieter Brueghel the Elder (1525–69), whose earthy genius no foreign influence could tame. While the great age was passing elsewhere, however, the setting sun of the Renaissance cast a last glow of brilliant color across the lagoons of Venice. Always independent in its relations with the papacy, Venice escaped the dampening effect of the Counter-Reformation and also its religious enthusiasm. In these years, when their economic activity was declining, when Venice spent what Venice earned, the citizens of the commercial republic spent their inherited wealth to indulge a sensuous taste for color, a taste richly satisfied during a long lifetime by Titian (1477–1576) and by his equally colorful contemporaries, Tintoretto (1518–94) and Veronese (1528–88).

The Counter-Reformation. In most parts of Catholic Europe, the Counter-Reformation had a more direct impact on aesthetic culture than in Venice. Its reassertion of rigid orthodoxy, reinforced by the repressive action of Inquisition and Index, hastened the decline of the Renaissance in Italy by discouraging the free and secular spirit that had inspired it, although the decline was probably inevitable in any case

Miguel de Cervantes, the creator of Don Quixote, was the towering literary figure of Spain's "Golden Age." This portrait, by Juan de Jáurequi, was painted in 1600.

as the result of other causes. The Counter-Reformation was, however, by no means an entirely negative force. It also inspired a positive religious fervor, embodied in the young Society of Jesus, in the renewed authority of the Roman papacy, and in the intense if narrow zeal of Philip II. As we shall see, it shaped the music of Palestrina and gave birth to Baroque architecture. And in Spain, one aspect of its spirit inspired the painting of El Greco (1541–1614). Born in Crete and trained in Venice and Rome, "The Greek" combined something of the rigid formalism of Byzantine painting with the Venetian use of masses of color, but it was in the Spain of Philip II that he found his spiritual home. In his somber paintings line and color heighten the emotional intensity and express a religious sentiment that was in the main morbidly ascetic.[1] There were other sides to the Counter-Reformation, but none was so completely represented in the work of one artist.

[1] See above, pages 382, 387, and 389.

The Baroque style. Around the year 1600, new styles in art and music opened a new era generally designated by the term Baroque, a period which lasted for about a century and a half. Within that period there were many conflicting tendencies, so that it is difficult to define exactly what is meant by Baroque style, although anyone who has paced the endless corridors of the Louvre or has entered the churches built in that period from Rome to Montreal will recognize it when he sees it. The Counter-Reformation had lost both the enthusiasm and the morbid piety that had characterized its first half-century, but the feeling for the authority, the might and power of the Church Eternal, which the Jesuits and the Council of Trent inspired, still remained and found expression in the building of churches of unparalleled magnificence. Almost everywhere in continental Europe, too, this was an age of absolute monarchy, and the cultural tone was set by royal or princely courts, which existed solely for the purpose of enhancing the prestige of the sovereign. It was an age that revered power and authority, and art both served and expressed what the age admired. Grandiloquent design, complex ornamentation filling every inch of space, a general effect of opulence, and great virtuosity in execution were all characteristic of Baroque architecture, sculpture, and painting and, in somewhat different terms, of Baroque music also. But though this was an age that loved authority, there were religious and intellectual cross-currents which robbed it of complete assurance, and the impression one receives from the excessively ornamented buildings and the swirling draperies and violent movement that characterize much of Baroque painting is one of restlessness and turbulence.

Baroque painting. Italy was still the schoolmaster of Europe in the Baroque age, and the painters who seem most typical of the period show strong evidence of Italian influence. This is notably true of Peter Paul Rubens (1577–1640), the Flemish artist whose opulent and voluptuous paintings express the quintessence of the Baroque spirit. Choosing dramatic themes for his pictures, Rubens filled them with massive figures in violent motion, not clearly outlined but built up out of color and light. Something of the same dramatic quality is seen in the works of his Spanish contemporary, Diego Velasquez (1599–1660). But Velasquez, like so many of the painters of this age of absolute monarchy, was forced to spend a great deal of time painting the portraits of kings and their families, and in these figures we see another aspect of the Baroque age, the rigid formality, the pomp and circumstance that surrounded royalty. On the whole, Baroque art flourished best in Catholic countries, in Italy, Spain, Flanders, and France. Pictorial art in this period was almost nonexistent in Puritan England except as an importation, and Protestant Germany produced little after Holbein and Cranach. In Protestant Holland, on the other hand, the taste of a rich, bourgeois society, very different from that of the royal courts, was met by a series of masterly painters in a style that had little in common with the rest of Europe. Here Frans Hals (1580–1666) painted informal portraits of soldiers and burghers, and Jan Vermeer (1632–75) and a whole school of genre painters produced the charming little domestic scenes that more than anything else reveal to us the social atmosphere of seventeenth-century Holland. And here, too, the incomparable Rembrandt van Rijn (1606–69) created his own style and painted pictures out of a stark genius that was too much for his own age, and would be appreciated at its true worth only by later generations.

Music of the late Renaissance. In contrast to the sense of failing vitality that characterizes a good deal of the pictorial art between the High Renaissance and the Baroque, the music of the late Renaissance carried on the developments of the preceding period with undiminished vigor. Although the great age of the northern French and Flemish composers passed with the death of Josquin des Prez in 1521, their influence had by then revivified Italian music and for the rest of the century, while the other arts were declining there, Italy took the lead in musical composition and in turn reinvigorated the music of the North. The music of the late Renaissance, like that of the preceding period, was essentially polyphonic, but characterized by an increasing integration of the whole composition through the use of imitation and occasionally by chordal writing.[1]

[1] See above, page 338.

"The Peasant Dance" is an excellent example of the style of Pieter Brueghel the Elder. This Dutch painter portrayed scenes of peasant life with a realism and zest that owed little to traditional styles.

Together with this closer integration went a great expansion of the tonal range between the lower and the upper voices, a development fostered perhaps by the increasing use of mixed choirs. Throughout the century, the polyphonic mass continued to be the dominant form of church music and to it men of every country contributed — the Italianate Fleming, Orlando de Lassus (1530–94); the English Catholic, William Byrd (1542–1623); the Spaniard, Tomás Luis de Victoria (1535–1611), who spent most of his life in Rome; and finally, that noblest Roman of them all, Giovanni Pierluigi da Palestrina (1525–94), whose monolithic masses were the most perfect expression of the spirit of the Council of Trent and still possess a comparable authority.

Chansons and madrigals. While polyphonic music in the grand manner was still largely devoted to the service of the church, the late Renaissance produced an immense number of secular chansons and madrigals for the delectation of the courts of princes and the households of nobles and burghers. These delicate and artistically conceived pieces form one of the most important musical developments of the age and retain for us an intimate charm possessed by no other form of vocal polyphony. The chanson was primarily a French form, a polyphonic setting of poetry which was generally simple enough to be performed by amateurs. The Italian madrigal, on the other hand, although influenced by the French chanson as well as by earlier native popular and courtly forms, was a more sophisticated product, frequently intended to be sung by professionals in the princely courts. It grew up in the early sixteenth century under the influence of the Italian literary revival that followed the age of humanism, and its inspiration was primarily literary. What the composers aimed to achieve was a musical setting perfectly adapted in all voices to express the sense and the imagery of poems by such great masters as Petrarch, Ariosto, and Tasso. Toward the end of the sixteenth century, the madrigal was introduced, with other elements of Italian culture, into England, where it became thoroughly naturalized and forms one of our most cherished legacies from the Elizabethan age. Here, madrigals were composed primarily for the music, the verses, however charming, being of secondary importance, and they were intended to be performed by amateurs as household music. While demanding a degree of musical ability beyond the reach of most untrained singers today, they were well adapted to performance by a small social group, each voice having its share of melodic line. The popularity of both chansons and madrigals is attested by the large number of collections published by contemporary printers — some 270 collections of Italian madrigals alone between 1550 and 1600 — and also by the number of composers who contributed to them. Nearly all the great composers of the sixteenth century wrote madrigals, and some of the most distinguished Elizabethans, including Thomas Morley (1577–1602), John Wilbve (1573–1638), and Thomas Weelkes (1575–1623) are known chiefly as madrigalists.

Early Baroque music. Around the year 1600 a distinct change in musical style, beginning in Italy and spreading to the North, marked the transition apparent within the musical production of Claudio Monteverdi (1567–1643), who was at once the last of the great Italian madrigalists and one of the founders of the opera. One of the most notable elements in the new style was a reaction against polyphony, inspired in part by the need for dramatic expression of passionate emotion in opera and oratorio, both newly invented forms in the last years of the sixteenth century. Here the words of a dramatic text were given to a single voice in recitative or aria, with instrumental accompaniment in harmonic chords. Although polyphonic music continued, reaching its culmination at the end of the Baroque era in the fugues and choral works of Johann Sebastian Bach (1685–1750), the most characteristic form of Baroque music was chordal harmony. The voices in this type of music were no longer of equal melodic importance, for the upper voice carried the melody and the lower voices merely supplied the chords founded on the bass. This was a period, too, of great virtuosity in performance of both instrumental and vocal music. Operas and ora-

torios made unprecedented demands on the solo voice, and the composition of music for specific instruments, which was rare in the preceding period except for lute and keyboard instruments, went hand in hand with an immense improvement in the instruments themselves, especially those of the violin family, and with an equivalent development of virtuosity in the performers.

3. The Scientific Revolution

The background. Viewed in retrospect from our own scientifically oriented age, the pre-eminent characteristic of the period we have been discussing may well seem to be the revolution in scientific thought which laid the foundation for the distinctively modern conception of the natural sciences. To this age we owe the discovery of a great many of the basic principles which, when further developed and applied, have enabled modern men to master the forces of nature and to use them, for good and ill, in ways that have transformed our civilization. The rise of modern science was a late fruit of the transition from medieval to modern civilization, but like so many other developments of that age, it had its roots in the past. Many of those roots extended back to antiquity and drew nourishment from the speculations of Greek mathematicians, physicists, and astronomers. The legacy of the inquiring Greek mind, as we saw in Chapter 20, was partially recovered by the scholastic philosophers in the twelfth and thirteenth centuries, aided by Arabic intermediaries. In the early fourteenth century, under the influence of the Nominalist school of philosophy, promising beginnings were made at the universities of Paris and Oxford in the direction of experiment and the observation of individual phenomena. That movement, however, soon lost its way in a maze of logical subtleties, and although it influenced later thinkers, it bore little immediate fruit.

Influence of the Renaissance. While scholastic thought was thus declining, the rising movement of classical humanism was inadvertently serving the cause of science. The humanists, who were primarily men of letters, had no great interest in science themselves, but they were interested in anything written in the age of classical antiquity. They therefore corrected and published all the works of the ancient scientists they could find and so gave new inspiration to scientific thought. Inspiration of a very different kind came also from the Renaissance artists, engineers, technicians, and inventors, who carried on practical experiments in an effort to solve their professional problems. The invention of printing by itself deserves much of the credit for the scientific advances of the following centuries, for it enabled scientists to communicate their ideas widely and rapidly, and made it possible for them to profit almost immediately from the work done by other scientists. Many books on science were illustrated with copper engravings, the accuracy of which owed much to the realistic technique developed by the Renaissance artists. Finally, the cultural and social movements of the Renaissance created an atmosphere in many ways favorable to the natural sciences. The spread of education among laymen broke the monopoly on learning held by the clergy in the Middle Ages and enlarged the secular content of culture. The men of the sixteenth century were certainly not irreligious, but their thought was less exclusively confined within the sphere of theology and metaphysics than was that of the churchmen who dominated the culture of the Middle Ages. Burckhardt's characterization of the Renaissance as "the discovery of the world and of man" may be something of an exaggeration; but the Renaissance did bring a shift in emphasis from the spiritual to the physical world, from the infinite future to the finite present.

The revolt against Aristotle. The essential factor in the scientific revolution that began in the late Renaissance was a gradual but fundamental change in men's ideas about the character of matter and the causes of change and motion. They learned to think of matter as purely material, moved or changed by objective forces. This involved a revolt not only against the medieval theology which had peopled the universe with spirits, but still more against the teaching of Aristotle, whose conception of the nature of the physical universe dominated the thought of the scholastic scientists and continued to exert a powerful influence on scientific thought till the seventeenth century. The Aristotelian system of physics and cosmology is too complicated to be described briefly. It may be enough to say that it explained the behavior of physical things in accordance with the qualities supposed to be inherent in the nature of the thing, which gave it a natural "disposition" to certain kinds of action. For example, flames rise because fire aspires to reach its natural home in the sphere of fire which surrounds the earth beyond the sphere of air. And, conversely, solid objects in which the element of earth predominates, are heavy because they seek to find rest in their natural home at the center of the earth, and when falling freely they accelerate because they are rushing more eagerly as they approach their destination. Crude examples of this kind are unfair to the large amount of practical common-sense observation, however erroneous, contained in Aristotle's system, but the tendency of Aristotelian thought was to make the scientist ask first what was the "essence" of a thing and then deduce from that premise how it would behave. The advances made during the scientific revolution, on the other hand, were made by men who asked first *how* a thing behaved and who then, after observing and experimenting, after measuring, weighing, and counting, induced an hypothesis to explain its behavior without reference to inherent qualities or dispositions. The new science, in short, abandoned the search for unmeasurable qualities and concentrated attention on quantities and measurable forces. And more often than not the laws it discovered were expressed in the language of mathematics.

Advances in mathematics. Mathematics, experiment, and measurement were the intellectual tools of the new science, and the most important of these was mathematics, for by means of it men manipulated the data and formulated the results drawn from the other two. As scientists began to think of the relations of things in terms of mathematical order — numbers, ratios, and geometrical figures — their interest led to great advances in every branch of the mathematical sciences. At the same time, without such advances the scientific revolution could not have progressed as it did.

René Descartes, the great mathematician and philosopher, as painted by Frans Hals, one of the most realistic of the Baroque painters.

At the beginning of the sixteenth century, mathematicians had at their disposal the basic forms of arithmetic, greatly simplified by the adoption of Arabic numerals during the Later Middle Ages, Euclidian geometry, which was made more widely available by the publication of a Latin translation of Euclid in 1505, and elementary algebra — in short, about the amount of mathematics to which the average high school student is now exposed. The publication of Girolamo Cardano's epoch-making book on algebra, *The Great Art* (1545), added immensely to this store of knowledge, and in the following years further advances in algebra were made, including the gradual adoption of a system of internationally recognized symbols, so that by the early seventeenth century algebra had assumed pretty much its modern form. Among Cardano's original contributions, his use of negative and imaginary numbers was especially important as opening up a whole new field. Meanwhile, arithmetical calculation involving large numbers, fractions, and trigonometrical functions was greatly facili-

tated by the invention of decimals by the Flemish scientist, Simon Stevin (1548–1620), in 1585 and of logarithms by the Scottish mathematician, John Napier (1550–1617), in 1614. Although much work on angles was done earlier, chiefly in relation to astronomy, trigonometry did not emerge as an independent science till the sixteenth century. The calculus of probabilities was more clearly an innovation, making its appearance in Cardano's work on algebra, but its full development came only a century later, when the French scientist, Blaise Pascal (1623–62), undertook to work out the mathematical laws of chance for the benefit of a gambling friend. Analytical geometry, the process by which any algebraic equation can be plotted out in a geometrical figure and any geometrical figure can be expressed in an algebraic equation, was invented by the French philosopher-scientist, René Descartes, and published in 1637 as a sequel to his great philosophical *Discourse on Method*. Descartes (1596–1650) was one of the most revolutionary thinkers of the seventeenth century, and his influence gave new impetus to the tendency of scientists to reduce all science to mathematical abstraction, although in the long run his method, which depended largely on deductive logic, proved less fruitful than the more purely experimental science championed by his English forerunner, Francis Bacon (1561–1626). The invention of infinitesimal calculus by both Sir Isaac Newton and the German philosopher, Leibniz, working independently, came later than the period with which this chapter is concerned, but should be mentioned here as the culminating triumph of seventeenth-century mathematics.

Instruments of measurement. The mathematical approach to science, because it depended on consideration of such quantities as distance, volume, heat, weight, and acceleration, required accurate measurement to bring satisfactory results; and that demand was met by improvements in the known instruments of measurement and by the invention of new ones. Careful workmanship was all that was required to improve the ordinary instruments for measuring weight and distance, and the interest of merchants in the accurate measurement of the goods they bought and sold had already led to much improvement in the Later

Middle Ages. Instruments for astronomical measurement had also been improved to meet the practical needs of navigators, but those in use during the period of exploration were still too small to give accurate readings. Toward the end of the sixteenth century, the Danish astronomer, Tycho Brahe (1546–1601), set a new standard for accuracy by constructing much larger instruments which greatly decreased the margin of error. The new instruments invented during the first half of the seventeenth century — the telescope and the microscope, the barometer and the thermometer, and the pendulum clock — advanced science by making it possible to see or to measure things which before could only be guessed at or which were beyond the reach of the unaided senses. It is worth noting, however, that these new instruments were themselves the products

of the scientific revolution, having been made possible by the application of newly discovered principles. It is a remarkable fact that many of the most important discoveries of this period were made without the instruments which modern scientists regard as indispensable.

Astronomy. The first great scientific discovery of the sixteenth century, the Copernican hypothesis which revolutionized astronomy, certainly falls within this category and bears out the thesis that the essential fact in the scientific revolution was a new way of looking at nature rather than more accurate observation. To appreciate the immense mental leap that Copernicus must have made to reach his hypothesis, one must bear in mind the conception of the universe held in western Europe since the introduction of Greek science in the High Middle Ages. It was a conception based

This painting of a Dutch geographer and map-maker by Jan Vermeer reminds us of the importance of maps in the century when the European nations were fighting for colonies and world trade.

on Aristotle's description of the cosmos, as revised and brought into closer relation to the observed movements of the planets by the Alexandrian astronomer Ptolemy, in the second century A.D., and as later given a Christian coloring by the medieval schoolmen. For the modern student the most vivid medieval description of the Ptolemaic system is to be found in Dante's *Divine Comedy.* According to this theory, the earth is a stationary sphere at the center of the universe, and about it the planets — the moon, Mercury, Venus, the sun, Mars, Jupiter, and Saturn — and beyond them the fixed stars move in a series of concentric circles. Aristotle assumed that each planet was carried at a uniform speed in a perfect circle by a crystalline sphere, which fitted into the sphere outside it. These spheres were moved about the earth by Intelligences, which the Christian philosophers translated into angelic spirits, and the whole apparatus received its initial movement from an invisible outer sphere called the Primum Mobile or first mover, beyond which Christian thought placed the motionless heaven which is the abode of God.

The heliocentric theory of Copernicus, an illustration from his book, Concerning the Revolutions of the Heavenly Bodies.

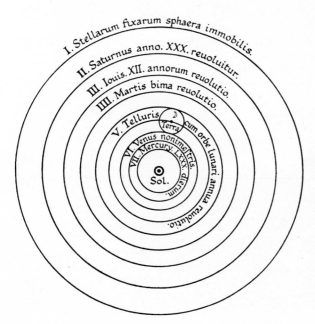

Even before Ptolemy's time, it became evident that this beautifully simple system did not fit all the observed movements of the planets. Ptolemy found it necessary to add epicycles to the spheres, i.e., to assume that the planets moved in a small cycle around a point fixed upon the moving sphere, and later observers were forced to add further epicycles, and even epicycles on the epicycles. By the sixteenth century the system required some eighty cycles in all. It was apparently a conviction that there must be some simpler way of accounting for the movements of the planets that led Copernicus to his epoch-making discovery.

Copernicus. Nicolaus Copernicus (1473–1543) was a Polish scholar of wide intellectual interests. During a ten-year stay in Italy, he studied medicine, mathematics, astronomy, and canon law, and then retired to a life of peaceful speculation in his native country as a canon in the cathedral at Frauenburg. Just when he hit upon the solution of the problem presented by the bewildering complexity of Ptolemaic epicycles is not certain. The results, at any rate, were published only after some thirty years of study in a book entitled *Concerning the Revolutions of the Heavenly Bodies,* which appeared just before his death in 1543. The whole approach of Copernicus to the problem was that of a mathematician. He made few independent observations and depended almost entirely on data already known, merely shuffling them about into new combinations. Although he may have profited by hints contained in the recently published works of ancient astronomers, his hypothesis was in fact an original creation, the first heliocentric system worked out in mathematical detail. Once having made the assumption that the sun is the center of the universe, about which all the planets including the earth revolve, and that the apparent revolution of the whole system about the earth is actually caused by the daily rotation of the earth on its own axis, he found that all the pieces of the gigantic puzzle fell into place. Or almost all of them, for, after rejecting so much of Aristotle, Copernicus still clung to the Aristotelian notion that all planetary motions must be circular, and so his theory did not in fact fit all the observed phenomena, nor could it be made to do so until it had been altered by Kepler's theory of elliptical motion.

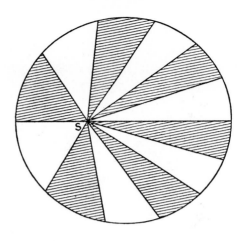

Kepler's first and second laws stated that (1) each planet moves about the sun in an ellipse of which the sun is one focus; and (2) the speed of a planet varies with its position in its orbit — faster when nearer the sun. If the shaded areas are equal, it will travel the outer edge of each in exactly the same time.

Kepler. It was not his errors, however, which were chiefly responsible for delaying the general acceptance of Copernicus' hypothesis. Other objections, quite reasonable in the light of the knowledge available at the time, prevented most scientists from accepting it until well into the seventeenth century as anything but a technique for facilitating calculation. Meanwhile, theologians rejected it as contrary to the teaching of the Bible, and ordinary folk as contrary to simple observation and common sense. New evidence gained by more accurate observation and new discoveries which tended to discredit the Aristotelian system in other sciences, however, worked in its favor, and in the long run the appeal of the Copernican system to the mathematically minded proved irresistible. Copernicus' cosmos was so much simpler than that of Ptolemy; could it not be made simpler still and could not the whole system of planetary motion be reduced to a mathematical formula? This was the dream which inspired the German astronomer, Johann Kepler (1571–1630), through years of arduous calculation. Kepler was aided by the improved instruments and systematic observations provided by Tycho Brahe and also by the advances made in mathematics since the death of Copernicus; but equally important was his conviction that the movements of the heavenly bodies *must* conform to mathematical order. His search for mathematical harmony in the universe led Kepler down many blind alleys before he discovered the three "laws" ever since connected with his name. The first is that the planets move about the sun in an ellipse, of which the sun is one focus. The second is that each planet moves more rapidly as the ellipse brings it closer to the sun, its relative speed being such that a line drawn from the sun to the planet would sweep equal areas in equal times. Ten years of further calculation led Kepler to his third law, published in 1619. Copernicus had noted that the planets near the sun revolved in a shorter time than those further away. Kepler now discovered that the squares of the periods of revolution of the planets are proportional to the cubes of their mean distance from the sun.

Galileo. While Kepler thus corrected and supported the Copernican hypothesis by discoveries in the realm of abstract mathematics, the brilliant Florentine scientist, Galileo Galilei (1564–1642), was bringing to the attention of the reading public new and more concrete evidence in its favor. Having constructed a telescope in 1609 that would magnify by thirty diameters, Galileo discovered many things in the heavens that could not be seen with the naked eye, and all were in accord with the Copernican system. His findings, communicated to the world in a readable book entitled *The Messenger of the Stars* (1610), did more to convince people than could any amount of abstruse mathematics. Theologians became alarmed, now that they could no longer ignore the possible truth of the Copernican hypothesis, and launched a campaign against it. Galileo was warned by the Inquisition in 1616 and again in 1633, after he had published a second work defending the Copernican system. Religious people resented the new theory, not only because it seemed contrary to the teaching of the Bible and the tradition of the church, but also because it removed the earth from the center of the universe, the place proper for it as the stage on which was enacted the divine drama of man's creation, fall, and redemption. In fairness to the theologians, it must be noted that the case for the Copernican hypothesis was not fully proven nor all the objections removed until the new system was completed by

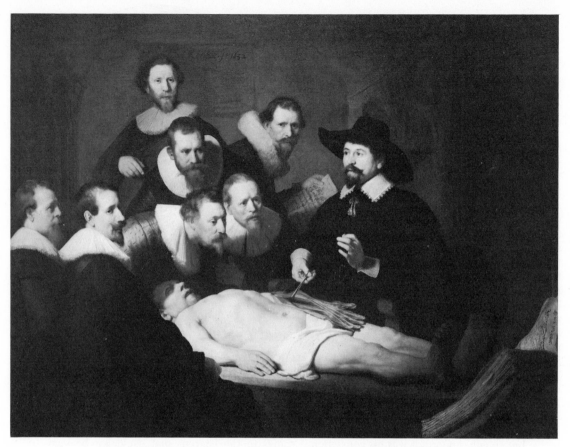

"The Anatomy Lesson," a striking picture by Rembrandt van Rijn, illustrates not only the Baroque style but also the scientific interests of the age.

Newton's discovery of the law of gravity toward the end of the seventeenth century.

Physics and chemistry. Though less shocking in their implications for the general public, the discoveries in the field of physics during this period were equally revolutionary and more numerous. The science of physics, which deals largely with the behavior of inanimate objects, was especially susceptible to the experimental and mathematical approach characteristic of the new science. It was in physics, too, that Aristotle's combination of inaccurate observation with explanation in terms of inherent qualities had led to the most numerous errors. Galileo was here the most important figure. To an unusual degree he combined the ability to set up mechanical experiments with the mental power to induce from them valid generalizations. The discoveries he made con-

cerning the motion of falling bodies, the oscillation of the pendulum, the theories governing mechanical action, and the cohesive power of solids were so numerous and of such fundamental importance that he may be said to have laid the foundation of modern physics. He was, however, but one, if the most brilliant, of the scientists who added to knowledge in this field in what has been called "the century of genius." The two Netherlanders, Simon Stevin and Christian Huygens (1629–95) made contributions to mechanics that were of great practical as well as theoretical value; Kepler and Descartes worked out the theories of the refraction of light; William Gilbert (1540–1603) laid the foundations for the study of magnetism; and there were many others. Compared with physics, chemistry made relatively little advance during this period. Aristotelian theories which explained the action of chemical elements by their inherent qualities and dispositions could not be easily overthrown without more accurate instruments than were yet available. Robert Boyle (1627–91), best known for his discovery that the volume of air varies inversely as the pressure imposed upon it, made important contributions to chemistry, but he was an isolated figure in the seventeenth century. The real revolution in chemistry was to come in the eighteenth century.

Biology and anatomy. In the biological sciences, the new interest in accurate observation and measurement produced few advances in theory, but much in the way of description and classification. During the sixteenth and seventeenth centuries, a number of encyclopedic books were published, with illustrations drawn by competent artists, describing and classifying thousands of species of plants and animals. This was work that had to be done before there could be any further advance in either botany or zoology. The combination of the scientist's observation with the artist's skill in portrayal also served the science of descriptive anatomy. In this field the most important contribution in the sixteenth century was made by Andreas Vesalius of Brussels (1514–64), whose book *On the Construction of the Human Body* (1543) was based on surgical dissection and illustrated with remarkably accurate drawings. Vesalius was willing to believe the evidence of his eyes, even when it contradicted the opinion of the Greek anatomist, Galen, but reverence for Galen was still strong enough

in the sixteenth century to be a real obstacle to further progress. Further progress, too, was almost impossible so long as anatomists had no understanding of the function of the heart or the circulation of the blood. This very basic problem was finally solved by William Harvey (1578–1657), who demonstrated in a book published in 1628 that the blood is pumped out of the heart through the arteries and returns through the veins in a constant circular motion.

Conclusion. By 1660, the scientific revolution had gained a momentum that could not be checked. And the achievements of science had already begun to attract the interest of educated people everywhere, though many people still found them disturbing in their implications. Revolutions are always disturbing, and those which overthrow men's long-established ideas are perhaps most disturbing of all. The Copernican picture of the universe was a shock not only to men's religious beliefs but also to their ideas about the world in which they lived. Kepler and Descartes, both profoundly religious men, believed that in demonstrating mathematical order throughout the universe they were glorifying the supreme rationality of God. But some men began to feel that there was no need for Divine Providence in a mechanical universe which operated like a gigantic clockwork. The full impact of the new science, however, was not felt until the eighteenth century, when it produced the broader "intellectual revolution" of the Age of Reason.

Appendixes

Genealogical Table

A List of European Rulers to the Middle
of the Seventeenth Century

Suggestions for Further Reading

Acknowledgments and Credits

GENEALOGICAL TABLE

*The Patrimony of Charles V, Showing the Ancestors
from whom he Inherited his Lands*

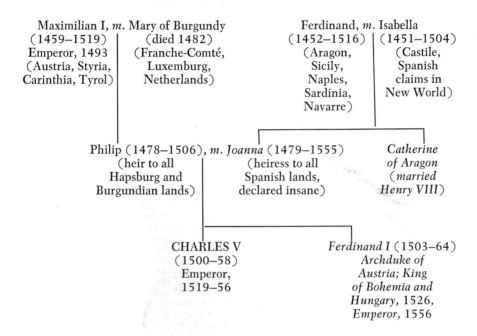

Maximilian I, *m.* Mary of Burgundy
(1459–1519) (died 1482)
Emperor, 1493 (Franche-Comté,
(Austria, Styria, Luxemburg,
Carinthia, Tyrol) Netherlands)

Ferdinand, *m.* Isabella
(1452–1516) (1451–1504)
(Aragon, (Castile,
Sicily, Spanish
Naples, claims in
Sardinia, New World)
Navarre)

Philip (1478–1506), *m. Joanna* (1479–1555)
(heir to all (heiress to all
Hapsburg and Spanish lands,
Burgundian lands) declared insane)

*Catherine
of Aragon
(married
Henry VIII)*

CHARLES V
(1500–58)
Emperor,
1519–56

Ferdinand I (1503–64)
*Archduke of
Austria; King
of Bohemia and
Hungary, 1526,
Emperor, 1556*

A LIST OF EUROPEAN RULERS

To the Middle of the Seventeenth Century

RULERS OF THE CAROLINGIAN FAMILY

Pepin of Heristal, Mayor of the Palace, 714
Charles Martel, Mayor of the Palace, 715–41
Pepin I, Mayor of the Palace, 741, King, 751–
68
Charlemagne, King, 768, Emperor, 800–14
Louis "the Pious," Emperor, 814–40

WEST FRANKISH KINGDOM

Charles "the Bald," King, 840–77, Emperor,
875
Louis II, King, 877–79
Louis III, King, 879–82
Carloman, King, 879–84

MIDDLE KINGDOMS

Lothair, Emperor, 840–55
Louis (Italy), Emperor, 855–75

Charles (Provence), King, 855–63
Lothair II (Lorraine), King, 855–69

EAST FRANKISH KINGDOM

Louis "the German," King, 840–76
Carloman, King, 876–80
Louis, King, 876–82
Charles "the Fat," Emperor, 876–87

EMPERORS OF THE HOLY ROMAN EMPIRE

SAXON EMPERORS
Otto I, King, 936, Emperor, 962–73
Otto II, 973–83
Otto III, 983–1002
Henry II, 1002–24
FRANCONIAN EMPERORS
Conrad II, 1024–39
Henry III, 1039–56

Henry IV, 1056–1106
Henry V, 1106–25
Lothair III (of Saxony), 1125–37

Hohenstaufen Emperors
Conrad III, 1138–52
Frederick I "Barbarossa," 1152–90
Henry VI, 1190–97
⎰ Philip of Swabia, 1198–1208
⎱ Otto IV (Welf), 1198–1215
Frederick II, 1211–50
Conrad IV, 1250–54

Interregnum, 1254–73

Emperors from Various Houses
Rudolf I (Hapsburg), 1273–91
Adolf (Nassau), 1292–98
Albert I (Hapsburg), 1298–1308
Henry VII (Luxemburg), 1308–13
Louis IV (Wittelsbach), 1314–47
Charles IV (Luxemburg), 1347–78
Wenceslas (Luxemburg), 1378–1400
Rupert (Wittelsbach), 1400–10
Sigismund (Luxemburg), 1410–37

Hapsburg Emperors
Albert II, 1438–39
Frederick III, 1440–93
Maximilian I, 1493–1519
Charles V, 1519–56
Ferdinand I, 1556–64
Maximilian II, 1564–76
Rudolf II, 1576–1612
Matthias, 1612–19
Ferdinand II, 1619–37
Ferdinand III, 1637–57
Leopold I, 1658–1705

HAPSBURG KINGS OF SPAIN

Charles V, 1516–56
Philip II, 1556–98
Philip III, 1598–1621
Philip IV, 1621–65

KINGS OF FRANCE FROM HUGH CAPET

Capetian Kings
Hugh Capet, 987–96
Robert II, 996–1031
Henry I, 1031–60
Philip I, 1060–1108
Louis VI, 1108–37
Louis VII, 1137–80
Philip II "Augustus," 1180–1223
Louis VIII, 1223–26
Louis IX (Saint Louis), 1226–70
Philip III, 1270–85
Philip IV "the Fair," 1285–1314

Louis X, 1314–16
Philip V, 1316–22
Charles IV, 1322–28

Valois Kings
Philip VI, 1328–50
John, 1350–64
Charles V, 1364–80
Charles VI, 1380–1422
Charles VII, 1422–61
Louis XI, 1461–83
Charles VIII, 1483–98
Louis XII, 1498–1515
Francis I, 1515–47
Henry II, 1547–59
Francis II, 1559–60
Charles IX, 1560–74
Henry III, 1574–89

Bourbon Kings
Henry IV, 1589–1610
Louis XIII, 1610–43
Louis XIV, 1643–1715

KINGS OF ENGLAND FROM THE NORMAN CONQUEST

Norman Kings
William I, 1066–87
William II, 1087–1100
Henry I, 1100–35
Stephen, 1135–54

Angevin Kings
Henry II, 1154–89
Richard I, 1189–99
John, 1199–1216
Henry III, 1216–72
Edward I, 1272–1307
Edward II, 1307–27
Edward III, 1327–77
Richard II, 1377–99

Lancastrian Kings
Henry IV, 1399–1413
Henry V, 1413–22
Henry VI, 1422–61

Yorkist Kings
Edward IV, 1461–83
Edward V, 1483
Richard III, 1483–85

Tudor Kings
Henry VII, 1485–1509
Henry VIII, 1509–47
Edward VI, 1547–53
Mary, 1553–58
Elizabeth I, 1558–1603

Stuart Kings
James I, 1603–25
Charles I, 1625–49

Interregnum, 1649–60

SUGGESTIONS FOR FURTHER READING

PART ONE

The first section includes basic reference works and texts dealing with major periods of history. More specialized studies are given under separate chapter headings. Although they have not generally been repeated, books suggested for one chapter frequently may be useful for other chapters as well.

Many of the books cited are available in paperbound editions. However, the rapid increase in the number of paperbound books makes it impracticable to attempt to indicate which titles have been published in paperbound form.

ANCIENT HISTORY

Cambridge Ancient History (1926–39)
W. E. Caldwell, The Ancient World (1947)
V. Scramuzza and P. MacKendrick, The Ancient World (1958)
C. Starr, A History of the Ancient World (1965)
C. Roebuck, The World of Ancient Times (1966)
A. A. Trevor, History of Ancient Civilization, 2 vols. (1936–39)
C. E. Van Sickle, A Political and Cultural History of the Ancient World (1947)
M. I. Rostovtzev, History of the Ancient World, 2 vols. (1926–28)
J. W. Swain, The Ancient World, 2 vols. (1950)

MEDIEVAL HISTORY

The Cambridge Medieval History, 8 vols. (1911–36)
Cambridge Economic History of Europe, 3 vols. (1941–63, Vol. I revised 1966)
R. S. Hoyt, Europe in the Middle Ages (1957)
C. Stephenson, Medieval History (1935)
S. Painter, A History of the Middle Ages (1953)
J. R. Strayer and D. C. Munro, The Middle Ages (1942)
H. A. L. Fisher, A History of Europe, Vol. I (1935)
R. W. Southern, The Making of the Middle Ages (1963)

J. L. La Monte, The World of the Middle Ages: a Reorientation of Medieval History (1949)
F. Heer, The Medieval World, 1100–1350 (1962)
C. Dawson, The Making of Europe (1932)
F. B. Artz, The Mind of the Middle Ages (1954)
H. O. Taylor, The Medieval Mind, 2 vols. (1925)
G. C. Crump and E. F. Jacob, eds., The Legacy of the Middle Ages (1926)

RENAISSANCE, REFORMATION, AND WARS OF RELIGION

New Cambridge Modern History, Vols. 1–2 (1957–58)
W. K. Ferguson, Europe in Transition, 1300–1520 (1962)
R. Ergang, The Renaissance (1967)
M. P. Gilmore, The World of Humanism (1952)
V. H. H. Green, Renaissance and Reformation (2d ed., 1964)
P. Smith, The Age of the Reformation (1920)
J. H. Thompson, Renaissance and Reformation (1962)
H. J. Grimm, The Reformation Era, 1500–1650 (1954)
D. Hay, The Fourteenth and Fifteenth Centuries (1966)

SOURCE BOOKS

P. J. Alexander, The Ancient World to A.D. 300 (1968)
N. F. Cantor, The Medieval World (1968)
G. R. Elton, Renaissance and Reformation, 1300–1648 (1968)
G. H. Knoles and R. K. Snyder, eds., Readings in Western Civilization (1954)
F. LeV. Baumer, Main Currents of Western Thought (1952)
K. M. Setton and H. R. Winkler, eds., Great Problems of European Civilization (1954)
T. C. Mendenhall, B. D. Henning, and A. S. Foord, Ideas and Institutions in European History, 800–1715 (1948)

J. B. Ross and M. M. McLaughlin, *The Portable Medieval Reader* (1949)

HISTORICAL ATLASES

W. R. Shepherd, *Historical Atlas* (rev. ed., 1956)

E. W. Fox, *Atlas of European History* (1957)

R. Muir and G. Philip, *Putnam's Historical Atlas* (1927)

INTRODUCTION

(1) The Study of History

T. R. Tholfsen, *Historical Thinking* (1967)

C. Becker, *Everyman His Own Historian* (1935)

R. G. Collingwood, *The Idea of History* (1946)

L. Gottschalk, *Understanding History* (1950)

————, ed., *Generalization in the Writing of History* (1963)

M. C. Bloch, *The Historian's Craft* (1953)

(2) The Prehistoric Background

W. W. Howells, *Mankind in the Making* (rev. ed., 1967)

————, *Back of History* (1954)

F. Boas, *The Mind of Primitive Man* (1938)

M. Burkitt, *Old Stone Age* (1963)

C. W. Ceram, *Gods, Graves, and Scholars* (1951)

V. G. Childe, *What Happened in History* (1954)

H. Movius, Jr., *Old World Prehistory* in A. L. Kroeber, ed., *Anthropology Today* (1953)

J. G. D. Clark, *Prehistoric Europe: The Economic Basis* (1952)

R. J. Braidwood, *Prehistoric Man* (1951)

1. THE ANCIENT MIDDLE EAST

R. J. Braidwood, *The Near East and the Foundations of Civilization* (1952)

G. Contenau, *Everyday Life in Babylon and Assyria* (1954)

H. W. F. Saggs, *The Greatness that was Babylon* (1966)

A. T. Olmstead, *History of Assyria* (1923)

P. Montet, *Everyday Life in Egypt in the Days of Ramses the Great* (1958)

H. Frankfort, *Kingship and the Gods* (1949)

W. C. Hayes, *The Scepter of Egypt* (1953)

G. Steindorff and K. C. Seele, *When Egypt ruled the East* (1942)

J. A. Wilson, *The Culture of Ancient Egypt* (1956)

H. E. Winlock, *The Rise and Fall of the Middle Kingdom in Thebes* (1947)

J. Černý, *Ancient Egyptian Religion* (1952)

B. L. Ullman, *Ancient Writing and its Influence* (1932)

O. Neugebauer, *The Exact Sciences of Antiquity* (1952)

P. K. Hitti, *History of Syria* (1951)

H. J. Kantor, *The Aegean and the Orient in the Second Millennium B.C.* (1947)

O. R. Gurney, *The Hittites* (1952)

H. M. Orlinsky, *Ancient Israel* (1954)

SOURCES:

J. B. Pritchard, ed., *Ancient Near Eastern Texts relating to the Old Testament* (1950)

2. ANCIENT GREECE

H. N. Couch, *Classical Civilization: Greece* (2d ed., 1951)

H. D. F. Kitto, *The Greeks* (1951)

S. Barr, *The Will of Zeus* (1961)

G. W. Botsford, *Hellenic History* (1948)

M. Finley, *The World of Odysseus* (1954)

G. Glotz, *The Greek City and its Institutions* (1930)

————, *Ancient Greece at Work* (1926)

A. Andrewes, *The Greek Tyrants,* (1956)

H. Mitchell, *The Economics of Ancient Greece* (1940)

C. E. Robinson, *Everyday Life in Ancient Greece* (1933)

R. W. Livingston, ed., *The Legacy of Greece* (1922)

G. Murray, *Five Stages of Greek Religion* (1925)

B. Farrington, *Greek Science,* 2 vols. (1949)

SOURCES:

Good modern translations of all major Greek authors are available in the Penguin Classics.

3. THE HELLENISTIC AGE

M. Cary, *History of the Greek World from 323 to 146 B.C.* (1952)

M. I. Rostovtzev, *Social and Economic History of the Hellenistic World* (1941)

W. W. Tarn, *Hellenistic Civilization* (1952)

P. Jouguet, *Macedonian Imperialism and the Hellenization of the East* (1928)

A. J. Toynbee, *Hellenism: The History of a Civilization* (1959)
C. H. Robinson, *Alexander the Great* (1947)
W. W. Tarn, *Alexander the Great* (1948)

SOURCES:

W. J. Oates, *The Stoic and Epicurean Philosophers* (1940)

4. THE ROMAN REPUBLIC

R. H. Barrow, *The Romans* (1951)
L. P. Homo, *Roman Political Institutions from City to State* (1930)
F. B. Marsh, *A History of the Roman World from 146–30 B.C.* (1935)
H. Scullard, *From the Gracchi to Nero, a History of Rome from 133 B.C. to 68 A.D.* (2d ed., 1959)
T. Frank, *An Economic History of Rome* (1927)
J. Carcopino, *Daily Life in Ancient Rome* (1940)
F. E. Adcock, *The Roman Art of War under the Republic* (1940)
R. Syme, *The Roman Revolution* (1939)
D. Dudley, *The Civilization of Rome* (1960)
J. Whatmough, *The Foundations of Roman Italy* (1937)
M. Hadas, *A History of Latin Literature* (1952)

SOURCES:

N. Lewis and M. Reinhold, *Roman Civilization* (1951)
Good modern translations of all major Latin authors are available in the Penguin Classics.

5. THE ROMAN WORLD IN THE FIRST TWO CENTURIES OF THE EMPIRE

M. P. Charlesworth, *The Roman Empire* (1951)
M. Hammond, *City State and World State* (1951)
M. Grant, *The World of Rome* (1960)
E. M. Salmon, *A History of the Ancient World from 30 B.C. to A.D. 138* (1945)
C. Starr, *Civilization and the Caesars* (1965)
M. I. Rostovtzev, *Social and Economic History of the Roman Empire* (1926)
S. Dill, *Roman Society from Nero to Marcus Aurelius* (1920)

M. P. Charlesworth, *Trade Routes and Commerce of the Roman Empire* (1924)
C. Bailey, ed., *The Legacy of Rome* (1924)
J. W. Duff, *Literary History of Rome from the Origins to the Close of the Golden Age* (1928)
———, *Literary History of Rome in the Silver Age* (1930)

FICTION:

M. Yourcenar, *Hadrian's Memoirs* (1954)

6. DECLINE OF THE ROMAN EMPIRE

S. Katz, *The Decline of Rome and the Rise of Medieval Europe* (1955)
F. Lot, *The End of the Ancient World and the Beginning of the Middle Ages* (1931)
S. Dill, *Roman Society in the Last Century of the Western Empire* (2d ed., 1925)
A. H. M. Jones, The Later Roman Empire, 2 vols. (1964)
———, *The Decline of the Ancient World* (1966)
W. W. Fowler, *The Religious Experience of the Roman People* (1911)
C. Starr, *The Emergence of Rome as the Ruler of the Western World* (2d ed., 1953)

SOURCES:

Ammianus Marcellinus, *Roman History,* trans. by J. C. Rolfe, 3 vols. (Loeb Classical Library, 1925–39)

7. THE CHRISTIAN CHURCH IN THE ROMAN EMPIRE

K. Latourette, *History of Christianity* (1953)
C. T. Craig, *Beginnings of Christianity* (1943)
J. Lebreton and J. Zeiller, *A History of the Christian Church* (1949)
R. H. Bainton, *Early and Medieval Christianity* (1962)
T. R. Glover, *The Conflict of Religions in the Early Roman Empire* (1960)
J. Lebreton and J. Zeiller, *A History of the Church* (1938)
E. R. Goodenough, *The Church in the Roman Empire* (1931)
M. Burrows, *The Dead Sea Scrolls* (1955)
C. N. Cochrane, *Christianity and Classical Culture* (1940)
M. L. W. Laistner, *Christianity and Pagan Culture in the Later Roman Empire* (1951)

H. B. Workman, *Evolution of the Monastic Ideal* (1913)

J. Chapman, *St. Benedict and the Sixth Century* (1929)

M. A. Schroll, *Benedictine Monasticism with Commentaries on the Rule* (1941)

SOURCES:

St. Augustine, *The Confessions* (Modern Library, 1949)

H. S. Bettenson, *Documents of the Christian Church* (1947)

8. THE BARBARIAN INVASION OF THE EMPIRE

J. B. Bury, *The Invasions of Europe by the Barbarians* (1928)

F. Lot, *The End of the Ancient World and the Beginning of the Middle Ages* (1931)

E. S. Duckett, *The Gateway to the Middle Ages* (1938)

H. S. B. Moss, *The Birth of the Middle Ages* (1935)

H. M. Barrett, *Boethius* (1940)

SOURCES:

Boethius, *The Consolation of Philosophy* (numerous editions)

Tacitus, *On Britain and Germany,* trans. by H. Mattingly (Penguin Classics, 1957)

Jordanes, *Origins and Deeds of the Goths,* trans. by C. C. Mierow (1915)

9. THE EASTERN EMPIRE BECOMES BYZANTINE

A. A. Vasiliev, *History of the Byzantine Empire* (1952)

N. H. Baynes and H. B. Moss, *Byzantium* (1948)

J. B. Bury, *History of the Later Roman Empire,* 2 vols. (1923)

C. Diehl, *Byzantium; Greatness and Decline* (1957)

R. Jenkins, *Byzantium: The Imperial Centuries, A.D. 610–1071* (1966)

G. Ostrogorsky, *History of the Byzantine State* (1957)

J. M. Hussey, *The Byzantine World* (rev. ed., 1961)

A. Grabar, *Byzantine Painting* (1953)

S. Runciman, *Byzantine Civilization* (1933)

P. N. Ure, *Justinian and His Age* (1951)

FICTION:

R. Graves, *Count Belisarius* (1936)

10. THE RISE OF ISLAM AND THE EXPANSION OF THE MOSLEM EMPIRE

B. Lewis, *The Arabs in History* (1950)

C. Brockelmann, *History of the Islamic Peoples* (1947)

P. K. Hitti, *History of the Arabs* (1951)

T. W. Arnold, ed., *The Legacy of Islam* (1931)

A. J. Wensinck, *The Muslim Creed* (1932)

G. E. von Grunebaum, *Medieval Islam: A Study in Cultural Orientation* (1946)

H. A. H. Gibb, *Mohammedanism: An Historical Survey* (1953)

R. A. Nicholson, *A Literary History of the Arabs* (1930)

T. Andrae, *Mohammed* (1936)

E. Dermenghem, *Life of Mohammed* (1930)

SOURCES:

The Koran (numerous editions)

J. Campbell, ed., *Portable Arabian Nights* (1952)

11. THE FRANKS, THE LOMBARDS, AND THE PAPACY

F. Lot, *The End of the Ancient World and the Beginning of the Middle Ages* (1931)

S. Dill, *Roman Society in Gaul in the Merovingian Age* (1926)

J. M. Wallace-Haddrill, *The Barbarian West, 400–1000* (1961)

E. K. Rand, *The Founders of the Middle Ages* (1928)

M. L. W. Laistner, *Thought and Letters in Western Europe, A.D. 500–900* (1931)

H. O. Taylor, *The Classical Heritage of the Middle Ages* (1901)

J. Chapman, *Studies in the Early Papacy* (1928)

P. Batiffol, *Saint Gregory the Great* (1929)

SOURCES:

Gregory of Tours, *History of the Franks,* ed. D. M. Dalton (1927)

The Venerable Bede, *The Ecclesiastical History of the English People*

12. THE CAROLINGIAN EMPIRE AND THE NORTHMEN

H. Pirenne, *Mohammed and Charlemagne* (1939)

H. Fichtenau, *The Carolingian Empire: the Age of Charlemagne* (1957)

M. W. Williams, *Social Scandinavia in the Viking Age* (1920)

H. Arbman, *The Vikings* (1961)

P. H. Sawyer, *The Age of the Vikings* (1961)

E. S. Duckett, *Alcuin, Friend of Charlemagne* (1951)

————, *Alfred the Great* (1962)

R. Winston, *Charlemagne: From the Hammer to the Cross* (1954)

SOURCES:

Einhard, *Life of Charlemagne,* trans. by S. E. Turner (1880)

13. THE FEUDAL SYSTEM

F. L. Ganshof, *Feudalism* (3d ed., 1965)

C. Stephenson, *Medieval Feudalism* (1942)

M. Bloch, *Feudal Society* (1961)

S. Painter, *Studies in the History of the English Feudal Barony* (1943)

C. E. Odegaard, *Vassi and Fidèles in the Carolingian Empire* (1945)

P. Boissonade, *Life and Work in Medieval Europe* (1927)

G. G. Coulton, *The Medieval Village* (1926)

N. S. B. Gras, *A History of Agriculture* (1925)

H. S. Bennett, *Life on the English Manor* (1937)

14. THE FOUNDING OF THE FEUDAL KINGDOMS AND THE REVIVAL OF THE EMPIRE

C. Brooke, *Europe in the Central Middle Ages, 962–1154* (1964)

J. R. M. MacDonald, *History of France* (1915)

F. M. Stenton, *Anglo-Saxon England* (rev. ed., 1961)

P. H. Blair, *An Introduction to Anglo-Saxon England* (1956)

J. Bryce, *The Holy Roman Empire* (1886)

G. Barraclough, *Medieval Germany,* 2 vols. (1948)

C. H. Haskins, *The Normans in European History* (1915)

FICTION:

H. Muntz, *The Golden Warrior* (1949)

15. THE STRUGGLE BETWEEN THE EMPIRE AND THE PAPACY

G. Barraclough, *Origins of Modern Germany* (1946)

T. F. Tout, *The Empire and the Papacy* (1898)

F. W. Butler, *The Lombard Communes* (1906)

A. J. MacDonald, *Hildebrand, a Life of Gregory VII* (1932)

E. Kantorowicz, *Frederick the Second* (1931)

A. L. Poole, *Henry the Lion* (1912)

SOURCES:

Otto of Freising, *Deeds of Frederick Barbarossa*

16. THE GROWTH OF THE MONARCHIES IN FRANCE AND ENGLAND

C. Petit-Dutaillis, *Feudal Monarchy in France and England* (1936)

M. L. Labarge, *Louis IX* (1968)

A. Luchaire, *Social France in the Time of Philip Augustus* (1929; new ed., 1957)

R. Fawtier, *The Capetian Kings of France; Monarchy and Nation* (1960)

F. M. Stenton, *The First Century of English Feudalism* (1932)

A. L. Poole, *From Domesday Book to Magna Carta* (1951)

M. Powicke, *The Thirteenth Century* (1953)

B. D. Lyon, *A Constitutional and Legal History of Medieval England* (1960)

G. O. Sayles, *The Medieval Foundations of England* (1948)

F. Barlow, *William I and the Norman Conquest* (1965)

————, *The Feudal Kingdom of England, 1042–1216* (1955)

D. C. Douglas, *William the Conqueror: The Norman Impact upon England* (1964)

J. E. A. Jolliffe, *The Constitutional History of Medieval England* (1954)

C. H. Haskins, *Norman Institutions* (1918)

D. M. Stenton, *English Society in the Early Middle Ages, 1066–1307* (1951)

S. Painter, *The Reign of King John* (1949)

————, *William Marshal* (1933)

A. Kelly, *Eleanor of Aquitaine* (1950)

17. THE CRUSADES AND THE EXPANSION OF CATHOLIC EUROPE

S. Runciman, *A History of the Crusades,* 3 vols. (1951–54)

J. L. La Monte, *Feudal Monarchy in the Latin Kingdom of Jerusalem* (1932)

A. S. Atiya, *The Crusade in the Later Middle Ages* (1938)

————, *Crusade, Commerce and Culture* (1962)

K. M. Setton, ed., *A History of the Crusades,* Vol. I, *The First Hundred Years* (1955)

D. C. Munro, *The Kingdom of the Crusaders* (1936)

R. A. Newhall, *The Crusades* (1927)

A. C. Krey, *The First Crusade, the Accounts of Eye-witnesses and Participants* (1921)

SOURCES:

Fulcher of Chartres, *Chronicle of the First Crusade,* trans. by M. E. McGinty (1941)

William of Tyre, *A History of Deeds done beyond the Sea,* trans. by E. A. Babcock and A. C. Krey, 2 vols. (1943)

Villehardouin and de Joinville, *Memoirs of the Crusades,* trans. by F. T. Marzials (Everyman's Library, 1908)

18. FEUDAL SOCIETY — THE PEASANTS AND THE NOBLES

M. Bloch, *Feudal Society* (1961)

————, *Land and Work in Medieval Europe* (1967)

B. D. Lyon, *From Fief to Indenture* (1957)

U. T. Holmes, *Daily Living in the Twelfth Century* (1952)

S. Painter, *Medieval Society* (1951)

————, *French Chivalry* (1940)

G. G. Coulton, *Medieval Panorama* (1938)

G. C. Homans, *English Villagers of the Thirteenth Century* (1940)

H. S. Bennett, *Life on the English Manor* (1937)

E. Power, *Medieval People* (1924)

J. Evans, *Life in Medieval France* (rev. ed., 1957)

M. W. Labarge, *A Baronial Household of the Thirteenth Century* (1966)

W. S. Davis, *Life on a Medieval Barony* (1923)

A. L. Poole, *Obligations of Society in the xii and xiii Centuries* (1946)

L. White, *Medieval Technology and Social Change* (1962)

SOURCES:

C. W. Jones, ed., *Medieval Literature in Translation* (1950)

19. THE CITIES AND THE MIDDLE CLASS — COMMERCE AND INDUSTRY

H. Heaton, *Economic History of Europe* (1936)

H. Pirenne, *Economic and Social History of Medieval Europe* (1937)

————, *Medieval Cities* (1925)

P. Boissonade, *Life and Work in Medieval Europe* (1927)

E. M. Carus-Wilson, *Medieval Merchant Venturers* (1954)

L. F. Salzman, *English Industries in the Middle Ages* (1923)

————, *English Trade in the Middle Ages* (1931)

E. Lipson, *The Economic History of England,* Vol. I, *The Middle Ages* (1929)

J. Tait, *The Medieval English Borough* (1936)

C. Stephenson, *Borough and Town, a Study of Urban Origins in England* (1933)

B. N. Nelson, *The Idea of Usury* (1949)

G. Renaud, *Guilds in the Middle Ages* (1918)

SOURCES:

R. S. Lopez and I. W. Raymond, eds., *Medieval Trade in the Mediterranean World. Illustrative Documents* (1955)

20. THE CHURCH, RELIGION, AND CULTURE

M. W. Baldwin, *The Medieval Church* (1964)

J. R. Moorman, *Church Life in England in the Thirteenth Century* (1945)

G. G. Coulton, *Five Centuries of Religion,* 4 vols. (1929–50)

E. Power, *Medieval English Nunneries* (1922)

D. Knowles, *The Monastic Orders in England* (1940)

————, *The Religious Orders in England,* 2 vols. (1948–55)

C. H. Haskins, *The Rise of the Universities* (1923)

————, *The Renaissance of the Twelfth Century* (1927)

H. Rashdall, *The Universities of Europe in the Middle Ages,* 3 vols. (1936)

H. Wieruszowski, *The Medieval University* (1966)

L. J. Daly, *The Medieval University* (1961)

D. Knowles, *Evolution of Medieval Thought* (1962)

M. H. Carré, *Phases of Thought in England* (1949)

———, *Realists and Nominalists* (1946)

E. Gilson, *The Spirit of Medieval Philosophy* (2d ed., 1950)

———, *Reason and Revelation in the Middle Ages* (1938)

G. Leff, *Medieval Thought from St. Augustine to Ockham* (1958)

P. Sabatier, *Life of Saint Francis of Assisi* (1922)

H. Waddell, *The Wandering Scholars* (rev. ed., 1934)

———, *Peter Abelard* (1959)

E. Panofsky, *Gothic Architecture and Scholasticism* (1951)

N. Pevsner, *An Outline of Medieval Architecture* (7th ed., 1963)

P. H. Láng, *Music in Western Civilization* (1941)

SOURCES:

R. L. Poole, *Illustrations of the History of Medieval Thought and Learning* (1920)

21. GERMANY AND EASTERN EUROPE

R. Lodge, *The Close of the Middle Ages* (1924)

W. T. Waugh, *A History of Europe from 1378 to 1494* (1932)

G. Barraclough, *The Origins of Modern Germany* (1947)

W. Stubbs, *Germany in the Later Middle Ages* (1908)

V. Valentin, *The German People* (1946)

J. Curtin, *The Mongols* (1908)

G. Vernadsky, *The Mongols and Russia* (1953)

S. Runciman, *The Fall of Constantinople, 1453* (1965)

P. Wittek, *Rise of the Ottoman Empire* (1931)

22. FRANCE AND ENGLAND TO THE END OF THE HUNDRED YEARS' WAR

W. E. Lunt, *History of England* (1946)

M. McKisack, *The Fourteenth Century, 1307–1399* (1959)

E. F. Jacob, *The Fourteenth Century, 1399–1485* (1961)

S. B. Chrimes, *Introduction to the Administrative History of Medieval England* (1952)

A. R. Myers, *England in the Late Middle Ages* (1952)

B. Wilkinson, *Constitutional History of Medieval England,* 2 vols. (1948–52)

J. L. A. Calmette, *The Golden Age of Burgundy* (1963)

R. Vaughan, *John the Fearless: the Growth of Burgundian Power* (1966)

E. Perroy, *The Hundred Years' War* (1951)

A. A. Burne, *The Crécy War* (1955)

———, *The Agincourt War* (1956)

V. Sackville-West, *Saint Joan of Arc* (1948)

J. Froissart, *Chronicles* (Everyman's Library, 1906)

FICTION:

A. Conan Doyle, *The White Company* (numerous editions)

23. THE DECLINE OF THE PAPACY IN THE LATER MIDDLE AGES

E. Binns, *History of the Decline and Fall of the Medieval Papacy* (1934)

W. Ulmann, *The Origins of the Great Schism* (1948)

G. Mollat, *The Popes at Avignon, 1305–1378* (1963)

P. Hughes, *A History of the Church,* Vol. III (1947)

W. A. Pantin, *The English Church in the Fourteenth Century* (1955)

W. E. Lunt, *Papal Revenues in the Middle Ages,* 2 vols. (1934)

G. Barraclough, *Papal Revenues* (1935)

A. H. Thompson, *The English Clergy and their Organization in the Later Middle Ages* (1947)

G. Leff, *Heresy in the Later Middle Ages,* 2 vols. (1967)

G. M. Trevelyan, *England in the Age of Wyclif* (1925)

B. L. Manning, *The People's Faith in the Time of Wyclif* (1919)

H. Kaminsky, *A History of the Hussite Rebellion* (1957)

K. B. McFarlane, *John Wycliffe and the Beginning of English Nonconformity* (1952)

C. H. McIlwain, *The Growth of Political Thought in the West* (1932)

24. MEDIEVAL ECONOMY IN TRANSITION

H. Heaton, *Economic History of Europe* (1936)

C. M. Cipolla, *Money, Prices and Civilization in Mediterranean Europe* (1956)

F. C. Lane, *Venetian Ships and Shipbuilding of the Renaissance* (1934)

———, *Andrea Barbarigo, Merchant of Venice, 1418–44* (1945)

I. Origo, *The Merchant of Prato* (1957)

R. de Roover, *Money, Banking, and Credit in Medieval Bruges* (1948)

———, *The Rise and Decline of the Medici Bank* (1963)

A. P. Usher, *The Early Days of Deposit Banking in Mediterranean Europe* (1943)

R. Ehrenberg, *Capital and Finance in the Age of the Fuggers* (1928)

E. Power and M. M. Postan, *Studies in English Trade in the Fifteenth Century* (1933)

E. Power, *The Wool Trade in English Medieval History* (1941)

S. Thrupp, *The Merchant Class of Medieval London* (1948)

25. THE AGE OF THE RENAISSANCE IN ITALY

J. Burckhardt, *The Civilization of the Renaissance in Italy* (numerous editions)

D. Hay, *The Italian Renaissance in its Historical Background* (1961)

E. P. Cheyney, *The Dawn of a New Era* (1936)

W. K. Ferguson, *The Renaissance in Historical Thought* (1948)

———, *The Renaissance* (1940)

D. Waley, *Medieval Orvieto, the Political History of an Italian State* (1952)

F. Schevill, *History of Florence* (1936)

G. A. Brucker, *Florentine Politics and Society, 1343–78* (1962)

L. Martines, *The Social World of the Florentine Humanists 1390–1460* (1963)

———, *Lawyers and Statecraft in Renaissance Florence* (1968)

P. Muir, *History of Milan under the Visconti* (1924)

L. Collison-Morley, *The Story of the Sforzas* (1933)

D. Herlihy, *Pisa in the Early Renaissance* (1958)

F. Chabod, *Machiavelli and the Renaissance* (1958)

F. Gilbert, *Machiavelli and Guicciardini* (1965)

H. Butterfield, *The Statecraft of Machiavelli* (1940)

P. O. Kristeller, *The Philosophy of Marsilio Ficino* (1943)

L. Olschki, *The Genius of Italy* (1949)

J. H. Plumb, *The Penguin Book of the Renaissance* (1964)

B. Berenson, *The Italian Painters of the Renaissance* (1930)

SOURCES:

N. Machiavelli, *The Prince* (numerous editions)

B. Castiglione, *The Book of the Courtier,* trans. by L. E. Opdycke (1901)

Vespasiano, *Renaissance Princes, Popes and Prelates* (1963)

H. H. Blanchard, *Prose and Poetry of the Continental Renaissance in Translation* (1949)

FICTION:

S. Shellabarger, *The Prince of Foxes* (1947)

26. THE WANING OF THE MIDDLE AGES AND THE RENAISSANCE IN THE NORTH

J. Huizinga, *The Waning of the Middle Ages* (1924)

H. S. Bennett, *The Pastons and their England* (1951)

H. M. Smith, *Pre-Reformation England* (1941)

G. M. Trevelyan, *English Social History,* Vol. I (1949)

R. L. Kilgour, *The Decline of Chivalry* (1937)

A. Hyma, *The Christian Renaissance* (1925)

M. M. Phillips, *Erasmus and the Northern Renaissance* (1950)

P. Smith, *Erasmus* (1923)

W. E. Campbell, *Erasmus, Tyndale, and More* (1949)

R. Weiss, *Humanism in England During the Fifteenth Century* (1941)

R. W. Chambers, *Thomas More* (1935)

J. H. Hexter, *More's Utopia* (1952)

E. P. Goldsmith, *The Printed Book of the Renaissance* (1950)

A. Hyma, *The Brethren of the Common Life* (1950)

E. Panofsky, *Early Flemish Painting* (1952)

P. H. Láng, *Music in Western Civilization* (1941)

G. Reese, *Music in the Renaissance* (1954)

SOURCES:

Erasmus, *The Praise of Folly* (numerous editions)

T. More, *Utopia* (numerous editions)

Thomas à Kempis, *The Imitation of Christ* (World's Classics, 1903)

27. THE STATES OF EUROPE AT THE DAWN OF THE MODERN AGE

W. T. Waugh, *A History of Europe from 1378–1494* (1932)

R. B. Merriman, *The Rise of the Spanish Empire*, Vols. I and II (1918)

A. Castro, *The Structure of Spanish History* (1954)

J. S. C. Bridge, *History of France from the Death of Louis XI*, 4 vols. (1921–29)

J. R. Lander, *The Wars of the Roses* (1965)

P. M. Kendall, *The Yorkist Age* (1962)

A. R. Myers, *England in the Late Middle Ages* (1952)

J. N. L. Baker, *A History of Geographical Discovery and Exploration* (1931)

J. E. Gillespie, *A History of Geographical Discovery* (1933)

A. P. Newton, ed., *The Great Age of Discovery* (1932)

S. E. Morison, *Admiral of the Ocean Sea: A Life of Christopher Columbus*, 2 vols. (1942)

E. Sanceau, *Henry the Navigator* (1947)

FICTION:

S. Shellabarger, *Captain of Castile* (1945)

28. THE REFORMATION AND THE FOUNDING OF THE PROTESTANT CHURCHES

H. J. Grimm, *The Reformation Era, 1500–1650* (1954)

G. R. Elton, *Reformation Europe, 1517–59* (1963)

G. L. Mosse, *The Reformation* (1953)

R. H. Bainton, *The Reformation of the Sixteenth Century* (1952)

T. M. Parker, *The English Reformation to 1558* (1950)

J. Lartz, *How the Reformation Came* (1964)

G. H. Williams, *The Radical Reformation* (1962)

P. Hughes, *The Reformation in England*, 2 vols. (1951–54)

O. Chadwick, *The Reformation* (1964)

M. H. Smith, *Henry VIII and the Reformation* (1948)

J. Ridley, *Thomas Cranmer* (1962)

R. Smithson, *The Anabaptists* (1935)

R. H. Bainton, *Here I Stand: A Life of Martin Luther* (1950)

H. Holborn, *Ulrich von Hutten and the German Reformation* (1937)

J. Rilliet, *Zwingli, Third Man of the Reformation* (1964)

F. Hildebrandt, *Melanchthon: Alien or Ally* (1946)

J. T. McNeill, *The History and Character of Calvinism* (1954)

G. Harkness, *John Calvin, the Man and his Ethics* (1931)

F. Wendel, *Calvin, the Origins and Development of his Religious Thought* (1963)

G. Mattingly, *Catherine of Aragon* (1941)

SOURCES:

P. Smith, *Luther's Correspondence*, 2 vols. (1913–18)

B. L. Woolf, *Reformation Writings of Martin Luther* (1953)

R. H. Bainton, *The Martin Luther Christmas Book* (1948)

29. THE STATES OF EUROPE IN THE AGE OF CHARLES V

A. J. Grant, *A History of Europe from 1494 to 1610* (5th ed., 1957)

J. H. Elliot, *Imperial Spain, 1469–1716* (1964)

R. B. Merriman, *The Rise of the Spanish Empire*, Vol. II (1918)

B. Chudoba, *Spain and the Empire* (1952)

R. T. Davies, *The Golden Century of Spain* (1937)

W. L. McElwee, *The Reign of Charles V* (1936)

J. R. M. MacDonald, *History of France* (1915)

J. R. Major, *Representative Institutions in Renaissance France* (1960)

G. R. Elton, *England Under the Tudors* (1955)

———, *The Tudor Revolution in Government* (1953)

S. T. Bindoff, *Tudor England* (1950)

J. D. Mackie, *The Earlier Tudors* (1952)

C. Morris, *The Tudors* (1957)

R. B. Wernham, *Before the Armada: The Emergence of the English Nation, 1485–1588* (1966)

W. G. Zeeveldt, *Foundations of Tudor Policy* (1948)

J. J. Scarisbrick, *Henry VIII* (1968)

K. Brandi, *The Emperor Charles V* (1939)

H. Holborn, *A History of Modern Germany*, Vol. I (1959)

30. THE CATHOLIC OR COUNTER-REFORMATION

H. Daniel-Rops, *The Catholic Reformation* (1962)

B. J. Kidd, *The Counter-Reformation* (1933)

P. Janelle, *The Catholic Reformation* (1949)

H. Jadin, *A History of the Council of Trent*, 2 vols. (1957–60)

Fr. Cuthbert Hess, *The Capuchins*, 2 vols. (1939)

J. Broderick, *The Origins of the Jesuits* (1940)

M. P. Harney, *The Jesuits in History* (1941)

Fr. P. Dudon, *St. Ignatius Loyola* (1950)

P. Van Dyke, *Ignatius Loyola, the Founder of the Jesuits* (1926)

F. S. Betten, *The Roman Index of Forbidden Books* (1935)

A. S. Turberville, *The Spanish Inquisition* (1932)

SOURCES:

J. F. X. O'Connor, ed., *The Autobiography of Saint Ignatius* (1900)

H. J. Schroeder, ed., *Decrees of the Council of Trent* (1941)

31. THE STATES OF EUROPE IN THE AGE OF PHILIP II

C. J. Cadoux, *Philip of Spain and the Netherlands* (1947)

P. Geyl, *The Revolt of the Netherlands* (rev. ed., 1962)

C. Petrie, *Philip II* (1963)

C. V. Wedgwood, *William the Silent* (1944)

J. E. Neale, *The Age of Catherine de Medici* (1943)

F. C. Palm, *Calvinism and the Religious Wars* (1932)

O. Zoff, *The Huguenots* (1942)

J. B. Black, *The Reign of Elizabeth* (2d ed., 1959)

A. L. Rowse, *The England of Elizabeth* (1951)

———, *The Expansion of Elizabethan England* (1955)

J. E. Neale, *Queen Elizabeth* (1934)

———, *The Elizabethan House of Commons* (1950)

———, *Elizabeth I and her Parliaments* (1953)

C. Read, *Mr. Secretary Cecil and Queen Elizabeth* (1955)

———, *Lord Burghley* (1960)

H. F. M. Prescott, *Mary Tudor* (1954)

W. Haller, *The Rise of Puritanism* (1939)

G. Mattingly, *Renaissance Diplomacy* (1955)

———, *The Armada* (1959)

32. THE ESTABLISHMENT OF ABSOLUTE MONARCHY IN FRANCE

New Cambridge Modern History, Vol. V (1961)

D. Maland, *Europe in the Seventeenth Century* (1966)

J. Lough, *Introduction to Seventeenth Century France* (1954)

J. Boulenger, *The Seventeenth Century* (1920)

J. B. Perkins, *Richelieu and the Growth of French Power* (1926)

C. Hugson, *Social France in the Seventeenth Century* (1911)

C. V. Wedgwood, *Richelieu and the French Monarchy* (1949)

A Bailly, *The Cardinal Dictator: A Portrait of Richelieu* (1936)

P. O. Doolin, *The Fronde* (1935)

33. THE DECLINE OF THE MONARCHY IN ENGLAND

G. M. Trevelyan, *England under the Stuarts* (1914)

M. Ashley, *England in the Seventeenth Century* (3d ed., 1961)

G. Davies, *The Early Stuarts* (1937)

C. V. Wedgwood, *The King's Peace, 1637–41* (1955)

———, *The King's War, 1641–47* (1958)

C. Hill, *The Century of Revolution* (1961)

———, *Puritanism and Revolution* (1958)

D. Mathew, *The Age of Charles I* (1951)

W. Notestein, *The Winning of the Initiative by the House of Commons* (1925)

J. H. Hexter, *The Reign of King Pym* (1941)

D. H. Willson, *King James VI and I* (1956)

C. V. Wedgwood, *Strafford* (1935)

———, *Oliver Cromwell* (1939)

M. James, *Social Problems and Policy during the Puritan Revolution* (1948)

SOURCES:

T. Carlyle, *Oliver Cromwell's Letters and Speeches*, 5 vols. (1871–72)

J. R. Tanner, *Constitutional Documents of the Reign of James I* (1930)

34. THE THIRTY YEARS' WAR

D. Ogg, *Europe in the Seventeenth Century* (1925)

C. V. Wedgwood, *The Thirty Years' War* (1939)

S. H. Steinberg, *The Thirty Years' War and the Conflict for European Hegemony* (1966)

H. Holborn, *A History of Modern Germany,* Vol. I (1959)

E. A. Beller, *Propaganda in Germany during the Thirty Years' War* (1940)

F. Watson, *Wallenstein* (1938)

M. Roberts, *Gustavus Adolphus* (1953)

35. THE COMMERCIAL REVOLUTION AND OVERSEAS EXPANSION

F. L. Nussbaum, *History of the Economic Institutions of Modern Europe* (1933)

L. B. Packard, *The Commercial Revolution* (1927)

N. S. B. Gras, *Business and Capitalism* (1939)

R. H. Tawney, *Religion and the Rise of Capitalism* (1926)

E. F. Hecksher, *Mercantilism*, 2 vols. (1935)

E. Lipson, *The Economic History of England,* Vols. II and III (1930–31)

E. J. Hamilton, *American Treasure and the Price Revolution in Spain* (1934)

J. B. Brebner, *Explorers of North America* (1933)

W. Notestein, *The English People on the Eve of Colonization* (1954)

W. C. Abbott, *The Expansion of Europe* (1938)

J. N. L. Baker, *A History of Geographical Discovery and Exploration* (1937)

J. H. Parry, *Europe and a Wider World, 1415–1715* (1949)

W. P. Webb, *The Great Frontier* (1952)

H. C. Herring, *A History of Latin America from the Beginning to the Present* (1955)

F. A. Kirkpatrick, *The Spanish Conquistadores* (1934)

W. Roscher, *The Spanish Colonial System* (1944)

L. B. Simpson, *The Encomienda in New Spain* (1950)

36. THE CULTURE OF THE EARLY MODERN PERIOD

P. Smith, *History of Modern Culture, Vol. I* (1930)

G. N. Clark, *The Seventeenth Century* (1931)

B. Willey, *The Seventeenth Century Background* (1953)

C. J. Friedrich, *The Age of the Baroque, 1610–1660* (1952)

J. W. Allen, *A History of Political Thought in the Sixteenth Century* (1928)

D. Bush, *The Renaissance and English Humanism* (1939)

L. B. Wright, *Middle Class Culture in Elizabethan England* (1935)

E. M. W. Tillyard, *The Elizabethan World Picture* (1944)

H. Butterfield, *The Origins of Modern Science* (1949)

C. Singer, *A Short History of Scientific Ideas to 1900* (1959)

H. T. Pledge, *Science since 1500* (1947)

A. Wolf, *A History of Science, Technology, and Philosophy in the 16th and 17th Centuries* (1951)

A. R. Hall, *The Scientific Revolution, 1500–1800* (1954)

A. C. Crombie, *Augustine to Galileo* (1952)

A. Castiglioni, *A History of Medicine* (1947)

A. Armitage, *Copernicus* (1938)

T. S. Kuhn, *The Copernican Revolution: Planetary Astronomy in the Development of Modern Thought* (1957)

ACKNOWLEDGMENTS AND CREDITS

Sources for Illustrations

xvii

Sources for Chapter-head Quotations

Chapter

1   James Henry Breasted, *Ancient Records of Egypt* (Chicago, 1906–27), III, 176.
2   Andrew R. Burn, *Pericles and Athens* (New York, 1949), p. 216.
3   Charles A. Robinson, Jr., "The Two Worlds of Alexander" in *Horizon,* I, No. 4 (March, 1959), 58.
4   Gaius Suetonius Tranquillus, "Julius Caesar," *Lives of the Twelve Caesars.* Quoted in Daniel G. McGarry and Clarence L. Hohl, Jr., *Sources of Western Civilization* (Boston, 1962), I, 45–46.
5   Suetonius, "Divus Augustus," *Lives of the Twelve Caesars.*
6   Marcus Aurelius Antoninus, *Meditations,* Book II. There are numerous editions and translations.
7   Saint Benedict of Nursia, *Regula Monachorum,* Chapter 48.
8   Flavius Magnus Aurelius Cassiodorus, *Variae,* Theodor Mommsen, ed., *Monumenta Germaniae Historica: Auctores Antiquissimi,* XII. Thomas Hodgkin edited an abridged English translation (London, 1886).
9   T. C. Sanders, *The Institutes of Justinian* (London, 1883), pp. 1–2.
10 The *Koran* (or *Quran*), Chapter (*Sura*) 4.
11 *Monumenta Germaniae Historica: Auctores Antiqui,* XI, 361. Quoted in Lynn White, *Medieval Technology and Social Change* (New York, 1962), p. 136.
12 Einhard, *Vita Caroli Magni,* Georg Heinrich Pertz and Georg Waitz, eds. (Hannover, 1896), p. 112.

13 S. H. Gem, *An Anglo-Saxon Abbot, Aelfric of Eynsham* (Edinburgh, 1912) includes the Colloquy, pp. 183–191. The passage may be found in Hutton Webster, *Historical Selections* (Boston, 1929), p. 614.

14 Alice J. Robertson, *The Laws of the Kings of England from Edmund to Henry I* (Cambridge, 1925), p. 239. Quoted in Webster, *Historical Selections*, p. 508.

15 J. W. Bowden, *The Life and Pontificate of Gregory the Seventh* (London, 1840), II, 108. Quoted in Webster, *Historical Selections*, p. 460.

16 Dana G. Munro and G. C. Sellery, *Medieval Civilization*, 2d ed. (New York, 1907), pp. 367–68. Quoted in Webster, *Historical Selections*, p. 520.

17 J. C. Morison, *The Life and Times of Saint Bernard*, 2d ed. (London, 1868), pp. 142–43. Quoted in Webster, *Historical Selections*, p. 481.

18 Achille Luchaire, *Social France at the Time of Philip Augustus* (New York, 1929), p. 254.

19 *Translations and Reprints from the Original Sources of European History* (Philadelphia, 1895), II, 7–8. Reprinted in Webster, *Historical Selections*, p. 552.

20 Saint Thomas Aquinas, *Summa Theologica*, I.

21 *Encyclopedia Britannica* (Chicago, 1965), IX, 824.

22 V. Sackville-West, *Saint Joan of Arc* (London, 1936), p. 134.

23 Pope Boniface VIII, *Unam Sanctam*, issued 18 November 1302.

24 Iris Origo, *The Merchant of Prato, Francisco di Marco Datini* (London, 1957), p. 114. Quoted in Wallace K. Ferguson, *Europe in Transition, 1300–1520* (Boston, 1962), p. 104.

25 James Harvey Robinson and Henry W. Rolfe, *Petrarch: The First Modern Scholar and Man of Letters. A Selection from his Correspondence.* Quoted in McGarry and Hohl, *Sources of Western Civilization*, I, 285.

26 Erasmus, *Enchiridion Militis Christiani.*

27 Niccolò Machiavelli, *The Prince*, Chapter XVIII. There are many editions.

28 Preserved Smith, *The Life and Letters of Martin Luther* (New York, 1911), p. 118.

29 *Oxford Dictionary of Quotations*, 2d ed., 4th Impression (New York, 1959), p. 136.

30 J. F. X. O'Connor, S.J., ed., *The Autobiography of St. Ignatius: The Account of His Life Dictated to Father Gonsález by St. Ignatius* (New York, 1900). Quoted in McGarry and Hohl, *Sources of Western Civilization*, I, 438.

31 Milton Waldman, *Queen Elizabeth* (London, 1952), p. 137.

32 Armand du Plessis, Cardinal Duc de Richelieu, *Testament politique*, Chapter 1. Quoted in Orthon Guerlac, ed., *Les Citations françaises: Recueil de Passages célèbres, Phrases familières, Mots historiques*, 2d ed. (Paris, 1933), p. 260.

33 *The Workes of the Most High and Mightie Prince, James . . . King of Great Britaine* (London, 1616), p. 529. Quoted in Stearns, *Pageant of Europe*, p. 216.

34 C. V. Wedgwood, *The Thirty Years' War* (New Haven, 1939), p. 513.

35 Willis F. Johnson, *Four Centuries of the Panama Canal* (New York, 1906), p. 29.

36 James Spedding, Robert L. Ellis, and Douglas Heath, eds., *The Works of Francis Bacon* (Boston, 1861), VIII, Aphorism 95.

Indexes

LIST OF MAPS

INDEX OF PLACE NAMES ON MAPS

GENERAL INDEX

Note: *Italic page numbers refer to illustrations*

Abbas, uncle of Mohammed, 126
Abbasids. *See* Caliphate, Abbasid
Abelard, Peter, 250, 253, 254
Absolutism: in the ancient world, 17–19, 23, 44, 63; in England, 201–202, 282–283, 414–415, 419–420, 421; in France, 197, 198, 272–273, 282, 286, 343–344, 406–413; in Spain, 341, 392–393
Abu Bakr, 123, 125, 126
Abu Simbel, temple of Ramses II at, *18*
Academy: Platonic, 320–321; French, 449
Acre, siege of (1191), 208
Acropolis, *10, 34,* 35
Acts of the Apostles, 85
Adelaide, Queen of Italy, 166
Aden, 130
Administration. *See* Government and administration
Adolf of Nassau, Holy Roman Emperor, 263
Adrian I, Pope, 142
Adrian IV, Pope, 181
Adrianople, battle of (378), 102
Adriatic Sea, 315
Aegean Islands, 30, 31
Aeneid, 71
Aeschylus, 36
Aëtius, 105, *106*
Africa, exploration of, 350–351
Africa, North: Carthaginian empire in, 53–54; Roman province of, 74–75, 87; Vandals invade, 103–104, 109; Justinian conquers, 114; Moslem expansion into, 126, 131; Turks conquer, 271
Agamemnon, 25
Agincourt, battle of (1415), 280, 283
Agriculture: prehistoric, 9; in the ancient world, 12–13, 16, 25, 26, 32, 44, 50–51, 55, 70, 74–75; early Germanic, 98, 100; manorial, 154–156, 214, 217, 307; in France, 408; capital in, 436–437; in the New World, 442. *See also* Tools
Akkad, 13
Alamanni, 100, 132
Alaric, 103
Albania, 270
Albert I, Holy Roman Emperor, 263
Albert II, Holy Roman Emperor, 265, 347
Albertus Magnus, Saint, 250
Albigenses, 210, 246–247. *See also* Crusade, Albigensian
Albret, Jeanne d', 398
Albuquerque, Alfonso de, 440
Alcuin of York, 144–145, 150
Alençon, Francis, Duke of, 401
Alessandria, 182
Alexander III, Pope, 182, 183, 190
Alexander V, Pope, 294
Alexander VI, Pope, 314, 317, 345, 353

Alexander of Hales, 250
Alexander the Great, 40–42
Alexandria, 44–45, 47, 72; patriarchate of, 91
Alexius Comnenus, Byzantine Emperor, 204–206
Alfonso II, King of Naples, 345
Alfred the Great, 150, 169
Ali, cousin of Mohammed, 123, 124, 126
Allah, 123
Alphabet: introduction of, 14; Phoenician, 22; Gothic, 101; Greek, 121. *See also* Writing
Alva, Fernando, Duke of, 377, 396
Ambrose, Saint, 92
Americas: North — Vikings reach, 148; exploration of, 351, 352, 443–444; Calvinism in, 366; Central — Spanish colonies in, 374, 441–443; South — Spanish colonies in, 441–443. *See also* Brazil; Canada, England, colonies of; Mexico; Peru; Portugal, colonies of; Spain, colonies of; Venezuela
Ammianus Marcellinus, 80, 93
Amorites, 13
Amsterdam, 435
Anabaptists, 363, 395
Anabasis, 38
Anagni, 289
Anatomy, *460, 461*
Angles, 100, 108
Anglican Church, 369, 401–403, 416, 420. *See also Book of Common Prayer*
Anglo-Saxon Chronicle, 148, 150
Anglo-Saxons, 108–109, 150
Anjou: county of, 169, 187, 189, 195, 198; House of, 189, 190, 317, 372
Anne, Duchess of Brittany, 344
Anne of Austria, Queen of France, 412
Anne of Beaujeu, 344
Anselm, Saint, 253
Anthony, Saint, 95
Anthony of Bourbon, King of Navarre, 398
Antigonus Gonatus, 42
Antilles, Greater, 351
Antioch: patriarchate of, 91; principality of, 206
Antiochus III, King of Syria, 54
Antiquity: classical, 119–120, 145, 166; Christian, 145, 333, 335; revival of, 270, 319–321, 333
Antwerp, 302, 306, 397, 435
Appian Way, *70*
Aquinas, Thomas, Saint, 250, 253, *253,* 254
Aquitaine: in the early Middle Ages, 134, 140, 142, 169; duchy of, 187, 188, 195, 197, 277
Arabia, 122–124, 126, 129
Arabian Nights, 128, 130
Arabs, 117, 122–131. *See also* Egypt; Moslems; Syria

Aragon: kingdom of, 212, 340, 347–348; House of, 317, 340, 345
Arcadius, Emperor, 103
Archimedes, 47
Architecture: Greek, *10,* 34–35, 73; Egyptian, 18; Minoan, 20; Roman, *60, 67, 68, 70,* 73, 80, *81, 82, 95;* Byzantine, *118,* 120–121, *144;* Moslem, *125,* 130; Romanesque, *144, 245,* 256; Gothic, *254, 256–257;* Renaissance, 325; Baroque, 452. *See also* Castles, medieval; Cathedrals; Churches
Argos, 32
Arianism, 89–91. *See also* Christianity, Arian
Ariosto, Ludovico, 322, 450
Aristocracy: Greek, 29; Roman, 50–51, 63, 68–69, 78, 79; feudal military, 152–153, 157–158. *See also* Lords; Nobles
Aristophanes, 37
Aristotle, 39; in the Middle Ages, 129, 252, 253; and the scientific revolution, 455, 458, 460
Arius, 89
Armagnac, Bernard, Count of, 280
Armor, medieval, *205, 223–224, 279*
Army: Roman, 76, 77; New Model, 422–423. *See also* War; Warfare, feudal; Wars
Arnold of Brescia, 181
Arnulf, King of Germany, 149
Arras, Treaty of (1579), 397
Art: prehistoric, 8, 13; Egyptian, *18, 19;* Minoan, *20;* Mycenaean, *21;* Persian, *23;* Greek, 27, *30, 34, 35;* Hellenistic, *45, 46, 48;* Etruscan, *50;* Roman, *57, 58, 66, 72, 73, 80;* early Christian, *87, 90;* early German, *99, 102;* Byzantine, *119;* Moslem, *129,* 130; Renaissance, *249,* 322–324, 451; religious, 256–257; Baroque, 452. *See also* Architecture; Mosaics; Painting; Sculpture
Arte di Lana, 301
Arthur, King, 226
Arthur, Prince, son of Henry VII, 343, 368
Arthur, son of Geoffrey of Anjou, 195
Articles of Religion: Forty-two, 369; Thirty-nine, 402
Artois, county of, 195, 198, 372, 433
Asceticism, 94, 95, 204–205, 359. *See also* Monasticism
Asia, 269, 349, 350, 353. *See also* China; India
Asia Minor: Greek cities in, 21, 24, 26, 30, 31; in crusades, 205–209
Assyria, 13–14
Astronomy: ancient, 14, 47; early modern, 457–459. *See also* Science
Athanasius, Saint, 90, 96
Athens, 27, 28–29, 30–31, 33–39
Attica, 31

Oslo
SCANDINAVIAN PENINSULA
BRITISH ISLES
SCOTLAND
Edinburgh
NORTH SEA
IRELAND
Dublin
Copenhagen
ENGLAND
ELBE
Berlin
London
Amsterdam
English Channel
Brussels
Bonn
SEINE
MEUSE
RHINE
Paris
BOHEMIAN BASIN
DANUBE
LOIRE
Vienna
BAY OF BISCAY
Berne
MASSIF CENTRAL
ALPS
GARONNE
RHÔNE
PO
ADRIATIC
PYRENEES MTS.
APENNINE MTS.
EBRO
IBERIAN PENINSULA
Lisbon
TAGUS
Madrid
CORSICA
Rome
BALEARIC IS.
SARDINIA
GUADALQUIVIR
Strait of Gibraltar
MEDITERRANEAN
SICILY
ALGERIAN PLATEAU
Europe
AFRICA